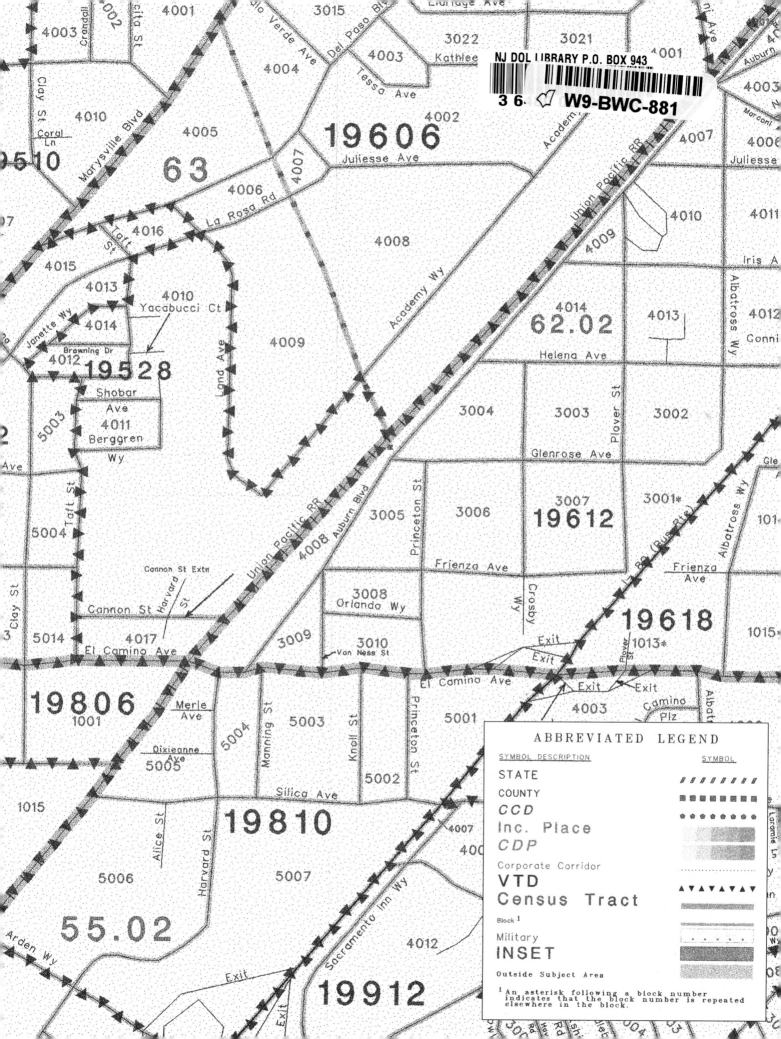

Encyclopedia of the U.S. Census

Encyclopedia of the U.S. Census

Margo J. Anderson, Editor in Chief

CQ PRESS

A Division of Congressional Quarterly Inc.
Washington, D.C.

CQ Press
A Division of Congressional Quarterly Inc.
1414 22nd Street, N.W.
Washington, D.C. 20037

202-822-1475; 800-638-1710

www.cqpress.com

CQ Press Staff, *Encyclopedia of the U.S. Census*

Executive Editor: David R. Tarr
Assistant to the Executive Editor: Grace Hill
Managing Editor, Textbook and Reference: Ann Davies
Electronic Composition Manager: Paul P. Pressau
Print Buyer: Liza Sanchez
Senior Editors: Christopher Karlsten, Jon Preimesberger, Jerry Orvedahl
Project Editor: Talia Greenberg
Production Editors: Belinda Josey, Thomas Roche
Editorial Assistant: Scott Kuzner

Encyclopedia of the U.S. Census was designed and typeset by
Karen W. Doody.

Cover Design: Naylor Design Inc.

Printed and bound in the United States of America

04 03 02 01 00   5 4 3 2 1

Library of Congress Cataloging-in-Publication Data

Encyclopedia of the U.S. census / Margo J. Anderson, editor
       p. cm.
  Includes bibliographical references and index.
  ISBN 1-56802-428-2
   1. United States—Census—Encyclopedias. I. Title: Encyclopedia of the U.S. census. II. Anderson, Margo J., 1945–

HA37.U55 C66 2000
304.6'07'23—dc21   00-030522

About the Editors

EDITOR IN CHIEF

MARGO J. ANDERSON specializes in the social history of the United States in the nineteenth and twentieth centuries. With Stephen E. Fienberg she recently published *Who Counts? The Politics of Census-Taking in Contemporary America* (1999). She is also the author of *The American Census: A Social History* (1988) and *The United States Census and Labor Force Change* (1980) as well as the coeditor with Maurine Greenwald of *Pittsburgh Surveyed* (1996). Anderson teaches women's history and quantitative methods for historians and is working on a history of statistics and the formation of American social policy. She is a fellow of the American Statistical Association, serves as the chair of the Council of the Interuniversity Consortium for Political and Social Research, and has served as chair of the History Department and of the Executive Committee of the Faculty at the University of Wisconsin—Milwaukee. She holds M.A. and Ph.D. degrees in history from Rutgers University.

JORGE CHAPA is professor and founding director of Latino Studies at Indiana University—Bloomington. His many publications reflect his research focus on the low rates of Hispanic educational, occupational, and economic mobility and on the development of policies to improve these trends. Much of his research has been based on the analysis of data produced by the Census Bureau. In 1994 Secretary of Commerce Ron Brown appointed Chapa to serve as a member of the Census Bureau's Advisory Committee on the Hispanic Population. He was reappointed to the committee in 1996 by Secretary Mickey Kantor and in 1998 and 2000 by Secretary William Daley. This committee made several substantive recommendations that were adopted by the Census Bureau as important improvements in the bureau's proposed plans and procedures. Chapa received a B.A. with honors from the University of Chicago and graduate degrees in sociology and demography from the University of California, Berkeley.

CONSTANCE F. CITRO is a senior program officer for the Committee on National Statistics at the National Academy of Sciences/National Research Council. She is a former vice president of Mathematica Policy Research, Inc., and of Data Use and Access Laboratories (DUALabs) and was an American Statistical Association/National Science Foundation research fellow at the Bureau of the Census. For the Committee on National Statistics she has served as study director for numerous panels, including the Panel on Estimates of Poverty for Small Geographic Areas, the Panel on Poverty and Family Assistance, the Panel to Evaluate the Survey of Income and Program Participation, and the Panel on Decennial Census Methodology. Her research has focused on the quality and accessibility of large, complex microdata files and analysis related to income and poverty measurement. She is a fellow of the American Statistical Association and a past president of the Association of Public Data Users. She received M.A. and Ph.D. degrees in political science from Yale University.

JOSEPH J. SALVO is director of the Population Division at the New York City Department of City Planning, where he has worked for the past eighteen years. The Population Division is one of the largest public sector users of decennial census data in the nation and has a long history of involvement with all aspects of the decennial census. Salvo's recent research includes studies on immigration and population change, census address list issues, small-area data quality issues pertaining to the American Community Survey, and local-area population estimates. He is a former president of the Association of Public Data Users, and he serves on the Advisory Board of the Center for Migration Studies, the Commerce Department secretary's 2000 Census Advisory Committee, and the National Academy of Sciences/National Research Council Panel on Future Census Methods. In 1995 he was a recipient of the Sloan Public Service Award from the Fund for the City of New York. He holds M.A. and Ph.D. degrees in sociology from Fordham University.

Contents

Introduction by *Margo J. Anderson*   ix

Alphabetical List of Articles   xvii

Contributors   xxi

THE ARTICLES   3–371

Photo Insert, *following page 184*

Appendix

Census Leadership, 1850–2000   374

U.S. Population and Area, 1790–2000   375

Center of Population, 1790–1990   376

Congressional Apportionment, 1789–1990   378

Percentage of the House of Representatives for Each State

     After Each Apportionment   379

Methods of Congressional Apportionment   381

Chronology of the States of the Union   382

Growth of the Decennial Census, 1790–1990   383

Cost of Taking the Census, 1790–2000   384

Census 2000 Questionnaires: Short and Long Forms   385

Standards for the Classification of Federal Data on Race and Ethnicity   400

Census on the Internet   403

Glossary   406

Index   411

Introduction

The *Encyclopedia of the U.S. Census* is a comprehensive, one-volume work that offers ready reference information on the U.S. decennial census. It describes the concepts, politics, and history of the decennial census while also offering clear, accessible information on current census methods and results. In short, the encyclopedia provides concise and accurate answers to questions about census taking in the United States, past and present.

The essays in this volume are organized alphabetically and identify the principal techniques, terms, processes, issues, and concepts of census taking. The underlying logic of the volume is based on the logic of census taking in the United States. We include essays on the mechanics of the census: the procedures for preparing the questionnaire, printing and mailing the forms, and retrieving the information from American households. We discuss the data produced from the census: the demographic results, how to get access to the information, and who makes use of the data. Other essays discuss the decennial census in the context of public policy, including its origins in the federal Constitution as a mechanism for apportioning seats in the House of Representatives. We include short articles that provide a snapshot of the nation at each of the decennial censuses from 1790 to the present. And we address census controversies, both historical and current, including the legal controversies surrounding census taking, the apportionment of Congress, the privacy of census information, and the propriety and usefulness of particular questions on such sensitive issues as income, race, and family status.

The encyclopedia includes 120 signed articles by prominent scholars, professionals, and other census experts. The articles have been written to be accessible to students, scholars, and general readers, and the book is structured in such a way as to facilitate retrieval of information. Accompanying each article are cross-references to related articles and a brief bibliography that suggests further reading. A detailed index guides readers to the information they need. Moreover, we asked our contributors to integrate cross-cutting issues into their entries.

In addition to the articles, the encyclopedia includes a wide assortment of maps, tables, and figures. A sixteen-page photo gallery documents the history of census taking in America. The appendix contains useful tabular data and other supplementary materials, such as a glossary of terms; the budget for taking the census; a list of Census Bureau directors; examples of census forms and questions; a center of population map and U.S. population totals from each census taken since 1790; information on the apportionment of Congress, including apportionment methods and formulas; and a compilation of census-related Internet sites, among other reference materials. The sites listed in the appendix and elsewhere in the book were current as of July 2000.

Census taking may be one of the most routine and ordinary functions of the federal government, yet it is little understood. It is also one of the oldest activities of the federal government, dating, like postal service and tax collection, to the birth of the Republic in 1789. But unlike these other venerable government activities, the census is infrequent, arriving on the public scene only once a decade and then receding from public consciousness between counts.

Definitions: What Is a Census?

A census is a count of the population of a country as of a fixed date. National governments conduct censuses to determine how many people live in different areas of the country; to assess whether the population is growing, stable, or declining in the country as a whole and in particular parts of the country; and to describe the characteristics of the population in terms of age, sex, ethnic background, marital status, income, and other variables. Generally, governments collect the information by sending a questionnaire in the mail or an interviewer to every household or residential address in the country. The questionnaire asks the head of the household or a responsible adult in the household (the respondent) to list all of the people who live at the address as of a particular date and to answer a series of questions about each of them. The respondent or the interviewer is then responsible for sending the answers back to the government agency, which in turn tabulates or aggregates the answers for the country overall and for political subdivisions such as states or provinces, cities, counties, or other civil divisions. The agency usually reports the results to the public a few months or years after the census; the results are considered "news" and are reported by the media.

Because censuses aim to count the entire population of a country, they are very expensive and elaborate administrative operations and thus are conducted relatively infrequently, generally at five- or ten-year intervals. Between censuses, governments estimate the size and characteristics of the population, either by extrapolating the trends identified in the census into the future, by estimating the population from other data systems such as vital statistics or tax records, or by conducting periodic sample surveys to collect information about the population. Researchers also can use representative probability samples to collect information from a small portion of the population; these can be conducted frequently, even monthly. In the United States the Current Population Survey of about 50,000 households is conducted monthly. (See *American Community Survey; Federal household surveys.*)

National governments also conduct other types of censuses, particularly of economic activity, such as agriculture, manufacturing, or business. Such censuses collect information on the number and characteristics of farms, businesses, or manufacturing firms. In the past, such censuses were conducted at the same time as the population census. Today, the economic censuses are generally conducted on a different schedule from the population census. (See *Agricultural censuses; Censuses in other countries; Economic censuses.*)

Censuses have been taken since ancient times. Emperors and kings used them to assess the strength of their realms. These early censuses were conducted sporadically and generally served to measure the tax or military capacity of a particular area. Unlike modern censuses, they tended to count only adult men, men liable for military service, or tithables (people liable to pay taxes). The modern census of all persons dates from the seventeenth and eighteenth centuries, when the colonial powers of western Europe sought to determine the success of their overseas colonies. (See *Colonial censuses.*)

The American Experience

The U.S. decennial census was mandated in the 1787 federal Constitution as a mechanism for determining the political representation for each state in the House of Representatives. Article 1 of the Constitution created Congress (the House of Representatives and the Senate) and defined its membership and capacities. Paragraph three of section 2 described the method of constituting the House:

> Representatives and direct Taxes shall be apportioned among the several States which may be included within this Union, according to their respective numbers, which shall be determined by adding to the whole Number of free Persons, including those bound to Service for a Term of Years, and excluding Indians not taxed, three-fifths of all other Persons. The actual Enumeration shall be made within three Years after the first Meeting of the Congress of the United States, and within every subsequent Term of ten Years, in such Manner as they shall by Law direct.

Section 9 of Article 1 included the only other mention of the census in the Constitution: "No capitation, or other direct, Tax shall be laid, unless in Proportion to the Census or Enumeration herein before directed to be taken." The language of Article 1 provided the solution to one of the fundamental political controversies of the American revolutionary era: how to allocate representation in legislative assemblies. Before the American Revolution, the colonists had protested their lack of representation in the British Parliament. They had also objected to the existence of rotten boroughs—legislative districts with few or no people living in them. A legislator from such a district cast the same single vote as a representative from a city with thousands of people.

After declaring their independence in 1776, the newly united thirteen colonies struggled over the problem of equitably distributing the burdens and resources of the national government among large and small states. In the Continental Congress and under the Articles of Confederation during the 1770s and 1780s, states had voted as units, regardless of their wealth or population. This system was opposed by the larger states and was one element of the government that they sought to reform in the 1787 Constitution.

The framers of the Constitution resolved the dispute between large and small states by allocating representation in the House according to population and in the Senate by state. In the Senate each state, regardless of size, had two members. Since the framers also intended for "direct taxes" to be allocated among the states according to population, the large states would gain greater House representation but would pay higher taxes to the federal government. The strength of each state in the electoral college would be determined by summing its Senate and House members. Finally, the framers were well aware that populations—and especially the American population—grew and shifted over time and that no legislative apportionment could be permanent.

The census and apportionment mechanisms of the federal Constitution were crucial pieces of the Great Compromise among the large and small states that made a new national government possible. The United States became the first nation in the world to take a regular population census and to use it to apportion legislative seats. Since then, the decennial census and reapportionment, like regular elections, have facilitated the always difficult process of transferring political power among the various elements of the population.

The logic of the new census system flowed from the experience and conceptions of the framers. The framers had debated various methods of allocating political power and tax burden during the Constitutional Convention. They discussed apportionments based on land assessments, other measures of wealth, and population. They agreed that, theoretically, political power should be allocated on the basis of population and that tax capacity derived from wealth. Everyone also agreed, however, that population was much easier to measure than wealth and that wealth was highly correlated with population. So population would be the apportionment measure.

The issue of allocating representation based on population was complicated further by the institution of racial slavery and the relationships between the Euro-American majority and American Indians. At the time of the Revolution, about 20 percent of the American population was enslaved. If population were the apportionment measure, should the southern states be granted political representation for their African American slaves? Should the slaves be considered "property" for purposes of tax assessments? Northern states were already beginning to abolish the institution of slavery and were wary of writing any support for the system into the Constitution. Southerners insisted that the slaves be counted as part of the population. The framers decided to base both representation and direct taxes on population. The rather clumsy solution to the slavery dilemma was the three-fifths compromise. Slaves would be counted in the census but would be "discounted" to 60 percent of a free person when calculating the state population totals for apportionment.

At the time of the American Revolution, Indian tribes were considered sovereign powers. The Constitution gave Congress the power to "regulate Commerce...with the Indian Tribes" and created the category of "Indians not taxed," that is, American Indians who lived within the boundaries of the United States but did not owe taxes to the United States since they maintained allegiance to their tribe. "Indians not taxed" thus became the one population group within U.S. territory specifically excluded from enumeration in the decennial census. Thus, until passage of the Fourteenth Amendment in 1868, the census recognized three different civil statuses: free, slave, and nontaxed Indian. The amendment, which granted full civil and political rights to the former slaves, retained the exemption from enumeration for nontaxed Indians.

Since the purpose of the census was to distribute House seats among the states, Congress mandated that the census count the population by geographic area so that it could allocate political representation. The states, too, began to use census data to allocate representation to particular geographic areas.

Implementing the System

The censuses from 1790 to 1840 were simple counts of the people in each household or family. Congress instructed the U.S. marshals to appoint assistants, who in turn were supposed to contact each household head to find out how many people in particular age, race, and sex categories lived in the household. The assistant totaled the household counts and transmitted them to the U.S. marshal, who in turn totaled the assistants' counts and transmitted them to Washington. The secretary of state and a clerk or two added the numbers obtained from all U.S. marshals and submitted them to Congress. No bureaucracy existed to check the coverage or accuracy of the enumeration. Neither the federal government nor the marshals were required to map their local areas. Congress required that the census workers take an oath that they had faithfully counted everyone; returns were posted in a public place so that people could check them. The major concern of government officials in those early years of the census was that the returns be collected at all. In the sparsely settled nation, it took about a year to conduct the census, and Congress routinely had to legislate extra time for the marshals to collect the information.

Despite these difficulties, by the early nineteenth century the census had developed a successful record. The population was counted, and Congress was reapportioned. Congress experimented with direct-tax measures based on the census in the late 1790s and again during the War of 1812 but found that the tariff was a more efficient source of federal revenue and thus let this provision of the Constitution fall into disuse. The country at the time was overwhelmingly agricultural and rural. The U.S. population was also growing rapidly—at the rate of 30 to 35 percent a decade. In a society where the prime issues were integrating new states into the Union and accounting for growth based on the settlement of western land, the census proved to be an effective mechanism of allocating and reallocating political power each decade.

Today we know what nineteenth-century Americans were just beginning to realize: the United States has one of the most heterogeneous and flourishing populations in the history of the world. From a mere 3.9 million rural residents spread along the East Coast in 1790, the population has grown to more than 275 million spread from coast to coast. Racially and ethnically the population was and is diverse. Until the early twentieth century the nation was predominantly rural; now it is overwhelmingly urban. That the American political system has absorbed the shocks of these demographic and economic changes is remarkable.

The census has been one of the chief mechanisms for absorbing the shocks because it guarantees that geographic areas receive political representation in proportion to their population. Over time, states with populations that grew relative to the rest of the nation received relatively more representation in Congress. Those with stable or declining populations lost representation. By 1820 several of the original thirteen states began to lose seats in the House. By the Civil War, in 1861, the original thirteen states no longer held a majority of House seats.

Once Americans had acquired several decades of experience with census taking, they began to ask questions about technical issues of counting the population and the meaning of rapid population growth. Almanacs began to publish census figures for local areas. Local boosters in western states used these figures to encourage further settlement. On the downside, political leaders from parts of the country that were not growing as fast as others began to realize that slower relative population growth meant their political power would erode after the next reapportionment.

Over time, states that thought of themselves as "losing" in the population growth game began to object to a system that rewarded growth so relentlessly and began to scrutinize the underlying census results. Although their objections never disrupted the functioning of the census, at several points in the past two centuries the decennial census and reapportionment process brought into sharp relief other political controversies. The first major controversy arose during the Civil War era and reflected the growing conflict between North and South over the future of slavery and control of the national government. The second occurred in the 1920s, as the rural areas of the country refused to relinquish control of legislative bodies to the new urban majority. The third began with the Supreme Court decisions of the 1960s mandating the one-person, one-vote rule for legislative apportionment. That controversy continues today over the accuracy of the census. As the census was politicized, it lost its major original function as a mechanism to defuse the contentiousness surrounding the allocation of political power among the constituent elements of the population. And in all three eras—the 1860s, the 1920s, and the 1960s—the controversies surrounding the census led to technical and administrative reforms of the census-taking process, which in turn have provided Americans with ever greater amounts of information about their society.

Demographic Challenges and the Engine of Census Innovation

Western population growth did not pose a dangerous challenge to American governmental stability because there was a general consensus that western expansion was a good thing. However, other shifts in population were more problematic. By the 1820s it was clear that the southern population was not growing as fast as the northern. Each census and reapportionment therefore weakened southern power in the House and hence made control of the Senate and the presidency that much more important. The growing demographic imbalance between North and South also drew increasing attention to the census process. The first major effort to reform the census took place in the same session of Congress that debated the Compromise of 1850. (See *1850 census*.) Congress created the post of census superintendent and authorized a large, temporary office in the Interior Department to tally and publish the census. Congress required that each person in the country have a separate line on the census form. In other words, the individual rather than the household became the unit of analysis. Many new questions were added to the census schedule.

Further changes were made during the Civil War years. The southern states began to secede after Abraham Lincoln's election in November 1860, as the 1860 census was completed and reports of the continuing decline of the relative strength of the southern population were appearing in the press. As southerners looked to the future, they saw that they would face more losses in the House. The relentless, recurring process of census taking and reapportionment exacerbated the sectional crisis. Northern abolitionist Horace Bushnell gleefully commented that slavery would ultimately end because "the laws of population are themselves abolitionists." Northerners endorsed the census and apportionment process because they worked to the North's political advantage. As Lincoln and the Republicans took over the government, they were unconcerned that the simple constitutional mechanism of awarding power in accordance with population did not take account of the dislocation faced by regions that lost in the race of relative growth.

Northern Republicans realized that the census and reapportionment would work to their political *dis*advantage after the Civil War and Reconstruction. The Thirteenth Amendment to the Constitution, which abolished slavery, also implicitly ended the three-fifths compromise. (The Fourteenth Amendment would abolish the three-fifths formula explicitly.) With its demise, the southern states would gain a windfall of increased representation in Congress. However, since few policymakers expected the freed slaves to be able to vote initially, they realized that a disfranchised free black population would strengthen the white-led southern states and permit the Democrats to come dangerously close to gaining control of the presidency as early as 1868.

The logic of population counting and apportionment, therefore, was one of the major forces driving Congress to extend further political and civil rights to the freedmen. The Fourteenth Amendment extended citizenship, due process, and equal protection of the laws to all "persons born or naturalized in the United States." It also contained a provision—never enforced—to reduce the representation of a state that disfranchised any portion of its male citizenry. The ambiguity of that sanction led to passage of the Fifteenth Amendment, which declared that the right to vote "shall not be abridged by the United States or by any State on account of race, color, or previous condition of servitude."

In the years after the Civil War, the American population continued to grow and spread rapidly, by world standards, but never again would it achieve a national rate of 30 percent a decade. By 1890 the census superintendent announced the closing of the frontier. At the same time, the census takers documented the rapid urban growth in the nation. Cities had replaced the rural West as the locus of the most rapid growth, and European immigrants as well as native-born Americans were flocking to the new jobs and opportunities the cities offered.

As the twentieth century dawned, the census takers could see political power shifting again—this time to the rapidly urbanizing and industrializing states in the Northeast and Midwest, with their growing polyglot populations. From the Civil War until World War I, Congress solved the decennial problem of reallocating political power among the states by increasing the size of the House of Representatives. From 1880 to 1910, no state lost a seat. In 1860 the House comprised 243 members; by 1910 there were 435. Areas with slow-growing or declining populations lost relative, but not absolute, political power in the House.

In the late nineteenth and early twentieth century Congress expanded the administrative capacity of the census office. In 1880 the census superintendent received the authority to map the country, appoint local census supervisors, and test the enumerators for basic competency at their jobs. In 1890 the Census Office pioneered the machine tabulation (see *Pre-computer tabulation systems*) of census results. In 1902 the office became a permanent government bureau, and it joined the new Department of Commerce and Labor in 1903.

After the 1920 census, another apportionment crisis arose. The statisticians announced that a majority of Americans lived in urban areas, a development that threatened to undermine the rural states' domination of national politics and the rural towns' domination of state politics. The strikes and violence that erupted at the end of World War I were generally centered in the big cities, the home of immigrants and industrial workers, and such behavior deeply disturbed small-town and rural Americans. As the nation turned in revulsion from all things foreign, particularly European, Congress moved to restrict immigration and to delay reapportionment.

Congress had vowed in 1910 not to increase the size of the House beyond 435 members. When the census results showed that the great gainers from congressional reapportionment would be the large urban states—primarily in the Northeast and Midwest—Congress balked at passing an apportionment bill. Leaders from the predominantly rural states of the nation refused to surrender political power to the large urban states. They argued that geography was the true basis for representation, that the urban states did not deserve representation for their noncitizen, foreign-born populations, and that urban political machines were corrupting traditional republican institutions. They also argued that because the census was taken in the immediate aftermath of World War I and in January—a month when farm workers were often absent from their land—the bureau had incorrectly allocated rural residents to cities where they were temporarily employed. For the remainder of the 1920s no bill passed, and for the only time in the history of the Republic, Congress was not reapportioned.

In 1929 Congress finally passed a prospective bill, which would reapportion Congress in 1932 using the results of the 1930 census. But as part of the difficult compromise that made the bill possible, Congress removed the existing requirement that congressional districts be substantially equal in size. In short, Congress redistributed political power among the states but quietly permitted malapportioned districts within states in order to preserve rural and small-town dominance of Congress. By the early 1930s it was not uncommon for congressional districts in large urban areas to encompass seven or eight times more people than those in rural areas. A similar pattern of apportionment held true at the local and state government level.

Malapportionment would remain the norm until the 1960s. In the meantime, the census was redirected to address new issues. The Census Bureau pioneered the collection of new information to cope with the problems of depression and war in the 1930s and 1940s. It used the first nondefense computer in the 1950s. With the growth of population-based federal aid and grant programs, census numbers came to be employed in a wide variety of laws and funding allocations at all levels of the federal system. The Census Bureau also developed sample surveys to collect information between decennial counts, quality control procedures, and methods to measure the accuracy of the basic census count and the quality of responses to individual questions.

By the 1960s it was clear that the compromises of the 1920s had built major distortions into the apportionment and districting systems of the nation. Substantial numbers of Americans in urban and suburban areas were under-represented in their state legislatures and in Congress. Older cities were losing population and no longer seemed to threaten the future of the Republic. Nevertheless, legislatures dominated by rural members were unwilling to reapportion or redistrict. Thus, a series of carefully crafted test cases made their way through the court system.

In 1962 the Supreme Court ruled in *Baker v. Carr* that individuals could challenge the constitutionality of a malapportioned state legislature in court. The case led to a series of decisions which declared that state legislatures, local legislative bodies, and congressional districts had to be apportioned according to the rule that came to be called "one-person, one-vote." Citing the equal protection clause of the Fourteenth Amendment and the language of Article 1, section 2 of the Constitution, the Court ruled that states must draw legislative districts such that they encompass an equal number of people as counted in the decennial census. Other methods of drawing legislative districts, which might use political or geographic boundaries, were invalid if those districts were not equal in population. As Chief Justice Earl Warren noted in his impassioned ruling in *Reynolds v. Sims* (1964), which restored population as the apportionment measure:

> Legislators represent people, not trees or acres. Legislators are elected by voters, not farms or cities or economic interests. As long as ours is a representative form of government, and our legislatures are those instruments of government elected directly by and directly representative of the people, the right to elect legislators in a free and unimpaired fashion is a bedrock of our political system.

Thus, he concluded, "the right of suffrage can be denied by a debasement or dilution of the weight of a citizen's vote just as effectively as by wholly prohibiting the free exercise of the franchise." Since legislatures should be apportioned on the basis of one-person, one-vote, such "dilution" was unconstitutional. By the late

1960s congressional and legislative districts around the country had been redrawn to meet the new guidelines, and the under-represented areas—mainly urban and suburban areas—increased their level of legislative representation dramatically.

The Supreme Court requirement for legislative districts equal in population drew new attention to the quality of census data. Statisticians and demographers knew that the census counted some groups in the population more accurately than others, and demographers had developed a substantial technical literature on under-enumeration and census accuracy. Minorities, the poor, and urban dwellers were counted less accurately than those people living in suburbs and middle-class areas of the country. Once local officials began to understand the implications of the one-person, one-vote decisions, they and Congress began to look much more closely at the quality of local-area census data. Officials in local areas that were undercounted or miscounted sought to improve the data, and census officials began to see interest in better data not only from demographers but also from ordinary citizens unschooled in the niceties of advanced statistical methods.

For most of the 1970s and 1980s the census was embroiled in a complex set of controversies about improving the count. Congress, statisticians, local officials, and minority representatives demanded that the bureau count the population better in the first place and that they make plans to adjust the census in light of the inevitable undercounts. The bureau began to develop methods to improve the count and to experiment with adjustment methods to correct for undercounts. The budget for the census grew dramatically. New advisory committees worked on the planning efforts. The bureau successfully defended itself against fifty-four lawsuits after the 1980 census that accused the bureau of using improper and inadequate methods.

In the late 1980s the Census Bureau developed what it hoped would be a statistically defensible method of adjusting the decennial census for the undercount, but it faced political resistance to implementing the new methods. Since the late 1980s Republicans generally have opposed adjusting for the undercount. Democrats, on the other hand, have supported it, since much of the undercount occurs in traditionally Democratic strongholds—big cities—and among traditionally Democratic constituencies—minorities and immigrants. That control of the executive and legislative branches of the federal government has been split between the two parties has hampered resolution of the issue. Both parties have used their power in Congress or the executive branch to shape the census. In the late 1980s Commerce officials in the administrations of Ronald Reagan and George Bush canceled the implementation of the new adjustment methods. In response, New York City and a coalition of other cities, states, and civil rights organizations sued the Census Bureau, demanding that it proceed with the new methods. The courts mandated that the new methods be implemented in 1990 but that the commerce secretary decide whether to use the corrected data as the official results. Republican commerce secretary Robert Mosbacher decided not to use the adjusted data; his decision was upheld in the courts. In the 1990s the administration of Bill Clinton took the opposite tack, proposing adjustment of the 2000 census. Republican members of Congress and the Southeastern Legal Foundation sued to stop the Clinton plan. In *Department of Commerce v. United States House* (1999) the Supreme Court ruled that the current census statute prevents the use of sampling methods for reapportioning congressional seats after the 2000 census. The Clinton administration interpreted the ruling as authorizing the use of sampling and adjusted census results for other uses of census data.

The 2000 census results are still framed in controversy. How Americans will come to understand these results is not yet clear, but the 2000 results and the controversy surrounding them will encourage Americans to ponder the original purpose of the census. The census was and is a mechanism for distributing political power and economic resources among the various elements of the population. The founders created it because they needed a simple, automatic mechanism for apportioning legislative seats that was acceptable to all political factions. If we recognize this function, perhaps we can also set standards for resolving controversies and shaping technical improvements in the census.

Margo J. Anderson

Acknowledgments

Several people contributed to the success of this innovative encyclopedia. More than eighty distinguished editors and contributors appear as authors of entries. In addition, many others made the success of the volume possible, including our editors at CQ Press. Shana

Wagger conceived of a volume that would extend CQ's long experience with accessible reference books on the workings of government, particularly Congress, to produce such a book on the history, politics, techniques, and administration of America's premier statistical enterprise, the decennial census. Paul McClure worked tirelessly with the editorial board to make that vision a reality. Dave Tarr and Christopher Karlsten managed the final production of the volume and the myriad details of design and composition that result in an elegant book. Throughout, Grace Hill provided the administrative support necessary for a large project with many writers.

The project could not have been accomplished without the help and support of officials and experts at the U.S. Census Bureau. Several current and former bureau staffers wrote for the encyclopedia, and many others provided reference support and good words for the project. Particular thanks go to Carolee Bush, Susan Miskura, Jorge del Pinal, Roderick Harrison, David Pemberton, Paula Schneider, and Stephanie Shipp. The editors also wish to thank bureau staffers Laura Schebler, Victor Romero, and Michael Morgan for providing many of the photos that appear in the photo insert.

Alphabetical List of Articles

A

Accuracy and coverage evaluation
HOWARD HOGAN

Address list development
DONALD HIRSCHFELD

Advertising the census
MARGO J. ANDERSON

Advisory committees
CONSTANCE F. CITRO

African-origin population
CLAUDETTE BENNETT

Age questions in the census
GRETCHEN A. STIERS

Agricultural censuses
RICH ALLEN

American Community Survey
CHARLES ALEXANDER

American Indians and Alaska Natives
C. MATTHEW SNIPP

Americans overseas
DAVID McMILLEN

Apportionment and districting
DAVID McMILLEN

Archival access to census data
ERIK W. AUSTIN

Asian and Pacific Islander Americans
SHARON LEE

C

Capture-recapture methods
STEPHEN E. FIENBERG

Census law
J. PATRICK HEELEN

Census of Puerto Rico
JONATHAN SPERLING

Census testing
BARBARA A. BAILAR

Census tracts
JOSEPH J. SALVO

Censuses in other countries
BENOIT LAROCHE

Center of population
MARGO J. ANDERSON

Civil War and the census
J. DAVID HACKER

Colonial censuses
ROBERT V. WELLS

Composition of the population
BARRY EDMONSTON

Confidentiality
GERALD W. GATES

Congress and the census
TERRI ANN LOWENTHAL

Content
CONSTANCE F. CITRO

Content determination
CONSTANCE F. CITRO

Coverage evaluation
MICHAEL COHEN

Coverage improvement procedures
CONSTANCE F. CITRO

D
Data capture
JOSEPH J. SALVO

Data dissemination and use
DEIRDRE A. GAQUIN

Data products: evolution
JUDITH S. ROWE

Decennial censuses
PATRICIA C. BECKER (1970 census, 1980 census)
BARBARA EVERITT BRYANT (1990 census)
PATRICIA CLINE COHEN (1830 census, 1840 census)
EDWIN D. GOLDFIELD (1950 census, 1960 census)
J. DAVID HACKER (1850 census, 1860 census, 1870 census)
ROBERT M. JENKINS (1940 census)
DIANA L. MAGNUSON (1880 census, 1890 census,
    1900 census, 1910 census, 1920 census, 1930 census)
DAVID M. PEMBERTON (1950 census, 1960 census)
MARTHA FARNSWORTH RICHE (2000 census)
DANIEL SCOTT SMITH (1810 census, 1820 census)
ROBERT V. WELLS (1790 census, 1800 census)

Demographic analysis
J. GREGORY ROBINSON
KIRSTEN K. WEST

Depository libraries
MICHAEL LAVIN

Disability
MARGO J. ANDERSON

Dissemination of data: electronic products
ALBERT F. ANDERSON
LISA NEIDERT

Dissemination of data: printed publications
JANICE S. FRYER

Dissemination of data: secondary products
ANN S. GRAY

Dress rehearsal
MARGO J. ANDERSON

E
Economic census
PAUL T. ZEISSET

Editing and imputation
CONSTANCE F. CITRO

Education: changing questions and classifications
ROBERT KOMINSKY

Enumeration: field procedures
PATRICIA C. BECKER

Enumeration: special populations
CONSTANCE F. CITRO

Errors in the census
EUGENE P. ERICKSEN

F
Family and household composition of the population
LYNNE M. CASPER
MARTIN O'CONNELL

Federal administrative records
JOHN CZAJKA

Federal agency uses of census data
CONSTANCE F. CITRO

Federal household surveys
PAT DOYLE

Foreign-born population of the United States
ARUN PETER LOBO
ELLEN PERCY KRALY

G
Genealogy
PAUL McCLURE

Geography: distribution of the population
LARRY LONG

Grassroots groups
DEBORAH A. GONA

H

Hispanic population
JORGE CHAPA

Hispanic/Latino ethnicity and identifiers
JORGE CHAPA

Housing
PATRICIA C. BECKER

I

Immigration
JEFFREY S. PASSEL

Income and poverty measures
CONSTANCE F. CITRO

International coordination in population censuses
WILLIAM SELTZER

IPUMS (Integrated Public Use Microdata Series)
STEVEN RUGGLES

L

Litigation and the census
MARGO J. ANDERSON

Local involvement in census taking
JOSEPH J. SALVO

Long form
CONSTANCE F. CITRO

M

Media attention to the census
TERRI ANN LOWENTHAL

Metropolitan areas
RICHARD L. FORSTALL

N

National Archives and Records Administration
   (NARA)
MARGARET O'NEILL ADAMS, with Thomas E. Brown,
Barbara Lewis Burger, Charles DeArman, Theodore J.
Hull, Constance Potter, Rodney A. Ross, Richard H.
Smith, and Aloha South

Not-for-profit organizations
DEBORAH A. GONA

O

Occupation and education
MARY G. POWERS

Organization and administration of the census
JOHN H. THOMPSON

P

Population estimates and projections
CONSTANCE F. CITRO, assisted by Meyer Zitter

Post-enumeration Survey
MARY H. MULRY

Pre-computer tabulation systems
DIANA L. MAGNUSON

Private sector
EDWARD J. SPAR

PUMS (Public Use Microdata Samples)
NANCY E. DUNTON

R

Race: questions and classifications
CLAUDETTE BENNETT

Related data sources
CONSTANCE F. CITRO

Rural areas
PAUL R. VOSS

S

Sampling for content
CONSTANCE F. CITRO

Sampling for follow-up of nonresponding households
TOMMY WRIGHT

Sampling in the census
CONSTANCE F. CITRO

Small Area Income and Poverty Estimates (SAIPE)
PAUL SIEGEL

Staffing
JAY K. KELLER
JOHN M. STUART

State and local censuses
MARGO J. ANDERSON

State and local governments: legislatures
DEBORAH A. GONA

State and local governments: use of census data
LEONARD M. GAINES
LINDA GAGE
JOSEPH J. SALVO

State data centers
ROBERT SCARDAMALIA

Statistical policy and oversight
HERMANN HABERMANN
FRANKLIN S. REEDER

Summary Tape Files
DEIRDRE A. GAQUIN

T
Tabulation geography
PATRICIA C. BECKER

Three-fifths Compromise
MARGO J. ANDERSON

U
Urban areas
RICHARD L. FORSTALL

U.S. insular areas
MICHAEL J. LEVIN

Uses of census data by the private sector
JOAN NAYMARK
KENNETH HODGES

V
Veterans' status
STEPHEN J. DIENSTFREY

Vital registration and vital statistics
DOROTHY S. HARSHBARGER

W
White or European-origin population
MONICA McDERMOTT

White population of the United States
MONICA McDERMOTT

Women in the decennial census
GRETCHEN A. STIERS

Contributors

ADAMS, MARGARET O'NEILL
National Archives and Records Administration
National Archives and Records Administration (NARA)

ALEXANDER, CHARLES
U.S. Bureau of the Census
American Community Survey

ALLEN, RICH
U.S. Department of Agriculture
Agricultural censuses

ANDERSON, ALBERT F.
Public Data Queries, Inc.
Dissemination of data: electronic products

ANDERSON, MARGO J.
University of Wisconsin—Milwaukee
Advertising the census
Center of population
Disability
Dress rehearsal
Litigation and the census
State and local censuses
Three-fifths Compromise

AUSTIN, ERIK W.
University of Michigan
Archival access to census data

BAILAR, BARBARA A.
National Opinion Research Center, University of Chicago
Census testing

BECKER, PATRICIA C.
APB Associates/Southeast Michigan Census Council
Enumeration: field procedures
Housing
1970 census
1980 census
Tabulation geography

BENNETT, CLAUDETTE
U.S. Bureau of the Census
African-origin population
Race: questions and classifications

BRYANT, BARBARA EVERITT
University of Michigan
1990 census

CASPER, LYNNE M.
National Institute of Child Health and Human Development
Family and household composition of the population

CHAPA, JORGE
Indiana University
Hispanic population
Hispanic/Latino ethnicity and identifiers

CITRO, CONSTANCE F.
National Academy of Sciences/National Research Council
Advisory committees
Content
Content determination
Coverage improvement procedures
Editing and imputation
Enumeration: special populations
Federal agency uses of census data
Income and poverty measures
Long form
Population estimates and projections
Related data sources
Sampling for content
Sampling in the census

COHEN, MICHAEL
National Academy of Sciences/National Research Council
Coverage evaluation

COHEN, PATRICIA CLINE
University of California, Santa Barbara
1830 census
1840 census

CZAJKA, JOHN
Mathematica Policy Research, Inc.
Federal administrative records

DIENSTFREY, STEPHEN J.
Schulman, Ronca, & Bucuvalas, Inc.
Veterans' status

DOYLE, PAT
U.S. Bureau of the Census
Federal household surveys

DUNTON, NANCY E.
Midwest Research Institute
PUMS (Public Use Microdata Samples)

EDMONSTON, BARRY
Portland State University
Composition of the population

ERICKSEN, EUGENE P.
Temple University
Errors in the census

FIENBERG, STEPHEN E.
Carnegie Mellon University
Capture-recapture methods

FORSTALL, RICHARD L.
Consultant
Metropolitan areas
Urban areas

FRYER, JANICE S.
Iowa State University
Dissemination of data: printed publications

GAGE, LINDA
State of California Department of Finance
State and local governments: use of census data

GAINES, LEONARD M.
Empire State Development and SUNY—Empire State College
State and local governments: use of census data

GAQUIN, DEIRDRE A.
Consultant
Data dissemination and use
Summary Tape Files

GATES, GERALD W.
U.S. Bureau of the Census
Confidentiality

GOLDFIELD, EDWIN D.
Committee on Statistics, National Academy of Sciences
1950 census
1960 census

GONA, DEBORAH A.
Gona & Associates
Grassroots groups
Not-for-profit organizations
State and local governments: legislatures

GRAY, ANN S.
Cornell University
Dissemination of data: secondary products

HABERMANN, HERMANN
United Nations Statistics Division
Statistical policy and oversight

HACKER, J. DAVID
California Institute of Technology
Civil War and the census
1850 census
1860 census
1870 census

HARSHBARGER, DOROTHY S.
Alabama Department of Public Health
Vital registration and vital statistics

HEELEN, J. PATRICK
U.S. Bureau of the Census
Census law

HIRSCHFELD, DONALD
U.S. Bureau of the Census (retired)
Address list development

HODGES, KENNETH
Claritas Inc.
Uses of census data by the private sector

HOGAN, HOWARD
U.S. Bureau of the Census
Accuracy and Coverage Evaluation

JENKINS, ROBERT M.
University of North Carolina at Chapel Hill
1940 census

KELLER, JAY K.
U.S. Bureau of the Census
Staffing

KOMINSKY, ROBERT
U.S. Bureau of the Census
Education: changing questions and classifications

KRALY, ELLEN PERCY
Colgate University
Foreign-born population of the United States

LAROCHE, BENOIT
Statistics Canada
Censuses in other countries

LAVIN, MICHAEL
Lockwood Library, State University of New York at Buffalo
Depository libraries

LEE, SHARON
Portland State University
Asian and Pacific Islander Americans

LEVIN, MICHAEL J.
U.S. Bureau of the Census
U.S. insular areas

LOBO, ARUN PETER
New York City Department of City Planning
Foreign-born population of the United States

LONG, LARRY
U.S. Bureau of the Census
Geography: distribution of the population

LOWENTHAL, TERRI ANN
Consultant
Congress and the census
Media attention to the census

MAGNUSON, DIANA L.
Bethel College & Seminary
1880 census
1890 census
1900 census
1910 census
1920 census
1930 census
Pre-computer tabulation systems

McCLURE, PAUL
World Bank
Genealogy

McDERMOTT, MONICA
Harvard University
White or European-origin population
White population of the United States

McMILLEN, DAVID
Office of Rep. Henry A. Waxman, D-Calif.
Americans overseas
Apportionment and districting

MULRY, MARY H.
M/A/R/C Research
Post-enumeration Survey

NAYMARK, JOAN
Target Corporation
Uses of census data by the private sector

NEIDERT, LISA
University of Michigan
Dissemination of data: electronic products

O'CONNELL, MARTIN
U.S. Bureau of the Census
Family and household composition of the population

PASSEL, JEFFREY S.
Urban Institute
Immigration

PEMBERTON, DAVID M.
U.S. Bureau of the Census
1950 census
1960 census

POWERS, MARY G.
Fordham University
Occupation and education

REEDER, FRANKLIN S.
United Nations Statistics Division
Statistical policy and oversight

RICHE, MARTHA FARNSWORTH
Farnsworth Riche Associates
2000 census

ROBINSON, J. GREGORY
U.S. Bureau of the Census
Demographic analysis

ROWE, JUDITH S.
Princeton University (retired)
Data products: evolution

RUGGLES, STEVEN
University of Minnesota
IPUMS (Integrated Public Use Microdata Series)

SALVO, JOSEPH J.
New York City Department of City Planning
Census tracts
Data capture
Local involvement in census taking
State and local governments: use of census data

SCARDAMALIA, ROBERT
New York State Department of Economic Development
State data centers

SELTZER, WILLIAM
Fordham University
International coordination in population censuses

SIEGEL, PAUL
U.S. Bureau of the Census
Small Area Income and Poverty Estimates (SAIPE)

SMITH, DANIEL SCOTT
University of Illinois—Chicago
1810 census
1820 census

SNIPP, C. MATTHEW
Stanford University
American Indians and Alaska Natives

SPAR, EDWARD J.
Council of Professional Associations on Federal Statistics
Private sector

SPERLING, JONATHAN
U.S. Bureau of the Census
Census of Puerto Rico

STIERS, GRETCHEN A.
U.S. Bureau of the Census
Age questions in the census
Women in the decennial census

STUART, JOHN M.
U.S. Bureau of the Census
Staffing

THOMPSON, JOHN H.
U.S. Bureau of the Census
Organization and administration of the census

VOSS, PAUL R.
University of Wisconsin—Madison
Rural areas

WELLS, ROBERT V.
Union College
Colonial censuses
1790 census
1800 census

WEST, KIRSTEN K.
U.S. Bureau of the Census
Demographic analysis

WRIGHT, TOMMY
U.S. Bureau of the Census
Sampling for follow-up of nonresponding households

ZEISSET, PAUL T.
U.S. Bureau of the Census
Economic census

Encyclopedia of the U.S. Census

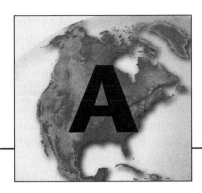

Accuracy and Coverage Evaluation

The Accuracy and Coverage Evaluation (ACE) is the program the Census Bureau uses to measure and correct for the net undercount in Census 2000. The ACE program uses the concepts of statistical sampling. It measures the proportion of people missed by the census, that is, the gross undercount or gross omissions rate. It also estimates the proportion of census records that were included in error, that is, the gross overcount or erroneous enumerations rate. These proportions are combined to measure the net undercount. The undercount is measured not just nationally but also by geographic area and demographic group. The Census Bureau then uses this information to compute corrected population estimates for all blocks and all groups in the nation.

Background

The Census Bureau has long recognized that it is not possible to enumerate all the people in the census. The census misses some people. These omissions constitute the gross undercount. In addition, the Census Bureau recognized that it sometimes counts the same person twice, counts babies born after the official census reference date, and so forth. Indeed, some census records do not refer to real people at all but instead refer to people made up by the census taker or by the respon-

dent. These erroneous inclusions constitute the gross overcount.

However, beginning in the 1960s, the Census Bureau had increasing evidence that the undercount was relatively larger for African Americans and other minorities. This relative difference in the undercount constitutes the differential undercount. About the time of the 1980 census, the differential undercount became both a political issue and the subject of litigation.

Until the 1980s, although the Census Bureau recognized the problem of the differential undercount, it lacked the statistical tools that would allow it to correct the problem. However, during the 1980s the Census Bureau developed improved tools to measure the number of people missed by the census for relatively large areas and large groups. Equally important, the Census Bureau developed methods to incorporate the adjustments into the detailed census tabulations.

These techniques were first carried out in the 1990 post-enumeration survey (PES). The 1990 PES measured the undercount and prepared corrected population measures for all areas within the United States. However, the results of the 1990 PES were not available until the spring of 1991, well after December 31, 1990, the legal deadline for the census to provide state population counts to the president and the Congress for use in congressional apportionment. Congressional apportionment is the process by which the members of Congress (currently 435) are divided among the states. The corrected population numbers were also produced after the legal date of April 1, 1991, when the Census Bureau was required to release to the states detailed block-level population counts to be used for drawing congressional, state, and local political boundaries, a process called redistricting.

Planning for Census 2000

In planning for Census 2000, the Census Bureau had hoped to produce corrected population counts in time to deliver to the president on December 31, 2000. The basic census enumeration and the sample-based post-enumeration survey procedures were designed to work together to produce the most accurate population measures possible in time for this legal deadline, as well as the later April 1 "redistricting" deadline. Because of this combined approach, the survey was called the Integrated Coverage Measurement, or ICM. It was also sometimes referred to as the quality check, because it was meant as a method to check and improve the quality of the basic enumeration.

The Census Bureau implemented the ICM approach in its final "dress rehearsal" for Census 2000, conducted in two sites: Sacramento, California, and Menominee County, Wisconsin. The Census Bureau succeeded in completing the process on schedule. Specifically, the ICM produced the population totals needed for "apportionment" (although obviously restricted to the two sites in this dress rehearsal) in the required time period of nine months after census day.

However, in January 1999, the Supreme Court ruled that the law governing the census, Title 13 of the U.S. Code, prohibits the use of sampling techniques to determine the state population used to apportion Congress. Because the ICM plan relied on sampling to produce the apportionment counts, the Census Bureau had to develop a different approach to Census 2000.

The approach that the Census Bureau adopted added several programs to improve the census enumeration in order to produce the most accurate state population counts possible by December 31, 2000, but without the use of sampling techniques. In addition, the Census Bureau conducted a post-enumeration survey and will use the results of that survey to produce population counts by block and demographic group, corrected for the undercounts, for release to the states by the April 1, 2001, deadline. This survey and the associated correction process together make up the ACE program.

Measuring the Undercount

The ACE program uses post-enumeration survey and capture-recapture methodology to measure and correct for the undercount. The process begins by taking a random sample of census blocks. A block can be an ordinary city block bounded by four streets. It can also be a "country block" bounded by a dirt road, a creek, and an irrigation ditch. In all cases, it is a small unit of land bounded by visible features. If the blocks have only a few housing units each, they are grouped with neighboring blocks to form block clusters.

Although the sampling procedure is fairly complex, it selects enough block clusters to obtain approximately 300,000 housing units for interview. The sample is designed to include sample households from all fifty states, the District of Columbia, as well as Puerto Rico. Since an important goal of the ACE program is to measure and correct for the differential undercount, the sample is selected to ensure that all demographic groups are properly represented, including historically undercounted groups such as blacks, Hispanics, Asians, Native Hawaiians, and American Indians.

In these blocks or block clusters, all the ordinary census activities take place: census address listing, questionnaire delivery, nonresponse follow-up, coverage improvement, and the like. It is important that these blocks are enumerated with the same procedures and the same accuracy as any other similar census block.

The ACE program began by preparing blank maps of these blocks. Although these "blank" maps showed roads and physical features, they did not show any of the housing units already listed by the main census address-listing procedures. The ACE program's field interviewers visited each of these blocks in the fall of 1999 and prepared an independent listing of all housing units in the blocks. "Independent" means that they did not use any of the information already gathered by the main census address-listing procedures.

In July 2000, after the census enumeration was largely completed, ACE interviewers began visiting each housing unit in the sample blocks. During this interview, they determined who was living there on April 1, census day. They also gathered basic demographic information such as age, race, and Hispanic origin. The people interviewed during this process constitute the population, or P-sample.

The ACE program is designed to measure the undercount of the people who live in housing units.

The P-sample excludes those living at college, in prison, in hospitals, in homeless shelters, on the street, or in other unusual housing arrangements.

The ACE interviews are conducted using portable computers, in what is known as Computer-Assisted Personal Interviewing (CAPI). The information is transmitted electronically to census headquarters in Suitland, Maryland.

When both the census enumeration and the ACE interviewing are complete, the two lists of census day residents will be compared, or "matched." The matching is done using both computer matching software and computer-assisted clerical matching. People that the ACE workers interviewed, but that the census did not list, constitute the census gross omissions in those blocks. Sometimes, the ACE work is rechecked to make sure that these were true census omissions. After follow-up, the ACE cases, that is, the P-sample, are classified as either enumerated or missed by the census.

Since the net undercount is the difference between the number missed by the census and the number counted in error, the ACE workers must also check a sample of census enumerations to see if they were correctly included. This enumeration, or E-sample, is drawn from the same sample of blocks as the population sample.

The ACE program checks to see if the E-sample includes duplicate, fictitious, or other erroneous enumerations. All E-sample (census) records that match to P-sample (ACE) records are assumed to be verified and correct. Census records that do not match to ACE records must be verified in the field. Some of these may be erroneous enumerations in the census. Others may simply be people missed by the ACE workers. Interviewers return to the field to determine which are correct and which are erroneous. This is done at the same time as the P-sample follow-up to check on census omissions. After the follow-up interviewing is completed, census enumerations in these blocks, that is, the E-sample, are classified as either correctly or erroneously enumerated.

At the end of this process, the ACE will have estimated, within the sample blocks, the proportion of people missed by the census and the proportion of census records that are erroneous. This information is combined with the known census results into corrected estimates of the total population using the capture-recapture or dual-systems estimate.

The estimation is done separately for distinct groups

of people known as poststrata. The poststrata are defined based on factors known to affect the undercount, such as age, sex, race, and Hispanic origin. The poststrata definitions also consider other variables, such as region of the country and size of the town the person lives in. Because, historically, families that own their own home are easier to count than those who rent, this characteristic is also taken into account. A poststratum might be, for example, Hispanic females, eighteen to twenty-nine years old, living in rented housing units in rural areas in the West.

Because the census results are tabulated for small areas and for detailed demographic categories, the ACE program must distribute the undercount to the blocks by detailed demographic group. This is done for all poststrata and all blocks in the nation. To do this, the ACE increases the count of a block proportionally to the number of people in each poststrata in each block. For example, if the ACE-corrected population was 10 percent higher than the census for a poststratum, then the count of all people in this poststratum in all blocks would be increased by 10 percent. If this results in a whole number of people plus a fraction, as it usually will, the ACE process rounds the population count to a whole number of people.

The ACE program will also conduct a similar process to correct the census counts for the number of housing units. The Census Bureau believes that the result of the ACE will be improved population statistics for the nation's decision makers and scholars.

See also *Errors in the census; Post-enumeration Survey.*

■ Howard Hogan

Bibliography

Hogan, Howard. "The 1990 Post-Enumeration Survey: An Overview." *The American Statistician* 46 (1992): 261–269.

———. "The Post-Enumeration Survey: Operations and Results." *Journal of American Statistical Association* 88, no. 423 (1993).

Marks, E. S. "The Role of Dual System Estimation in Census Evaluation." In *Recent Development of PGE,* ed. K. Krotki. Edmonton, Canada: University of Alberta Press, 1979.

Wolter, K. M. "Some Coverage Error Models for Census Data." *Journal of the American Statistical Association* 81 (1986): 338–346.

Wright, T., and H. Hogan. "Census 2000: Evolution of the Revised Plan." *Chance Magazine* 12 (2000): 11–19.

Address list development

The Census Bureau's address list and geographic information must be as accurate and current as possible if the modern census is to be taken efficiently and economically. In addition, they must be interrelated in a computer-based environment. The resultant database enables the bureau to tabulate census data and produce maps.

The Traditional Census

As recently as the 1960 census, the Census Bureau enumerated the nation's population by the traditional door-to-door method, generally referred to as "conventional enumeration." This involved assigning a specific geographic area to an enumerator, who was responsible for accounting for all housing units and completing a census questionnaire for each unit and its occupants, if any. The enumerator was given a manually prepared census map of the assigned area and questionnaires to complete in face-to-face interviews with the residents of the assigned area. The bureau first used such maps nationwide for the 1890 census.

With a growing population to enumerate, a shrinking labor pool as a source for its temporary census-taking staff, and the availability of computers to record and keep track of a variety of complex information, such labor-intensive efforts were no longer appropriate as the primary way to take a modern-day census. Also, more and more homes were receiving their mail at city-style addresses—that is, they had a house number and street name that were recognized by the U.S. Postal Service (USPS)—which would make it easier to identify and geographically code (geo-code) their locations.

The Mail Census

After the 1960 census, the bureau decided that it would be effective to take much of the decennial census by mail. Taking the census based on a mailing list would ensure a more accurate count; identify those housing units that required follow-up because the bureau had not received a questionnaire; enable the bureau, in areas with city-style mailing addresses, to code housing units based on the addresses identified on each side of each street in relation to a geographic boundary; and use the USPS to deliver questionnaires to specific housing units in such areas.

To take much of the census by mail, the bureau needed a list of city-style residential mailing addresses to which it could send its questionnaires. This list had to be as accurate, complete, and current (as of census day) as possible to ensure that a questionnaire could be delivered to every housing unit with a specific city-style mailing address; the bureau refers to this type of enumeration as "mail-out, mail-back." The bureau also needed to link each address to a geographic database so it could be geo-coded automatically by computer to the appropriate geographic entities used to collect census information, and then to tabulate the data for appropriate legal and statistical entities. For areas where city-style addresses were not used for mail delivery, each address had to be related to the location of its living quarters. This allowed the bureau to assign every housing unit and group quarters to its census geography, deliver a questionnaire to or find it to enumerate its residents (if any), and follow up to resolve problems and provide quality control. Thus, in addition to the geo-coding and delivery aspects of the census, the bureau's list of residential addresses would serve as a device to control the enumeration, ensure complete coverage of all living quarters, identify which housing units should receive sample questionnaires, and record which ones would require follow-up field visits.

Early Coding Efforts

Computerized geographic coding systems were being developed in the late 1950s by transportation and urban-planning agencies. To use address files for a decennial census, however, required a more complex and extensive system. The bureau's first effort to use an address list for census purposes took place in 1962 to support a mail-out, mail-back test census of Fort Smith, Arkansas, and Skokie, Illinois. Using punched cards, the bureau created a list using the 1960 census addresses for Skokie, the information from a 1961 address-listing test for Fort Smith, and updates from building permits for both places. The list was then given to the USPS to review and correct. In 1963 a test census in Huntington, New York, used a similarly constructed file, recorded on magnetic tape. Also in 1963 the bureau began exploring the availability and usability of computer-based address lists and found that a commercial mailing list would serve its needs better than city directories.

For the 1963 economic censuses, the bureau identified the address ranges for all streets in incorporated places with a population of 25,000 or more. The last address on each side of each street where it crossed the place boundary identified whether an establishment with a city-style address was inside or outside the place. The list was based on an address file purchased from a commercial vendor. (For the 1967 economic censuses, the bureau expanded the file to cover places with a population of at least 2,500.) For a 1965 test census in Cleveland, the bureau used a commercial mailing list whose addresses were geo-coded by matching them against a rudimentary address-coding guide (ACG). Basically, an ACG was a computerized address geo-coding system that consisted of address-range records for each side of each street segment within an area, with each record associated with a census block. In 1967, to take a census of New Haven, Connecticut, the bureau used a more refined ACG that linked individual addresses to census geography. The procedures were further refined for the dress rehearsal censuses in preparation for the 1970 census.

For that census the bureau, in cooperation with local and regional government agencies, created ACGs for the 145 largest metropolitan areas. Because the files covered multiple jurisdictions, if a street segment was split between two jurisdictions, the database was refined to record a separate address-range record for each segment. The combination of three factors—the geographic extent of the coverage of each ACG, the geographic extent of the USPS's city—delivery routes, and the availability of an address source—enabled the bureau's Geography Division manually to identify a boundary within which the bureau could prepare a computerized list of geo-coded, mailable addresses. This boundary was called the "blue line" (simply because it had been drawn in blue pencil); the area it covered was referred to as the Tape Address Register (TAR) area because the geo-coded addresses were maintained on magnetic tape. TAR areas covered the urban cores that had ACGs, estimated to contain about half the nation's population. The ACGs enabled the bureau to automate the assignment of 31.4 million city-style mailing addresses to their census geography.

The streets and areas recorded in the ACGs were related to a set of hand-drawn maps, called the Metropolitan Map Series. These maps showed the streets represented in the ACGs, as well as other geographic features that were not. They also showed census tract and block numbers, to which each address range—and, therefore, every address within that range—was

assigned, together with the boundaries of higher-level geographic entities. To make the system work, the bureau, for the first time, assigned a number to every block covered by the ACG (as well as to the adjacent blocks that appeared to contain urban development); previously, blocks were numbered only in areas that had contracted with the bureau for data at the block level (beginning with the 1940 census of housing).

The mailing addresses that the bureau recorded for the TAR areas came from two sources:

- A file of residential mailing addresses, which the bureau purchased from a single vendor. The vendor limited the file to residential addresses that were located in zip codes the bureau had identified as being within the blue line. Because TAR areas used city-style addresses for the delivery of mail, each mailing address had to consist of a house number and street name. It also could include a unit designation, such as an apartment number or a location identification (for example, "basement," "right front"). The addresses had to be in a format that could be recognized by the database and then by the USPS so its letter carriers could deliver each questionnaire to the correct housing unit. The bureau geo-coded the addresses by matching them to the ACGs. Some addresses did not match the information in the ACGs, so the bureau tried to geo-code as many of them as it could using both office and field operations.
- The USPS. The bureau produced address labels for the geo-coded vendor addresses and affixed them to cards. In mid-1969, it delivered the cards to appropriate post offices, where letter carriers "cased" the cards in their delivery slots—hence, the term *casing check*—for an *advance post office check*. The carriers corrected errors, noted nonexistent addresses, and filled out "add cards" for missing residential addresses. Field staff tried to locate the added addresses so they could assign the proper geo-codes. Within a month before census day, letter carriers again completed add cards to report residential addresses that were missing when they cased the preaddressed questionnaires. They did this yet one more time when they actually delivered the questionnaires for the census—the *time-of-delivery check*.

The address file for the 1970 census included all the geo-coded addresses from the commercial mailing list plus the first postal check. The addresses were processed against the ACGs, resulting in a geo-coded address control file (ACF) that the bureau could use for the census.

In addition to the TAR areas, the bureau sent enumerators out to list addresses in adjacent suburban areas that had a preponderance of city-style mailing addresses but were not within the parameters noted above that would have allowed them to be included in the TAR area—an operation referred to as "prelist." As in previous censuses, field staff recorded the address and other basic information for each living quarters in a book, now called an address register. Enumerators also assigned a number to each residential structure in the register and showed its location on a census map by "map spotting" the number; this helped field staff find the unit for subsequent operations. However, the bureau did not add these addresses to the address file at this time, so the addresses were clerically geo-coded and the questionnaires were addressed manually for mail-out. These addresses were subjected to the late post office checks. The bureau estimated that the mail-out, mail-back census covered about 60 percent of the population of the United States.

In areas that did not use city-style addresses for mail delivery—that is, where most residents used a postal route address or picked up their mail at a local post office—each housing unit was visited and enumerated. When the enumerator obtained or completed a questionnaire at each housing unit, he or she recorded the block number, address, and, if it was not a city-style address, a location and physical description for the unit in an address register; the enumerator also map-spotted the location of the unit on a census map. The block number was the basis for geo-coding the questionnaire for data tabulation. The bureau did not record either the addresses or the map spots in a database.

GBF/DIME-Files

After the 1970 census, the bureau improved on the ACGs by converting them to a technically better system, the Geographic Base Files/Dual Independent Map Encoding Files (GBF/DIME-Files). The technical improvements involved the application of the topological principles of points, lines, and areas having a mathematical relationship that linked them together, whereas the ACGs were simply a collection of records with no linkage other than identification of the census tract and block number that were associated with the address range along one side of a street segment. Also, the lines in the GBF/DIME-Files represented all map

features—railroads, streams, invisible boundaries, and the like—not just streets and roads. The bureau expanded the coverage of the mail-out, mail-back census by creating files for additional areas, again with the cooperation of local governments. The files included the urban cores of 276 metropolitan areas for the 1980 census.

Addresses for the 1980 Census

The 1980 census did not retain the addresses from the 1970 census. Instead, the bureau obtained a new set of addresses using essentially the same basic methodology as it used for the 1970 census, but this time it purchased the addresses from three vendors. The bureau used the GBF/DIME-Files to geo-code the addresses. However, rather than relying solely on the advance post office check to report missing and erroneous addresses and to identify miscoded ones, the bureau decided to perform its own field check in the TAR areas—an operation referred to as "precanvass." Based on the information in its database, the bureau printed the addresses for each census block in address registers that covered one or more blocks. Using a census map, field staff visited each block to verify, correct, and update the list of TAR addresses and the information shown on the census maps. The bureau then revised the GBF/DIME-Files and the ACF to reflect the additions and changes.

The bureau also expanded the area covered by the prelist. It added these addresses to the ACF, thereby enabling it to use the residential addresses in prelist areas in the same way that it did in TAR areas. The enumerators also map-spotted residential structures outside of TAR areas; again, the map spots were not carried to a database. Both TAR and prelist addresses were subjected to a late casing check and a time-of-delivery check by the USPS, requiring the bureau to geo-code added addresses at the last minute. The bureau estimated that the mail-out, mail-back census covered about 95 percent of the nation's population.

The *TIGER* Database

For both the 1970 and 1980 censuses, the ACGs and the GBF/DIME-Files, the census maps (the files could not be used to produce maps), and the lists of geographic entities ("geographic reference files") were developed separately. The result was that information in the different files could be out of sync with one another, so that a map might display information differently from the data, or a geographic code in one file might not match the code for the same area in another file. Furthermore, the census maps, as in previous censuses, were drawn by hand or obtained from local sources. If an operation required maps that covered smaller or larger areas, they were copied as reductions or enlargements of the basic maps. Many maps had to be re-used in the field for several operations, because they contained the annotations and updates from previous operations. Also, the area assigned to each enumerator generally was used for all census operations, even though this might mean that some assignments in late operations were too small, and therefore reasonable assignments had to be pieced together. And finally, the geographic coverage of both the ACGs and GBF/DIME-Files was less than 2 percent of the nation's land area.

The bureau decided that for the 1990 census and beyond, it had to have a single, integrated, automated geographic database that covered the entire United States and its territories. This computer file needed to have the ability to link every housing unit and group quarters to its correct geographic entities; to provide the maps and geographic controls needed for the bureau's collection, tabulation, and dissemination of census data; and to be updated quickly and easily to reflect new information needed for various operations. The result was the *Topologically Integrated Geographic Encoding and Referencing (TIGER)* database (at that time referred to as the *TIGER* file). Basically, this is a computer-readable, seamless map of the United States and its territories that the bureau can use to

- catalog and identify the relationships between and attributes of the geographic entities for which it collects, tabulates, and disseminates data
- geo-code addresses so they are assigned to these entities
- produce a variety of maps that display that exact same census geography or specially selected items.

The bureau derived part of the *TIGER* file from the GBF/DIME-Files. However, as noted above, these usually included only large urban centers, which covered only a small portion of the United States. In order to include map features and their attributes for the rest of the area covered by the bureau's periodic censuses and surveys, the bureau initiated a cooperative arrangement with the U.S. Geological Survey to integrate their computerized map files into the new database for the continental United States. For Alaska, Hawaii, and the territories, the bureau developed this information in a separate operation. In addition to recording basic map features in their correct locations, the file had to

- include the names of named features
- contain city-style address ranges for those street segments whose living quarters get their mail delivered to such addresses
- identify, and delineate the boundaries of, every geographic entity for which the bureau collects and tabulates data.

The *TIGER* database is part of the larger TIGER System (see Figure 1), which also includes the applications, specifications, procedures, computer programs, and related source materials required to build, use, and maintain the database.

Addresses for the 1990 Census

Once again, the bureau did not retain the addresses from the previous census. The address acquisition process was essentially the same as for the previous two censuses, except that this time, two vendors provided the addresses for the TAR areas. For the purchased addresses that did not match the *TIGER* file, the bureau undertook a massive clerical geo-coding operation. Many of the prelist addresses, as well as all the TAR addresses, were subjected to an advance post office check. The USPS conducted a late casing check of all mailing addresses covered by the mail-out, mail-back census a few weeks before census day; however, this time there was no time-of-delivery check.

To develop, maintain, update, and finally use the address list for the census, the bureau used the ACF to identify uniquely every living quarters for the 95 percent of the nation's population included in the mail-out, mail-back and update/leave (new for the 1990 census) enumeration areas. In update/leave areas, bureau field staff, rather than the USPS, delivered the census questionnaires to the specific units identified by the prelist operation, because the addresses recorded for a significant number of housing units did not uniquely identify the intended unit. Therefore, it was more effective to have field staff, with copies of the annotated prelist maps and the information recorded by the listers in hand, deliver the questionnaires. Furthermore, at the same time, the field staff could update and correct the maps and the list of living quarters, simultaneously dropping off a questionnaire at each housing

Figure 1. Census 2000 Map Produced from the TIGER System

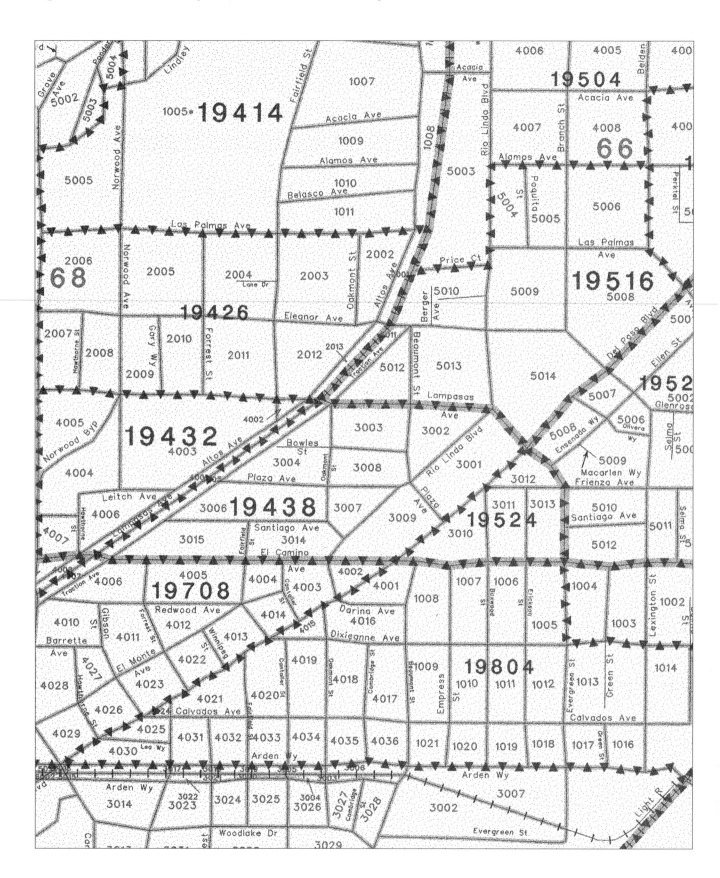

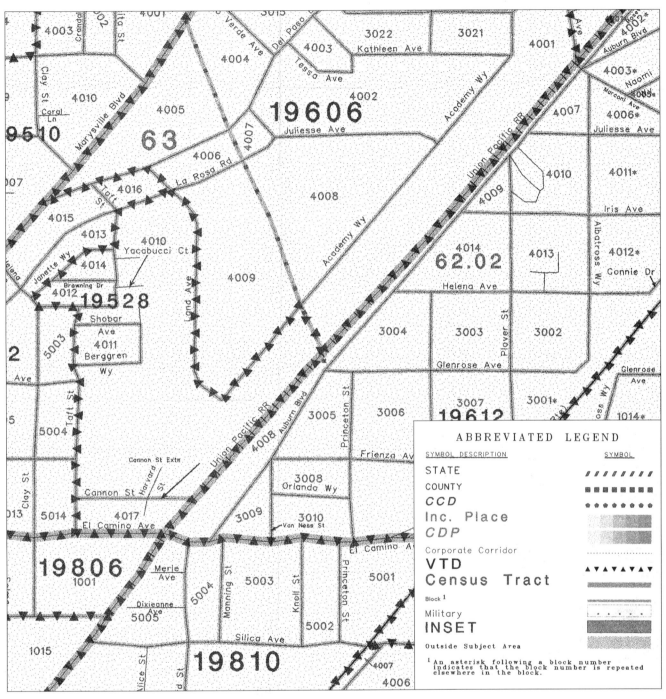

Notes: Map of part of Sacramento, California, produced from the Census Bureau's TIGER (Topologically Integrated Geographic Encoding and Referencing) System, a digital database of geographic features, such as roads, railroads, rivers, lakes, political boundaries, and census statistical boundaries covering the United States. The bureau uses TIGER to support its mapping and related geographic activities required by the decennial census and sample survey program. *Census county division (CCD):* a subdivision of a county that is a relatively permanent statistical area established cooperatively by the Census Bureau and the local government authorities. *Census designated place (CDP):* a statistical area defined for a census as a densely settled concentration of population that is not incorporated but which resembles an incorporated place in that it can be identified with a name. *Voting district (VTD):* any of a variety of types of areas, such as election districts, precincts, wards, and legislative districts, established by state and local governments for purposes of elections.

unit and identifying problem addresses (such as "burned down," "not a housing unit"). After the census, the bureau keyed into the ACF the approximately 5.5 million addresses the bureau collected in the areas covered by conventional enumeration procedures (called list/enumerate) for the 1990 census, as well as additions and corrections recorded in update/leave areas. It also added addresses obtained by the Local Review Program and the Count Question Resolution operation offered to local officials so they could point out problems with the counts for their jurisdictions.

Improvements to *TIGER* for Census 2000

For Census 2000 the bureau took several steps to improve the content of and products from the *TIGER* database and to create the most complete list of addresses and residential locations possible. To this end, the bureau for the first time retained a substantial number of the addresses it had recorded and geo-coded for the previous census. It did this by carrying forward to a restructured Master Address File (MAF) all the city-style mailing addresses recorded in the 1990 census's ACF. In addition, Public Law 103-430, the Census Address List Improvement Act of 1994, directed the USPS to provide the bureau with the information it needs to carry out its periodic censuses and surveys, and it enabled the bureau to allow people who are not employees to look at its list of addresses. To accomplish this, the USPS provided the bureau with its list of all known mailing addresses, the Delivery Sequence File. Rather than accepting every monthly list, the bureau chose to obtain the lists on an as-needed basis. To facilitate the bureau's use of these files and obviate the need for a casing check in zip codes with city-style mailing addresses, the USPS undertook two special efforts to ensure that its local post offices reported address updates on a timely basis.

In addition to adding the Delivery Sequence File addresses to the MAF, the bureau matched this file against the street name and address range information in the *TIGER* database. Geographic staff in the bureau's twelve regional offices—and, after their establishment from December 1997 to April 1998, the census-related regional census centers—investigated unmatched cases by obtaining and reviewing reference materials in the office and visiting areas to resolve residual unmatched address ranges. It also offered to have local governments resolve unmatched cases by providing them with *TIGER*-derived maps and lists of address ranges (the *TIGER* Improvement Program). To ensure the completeness and accuracy of the addresses and their geo-coding within the blue line—the mail-out, mail-back areas—the bureau had field staff check the addresses in a precanvass-like operation now called "block canvassing."

In all but the most sparsely settled areas of the nation, and including Puerto Rico, the bureau listed and map-spotted addresses outside the blue line. All the addresses were keyed into the MAF, and the map spots and numbers also were inserted into the *TIGER* database. As a result, the bureau could print maps that showed the location of each residential structure—extremely useful when the map spots were referenced in later operations.

In recent years, many government agencies and commercial sources created and maintained computer-based map files, which include roads and streets, their names, address ranges (where applicable), and zip codes. The Geography Division identified and, where acceptable, obtained such digital exchange files to compare with and improve the information in the *TIGER* database.

With Public Law 103-430 requiring the bureau to let local and tribal government officials look at its addresses, it established an address list review program called Local Update of Census Addresses (LUCA). This program allowed those officials who had sworn to maintain the confidentiality of the addresses to review the completeness of the address list for their jurisdictions. At the same time, they could update the maps. In areas within the blue line, they were asked to identify missing addresses; outside, they were asked to identify blocks with incorrect housing unit counts. In both cases, the bureau followed up with field checks, and then updated its database and the MAF with its findings.

In order to ensure that it had current address and street information on census day, the bureau initiated the New Construction program, which asked local and tribal governments whose jurisdictions were within the blue line to inform the bureau of any new housing units built between the bureau's last update of their address information and April 1, 2000. Outside the blue line, census enumerators canvassed every block, generally beginning in mid-March 2000, to ensure the completeness of the address list and maps as they delivered a questionnaire to or enumerated each housing unit. Again, all updates of addresses and maps, including map spots, were carried to the database and the MAF.

As a result of improvements to its mapping capabilities, the bureau could create a variety of maps, at an appropriate size and scale, reflecting updates from previous operations, for every field and local input operation. Furthermore, these maps could now be printed at the regional census centers and the local census offices, on an as-needed basis. The same mapping capabilities enabled the bureau to print maps needed to accompany the data, and also to make available to data users the ability to print their own maps from an extract of the *TIGER* database.

For Census 2000 every geographic entity for which the bureau tabulated data is represented by one or more census blocks. With every residential address in the MAF assigned to its census block in the *TIGER* database, the bureau can allocate each response from a housing unit, group quarters resident, and other special populations to its census block, which in turn can be related to the higher-level geography associated with that block, in order to tabulate the data for Census 2000.

See also *Enumeration: field procedures; Geography: distribution of the population; Tabulation geography.*

■ Donald Hirschfeld

Bibliography

U.S. Bureau of the Census. *1963 Economic Censuses: Procedural History.* Washington, D.C.: U.S. Government Printing Office, 1968.

———. *1970 Census of Population and Housing: Procedural History.* PHC(R)-1. Washington, D.C.: U.S. Government Printing Office, 1976.

———. *1980 Census of Population and Housing: History.* PHC80-R-2. Washington, D.C.: U.S. Government Printing Office, 1986–1989.

———. *1990 Census of Population and Housing: History.* 1990 CPH-R-2. Washington, D.C.: U.S. Government Printing Office, 1993–1996.

———. *2000 Census of Population and Housing: History.* Washington, D.C.: U.S. Government Printing Office, forthcoming.

Advertising and the census

The census outreach and promotional campaign is designed to raise public awareness of the count and to encourage prompt and voluntary participation. The Census Bureau organizes a partnership program with state and local government and voluntary organizations, the private sector, and schools. It develops media materials to promote the census and conducts a direct mail campaign consisting of an advance letter, questionnaire, and reminder card sent to all households; it also organizes media events and special programs to raise public awareness. The 2000 census added a new feature to these activities and employed a paid advertising campaign, budgeted at $167 million, to promote census awareness and participation. The campaign was designed to expose each American to an average of three dozen advertisements for the census before April 2000. Hard-to-count populations were targeted for special advertising and were to be exposed to up to 100 ads by April 2000.

From 1950 to 1990 the bureau worked with the Advertising Council to produce radio and television commercials and print material to advertise the census. The advertising campaign also generated billboards, buttons, coffee mugs, signs, posters, brochures, pencils, and other memorabilia. An official logo was designed. During the 1990s the World Wide Web became an important advertising venue.

The advertising campaign has become increasingly elaborate and important to the overall design of the census plan since 1970, when the mail census first required residents to recognize and fill out a census form voluntarily and promptly. Before the development of the mail census in 1970, the enumerators who went door-to-door bore the primary burden of explaining the process to household heads as they recorded the information. Since 1970 the mail census method has presumed that Americans are already aware of the census and are prepared to fill out the form when it arrives in the mail and, furthermore, that they know how to fill it out and send it in. At the household level, there are few incentives to fill out the form promptly and completely. Respondents receive little immediate direct benefit when they fill out the form, and the penalty for not filling it out is rarely invoked.

Householders can easily lose the form in piles of junk mail, or they may hesitate to fill it out because they are suspicious of the government's request for the information. The ad campaign is designed to educate and encourage participation.

Response rates to the mail census declined from the 1970 level of 78 percent to 65 percent in 1990, and Congress provided funding for advertising in the hope of reversing that slide for 2000. The advertising campaign for the 1970 census was the first to target ads to hard-to-count populations and minorities, and each decade such targeted advertising has increased. Before the 1980 census the bureau considered asking Congress for a $40 million appropriation for a paid advertising campaign but decided that it would continue working with the Advertising Council. Ogilvy and Mather served as the lead agency working on the campaign in 1980, which was considered a success. The bureau renewed its relationship with the Advertising Council and Ogilvy and Mather and related agencies in 1990, but the campaign was considered less successful than in 1980. In 2000 Young and Rubicam, the main advertising firm in charge of the campaign, worked with four additional advertising firms that specialize in advertising for Hispanic, African American, African and Caribbean, Asian, American Indian, and recent immigrant groups. The campaign ran from October 1999 to the spring of 2000 and included high-profile advertising, such as spots during the Super Bowl.

In earlier censuses, public service ads were donated by the advertising industry and were displayed and broadcast as time and space permitted. The 2000 census advertising campaign was designed to guarantee coverage and to make an explicit claim for civic participation in the census. Advertisements described the benefits to local communities of good census data, the mechanics of the count, and how to fill out the form.

From mid-March to mid-April 2000, after the census forms had been mailed to all residential addresses, the Census Bureau used its Web site to publish daily reports of response rates for states and all local jurisdictions in the country. The bureau designed the advertising campaign to generate a 5 percent increase in the 61 percent national response rate initially expected. The bureau also set targets for local areas to increase their response rates from those in 1990; it listed those targets on the Web site, in the hope that competition between areas would be "news" and encourage local leaders to promote response.

It is too soon to tell if the 2000 census advertising campaign contributed to dramatically transformed public perceptions of the census. The increased visibility of the census may also lead to unforeseen consequences. In early spring 2000, radio talk shows introduced extensive discussion of the count with a different message from the one the Census Bureau was promulgating. The talk show coverage spilled over into the print and TV national electronic media in March and April of 2000. It questioned why, if the census was mandated in the Constitution to provide a simple count of the population for political apportionment and legislative redistricting, householders had to provide additional detailed answers to the questions on the long form. These additional questions were challenged as an invasion of privacy, and many callers claimed they would not answer them. The response rate to the census reached 65 percent as of April 19, 2000.

■ Margo Anderson

Bibliography

Bryant, Barbara Everitt, and William Dunn. *Moving Power and Money: The Politics of Census Taking.* Ithaca, N.Y.: New Strategist Publications, 1995.

U.S. Bureau of the Census. "The Census Promotion Program." *1980 Census of Population and Housing: History, Part B.* PHC80-R-2B. Washington, D.C.: U.S. Government Printing Office, 1986.

———. "The Census Promotional Program." *1990 Census of Population and Housing: History, Part B.* 1990 CPH-R-2B. Washington, D.C.: U.S. Government Printing Office, 1995.

———. "The Public Information Program." *1970 Census of Population and Housing: Procedural History.* PHC(R)-1. Washington, D.C.: U.S. Government Printing Office, 1976.

Advisory committees

Advisory committees provide input to planning and evaluation of the decennial census from groups of people not directly employed by the Census Bureau who are chosen for their particular expertise or perspective and who serve on a volunteer basis. Since 1973, all advisory committees appointed by the executive branch have operated under the 1972 Federal Advisory Committee Act (FACA), which provides for open deliberations and advance notice of meetings in the *Federal Register.*

For the 2000 census, advisory groups were formed that report to the Secretary of Commerce and to the U.S. Congress, in addition to groups that report to the Census Bureau. Also, as in past censuses, input was provided by committees or groups responsible to private organizations. Examples from recent censuses include the continuing Committee on Population Statistics of the Population Association of America, first established in 1956; several committees appointed by the American Institute of Planners to review plans for information systems and data series for the 1960 and

1970 censuses; and an ad hoc Technical Panel on the Census Undercount appointed by the American Statistical Association in 1982.

Early Advisory Efforts

Outside experts were first used to advise on census planning in 1849 at the behest of Joseph Kennedy, secretary of a newly created Census Board, consisting of the secretary of state, the attorney general, and the postmaster general, that was charged to draft legislation for the 1850 census. Kennedy invited Lemuel Shattuck of the American Statistical Association and Archibald Russell of the American Geographical and Statistical Society to Washington to help draw up the schedules for the census (the forms for obtaining data items), hitherto a function undertaken entirely by Congress. They recommended that the census schedules be expanded and restructured to collect data for each individual instead of summaries for each household. Also, they recommended that different schedules be developed for different elements of the census, such as free persons, slaves, people who had died in the preceding year, agriculture, manufacturing, and other "social" statistics (e.g., information on schools, libraries, crime, religion). After extensive debate, Congress adopted most of the recommendations.

In November 1918 the first continuing formal advisory committee was appointed for the census: the Census Advisory Committee of the American Statistical Association (ASA) and the American Economic Association (AEA). It consisted of people who had worked on the census and on obtaining statistics needed for mobilization of the economy for World War I. It continued as a joint ASA-AEA committee until 1937 and as an ASA committee subsequently.

During the early years of the joint committee, committee members contributed substantially to policy making for the census: they developed the form and content of census schedules, set priorities for special census studies, analyzed census data, and testified before Congress. For example, during a period of intense controversy over restricting foreign immigration in the 1920s, the Census Advisory Committee helped commission a study by the American Council of Learned Societies to revise key census estimates of the national origins of the population. The committee also participated in a debate on whether to conduct a second census in 1931 to measure unemployment, for which the 1930 census statistics were believed to be inadequate. Such a census was not conducted, but in 1937 Congress authorized voluntary registration of the unemployed, obtained by having postal carriers deliver forms to all residential addresses for unemployed workers to fill out and mail back. Later in 1937, at the behest of professional statisticians, postal carriers enumerated a 2 percent sample of households to ask about unemployment. The sample survey produced a 40 percent higher estimate of unemployed workers than did the voluntary registration.

Also providing considerable oversight and review of census issues during the early 1930s was the Committee on Government Statistics and Information Services (COGSIS), established by ASA and the Social Science Research Council. Meeting from 1933 to 1935, COGSIS helped promote professionalization of the Census Bureau's staffing, the introduction of new sampling methods for censuses and surveys, and the development of research and experimentation capabilities within the Census Bureau. The first chair of COGSIS, Stuart Rice, then president of ASA, became assistant director of the Census Bureau to help spearhead these changes.

Professional Advisory Committees

Since 1940 the advisory committee structure for obtaining outside professional review of census plans and results has expanded from the original joint ASA-AEA Census Advisory Committee. In 1946, a Census Advisory Committee of the American Marketing Association was established to review publicity and outreach plans for the census and data products for the user community. In 1960, a Census Advisory Committee of the American Economic Association was established to reforge a formal link with economists, who had not been represented on the ASA Census Advisory Committee after 1937. A Census Advisory Committee on Population Statistics was established in 1965, subsequently renamed the Census Advisory Committee of the Population Association of America. Over time, steps were taken to integrate the work of these four advisory committees (AEA, AMA, ASA, and PAA); currently, they meet as a single Census Advisory Committee of Professional Associations with four subcommittees.

Other census advisory committees for specific areas have included the Census Advisory Committee on Privacy and Confidentiality, which met from 1972 to 1975, and the Census Advisory Committee on State and Local Area Statistics, which operated from 1964 to

1976. (These committees were disbanded as part of a government-wide effort to reduce the number of public advisory committees.)

Another professional advisory committee of note was appointed by the Secretary of Commerce in 1989 pursuant to an agreement between the parties in a lawsuit challenging the Commerce Department's 1987 decision that a post-enumeration survey would not be used to adjust the 1990 census counts for population undercoverage. The Special Advisory Panel consisted of eight members, four appointed from a list of experts recommended by the plaintiffs (New York City and other local governments and citizen groups) and four from a list developed by the Commerce Department. The panel was to advise on adjustment-related issues. The four members appointed by the plaintiffs issued a report that supported statistical adjustment; the other four members issued a contrary report. Although the Census Bureau Director recommended adjustment, the Secretary of Commerce ultimately decided not to adjust the 1990 census counts.

Minority Advisory Committees

The Census Bureau first established formal advisory committees for the 1980 census to advise on ways to reach minority groups and improve coverage for them. Beginning with informal discussions in 1971, by 1976 three Census Advisory Committees were chartered for the African-American, Asian and Pacific Islander, and Hispanic communities. (The Asian and Pacific Islander Committee was subsequently renamed the Asian, Native Hawaiian, and Other Pacific Islander Committee.) The American Indian and Alaska Native communities decided not to have a formal advisory group; instead, the Census Bureau held a series of regional meetings with these groups to explain the census plans and request input for improving the count. The three minority advisory committees met from 1975 to 1981. They were reconstituted in 1985 and a fourth committee was added for the American Indian and Alaska Native populations at that time.

National Academy of Sciences Review Panels

In addition to standing advisory committees, committees and panels of experts convened by the National Academy of Sciences/National Research Council (NAS/NRC) have reviewed census methods and results and have made recommendations for future censuses.

The NAS is an independent, nonprofit honorific membership organization, chartered by Congress in 1863 to provide scientific advice to the government upon request. The NRC, established by presidential executive order in 1916 to involve the broader scientific community in advisory studies, is the principal operating arm of the NAS. Experts appointed to serve on NAS/NRC study committees serve as volunteers; government agencies requesting studies by the NAS/NRC pay for committee members' travel and staff costs. Since 1997, NAS/NRC committees have operated under an amendment to the Federal Advisory Committee Act, which provides for fully open meetings when committees are gathering information but permits closed meetings to deliberate on recommendations and to draft report text.

The first involvement of the NAS/NRC with census issues concerned the formula used to reapportion the U.S. House of Representatives on the basis of census counts for each state. The Speaker of the House asked the NAS/NRC in 1928 to advise on the relative merits of two different methods of apportionment to help in framing a reapportionment bill. (For the only time in U.S. history, the Congress did not reapportion the House of Representatives after the 1920 census.) The NAS committee recommended a method of "equal proportions" (known as Hill's method), but legislation passed in 1929 continued the method of "major fractions" (known as Webster's or Willcox's method) that was used for reapportionment after the 1910 census. The reapportionment method was changed to Hill's method following the 1940 census (largely because that method would result in one more seat for the Democratic majority). Reapportionment scholars have criticized the NAS arguments supporting Hill's method.

The NAS/NRC was not asked to consider census issues again until 1969, when it convened a Committee on Problems of Census Enumeration at the request of the Census Bureau, the U.S. Office of Economic Opportunity, and the Manpower Administration of the U.S. Labor Department. The committee was charged to provide advice on ways to improve coverage of the population in the census and household surveys. Research dating back to the 1940s had documented that the census did not count everyone and that it disproportionately missed minorities, men, and people in younger age groups. In the 1960s interest in coverage problems increased due to the growing importance of census and household survey data for civil rights enforcement (including equal representation under the

Voting Rights Act of 1965), allocation of federal funds to states and localities, the documentation of conditions in cities, and related uses.

The Committee on Problems of Census Enumeration focused on ways to understand, measure, and reduce undercoverage in the census and surveys. Its 1972 report, "America's Uncounted People," also recommended research on methods to adjust small-area census counts to account for coverage errors.

In 1977 the Census Bureau asked the Committee on National Statistics (CNSTAT, a standing NAS/NRC committee, established in 1972) to convene a panel to review the design and procedures for the 1980 census. The Panel on Decennial Census Plans, chaired by demographer Nathan Keyfitz of Harvard University, was charged to examine census coverage improvement plans; review proposed procedures for handling contested census counts; investigate the feasibility and implications of adjusting census counts, and subsequent population estimates, for undercoverage; and review the evaluations planned for the 1980 census.

This panel was the first to recommend not only research about undercoverage, but also adjustment of the census counts for coverage errors for some purposes. In its 1978 report, "Counting the People in 1980: An Appraisal of Census Plans," the panel concluded that it would be feasible and desirable to adjust the population totals for states and local areas for the purpose of allocating federal funds.

Subsequently, the Census Bureau requested a series of CNSTAT panels on the census. These panels were asked not only to address issues of coverage and possible adjustment for coverage errors, but also to consider methods that could potentially improve the accuracy and reduce the costs of census operations. (Such methods included sampling for follow-up of households that did not mail back a questionnaire and the use of administrative records to obtain census data.) These panels were the following:

- Panel on Decennial Census Methodology: 1984–1985, extended through 1988; chaired by John Pratt, Harvard Business School, and, later, Benjamin King, Florida Atlantic University; report issued 1985, "The Bicentennial Census: New Directions for Methodology in 1990."
- Panel to Evaluate Alternative Census Methods: 1992–1994; chaired by Norman Bradburn, University of Chicago; report issued 1994, "Counting People in the Information Age."

- Panel on Census Requirements in the Year 2000 and Beyond: 1992-1994; chaired by Charles Schultze, Brookings Institution; mandated by Congress in the Decennial Census Improvement Act of 1991; report issued 1995, "Modernizing the U.S. Census."
- Panel on Alternative Census Methodologies: 1996-1999; chaired by Keith Rust, Westat, Inc.; report issued 1999, "Measuring a Changing Nation-Modern Methods for the 2000 Census."

While these panels differed in aspects of their scope and focus, several common threads characterized their reports. They generally concurred on the following points: the potential for using statistical methods (specifically, dual-system estimation based on matching responses from a coverage evaluation survey to the census) to adjust census counts in order to make the data more accurate for many purposes; the high costs and errors introduced by trying to achieve more complete coverage through special field operations; the potential cost-effectiveness from using sampling in field operations; the difficulties of using administrative records for the census; and the need for more research and data collection to inform planning and testing of methods for future censuses (e.g., tracking a sample of housing units through the census process).

Currently, there are two CNSTAT panels that are studying census issues: the Panel to Review the 2000 Census, chaired by Janet Norwood, former commissioner of the U.S. Bureau of Labor Statistics; and the Panel on Research on Future Census Methods, chaired by Benjamin King, which is looking ahead to the 2010 census.

Advisory Committees for 2000

An elaborate structure of advisory committees was established for the 2000 census because of concerns about rising census costs and the perceived high stakes for Congress over the issue of whether to use statistical techniques to adjust the census results for population undercount. The Census Bureau's own advisory structure, consisting of the Census Advisory Committee of Professional Associations, with members nominated by the AEA, AMA, ASA, and PAA, and the Minority Advisory Committees, continued from the past. The Census Bureau also asked the NAS Committee on National Statistics to convene a Panel to Review the 2000 Census (see above).

The U.S. Department of Commerce set up an advisory structure for 2000 as well. The Department's Inspector General carried out several studies of census plans. In addition in late 1991, the Secretary of Commerce appointed a 2000 Census Advisory Committee with representatives from a wide range of organizations representing private-sector users; minority groups; professional associations; state, local, and tribal governments; and others. (Just some of the organizations represented are the American Civil Liberties Union, American Legion, American Sociological Association, Association of Public Data Users, Business Roundtable, Council of Chief State School Officers, Mexican American Legal Defense and Education Fund, National Association of Counties, and the National Governors' Association.) The committee also includes ex-officio, nonvoting members, including representatives of the congressional committees that handle oversight and appropriations for the census. The Secretary's committee has met several times a year since it was first chartered and has reviewed and made recommendations on all aspects of census planning.

Finally, in addition to continuing its practice in past censuses of holding frequent oversight hearings and periodically asking the U.S. General Accounting Office to study census plans and budget proposals for 2000, Congress also established a 2000 Census Monitoring Board. The provision for the Monitoring Board was part of legislation passed in fall 1997 that represented a compromise between Congress and the Clinton administration on census issues. (The legislation called for the Census Bureau to plan a census both with and without sampling for nonresponse follow-up and coverage adjustment and provided for expedited judicial review of the constitutionality of using sampling to produce census counts for congressional reapportionment.) The Monitoring Board consists of eight members, four appointed by House and Senate Republican leaders and four by the president in consultation with House and Senate Democratic leaders. The congressional and presidential appointees each have their own budgets and staffs and are charged to issue periodic reports to Congress on the progress of the census through fall 2001.

See also *Apportionment and districting; Congress and the census; Content determination; Coverage evaluation; Sampling in the census; Statistical policy and oversight.*

■ Constance F. Citro

Bibliography

Anderson, Margo J. *The American Census: A Social History.* New Haven: Yale University Press, 1988.

Anderson, Margo J., and Stephen E. Fienberg. *Who Counts? The Politics of Census-Taking in Contemporary America.* New York: Russell Sage Foundation, 1999.

Bureau of the Census. *1970 Census of Population and Housing Procedural History.* Washington, D.C.: U.S. Department of Commerce, 1976.

Bureau of the Census. *1990 Census of Population and Housing History.* Part B, Chapter 2, Planning the Census. Washington, D.C.: U.S. Department of Commerce, 1995.

Goldfield, Edwin D. *Review of Studies of the Decennial Census of Population and Housing: 1969-1992.* Paper prepared for the Panel on Census Requirements in the Year 2000 and Beyond, Committee on National Statistics, National Research Council, Washington, D.C., 1992.

African-origin population

Blacks or African Americans (the terms are used interchangeably here) have been in America since the founding of the colonies. The first Africans (about twenty) came to Virginia in 1619 as indentured servants. However, emigrant Africans arriving as indentured servants quickly gave way to imported Africans arriving as slaves. While the importation of slaves was banned by 1808, slavery continued on through the Civil War, finally ending with the enactment of the Thirteenth Amendment to the Constitution on December 18, 1865.

Slaves were brought to the American colonies primarily to work in the fields of southern farmers. In 1649 there were 300 black slaves in the Virginia colony; by 1671 there were 2,000. In 1700 the slave population of the American colonies was estimated at 28,000, with 23,000 residing in the South. In 1750 there were 236,000 black slaves in the American colonies, and 87 percent of those lived in the South. At this time blacks composed about 20 percent of the population of the colonies, though they accounted for fully 40 percent of the population of Virginia.

The slave labor system in America stood in stark conflict with the ideals of freedom and equality proclaimed by the colonists and provoked great controversy. The presence of a large number of racially distinct people held in bondage created economic, social, and military problems, and many white Americans wanted to rid the country of both the "peculiar institution" of slavery and slaves themselves. Slavery in the United States forced ideological debates about whether slaves should be returned to Africa or integrated into American life as free persons. The uncertainty over what to do with slaves and free blacks is reflected in the Constitution. For example, Article I, Section 2 apportioned representation and taxation using a formula that counted the slave population as three-fifths of the free population. It also required the decennial census to collect population information distinguishing the slave and the free population.

In 1790, when the first census of the United States was conducted, there were 757,000 blacks in the United States, representing about 19 percent of the total population. At no other time in the history of the United States has the black population approached this percentage. In 1790, 60,000 blacks (9 percent) were "free persons of color." The terms used in the decennial censuses to categorize the African American population have changed at almost each census. Census 2000 and its questions on race continued this pattern of change.

1790 to 1860

The censuses from 1790 to 1840 were household censuses: only the names of household heads appeared on the schedule. Data on race or color were collected based on the observation of enumerators, who were assistants to United States Marshals. In 1790, the enumerators asked six questions, including the name of the head of the family and the number of persons in each household of the following descriptions: free white males of sixteen years and upward, free white males under sixteen years, free white females, all other free persons, and slaves.

In 1850, the Census Bureau began to use a schedule that separately identified each person. Officials created two separate forms, one for free persons and one for slaves. The enumerators listed each free individual by name and under the heading of "Color" identified him or her as "White," "Black," or "Mulatto." Slaves were listed by number and categorized as black or mulatto.

From 1790 to 1860 the black population grew from 757,000 to 4.4 million. In 1860, blacks represented 14 percent of the total population. One in ten African Americans was free in 1860. In 1790 four states (Maryland, North Carolina, South Carolina, and Virginia) contained 87 percent of the slave population; by 1860 this proportion had declined to 33 percent.

1870 to 1920

After the Civil War, the decennial census continued to collect data on the African American population. A column headed "Color" was used consistently. Beginning with the 1850 census, enumerators were provided specific instructions on how to fill in the "Color" column, and attempts were made to differentiate the black population into full-blooded blacks and mulattoes. Enumerators in 1870, for example, were cautioned to "be particularly careful in reporting the class mulatto," including "all persons having any perceptible trace of African blood."

The term "Race" was added to the column in the 1890 census, and additional instructions were provided to the enumerators to categorize "black." The 1890 census was the first to categorize the African American population by blood quantum. Instructions were given to enumerators specifying the appropriate classification of "black" (those who had three-fourths or more black blood), "mulatto" (those who had three-eighths to five-eighths black blood), "quadroon" (those who had one-fourth black blood), and "octoroon" (those who had one-eighth or any trace of black blood).

The 1900 census was the first in which the category "Negro or of Negro descent" appeared. Enumerators indicated the race of the respondent as black if he or she was a Negro or of Negro descent. The category "Mulatto" was dropped in 1900, but reintroduced in 1910 and used again in 1920. In the 1910 and 1920 censuses, the heading "Color or Race" continued to be used on the schedules to capture data on race.

The African American population grew from 4.9 million in 1870 to 10.5 million in 1920. Blacks composed about 13 percent of the total U.S. population in 1870; by 1920 this proportion had declined to about 10 percent. The country continued to be composed primarily of individuals of African and/or European descent. Native Americans and people of other races composed less than 5 percent of the total population in the United States.

1920 to 1960

The African American population of the United States became more diverse by residence and origin in the twentieth century. In the early years of the century, blacks began to leave the South for other regions. Blacks from Jamaica, Barbados, and Trinidad began to move to America in small numbers, though restrictive immigration laws in the 1920s halted this trend.

The categories used by the Census Bureau to collect information on the race of the population from 1930 to 1960 continued to be listed in the column "Color or Race." However, changes were made in the categorization of the population. In 1930 the mulatto category was eliminated and the "one drop rule" or hypo-descent rule was used to categorize the black population by race. Enumerators were instructed to record "a person of mixed White and Negro blood as a Negro, no matter how small the percentage of Negro blood." Respondents who were part American Indian and part African American were recorded as Negro unless the American Indian blood predominated and the person was accepted as such in the American Indian community.

In the 1940 and 1950 censuses "Negro" was the term used on the census form to refer to the black population. It was also used in the 1960 census, though the question format was changed. Prior to 1960 self-enumeration had been used on a very limited scale; with the 1960 census, however, it became a major aspect of the decennial census. As a result of the use of self-identification, the format of the question on race changed. The question on race asked, "Is this person White, Negro, American Indian, Japanese, Chinese, Filipino, Hawaiian, Part Hawaiian, Aleut, Eskimo, (etc.)?"

The definition of "Negro" in the 1960 census was similar to that used in the 1930 census. Individuals of mixed African and European descent were considered Negro, and those of mixed African and American Indian descent were also considered Negro unless they were recognized as American Indian by that community. People of mixed racial parentage were classified according to the race of the "nonwhite" parent, and mixtures of nonwhite races were classified according to the race of the father.

The African American population grew from 11.9 million in 1930 to 18.9 million in 1960. According to the 1960 census, blacks represented about 10.5 percent of the total U.S. population, up from 9.7 percent in 1930. The majority of the growth in the black population was attributable to natural increase (births minus deaths).

1970 to 1990

For the 1970 census, about 60 percent of U.S. households (mostly urban) received a questionnaire in the mail, which they were to complete and return. In the remaining areas the data were collected by enumerators. When a respondent failed to return a questionnaire, data on race were obtained by an enumerator who showed the respondent a flashcard from which to choose the appropriate race. During personal visits and telephone interviews, enumerators asked respondents, "What is ——'s race?" In such cases, the respondent's race was assumed for all other related members of the household unless the enumerator learned otherwise. Data collected by self-identification were thought to be of higher quality than that obtained through enumerator observation.

The 1970 census question on race contained language that had been used in the past, and the racial categories were only slightly modified. The wording of the category "Negro" was changed to "Negro or Black" after a review of responses to the "Color or Race" item in several 1970 census pretests and after consultation with a number of national and regional organizations and individuals concerned with race relations in the United States. The term "Afro-American" was also considered, but was found to be less widely used than "Black."

The 1980 census employed self-enumeration to collect racial data. Unlike the previous census, the heading "Color or Race" was not used. The definition of the race groups was expanded to comply with the Office of Management and Budget's (OMB) standards for federal data on racial and ethnic populations. In 1977 the OMB issued standards that all federal agencies were to use to collect, tabulate, and present data on race. These standards identified four race groups: White, Black, American Indian or Alaskan Native, and Asian or Pacific Islander. The directive also stated that additional race groups could be used to collect data if the additional groups could be collapsed back into the four minimum race groups.

For census purposes, the category "Black" included respondents who indicated their race as black or Negro, as well as respondents who did not classify themselves in one of the specified race categories on the questionnaire but wrote in entries such as Black Jamaican, Black Puerto Rican, Black West Indian, Black Haitian, or Black Nigerian.

The 1990 census question on race, much like the 1980 question, included a number of sociocultural (or national origin) groups. It also included the heading "Race," and the instructions were improved to make the intent of the question clearer. The response category for blacks changed from "Negro or Black" to

"Black or Negro" to reflect the increased use of the term black and the diminished use of the term Negro.

The African American population grew from 22 million in 1970 to 30 million in 1990. (The estimated undercount of the black population in the 1990 census was 4.4 percent.) Blacks composed about 12 percent of the total population, up from 11 percent in 1970. Changes in immigration laws allowed more immigrants to come from the African continent. Immigration also increased from the Caribbean and the West Indies. However, the growth of the black population was still due mainly to natural increase.

Between 1970 and 1980 migration patterns of blacks changed. During the 1940s, 1950s, and 1960s, millions of blacks left the South. After 1970, however, the trend reversed as more blacks stayed in the South and others returned to the South. By 1990 a majority of all blacks still lived in the southern region of the United States.

Census 2000

After the 1990 census, OMB conducted a review of the statistical standards used to collect and tabulate federal data on race and ethnicity in response to criticism that the standards no longer accurately reflected the racial and ethnic diversity of the country. Children of interracial unions and their parents criticized standards that forced them to identify with only one race category. Others suggested that changes be made to the particular race categories identified in the standards. Some groups even questioned the need of the federal government to collect and tabulate data on race, stating that doing so promoted racism.

A number of significant innovations in the question on race appeared on Census 2000, including changes in the formatting and terminology of the question. Most notably, respondents were able to report themselves in one or more categories of race. These changes were the result of an extensive research and consultation process that began with an international conference convened by the Census Bureau and Statistics Canada in 1992, congressional hearings held in 1992 and 1993, and the OMB review of the statistical standards used by all federal agencies to collect, tabulate, and present data on race and ethnicity that began in 1993.

The question on race for Census 2000, much like the question on race in previous censuses, was asked of all respondents. It included fifteen response categories:

White; Black, African Am., or Negro; American Indian or Alaska Native; Asian Indian; Chinese; Filipino; Japanese; Korean; Vietnamese; Other Asian; Native Hawaiian; Guamanian or Chamorro; Samoan; Other Pacific Islander; and Some other race. Respondents who marked the "American Indian or Alaska Native" category were asked to provide the name of their enrolled or principal tribe. People who reported "Other Asian," "Other Pacific Islander," or "Some other race" were also asked to write in their race.

Changes were made to the black response category on the race question as a result of consultation with community and national organizations. During the latter part of the 1980s, some members of the African American community suggested that the response category be changed to reflect the increased use of the term African American. Others suggested that "African American" be used alongside "Black," and that "Negro" be dropped altogether. These suggestions came too late to be effectively tested and implemented in the 1990 census. However, after extensive research, "Black, African Am., or Negro" became the response category for blacks for Census 2000.

The U.S. government has collected data on the black population since it began its census-taking activities in 1790. Over time the terminology for the response categories has changed considerably, from "free person" or "slave" to "Black," "Mulatto," "Quadroon," or "Octoroon" to "Negro" to "Black or Negro" to "Black, African Am., or Negro." The African American population grew from less than one million in 1790 to nearly 30 million in 1990. Unlike many other groups in this country, immigration has not been a major factor in the growth of the black population. Historically, about 85 percent to 90 percent of the growth in the black population since its inception in the United States has been due to natural increase. The censuses of years past have permitted the black population to identify with only one race group, albeit with some attempts to differentiate between full-blooded and mixed-blood descent. The Census 2000 option that allowed respondents to mark one or more racial group more clearly permitted blacks, as well as other racial groups, to identify their mixed racial heritage.

See also *Appendix, Standards for the Classification of Federal Data on Race and Ethnicity; Race: questions and classifications.*

■ Claudette Bennett

Bibliography

Bureau of the Census. Historical Statistics of the United States, Colonial Times to 1970. Bicentennial ed., Part 2. Washington, D.C.: Government Printing Office, 1975.

———. Negro Population 1790–1915. Washington, D.C.: Government Printing Office, 1918.

———. The Social and Economic Status of the Black Population in the United States, 1790–1978. P23, No. 80. Washington, D.C.: Government Printing Office, 1980.

Joint Center for Political and Economic Studies. Annual Report. Washington, D.C.: Joint Center for Political and Economic Studies, 1992.

Lavraska, Paul, et al. "The Use and Perception of Ethno-Racial Labels: 'African American' and/or 'Black.'" Paper presented at the Bureau of the Census Annual Research Conference and CASIC Technologies Interchange, Arlington, Va., March 20–23, 1994.

Ploski, Harry A., and James Williams. The Negro Almanac: A Reference Work on the African American. 5th ed. Detroit: Gale Research Inc., 1989.

Age questions in the census

Since its beginnings in 1790, the decennial census has gathered information on age and as such has served for over 200 years as a basic source of information on the age structure and changing distribution of ages in the U.S. population. The first census recorded the numbers of free white males under age sixteen years and those age sixteen years and over. Congress limited age categories to white men because it was interested in assessing the number of them who were able to work and eligible for military service. The 1800 and 1810 censuses expanded the age information collected for white men and also white women: these two censuses counted the number of free white women and men under age ten years; those age ten to under sixteen years; those age sixteen to under twenty-six years, including heads of families; those age twenty-six years to under forty-five years, including heads of families; and those forty-five years and over, including heads of families. Between 1820 and 1840, these age categories were expanded to thirteen different age groups, which signified an increased awareness that the U.S. population was aging. The 1820, 1830, and 1840 censuses also counted the number of free "colored" persons and slaves for a number of age categories. Starting in 1850, the census recorded the characteristics, including age, of individuals living in each household. Date of birth was not permanently added to the census schedule until 1960 (although it was included in the 1900 census).

In Census 2000, respondents were asked the following question for every household member: "What is this person's age and what is this person's date of birth? Print numbers in boxes. Age on April 1, 2000. Month, Day, Year of Birth." This question was asked in two parts to ensure that ages were reported accurately. Demographers have long been aware that people have a tendency to round their ages to a number ending in five or zero in response to a single question on age, a phenomenon known as *age heaping*. Thus the question on date of birth provides a second piece of information to use in evaluating the answer to the question on age.

Data can be analyzed by any designated age categories, for example, data on income can be analyzed to examine the degree to which income levels vary by age. Data users also combine the answers to census questions to create age cohorts or average patterns by age. Current census data on age composition is useful because it can be aggregated in any cohorts of interest, to describe the patterns of living for a wide variety of groups, for example, children, teenagers, young adults, the middle aged, the elderly, the young old, the oldest old, to name just a few currently used cohorts. Alternatively, characteristics of the population can be described by a single point estimate based on age, for example, a mean age at marriage or the median age of the population.

Many federal agencies, including the Departments of Commerce, Education, Labor, and Justice, use decennial census information on age. Numerous federal statutes require the Census Bureau to collect information on age in order to implement and evaluate social programs. Community planners at both the state and local levels also use census data, broken down by age, to evaluate future needs for child care, education, and employment. At all levels of government, this information is used for equal opportunity purposes specified by the Age Discrimination and Employment Act and the Older Americans Act.

Over the course of U.S. history, the age composition of the population has changed dramatically. In 1800 the median age of the population was around sixteen years; now it is around thirty-four years. Life expectancy at birth has increased from about age forty years in 1800 to about age seventy-five years today.

■ Gretchen A. Stiers

Bibliography

U.S. Bureau of the Census. *General Population Characteristics: Part I, United States Summary.* Washington, D.C.: Government Printing Office, 1983.

U.S. Bureau of the Census. *Planning for Census 2000: Questions Planned for Census 2000, Federal Legislative and Program Uses.* Washington, D.C.: Government Printing Office, 1998.

U.S. Bureau of the Census. *Twenty Censuses: Population and Housing Questions, 1790–1980.* Washington, D.C.: Government Printing Office, 1978.

Wright, Carroll D., and William C. Hunt. *The History and Growth of the United States Census.* Washington, D.C., Government Printing Office, 1900.

Agricultural censuses

Censuses of agricultural production have been conducted in the United States at least every ten years since 1840. These censuses, more than any other census efforts, combine demographic and economic information. Detailed information is collected on land use, total production of crops and livestock, value of sales, and farming practices of broadly defined American agricultural operations. Data on farm operation types and each operator's age, race, ethnicity, and sex are also collected. These periodic censuses are the only attempts to collect information from all farms in the United States and provide comprehensive data for all states and counties—data not available from any other source.

Each census of agriculture covers Puerto Rico, Guam, and the U.S. Virgin Islands as well as all fifty states. The Northern Mariana Islands and American Samoa have usually been included also. Farm size, questions, timing, and survey procedures are adapted to local needs in conducting the censuses for these outlying areas. Specific agreements are normally written with the local government for assistance in list preparation, data collection, and other aspects of the census.

In addition to the basic agricultural census data collection from all farms, subsidiary special censuses or surveys have been conducted since 1890 to collect additional information about certain practices or specific economic factors. The regular agricultural census collection serves to identify a current frame for follow-on surveys. The first such collection was the 1890 census of horticulture, which has been repeated seven times, including after the 1997 census of agriculture. Special irrigation surveys were conducted every decade starting in 1910 and have been a feature of each agricultural census since 1984. Other special studies have included censuses of drained lands and surveys of farm mortgage indebtedness, farm workers, hired farm workers, nonfarm income and source, farm energy use, and farm finances. An additional follow-on survey conducted after the 1987 census, and planned to follow the 1997 census, is the Agricultural Economics and Land Ownership Survey, which includes questions addressed to farm landlords as well as the selected farmers. A census of aquaculture was conducted for the first time following the 1997 census.

The Questionnaire

Since agriculture in the United States varies so greatly—from alligator farms to intensive herb-growing operations located in cities to large crop and livestock farms—the agricultural census questionnaire must include many different categories. The basic questionnaire contains about 300 answer cells, but the median number of positive answer cells in the 1997 census of agriculture was only 37. One additional page of detailed production expenditure categories is included for approximately one of every six operations. Sampling rates are adjusted by state and county to ensure a reasonable sample in every county for expanding these sample data.

The first agricultural census, in 1840, was conducted to answer the need for a better understanding of the U.S. economy. In 1838 President Martin Van Buren called for expansion of the 1840 census of population to collect information "in relation to mines, agriculture, commerce, manufactures, and schools." More than 70 percent of the U.S. population was involved in agriculture at the time.

The first agricultural census included 37 questions asked in face-to-face interviews with all people who indicated any agricultural operations on the population census. The agricultural census questionnaires for 1850, 1860, and 1870 included 46, 48, and 52 questions, respectively. The number of questions increased substantially in 1880 (108 questions) and 1890 (255 questions). The 1840 questionnaire collected crop production data but no information on the area from which each crop was harvested, which greatly limited comparison with surveys conducted between censuses. This weakness continued until 1880, although questions were added in 1850 and 1860 to determine if production levels in those years correctly represented a typical production year.

Because of the broad interest in agriculture and the relatively rapid changes in crop acreage, livestock production patterns, and price levels, interest was often expressed in collection of agricultural data more often than every ten years. In 1896 Col. Carroll D. Wright, the commissioner of labor, called for an annual survey of agriculture and manufacturing. In 1909 Congress mandated that the Department of Commerce conduct a mid-decade agricultural census. The 1915 census was not conducted, however, because the country was preparing for World War I. The 1925 census was the first mid-decade census and agricultural censuses have been collected at approximately five-year intervals ever since.

Until 1997 each agriculture census was conducted by the Bureau of the Census, or its predecessor organizations. However, the census staff and officials at the Department of Agriculture (USDA) usually worked in close cooperation. In some cases, individuals transferred from the USDA to take over as statisticians in charge of the agricultural census activities. The USDA helped with the hiring of census enumerators, in cases where the population and agricultural collections were not combined, and USDA staff often assisted in the editing and final review of agricultural census results as well as coverage evaluation studies.

Face-to-face interviews continued to be the way agricultural censuses were conducted until 1950. In that year questionnaires, written in a personal interviewer style, were mailed out ahead of time. Farmers were asked to fill out the questionnaires and hold them for enumerators. This approach was used for most data collection through 1964. In 1969 farmers were asked to mail back the questionnaires for the first time. To ensure returns, the Census Bureau sent out many follow-up mailings. In the 1970s a decision was made to coordinate agricultural census data collection on the same dates as other economic censuses. The shift was accomplished by conducting two four-year censuses in 1978 and 1982. Reference dates since have been for years ending in 2 and 7.

The major difficulty with a mail-out census collection is the development of the original mailing list. Many list sources have been used to create as complete a census mail list as possible, including lists from other government agencies and specialty agriculture association producer lists. However, many small farming operations do not appear on any lists. Coverage evaluation studies have been conducted since 1945, mainly using independent area frame survey results from the

National Agricultural Statistics Service (NASS). In area frame surveys, random sections of land are chosen and the operators of that land are interviewed rather than choosing random addresses from a mail list. Although these studies have shown that coverage of all farm operations has ranged from 85 to 93 percent, the coverage of total agricultural production has always exceeded 95 percent. Therefore, the farms that are missed are generally smaller farms. Follow-up telephone calls to at least large farms from which a response to the census has not been received have been made since the 1969 census. Priority is given to large operations and counties with low response rates to ensure that all counties maintain a response rate that provides quality statistics. For the 1997 census NASS used experienced telephone staffs in their state offices and a computer-assisted data collection instrument to increase the number of follow-up telephone calls. Because response rates for the 1997 census were higher than expected, NASS began telephone calls earlier than originally scheduled and canceled planned third and fourth follow-up mailings.

Definition of Farms

Department of Commerce funding concerns led to announcement of a plan to change the farm definition from $1,000 in sales to $10,000 for the 1997 census of agriculture. That would have reduced the number of "farms" in the United States by 50 percent and removed as many as 80 percent in some states such as West Virginia. Reaction from states and from Congress was immediate and forceful. Funding authority was changed to NASS for fiscal year 1997 and full legislative authority was shifted to the USDA in the Census of Agriculture Act of 1997, signed into law on November 21, 1997. NASS conducted the 1997 census of agriculture but contracted with the Bureau of the Census for sending and receiving mail, data entry, and basic editing. The NASS State Statistical Offices performed detailed editing, follow-up, and analysis steps.

The first agricultural census, in 1840, did not include any definition of a farm; but every collection since, except for that in 1900, has used some definition. Those definitions normally used some dollar value of sales or production. They also often used certain acreage thresholds in order to include agricultural holdings that did not have qualifying production or sales. For example, the definition of a farm used from 1959 to 1974 was any place that had ten or more acres and $50 or more value of agricul-

Figure 1. Percentage of Farms and of Market Values of Agricultural Products Sold: 1997

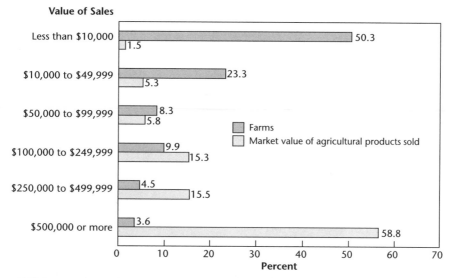

Source: 1997 Census of agriculture, National Agricultural Statistics Service, U.S. Department of Agriculture

Figure 2. Farms by Market Value of Agricultural Products Sold: 1969 to 1997

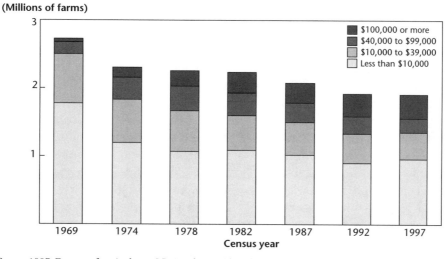

Source: 1997 Census of agriculture, National Agricultural Statistics Service, U.S. Department of Agriculture

tural production or a place of any size with $250 or more value of agricultural production. Since 1978 the farm definition has been any place that had, or normally would have had, $1,000 or more total value of agricultural production. (See Figures 1 and 2.) That definition has often been questioned because of increases in cost-of-living indexes. However, values that farmers receive for their products have varied considerably during that period and have not moved with the level of inflation. The 1998 annual index of prices *received* by farmers compared with the 1975-1984 average was only 114 percent, whereas the 1998 index of prices *paid* by farmers was 169 percent of the corresponding 1975–1984 average.

The census of agriculture has been independent of the census of population since 1950. The population census has retained a question on its long form asking whether each residence is located on a farm. That question provides an estimate of the population living on farms that is not collected by the census of agriculture. The agricultural census focuses only on economic and demographic characteristics of the farm operator; no household or family information is collected.

Availability and Uses of Census Data

Census of agriculture data are available free on the Internet, as well as at Federal Depository Libraries, State Data Centers, and many land grant colleges and universities. Printed publications and CD-ROMs can be purchased. Reports for each of the fifty states include county and state data, whereas the *United States Summary* report includes data for each state with national totals. The CD-ROM includes all data for every county and state and the United States as a whole and provides statistics for three census periods for most data items.

Uses of census of agriculture data are quite varied. State and local government bodies have always used published data for a wide range of analyses. In recent years, many government units have been interested in the data for farm land preservation and taxation issues. Census of agriculture data are also used for research by sociologists, economists, and business analysts. All elected officials are interested in the makeup and economic attributes of their constituents. Special congressional district tabulations and products such as the *Agricultural Atlas of the United States, Zip Code Tabulation of Selected Items*, and the *Rankings of States and Counties* are in high demand.

Results from each agricultural census serve as part of a complete review of all NASS survey and administrative data for the years since the previous census. Thus, the census totals are used not only as a benchmark but also as another indication that must be interpreted in light of any changes in census definitions, response rates, data collection procedures, and so forth. Now that agricultural census and current survey responsibility are vested in the same organization, NASS should be able to use agricultural census information for improving the sampling and conduct of surveys during the period between censuses. In addition, NASS can maximize the value of the entire agricultural census and survey program by streamlining procedures, questionnaires, and data products. This will help reduce the burden on farmers and ranchers who are surveyed and provide unified service and products to all customers of agricultural statistics.

See also *Rural areas.*

■ Rich Allen

Bibliography

Allen, Rich, Vickie J. Huggins, and Ruth Ann Killion. "The Evolution of Agricultural Data Collection in the United States." In *Business Survey Methods*, edited by Brenda G. Cox, David A. Binder, B. Nanjamma Chinnappa, Anders Christianson, Michael J. Colledge, and Phillip S. Kott, 609–631. New York: Wiley, 1995.

Clark, Cynthia Z. F., and Elizabeth A. Vacca. "Ensuring Quality in U.S. Agricultural List Frames." *Proceedings of the International Conference on Establishment Surveys*, 352–361. Alexandria, Va.: American Statistical Association, 1993.

Taylor, Henry C., and Anne D. Taylor. *The Story of Agricultural Economics in the United States, 1840-1932.* Ames, Iowa: Iowa State College Press, 1952.

U.S. Bureau of the Census. *1992 Census of Agriculture-History.* Vol. 2, part 4. Washington, D.C.: U.S. Department of Commerce, 1996.

Wright, Carroll D., and W. C. Hunt (1900). *History and Growth of the U.S. Census: 1790–1890.* Washington, D.C.: U.S. Government Printing Office.

American Community Survey

The American Community Survey, or ACS, is a large ongoing survey to provide detailed information about communities in the United States, based on a sample of addresses whose occupants are interviewed each month. Planned to be implemented nationwide after the 2000 census, the ACS will provide annual data to update the 2000 census and to replace the long form and the information it generates in the 2010 census. Before 1996 the ACS was known as the "continuous measurement" program. That name is still used for the broader program that also encompasses uses of ACS data to improve other statistical programs and field operations to improve the address list from which the ACS sample is selected.

The Development of the ACS

The need for more frequent census-type information for "communities," including both geographic areas and population subgroups, has been discussed at least as far back as a 1941 proposal by Philip Hauser, former deputy director of the Census Bureau, for an "annual sample census." In 1981, congressional hearings considered a proposal by Leslie Kish, of the Institute for Social Research, at the University of Michigan, for a survey similar to the ACS, along with a competing proposal for a "quinquennial" (every five years) census.

The law authorizing a mid-decade census in 1985 and every ten years thereafter was passed in 1976, but funding was never provided; Canada began a quinquennial census in 1956. A different design for an ongoing "Decade Census Program," was proposed by Roger Herriot, chief of the Population Division at the Census Bureau, and several colleagues in 1988.

After the 1990 census there was renewed interest by Congress in updating the census long form information used in allocating federal program funds. There were also concerns about the effect of the long-form on census coverage. A "continuous measurement" option, originally to replace the 2000 long form, was included as one of the topics for the 1992–1994 research on new methods for the 2000 census. A staff was formed in 1994 to implement the proposed continuous measurement design in a few test sites, so that it could be evaluated as a replacement for the 2000 long form.

The ACS was implemented in four counties in 1996. The development process included "town meetings" with potential ACS data users in each test site, to explain the ACS plan and get comments. These meetings identified many potential uses of the data by state, local, and tribal governments and other community decision makers. At the advice of the data users, the census long form was retained in 2000, and the ACS was implemented gradually, to replace the 2010 long form after further testing and evaluation. The four test sites in 1996 were increased in stages to thirty-one sites for the years 1999–2001, so that the ACS could be compared with the long form in a variety of areas. Full implementation of the ACS was delayed until 2003, allowing the program time to prove itself, before replacing the long form.

The ACS is a mail survey with telephone follow-up if there is no response and if the telephone number can be determined; personal follow-up is conducted for a random sample of one-third of the remaining nonrespondents. The mail operations were modeled on the 1990 census, with improvements based on research for the 2000 census. The follow-up operations were modeled on the Census Bureau's ongoing national household survey operations, using a permanent interviewing staff. The interviews take place throughout the year, and people are included at their "current residence" at the time of the interview, which means wherever they are "living or staying" at the time, excepting only short stays away from a usual residence. For areas with many seasonal residents, this can lead to differences between the ACS annual average estimates and census estimates, which count people at their "usual" residence as of census day.

When the full ACS program starts in 2003, the ACS will be mailed to 3 million addresses each year, evenly spread over the twelve months. Each address is in the sample at most once in any consecutive five years, so that over a five-year period the survey is sent to 15 million addresses. This five-year sample size was chosen to come close to the census long-form sample size.

The addresses for the ACS sample come from the Census Bureau's Master Address File. This file is created by matching the current census address list with the U.S. Postal Service address files and adding the new addresses found. To improve the coverage of the Master Address File for the ACS, there will be an ongoing field operation called the Community Address Updating System. This system will use a combination of centralized administrative records systems and local sources to target addresses not on the Master Address File. Field staff, working closely with community governments, will list the targeted areas to locate the new addresses. This operation, started in 1997, is scheduled to be implemented nationwide in 2002.

The ACS Data and Its Impact

As with any survey, ACS data users must consider the sample size upon which each community's estimates are based and what it implies about the precision of the estimates. When the sample is too small, it may not be possible to measure small or moderate differences between communities or between time periods for a particular community. For small communities, below 20,000 population, the recommended estimate for most purposes is the average based on the previous five years. For example, in 2008, the 2003–2007 average would be used, and in 2009, the 2004–2008 average would be available. These averages will have nearly the same sample size as the census long form, with the advantage that five-year averages are regularly updated. For larger communities, the sample is sufficient to use averages based on fewer than five years. For states, the ACS provides good estimates of change from one year to the next, using the one-year average.

The variety of estimates available from the ACS data gives the survey the flexibility to be used for many purposes. For communities of all sizes, the most recent five-year average gives a profile of the community similar to what is given by a census long form, but always available for the most recent five-year period. The series of successive five-year averages tracks the general trends in the characteristics of the community.

The annual estimates can be used to identify when and where sudden changes occur, although for small communities, the smaller sample size means that the exact magnitude of the change from one year to the next cannot be measured precisely. For large communities, the annual estimates are based on a big enough sample to measure year-to-year change quite precisely. For states, this means that considerable detail can be provided. For example, useful measures of the changes in the number of children living with both parents can be made for all states. These new capabilities open up new applications, ranging from community planning for small communities to monitoring the progress of state welfare programs.

When the ACS was first proposed, there was extensive discussion of the interpretation of "the average over a period of several years," as compared with "the point-in-time estimate" given by a census long-form sample, whether for describing the characteristics of one community or for comparing two communities. The average describes the general tendency over a period of years, rather than the value at one particular moment. This may be an advantage when the characteristics of the communities fluctuate from year to year. For many descriptive and comparative purposes, there is little difference in interpretation, although special treatment such as the need to adjust for price inflation for dollar amounts, is sometimes needed.

Information from the ACS will be employed to improve the statistical models that are used to generate the Census Bureau's intercensal population estimates and the Small Area Income and Poverty Estimates, as well as similar statistical models at other federal statistical agencies. The ACS will also likely improve the geographic and demographic detail available from other federal surveys that cover topics such as unemployment or crime victimization, by, for example, identifying households in population groups in which a larger sample is needed, so that these households can be added to the other surveys' samples and be interviewed by workers in those surveys. The combination of these other statistical programs and the ACS will likely provide more detailed and accurate information than any of the programs, or the ACS, can provide on its own.

The ACS is expected to have a substantial effect on the 2010 census, creating opportunities for procedures to help with complete enumeration of the population.

The ACS will create a database of problems encountered during ACS interviews, keeping track of special techniques or helpful community contacts used by ACS interviewers. This will help the surveyors refine techniques to improve the completeness of 2010 census coverage in "hard-to-enumerate" areas; the database will also help them identify situations in which special techniques are needed. The work will be supported throughout the decade by community contacts, involved in updating the Master Address File and reviewing and reacting to ACS estimates. Eliminating the long form will simplify many census operations, and will permit census enumerator training to focus on the short-form enumeration.

■ Charles Alexander

Bibliography

Alexander, C. H. "The American Community Survey: Design Issues and Initial Test Results." *Symposium 97: New Directions in Surveys and Censuses: Proceedings.* Ottawa, Canada: Statistics Canada, 1997, 187–192.

Herriot, R., D. B. Bateman, and W. F. McCarthy. "The Decade Census Program—New Approach for Meeting the Nation's Needs for Sub-National Data." *Proceedings of the American Statistical Association Social Statistics Section* (1989), 351–355.

Kish, L. "Population Counts from Cumulated Samples." In *Using Cumulated Rolling Samples to Integrate Census and Survey Operations of the Census Bureau.* Washington, D.C.: U.S. Government Printing Office, June 26, 1981, 5–50.

Kish, L. "Rolling Samples and Censuses." *Survey Methodology* 16, no. 1 (1990): 63–79.

Kish, L. "Space/Time Variations and Rolling Samples." *Journal of Official Statistics* 14, no. 1 (1998): 31–34.

U.S. Bureau of the Census. *The American Community Survey.* Washington, D.C., June 1999. Internet address: www.census.gov/acs.

American Indians and Alaska Natives

As the first inhabitants of what is now the United States, American Indians and Alaska Natives are a legally, politically, and culturally unique part of the nation. No other group is explicitly recognized in the Constitution. An entire volume of the Code of Federal Regulations (CFR 25) is devoted to American Indian law; two congressional committees—one each for the House and the Senate—oversee relations with American Indians; and an agency within the executive branch is solely responsible for American Indians (the Bureau of Indian Affairs within the Department of the Interior).

In light of the special relationship that exists between American Indians and the federal government, it may be surprising that American Indians were not included in the early censuses of this country. For decades the United States government regarded American Indians as belonging to nations apart, and to some extent it continues to do so today. As a result, the decennial census did not enumerate American Indians until 1860 and paid virtually no attention to American Indian population characteristics until 1890.

The census clearly illustrates the peculiar status that American Indians have occupied throughout this country's history. The first census that counted American Indians (1860) distinguished "Indians taxed" from "Indians, not taxed." "Indians taxed" were individuals who had settled in or near Anglo-American communities, had adopted Anglo-American livelihoods and lifestyles, and had more or less assimilated themselves into Anglo-American society. They resembled Anglo-Americans enough to be considered "citizens" and they could be taxed. "Indians, not taxed" were precisely the opposite. They were Indians who lived among their kinsmen in tribal communities, refused to adopt Euro-American customs, and, because they were not "citizens" of the United States, were not called upon to pay taxes. This distinction was eventually discarded in the late nineteenth century, when many American Indians were made citizens, and finally in 1924 the Indian Citizenship Act made all American Indians eligible for taxation.

Data Sources

Modern anthropology had an important influence on the types of information the Census Bureau first collected about American Indians. Anthropologists of this era were convinced, as were many others, that American Indians were destined for extinction. Guided by this belief, anthropologists in the late nineteenth century set out to observe, document, and collect every conceivable detail connected with the lifestyles and cultures of American Indians. This effort has come to be known as "salvage ethnography."

The Census Bureau issued its first major report devoted to American Indians in 1894, as part of the eleventh decennial census in 1890. The report, titled *Report on Indians Taxed and Not Taxed in the United States, Except Alaska* (volume 17), was a remarkable document for at least two reasons. One is that it was the first significant effort ever made to enumerate and collect data about the American Indian population. Second is that this document was an exercise in salvage ethnography. In addition to the usual statistical data, this report also includes maps, drawings, photographs, and detailed narrative accounts of tribal culture. It is perhaps the most unique publication ever produced by the bureau.

In each decade since 1890, "American Indians" have been a more or less regular feature in the decennial census. This does not mean, however, that data for American Indians improved significantly throughout the twentieth century. In fact, a great deal of information was available for American Indians at the century's end, somewhat less at the beginning of the century, and relatively little for the mid-century decades.

Nonetheless, the decennial census has been and continues to be the preeminent source of data about the American Indian population. No other source contains as much information for the American Indian population in its entirety—urban and reservation—for so many different characteristics. This information can be found in two forms: special reports devoted to the American Indian population and in tabulations for the general population.

In the early part of the twentieth century, the Census Bureau published two special reports devoted to American Indians; one in 1915 and another in 1937, based on the 1910 and 1930 decennial censuses, respectively. These reports also contained a small amount of information about Alaska Natives. In 1940, 1950, and 1960 American Indians were enumerated in the census but virtually disappeared from most Census Bureau publications. Data for American Indians did not appear in the main publications for states and other localities. In most instances, they were subsumed within the "Other Races" category of the bureau's racial classification. Data for American Indians (and other ethnic minorities) were published in special reports on the "non-white population" published in 1943, 1953, and 1963.

Likewise, American Indians were missing from most of the reports produced from the 1970 census. However, the Census Bureau produced a special report devoted exclusively to American Indians and, to a lesser extent, Alaska Natives. The publications from the 1980 census were the first regularly to include American Indians and Alaska Natives in tabulations of racial characteristics. The Census Bureau also produced in 1983 a special subject report for American Indians and Alaska Natives, resembling the 1970 special report but containing much more detail. In addition to the regular census, a special supplementary questionnaire was distributed to reservation households. The results of this survey were published in yet another special report. The Census Bureau did not sponsor a special reservation survey in the 1990 census. It did publish two special reports, however, one tabulated for reservations and another tabulated for tribes, in addition to including American Indians in all tabulations of racial characteristics.

Population Characteristics

The content of information published about American Indians has varied substantially across the century. In the early decades of the century, the Census Bureau paid considerable attention to the topic of "stock." "Stock" referred to tribal, linguistic, and blood quantum characteristics of the population. Blood quantum was of special concern to the Census Bureau because of the government's long-standing interest in the so-called civilization and assimilation of American Indians. Blood quantum was a convenient measure of the Indian's progress toward being fully assimilated into the population at-large. In particular, full-blood American Indians were considered to be backward and uncivilized, whereas persons with less than one-fourth blood quantum were considered to be fully civilized individuals, lacking any residual traces of American Indian cultural traits.

As the century passed, ideas about cultural inheritance receded in popularity. By mid-century, eugenics and its association with scientific racism were in disrepute and the Census Bureau discontinued its publication of these data. Nonetheless, enumerators for the 1950 census were instructed to include as American Indians anyone who was one-quarter or more blood quantum. These instructions did not specify how blood quantum was to be ascertained.

The 1950 census was the last enumeration in which census workers ascribed racial ancestry to respondents. In the 1960 census, respondents themselves were asked to identify their racial background. For American Indians, this was perhaps the most significant innovation of the twentieth century. The importance of this change in procedure was reflected in growing numbers of persons reporting their race as American Indian.

From 1900 to 1950 the rate of growth in the American Indian population was slow and relatively stable. In 1900 American Indians numbered approximately 237,000. By mid-century, the population had grown 50 percent, reaching a total of 357,000. Compared with coming decades, this growth rate was very low. One reason is that although the American Indian population had a relatively high birth rate, they also had a high death rate. In 1940 the life expectancy at birth for American Indians was fifty-one years for males and fifty-two years for females. Another reason is that census coverage of American Indians was poor in many areas of the country, especially in urban areas. An evaluation of the 1940 census concluded that in areas in which there were concentrations of American Indians, such as reservations, the count of American Indians was reasonably acceptable. In other areas, it was most likely poor, with many persons of mixed American Indian ancestry misclassified by census enumerators.

The introduction of racial self-identification eliminated enumerator errors and significantly improved the coverage of the American Indian population. Between 1950 and 1960, the American Indian and Alaska Native population grew from 377,000 to nearly 552,000, an increase of 51 percent in a single decade. This growth continued in the next decades with the Native American population expanding to 827,000 in 1970 (50 percent increase), 1.4 million in 1980 (71 percent increase), and 2.0 million in 1990 (43 percent increase).

Besides changes in census procedures, there are many possible reasons for these spectacular growth rates. One is that life expectancies increased dramatically for American Indians after World War II. The other is that the stigma attached to identifying with any race other than white diminished in the years after 1960, especially for persons with American Indian or Alaska Native heritage. Growing ethnic pride and awareness prompted many mixed race persons who could have identified otherwise to choose instead to affiliate themselves with their American Indian ancestry. It is virtually impossible to ascertain the numbers of persons who changed their racial affiliation between the decennial censuses, but such individuals accounted for a substantial portion of the population growth for American Indians after 1960.

As this was written, it was not clear what data would be available for American Indians in the 2000 census; this census was still in the final planning stages. Given the technological innovations that were introduced to distribute census data via electronic networks, the volume of this information is almost certain to be more extensive than in past censuses. For the first time, census respondents were given the opportunity to select one or more categories for their racial heritage. It is not clear how this change will affect the comparability of these data with data from earlier censuses. Because the American Indian population includes a large number of persons with multiracial heritage, it is possible that a sizable number of these individuals will report more than one race.

■ C. Matthew Snipp

Bibliography

Sandefur, Gary D., Ronald R. Rindfuss, and Barney Cohen, eds. *Changing Numbers and Changing Needs: American Indian Demography and Public Health.* Washington, D.C.: National Academy Press, 1996.

Shoemaker, Nancy. *American Indian Population Recovery in the Twentieth Century.* Albuquerque: University of New Mexico Press, 1999.

Snipp, C. Matthew. *American Indians: The First of This Land.* New York: Russell Sage, 1989.

Thornton, Russell. *American Indian Holocaust and Survival.* Norman: University of Oklahoma Press, 1987.

Americans overseas

Each census must arrive at a count of the total population, and it must also place each person at a specific location. For apportionment, that location needs only to be within a specific state. For drawing legislative districts, much more detailed information is required. The census thus must provide a precise and accurate count of each and every block in the nation. Consequently, "who gets counted where" is critically important and, in census terms, is defined as rules about residency.

The basic residency rule is that people should be counted at their "usual place of residence." Those away from home on census day are counted at their usual home. Similarly, those visiting the United States from other countries are not counted. However, those from other countries living in the United States on census day, regardless of citizenship, are counted.

People with two residences are counted at the residence where they stay "most of the time." Interpreting that seemingly straightforward rule can become difficult, however. For example, some small children spend equal time with their divorced parents who have joint custody. Members of Congress, meanwhile, are counted in their home district or state, even though they live and work in Washington, D.C., during the week. Residency rules are not so simple after all, and counting Americans overseas, who often have no U.S. residence, strains the system.

Since 1790, the census has been conducted by counting the persons living in each house. In 1790, determining who lived where was simple compared with today, but nonetheless was a complicated undertaking. As the population increased and society became more complex, determining who lives where became more difficult, and rules determining who gets counted where have become more important. A 1987 conference sponsored by the Council of Professional Associations on Federal Statistics produced a 375-page volume discussing census residency rules. Among the issues covered were where to count college students, students away at school below the college level, children in shared custody, and Americans overseas. In 1990 the Census Bureau produced a document specifying more than thirty rules for where individuals should be counted.

The complexity of determining who lives where results in some people not getting counted anywhere. Seventy percent of those missed in the 1990 census, and 80 percent of African Americans missed in that census, were in households that were counted. Many of these errors resulted from the incongruence between census residency rules and the public's sense of who lives where.

The inclusion in the census count of Americans overseas has become more controversial as the uses of census data have become more politically charged. Procedures for counting Americans overseas have evolved from relatively simple ones for counting "men at sea" in the mid-nineteenth century to the elaborate system of administrative procedures used in 1990 and 2000. In the early nineteenth century the census counted merchant seamen and military serving at sea or abroad. For most of the nineteenth century, when the overseas were counted, they were enumerated at their stateside home. The twentieth-century count of Americans overseas grew progressively more complicated and began to include private citizens as well as the military and merchant seamen. Controversy surrounded the plans for including Americans living overseas in the 2000 census.

Instructions for the inclusion of Americans overseas in the censuses from 1860 to 1990 are summarized in Table 1. While the tabulations from the 1830 and 1840 censuses show totals for Americans overseas, the first record of instructions for counting Americans overseas accompanies the 1860 census. Four conceptual categories are used to group Americans overseas: (1) merchant seamen, (2) military at sea and land-based armed forces, (3) civilians working for the government, and (4) private citizens.

Counting Procedures

How Americans overseas are counted has varied considerably. For 1860 through 1880, census-takers were instructed to include merchant seamen and overseas military as residents of their stateside home. In 1890 no

Table 1. Instructions for Inclusion of Americans Overseas in Census, 1860–1990

Census	Merchant seamen	Military at sea and land-based armed forces	Federal civilian employees	Private citizens
1860	Enumerated at stateside home	Enumerated at stateside home	Not included overseas or stateside	No instructions provided
1870	Enumerated at stateside home	Enumerated at stateside home	Not included overseas or stateside	No instructions provided
1880	Enumerated at stateside home	Enumerated at stateside home	Not included overseas or stateside	No instructions provided
1890	No instructions provided	No instructions provided	No instructions provided	No instructions provided
1900	No instructions provided	Enumerated at stateside home	Enumerated at stateside home	No instructions provided
1910	Enumerated at stateside home	Included in overseas population	Included in overseas population	Enumerated at stateside home
1920	Enumerated at stateside home	Included in overseas population	Included in overseas population	Enumerated at stateside home
1930	Officers reported at home; crew reported at home port	Included in overseas population	Included in overseas population	Enumerated at stateside home
1940	Officers reported at home; crew reported at home port	Included in overseas population	No instructions provided	Enumerated at stateside home
1950	Included in overseas population if vessel at sea or in a foreign port	Included in overseas population	Included in overseas population	No instructions provided
1960	Included in overseas population if vessel at sea or in a foreign port	Included in overseas population	Included in overseas population	Included in overseas population
1970	Included in overseas population if vessel at sea with a foreign port as its destination or in a foreign port	Included in overseas population	Included in overseas population	Included in overseas population
1980	Not included in overseas population	Included in overseas population	Included in overseas population	Not enumerated
1990	Included in overseas population if in a foreign port or sailing from one foreign port to another	Included in overseas population	Included in overseas population	Not enumerated

instruction was provided for counting Americans overseas. In 1910 military and federal civilian employees were counted in the overseas population, but merchant seamen and private citizens overseas during the census were included at their stateside home. As the twentieth century progressed, the rules for the inclusion of Americans overseas were modified from census to census. In 1990 and 2000 the count of Americans overseas included federal military and civilian employees and their dependents. Merchant seamen were not included in the 1990 and 2000 counts.

When Americans overseas have been included in the census, they have been counted as a separate population and reported separately (see Table 2). A major exception was made in both 1970 and 1990 when federal military and civilian employees were included in the population of the states used for apportionment. In both cases, the Census Bureau yielded to pressure from Congress to change its procedures to forestall the passage of undesirable legislation. In 1970 the Census Bureau sought to avoid being embroiled in the debate over the Vietnam War. In 1990 the Census Bureau did not want to link the counting of Americans overseas with excluding undocumented aliens from the census.

Since 1995, groups representing Americans living overseas have lobbied the Census Bureau, without success, to count not just federal military and civilian employees overseas, but all Americans overseas. The exceptions of 1970 and 1990, while well intentioned, have made it difficult for the Census Bureau to argue convincingly against the inclusion of all Americans overseas in the census. Proponents of counting private citizens overseas ask "How can counting employees for the Department of Energy, and not Americans working for ExxonMobil, be justified?" "Why include the fifteen Americans working for the Overseas Battlefield Memorial Commission and not the thousands of Americans working overseas for the Red Cross?"

No basis exists for differentiating between federal military and civilian employees and private citizens overseas other than ease of counting. For those Americans overseas who want to be included in the census, ease of counting does not justify being left out. The Census Bureau, however, argues that it can use administrative records for enumerating federal military and civilian employees, and thus some measure of completeness of the count. The Census Bureau has no such records for private citizens overseas, and hence no way to measure completeness. Those wishing to be counted point to the weakness of those administrative records to mitigate that difference.

Table 2. Americans Overseas, 1900–1990 Censuses

Census	U.S. population abroad	Total U.S. population	Percentage abroad
1900	91,219	75,994,595	0.12%
1910	55,608	91,972,266	0.06%
1920	117,238	105,710,620	0.11%
1930	89,453	122,775,046	0.07%
1940	118,933	131,669,275	0.09%
1950	481,545	150,697,361	0.32%
1960	1,374,421	179,323,798	0.77%
1970	1,737,836	203,302,031	0.85%
1980	995,546	226,542,199	0.44%
1990	925,845	248,718,301	0.37%

Role of Administrative Records

In 1990 the Census Bureau used administrative records from the State Department and the Defense Department to count Americans overseas. No comparable record system exists that could be used to account for private citizens overseas. Evaluation of the count of Americans overseas in 1990 revealed problems in the administrative records used. While military records show the number of dependents for military serving overseas, those records do not indicate the location of those dependents. The assumption was made to include all dependents as part of the overseas population. Some dependents not living overseas were likely counted twice. Similarly, the quality of information from federal agencies other than the Defense Department varied considerably. While the use of administrative records may have simplified the task for the Census Bureau, the accuracy of that count left much to be desired.

The controversy over the inclusion of Americans overseas in the apportionment population likely will continue into the 2010 census. Those advocating the inclusion of all Americans overseas probably will not relent. However, the most likely methodologies to count private citizens overseas involve some use of statistical methods, and that would preclude the use of the count for apportionment. The Census Bureau is not expected to step back from the inclusion of federal military and civilian employees and their dependents in the apportionment count.

■ David McMillen

Apportionment and districting

The distinction between apportionment and districting is central to one of the controversies surrounding the 2000 census. The 1999 Supreme Court decision in *Clinton v. Glavin* stated that Section 195 of Title 13 of the U.S. Code prohibited the use of sampling for apportionment purposes. Justice Sandra Day O'Connor went on to point out that the 1976 amendment to Section 195 changed that section from one that allowed the use of sampling for purposes other than apportionment to one that *required* the use of sampling for all other purposes. Those two points allow both sides to claim victory. Supporters of sampling point to the 1976 amendment and claim that Section 195 required the use of sampling to produce the data used to draw congressional districts. Opponents of sampling argue that drawing congressional districts is simply an extension of the apportionment process, and the use of sampling is prohibited.

Political dictionaries like Congressional Quarterly's 1993 *Encyclopedia of American Government* or its 1991 *American Congressional Dictionary* define *apportionment* as the allocation of seats and *districting* as the drawing of geographic boundaries. Similarly, Justice Lewis F. Powell Jr., in *David v. Bandemer*, writes, "technically, the words 'apportionment' and 'reapportionment' apply to the 'allocation of a finite number of pre-established areas,' while 'districting' and 'redistricting' refers to the drawing of district lines."

The dynamics of apportionment played out between 1790 and 1940. Since 1940 there has been little controversy over apportionment. Districting, in contrast, has been increasingly controversial since 1940. The issue of drawing districts for state houses has been as important as that of congressional districting in developing the current standards used by the courts. One of the most interesting controversies in the legal battling over state houses is whether or not the Constitution permits states to adopt the federal model with one house based on population and one based on political boundaries. In general, the courts have insisted that both houses be based on population, although, in some cases they have allowed political boundaries to be a part, but not the sole determinant, of the districting process.

Apportionment from 1790 to 1910

Apportioning the seats in the House of Representatives according to the population of each state as measured by the census every ten years is part of what makes American democracy unique. The issue was central enough to making the new government work that the census was created in the first Article of the Constitution. But not long after the census of 1790, Congress realized that although the Constitution directed Congress to apportion the seats among the states, it did not say how to do it. Thus was born the first census controversy as opposing sides lined up behind separate formulas for apportioning seats—one proposed by Alexander Hamilton, a Federalist from New York, and one supported by Thomas Jefferson, a Republican from Virginia. Indeed, President George Washington used the first presidential veto on the apportionment bill passed by Congress. His veto forced Congress to change the formula used for apportionment. This battle between North and South, between political parties, between geographic areas with large populations and those with small populations, or between urban and rural areas, is central to nearly all controversy over apportionment and districting from 1790 to the present.

The conflict between the methods of Hamilton and Jefferson is the beginning of the politics of numbers in America as well as illustrative of the extent politicians will go to get their way when even one seat is at stake. Hamilton and his supporters proposed a House of 120 seats, up from the 65 apportioned in the Constitution, arrived at by dividing the total population of 3,615,920 by 30,000, the minimum number of persons per representative set in the Constitution. They then apportioned those 120 seats among the states by dividing the state population by 30,132, a number chosen so that the state quotas (population divided by 30,132) summed to 120. Of course, this left each state with a whole number of representatives and a fraction, or remainder (see Table 1). Each state was then apportioned the whole number from the quota, which apportioned 111 of the 120 seats. To distribute the remaining 9 seats, Hamilton gave 1 seat to each of the nine states with the largest fraction. Thus, Connecticut, Delaware, Massachusetts, New Hampshire, New Jersey, North Carolina, South Carolina, Vermont, and Virginia each got 1 extra seat. The other six states got none, despite the size of the fraction or remainder.

Jefferson argued that awarding the "extra" seats to some of the states based on the fractions remaining, in

Table 1. Apportionment Formulas Proposed by Hamilton and Jefferson

State	Hamilton		Jefferson	
	quota	apportionment	quota	apportionment
Connecticut	7.860	8	8.310	8
Delaware	1.843	2	1.949	1
Georgia	2.351	2	2.485	2
Kentucky	2.280	2	2.411	2
Maryland	9.243	9	9.772	9
Massachusetts	15.774	16	16.678	16
New Hampshire	4.707	5	4.976	4
New Jersey	5.959	6	6.301	6
New York	11.004	11	11.635	11
North Carolina	11.732	12	12.404	12
Pennsylvania	14.366	14	15.189	15
Rhode Island	2.271	2	2.402	2
South Carolina	6.844	7	7.236	7
Vermont	2.839	3	3.001	3
Virginia	20.926	21	22.125	22
Total	**120.000**	**120**	**126.874**	**120**

effect, resulted in two apportionment ratios—one for those states with the extra seats, and one for all others. He argued that fairness called for each state to be apportioned with the same ratio, and thus proposed a divisor of 28,500 (see Table 1). In effect, the Jefferson method simply drops all fractions, awarding only the whole number of seats. The divisor is selected to sum to the predetermined size of the House, in this case 120 seats. After listening to the arguments in support of the congressional apportionment from Hamilton, and arguments against that bill from Jefferson, President Washington vetoed the bill and sent Congress back to work. The attempt to override the veto failed, and Congress sent the president a bill apportioning 105 seats (as originally proposed by the Senate), using the Jefferson method. The Jefferson method remained the method used through the apportionment following the 1830 census.

By 1830 the bias in the Jefferson method was well known. Jefferson's method systematically gave preference to large states over small ones. Between 1790 and 1830 Delaware routinely had remainders over one-half but received two seats in only one of the five apportionments. New York, in contrast, was awarded a seat more than its whole number in each apportionment. As the debate began over the 1830 apportionment, many alternative methods for apportioning the seats in the House of Representatives were proposed, as were many different sizes for the House. It was Daniel Webster

who became the champion of change. He proposed what is today considered the method with the fewest problems, although not the method in use today.

In 1830 Daniel Webster was one of the most revered public figures. Many regarded him as the greatest man in America. His eloquence and power as an orator live today in folktale and song. Although Webster did not prevail in the 1830 debate, by 1842 (when the apportionment using the 1840 census actually became law) dissatisfaction with the Jefferson method, and with the ever-expanding House, resulted in the passing of a Senate bill that apportioned 223 seats using Webster's method (see Table 2). The 1840 apportionment is the only time in history that Congress has reduced the size of the House.

Prior to the 1850 census Rep. Samuel Finley Vinton, a Whig from Ohio, proposed a bill that would make the apportionment formula permanent law rather than the subject of partisan debate once the results were known. He proposed the Vinton method, a restatement of the method put forward by Hamilton, in which the size of the House was fixed and a divisor chosen. Seats were then allocated for the whole number for each state's quota. Any remaining seats were allocated to the largest remainders until all seats were apportioned. Between 1850 and 1900, the Vinton, or Hamilton, method was the law of the land, although it was never followed.

Table 2. U.S. House Size, Population, and Methods of Apportionment, 1790–2000

Census	House size	Population (in 000s)	Average pop. per district	Method of apportionment[a]	Statutes at Large cit.
1790	105	3,929	37,419	Jefferson	1 Stat. 253
1800	141	5,308	37,645	Jefferson	2 Stat. 128
1810	181	7,240	40,000	Jefferson	2 Stat. 669
1820	213	9,638	45,249	Jefferson	3 Stat. 213
1830	240	12,866	53,608	Jefferson	4 Stat. 516
1840	223	17,069	76,543	Webster	5 Stat. 491
1850	234	23,192	99,111	Webster/Vinton	9 Stat. 428 and 10 Stat. 25
1860	241	31,443	130,469	Webster/Vinton	12 Stat. 353 and 12 Stat. 572
1870	292	39,818	136,363	Webster/Vinton	17 Stat. 28 and 17 Stat. 192
1880	325	50,156	154,326	Webster/Vinton	22 Stat. 5
1890	356	62,948	176,820	Webster/Vinton	25 Stat. 735
1900	386	75,995	196,878	Webster/Vinton	31 Stat. 733
1910	433	91,972	212,406	Webster	37 Stat. 13
1920	435	105,711	243,014	—	—
1930	435	122,775	282,241	Webster/Hill	46 Stat. 21
1940	435	131,669	302,687	Hill	54 Stat. 162 and 55 Stat. 761
1950	435	151,326	346,430	Hill	
1960	435	179,323	412,237	Hill	
1970	435	203,302	467,361	Hill	
1980	435	226,542	520,786	Hill	
1990	435	248,718	571,766	Hill	
2000	435	275,000	631,343	Hill	

Notes: There was no reapportionment in 1920. Population figures for 2000 are estimates.

[a] For brief explanations of apportionment methods, see Appendix, Methods of Congressional Apportionment.

In 1850 the Vinton bill called for a house of 233 seats, but 234 seats were apportioned, with the extra seat given to California because of the rapid growth brought on by the gold rush. It was also the case that at 234, the methods of both Hamilton and Webster gave the same results. In 1860 the Hamilton/Vinton method was used to apportion 233 seats, and then 8 additional seats were distributed to northern states. In 1870 a House size of 283 was chosen, because at that point the Webster and Hamilton methods agreed. A few months later, an additional 9 seats were distributed without the benefit of formula. The distribution of those additional seats proved to be the margin of presidential victory for Rutherford B. Hayes over Samuel J. Tilden in the electoral college, even though Tilden had received more popular votes. Had the House been apportioned according to Hamilton's formula, as the law required, Tilden would have carried the electoral college.

The 1870 apportionment was also the first observation of what became known a decade later as the Alabama Paradox, in which an increase in the size of the House results in a decrease in the number of seats allotted to a state. Rep. Ulysses Mercur (R-Pa.), in examining the apportionment of House sizes from 241 to 300, noted that in a House of 270 members Rhode Island received two seats, whereas in a House of 280 members it received only one—an increase in the size of the House should not result in one state losing a seat. He cited this paradox as yet another reason for favoring the Webster method, but at the time, his argument was ignored.

The Alabama Paradox was so named by the head of the census as materials were prepared for the 1880 apportionment. He noted that, using the Hamilton method, Alabama dropped from 8 seats to 7 between House sizes of 299 and 300 members. He proposed a variant of the Jefferson method as an alternative, but the large-state bias in his method was quickly noted, and the proposal rejected. In the meantime, however, Congress had been alerted to one of the major flaws of the Hamilton method. In the end, a compromise was reached at a House size of 325—the point at which Hamilton and Webster agreed on the distribution of seats. A similar compromise was reached in 1890. A House of 356 seats was created because the two methods agreed on the distribution of those seats among the states, and at that size no state lost a seat.

Politics and the Alabama Paradox were the final undoing of the Hamilton method in 1900. Rep. Albert Jarvis Hopkins (R-Ill.), chairman of the Select Committee on the Twelfth Census, submitted a bill for apportioning a House of 357 seats. In every House size between 350 and 400 Colorado got 3 seats, except for a House of 357, at which point it got 2 seats. Colorado was a populist state, and Hopkins was an anti-populist. Congress passed an apportionment bill distributing 386 seats using Webster's formula. At 386 seats, no state lost a seat in the new apportionment. Michael L. Balinski and H. Peyton Young have identified two other paradoxes in apportionment formulas: the population paradox, in which a faster-growing state loses a seat to a slower-growing state, and the new state paradox, in which a seat shifts between two states when a new state is admitted.

Apportionment in the Twentieth Century

The 1910 apportionment was carried out using Webster's method. In 1911 Congress passed an apportionment bill that distributed 433 seats among the states, and provided for 1 additional seat each for Arizona and New Mexico should they be admitted to the Union. (They were admitted in 1912.) A House of 433 members was chosen because that was the size at which no state would lose a seat.

Between 1910 and 1930 two sets of activities played out to remove apportionment from the controversy that characterized the nineteenth century. Following the 1920 census, which showed that for the first time in the country's history more people lived in cities than in rural areas, Congress was unable to agree on an apportionment formula. Congress complained bitterly about the quality of the census, arguing that the results could not possibly be correct. At the same time, there was heated debate within the academic community over the "best" method for apportion-

ment. Those two sets of events led to the system that is in place today.

A reapportionment of the 435 seats in Congress by the Webster method in 1920 would have resulted in ten rural states losing 11 seats. California would have gained 3 of those seats, and Michigan and Ohio would have gained 2 each. This shift of power from rural to urban centers was strongly opposed by the rural interests in both the House and the Senate. It is difficult to exaggerate the rancor of this debate. Members criticized the Census Bureau for taking the census in January, when there was no work on the farm. They blamed the 1920 recession and World War I, and they claimed that the farms were undercounted. Members opined on the superiority of rural inhabitants and the evils of the city. The cities were, after all, full of immigrants, they said. In the end, these interests conspired to prevent the reapportionment of the House—the only time in the 210-year history of apportionment that such has happened.

At the same time that politicians were arguing the merits of rural versus urban settings, rival factions of scholars were warring over apportionment methodology. One group, led by Walter Willcox, a professor at Cornell University, argued that Webster's method, or the method of "major fractions," as he called it, was the best approach. Willcox served as president of the American Statistical Association, the American Economic Association, and the American Sociological Association. These three groups represented the vast majority of professionals with expertise to bring to bear on apportionment methods. The opposing group, led by Edward Huntington, a professor of mechanics at Harvard University, pushed the "method of equal proportions" first proposed by a classmate of his, Joseph Hill, then assistant director of the Bureau of the Census.

Willcox argued that Webster's method should be adopted because it met the fundamental constitutional objective of treating small and large states the same, and it had been the actual method used since at least 1860. Hill's method, Willcox argued, was biased in favor of small states. Huntington made the opposite claim. He argued that Hill's method was unbiased and that Webster's method favored large states. Confused by conflicting testimony, Congress turned to the National Academy of Sciences for advice. In 1929 the academy reported its support for Hill's method of equal proportions. The fundamental difference between the two methods is in what is used to measure the inequality between states. Huntington argued that the appropriate measure was the proportional difference in per capita representation, whereas Willcox advocated the use of the absolute difference in per capita representation. Balinski and Young argue that both Huntington and the National Academy were wrong in characterizing Hill's method as neutral, or sitting in the middle of the five possible methods of apportionment. They point out, as did Willcox, that there are an infinite number of apportionment formulas, and that Hill's and Webster's methods are both in the class they call divisor methods, as are the methods of Jefferson and others. They argue that of the possible divisor methods, Webster's method is "the only one that is perfectly unbiased."

In 1929 Congress was still apportioned on the basis of the 1910 census, despite a 34 percent increase in the population. Still, the controversy over reapportionment, and the sectional split between rural and urban representatives, remained. That year, the Senate passed a permanent reauthorization bill, but rather than specify a given method, the bill simply directed that the apportionment be done by the method used in the preceding census. Rural forces in the House seized on Huntington's criticisms of Webster's method as biased and unscientific in hopes of thwarting any apportionment bill. In the end, however, they only managed to modify the Senate bill to require that the president transmit to Congress the population of the states, the apportionment of representatives using the method used in the preceding apportionment, and the apportionment using both Webster's and Hill's methods. If Congress failed to act, then the apportionment based on the previous method would become law.

As it turned out, the apportionment of 435 seats based on the 1930 census resulted in no difference between Webster's and Hill's methods. The 1940 census was a different story. Using that census, the two methods differed only in the apportionment for Michigan and Arkansas. Hill's method gave Michigan 17 seats and Arkansas 7, whereas Webster's method gave Michigan 18 seats and Arkansas 6. Not surprisingly, an Arkansas representative introduced a bill calling for apportionment using Hill's method. That bill was supported by all Democrats except those from Michigan and opposed by all Republicans. By the end of 1941 Congress passed, and the president signed, legislation apportioning the House using Hill's method. Once again, politics won out over science, and the majority party in Congress voted for the method that would give it one more seat. The method of equal proportions has been used ever since and the House size has remained set at 435 members.

It was a large concession for Congress to pass a permanent apportionment bill in 1929, but that act is important as much for what was left out as for what was said. Prior to 1929 Congress had included in apportionment bills the requirement that congressional districts be of roughly equal size, contiguous, and compact. That language was omitted from the 1929 bill, and the result was the redistricting mischief that prevailed for the next thirty years. The 1931 apportionment corrected the huge disparity in congressional district size that had grown from population growth and shifts between 1910 and 1930. By the time the Supreme Court ruled in *Baker v. Carr*, however, that disparity had returned.

Drawing Congressional Districts

By and large, Congress has left the process of creating congressional districts within states to the state legislatures. In 1842, however, Congress passed legislation requiring states with more than one representative to divide the state into districts with one representative for each district, commonly known as single-member districts. During the second half of the nineteenth century the requirements of compactness and equal size were added. All these requirements died in 1929 when Congress passed the permanent apportionment act without such language. The requirement for single-member districts was reintroduced in 1967. Thus, the history of redistricting can be separated into three distinct phases: 1790 to 1930, a period of modest federal guidance; 1930 to 1964, a laissez-faire period; and 1964 to the present, the period of the courts.

Between 1930 and 1964 neither Congress nor the courts would address the issue of equity of representative districts for either state governments or for the U.S. House of Representatives. As a consequence, the size and shape of districts were at the whim of those creating them—in most states, the state legislature. The result was congressional districts of widely varying size. In many states, the rural/urban divide that immobilized the U.S. House of Representatives during the 1920s dominated the state legislature throughout this period.

The first challenge to the disparity in size of congressional districts came in 1946. Kenneth Colgrove, a political science professor at Northwestern University, argued that he was denied equal protection of the law

(Fourteenth Amendment) because as a resident of the Seventh Congressional District in Chicago he was among 900,000 people represented by a single member of Congress, whereas the Fifth Congressional District contained only about 100,000 people. Justice Felix Frankfurter wrote the opinion dismissing the case in an opinion that would prevail for almost twenty years. Justice Frankfurter wrote, in *Colgrove v. Green* (328 U.S. 549 [1946]), that the question of district size was outside the jurisdiction of the Court because it was an issue of "peculiarly political nature." After the *Colgrove* decision, the problem for the proponents of equal representation became one of framing the argument in a way that compelled the Supreme Court to recognize the inequity as a constitutional issue.

In 1962 the Supreme Court reversed the Frankfurter decision and ruled that state legislatures of unequal size violated the equal protection clause of the Fourteenth Amendment. In 1964 the Supreme Court ruled that U.S. congressional districts should be of equal size and began the era of one-person, one-vote. At that time, Michigan had the smallest congressional district with a population of 177,431, and Texas had the largest with a population of 951,527 (a difference of 774,096). Texas also had the largest disparity between congressional districts, with a difference of 735,156 between the largest and the smallest district. The Supreme Court decision in *Baker v. Carr* (369 U.S. 186) in 1962 addressed the size of districts for state legislatures, whereas the decision in *Wesberry v. Sanders* (376 U.S. 1) in 1964 addressed the size of districts for the U.S. House of Representatives. A second difference between these cases is that *Baker v. Carr* relied on the Fourteenth Amendment, whereas *Wesberry v. Sanders* cited Article I, Section 2, of the Constitution, which states that representatives should be "apportioned among the several States . . . according to their respective Numbers." The Court thus held that in a House election, one person's vote should be worth as much as another's.

These decisions set in place the restructuring of legislative districts throughout the country. Congressional districts, which had a difference of more than 700,000 people between the largest and smallest in the 88th Congress (1963–1964), had a difference of less than 50,000 people by the 93d Congress (1973–1974). By the 103d Congress (1993–1994) the difference had dwindled to about 5,000.

Although these lawsuits established the Court's jurisdiction over the size and shape of legislative districts, and established the principle of one-person, one-vote, much was left unspecified, and Court decisions have refined the concept. This change in law has affected the census and the Census Bureau.

One Person, One Vote: The Pressure for Accuracy. The census is required by the Constitution for apportioning the seats in the House of Representatives among the states, but there is no requirement either in the Constitution or federal law that census numbers be used to draw congressional or state district boundaries. Some states, as late as 1980, used voter registration data to define congressional districts, whereas other states, like Massachusetts, conducted their own census to be used for districting. Other states took census data from the U.S. census and modified it for districting purposes. Kansas, disapproving of the Census Bureau's practice of counting college students at their college or university, adjusts census data to remove these students prior to redistricting.

Nonetheless, the requirement that congressional districts be of equal size has put increased pressure on the census. Issues of census geography and census accuracy became intertwined in the political battles over drawing districts to give one side or the other a competitive advantage. As state legislatures struggled to create districts that would pass muster with the courts, they simultaneously struggled to maintain existing power structures and the integrity of existing political boundaries. That led to a need for more and more detail from the census.

The boundaries of states are relatively simple to deal with. No congressional district crosses state lines, and census geography always allows separate totals for each state. Below the state level, however, political boundaries and census geography often conflict. As a result of these demands, during the Ninety-fourth Congress (1975–1976) a law was passed (Public Law 94-171) requiring the Census Bureau to provide to the states the age, sex, and race data for each census block within the state to be used in the redistricting process. These data files, or computer tapes as they were then, became commonly known as the P.L. 94-171 tapes, or the redistricting files. Drawing on this mandate, the Census Bureau began a program to work with the states to ensure that the geographic boundaries used for census data were similar to those used by the state. Representatives from the Census Bureau visited each state legislature to explain census geography and urge the state to use similar boundaries to define units within the state.

Defining a census block within a city is usually a simple task. However, even city blocks do not always conform to other boundaries. In some cases the boundary of a political jurisdiction runs down the middle of a street, splitting the block between two jurisdictions. As houses become more and more spread out, defining the boundaries of a block becomes increasingly difficult, and in most rural areas the concept of a block just does not exist. For the 1970 census, a large proportion of the country was not defined in terms of blocks, but only in terms of larger geographical units—census tracts, places, census-designated places, minor civil divisions, cities, counties, and states. Since 1970, the Census Bureau has defined "blocks" for more and more of the United States. In 2000 the Census Bureau defined blocks for the entire country. By doing so, the Census Bureau made the block the basic building block from which all other units can be constructed.

The process of building congressional districts varies from state to state, but as computers have become more powerful, more and more states have relied on them to draw and examine the effect of district boundaries. In 1970 the computing power needed to manipulate the geographic and census data necessary to draw congressional district boundaries was available to only a few. Many states still relied on paper maps, colored pencils, and books of tables. The desktop computers of 1980 were more powerful than the mainframes used to process the 1960 census. Nevertheless, they did not have nearly enough power to be useful in the redistricting process. Today's personal computer is still not sufficient to handle both the amount of data and the demand for rapid turnaround needed for redistricting in most states; still, the cost of sufficient computing power is well within the reach of every state and political party, and the need has spawned a healthy redistricting consulting business. The necessity for massive computer power has been driven primarily by the demands put on redistricting by both politicians and the courts.

Legal Developments since 1962. In addition to the Supreme Court decisions of 1962 (*Baker v. Carr*) and 1964 (*Wesberry v. Sanders*), the Voting Rights Act was passed by Congress in 1965 to protect the voting rights of minorities. Sections 2 and 5 of the Voting Rights Act are of particular importance to this discussion. Section 2 creates the right for individuals to challenge an apportionment plan and was amended in 1982 to allow individuals to prevail if they could prove that the effect of the districting was discriminatory regardless of the intent. Section 5 requires sixteen states (Alabama, Alaska, Arizona, California, Florida, Georgia, Louisiana, Michigan, Mississippi, New Hampshire, New York, North Carolina, South Carolina, South Dakota, Texas, and Virginia) to have their redistricting plans reviewed by the Department of Justice before they become effective. In addition, Section 5 requires "no retrogression" after redistricting. That is to say, no minority could be worse off after redistricting than it was before. Even if the minority could not prove to the court that retrogression had occurred, it could prevail if it could prove to the courts that the redistricting plan had a discriminatory purpose. The review by the Department of Justice proved to have as great an effect on redistricting as the provision of the act itself.

Although the Supreme Court laid out the principle of one person, one vote in 1964, it did not define just what that meant. In the ensuing years, defining the standards of one person, one vote has occupied a considerable amount of the intellectual energy of the courts. It should be noted that the Supreme Court resisted entering the political fray of redistricting for the first twenty years and has moved very cautiously even after changing course. As a result, the Court often has been vague in explaining what would and would not constitute acceptable districting, and at times it has stepped back and changed direction.

Three issues have emerged as central to understanding what the Supreme Court will and will not accept in defining legislative districts: numerical equality among districts within a state; the use of "other" information, like existing political boundaries; and majority-minority districts, or congressional districts in which the majority of voting-age residents were minorities, such as African American or Hispanic.

Supreme Court decisions in the late 1960s, the 1970s, and the 1980s pushed states toward greater and greater equality among congressional districts. In *Kirkpatrick v. Preisler* (394 U.S. 526 [1969]) the Court held that a Missouri reapportionment with a difference of approximately 35,000 between the smallest and largest was too great to provide equal representation. The same Court, in *Wells v. Rockefeller* (394 U.S. 542 [1969]), threw out a New York redistricting plan that had a difference of approximately 53,000 persons from the smallest to the largest congressional district. Following the 1970 census, the Court invalidated a Texas redistricting plan in which the difference was only approximately 19,000 persons, or 4.1 percent (*White v. Weiser*, 412 U.S. 783 [1973]). Finally, in 1983, in *Karcher v. Daggett* (462 U.S.

725 [1983]), the Supreme Court invalidated a New Jersey plan in which the difference was less than 5,000 persons, and a difference of less than one-quarter of 1 percent from the ideal.

This series of Supreme Court decisions pushed state redistricting committees to greater and greater numerical equality between districts. The implication for state redistricting committees was that they had to use smaller and smaller geographic units to achieve this equality and simultaneously to achieve their political goals. For the Census Bureau these court cases meant increased political tension focused on census numbers, and increased attention to errors in the census.

As the 1990 census approached, the Department of Justice pushed the sixteen Section 5 states to create,

wherever possible, majority-minority districts. The basis for this push was the Supreme Court's 1986 decision in *Thornburg v. Gingles* (478 U.S. 30 [1986]), in which the Court set out three standards necessary to prove that retrogression had occurred: the minority group must be able to demonstrate that it is sufficiently large and geographically compact to constitute a majority in a single-member district; the minority group must be able to demonstrate that it is politically cohesive; and the minority group must be able to show that the white majority votes sufficiently as a bloc to enable it to defeat the minority's preferred candidate.

The push for majority-minority districts, coupled with the Court's focus on numerical equality, produced in many states districts so oddly shaped that Elbridge

Figure 1. Gerrymandering in the 1990s: North Carolina's First and Twelfth Districts

After the 1990 census (1992)

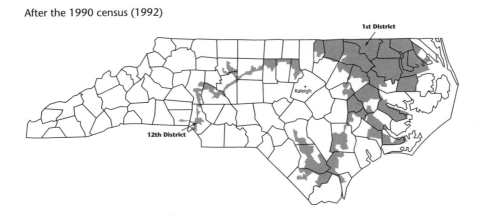

Two remaps later, after federal court decisions (1998)

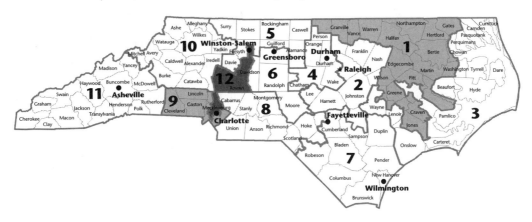

Sources: Congressional Districts in the 1990s: A Portrait of America (Washington, D.C.: Congressional Quarterly, 1993), 548; and *Congressional Quarterly Weekly Report*, April 5, 1997, 810.

Note: North Carolina's First and Twelfth Districts were drawn to give the state its first black representatives in ninety-three years. Elected in 1992, the two representatives were reelected in 1994 and 1996.

Gerry's salamander from 1812 looked prosaic. The Supreme Court was still developing just what it would accept, and oddly shaped districts swelled their suspicion. In *Shaw v. Reno* (113 S.Ct. 2816 [1993]) the Court said, "we believe that reapportionment is one area in which appearances do matter. A reapportionment plan that includes in one district individuals who belong to the same race, but who are otherwise widely separated by geographical and political boundaries, and who may have little in common with one another but the color of their skin, bears an uncomfortable resemblance to political apartheid." (For an illustration of the majority-minority districts reviewed by the Court in *Shaw*, which examined North Carolina's First and Twelfth Districts, see Figure 1.)

It is useful to look at the experience in California and Florida following the 1990 census to understand the position the Court has laid out. In both cases the redistricting plan was drawn by a special master appointed by the Court. In California the special master used census tracts as building blocks and focused on creating compact districts. The result was districts that were not numerically equal in size (the disparity in numerical equality in California actually increased from 1980 to 1990) but that were acceptable to the Court. In Florida the special master focused on numerical equality and produced many oddly shaped districts that were eventually rejected by the courts.

Politics and the Census. Not surprisingly, the controversy over numerical equality of districts and the appropriate building blocks affects the controversy over the census. With the redistricting battles as a background, it is easier to understand why one of the principal attacks on sampling by Republicans has been the issue of accuracy at the block level. The demand for accuracy at the block level is made knowing that it is impossible for the Census Bureau to meet the test of producing more accurate data for all blocks through statistical adjustment. Similarly, it is much easier to draw congressional districts that meet both the test of numerical equality and maintain political advantage for one party or the other using census blocks as the basic unit of geography.

The census will be subject to political pressure as long as census data form the basis for political representation. As history shows us, that pressure will ebb and flow as the nation pays more or less attention to issues of fairness and equality. The population shift from rural to urban revealed in the 1920 census is still reverberating today. That shift led to the failure of Congress to reapportion, which led to the repeal of nearly all congressional requirements on the size and shape of districts in 1929. That freedom, in a very short period of time, led to congressional districts of such widely disparate size that pressure for change began to mount. It took nearly twenty years for the Supreme Court to act, and it is not coincidental that the Court action came during the civil rights movement of the 1960s. But the courts are a blunt instrument to forge equality, and the struggle to define "legal" remedies for politically motivated districts continues. It is the case, however, that politicians ultimately derive both their power and their motivation from the public. Without public involvement in the drive for fair and reasonable congressional districts, there will always be those who attempt to manipulate the system for personal gain.

See also *Congress and the census; Tabulation geography.*

■ David McMillen

Bibliography

Balinski, Michel L., and H. Peyton Young. *Fair Representation.* New Haven: Yale University Press, 1982.

Hanson, Royce. *The Political Thicket: Reapportionment and Constitutional Democracy.* Englewood Cliffs, N.J.: Prentice-Hall, 1962.

U.S. Bureau of the Census and the Association of Public Data Users. *A Guide to State and Local Geography.* CPH-I-18. Washington, D.C.: U.S. Government Printing Office, 1990.

Archival access to census data

There are several major sources of information from recent and past censuses. Two of these are recognized archives whose mission is to preserve and provide access to census information. Using one or more of these sources, individuals may examine data from all of the nation's censuses, from the first in 1790 to the most recent.

Types of Census Information

Information from the decennial censuses is available in three forms: printed, microform, and electronic. Here we will concentrate on the third form in which census data are available, the electronic format. Although the Census Bureau began using electronic data-processing equipment for its tabulations as early as 1890, it was not until the 1960s that census information became publicly available in electronic form. Beginning with the 1970 census, electronic data products were routinely prepared and distributed by the Census Bureau for each decennial census. Those products took two forms: information on individuals (names were withheld to prevent identification) and summary or aggregate information. These are commonly known as Public Use Microdata Samples (PUMS) and Summary Tape Files (STFs), respectively. For the censuses before 1970, electronic census information was created from the printed and microform products of earlier censuses, not by the Census Bureau but by several academic organizations, often working in conjunction with the bureau. For those years the same two formats of information, individual-level and summary, were created.

The chief advantage of census information in electronic form is the ability to manage, search for, and manipulate these massive data resources with the aid of computers. Additionally, users can access or obtain electronic census information remotely, without having physically to travel to a site where the information is located or stored (such as a library or other repository). Finally, a dispersed network of organizations provides convenient access to electronic census information, providing choices for those who wish to use data in this form.

Major Sources of Census Information

The first major source of electronic census information is the U.S. Bureau of the Census, which maintains a large number of data files, chiefly from the most recent decennial census. Copies of these data files can be acquired from the bureau. In addition, the bureau's World Wide Web site (http://www.census.gov) facilitates search and display of discrete items of census information for all areas of the country. The Census Bureau's network of State Data Centers, located in each state, affords yet other means of access to (mostly current) census information in electronic form.

The Census Bureau is required by law to deposit its official electronic products (as well as other material) with the U.S. National Archives and Records Administration (NARA). NARA is the official federal government repository for census data, with a mission to pre-

serve those data as official records of the U.S. government. This organization is therefore a second source for electronic census information. NARA's holdings of electronic material are chiefly concentrated in the period since 1960. Its Web site (http://www.nara.gov) provides information on how to obtain copies of electronic census data files.

A third source of electronic census data preserves and provides access to both contemporary and historical information from the first census in 1790 to the present. That is the Inter-university Consortium for Political and Social Research (ICPSR) at the University of Michigan. This repository contains both individual-level (PUMS) and aggregated (summary file) data. PUMS files in the ICPSR archive were either obtained from the Census Bureau (1960–1990) or key entered by scholars from original census questionnaires (1880–1920, 1940–1950). Summary (aggregate) information was similarly key entered by academic project members from the printed reports for the 1790–1960 censuses or purchased from the Census Bureau (1970–1990). The ICPSR holdings of historical and contemporary census data are accessible online (http://www.icpsr.umich.edu) for downloading by personal computers; copies of specific data files can also be provided, upon request, on removable media such as diskettes or CD-ROMs. In addition, the ICPSR Web site provides links to related sites that provide other forms of access to census data.

Format of Electronic Census Data

Census information in electronic form is most commonly stored in "data files" that record characteristics of persons and households (for PUMS files) or tabulations of census-gathered characteristics that are summarized and recorded for geographic areas (summary files). These data files are largely numeric and require the use of computer software to interpret and display the information contained in the files. Ubiquitous packages of such computer software can be instructed to "read" census data files, and either display items or perform statistical analysis on the files. Two forms of ancillary information accompany most or all of the available census data files. The first is a collection of *technical documentation* describing each data file. This textual material describes the data file and its contents, permitting a user to understand the data storage format and all of the items of information contained in the file. A second set of information, called a *database dictionary or format statements,* is used to instruct computer software how to read the data file. Census files obtained from the Census Bureau or NARA will usually be accompanied by technical documentation in paper form, with database dictionaries often supplied in electronic form.

The census data files maintained by ICPSR are less well known to nonspecialists. They include summary data files for the censuses of 1790–1960 that contain some 8,300 indicators, recorded for every state and for each of the 3,400 counties or county equivalents that have ever existed across the nation's history. These historical census data, key entered from printed census reports, record social, demographic, and economic characteristics of the population. Also included in this collection are statistics describing economic activities (farming, manufacturing), information on churches and church membership, and country of origin of immigrants. U.S. Technical documentation and database dictionaries, both in electronic form, accompany the ICPSR historical census data files. (ICPSR also maintains copies of census data files for the 1970–1990 decennial censuses, with electronic technical documentation.)

Access to Census Data Files

Copies of census data files can be purchased from many sources. The Census Bureau and NARA impose a small charge per file (essentially the cost of reproduction of the file), whereas commercial firms specializing in census data typically charge higher fees. Census files in the ICPSR holdings are available without charge to students, faculty, and staff at more than 350 colleges and universities worldwide, and to others for a small fee.

Another form of access to electronic census data is through online information utilities reached through the World Wide Web. The Census Bureau's main Web site permits free browsing of 1990 census data, which is particularly useful for individuals interested in looking up discrete facts or rapidly obtaining a statistical profile of any area in the country. Many of the bureau's State Data Centers also provide this type of online access to the most recent census, and numerous commercial firms provide similar services for a fee. A similar facility exists for accessing the ICPSR historical census data files, through the Historical Census Data Browser, maintained at the University of Virginia. (This facility is available free-of-charge.)

Issues of Using Archival Census Data

Census data covering two hundred years of the nation's history provide an unmatched resource for research and discovery of a wealth of topics. The electronic data files in particular permit examinations of changes over time in the size, distribution, and characteristics of the U.S. population. Several caveats, however, should guide the use of these collections of information. First is the number and size of available census data files. Several thousand discrete files have been prepared from the U.S. decennial censuses. Many of them are immense, containing millions of data records or thousands of observations at a single point in time. Consultation with experts in using such files is often necessary to avoid time-consuming and frustrating searches for needed information and its extraction from such large files.

Three methodological issues complicate the use of census data, particularly the comparison of such data over time. The first is the changing definitions of terms used in different censuses for measuring concepts and describing population characteristics. Care needs to be paid to the varying definitions of attributes or categories of information over the years, including such basic concepts as "race," "occupation," and "ethnicity." Those who examine summary data recorded for various geographic areas will confront a second issue, changing territorial or geographic boundaries. The nation's counties (and even states) have frequently changed their boundaries, and smaller geographic units have been even more volatile. A third methodological issue is census "underenumeration," or the failure to count and then record information for all persons residing in the country at the time of a census. Progressively better census-taking methods have reduced the undercounting, although undercount rates remain high for some groups. Yet for all censuses, researchers interpreting reported figures must contemplate the effect of persons missed or left out of the tabulations.

See also *Data dissemination and use; Dissemination of data: printed publications; National Archives and Records Administration.*

■ Erik W. Austin

Bibliography

Anderson, Margo. *The American Census: A Social History.* New Haven, Conn.: Yale University Press, 1988.

Clubb, Jerome, Erik W. Austin, and Michael W. Traugott. "Demographic and Compositional Change." In *Analyzing Electoral History: A Guide to the Study of American Voter*

Behavior, edited by Jerome M. Clubb, William H. Flanigan, and Nancy Zingale, 105–136. Beverly Hills, Calif.: Sage Publications, 1981.

Sharpless, John B., and Ray M. Shortridge. "Biased Under-enumeration in Census Manuscripts: Methodological Implications." *Journal of Urban History* 1 (August 1975): 409–439.

U.S. Bureau of the Census. *Twenty Censuses: Population and Housing Questions, 1790–1980.* Washington, D.C.: 1978.

Asian and Pacific Islander Americans

Americans of Asian and Pacific Islander (API) descent include people who trace their origins to an Asian country (for example, China, Japan, or India) or one of the Pacific Islands (for example, Hawaii or Guam). The implementation of Statistical Policy Directive 15 after 1976 led to the collection and presentation of racial data that combined Asian and Pacific Americans into a single "race." Beginning with the 2000 census, however, racial statistics were collected separately for Asian Americans and Pacific Islanders.

Population Size and Growth

Pacific Islanders are usually considered part of the native peoples of the United States, whereas the majority of Asian Americans are descendants of immigrants from many Asian countries. About 95 percent of the API population are Asian Americans. The API population is relatively small, representing about 4 percent of the U.S. population as of 1997 (see Table 1). Still, the

API population has increased rapidly in recent years, primarily as a result of changes to U.S. immigration policies after 1965. Much of this growth is due to an immigration-related surge in the Asian American population. Between 1970 and 1980 the API population grew 104 percent. The 1980s saw another doubling of the Asian and Pacific Islander population to more than 7 million, according to the 1990 census. The rate of growth slowed down during the 1990s to about 40 percent, but this is still faster than that of other racial and ethnic populations.

The Role of Immigration

Prior to the 1960s, Asians in the United States were mostly descendants of three earlier streams of immigrants. The first group consisted of Chinese men who arrived from the 1850s to the 1880s to join in the Gold Rush. Many stayed on to work in building the railroads that would connect the West to the rest of the country. Intense discrimination against these immigrants led to the passage of the Chinese Exclusion Act in 1882. This act was renewed several times until World War II, severely curtailing immigration from China. The Chinese American population therefore remained very small until recent years.

The second wave of Asian immigration consisted mostly of Japanese men who arrived to work in agriculture. Beginning in the 1880s, they first went to Hawaii, then to the West Coast. Opposition to Japanese immigration led to the 1907 "Gentlemen's Agreement." In this pact between the U.S. and Japanese governments, Japan agreed to restrict Japanese labor migration to the United States. However, the traditional Japanese system of "picture brides" allowed the entry of Japanese women as brides of men who were

Table 1. Growth of the Total U.S. and Asian and Pacific Islander (API) Population, 1970 to 1997 (numbers in thousands)

| | 1970 | | 1980 | | 1990 | | 1997 | | Percentage Increase | | |
	No.	%	No.	%	No.	%	No.	%	1970–1980	1980–1990	1990–1997
Total	205,567	100.0	226,625	100.0	248,712	100.0	266,792	100.0	10.2	10.0	7.0
API	1,800	0.9	3,726	1.6	7,274	2.9	10,046	4.0	107	95.0	38.0

Sources: J.S. Passel and Barry Edmonston, "Immigration and race: recent trends in immigration to the United States," in *Immigration and Ethnicity: The Integration of America's Newest Arrivals,* 31–71, ed. B. Edmonston and J.S. Passel. (Washington, D.C.: Urban Institute Press, 1994); S.M. Lee, "Asian Americans: Diverse and Growing," *Population Bulletin,* vol. 53, no. 2, table 3 (Washington, D.C.: Population Reference Bureau, 1998).

already in the United States prior to the Gentlemen's Agreement. The establishment of families meant that the Japanese American population was able to increase slowly but steadily as new generations were born in the United States.

The third wave of early Asian Americans can be traced to Filipinos who were recruited to work in sugar plantations in Hawaii. Other Filipinos worked in agriculture in California. Filipinos were considered U.S. nationals following the annexation of the Philippines in 1898, when the United States prevailed in the Spanish-American War. As Asians, however, Filipinos also encountered discrimination, and immigration of Filipinos was essentially ended with the 1934 Tydings-McDuffie Act.

Restrictive immigration policies directed at Asians meant that the Asian American population remained small and grew very slowly through the 1960s. After 1965 immigration from Asia was transformed by the 1965 Immigration and Nationality Act Amendments (which ended discriminatory limits on Asian immigration) and the end of the Vietnam War (which generated a new and large flow of refugees-turned-immigrants from Vietnam, Cambodia, and Laos). As shown in Table 1, the largest increases in the API population occurred during the 1970s and 1980s. The API population continued to grow faster than the total U.S. population during the 1990s, although the rate of increase had slowed somewhat.

Changing Ethnic Composition

The dramatic growth of the API population since the early 1970s has been accompanied by significant changes in the ethnic composition of the population, as shown in Table 2.

As recently as 1980, Chinese, Japanese, and Filipino Americans were the largest ethnic groups in the API population. By the 1990 census, however, two new groups—Korean and Asian Indians—had become as large as the Japanese American community. Continuing trends in the 1990s indicate that Vietnamese and other Southeast Asian Americans (Cambodian and Laotian) are now about 23 percent of the Asian American population, just behind Chinese Americans (24 percent), and ahead of Filipino Americans (21 percent), Indian Americans (13 percent), and Japanese and Korean Americans (at 10 percent each). The increased diversity of the Asian American population is an important factor in examining its demographic, sociological, economic, and political experiences.

The role of immigration has been central in the recent growth of the Asian American population and in altering its ethnic composition. During the 1980s and through the mid-1990s, immigration from Asia amounted to 40 to 44 percent of all legal immigration to the United States. China, the Philippines, Vietnam, India, and Korea were the leading countries of origin for Asian immigrants during these years; immigration

Table 2. Changing Ethnic Composition of the Asian American Population, 1980 to 1997 (numbers in thousands)

Ethnic Group	1980 No.	1980 %	1990 No.	1990 %	1997 No.	1997 %
Total API	3,726	100.0	7,274	100.0	10,046	100.0
Chinese	812	23	1,649	24	2,268	24
Filipino	782	23	1,420	21	1,995	21
Japanese	716	21	866	13	925	10
Asian Indian	387	11	787	11	1,215	13
Korean	357	10	797	12	982	10
Vietnamese	245	7	593	9	1,045	11
Other Southeast Asian	69	2	391	6	444	5
Other Asian	97	3	374	5	695	7
Pacific Islander	269	7	398	5	478	5

Source: S. M. Lee, "Asian Americans: Diverse and Growing," *Population Bulletin*, vol. 53, no. 2, table 3 (Washington, D.C.: Population Reference Bureau, 1998).

from Japan was negligible. As the new immigrants settle down, future generations of Asian Americans will continue to display the changed ethnic composition of the Asian American population. More of the U.S.-born Asian American population will consist of Korean, Indian, and Southeast Asian Americans.

Place of Birth or Nativity and Generational Status

The important role of immigration in the growth and diversification of the API population means that place of birth and generational status are important dimensions in describing this population. Demographers speak of the first generation, which refers to the foreign-born generation, and the second generation, which refers to the U.S.-born children of immigrants. Third and higher generations refer to the grandchildren and subsequent descendants of the original immigrants. The majority of Pacific Islanders are native to the United States, so generational status and place of birth are not appropriate dimensions to describe Pacific Islanders. Immigration has been the main force behind recent growth of the Asian American population, however, and Table 3 shows the percentage of Asian Americans who are first generation (foreign-born), second generation, and third and higher generation. Census data distinguish only between the native- and foreign-born; detailed nativity and generational status of the API population in 1990 are shown in Table 3, with projections to 2040. In 1990 more than two-thirds of Asian Americans were foreign-born (first generation).

Among the native-born, the majority were second generation. By 2040, the percentages of foreign- and native-born will be about even, almost 40 percent of Asian Americans will be second-generation Americans, and there will be a small increase in the third and later generations.

Age and Sex

Age and sex are basic variables in describing any population. The API population is younger than the total population. Data from the March 1997 Current Population Survey, published by the Census Bureau in 1998, show that the median age of Asian and Pacific Islander Americans is thirty-one, compared with thirty-four for the total population. The percentage of APIs who are under twenty years is 32 percent (higher than the 30 percent for the total population), and the percentage over sixty-five (6 percent) is lower than in the total population (12 percent). The API sex ratio (number of males for every 100 females) is 97, and is similar to the sex ratio observed in the total population.

Regional and Metropolitan Area Distribution

Compared with the U.S. population as a whole, the API population is distinctive in its concentration in the West, and in metropolitan areas. Over half the API population reside in the western region, compared with 22 percent of the total population. California, Hawaii, and Washington are three western states with large API populations. Just 10 percent of the API population

Table 3. U.S. and Asian and Pacific Islander Population by Nativity and Generation, 1990 and 2040

Year	Total (in millions)	Percentage foreign Born	Percentage native-born	Native Born Population	
				% Second generation	% Third and higher generation
Total Population					
1990	248.8	8.6	91.4	9.7	81.7
2040	355.5	14.2	85.8	12.9	72.9
Asian and Pacific Islanders					
1990	7.3	66.3	33.7	21.6	12.0
2040	34.5	49.4	50.6	36.8	13.8

Source: Barry Edmonston and J.S. Passel. "The Future Immigrant Population of the United States," in *Immigration and Ethnicity: The Integration of America's Newest Arrivals*, 317–353, table 11.7, ed. B. Edmonston and J.S. Passel (Washington, D.C. : Urban Institute Press, 1994).

reside in the Mid-west, however, compared with 23 percent of the total population. The API population is also highly urbanized, with 95 percent living in metropolitan areas, compared with 80 percent of the U.S. population. Within metropolitan areas, a higher percentage of Asian and Pacific Islanders live inside central cities (46 percent), compared with 30 percent of the total metropolitan population. This suggests that the API population is less suburbanized than the total population, although almost half of the urban API population live outside central cities.

Future Prospects

Despite remarkable growth in recent years, the API population will remain a relatively small percentage of the U.S. population for many years. Continued immigration and the growth of the second generation will sustain relatively high growth of the API population. By 2050, the API population may be as large as 8 percent of the U.S. population. The increased ethnic diversity and distinctive characteristics of the API population (for example, regional and metropolitan area concentration) and other characteristics described elsewhere in this volume (high educational attainment, intermarriage rates, and the like) ensures that the API population will have significant and extensive impact on future population trends in the United States.

See also *Race: questions and classifications.*

■ Sharon Lee

Bibliography

Edmonston, Barry, and J. S. Passel. "The Future Immigrant Population of the United States." In *Immigration and Ethnicity: The Integration of America's Newest Arrivals,* 317–353, edited by B. Edmonston and J. S. Passel. Washington, D.C.: Urban Institute Press, 1994.

Lee, Sharon M. "Asian Americans: Diverse and Growing." In *Population Bulletin,* vol. 53, no. 2. Washington, D.C.: Population Reference Bureau, 1998.

Smith, James P., and Barry Edmonston, eds. *The New Americans; Economic, Demographic, and Fiscal Effects of Immigration.* Washington, D.C.: National Academy Press, 1997.

U.S. Bureau of the Census. *Population Profile of the United States: 1997.* Current Population Reports, Series P23-194. Washington, D.C.: U.S. Government Printing Office, 1998. (http://www.census.gov/population/socdemo/race/api97/table01.txt).

U.S. Bureau of the Census. *Selected Social Characteristics of the Population, by Region and Race: March 1997.* Washington, D.C., 1998.

Black Americans

See *African-origin population.*

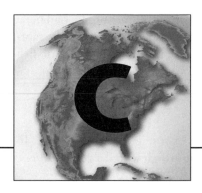

Capture-recapture methods

The U.S. decennial census process produces what is commonly referred to as a "complete count." The Bureau of the Census has traditionally dealt with counting problems by building many follow-up and checking procedures into the census process to catch errors and make sure that households are counted.

Considerable evidence, accumulated over decades, supports the existence of a systematic undercount in the decennial census, one that differentially affects different population groups. For the 1980 census the bureau determined that there were at least 6 million erroneous enumerations in the census, of which as many as 1 million were fabrications and as many as 2.5 million people were erroneously included twice at the same location, as Robert E. Fay reports. Given the bureau's report of a net undercount of 1.4 percent, or 3.2 million people, in 1980, an estimated 9.2 million people were omitted from that year's census count. By adding omissions to erroneous enumerations we get a total of 15.2 million gross errors in counting individuals, which corresponds to almost 7 percent of the official 1980 census total. For 1990 the estimates of gross error ran even higher than in 1980, with about a 10 percent gross error being cited by Eugene P. Ericksen and Teresa K. DeFonso as well as many others.

The controversies surrounding the differential undercount of blacks and other minorities have made the flaws in the counting systems painfully clear and have led to proposals for fundamentally new ways to count, derived from different statistical traditions. This new methodology involves a form of systematic double counting, not just checking to make sure that the count is accurate, and it uses sampling. The traditional methods rely for their validity on careful bureaucratic procedures, the administrative chain of command, legal sanctions for nonresponse, and public cooperation of respondents. The new methods rely on the principles of statistical theory and probability for validity. Dual-systems estimation was the method of choice adopted by the methodologists at the Census Bureau for the 1990 decennial census. Its basic premise is the use of two sources of information to arrive at a better estimate of the population than could be obtained from one source alone. The procedure is an old one, widely accepted among statisticians, and has been used for a host of different practical population estimation problems. It is most familiar in the context of estimating the size of wildlife populations, in which it is known as the capture-recapture technique. A hypothetical example of fish counting adapted from Margo Anderson and Stephen E. Fienberg shows how the technique can be applied to a counting problem associated with public policy.

Fish in a Lake

State X has only two types of fish in its lakes, red fish and blue fish (with apologies to a favorite author, Dr. Seuss), and we would like to know how many of each there are and how they are distributed across the lakes in the state. We begin by going to one lake where we attempt to catch and count each fish in the lake on two successive occasions. To keep track of which fish were counted the first time, we mark each fish caught before releasing it. As the fish are caught the second time, we can then determine, for each fish, whether it had been counted in the first attempt. We can use the information from these two counts to derive a more accurate estimate of the size of the fish population than the ones we made from either of the two counts alone. It turns out that the first time we went out was sunny and the fish were somewhat difficult to catch. As a result, we counted only 150 fish. The second day was cloudy and the fish were easier to catch; as a result we were able to catch 200 fish. Further, of the 200 fish counted the second time, 125 bore marks indicating that they had been among the 150 fish counted the first time. There are thus three distinct classes of fish that have been counted: fish caught both the first time and the second time (which in this example number 125), fish caught the first time but not the second (25 in this example, or the total number of fish caught the first time minus the number of marked fish recaught the second time), and fish caught the second time but not caught the first time (75 here, equaling the total number caught the second time minus the number of marked fish caught the second time). The total number of fish in the three classes is 225. Note that we have observed all 225 fish directly and that this number exceeds the number of fish observed in either of the two counts separately. A convenient way to display the data is in the form of a 2×2 table with rows corresponding to presence and absence in the first attempt and columns corresponding to presence and absence in the second attempt (see Table 1).

The task at hand is to estimate those not caught either time. This can be done as long as the two fish counts are independent random samples. A random sample by its nature permits us to estimate the incidence of any observable characteristic in the larger population from which the sample is drawn. In this case, the characteristic of interest is that of having been captured in the first count. The examination of our random sample—the second count—showed that 125 out of 200 fish, or five-eighths of the sample, had been captured in the first count. Generalizing from the sample, we can conclude that the total number of fish counted the first time, 150, is five-eighths of the total population, that is,

$$150 = \frac{5}{8} \hat{N},$$

where $\hat{N}$ is the estimate of true population size N. To arrive at our estimate, a little high school algebra suffices:

$$\hat{N} = \frac{8}{5} \times 150 = 240.$$

Of this estimated 240 total population, 225 have been observed in one or the other or both of the two counts. Thus, we infer that there are 15 fish in the population that were not counted either time. We now observe that 30 red fish were counted the first day and 40 the second day; conversely, 120 blue fish were counted the first day and 160 counted the second day. We are interested in what would happen if we made separate calculations for red fish and blue fish. To do this, we work with a table divided into two parts, one for red fish and one for blue fish (see Table 2). By looking at the two parts of the table we see that

- red fish appear to be less numerous than blue fish (there are only 50 red fish observed but there are 175 blue fish).
- more fish, both red and blue, are caught on the cloudy second day than on the sunny first day (40 red fish on day 2 versus 30 on day one; 160 blue fish on day 2 versus 120 on day 1).
- on the sunny first day, the catchability rate for the red fish is less than for the blue fish (20/40 = 50 percent for red versus 105/160 = 65.6 percent for blue).
- on the cloudy second day, the catchability rate for the red fish is also less than for the blue fish (20/30 = 66.7 percent for red versus 105/120 = 87.5 percent for blue).
- the catchability rates for the cloudy day exceed those for the sunny day, for both red and blue fish.

If we now apply the same logic to the red and blue fish separately, we get

$$\hat{N}_r = \frac{40}{20} \times 30 = 60$$

and

$$\hat{N}_b = \frac{160}{105} \times 120 = 182.85.$$

Table 1

| | | Day 2: Cloudy | | |
		In	Out	Total
Day 1:	In	125	25	150
Sunny	Out	75	?	??
	Total	200	?	??

Table 2

Red Fish					Blue Fish				
		Day 2: Cloudy						Day 2: Cloudy	
		In	Out	Total				In	Out	Total
Day 1:	In	20	10	30	Day 1:	In	105	15	120
Sunny	Out	20	?	?	Sunny	Out	55	?	?
	Total	40	?	??		Total	160	?	??

Since our estimate for blue fish involves a fraction and we only count whole fish, we use $\hat{N}_b$ =182. We now have as our estimate of the total number of fish in the lake, $\hat{N} = \hat{N}_r + \hat{N}_b$ = 242. By taking into account the types of fish and the different patterns of "catching" fish, we learn that our original estimate of the total number of fish, 240, should be raised to 242. What will happen for a different lake where the proportions of red and blue fish are different? The same approach works no matter what the composition of the lake, but if catchability rates for red and blue fish vary according to the location of the lake (for example, in the northern as opposed to the southern part of the state), then we will need to gather separate data. Finally, we ask whether we really need to count all the fish in all the lakes twice to get an estimate of the total numbers of red and blue fish. One possibility is to carry out one count for all the lakes on the same day, but then on the second day use only a sample of the lakes for the north and a sample for the south. We can then apply the catchability rates from the second day's sample to the remaining lakes, separately for the two parts of the state, and separately for red and blue fish in each of the lakes.

Dual Systems and the Census Counting Problem

This method for counting fish can also be used to measure the size of a human population—in our case the first attempt to measure the population size is the census and the second is a special sample. For example, suppose we are trying to estimate the number of people living on a block in the Bedford-Stuyvesant neighborhood of Brooklyn, a neighborhood in New York City estimated to have one of the highest net undercounts in the nation in 1990; the congressional district that includes Bedford-Stuyvesant had a net undercount that ranked in the top ten nationwide. The first count of the population could be a list of the names and addresses of people counted in the census. Assume that 300 people were counted by the census on this particular block. For the second count of the population, let us imagine a specially commissioned, independent count carried out with even greater care than the census, and yielding 400 people. In the hypothetical Bedford-Stuyvesant block, this second count will surely include many of the same 300 people counted by the census (although the second count does not need to be bigger than the first for the method to work). We determine how many people were counted both times by comparing the list of names and addresses in the first count with the list of names and addresses in the second count, and matching those that are the same. Suppose that, through matching these two lists, we find that 250 people out of 400 counted in the second count on this block were also included in the census count. The three observed categories of the population, and their sizes, are thus the 250 counted both times, the 50 counted the first time but not the second, and the 150 counted the second time but not the first. Thus we have observed a total of 450 people. If the second count is a random sample of the population of the block as a whole, then the fraction of members of the second count included in the census (250 out of 400, or 5/8) is an estimate of the fraction of the total population of the block counted in the census. Finally, we can estimate that the total population is the number of people counted in the census, or 300, divided by 5/8. This yields an estimate of the total population of 480 people. Thus, the estimated census undercount in this hypothetical block is 180 people out of 480, or 3/8 of the population.

The numbers here are hypothetical, and they are the same as in the example of fish in the lake, except that all the counts are doubled. And just as there were red and blue fish in the lake, there are people from different population groups in our block in Bedford-Stuyvesant, for example, blacks and non-blacks, and so we will need separate estimates for the numbers of each group in this block. The breakdown this time might be quite different, as in Table 3.

This time, we have the vast majority of people in the block being black and the estimates for the total numbers of blacks and non-blacks in the block are:

$$\hat{N}_{black} = {}^{360}/_{214} \times 262 = 440.74,$$

and

$$\hat{N}_{non\text{-}black} = {}^{40}/_{36} \times 38 = 42.2.$$

Table 3

Black					Non-Black				
		Recount					Recount		
		In	Out	Total			In	Out	Total
Census	In	214	48	262	Census	In	36	2	38
	Out	146	?	?		Out	4	?	?
	Total	360	?	??		Total	40	?	??

Again, counting only the whole numbers of people, we get a total of 440 + 42 = 482. The result is slightly higher than our earlier estimate of 480 from the two groups combined because the catchabilities are so different and the numbers so disproportionate. There is a very serious differential undercount in this hypothetical block, however, 100 (1-262/440) = 40.5 percent of the blacks being missed compared with only 100 (1-38/42) = 9.5 percent of the non-blacks being missed.

Because the undercount rate varies among different kinds of blocks, we must estimate separate undercount rates for blacks and non-blacks for each of a sample of blocks. We would not, for example, expect our dual-systems estimate of the undercount rates of a block in Bedford-Stuyvesant to tell us very much about the undercount rates in an expensive suburb. Accordingly, in selecting the sample, one starts with a list of all the blocks or equivalent-size rural units in the United States, and groups the blocks into categories, or *strata*, according to their demographic characteristics. Such characteristics might include racial composition, proportion of homeowners to renters, and average household size. Rates of undercount are determined for each stratum by measuring the undercount of a sample of blocks within the stratum by dual-systems estimation. The undercount rate of these blocks is then applied to the other blocks throughout the country in the stratum. The actual correction of the census counts consists of adjusting the raw census count for each stratum to compensate for the estimated undercount in that stratum.

The Census Bureau itself was an early user of this type of methodology. In particular it matched the results from a sample to the census records for coverage evaluation in connection with the 1950 decennial census, although official reports did not provide a full implementation of the dual-systems estimation. In 1980 the bureau implemented a version of the dual-systems method using data from the Current Population Survey for the second count and not a specially designed post-enumeration survey. In 1990 the Census Bureau took an independent count of the populations of each of a large number of blocks nationwide and then matched those counted to the records of the census for those blocks. This second count was known as a "post-enumeration survey," or PES. C. Chandra Sekar and W. E. Deming, Karol J. Krotki, and Stephen E. Fienberg provide additional background and references to the original uses of the methodology and to technical details and discussions.

Dual-Systems Model Assumptions and Their Empirical Base

The dual-systems estimation method is based on a set of assumptions linked to a very explicit statistical model. The three assumptions most widely discussed are:

Perfect matching. The individuals in the first list can be matched with those in the second list, without error.

Independence of lists. The probability of an individual being included in the census does not depend on whether the individual was included in the second list.

Homogeneity. The probabilities of inclusion do not vary from individual to individual.

Perhaps the greatest problem with the dual-systems approach as it was used in conjunction with the 1980 census was the rate of matching errors (the failure of the "perfect matching" assumption). There are two kinds of matching errors: false matches and false nonmatches. False matches produce an underestimate of the population size. By contrast, if individuals in the sample cannot be matched with their records in the census, then the population size is overestimated.

The matching problem as it emerged in the context of the coverage evaluation program for the 1980 census was discussed at length in the analyses reported by Robert E. Fay and his colleagues and was the focus of a major research program in the 1980s, including the development of new computer-based matching algorithms by Matthew Jaro. Approximately 75 percent of the 1990 PES records were matched using these algorithms, and clerical matching then took care of most of the remaining records. Special features of the redesigned PES reduced other difficulties associated with the matching process. Yet there was still a residual group of nonmatches, some of which were real matches. Thus the bureau statisticians set about finding a suitable statistical approach to allocating the residual group to the match and nonmatch categories. Nathaniel Schenker describes the details of their approach.

The failure of the "independence of lists" assumption is known as correlation bias. In the presence of positive correlation bias (being missed in the census is positively correlated with being missed in the second list), the traditional capture-recapture population estimate tends to underestimate the actual population size but, as Howard Hogan suggests, the approach yields an improvement over the unadjusted value. The only direct statistical method available to measure the extent of correlation bias involves a generalization of the dual-systems approach to multiple lists and the estimation techniques developed for multiple-capture problems developed in works by Stephen E. Fienberg and in Yvonne M. M. Bishop, Stephen E. Fienberg, and Paul W. Holland cited in the Bibliography. This alternative is more complex and has been used only in the 1988 test census in analyses by Alan M. Zaslavsky and G. S. Wolfgang and not as part of the full-scale census process. As part of the coverage evaluation process for the 1990 census, William R. Bell of the Census Bureau produced several indirect estimates of correlation bias, all of which reaffirmed what had widely been assumed, that correlation bias appears to be positive.

Heterogeneity, or differences, of capture probabilities for both the census and the sample is clearly an issue in any real population setting. The issue is not so much whether the "homogeneity" assumption is violated, but the extent to which it is and the implications for the results of dual-systems estimation. What is quite clear is that the correlation between census and sample catchabilities and the effects of heterogeneity are confounded in the simple dual-systems estimation model, since in a 2×2 contingency table with a missing cell there are no degrees of freedom left over to separate the two. Only since the 1990 census have statisticians begun to address the precise nature of the effects of heterogeneity. Joseph B. Kadane, Michael M. Meyer, and John W. Tukey present an interesting and detailed model for heterogeneity and describe its implications.

Statisticians now understand that the problem of heterogeneity can be handled in at least two very different ways. One might model the effects of heterogeneity or one can attempt to reduce them directly by stratification or grouping the data into small, relatively homogeneous groups. The latter strategy, stratifica-

tion, was built into the design for the 1990 PES and it reduced but did not eliminate the concern at the Census Bureau about heterogeneity. The tricky thing here is that there is a trade-off between making the strata smaller and thus more homogeneous, on the one hand, and making sure that the counts in the 2×2 table used for dual-systems estimation are large enough to make the assumptions of the estimation statistically valid, on the other hand. As part of the follow-up to the PES, the Census Bureau examined several indirect measures of the effect of residual heterogeneity. A statistical modeling approach that actually attempts to account for individual-level heterogeneity is possible, but it requires matching three or more sources, rather than just the two in the dual-systems approach. John N. Darroch and his colleagues and Stephen E. Fienberg and his colleagues describe alternative approaches to the estimation of heterogeneity based on multiple lists, which may be of value in future censuses.

Modifying Dual-Systems Methods for the U.S. Decennial Census

Two major modifications to the basic dual-systems approach are required for it to be useful for census adjustment purposes. The traditional dual-systems method deals only with the problem of omissions and does not touch the problem of erroneous enumerations. In the 1970s and 1980s, the Census Bureau developed extensions to the basic methodology to allow for erroneous enumerations. The bureau counts erroneous enumerations by doing a check of those included in the census for the sample blocks and subtracts them out of the counts for dual-systems estimation.

If we break the block-level data down by racial and ethnic groups, which is a major goal of the dual-systems approach, the counts in the 2×2 table become very small. Thus we need to aggregate data across selected blocks according to some type of stratification scheme. To estimate the missing people for the nation as a whole we employ a complex stratified sample of blocks and so we need to "weight" the counts from different blocks according to the sample design when we combine them.

Because we take only a sample of such blocks, and it is only for them that we can produce adjustment factors based on dual-systems estimation, we need to be able to generalize from the sample, appropriately aggregated, to all the other blocks in the nation. This is a simple task in principle, but quite tricky in practice.

The method of choice has turned out to be a version of traditional regression estimation from sampling theory. In the traditional theory, one applies regression-based adjustments only to the units of the sample or their aggregates. For the 1990 census adjustment calculations these same adjustments were applied to blocks not in the sample as well. This has been labeled by some as the synthetic adjustment assumption. It not only provides a solution to the generalization problem but it also helps address the issue of how much to aggregate the sample data to form the strata for estimation purposes.

To some extent we have simplified the description of some of the basic ideas of the dual-systems estimation technique, and we do not wish to disguise the difficulties that some statisticians have claimed are inherent in the methodology. Lawrence D. Brown and his colleagues describe many of the concerns with and criticisms of the methodology as implemented in 1990. Nonetheless, the vast majority of assessments of the 1990 implementation of the method concluded that the results were superior for most purposes to the raw census counts. Mary H. Mulry and Bruce D. Spencer carried out the original analyses demonstrating the superiority of the adjusted data. Anderson and her colleagues provide a response to the critique of Brown and his colleagues. And the report from the National Research Council edited by M. L. Cohen, A. A. White, and K. F. Rust takes stock of the 1990 adaptation of the methodology for the 2000 census.

See also *Accuracy and Coverage Evaluation*.

■ Stephen E. Fienberg

Bibliography

Anderson, Margo, Beth Osborne Daponte, Stephen E. Fienberg, Joseph B. Kadane, Bruce D. Spencer, and Duane L. Steffey. "Sampling-Based Adjustment of the 2000 Census—A Balanced Perspective." *Jurimetrics*, to be published.

Anderson, Margo, and Stephen E. Fienberg. *Who Counts? The Politics of Census-Taking in Contemporary America.* New York: Russell Sage Foundation, 1999.

Bell, William R. "Using Information from Demographic Analysis in Postenumeration Survey Estimation." *Journal of the American Statistical Association* 88 (September 1993): 1106–1118.

Bishop, Yvonne M. M., Stephen E. Fienberg, and Paul W. Holland. *Discrete Multivariate Analysis: Theory and Practice.* Cambridge: MIT Press, 1975.

Brown, Lawrence D., Morris L. Eaton, David A. Freedman, P. Klein, Stephen, Richard A. Olshen, Kenneth W. Wachter, Martin T. Wells, and Donald Ylvisaker. "Statistical Controversies in Census 2000." *Jurimetrics* 39 (summer 1999): 347–375.

Chandrasekar, C., and W. E. Deming. "On a Method of Estimating Birth and Death Rates and the Extent of Registration." *Journal of the American Statistical Association* 44 (1949): 101–115.

Cohen, M. L., A. A. White, and K. F. Rust. *Measuring a Changing Nation: Modern Methods for the 2000 Census.* Washington, D.C.: National Academy Press, 1999.

Cowen, C. D., and D. J. Malec. "Capture-Recapture Models When Both Sources Have Clustered Observations." *Journal of the American Statistical Association* 81 (1986): 347–353.

Darroch, John N., Stephen E. Fienberg, Gary F. V. Glonek, and Brian W. Junker. "A Three Sample Multiple-Recapture Approach to Census Population Estimation with Heterogeneous Catchability." *Journal of the American Statistical Association* 88 (1993): 1137–1148.

Ericksen, Eugene P., and Teresa K. DeFonso. "Beyond the Net Undercount: How to Measure Census Error." *Chance* 6 (1993): 38–43.

Fay, Robert E. "Evaluation of Census Coverage from the 1980 Post Enumeration Program (PES): Census Population and Geocoding Errors as Measured by the Sample." In *1980 Preliminary Evaluation Results Memorandum*, vol. 119. Washington, D.C.: U.S. Bureau of the Census, 1988.

Fay, Robert E., Jeffrey S. Passel, J. Gregory Robinson, and Charles D. Cowan. *The Coverage of the Population in the 1980 Census.* Washington, D.C.: U.S. Bureau of the Census, 1988.

Fienberg, Stephen E. "The Multiple-Recapture Census for Closed Populations and the 2k Incomplete Contingency Table." *Biometrika* 59 (1972): 591–603.

———. "Bibliography on Capture-Recapture Modeling with Application to Census Undercount Adjustment." *Survey Methodology* 18 (1992): 143–154.

Fienberg, Stephen E., Matthew S. Johnson, and Brian W. Junker. "Classical Multilevel and Bayesian Approaches to Population Size Estimation Using Multiple Lists." *Journal of the Royal Statistical Society A* 162, Part 3 (1999): 383–405.

Gersh, Mark, and Ken Strasma. *1990 Census Undercount by Congressional District.* Washington, D.C.: National Committee for an Effective Congress, 1999 (http://www.ncec.org/census.cfm).

Hogan, Howard. "The 1990 Post-Enumeration Survey: Operations and Results." *Journal of the American Statistical Association* 88 (1993): 1047–1060.

Hogan, Howard, and Kirk M. Wolter. "Measuring Accuracy in a Post-Enumeration Survey." *Survey Methodology* 14 (1988): 99–116.

Jaro, Matthew. "Advances in Record-Linkage Methodology as Applied to Matching the 1985 Test Census of Tampa, Florida." *Journal of the American Statistical Association* 84 (1989): 414–420.

Kadane, Joseph B., Michael M. Meyer, and John W. Tukey. "Yule's Association Paradox and Stratum Heterogeneity in Capture-Recapture Studies. *Journal of the American Statistical Association* 94 (1999): 855–859.

Krotki, Karol J., ed. *Developments in Dual System Estimation of Population Size and Growth*. Edmonton: University of Alberta Press, 1978.

Mulry, Mary H., and Bruce D. Spencer. "Accuracy of the 1990 Census and Undercount Adjustments." *Journal of the American Statistical Association* 88 (September 1993): 1080–1092.

Schenker, Nathaniel. "Handling Missing Data in Coverage Estimation with Application to the 1986 Test of Adjustment Related Operations." *Survey Methodology* 14 (1988): 87–98.

Seuss, Dr. *One Fish Two Fish Red Fish Blue Fish*. New York: Random House, 1960.

Wolter, Kirt M. "Some Coverage Error Models for Census Data." *Journal of the American Statistical Association* 81 (1986): 338–346.

Zaslavsky, Alan M., and G. S. Wolfgang. "Triple System Modeling of Census, Post-Enumeration Survey and Administrative List Data." In *Proceedings of the Section on Survey Research*. Alexandria, Va.: American Statistical Association, 1990.

Census law

Census law, or the law pertaining to the decennial census of population, is grounded in the U.S. Constitution. The constitutional mandate to take a census every ten years is implemented by various acts of Congress that direct the manner of its conduct and the information to be collected.

The Constitution

The decennial census is the foundation on which our democratic system of government is built. The founding fathers realized that critical to the success of their efforts to create a new form of government was the development of processes for allocating political power among the states and for raising sufficient funds to support the federal government. Solutions to both representation and funding were reached through compromise.

The allocation of political power among the states was a particularly sensitive issue. The smaller states were concerned they would be dominated by the larger, faster growing states. This led to the Great Compro-

mise: The legislature would have two houses. In the House of Representatives, representation would be based on the size of a state's population, thereby protecting the interests of the larger states. In the Senate, each state would have two representatives, regardless of population size, thereby protecting the rights of the smaller states.

Given the differences among the states in population size, land mass, and natural and economic resources, a procedure was needed to determine each state's financial contribution to the federal government. The Framers of the Constitution quickly discovered that ability to contribute, or wealth, was an elusive concept. They were able to agree on neither the elements constituting wealth nor the manner of evaluating those elements. Eventually they decided to use population size as a proxy for wealth. This did not resolve the problem, however, because the southern states insisted that slaves should be included for purposes of representation. Again, a compromise was reached by agreeing to include three-fifths of the slave population. Thereafter, direct taxes (taxes on land and buildings primarily) were imposed in proportion to each state's population.

Having agreed on population as the basis for a state's political representation and its financial support of the federal government, the next challenge for the Framers was to agree on a means for determining the size of a state's population. After extensive debate, the Framers decided that a census of population should be taken every ten years (Article I, Section 2, Clause 3).

By basing both representation and funding on the size of a state's population, the Framers created a disincentive for states to inflate their census counts. Although a state would want its population count to be high for purposes of apportionment, the opposite would be true for determining the amount of its contribution through direct taxation by the federal government.

With the abolition of slavery and the adoption of the Fourteenth Amendment, the language requiring the inclusion of only three-fifths of the slaves was deleted. The adoption of the Sixteenth Amendment, providing for a personal income tax as a means of funding the federal government, resulted in two significant changes for the census. First, the size of a state's population would not affect the amount of its contribution through direct taxation by the federal government, thereby removing the disincentive against attempts to inflate a state's population count. Second, all residents, including Indians who formerly were not taxed, were to be counted.

Early Acts of Congress: Census Laws of 1790 to 1870

Since the first census, in 1790, Congress has passed laws directing how and by whom the census shall be taken. The first census law, the Act of March 1, 1790 (1 Stat. 101), set the tone and the parameters for censuses to follow. It established the residence rules (a person is to be counted where he or she usually resides), collected information beyond that needed to apportion the House, and made participation in the census mandatory.

Under the 1790 census law the information collected was limited in scope, asking for only the name of the head of the household; the numbers of free white males sixteen and up and those under sixteen; and the numbers of white females, all other free persons, and slaves. Indians not taxed were excluded. At the outset the census was used to collect information beyond that necessary to apportion the House. It was conducted by U.S. marshals and their assistants, under the direction of the secretary of state, Thomas Jefferson.

Persons were to be counted where they usually resided, those without a "settled place of residence" were to be counted where they resided on census day, and those "occasionally absent at the time of the enumeration" were to be counted as residing in their place of usual residence. This procedure for designating residence, essential to meeting the constitutional purpose of apportioning the House, has been carried forward to the present day, with minor revisions to reflect changes in living patterns.

Participation in the census was required. The law directed that every person over age sixteen years, whether or not the head of a family, must provide the information to the best of his or her knowledge, "on pain of forfeiting twenty dollars." Participation in the census continues to be mandatory to this day.

Subsequent early census laws expanded the scope of inquiries on a gradual basis and made moderate adjustments to the procedures for conducting the census. The 1800 census law, the Act of February 28, 1800 (2 Stat. 11), called for a breakdown of free white males and free white females into five age groups. The statute also specified that the census was to include the "territory of the United States northwest of the river Ohio, and of the Mississippi territory." Of particular interest to those concerned with privacy and confidentiality was the requirement that the marshals' assistants post a copy of census information, by name of family, "at two of the most public places within [his district], there to remain for the inspection of all concerned."

The 1810 census law, the Act of March 26, 1810 (2 Stat. 564), continued along the same lines as the 1800 census with the additional requirement that a personal visit be made to each dwelling. This requirement continued until the 1970 census.

The 1820 census law, the Act of March 14, 1820 (3 Stat. 548), extended the age breakdown to slaves and "free coloured persons" and required the designation of "persons in agriculture, commerce, and manufactures" and enumeration of "foreigners not naturalized."

The 1830 census law, the Act of March 23, 1830 (4 Stat. 383), called for a more extensive age breakdown and for data on persons who were "deaf and dumb" and those who were blind.

The 1840 census law, the Act of March 3, 1839 (5 Stat. 331), in addition to requiring information about those who were deaf and dumb and those who were blind, required information on those who were "insane and idiots," distinguishing those who were public charges. It also required information on those who were receiving pensions for revolutionary or military service. Further, information was to be collected "in relation to mines, agriculture, commerce, manufactures, and schools, as will exhibit a full view of the pursuits of industry, education and resources of the country."

The 1850, 1860, and 1870 censuses were all taken under the same law, the Act of May 23, 1850 (9 Stat. 428). This law moved the responsibility for conducting the census from the secretary of state to the secretary of the interior. The questions to be asked were no longer specified in the census law itself; rather the secretary of the interior was given discretion to do so. Although participation continued to be mandatory and a personal visit to each dwelling was required, posting of the census information was not required. Instead the marshals' assistants were required to provide the original census returns to the clerk of the county court and two copies were to be sent to the marshal.

The Era of Information Expansion: Census Laws of 1880 to 1920

A new law was passed for the 1880 census, the Act of March 3, 1879 (20 Stat. 473), which increased exponentially the number and kinds of questions asked, most notably in areas focusing on the nation's economy.

The 1850 census had included 15 subjects of inquiry and 138 questions seeking specific details. This scope held, with minor changes, for the 1860 and 1870 censuses. In contrast, the 1880 census included 23 subjects of inquiry and 13,010 questions seeking specific details under the various subjects. Most of these questions were inquiries about particular industries and were contained on separate census forms (for example, there were 5,779 inquiries about the insurance industry alone). Even so, more than 250 questions were inquiries about individuals or the institutions dealing with them.

Not only was the scope of the census expanded to encyclopedic proportions but the structure for conducting the census was changed radically. A census office was established in the Department of the Interior, to be headed by the superintendent of the census, who would be appointed by the president with the advice and consent of the Senate. The secretary of the interior was to appoint supervisors of the census within each state and territory. The supervisors were to employ enumerators "without reference to their political or party affiliations."

The 1880 census also introduced the first steps in ensuring the confidentiality of the respondents' information. The enumerator was required to take an oath that he would "not disclose any information...obtained by me to any person or persons, except to my superior officers." The law also provided a penalty for improper disclosure, making it a misdemeanor with a fine up to $500. These protections were limited, however, as reflected in the requirements of a subsequent modification, the Act of April 20, 1880 (25 Stat. 760), directing the enumerators to file a list of names (with age, sex, and color of all persons enumerated by him) with the county and to correct the enumeration "on such reliable information as he may obtain, all omissions and mistakes in such enumeration, and to that end he may swear and examine witnesses."

A personal visit to each dwelling was required, but for the first time authority was given to collect what has come to be known as last-resort information. If no one could be found at home, the enumerator could obtain the required information from neighbors.

The same scope and process pertained, for the most part, to the 1890 census law, the Act of March 1, 1889 (25 Stat. 760). A total of 13,161 separate inquiries were made, over 400 of which sought information about individuals or the institutions dealing with them. Again,

many of these inquiries were on separate census forms. The issue of privacy was again affected by a provision expressly authorizing the superintendent of the census to furnish incorporated municipalities, cities, towns, villages, and the like with a copy of the names (with age, sex, birthplace, and color or race) of all persons within these jurisdictions.

The 1900 census law, the Act of March 3, 1899 (30 Stat. 1014), called for a census office in the Department of the Interior but explicitly stated that it should not be considered as providing for a permanent census bureau. The director of the census was given "discretion as to the construction, and form and number of inquiries necessary to secure the information." Confidentiality was again qualified by further expanding the availability of the data. The law authorized release to the governors of the states and territories, as well as to municipal governments, of the names (with age, sex, color or race, and birthplace) of all persons within these jurisdictions.

The Act of March 6, 1902 (32 Stat. 51) established a permanent Census Office that continued to be located temporarily in the Department of the Interior. The 1910 census law, the Act of June 29, 1909 (36 Stat. 1), provided, in essence, that the Census Office would be in the Department of Commerce and Labor. This department was separated into two separate departments by the Act of March 4, 1913 (37 Stat. 736). For the 1920 census (Act of March 3, 1919 [40 Stat. 1291]), the Census Office was located in the Department of Commerce.

The Era of Methodological Innovation: Census Laws of 1930 to the Present

The 1930 census law, the Act of June 18, 1929 (46 Stat. 21), formed the basis for what was codified on August 31, 1954, as Title 13 of the U.S. Code, the Census Act (68 Stat. 1012). Although it ushered in what might be considered the modern era, the 1930 census law continued many of the provisions contained in earlier authorizing legislation. A personal visit to each dwelling was required, and the enumerators still had the authority to seek last-resort information. Participation was mandatory. Any enumerator who disclosed census information without authority from the director was subject to fines and imprisonment.

A major innovation came with the provision for confidentiality. Under previous statutes, only economic data were protected by a provision directing that the data be used solely for statistical purposes, prohibiting publication that would permit identification of data provided by a particular respondent, and permitting only sworn employees of the Census Office to examine the individual reports. This protection was now extended to all information collected under the census law. Complete protection was not afforded, however, because the provision authorizing release to governors of states and territories and courts of record, as well as to individuals for genealogical and other proper purposes, remained in effect. This apparent gap was corrected in a 1976 amendment (P.L. 94-521) that eliminated the authority to provide data to governors and courts of record and permitted release to individuals only if the requested data were their own or were requested by their authorized agent or in connection with their estate. Census confidentiality was upheld by the Supreme Court in *Baldrige v. Shapiro*, 455 U.S. 345 (1982).

Another milestone occurred in 1964 with the elimination of the requirement that the enumerators personally visit each dwelling (P.L. 88-530). This law permitted the first mail-out, mail-back census in 1970. Essential to the mail-out, mail-back procedure is development of a complete and correct address list. The Census Bureau works closely with the U.S. Postal Service to ensure that every reasonable effort is made to include all addresses in the country. For Census 2000 another improvement was added authorizing the Census Bureau to furnish state and local governments with a copy of the census address list and the opportunity to revise it (P.L. 103-430). The state and local government officials participating in this program are prohibited from using the information for any other purpose and are sworn to uphold census confidentiality.

Arguably, the most important innovation of the modern era is the authorization to use sampling in collecting census data. In sampling, only a portion of the total universe of respondents (for the census, the universe is all persons residing in the country) are queried. Information obtained from this portion (a systematic random sample) is used to make an estimate for the total universe. In 1957, Congress gave discretionary authority to the secretary of commerce to use sampling, if deemed appropriate, "except for the determination of population for apportionment purposes" (P.L. 85-207). This provision, codified as Sect. 195 of Title 13, U.S. Code, was amended by Congress in 1976 (P.L. 94-521) to require the secretary to use sampling, if

deemed feasible, with the caveat remaining that it could not be used for apportionment of the House. The Supreme Court held in *Department of Commerce v. House of Representatives*, 119 S.Ct. 765 (1999), that Sect. 195 precluded the use of sampling for apportionment of the House. Regardless of the limitation imposed by Sect. 195, sampling has permitted the Census Bureau to greatly reduce the burden placed on respondents in completing the census. In Census 2000 the vast majority of households (approximately five in six) received the short form, which asked for only very basic information (names, sex, race, and the like). Most of the demographic data collected in the census was asked on a sample basis using the long form. Thus sampling not only reduces the burden on respondents but also provides a substantial cost saving in data collection and processing.

See also *Confidentiality; Litigation and the census; Three-fifths Compromise.*

■ J. Patrick Heelen

Bibliography

Farrand, Max, ed. *The Records of the Federal Convention of 1787.* New Haven: Yale University Press, 1966.

Killian, Johnny H., ed., and Leland E. Beck, assoc. ed. *The Constitution of the United States of America. Analysis and Interpretation.* Washington, D.C.: U.S. Government Printing Office, 1987.

Bowen, Catherine Drinker. *Miracle at Philadelphia.* Boston: Back Bay Books, Little, Brown, 1966.

Rossiter, Clinton, ed. *The Federalist Papers.* New York: Mentor, NAL Penguin, 1961.

Wright, Carroll D. *The History and Growth of the United States Census.* Prepared for the Senate Committee on the Census. Washington, D.C.: Government Printing Office, 1900.

Census of Puerto Rico

Census 2000 marked the tenth consecutive decennial census of Puerto Rico conducted by the Census Bureau. Although a special census was conducted by the U.S. War Department in November 1899—one year after the island's acquisition from Spain following the Spanish-American War—it was not until the 1910 census that Puerto Rico was fully represented as a census area of the United States for the decennial censuses. Many counts and censuses of the island were taken in the previous 400 years under the auspices of the Spanish crown, but they were not taken with the same decennial regularity.

Since the 1910 census, and particularly during the past half century, Puerto Rico has become increasingly integrated into the bureau's statistical and geographic operations and products. Recent decennial census programs and operations in Puerto Rico generally have followed the same set of procedures as in the fifty states and the District of Columbia. All people whose usual place of residence is in Puerto Rico are counted by the bureau without regard to a person's legal immigration status or citizenship.

Similar to the District of Columbia and the noncontiguous territories of the United States, and in accordance with Title 13 of the U.S. Code, Puerto Rico is treated as a state equivalent for statistical purposes. Unlike other nonstate Island Areas, such as Guam and the U.S. Virgin Islands, but similar to the fifty states and the District of Columbia, the bureau conducts all aspects of the census in Puerto Rico. A 1958 Memorandum of Understanding (MOU), and its ongoing amendments, between the bureau and the government of the Commonwealth of Puerto Rico ensure close coordination and collaboration in the planning, conduct, and promotion of the Puerto Rico censuses.

The primary differences between census operations, activities, and products in Puerto Rico and the states result from many factors, such as its unique political status, social and economic planning needs, Spanish language and culture, geographic issues, and addressing system. Although the most apparent differences are language, culture, and political status, the primary technical obstacles to greater consistency with stateside programs and products during the past few censuses have been Puerto Rico's unique addressing system and its special data content needs. Puerto Rico's adoption of the stateside questionnaire for the first time in Census 2000, and the clarification and simplification of its geographic entities for the 1990 census, have left the addressing situation as the primary technical challenge to full integration with stateside programs and processes.

Data Content

Puerto Rico's unique status historically has caused the bureau to treat data content somewhat differently from its treatment in the states. Although census questionnaires used for previous decennial censuses generally have followed the stateside version (both the short and long forms), the bureau made some modifications to accommodate socioeconomic, cultural, language, and climatic differences according to provisions of the 1958 MOU between the commonwealth and the bureau. For Census 2000, the governor's office requested that the Census Bureau use the stateside questionnaire in Puerto Rico (albeit primarily printed and conducted in Spanish and with minor differences in terminology). Standardizing the questionnaire facilitates data processing and ensures greater consistency with stateside data delivery schedules and data products.

The adoption of the stateside questionnaire is one of the more significant differences between the 1990 and 2000 censuses that will affect data users and policymakers. All changes made for the stateside census questionnaire for Census 2000 applied to Puerto Rico. Because of the different questionnaires used by Puerto Rico for the 1990 and previous censuses, the cumulative changes for Puerto Rico were much greater than those for the states. For instance, sixteen subjects in the 1990 census were excluded for Census 2000 as opposed to only five stateside, and seven new subjects were included as opposed to only one for the stateside questionnaire. Puerto Rico no longer collected decennial data on ability to read and write or ability to speak Spanish and English, vocational training, and other questions traditionally used to measure foreign-born population and migration (for example, birthplace of parents, residence in the United States between decennial years). Housing questions on type of construction, condition of housing unit, number of bathrooms, type of water heater, type of cooking fuel, and whether or not there is air conditioning also were dropped. For the first time, Puerto Ricans were asked about Hispanic origin, ancestry, and language spoken at home. The question of race was asked for the first time since the 1950 census, and it was based on self-identification rather than enumerator observation.

Enumeration Methodology

For the past several censuses, data collection and processing methodologies in Puerto Rico generally have been much more labor intensive than their counterparts in the states. Although Puerto Rico contains metropolitan areas and urbanized areas with greater population densities than most similar areas stateside, the bureau continues to enumerate the island's population using canvassing methodologies it uses stateside only in very sparsely settled areas where mail delivery typically does not use house numbers and street names.

The primary reason for the use of data collection methodologies associated with sparsely settled areas in the United States is the existence of a street-naming and addressing system in Puerto Rico that is not compatible with Census Bureau address-matching requirements and current capabilities. For example, the U.S. Postal Service's addressing standards for Puerto Rico require an additional address line not used stateside to distinguish addresses with the same house number and street name in the same ZIP code. Other characteristics of the street-naming and addressing system in Puerto Rico that require special handling and additional computer-programming resources include variant street-naming and addressing conventions. As a result of these and other situations, data collection has been more costly and, due to the nature of highly labor-intensive operations, potentially more error-prone, than the mail-out, mail-back methodologies used in the states.

The 1990 and previous censuses used a list/enumerate methodology, whereby all housing units received an unaddressed short-form census questionnaire from the U.S. Postal Service. The 1990 census address list for Puerto Rico, called the Address Control File, was created at the time of enumeration. Census enumerators visited all housing units, listed their addresses in registers and marked their approximate location, and added missing streets and street names to Census Bureau maps. This served to geographically code each address to its census block, the basic unit for all decennial census data tabulations. They completed questionnaires for vacant housing units and interviewed respondents if the questionnaires were not complete. For one of every six housing units, enumerators were responsible for transferring the short-form responses to, and then completing, a long-form questionnaire.

Census 2000 used an update/leave methodology, whereby an addressed questionnaire—short or long form, as appropriate—is left at a housing unit by a census enumerator. The questionnaire is filled out by any adult household member and mailed to the local office of the Census Bureau. Nonresponding housing units, including those that are vacant, are visited and enumerated by census enumerators. Self-response, enabled by the new update/leave data collection methodology, has been shown, by census studies stateside, to yield higher-quality data than those obtained through enumerator interviews.

Using an update/leave operation for Census 2000 required the bureau to develop an address list prior to questionnaire delivery. This enhancement involved conducting an island-wide address-listing operation in 1998 to generate the Census 2000 address list, called the Master Address File (MAF). At the same time, and similar to stateside address-listing operations, all housing unit locations were annotated on census block maps and digitized into the *TIGER* database. The MAF was then used for census operations to control questionnaire delivery and return, and *TIGER* was used to generate maps with housing unit locations for follow-up operations. Linkage between the relative locations for all housing units in *TIGER* and the MAF for Puerto Rico enabled internal census staff to more easily check and review potential address-listing problems. For the first time, and similar to stateside operations, the bureau will generate mail-back response rates for Puerto Rico.

Unlike areas in the United States that have mail delivery to city-style addresses, the MAF for Puerto Rico was created entirely from the ground up by census field listers, and updated and corrected during the update/leave operation. Unlike in the states, the bureau did not use the 1990 Address Control File or the U.S. Postal Service's Delivery Sequence File of city-style addresses because of quality and coverage limitations and the inability of the bureau's address-matching software to deal with Puerto Rico's unique addressing conventions. As such, the creation and quality of the MAF were dependent on accurate listings and map updates by field staff. Although not specifically covered by Public Law 103-430, the Census Address List Improvement Act, which enables address list sharing between the bureau and local governments, all *municipio* (county equivalent) governments were invited, under Title 13 confidentiality provisions, to check the census address list and related maps to ensure coverage and quality; fifty of the *municipios* chose to participate in this process. The delivery of census questionnaires by census enumerators provided an additional opportunity to enhance the MAF and the *TIGER* database.

It is well known that, for a variety of reasons, large, labor-intensive clerical operations, in themselves, can lead to higher error rates than more automated operations. In Puerto Rico, this problem is compounded by language difficulties. Although supervisory and field staff in Puerto Rico are required to be Spanish-speaking, the information acquired in both map update and address-listing operations (sometimes illegible or difficult to understand even stateside) is transcribed and entered into computers in large, labor-intensive operations by staff that may know little, if any, Spanish or may not be cognizant of the unique aspects of census geography or postal addressing in Puerto Rico.

Geography

The bureau reports data by legal/administrative and statistical geographic entities. Legal/administrative entities include the commonwealth (state equivalent), *municipio*, barrio/barrio-pueblo (minor civil division equivalent), and subbarrio (no statistical equivalent stateside). Statistical areas are, for the most part, similar and conform to the same technical criteria as their stateside counterparts. *Zonas urbanas* and *comunidades* are census-designated places that are unique to Puerto Rico, which does not have legally incorporated places.

Puerto Rico's current legal/administrative geography is the result of historical factors and legal actions taken by the commonwealth legislature, whereas statistical geography is the result, in most cases, of the interaction of the bureau and the Puerto Rico Planning Board. Prior to both the 1980 and 1990 censuses, there was some confusion in understanding Puerto Rico's legal and statistical entities. This situation, which led to actual errors in the 1970 data tabulations for barrios, derived from several factors, such as alternative use of terms to define similar entities, use of same names to identify different entities, errors in original delineation or description of boundaries, and translations between English and Spanish.

Perhaps no other situation better dramatizes Puerto Rico's situation between two worlds and between past and present than the barrio geography. Barrios maintain a political and cultural function but they have no planning or economic function. The growing availability and use of data by ZIP code, census tract, block group, and block, and the growing unfamiliarity of urban Puerto Ricans with the sub-*municipio* barrio nomenclature, has led to several statistical and data collection concerns. In a growing number of cases, the original barrio boundaries no longer separate communities. Barrio boundaries often do not follow visible features, and the same name may exist for barrios in adjacent *municipios*. Unlike *municipios*, they are often not identified by signs, or even known by residents of the barrio. This situation is especially acute where there has been new suburban growth at the barrio boundary, residents are recent arrivals, or residents live in *urbanizaciones* (named housing developments).

Data Products

Prior to 2000, most data products offered to the fifty states and the District of Columbia also were available for Puerto Rico, including redistricting data files (although Puerto Rico is not covered by Public Law 94-171). However, data for Puerto Rico generally were not included in the nationwide products or summaries and, because of the addressing situation discussed earlier, some stateside data products (for example, the 1990 Summary Tape File 3B, which contains zip-code-level data) were not available for Puerto Rico. In 2000, however, Puerto Rico was treated as a state equivalent and included in all data products for which data were available, both electronic and hard copy. Barring congressional action, the U.S. national totals will continue to include only the fifty states and the District of Columbia.

Puerto Rico is fully integrated into most of the bureau's geographic data products. The only notable difference in products is related to the address limitations in the bureau's geographic files for Puerto Rico. As such, the Census Tract/Street Index and similar address-related products have not been available for Puerto Rico, and the *TIGER/Line* files do not have the same level and quality of attribute coding as stateside files with city-style addressing.

It is important that data users thoroughly acquaint themselves with the unique aspects of the geography of Puerto Rico before making use of the data. Of special concern is an understanding of the hierarchy of geographic designations, including *municipio*, *ciudad* (in census products prior to 1990), *zona urbana*, urbanized area, and metropolitan area. For example, data for San Juan can be referenced under all these headings, with each referring to a different geographic area.

Looking toward the Future

Data from the Census 2000 of Puerto Rico appears in all stateside census products and online through the census Web site. Online access for data from Puerto Rico includes a user-requested Spanish interface. This represents a change from 1990, when separate machine-readable and printed products were created for Puerto Rico and the outlying areas.

In an effort to achieve a more robust integration of Puerto Rico with stateside decennial census programs, operations, and products, problems arising from Puerto Rico's unique addressing conventions will be tackled and resolved through public and private partnerships begun during the 1990s. The enhancement and standardization of addressing by the U.S. Postal Service and *municipio* officials will be accompanied by the development of a continually updated MAF through cooperative efforts between the postal service, the bureau, the Puerto Rico Planning Board, the *municipio* governments, the island's emergency-911 program, and other public and private partners. Greater usage of signs on roads for legal boundaries by the commonwealth and *municipio* governments also will enhance the bureau's data collection efforts and resultant data quality as well as meet many local planning needs.

These developments, and a corresponding enhancement of the bureau's address-matching capability to handle Puerto Rico's unique addressing conventions, will make it easier to implement the American Community Survey (ACS) and other Census Bureau programs. The ACS will provide "long-form" demographic and economic data annually for geographic areas as small as the census block group and may replace the traditional census long-form questionnaire for 2010. Enhancing the MAF and the *TIGER* database also will enable Puerto Rico to participate fully in all future plans, procedures, and technology-based solutions implemented in the states.

The census of Puerto Rico serves many uses. It is essential for the redistricting of Puerto Rico's legislature and the distribution of billions of dollars in federal grants for social and economic programs. The census is the primary source of long-term reliable data for the government, business, and academic community. The 2000 census of Puerto Rico also offers the nation a statistical portrait of the commonwealth at the end of 100 years as a U.S. territory and at the birth of a new millennium.

■ Jonathan Sperling

Bibliography

Sperling, Jonathan. "Census Geography in Puerto Rico: A Technical Addendum to the 1990 Census." *Caribbean Studies* 23 (fall 1990): 111–130.

U.S. Bureau of the Census. "Puerto Rico, Virgin Islands, and the Pacific Island Territories." In *1990 Census of Population and Housing History*. Washington, D.C.: U.S. Government Printing Office, 1996.

Census testing

The Bureau of the Census has developed a strong testing program, starting with the 1940 census. It is divided into three parts: a series of census tests that occur between censuses, focused on techniques, technology, or methodology, that do not need to be tested in the midst of a census; dress rehearsals, or final tests before the census; and a series of experiments and tests in the Research, Evaluation, and Experimental (REX) Program of the census. One of the main criteria for a project to be included in the REX Program is the need for it to be conducted while the census is being taken.

The bureau's testing program has had seven major thrusts:

- Moving to a mailout-mailback census
- Increasing the use of sampling
- Improving census coverage
- Improving the measurement of census coverage
- Finding the right questionnaire wording and format for a variety of questions
- Using new technology
- Improving census processing

Because the testing program has been so extensive, the discussion that follows is illustrative only, not comprehensive.

Mailout- Mailback Census

The decision to change from an enumerator-based, canvassing-type census to a mailout- mailback census has dominated census testing. One can trace this effort from 1950 onward. Such problems as how to extend the mailout census to most of the country, how to deal with people who moved around the time of the census, and how to boost response rates to the mailed-out questionnaires had to be investigated. The first effort, in 1950, was an experiment carried out in Ohio and Michigan to measure the effect of enumerators. The results showed that enumerators added enough variability to the results that the census was no more accurate than a 25 percent sample. Thus, the experiment gave strong impetus to a mailout census that would lessen the enumerator effect. After a version of a mailout census was pretested, a census form was delivered in 1960 by the post office to each residential address to which mail was delivered. Residents were asked to fill it out and hold it for pickup by an enumerator. At the same time, as part of the REX Program, a post office coverage improvement study was conducted to identify households erroneously omitted and to test the feasibility of having field staff work with the post office to identify missed units. These kinds of post office checks were later built into the census.

Another experiment built into the 1960 census, the Response Variance Study, showed that the variance introduced by enumerators into census results had been reduced to about a quarter of what it had been in 1950. Although the mailout census had achieved one of its goals, it had to be extended to more of the United States.

Following the successful experience in 1960, the bureau tested the compilation of an address register, the mailback phase of a census, geographic coding, and the like. To extend the mailout, mailback procedure to rural areas, the bureau required an improvement in address listings in rural areas. Tests of addresses bought from commercial vendors and geographically coded by the bureau were also designed. Based on various tests, the mailout, mailback census was expanded from 60 percent of the population in 1970 to 95 percent in 1980.

Although the mailout-mailback census is now firmly established, alternative techniques for creating and updating a national mailing list were tested throughout the 1980s and 1990s. Buying commercial lists, using the post office list, updating the list from the last census, or, what may now be a possibility, updating the list on an ongoing basis through the use of the American Community Survey, a large-scale survey of 250,000 households a month that is being tested as an alternative to the census long form, have all been compared.

Sampling

The bureau first used sampling in the 1940 census when a set of supplemental questions were asked of a sample of individuals. Sampling soon became an accepted tool, and in 1950 most census questions were asked of only a sample of U.S. residents. During the next few decades, testing focused on the use of different sampling fractions, matrix sampling, and, now, the use of the American Community Survey as a possible replacement for the census long form.

Census Coverage

Census coverage became an important issue once the bureau learned how to measure it. Starting with the results of coverage evaluation in the 1950 census, a good part of the pretest program and the REX Program in every census has been devoted to testing methods to increase coverage. Studies to measure coverage of special groups, such as students in college and retired social security beneficiaries, were tested. In the 1970s, further innovations, such as making available a questionnaire in Spanish, were tested. A precanvass operation, used in selected areas of the United States in the 1970 census, was further tested in later decades. In areas not covered by a commercial mailing list, varieties of prelisting were tested. *Prelisting* is the listing of all the households in an area by census workers before the census starts. It was hoped that precanvassing would not be needed in 2000, but a census test showed that a precanvass would add to coverage so it became a part of the 2000 census.

Other attempts to improve coverage were aimed at reducing the differential undercount. Drivers' license records for young males were checked against the census. Post office checks, in which mail carriers took cards prepared by the bureau, put them in the right "cases," and then returned cards for missing addresses, were assessed and found valuable. The vacant/delete check, in which units originally classified as vacant or deleted were rechecked, was found to improve coverage. Although improvement had been expected, the check was done only on a sample basis for the 1970 census, when the counts of vacant units were high. Since then, it has been a part of every census. Also a local review program was tested. Each of these features is now part of the census procedures.

Much testing of coverage methods centered on different methods of compiling the address register. For more rural areas, the results of prelisting were compared with those of a post office listing.

Measurement of Coverage

As communities became aware of the effects of under-coverage in the census, there began a movement to adjust the census for an undercount. To do so meant the estimates of the undercount needed to be more accurate. The 1950 and 1960 censuses showed that a post-enumeration survey (PES) and demographic analysis yielded different results. Demographic analysis was thought to be the superior procedure but did not give results below the national level or for some large minority groups.

A reverse record check, patterned after the successful use of such a methodology in Canada, was tested to measure undercoverage in at least two censuses. The objective was to construct an independent sample of the population and to determine, by matching it to the census, what percentage of the population was missed. It was not successful because of the inability to match a large proportion of the sample with the census.

The 1970 REX Program included two studies designed to strengthen demographic analysis. One was a Medicare record check to strengthen the estimates for the population sixty-five years and older and to determine the effect on coverage estimates of misreporting age. The second study was a birth registration study because the estimates for a large part of the population are based primarily on registered births, with estimates corrected for underregistration.

In the 1980 census, demographic analysis and a PES were used to measure coverage. The PES was based primarily on a match between the Current Population Survey (CPS) and the census, supplemented by a sample from the census to estimate whether people had been counted correctly. For the first time, the bureau used dual-systems estimation to try to compensate for the fact that the CPS and the census could miss the same people.

In 1980 some administrative record check studies were also conducted to measure coverage. Again, matching problems and nonresponse were troublesome features.

The bureau began an early testing program right after the 1980 census to assure itself and the public that it would have more robust estimates in 1990 if there should be a decision to adjust the census for the persistent undercount. Early in the decade, the reverse record check and the PES were tested, resulting in a decision to improve the PES by reducing the amount of nonresponse and improving the matching process.

The 1986 test census had as one of its objectives the operations required to adjust census counts. Two alternatives were tested—a pre-enumeration survey and a post-enumeration survey. Based on results of the test, a post-enumeration survey was selected as the vehicle for measuring coverage in 1990. The PES was featured in the dress rehearsal in 1988 and was tested successfully.

Following 1990 and the decision not to adjust the census, the bureau tested additional procedures. However, once again the PES proved superior to alternatives and became a main feature of the 2000 census. The coverage measurement program for the 2000 census is called the Accuracy and Coverage Evaluation study (ACE).

Questionnaire Wording

Questionnaire wording and format have been of concern to the Census Bureau for a long time. One of the earlier experiments was the move from a person-based questionnaire to a household-based questionnaire. The latter has been a part of the census since 1960.

Between censuses, content tests determine the wording and format of new questions. Content error studies form part of the REX Program. In 1960 the question on age was changed from asking age at last birthday to asking date of birth, primarily because analysis showed that respondents tended to favor ages ending in 0 or 5. Other studies over the years have focused on wording for income questions and, especially, on the wording for questions on race and ethnicity.

To prepare for the 1970 census, two different FOS-DIC (Film Optical Sensing Device for Input into Computers) forms with different formats were mailed to a national sample. A second pretesting of content occurred later in the decade and focused on changes in the definitions for measuring employment and unemployment, as well as some questions on housing quality. Some new items were also tested. Most of the proposed new items were subsequently dropped. A questionnaire format test alternating four different formats was also tested during the decade.

The testing program for content always includes a National Content study in which some of the most pressing new content areas are tested or in which questions that have some problems are revised and tested. In the 1990s the National Content Test and other content tests focused on race and ethnicity, and led to the decision that respondents could select multiple categories.

Technology

The Census Bureau has long been an innovator for the use of new technology to speed up the processing of the census. Although part of the processing of the 1950 census was done by electronic computer, the 1960 census was the first in which the computer was fully featured. This was also the first census in which self-enumeration was the main data collection feature. Rather than keypunch all the data as in past censuses, the bureau designed questionnaires for which most of the information could be recorded by filling in a circle. When the questionnaires were microfilmed, the information was transferred to magnetic computer tape by means of FOSDIC electronic equipment. This equipment was developed by the National Bureau of Standards for the Census Bureau. The outcome of a census pretest with this type of questionnaire and equipment was very favorable and they were adopted for the 1960 census.

After 1960 the bureau turned its attention to speeding up the microfilming process. A test focused on the use of a motorized Plexiglas cover that held down the folds on the questionnaire and allowed the camera operator to have both hands free to move documents. It could also accommodate two pages at once. Camera production went from 2,500 questionnaires a day to 5,400.

The Census Bureau was interested in using a radio-navigational system as the basis for recording the location of rural residences listed in the field for the 1990 census. Testing of equipment went on before 1984, when the bureau decided not to invest in further funding for such a system, based on timing, precision, and cost.

During the 1980s, the bureau also tested automation of many of the data collection tasks. A major innovation tested was optical mark recognition (OMR) as a data conversion and data-processing technique. The new OMR system converted responses on the questionnaire directly to digital data, leading to the first use of concurrent processing in the census. Although the test results were favorable, OMR was not used in 1990. However, bar codes were read. Questionnaires were accepted and data captured as they arrived at the office rather than being held until all were received and put in geographic order. Testing of OMR continued and was used in 2000.

The bureau also experimented with portable computers in collecting addresses. A test comparing two independent staffs of twenty enumerators, one group with laptop computers and the other using pencils and address registers was conducted. Automation proved to be the more productive method. Even so, portable computers were not used in the 1990 census because of the cost of the laptops. Testing was continued again before the 2000 census. Laptops have been adopted for use in the ongoing surveys at the bureau and were used in the ACE study in 2000.

New technology for map generation was also tested. Maps were successfully generated by computer and printed on electronic plotters for the 1990 census.

The 1988 dress rehearsal included a full-scale systems test under census-like conditions of the family of minicomputers purchased for the 1990 data collection and data-processing offices. The automated system was used for data keying, questionnaire editing, address file updating, payroll processing, assignment control, and cost and progress reporting.

Editing and Coding

The millions of census forms need to be processed quickly and accurately. Using FOSDIC eliminated a clerical keying operation. However, the coding of the sample information in the 1960 census was a huge clerical operation. Over the years, ways to speed up or eliminate clerical operations, including coding, were tested.

When questionnaires were returned, they were checked for completeness in local offices. This editing function was costly, and incomplete questionnaires required follow-up. It was decided to try to make some of the repairs in the district office rather than send enumerators out. This method was tested before the 1970 census in several pretests and found to be successful. Telephone follow-up became a part of the census.

An innovation in the dress rehearsal for 1980 was the use of templates with instructions printed on them for editing the questionnaires. Having editing instructions on the template eliminated instruction booklets. The templates were eventually used in the census.

As part of the 1980 REX Program, processing operations were evaluated. Some had to do with the quality of the coding and its verification. Of particular concern was miscoding of income items, where 15 percent of the coders inadvertently shifted the decimal place in income responses to the left or right. Thus an entry of $3,000 by a respondent could be coded as $30,000 or $300. The bureau also had to deal with missing data in the census. A series of procedures was designed to deal with incomplete records. Research on editing and coding has continued with experiments testing the feasibility of automated coding.

Over the years, the census testing program has provided major assistance to the bureau in keeping up with new technology and new methods. Careful records are kept of cost, quality, and timing to ensure that new techniques are effective.

See also *American Community Survey*.

■ Barbara A. Bailar

Bibliography

Anderson, Margo J. *The American Census: A Social History.* New Haven: Yale University Press, 1988.

Choldin, Harvey. *Looking for the Last Percent: The Controversy over Census Adjustment.* New Brunswick, N.J.: Rutgers University Press, 1994.

Cresce, A., S. Lapham, and S. Rolark. "Preliminary Evaluation of Data from the Race and Ethnic Origin Questions in the 1990 Census." *1992 Proceedings of the Social Statistics Section.* Alexandria, Va.: American Statistical Association, 1992.

Edmonston, Barry, and Charles Shultze, eds. *Modernizing the U.S. Census.* Washington, D.C.: National Academy Press, 1995.

U.S. Bureau of the Census. *1960 Censuses of Population and Housing: Procedural History.* Washington, D.C.: General Printing Office, 1966.

Census tracts

Census tracts are small geographic units delineated for the presentation and analysis of decennial census data. They are a form of statistical geography, as opposed to geography created exclusively for legal, political, or administrative purposes. Census tracts are intended to permit meaningful analyses of small areas over time and, as such, have relatively permanent boundaries.

Origins

The census tract concept was conceived by Walter Laidlaw in the first decade of the twentieth century. At that time, many of the nation's cities were developing into major metropolitan areas, the result of huge immigrant flows. Social, religious, and government organizations were attempting to understand these changes and meet the needs of the burgeoning population. Laidlaw, an ordained Presbyterian minister, observed that little scientific knowledge existed about the neighborhoods of New York. Largely unaware of the changes occurring, the churches of the city were unable to take advantage of new opportunities. As director of the Population Research Bureau of the New York Federation of Churches, Laidlaw was sensitive to the dilemma faced by those attempting to gauge neighborhood change. In an article first published by the Federation of Churches and later summarized in the preface of the 1910 census tract report for New York, Laidlaw argued for a permanent geography not susceptible to the political manipulation of wards and assembly districts. He advocated a scientific map system, one capable of fitting addresses to new statistical areas that were small and similar in physical size with permanent boundaries that provided for comparisons from one census to another.

Laidlaw's efforts brought him to Washington, D.C., where he persuaded the Census Bureau to include a code for census tracts on the punched cards that would be created for the 1910 census. Eight cities would have census tract codes for 1910, but local organizations would have to supply funds and labor for the actual compilation and presentation of data. Laidlaw worked closely with the Census Bureau to compile data for New York City census tracts and presented these data as part of the 1910 census results. With the support of the Tenement House Department of New York City and the New York City Department of Health, Laidlaw worked on refinements to his tract concept over the next decade. The result was designation of more than 3,400 census tracts that would be the foundation for the 1920 census. In October 1919 the New York City Census Committee was formed, a broad group of business, government, religious, and social welfare organizations, of which Laidlaw was the executive director. The group raised more than $65,000 for the compilation, tabulation, and publication of tract data for 1920.

The work of the New York City Census Committee was a prototype for things to come. The two elements for what would later become the census tract program were falling into place: an interested local party and formal cooperation by the Census Bureau; however, the federal government still assumed no direct financial responsibility for the undertaking. Getting the Census Bureau to acknowledge that these data were essential to the national interest and should be made a part of the decennial census collection and publication program was the task at hand. It is at this juncture, in the 1920s, that Howard Whipple Green's work complemented Laidlaw's earlier efforts.

Green, a statistician, recognized the need for data from small areas when he attempted to study the movement of the black population in Cleveland in 1924. After examining data for wards from the 1910 and 1920 censuses, he quickly realized that boundary changes made such work impossible to carry out. Green had also heard the laments of the Cleveland Health Council about problems posed by the absence of base data from which to calculate mortality and morbidity rates over time for neighborhoods. After visiting with Laidlaw, Green was convinced that census tracts were the key to the future of small-area data analysis. Unable to obtain enough funds from the Health Council, Green garnered the interest of the *Cleveland Plain Dealer*, based on the business potential of census tracts in describing the market to potential advertisers. With Green's help, Cleveland went on to obtain tabulations from the 1910 and 1920 censuses. The Cleveland Health Council efforts also enhanced the state of the art by providing data for areas outside of the city and by publishing a census tract street index. Word of the efforts in Cleveland spread and other cities became interested in pursuing small-area data analysis. By 1930 eighteen cities had requested that decennial census data be coded at the census tract level.

Then, in 1931, the American Statistical Association (ASA) established the Committee on Census Enumeration Areas, with Howard Whipple Green as chair. Its assignment, unofficially sanctioned by the Census Bureau, was to promote census tract coding in all cities with more than 250,000 residents. The census tract movement now had organized support that would be reinforced in myriad meetings of the ASA and in other forums in which the ASA was a participant. This support was critical to the future of the program because the Great Depression strangled efforts by local organizations to come up with the dollars to support compilation of tract data. As a result of the movement promulgated by the ASA committee in general and Green in particular, it became clear that census tracts were here to stay and that the activity had become sufficiently broad in the range of its participants to warrant creation and administration of a formal program by the Census Bureau. In 1940 the Census Bureau, for the first time, coded and published census tract bulletins for sixty-four cities. The formal program that was created was based on a unique foundation of unprecedented federal-local cooperation. The task of delineating tracts and monitoring their boundaries from decade to decade was to be the work of local census tract committees, functioning in concert with Census Bureau geographers. Manuals, developed through federal-local cooperative efforts at several points in the 1930s, outlined the purpose of the program and suggested how local communities could participate.

As the program grew, it increasingly required national coordination. This was achieved in 1955 when the Census Bureau took responsibility for appointing local liaisons for the tract program. The idea was for a local committee to subdivide a jurisdiction into small areas as homogeneous as possible in population and housing. These subdivisions were submitted to the bureau, which then coded, tabulated, and published the data, along with a census tract map. Local committees also encouraged organizations to code their administrative records by census tract, originally through the use of locally prepared address coding guides and, more recently, through geographic information systems that permit electronic geo-coding.

Criteria and Use

When first established, census tracts were designed to be relatively homogeneous with respect to population characteristics, economic status, and living conditions and be in a certain population size range, most recently set at between 2,500 and 8,000 inhabitants. Visible permanent features are used to delineate boundaries of census tracts, that is, features that can be readily identified in the field and are not subject to change as a result of political or administrative considerations. Census tracts are almost always numbered consecutively within county boundaries.

Laidlaw's initial idea was to make census tracts of approximately equal area. Over time, however, this criterion proved to be impractical, as more and more of the nation became covered with tracts. In 1990 census tracts covered 80 percent of the nation's population but just 25 percent of its land area. Counties that did not have census tracts were covered with block-numbering areas (BNAs); the concept started in 1940 because the Census Bureau needed a way to group blocks in cities that did not have census tracts. In 1990 the Census Bureau created BNAs for all counties that did not have census tracts and published the same data for BNAs as for tracts. In 2000, for the first time, all counties in the nation were subdivided by census tract.

Covering the geography of the nation with census tracts means that the areal size of tracts will vary widely, depending upon the density of settlement. Although tracts are designed to be homogeneous from the standpoint of social, economic, and housing conditions when first delineated, there is little guarantee that this will continue over time, especially in areas with high population turnover. Although tracts are based on permanent features, physical changes in road and housing infrastructure, changes in street patterns (for example, street closings), or the absence of physical boundaries in large housing developments (for example, those consisting of cul-de-sacs and no continuous through streets) can all result in tracts with unusually large or small populations. Moreover, special conditions, such as the presence of ships in port, observations made during the actual enumeration that bring to light problems with tract boundaries (for example, errors in the bureau's tract boundary configuration), and requests by local jurisdictions to correct the location of misplaced census tract boundaries have all resulted in the creation of tracts with little or no population or housing.

Census tract boundaries do actually change in some cases; however, when tracts are added together or subdivided, the original boundaries are usually maintained. Tracts can be split because of large growth in population or housing or be combined, as when areas experience large population declines or housing losses that are not likely to be reversed. The guiding principle, however, is to maintain tract boundaries because tracts exist to chronicle population and housing change, holding geography constant. Thus, boundaries are altered in ways that permit them to be reconfigured for comparisons over time: a tract that was recently split into two parts can be reassembled into a single geographic unit for comparison with an earlier census; or a single census tract in the latest census, formed by combining two tracts from an earlier census, can then be compared with that combined area. Land use can change dramatically over time, as when formerly agricultural, industrial, or commercial areas are developed for residential use, causing the tract configuration to change. Areas may undergo rapid housing development, requiring a whole new template of census tracts to be created where a single census tract (or no census tract) may have existed earlier.

The mix of conditions that presents itself to local census tract liaisons is almost limitless. Thus, the decisions on tract delineation from census to census, although subject to criteria that attempt to achieve some level of standardization, need to be carefully evaluated with respect to the range of conditions present in a jurisdiction. The speed of population growth, level of housing development, changes in socioeconomic composition, and shifts in land use are just a few of the key conditions that need to be measured when evaluating how to configure and reconfigure census tracts.

See also *Local involvement in census taking; Tabulation geography.*

■ Joseph J. Salvo

Bibliography

Association of Public Data Users. *A Guide to State and Local Census Geography, 1990 CPH-I-18.* Washington, D.C.: U.S. Bureau of the Census, 1993.

Green, Howard Whipple. "A Period of Great Growth and Development, 1926–1946." Paper presented at the annual meeting of the American Statistical Association, Special Session on the Golden Anniversary of Census Tracts, Detroit, 1956.

Kaplan, Charles P., and Thomas L. Van Valey. *Census 80: Continuing the Factfinder Tradition.* Washington, D.C.: U.S. Bureau of the Census, 1980.

Laidlaw, Walter, ed. *Statistical Sources for Demographic Studies of Greater New York, 1910.* 2 vols. New York: New York Federation of Churches, 1913.

New York City 1920 Census Committee. *Statistical Sources for Demographic Studies of Greater New York, 1920.* New York City: City Census Committee, 1923.

Swift, Arthur L., Jr. "Doctor Laidlaw's Vision: The Early Years." Paper presented at the annual meeting of the American Statistical Association, Special Session on the Golden Anniversary of Census Tracts, Detroit, 1956.

U.S. Bureau of the Census. *Geographic Areas Reference Manual.* Washington, D.C., 1994.

Censuses, decennial

See *Decennial censuses.*

Censuses in other countries

Census taking has been used in all types of societies as a tool to understand better their physical and cultural dimensions. In the same way that representation of daily activities went from petroglyphs to live television coverage over the years, census methodology has evolved over time from rounding up people from a village to mail-out, mail-back technology, albeit at different paces from country to country.

In most countries, census taking is done by enumerators going from door to door asking the householder basic questions on the demographic and socioeconomic characteristics of the members of the household. In some countries, this operation is done in one day, whereas in others it is spread out over weeks. The enumerator records the information, which is then captured using different methods. For the 2000 round of censuses, the information gathered by the enumerators was transferred in many cases from imaged documents to computers by optical character recognition. Several countries also opt to compile population counts manually and produce them very quickly after census day. These counts are generally preliminary in nature and as such are subject to review once the questionnaires are processed. This door-to-door methodology is the only one applicable in countries where the rate of literacy is low, postal communication is not reliable, or communication with the householders is otherwise difficult. Most South American, African, and Asian countries used this methodology with slight variations in the conduct of their census.

In most Western countries, where postal communication is effective and the literacy rate relatively high, census questionnaires are either delivered to the household by an enumerator or sent by mail, the latter method requiring the existence of an accurate address register. Householders are asked to complete the questionnaire and return it to the enumerator (either by mail or by handing it back to the enumerator who comes back to pick it up). Missing questionnaires are followed up until an acceptable rate of response is achieved. Data are generally transferred to computers by imaging the questionnaires and by using a combination of optical character recognition, optical mark recognition, and keying techniques from the images.

In some European countries, mostly in northern Europe, population and demographic information is obtained from population registers created and maintained to administer the country. In some countries, such as Finland and Denmark, the information held in registers suffices, whereas in other countries, such as Norway, the register information needs to be completed by and combined with traditional basic census information.

India

In India the Census of India Act was placed in the statute book in 1948. The first census after independence was taken in 1951 and has been taken every ten years since. Prior to the 1971 census the data had been almost entirely sorted and tabulated manually except in 1961, when household economic data were processed on a sampling basis on computers. In 1971 the processing of data became largely computerized.

Enumerators visit the households and follow up with a second visit to verify and correct the data. In the snowbound and inaccessible areas of the country the census is taken earlier than in other areas. For the 1991 census 1.5 million enumerators were employed; for the 2001 census approximately 2 million enumerators will be used.

The census data are available on floppy disks, CD-ROMs, and as printed volumes. Following the 1991 census approximately 400 floppies and 750 printed volumes of three types were produced: those covering India as a whole, those covering individual states, and handbooks for each of the 452 districts.

New Zealand

New Zealand is required by legislation to take a census of population and dwellings every five years. For the 1996 census, traditional enumeration was undertaken with hand delivery and collection of questionnaires. Separate questionnaires were completed for each individual and each occupied dwelling. For the first time, New Zealand centrally processed the questionnaires using imaging technology and optical recognition for "tick boxes" and numeric responses. Publications from the census included regular media information with attached summary tabulations, a series of tabular reports on a range of topics, detailed analytical reports, and special tabular reports. A lot of 1996 tabulations were available on the Internet before the publications were released.

United Kingdom (UK)

The next census of population will be taken throughout the United Kingdom on April 29, 2001. The census will be the twentieth in a series carried out every ten years in Great Britain since 1801, except in 1941, and the eighteenth to be carried out in what is now Northern Ireland. The last census was carried out in April 1991.

The 1991 census forms were dropped off at households and the completed forms were picked up; the data were then keyed into computers. In 2001 enumerators will identify and visit every address and household in the country to deliver a census forms before census day. The United Kingdom will, for the first time, provide households with a preaddressed, prepaid envelope for the return of their completed forms by mail within a required time period. The 2001 census will count people where they are usually resident. Thus each household will be given a census form to complete, and the form will contain questions relating to each person resident in the household as well as to the household as a whole. Unlike the practice in previous censuses, only a head count of visitors to households on census night will be recorded. If these visitors are normally resident elsewhere in the United Kingdom, they will be required to supply full information at their usual residences.

A Census Coverage Survey (CCS) will be carried out throughout the United Kingdom three to four weeks after the census. It will be an independent sample survey of about 300,000 households, conducted on a voluntary basis to check on the coverage of households and people within households. The information obtained will be used, in conjunction with the census data, to produce a consistent set of census-based counts. These will form the new base for the series of annual mid-year population estimates for local and health authorities. It is intended, subject to successful testing, that the adjustments for undercoverage will be incorporated into the census database so that all census outputs reflect these adjustments.

The 1997 census test provided an opportunity to test the concept of using scanning and image recognition techniques, as well as automatic and computer-assisted coding of write-in responses. It was concluded that such techniques would be used for 2001.

A census rehearsal took place in April 1999 to assess the acceptability of the questions and to make sure that both the procedures for delivery and collection of the census forms, and the systems for processing the data and producing outputs, would be effective. It included a test of the CCS and the methods to be used to adjust the census counts for undercoverage.

Canada

In Canada national censuses were conducted at ten-year intervals starting in 1851 and at five-year intervals since 1956. The next census will be conducted on May 15, 2001.

The Canadian census is conducted as a household survey. Information with respect to all members of the private household and the dwelling are collected on a single questionnaire. Not all questions are collected on the basis of a complete enumeration. A small number of questions (seven out of fifty-five in 1996) is put to the entire population, the remaining questions being put to only one-fifth of all households, except in the Canadian north. There, in view of the sparse population, a complete enumeration is carried out using the long questionnaire in order to obtain reliable small area data for this region.

Canada employs self-enumeration as its method of data collection for over 98 percent of its population. The remainder, mostly in institutions, Indian reserves, and remote northern areas, are canvassed by enumerators. The self-administered questionnaires are hand delivered by enumerators and returned by mail by the respondents.

The propagation of electronic communications, such as the Internet, and the greater availability of electronic media, such as the CD-ROM, presented the opportunity to increase the amount of information disseminated while maintaining costs. Some paper publications were retained, however, because an important segment of data users still depends on paper to obtain information. The 2001 census will continue this transition from paper to electronic media.

Norway

The Norwegian population census is conducted every ten years. The last population census was taken in 1990.

The 1990 census was based partly on register data and partly on a sample survey. Register data on demography, income, and education had sufficient coverage and quality to form the basis for census statistics. Labor market data were available in existing registers but were not considered to have sufficient coverage and quality for statistical purposes. Little or no information on households and housing was available from existing registers. To increase the quality of data on the labor market and to add to the data on households and housing for the 1990 census, Norway collected questionnaires from a sample of the population. The sample fraction varied from full coverage of the smallest municipalities to samples of 8.5 percent of the largest, urban municipalities. To increase the quantity and quality of statistics for small areas, a statistical register for labor market data was established and used as a supplement when tables of labor market statistics were produced. In the 2000 census, data were collected from two different types of sources: registers for the population census and mail-out, mail-back questionnaires for the housing census. Questionnaires containing a preprinted family list were sent to a contact person in every family. The respondents were asked to correct the information and expand the lists to a household list. In addition the respondents were asked to answer the questions about dwellings and buildings.

See also *International coordination in population censuses.*
■ Benoit Laroche

Bibliography

Alonso, William, and Paul Starr. *The Politics of Numbers.* New York: Russell Sage Foundation, 1987.

Clark, Alex, and Ian White. "UK 2001 Census: Data Collection and Capture." Paper presented at the European Workshop on the Preparation of the Census Fieldwork. Rome, April 12–14, 1999.

Economic Secretary to the Treasury, the Secretary of State for Scotland, and the Secretary of State for Northern Ireland. "The 2001 Census of Population." White paper presented to Parliament by Command of Her Majesty. London, March 1999.

Laroche, Benoit. "1996 Census of Canada: Dissemination Aspects." Paper presented at Seminario Internacional sobre Censo de Poblacion y Vivienda del ano 2000 Cartagena de Indias—Colombia, January 26–31, 1998.

Nolan, Frank. "Planning for the 2001 Census of Population and Dwellings in New Zealand." International Seminar on Census Methodology. Portsmouth, United Kingdom, 1998.

Srivastava, S. C. *Census of India 1971.* Monograph series. Indian Census in Perspective. New Delhi: Office of the Registrar General, Ministry of Home Affairs, 1972.

Statistics Canada. *The 1996 Census Handbook.* Ottawa, Canada: Minister of Industry, 1997.

Statistics New Zealand. "Enumeration in the 2001 Census; Address Register." *International Forum for Census Dissemination—Statistics New Zealand.* Diffusion No. 15, April 1999.

Utne, Harald. "The Overall Design of the 2000 Census in Norway." Paper presented at the European Workshop on the Preparation of the Census Fieldwork. Rome, April 12–14, 1999.

———. "Two Methods for Data Capture in the 2000 Census." Paper presented at the European Workshop on the Preparation of the Census Fieldwork. Rome, April 12–14, 1999.

White, Ian. "UK 2001 Census Development Programme." Paper presented at the European Workshop on the Preparation of the Census Fieldwork. Rome, April 12–14, 1999.

Center of population

Census officials invented the concept of the center of population in the 1870s to illustrate trends in the distribution and migration of the American population over time (see map in appendix). Considered the center of population gravity, the center of population is the point on which the United States would balance if it were a plane without weight and its population were distributed on the plane as if each individual had the same weight. Each individual would exert on the central point a force proportional to the individual's distance from it. Calculating the point is complex and involves first allocating the population to square degrees of latitude and longitude and then determining where the United States would "balance" (for further details, contact the chief of the Geography Division, U.S. Bureau of the Census).

The center of population provided one of the first visual illustrations of population change in the census. Officials originally used the calculation in statistical maps published with tabular results of the census to illustrate the westward migration of the population. From the first census in 1790 to the ninth in 1870, the point moved from Maryland to southern Ohio. Officials saw its steady westward trajectory as natural. They continued the maps in later census publications and extended the concept to calculate centers of population for population subgroups, such as the white, foreign-born, and African-American populations.

In the twentieth century, as the nation industrialized in the Northeast and Midwest, the point's decennial migration slowed considerably. The center of population had moved to eastern Indiana by 1890 and remained in Indiana through 1940. Since then, rapid population growth in the South and Southwest has given the point a southwestern trajectory. In early 2000 the center of population rested in Missouri.

Americans have attributed symbolic meaning to the place where the center of population is located and have celebrated the site with commemorative markers. After the 1990 census, for example, a marker was erected in Steelville, Missouri, the Crawford County seat, 9.7 miles northwest of the true center of population.

Concepts related to the center of population include the median center of population and the geographic center of area of the United States. The median center is found at the intersection of two median lines: one a north-south line (a meridian of longitude) chosen so that half the population lives east of it and half west, and the other an east-west line (a parallel of latitude) selected so that half the population lives north of it and half south. The median center of population for the 1990 census resided in Indiana. The geographic center of area represents the point at which the surface of the United States would balance if it were a plane of uniform weight per unit of area. In early 2000 that point fell in Butte County, South Dakota, as it has since the 1960 census, after Alaska and Hawaii became states. The geographic center of the coterminous United States (forty-eight states and the District of Columbia) is in Smith County, Kansas.

See also *Geography: distribution of the population.*

■ Margo Anderson

Citizenship

See *Congress and the census; Foreign-born population of the United States; Immigration.*

Civil War and the census

The American Civil War and the growing sectional strife in the decades preceding it had an important influence on the census. Congressional debate over the 1850 census was concurrent with the acrimonious debate over the Compromise of 1850. Southern senators, keenly aware of the growing controversy over slavery and fearing detailed analyses of their "peculiar institution," were able to restrict the information the census collected on the nation's slave inhabitants. The final census bill approved by the Senate eliminated several questions from the proposed slave schedule that were deemed too sensitive, including each slave's name, birthplace, "degree of removal from pure blood," the number of children each woman had borne, and whether the children were living.

The war and its political ramifications also had a significant impact on several postwar censuses. The 1870 census included two questions on "Constitutional Relations" mandated by Section 2 of the Fourteenth Amendment, which was intended to reduce congressional apportionment in states restricting newly freed blacks' right to vote. In 1890 veteran groups and the growing federal commitment to support Union veterans and their widows with pensions convinced Congress to ask "Whether [the respondent was] a soldier, sailor, or marine during the civil war (U.S. or Confederate), or widow of such person" in the population schedule. An additional special schedule of inquiry was conducted to record the names, military units, and length of service of men in the Union forces who had survived to the 1890 census. The 1910 census asked whether the individual was a survivor of the Union or Confederate forces.

The 1860 Census Office played an important role in the conduct of the war. Following the bombardment of Fort Sumter in April 1861, Census Superintendent Joseph C. G. Kennedy prepared a report for President Abraham Lincoln on the number of men age eighteen to forty-five in the free states, the slave states, the "border" states, and the territories. The report showed the North had an overwhelming advantage in manpower— 69 percent of men of military age resided in the free states compared with just 9 percent in the slave states. The Census Office loaned clerks to the War Department for statistical work, conducted analyses of the Confederacy's ability to manufacture explosives, and prepared statistical maps for generals in the field showing local demographic and economic information. General William Tecumseh Sherman was able to make effective use of census maps during his march through Georgia in 1864. The 1860 census was also used to assess direct taxes to finance the war, prepare reports on the potential cost of paid emancipation, and help policymakers plan for the "reconstruction" of the postwar South.

However, on the most fundamental problem facing the postwar United States—the future of the freed slaves—the Census Office was of little help. In his introduction to the 1860 census, Kennedy, reflecting the racism of nineteenth-century white society, contended that competition with whites would lead to the "gradual extinction" of the black population.

The American Civil War was the most costly conflict in the nation's history. An estimated 618,222 military deaths occurred during the Civil War—roughly equal to the number of deaths suffered in all American wars through the Korean War combined. The human cost was borne most heavily by the South, which lost 18 percent of its white male population age thirteen to forty-three in 1860 to the North's 6 percent. The South also suffered a large but uncounted number of civilian deaths from famine, disease, and guerrilla warfare. Mortality was especially high among the white refugees who fled the advancing Union Army and the tens of thousands of blacks who escaped from slavery to enlist in the Union forces or to live in "contraband" camps behind army lines.

Postwar censuses also reveal a dramatic reduction in wartime fertility. Military mobilization, the death of hundreds of thousands of young men, and the economic disruptions of the war resulted in a deficit of approximately five hundred thousand to seven hundred thousand white births between 1862 and 1866 (8–11 percent of the expected total). The war also had a dramatic impact on the black population. For the first time, the nation's nearly four million slaves were able to form and maintain families without fear of disruption by owners and to live where they wanted. Although most blacks remained in their local area, many newly freed blacks chose to move to urban areas, swelling the population of many southern cities.

See also *1850 census; 1860 census; 1870 census; 1890 census.*

■ J. David Hacker

Bibliography

Anderson, Margo J. *The American Census: A Social History.* New Haven, Conn.: Yale University Press, 1988.

Hacker, J. David. "The Human Cost of War: White Population in the United States, 1850–1880." Ph.D. dissertation, University of Minnesota, 1999.

Magnuson, Diana Lynn. "The Making of a Modern Census: The United States Census of Population, 1790–1940." Ph.D. dissertation, University of Minnesota, 1995.

Vinovskis, Maris A. "Have Social Historians Lost the Civil War? Some Preliminary Demographic Speculations." *Journal of American History* 76 (1989): 34–58.

Colonial censuses

Residents of England's colonies in America acquired much experience with census taking before the first federal census of 1790. In all, 124 censuses were taken between 1623 and 1775, covering twenty-one colonies from Newfoundland in the north to Barbados in the Caribbean. Of these censuses, forty-six were for nine colonies that became part of the original thirteen states. Virginia was the first colony in which a census was taken (1623), though enumerating the people there would not last long into the eighteenth century. In contrast, New York first had its population counted in 1698, but then had nine more censuses by 1771. That colony was one of five to count its population in the 1770s. Other European countries also had censuses taken in their American colonies, as counts exist for territories originally under French and Spanish control that were eventually incorporated into the United States. Here, however, the focus will be on the English experience.

The censuses were intended to be enumerations of all the people living in a colony and were distinguished from estimates of population derived from militia rolls and tax lists, as well as pure guesses. Although colonial authorities in London often indicated an interest only in the growth or decline of populations and their racial composition, the censuses vary significantly in the scope and detail reported to England. Some provided little more than the total counted; others, such as the one taken in New Jersey in 1772 under the direction of Benjamin Franklin's son William, offered sophisticated compilations of data that went well beyond what the imperial authorities desired. Many included greater detail about the composition of populations than the 1790 census.

How the Censuses Were Taken

Every census taken in an American colony was the result of a request for information from England. In the seventeenth century, these requests frequently reflected a basic ignorance about what the colonies were like and how strong they were. Because the colonies were intended to profit the mother country, it was essential to learn who and what was there to be exploited. At the same time, the colonial censuses emerged at a time when men involved in public affairs were beginning to appreciate the value of accurate data collected in numerical form. Thus, censuses were often only one of many kinds of information requested.

Over the course of the seventeenth century, census taking became a more common part of colonial administration. The first censuses in Virginia (1623–1624, 1624–1625) were taken in response to concerns in England about the future of that colony. The results were not promising as the population was only just over twelve hundred, despite the migration of several thousand people since 1618. But as the survival of Virginia became more evident, counting the people subsided. In 1654 Thomas Povey, a prominent London merchant with interests in trade in the Caribbean, proposed a council of trade and plantations with responsibilities to collect data, including information on population. After 1670, a newly formed Council for Foreign Plantations elicited ten censuses in the next fourteen years. But the most impressive results for colonial censuses came with the creation of the Board of Trade in 1696, as 88.7 percent of all colonial counts occurred after the board assumed supervision of colonial affairs. In all, twenty censuses were taken between 1623 and 1700; another fifty-two date from between 1701 and 1750; the years between 1751 and 1775 saw an additional fifty-two censuses. As administrative control became better established, collection of information moved from a focus on one colony at a time to more general "queries" to all royal governors.

Most queries seldom asked about more than the size and growth of the population and its racial composition. The latter was a major concern regarding the economic and military viability of the Caribbean colonies. Governors were responsible for collecting the evidence and sending it back to England in a useable form. Over time, governors and their local legislative assemblies added categories into which the population was to be divided. The most common were to distinguish race (or between free and enslaved), as well as sex, and age, with sixteen and sixty the ages most often used to define different parts of the population. Broad age categories frequently were applied not only to white males, as in the 1790 census, but also to women and slaves. Censuses within a colony often were similar to those taken earlier in that colony. Although the final report sent to London was frequently only a table or two of results broken down by the major civil divisions in the colony, the process of taking a census could produce extraordinarily detailed findings. Some fragments of original manuscripts exist (most often in American archives), in which every member of a family or household is listed by name and age, allowing remarkably complex analysis of family structures and other relationships.

Most governors tried to respond promptly to requests from London, facing threats to their position if they were too slow in producing results. The governors had to rely on the cooperation of their colonists, from citizens responding to questions, to local officials recording and forwarding data, to legislatures agreeing

to pay for the process. This was not always easily obtained. William Franklin's 1772 census for New Jersey covered only the western half of the colony because the tax assessors in the east refused to do the job without pay. Occasionally the Old Testament story of a plague following King David's efforts to take a census was used to explain citizens' lack of cooperation. Suspicions over the possible use of censuses by tax collectors may have encouraged some to provide false information. Governor Archibald Hamilton of the Leeward Islands had to delay a census because of the presence of pirates who were too powerful for him to confront. Several times Pennsylvania governors used past apathy to excuse present dereliction of duty.

Once the data were collected, the governor had to send them to London in an appropriate form. Several years after the Board of Trade chided one Virginia governor that " 'Many' and 'Few' are too indeterminate expressions," it was forced to inform his successor that the lists he sent noting the names of every child and slave were "too particular and voluminous." But even when governors produced the right amount of detail, the uncertainty of colonial shipping could lead to the loss of a census. Lord Cornbury (Edward Hyde), governor of New York and New Jersey (1702–1708), seems to have had unusual trouble getting his censuses safely back to England, even though surviving fragments in American archives indicate he took at least some of them.

Using the Censuses

Throughout the seventeenth century, imperial officials made use of the censuses to determine what they had on the other side of the Atlantic and to ensure that their possessions were economically and militarily secure. Although early reports must have produced anxiety about the survival of some of the colonies, most settlements in America were thriving by 1700. Following the creation of the Board of Trade in 1696, English policymakers used the censuses as part of their effort to gain greater control over the colonies by emphasizing their economic potential. The most sophisticated analysis of census materials occurred in 1721, when a long report stressed the remarkably rapid growth of populations in America and, in conjunction with the belief that such growth meant economic benefit, offered suggestions on ways to sustain or even increase it. The report also took note of any groups of a population that might pose a potential threat in a given region. The same themes were repeated during the remainder of the colonial period, though often in a perfunctory fashion. In 1763, as England considered revisions in her colonial policies, two officials worried that rapid growth might eventually undermine the colonies' loyalty to the mother country.

By the middle of the eighteenth century, a number of Americans remarked with favor on the rapid growth that they, too, observed. Benjamin Franklin, Ezra Stiles, president of Yale College, and Edward Wigglesworth, Harvard College professor of divinity, all pointed with pride to such growth. They saw this as evidence that life was better in America than in England, even predicting that the colonies' population would be more numerous than England's by 1825. If not encouraging revolution, such views certainly made it conceivable.

The growth of the population in American colonies still attracts attention today, for it documents one of the most impressive population "explosions" in history, with numbers doubling approximately every twenty-five years from 1700 to 1860. At the same time, the censuses demonstrate the remarkable complexity of England's empire in America, with highly diverse populations in colonies from Canada to the Caribbean. The most obvious variation was the racial composition, as the proportion of people of African origin in each colony ranged from almost none to well over 90 percent. But the censuses have allowed historians to examine the age and sex composition in some detail and, in a significant number of instances, structures of the family and household.

■ Robert V. Wells

Bibliography

Dunn, Richard S. *Sugar and Slaves: The Rise of the Planter Class in the English West Indies, 1624–1713.* Chapel Hill.: University of North Carolina Press, 1972.

Greene, Evarts B., and Virginia D. Harrington. *American Population before the Federal Census of 1790.* New York: Columbia University Press, 1932.

Sutherland, Stella H. *Population Distribution in Colonial America.* New York: Columbia University Press, 1936.

Voorhies, Jacqueline K., compiler. *Some Late Eighteenth Century Louisianians: Census Records, 1758–1796.* Lafayette, La.: University of Southwestern Louisiana Press, 1973.

Wells, Robert V. *The Population of the British Colonies in America before 1776: A Survey of Census Data.* Princeton, N.J.: Princeton University Press, 1975.

Composition of the population

Population composition refers to the distribution within a population of one or more individually defined traits that influence population comparisons or demographic phenomena. The individual traits or variables to which population composition refers are usually those believed to have major significance for the uses of population data. Thus, while a large number of variables are of potential interest for study in demography, a limited number are relevant for use in compositional studies.

To a large degree, compositional elements relevant for study are those characteristics of individuals that are enumerable by conventional census-taking techniques. In earlier U.S. censuses, enumerable meant that nonprofessional census personnel could collect the information. In recent U.S. censuses, enumerable means that adults in a household are able to provide information on a questionnaire.

The individual characteristics to which composition generally refers include sex, age, marital status, place of birth, education, occupation, labor force status, industry, relation to head of household, and other such features.

Age

Age and sex are pivotal characteristics in analyses of composition. The distributions of other characteristics are usually contingent in one way or another on age and sex distributions. This results not only from the fundamental social and economic importance of sex and age but also from their independent variability. As inherent biological properties of individuals, sex and age do not determine marital status, education, or other demographic characteristics. But other demographic processes are often linked to the life cycle and, hence, develop a pattern that is revealed by the age and sex profiles.

A basic procedure in analyzing age structure is to learn what proportion of the population is at each stage of the life cycle, how these proportions have changed, how they differ from place to place, and what factors are responsible for the age composition and its changes.

The median age of the population—the age at which 50 percent of the population are above it and 50 percent are below it—gives a quick and approximate measure of the age of a population. The median age of the U.S. population was 16.7 years in 1820 and rose to 33.0 years in 1990 (see Figure 1). Thus, during a period of seventeen decades the median age increased by 16.3 years, or about one year per decade. The rise in the age was most rapid between 1900 and 1950, caused principally by fertility declines. Between 1950 and 1970 the trend of the previous 150 years was interrupted; the median age in 1960 and 1970 was lower than it was in 1950. The cause was the reversal in the long-term downward trend in fertility that took place starting in 1944 to 1946.

Even though median age is a useful measure for indicating generally the age level of a population, it cannot give detailed information about age structure or the distribution of the population among various stages of the life cycle. A more informative picture is to study the proportions of the population for a general set of age groups, such as childhood (age zero to eight), youth (age nine to seventeen), adulthood (age eighteen to sixty-four), and the elderly (age sixty-five and older).

The percentage distribution of the U.S. population by age is displayed in Table 1. In 1880 the U.S. population was young, with a larger proportion of the population in the childhood and youth ages, fewer in the adult years, and dramatically fewer in the elderly years. In 1990, about six out of ten residents are adults, about one out of four are children or youth, and about one out of eight are elderly.

If present low birth rates continue, the median age will increase and the absolute and relative population who are sixty-five years of age and older will expand. Current population projections indicate that the median age of the U.S. population will increase from thirty-three years in 1990 to thirty-eight years in 2050.

The U.S. population in 2050 will likely have slightly fewer relative persons in the childhood and youth years and fewer persons in the adult years. The decreases will be counterbalanced by unprecedented growth of persons in the elderly years, increasing to about one in five persons in the population.

Sex

Beginning in 1950, for the first time in its history, the United States had a preponderance of women. The

Figure 1. Median Age of the U.S. Population, 1820–2050

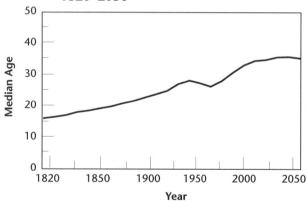

Source: Historical reconstruction of the U.S. population described in Jeffrey S. Passel and Barry Edmonston, "Immigration and Race: Recent Trends in Immigration to the United States," in Barry Edmonston and Jeffrey S. Passel, eds., *Immigration and Ethnicity: The Integration of America's Newest Arrivals*, chapter 2 (Washington, D.C.: Urban Institute Press, 1994); and population projection of the U.S. population described in Barry Edmonston and Jeffrey S. Passel, "The Future Immigrant Population of the United States," in Barry Edmonston and Jeffrey S. Passel, eds., *Immigration and Ethnicity: The Integration of America's Newest Arrivals*, chapter 11 (Washington, D.C.: Urban Institute Press, 1994).

Table 1. Percentage Distribution of the U.S. Population by Major Life Cycle Age Groups, 1880–2050

Major Stages of the Life Cycle	1880	1940	1990	2050
Childhood	24	14	13	12
Youth	19	16	13	12
Adulthood	54	63	61	56
Elderly	3	7	13	20

Source: Historical reconstruction of the U.S. population described in Jeffrey S. Passel and Barry Edmonston, "Immigration and Race: Recent Trends in Immigration to the United States," in Barry Edmonston and Jeffrey S. Passel, eds., *Immigration and Ethnicity: The Integration of America's Newest Arrivals*, chapter 2 (Washington, D.C.: Urban Institute Press, 1994); and population projection of the U.S. population described in Barry Edmonston and Jeffrey S. Passel, "The Future Immigrant Population of the United States," in Barry Edmonston and Jeffrey S. Passel, eds., *Immigration and Ethnicity: The Integration of America's Newest Arrivals*, chapter 11 (Washington, D.C.: Urban Institute Press, 1994).

extent of the imbalance is only slight. In 1990, for example, males were 48.7 percent of the total population.

A population's sex composition is conventionally described in terms of the sex ratio, or the number of males per 100 females. From 1820 to 1910 the sex ratio of the population of the United States fluctuated between 102 and 106. From 1910 to 1950 it declined steadily and dropped to 99 in 1950 (see Figure 2).

Both the native and foreign-born populations have had a distinctive sex-ratio history. The native-born population had a sex ratio near 100 between 1870 and 1950, and it was always below the general sex ratio for the nation. In 1950 its sex ratio was the same as the national average.

The sex ratio for the foreign-born population shows a preponderance of males until 1960. During the years of heavy immigration to the United States at the turn of the twentieth century, immigrants were predominantly male. Consequently, the sex ratio for the foreign-born population during that time was extraordinarily high. In 1850, for example, the foreign-born population had a sex ratio of 124. In 1910 it was 129. In the period from 1920 to 1960, as the volume of immigration was curtailed, the number of women immigrants came to equal and surpass that of men. By 1960 the sex ratio for the foreign-born had declined to 94.

Women will continue to outnumber men in future years, but the relative surplus of women will remain unchanged. The principal cause of the tendency of women to outnumber men is their greater longevity. If present demographic trends continue and if the gap in life expectancy narrows between women and men, the sex ratio of the overall population will remain at about 96 between 2000 and 2050.

The sex ratio for the overall population represents a balance between the sex ratios for the foreign-born and native-born components of the population. Because U.S. immigration includes a surplus of women, the foreign-born population will become more predominantly female as immigration continues and as the foreign-born population ages (a greater number of older women than men will survive). The sex ratio of the native-born population is expected to shift slightly upward, from 96 in 2000 to 98 in 2050, as the gap in life expectancy between males and females narrows.

Nativity

Nativity has a social significance that reaches into many spheres of study. The foreign-born have a distinctive age structure and tend to be selected from several major countries of origin. Furthermore, the foreign-born often have differences in English-language abilities, fertility, settlement patterns, and other social and economic characteristics.

Immigrants have arrived in the United States throughout its entire history, with a great deal of variation from the peaks of the 1900s and of the 1980s and 1990s to the valleys of the 1930s. Immigration increased steadily in the decades after World War II, because the United States enjoyed a high degree of political freedom and economic prosperity, compared with Europe and many other countries. The 1965 changes in U.S. immigration law prompted even further increases as the United States began to receive large numbers of new immigrants from Asia and Latin America.

Figure 3 displays the number of foreign-born persons in the United States, from 1850 to 2050. Immigrants affect the composition of the population in several ways. They change the racial and ethnic makeup of the population if they differ from the resident population. Immigrants always affect the generational

Figure 2. Sex Ratio of the U.S. Population by Nativity Groups, 1850–2050

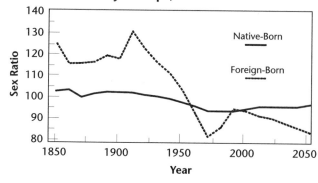

Source: Historical reconstruction of the U.S. population described in Jeffrey S. Passel and Barry Edmonston, "Immigration and Race: Recent Trends in Immigration to the United States," in Barry Edmonston and Jeffrey S. Passel, eds., *Immigration and Ethnicity: The Integration of America's Newest Arrivals,* chapter 2 (Washington, D.C.: Urban Institute Press, 1994); and population projection of the U.S. population described in Barry Edmonston and Jeffrey S. Passel, "The Future Immigrant Population of the United States," in Barry Edmonston and Jeffrey S. Passel, eds., *Immigration and Ethnicity: The Integration of America's Newest Arrivals,* chapter 11 (Washington, D.C.: Urban Institute Press, 1994).

composition, because they increase the size of first generation (that is, the foreign-born population). The foreign-born population derives principally from past levels of immigration but is also affected by emigration and mortality.

The size of the foreign-born population in the United States reflects the changing course of immigration over time. Approximately 2.2 million foreign-born persons resided in the United States in 1850, constituting 9.7 percent of the total population. With the continuing heavy volume of immigration in the late nineteenth century, the foreign-born population grew steadily, reaching a peak of 14.4 million in 1930. At the same time, the foreign-born population increased as a proportion of the U.S. population, reaching the peak proportion of 14.8 percent in 1890.

With the diminution of immigration from about 1918 to 1946, the foreign-born population decreased in both numbers and proportions as mortality reduced the aging wave of immigrants. By 1970, the foreign-born population had decreased to 10.5 million, accounting for only 5.1 percent of the total population.

The large increase in immigration that began in the 1960s produced a rapid turnaround in the forty-year decrease of the foreign-born population. By 1990, the number of foreign-born persons residing in the United States reached the highest levels in the history of the country, more than 20 million. Relative to the rest of the population, however, the foreign-born population is less than two-thirds of the highest levels attained from 1860 to 1920. Just over 8 percent of the population was foreign-born in 1990 versus 13 to 15 percent at the end of the nineteenth century.

Population projections suggest that the foreign-born population of the United States will increase from 21.3 million in 1990 to 28.4 million in 2000 and 56.5 million in 2050, assuming current trends in fertility, mortality, and international migration. Under similar assumptions for the growth of the native-born population, these projections forecast an increase of the foreign-born population, as a percentage of the total population, from 8.6 percent in 1990, to 10.2 percent in 2000 and 14.6 percent in 2050.

Race and Ethnicity

Race and ethnic characteristics of the U.S. population have long had special importance. Although "race" is

Figure 3. Foreign-Born Population of the United States and the Percentage of Foreign-Born Population of the Total Population, 1850–2050

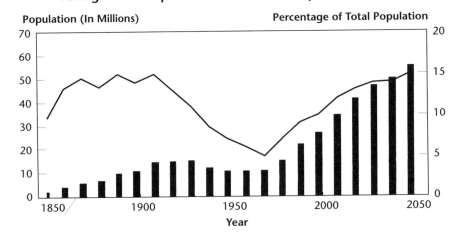

Note: The bars represent the total population with the scale shown on the left; the line represents the percent of the total population with the scale shown on the right.

Source: Historical reconstruction of the U.S. population described in Jeffrey S. Passel and Barry Edmonston, "Immigration and Race: Recent Trends in Immigration to the United States," in Barry Edmonston and Jeffrey S. Passel, eds., *Immigration and Ethnicity: The Integration of America's Newest Arrivals*, chapter 2 (Washington, D.C.: Urban Institute Press, 1994); and population projection of the U.S. population described in Barry Edmonston and Jeffrey S. Passel, "The Future Immigrant Population of the United States," in Barry Edmonston and Jeffrey S. Passel, eds., *Immigration and Ethnicity: The Integration of America's Newest Arrivals*, chapter 11 (Washington, D.C.: Urban Institute Press, 1994).

not now regarded as a meaningful biological concept, this fact should not overlook the social and economic correlates of self-reported racial and ethnic identity in U.S. society. Population statistics provide much of the basis for study of the conditions under which racial and ethnic groups live and the ways in which their relative positions are changing. For much demographic analysis of the U.S. population, ethnic and racial origin are basic variables that must be included as statistical controls before studying the effect of other variables.

Throughout most of its history, the United States has been essentially a biracial society, comprised of a white majority and a black minority (along with a small Native American population). In 1790 the United States' population was recorded as 81 percent white and 19 percent black (the U.S. census did not distinguish other racial groups until 1850). This situation is now changing. The United States is becoming a more diverse society. Figure 4 presents information on the percentage composition of the U.S. population, by race and Hispanic origin from 1850 to 2050.

Adequate data on the five current "racial" groups were developed in 1900. At the turn of the century the U.S. population was 87 percent white, 12 percent black, and about 1 percent other racial groups. The 1900 census counted about 240,000 Native Americans, 240,000 Asians (primarily Chinese, Japanese, and Hawaiians), and 660,000 Hispanics (predominantly Mexican-origin population).

All racial groups increased numerically from 1900 to 1960, although the relative shifts were small. By 1960, the white population's share had dropped only slightly from 87 to 85 percent. The proportion of blacks in the population had decreased slightly, from 12 to 11 percent. The other three racial and ethnic groups had increased their combined proportion from about 1 to 4 percent.

Since 1960, the shifts in origins of immigrants have led to substantial absolute and relative increases in the Asian and Hispanic populations. The combined proportion of Asians, Native Americans, and Hispanics increased from 4 percent in 1960 to 13 percent in 1990. These three groups, which accounted for just over one million people in 1900, had grown to a total of more than thirty-one million by 1990.

As a result of rapid growth of the Asian and Hispanic groups, the composition within the minority population is also changing. The minority population of the United States was almost exclusively black during the nineteenth century, with only a small number of persons of other races. While the black population has increased at a steady pace, the Asian and Hispanic

Figure 4. Racial Composition of the U.S. Population, 1850–2050

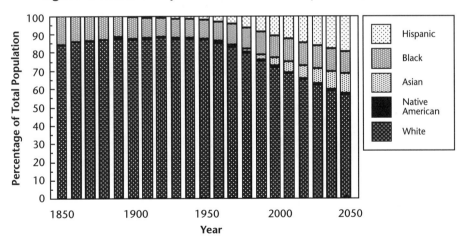

Source: Historical reconstruction of the U.S. population described in Jeffrey S. Passel and Barry Edmonston, "Immigration and Race: Recent Trends in Immigration to the United States," in Barry Edmonston and Jeffrey S. Passel, eds., *Immigration and Ethnicity: The Integration of America's Newest Arrivals*, chapter 2 (Washington, D.C.: Urban Institute Press, 1994); and population projection of the U.S. population described in Barry Edmonston and Jeffrey S. Passel. "The Future Immigrant Population of the United States," in Barry Edmonston and Jeffrey S. Passel, eds., *Immigration and Ethnicity: The Integration of America's Newest Arrivals*, chapter 11 (Washington, D.C.: Urban Institute Press, 1994).

groups have grown at much more rapid rates. Consequently, the proportion of minority population that is black has been dropping steadily, decreasing from 70 percent in 1960 to 48 percent in 1990.

With the current levels of immigration, the racial and ethnic composition of the United States will continue to change. Two groups are likely to experience substantial growth during the next half-century: Asians and Hispanics. The Asian population will grow at rates exceeding 1 percent for the next fifty years, increasing from seven million in 1990 to forty-one million in 2050. The Asian population will become about the same population size as the black population around 2050.

The Hispanic population—assumed to have the largest share of immigration, in part because of its predominant share of illegal immigration—will grow substantially over the next fifty years. The Hispanic population will increase from twenty-two million in 1990, or 9 percent of the total population, to thirty million in 2000. Growth will continue uninterrupted for the next five decades of the projection, at which time Hispanics would number 72.4 million, or 20 percent of the population. The Hispanic population will pass the black population to become the largest minority group in the nation shortly before 2010, under these assumptions.

See also *Asian and Pacific Islander Americans; Education: changing questions and classifications; Family and household composition of the population; Foreign-born population of the United States; Hispanic population; Occupation and education; Private sector; Race: questions and classifications; White population of the United States.*

■ Barry Edmonston

Bibliography

Edmonston, Barry, and Jeffrey S. Passel. "The Future Immigrant Population of the United States." In Barry Edmonston and Jeffrey S. Passel, eds., *Immigration and Ethnicity: The Integration of America's Newest Arrivals*, chapter 11. Washington, D.C.: Urban Institute Press, 1994.

Passel, Jeffrey S., and Barry Edmonston. "Immigration and Race: Recent Trends in Immigration to the United States." In Barry Edmonston and Jeffrey S. Passel, eds., *Immigration and Ethnicity: The Integration of America's Newest Arrivals*, chapter 2. Washington, D.C.: Urban Institute Press, 1994.

Confidentiality: keeping the promise

The Census Bureau's long-standing commitment to confidentiality in its laws, its policies, and its practices shows how strongly it believes that its core business depends on protecting confidentiality and privacy. Confidentiality is a component of employee training; it is emphasized in all communications with respondents; it is integrated into data-processing and transmission operations; and it is the first consideration in decisions about which data to release to the public.

Throughout the twentieth century, confidentiality has been tested by the courts, by congressional actions, and by actions of other government agencies. In each case, the Census Bureau has prevailed to maintain or strengthen its statutory protections. In its practices, the Census Bureau strives to improve its procedures and the products it disseminates while ensuring that confidentiality is not compromised. This often involves trade-offs between efficiency and data use on the one hand and confidentiality on the other.

Legal Protections

Legal confidentiality protections for census data are contained in Title 13 of the United States Code. Section 9 states that information provided by respondents to Census Bureau surveys and censuses can be used for statistical purposes only, that published information cannot identify a particular establishment or individual, and that no one other than sworn officers or employees can see individual reports. Section 214 provides for severe penalties, including large fines and up to five years in prison, for Census Bureau employees who breach confidentiality. One of the strongest confidentiality protections for any government agency, the current census law dates back to 1929, when it was amended to address concerns about the weaker protections afforded data on individuals compared with data on businesses.

Before the 1929 amendment, the confidentiality protections of the census law were less stringent. For example, in 1917 the Census director released transcripts of the 1910 census to the Department of Justice, to local draft boards, and to individuals in cases in which the individuals had been arrested for draft evasion. The census law at that time permitted such use of census records.

Perhaps the most notable and least accurately reported case is the War Department's request in 1942 for names and addresses from the 1940 census of Japanese-Americans living in western states. We are now aware that following the attack on Pearl Harbor, senior Census Bureau staff provided census tabulations that were implicated in the internment effort. What is unclear is whether the then-in-effect legal prohibitions against revealing individual census records were violated.

In 1947 a request by the attorney general to obtain census information on certain individuals suspected of being communist sympathizers resulted in the Census Bureau's refusal to comply. In 1950 representatives of the Secret Service approached a Census Bureau official seeking census records for a neighborhood in the northwest section of the District of Columbia, which was being considered for a temporary residence for President Harry S. Truman during a renovation of the White House. The Census official provided only tabulations that characterized the neighborhood, not the specific people residing there. During the summer of 1980, the Federal Bureau of Investigation (FBI), with a court order, showed up at the Colorado Springs Census District Office seeking access to all census records. This was in response to a former enumerator's allegation that questionnaires and payroll forms had been falsified. Following a tense standoff between Census Bureau and FBI personnel, the Census director called the FBI director and offered to assist the investigation in a way that ensured confidentiality of the census forms.

The courts have also played a role in defining and reshaping the census law. In 1961 the Supreme Court (*St. Regis Paper Co. v. United States*) ruled that copies of census forms retained by a respondent were not protected in the same way as the original forms submitted to the Census Bureau. This was in spite of the fact that the Census Bureau had asked its business respondents to retain completed file copies for future reference. As a result of this ruling, Congress strengthened the Census law to bring copies of completed forms under the same legal protections as the originals. In 1982 the Supreme Court (*Baldrige v. Shapiro*) ruled that census addresses collected and used by the Census Bureau were exempt from disclosure, either by way of civil discovery or the Freedom of Information Act. This ruling responded directly to suits filed by Essex County, New Jersey, and Denver, Colorado, to obtain the Census Bureau's address lists to compare with their own lists in support of their law suit alleging an undercount.

In a case that demonstrated the potentially harmful consequences of legislation that ignored existing statutes, the Illegal Immigration Reform and Immigrant Responsibility Act of 1996 gave the appearance that census records could be given to the Immigration and Naturalization Service (INS) to enforce the provisions of the act. Organizations representing minority groups expressed strong concerns that these groups would be reluctant to respond to the census if they felt law enforcement agencies could see their responses. Subsequently, the Department of Justice confirmed that census confidentiality prohibits release to the INS despite the new legislation, and the INS commissioner agreed not to seek or accept any confidential census information.

A legal exception to confidentiality of census records is the law that provides for the National Archives. Historically, the archivist has made available to genealogists and researchers many records on individuals after fifty years (later reduced to thirty years). Census records were precluded from release because of the strict interpretation of the confidentiality law. Beginning in 1952 the director of the Census Bureau and the archivist agreed that census records could be made publicly available after seventy-two years. This was later codified in the archives law (Title 44 of the United States Code). There is some disagreement about the significance of this time period. Most believe that it was the average life span of a person in 1950. Others argue that it is only significant as the time between the census of 1870 and its public release in 1942.

A more recent legal exception to census confidentiality is Public Law 103-430, the Census Address List Improvement Act of 1994. Under this law the Census Bureau is permitted to share its address register with state and local officials for the purpose of updating the census address list. Local officials who are designated as census liaisons are entitled to see only those addresses pertinent to their local jurisdictions. They are subject to the same confidentiality provisions and penalties as are regular census employees.

Providing Access to Data

Protecting confidentiality is paramount but must be accomplished within the basic mission of the Census Bureau—to provide data to inform the nation. This involves a trade-off between providing access to research data and ensuring confidentiality. Generally, the more detailed the data, the greater the risk of disclosure. Traditionally, the Census Bureau has provided census data in tabulations at the block level for only the few items on the short form and at the tract level for a sample of households using the long form. Beginning with the 1960 census, the Census Bureau began providing public-use microdata sample files representing a proportion of the population so that users could generate their own tables and estimate statistical models.

The technique for protecting confidentiality in census tabulations before 1990 involved cell suppression. Table cells with too few cases were made blank to protect the identity of the individuals with those characteristics. Data users did not like this approach because it left gaps in the data and severely limited their analysis. Beginning in 1990, for short-form data, the Census Bureau began using data swapping in tables of frequency data (the number or percentage of the population with certain characteristics). A sample of households is selected and matched on a set of selected key variables with households in neighboring geographic areas (census blocks or tracts) that have similar characteristics. The swapped households are similar (number of adults, number of children, and racial and Hispanic composition) to those they are replacing. Usually, the swap occurs within the tract, hence having no effect on tabulations at the tract level and above. With swapping, a user cannot be certain that the individual cell represents a particular person.

Microdata files from the census for public use consist of 1 percent and 5 percent samples of the population. This sampling adds considerable confidentiality protection. To protect confidentiality further, the Census Bureau removes individual identifiers (such as name and address), modifies distinguishing characteristics (such as high levels of income), and restricts geographic identifiers (such as name of city) to ensure that only population areas of at least 100,000 persons are identified. These disclosure limitation techniques are designed to protect against attempts by others to identify specific individuals on the file either directly or through links to other data sources.

The Internet

The Census Bureau is developing innovative ways to collect and disseminate data interactively over the Internet. Doing so is not without risk, however. Security is threatened by intruders who attempt to intercept data transmissions or break through security systems, or firewalls, to get to unprotected data. Beginning with Census 2000, respondents could file their census short forms over the Internet. Authentication was assured by requiring each household to enter its 23-digit control number from the mailed census form before entering the information through a firewall to a template on the Census Bureau's World Wide Web site. The data were encrypted and sent directly to Census Bureau computers where they were immediately brought behind a second firewall to ensure that hackers, should they get through the main firewall, could not get to the completed forms.

The American FactFinder (AFF) is the Census Bureau's online data retrieval system designed to allow users to extract tables from the confidential files. The AFF was developed to provide safe and easy access to data from the 2000 census and other Census Bureau programs. The AFF makes extensive use of firewalls to protect source data. It consists of three tiers: printed reports and press releases, summary tables, and custom tables. All data provided through AFF undergo a disclosure review and may be swapped to protect confidentiality. Data provided in tiers one and two are similar to the summary data products provided on paper and computer tapes in the 1990 census. Tier three (custom tabulations) provides the most innovative—and perhaps risky—advance over 1990 data products. At the time of this publication, the procedures have not been determined for limiting disclosure in tables generated from tier 3. The major issue to be addressed is the potential for users to make multiple queries of the source data to defeat the confidentiality protections.

The Census Bureau's reputation for protecting privacy is well known. Nevertheless, the external environment and the concerns raised by new technologies have led the bureau to examine the threat from the mere perception that confidentiality has not been adequately protected. Beginning in the early nineties, the Census Bureau began a research program focused on measuring the public's attitudes toward confidentiality. This research has shown that the public does value confidentiality but that it is cynical about the government's promises. Two general sentiments are prevalent: all government computers are connected and a law enforcement agency can get census data if it really wants it. In response to this public relations problem, the Census Bureau has set about to focus attention on its excellent record for protecting confidentiality, reinforcing its own "culture of confidentiality" internally, and undertaking an outreach and education program designed to change public opinion.

■ Gerald W. Gates

Bibliography

Bohme, Frederick G., and David Pemberton. "Privacy and Confidentiality in the U.S. Censuses-A History." Census Bureau paper presented at the annual meeting of the American Statistical Association. Atlanta, Ga., August 18–21, 1991.

Gates, Gerald, and Deborah Bolton. "Privacy Research Involving Expanded Statistical Use of Administrative Records." In *Proceedings of the Government Statistics Section.* Alexandria, Va.: American Statistical Association, 1998.

Griffin, Richard, Navarro, Alfredo, and Flores-Baez, L. "Disclosure Avoidance for the 1990 Census." In *Proceedings of the Section on Survey Research Methods.* Alexandria, Va.: American Statistical Association, 1989. 516–521.

Seltzer, William, and Margo Anderson. "After Pearl Harbor: The Proper Role of Population Data Systems in Time of War." Paper presented at the annual meeting of the Population Association of America. Los Angeles, Calif., March 23–25, 2000.

Congress and the census

The Constitution of the United States gives Congress the authority to determine how the census will be conducted. Congress also uses data collected in the census to assess the need for new policies and programs, administer and evaluate current programs, and allocate federal funds to state and local governments.

Article I of the Constitution establishes the legislative branch of the federal government, comprised of a Senate and a House of Representatives. Article I, Section 2 provides that the number of representatives for each state will be determined by a census every ten years. It also grants Congress the authority to enact laws governing how the census should be conducted. The inevitable tension between decisions affecting how the census will be conducted and the political consequences of the population count continues to influence congressional oversight of the census today.

Consistent with its constitutional mandate, Congress mandated that new information be collected. In 1850 Congress created a Census Office, headed by a superintendent of the census, which would prepare for the census every ten years in the manner that Congress directed. As time went on, Congress delegated more decision-making authority to the Census Office over field operations and for hiring workers to take the census. Finally, in 1902, Congress established a permanent agency responsible for taking the census and collecting other statistics as required by law. The Bureau of the Census, as the agency was called, initially was housed in the Department of the Interior. The agency was transferred to the Department of Commerce and Labor in 1903, currently the Department of Commerce, where it remains today. The agency reports to the undersecretary for economic affairs in the Economics and Statistics Administration.

Despite the establishment of a permanent census agency, Congress continued to pass laws in the first half of the twentieth century to implement the census. Congress did not enact the rules governing the modern-day census until 1954. Codified in law as Title 13 of the United States Code, the statutory requirements for the decennial census are broad and relatively brief. Congress vested responsibility for the census in the secretary of commerce, who in turn, by administrative order, has delegated authority to the director of the Census Bureau to plan, prepare for, and implement the once-a-decade population count. By granting broad authority to the commerce secretary (and, by implication, the Census Bureau director), Congress relieved itself of the burden of constructing an increasingly complex census process every ten years, a process that now requires ongoing research and development, planning, and preparation. Most technical and operational decisions are left to a world-renowned statistical agency, allowing members of Congress to focus their attention on policy-oriented questions of cost-efficiency, content, and, not surprisingly, the coverage of certain population groups for the purpose of determining the House's composition through the apportionment process. However, given its constitutionally prescribed roles as both manager and chief beneficiary of the census, Congress continues to direct specific census operations through changes in the law, even at times against the advice of experts at the Census Bureau and external scientific organizations. And when the Census Bureau believes that technical considerations outweigh political ones, battles fought at the highest levels of policymaking can ensue.

Because the primary consequences of the census are political in nature, some disputes in Congress over census methods or coverage of the population have been fought primarily along partisan lines. The landmark equal representation decisions handed down by the U.S. Supreme Court starting in the 1960s placed added burdens on the census, as state legislatures were required to draw congressional and other political district boundaries in a way that equalized the population of districts within each state. Suddenly, detailed data on the population of very small areas, including characteristics such as race and voting age, became essential for the decennial post-census exercise of redistricting. Already a process laced with partisan maneuvering, redistricting was elevated to an art form in the decades following the 1970 census, as rapid advances in technology allowed politicians to determine which neighborhoods—even which specific blocks—should be assigned to particular districts to benefit prospective candidates from one political party or the other. The instinct toward either individual or party preservation began to affect the way Congress perceived specific census methods, as opposed to the end results, particularly as the Census Bureau and outside experts began discussing the use of indirect scientific methods, such as sampling, to improve the accuracy of the count for historically undercounted groups.

Party allegiance started to emerge publicly and clearly in the years leading up to the 1990 census when, with backing from experts convened by the National Academy of Sciences, the Census Bureau announced that it planned to conduct a post-enumeration survey to measure the expected undercount and possibly adjust the initial results to improve the accuracy of the count. The Commerce Department, under the administration of Republican president Ronald Reagan, quickly moved to quash the idea, setting off protests from many Democratic lawmakers, who at the time controlled the leadership positions as the majority party in Congress. At the time, and throughout the 1990 census itself, both Republicans and Democrats in Congress refrained from accusing the other side of opposing or supporting a statistical adjustment to correct the disproportionate undercount of racial minorities and the poor, based on partisan interests. But a growing belief among party loyalists on both sides of the political aisle, that their political opponents viewed the debate over adjustment strictly in partisan, not scientific, terms, was simmering not far beneath the surface. When the controversy over the use of statistical methods to correct the census undercount resurfaced in 1996, with the Census Bureau's unveiling of its plan

for Census 2000, the political tables were turned; Democrat Bill Clinton was in the White House and Republicans were in control of both houses of Congress. This time around, the partisan accusations flew publicly. Republicans accused Democrats of supporting statistical methods to inflate the count of minorities and poor people, who they viewed as Democratic allies. Democrats said Republicans opposed scientific methods recommended by the nonpartisan Census Bureau because they feared political disadvantage from a more accurate count of those same populations. Census Bureau officials, rarely comfortable in the political arena that influenced so much of their domain, struggled to defend their plan while protecting what they viewed as the integrity of the scientific process from political interference.

But if party loyalties have shaped the opinions of some members of Congress, geographic interests on some issues affecting census methods and operations also played a significant role in several census controversies over the last forty years. Lawmakers from states with absolute or relative declines in their populations and states with significant minority populations have often viewed disputes over census methods in terms of the political and fiscal consequences for their home territory. As the secretary of commerce considered whether to statistically adjust the 1990 census numbers, for example, members of Congress from states that were in danger of losing a congressional seat tried to gauge how such a change would affect the apportionment outcome, before deciding whether to support or oppose the new method. A recurring controversy over whether to exclude undocumented residents from the census state totals used for apportionment was fought largely along geographic lines, with many Democrats and Republicans from states with large immigrant populations (such as California, New Mexico, and Texas) opposing such an exclusion, and lawmakers from states with relatively low numbers of immigrants (such as Indiana and Pennsylvania) supporting the change.

In addition to partisan and geographic concerns, interest group pressure has become an increasingly significant factor in determining how Congress views the Census Bureau's plans for each decennial census. Constituent and interest group involvement in the census decision-making process increased as more fiscal resources, enforcement of civil rights, and the promise of political representation became inextricably tied to the census results through the proliferation of formula-based government programs, Supreme Court decisions, and sweeping federal laws (such as the Voting Rights Act of 1965) designed to carry out the new rights that emerged from the Court's findings.

The series of hallmark desegregation, voting rights, and affirmative action cases in the 1950s, 1960s, and 1970s empowered more segments of the population and galvanized their advocates toward involvement in the legislative process as a way to ensure a fair share of resources for their communities. These advocates knew the importance of the census in determining the allocation of funds and guaranteeing equal representation. They used their newfound and growing political clout to urge legislative action that would ensure adequate funding for the census, new methods to address the chronic undercount, and the availability of demographic and economic data to track the progress of their communities.

At the same time, with the start of the so-called Information Age in the 1980s, businesses realized the need for detailed data to guide investment decisions and track the need for goods and services among different population subgroups, as industries grew and became more competitive. Already savvy players in the legislative process, business representatives also used their influence with both Congress and executive branch agencies to ensure the availability of useful data from the census.

Authorization and Oversight

Congress controls the conduct of the census through two basic legislative processes: authorizations and appropriations. The authorizing process involves enactment of laws that define what an agency must or can do, what it may not do, and how it should carry out its responsibilities. An authorization often sets a maximum funding level for a government activity, but the law governing the work of the Census Bureau includes no such restriction. This "open-ended authorization" has elevated the importance of the appropriations process in shaping the design and content of the decennial census. Congress has sanctioned or opposed census plans and methods in recent years by allocating or withholding funds in the annual bill that appropriates money for the Census Bureau, and by specifying how those funds can be spent.

Closely related to the authorizing process and usually carried out by the same committee is the oversight function of Congress. While not necessarily seeking to amend existing law or enact new ones, the authorizing committees and subcommittees often hold hearings to review the progress of federal activities, evaluate the success of programs, probe concerns about the misuse of funds or activities that may not be in accordance with the law, and assess the need for new programs or changes in the authorizing statutes governing federal activities.

Despite the enormous political consequences and high profile of the decennial census, Congress has not always afforded the census the level of attention an activity of such massive scope and cost usually receives. At times over the past several decades, the work of the Census Bureau appears to have been an afterthought in the organization of authorizing committees in both the House and Senate. In the House, the Committee on Post Office and Civil Service—established in 1946—had responsibility for overseeing activities of the Census Bureau until 1995, when a new Republican majority eliminated the entire panel and all its subcommittees. Since the 1970 census, jurisdiction over the Census Bureau's work shifted from one subcommittee to another as the committee reorganized from time to time. The census often competed for the attention of subcommittee members with other unrelated issues within the Post Office and Civil Service Committee's broader jurisdiction, including federal government workforce issues, postal employee concerns, and federal holidays. In the 1970s, the Subcommittee on Manpower and Human Resources was responsible for overseeing the census and authorizing its activities, as necessary. In the 1980s and early 1990s, a new Subcommittee on Census and Population signaled a desire to pay closer attention, on an ongoing basis, to census planning and preparation, as well as other statistical activities of the Census Bureau and federal government. In 1993, two years before the Post Office and Civil Service Committee's demise, the subpanels were reorganized once again, resulting in a new Subcommittee on Census, Statistics, and Postal Personnel.

The new Republican majority assumed control of all committee and subcommittee chairmanships in the 104th Congress (1995–1997), representing a sweeping change in how the House and Senate would be run. In the House, most of the standing committees were renamed and several were eliminated altogether. With the old Post Office and Civil Service Committee gone, responsibility for census authorization and oversight shifted to a renamed and reorganized Committee on Government Reform and Oversight (renamed the Committee on Government Reform in the 106th Congress).

Democrats had controlled the House for forty years as the majority party, and nearly all House Republicans had served only as minority party members in that chamber. Throughout the institution, including in the Senate, where Republicans also assumed majority status, Republican leaders had their hands full rearranging offices, hiring staff, and setting their policy agenda; Democrats were dealing with their loss of power and the institutional benefits that flow to the majority. (Majority control of the Senate had changed hands several times between 1970 and the late 1990s.) Hence, even though the Census Bureau was preparing for its final tests in 1995 before settling on a plan for the 2000 census, members of Congress had many other issues on their minds. Census planning was not a priority, and responsibility for overseeing the census process was tucked away, almost as an afterthought, in the Subcommittee on National Security, International Affairs, and Criminal Justice.

In early 1998, realizing that oversight of the upcoming census required more fiscal and personnel resources, House Republicans created the Subcommittee on the Census under the Government Reform and Oversight Committee. The jurisdiction for the new panel was limited to the work of the Census Bureau, allowing it to devote its resources to overseeing census preparations and considering legislative proposals to modify or add census operations.

By contrast, in the last several decades, the Senate took only sporadic interest in significant policy debates affecting the design, coverage, and content of the census. It followed an unwritten but traditional rule of deferring to the House in matters affecting reapportionment and redistricting, and, therefore, the composition of the House itself.

From the 1970s to the present, the Senate assigned authorizing responsibility for the census in much the same haphazard fashion as the House. Jurisdiction over the census rests with the Committee on Governmental Affairs. At times, the committee has elected to retain that responsibility, while at other times it has vested one of its subcommittees with jurisdiction over the census. As in the House, the census has sometimes been assigned to a subcommittee with jurisdiction over a wide range of unrelated government activities, making it difficult for members of the panel or their staff to devote significant time to the census. For example, in the 1970s, the Subcommittee on Energy, Nuclear Proliferation, and Federal Services was responsible for overseeing the census. In the late 1980s, after a com-

mittee reorganization, the census was assigned to a new Subcommittee on Government Information and Regulation (renamed the Subcommittee on Government Regulation and Information in the early 1990s), signaling a recognition that the census is part of a broader federal statistical system providing lawmakers with information to support policy decisions. However, in 1995, when Republicans took control of leadership posts and committee chairs as the new majority party, the Committee on Governmental Affairs decided not to assign the census to a subcommittee, giving members of the full panel a leading role in overseeing plans for the 2000 census.

Appropriations

Congress also has used the appropriations process to direct changes in the design and content of the decennial census that it could not accomplish through changes in the Census Bureau's authorizing statute. The practice became more prevalent in the mid-to-late 1990s, as the Republican-controlled Congress clashed with the Democratic administration over major aspects of the proposed 2000 census plan, making it more difficult to amend the law in the face of presidential veto threats.

Every year, Congress must pass and the president must sign spending bills that provide money to run all federal government activities in the next fiscal year. The government's activities are divided into thirteen broad budget accounts; a Committee on Appropriations in each chamber must steer the thirteen spending bills through the legislative process.

Funding for the Census Bureau is included in an appropriations bill covering the Departments of Commerce, State, and Justice, the federal Judiciary, and several independent agencies including the Legal Services Corporation and the Small Business Administration. (The Census Bureau is an agency of the Commerce Department.) Congress divides up the total amount of money available for spending on discretionary federal programs (for example, programs that are not entitlements, such as Social Security) among the thirteen budget accounts, in an annual budget resolution. Within each large budget category, diverse programs also must compete with each other for funds during the annual appropriations process.

The decennial census has not been immune from the competition for fiscal resources, despite its constitutional grounding. In the years between censuses, appropriators have been less generous in allocating funds for census research and planning, often preferring to spend available funds on other priority programs in the same budget account, such as the Justice Department's law enforcement initiatives and the Commerce Department's trade promotion activities. Congressional interest in the census heightens as serious preparations get under way for each count, usually two years before the census year. Even then, the Census Bureau is not guaranteed its full appropriation request. Preparations for the census require sharp increases in funding over a relatively short period (the years ending in "9," "0," and "1"), a cycle not well suited to a budget process that generally contemplates only modest annual increases, or no increases at all, in funding for existing programs.

Nevertheless, the "must-pass" nature of the annual funding bills makes them a logical vehicle for directing changes in census policy. If the administration disagrees strongly with the amount of appropriated funds or a restriction on census methods, the president must veto the entire funding bill, potentially delaying funds for equally important but unrelated federal programs.

Congress uses the annual Commerce appropriations bill to influence census plans by "earmarking" a portion of the funds for a specific activity, such as advertising, or by prohibiting the expenditure of funds on an activity. It also provides more detailed guidance to the Census Bureau in committee reports. Though legally nonbinding, the "report language" explains the intent of the bill and often includes more detail than the bill itself as to how the overall funding level for each program should be spent. Appropriators also express their views on the overall direction of census plans in the committee reports, noting their concern about the number of questions on the census long form or Census Bureau staffing levels, for example. Occasionally, the reports direct the Census Bureau to take certain steps, such as including American citizens living overseas in the census. However, the Census Bureau is legally required to comply only with bill language that is signed into law.

In 1997 the appropriations process became the battleground for the dispute between Republicans in Congress and the Clinton Administration over the proposed use of sampling methods in the 2000 census. Republican critics of the Census Bureau's plan to sample unresponsive households and statistically correct undercounts realized the futility of passing independent legislation to prohibit sampling in the face of

strong administration support for the plan. Instead, congressional leaders inserted a sampling prohibition in a mid-year emergency appropriations bill aimed primarily at helping flood victims in the Midwest and Northwest and supporting extended military operations in Bosnia. Despite the desperate situation in flood-ravaged communities, President Clinton vetoed the measure, citing his opposition to the sampling prohibition as one of two main reasons for rejecting the bill. Faced with fierce public criticism for their failure to provide the emergency funds, Republican leaders removed the antisampling provision before sending the measure back to the president for his signature.

Despite the temporary setback, sampling opponents continued to use the appropriations process to prevent the Census Bureau from carrying out its plan for the 2000 census. Later in 1997, they included an antisampling provision in the fiscal year 1998 Commerce Department spending bill over the president's objections, a showdown that delayed enactment of the measure for more than a month. Intense negotiations at the highest levels of Congress and the White House ultimately resulted in an extensive compromise agreement that essentially required the Census Bureau to prepare both for its original census plan and for a census without any sampling methods. It also authorized Congress to challenge the proposed sampling methods in court and created an eight-member Census Monitoring Board to oversee the census. Included as part of the fiscal year 1998 Commerce appropriations bill, the November 1997 agreement represents the most extensive use of the appropriations process to direct census plans since enactment of the modern census statute in 1954.

Independent Agencies and Organizations

Congress often turns to independent, nonpartisan agencies of the legislative branch, or other independent government organizations, to help it oversee and monitor the census process. Several of these organizations have helped legislators identify strengths and weaknesses in the census process. They also have recommended new methods for research or testing, evaluated the results of census tests, assessed the fiscal and political consequences of various census methods, and analyzed cost estimates of census operations.

The U.S. General Accounting Office (GAO) is the investigative and audit agency of the legislative branch. Primarily at the request of the census authorizing committees, the GAO has evaluated census plans and procedures, analyzed management practices, and monitored census operations in real time, for the past several decades. Its findings and recommendations are conveyed in testimony at congressional hearings or in written reports.

Congress also relies on the Congressional Research Service (CRS), an arm of the Library of Congress, for legal analyses of statutes governing the census, research into the uses of census data, and historical narratives of census methods and legislative activity affecting the count. CRS also monitors the effect of population change on congressional apportionment.

The National Academy of Sciences is a congressionally chartered, private, nonprofit corporation that advises the federal government on issues requiring technical and scientific expertise. At the request of Congress or federal agencies, the academy's National Research Council convenes panels of experts to study scientific aspects of policies and programs. Since the 1970s, the council's Committee on National Statistics has studied census methods and content requirements, and it has issued several exhaustive reports that include recommendations for new census methods and future research. In the early 1990s, two separate panels concluded that the Census Bureau could not reduce the persistent, differential undercount of racial minorities without employing sampling and statistical methods to supplement traditional counting operations. Congressional opponents of sampling, however, essentially discounted the panels' findings, a clear demonstration of Congress's ultimate authority to decide how the census should be conducted.

Determining Census Content

Another key decision that must be made for each census is the type and amount of information to be collected. For much of census history, Congress established the precise topics to be covered and the questions to be asked in the law enacted before each decennial count. As the nation grew and became more complex, Congress increasingly relied on the census for a wide range of demographic, social, housing, and economic information to help it evaluate conditions, assess need, and address both national and local problems. By 1940, the amount of desired data was so great that the Census Bureau applied new statistical sampling methods to collect some of the information from only a portion of the population. Starting in 1960, as the bureau came to rely increasingly on mailed questionnaires to conduct the census, it developed a second, longer form for a sample of households to gather information on topics that define the basic characteristics of the population in more detail, such as educational attainment, employment, ancestry, commuting patterns, and housing conditions.

As with much of the census planning process in recent history, Congress delegated more authority over content determination to the Commerce Department, but it retained clear lines of oversight through reporting mechanisms in the law. The Census Act of 1954 (Public Law 83-740) grants the secretary of commerce broad authority to conduct the census "in such form and content as he may determine." It also requires the secretary to report to Congress, no later than three years before Census Day, the subject matters that will be included in the next census. No later than two years before each census, the secretary must report the questions that will be included on the census forms. These reporting requirements have given Congress specific opportunities to review the proposed topics to be covered, as well as the questions that will appear on the census forms, before the questionnaires are finalized and printed in the year prior to the census.

However, while the law provides for notification to Congress of proposed census content, it does not explicitly require Congress to approve the topics or questions proposed by the Census Bureau. The absence of a formal approval process has given the Census Bureau some flexibility in deciding what data to collect and how to collect them. At times, Congress has been forced to pass legislation to add topics or modify questions when either the Census Bureau or the Office of Management and Budget, which is currently responsible for approving all federal data collection activities under the Paperwork Reduction Act of 1980 (Public Law 96-511), objected to the changes on technical or policy grounds.

For example, prior to the 1990 census, the Office of Management and Budget decided that some of the questions initially proposed by the Census Bureau on home heating fuel and other housing characteristics should be eliminated to reduce the burden of response on the public, much to the dismay of the utility and housing industries. In addition, in the standard question on race, the Census Bureau decided to ask Asian and Pacific Islander Americans to write in their specific country of origin, instead of providing a list of countries that respondents could simply check off, as it had in the 1980 census. The bureau informed Congress that its decision to modify the race question was based on extensive testing earlier in the planning process, which it said demonstrated that a write-in format would result in more accurate responses. Asian American advocacy and community-based organizations objected vigorously to the modified question, however, fearing that too many recent immigrants from Asian countries would be unable to fill in their country of origin easily or legibly.

Unable to convince the Census Bureau to revert to the previous race question format, Asian American groups turned to Congress for help. Lobbyists for the gas and oil industries, joined by their counterparts in the housing industry, also sought protection from Congress for the questions they wanted to preserve on the census forms. The stakeholders found a sympathetic ear among lawmakers interested in energy and housing issues, as well as among legislators with significant Asian American constituencies. In late 1988 Congress passed legislation to ensure the collection of particular information on home heating and plumbing and to require a check-off format for Asian Americans, as it had in the previous census. President Reagan, in the final months of his presidency, refused to sign the legislation, killing the initiatives with a pocket veto after the One Hundredth Congress had adjourned.

Despite its failure to force changes legislatively in the proposed content and wording of the 1990 census questionnaires, Congress prevailed. The Census Bureau apparently recognized that it made neither political nor public relations sense to thwart the will of Congress and undermine support for the census among Asian Americans and industry data users. When the 101st Congress convened in January 1989, the Census Bureau informed the relevant authorizing committees that it had decided to modify the race question, as set forth in the failed legislation, and to retain the questions on home heating equipment and plumbing facilities.

The eleventh-hour controversy over the 1990 census forms represented an extreme example of the precarious balance of power between Congress and the Census Bureau under the broad delegation of authority to the executive branch in the Census Act. But it demonstrates how the tension between the political interests of Congress and the technical or operational concerns of the Census Bureau (and other relevant executive branch agencies) can affect all aspects of census planning, preparation, and implementation. The 1990 content dispute also provides an example of how,

over the past several decades, Congress's modified role in determining census design and content is shaped by constituent and interest group pressure.

More often in recent decades, Congress has guided the content of the census forms without resorting to legislative battle with the Census Bureau. It has successfully expressed its interest in collecting certain information informally through consultations with the Census Bureau. For example, several legislators persuaded the Census Bureau to tabulate the number of Taiwanese Americans in the 1990 census, after overcoming State Department objections that designating Taiwanese as an independent national origin might undermine the United States' official position of not recognizing the independence of Taiwan from the People's Republic of China.

Congress also has guided the content determination process by including directives in the committee reports that accompany the Census Bureau's annual spending bill. Following the 1990 census, influential members of the House appropriations committee were convinced that the number of questions asked in the census (particularly on the long form) contributed to declining response rates. For several years, the committee's legislative reports included strong language directing the Census Bureau to reduce the amount of data collected in the census. That clear evidence of congressional intent, while not having the force of law, convinced the Census Bureau to scale back the length of both the short and long forms for the 2000 count.

But since delegating substantial authority over census design and content to the Census Bureau in the Census Act of 1954, Congress has influenced census content primarily through authorizing statutes for federal grant-in-aid programs, the number of which exploded in the post–World War II period. A significant number of these programs used population and other socioeconomic data to distribute funds to the states and cities; the census, or other government surveys that rely on the census to produce reliable estimates, was often the only source for the data.

Programmatic Uses of Census Data

Concerns about reapportionment and redistricting have been a primary but not exclusive factor driving congressional activity on census issues. The desire for a wide range of demographic, social, and economic information about the nation's population increased substantially in the latter half of the twentieth century.

Lawmakers sought information for increasingly smaller units of geography both to evaluate the need for federal resources or intervention at the state and local level and to distribute funds according to program formulas once they identified those needs.

According to the General Accounting Office, $185 billion in federal aid was distributed in 1998 to states or substate areas based in whole or in part on census data. Most population-based federal assistance is allocated according to formula grants. Large formula grant programs include Foster Care, Highway Planning and Construction, Employment and Training for Dislocated Workers, and Child Care and Development Block Grants; Medicaid reimbursements to states also rely on census population figures. Eligibility for some aid programs, such as Community Development Block Grants, is based on population size. Federal aid also is available through program grants, which fund specific projects such as research or planning. Examples of program grants that are distributed based on census data include Rural Development Grants and Head Start. Some direct lending and guaranteed lending programs, such as loans for rural electrification and water and waste disposal, depend at least in part on census data to establish eligibility.

While population is the most common factor in federal aid formulas, other characteristic data collected in the census are used to distribute funds or establish eligibility for grants. The number of people with incomes below the poverty level is a factor in some programs that target disadvantaged families or children, while census data on commuting patterns are used to allocate transportation funds. Other factors used to allocate funds or determine eligibility for funds are unemployment, per capita income, age, and counts of specific population subgroups, such as migrant children.

Typically, the authorizing statutes for federal grant-in-aid programs specify the source of the data to be used in determining the distribution of funds. Some programs require the use of decennial census data, while others require only the most recent data available. In the latter case, updated population estimates produced annually by the Census Bureau often are used, but characteristics data (such as journey to work or income data for some geographic areas) may be available only from the decennial census. Formulas that rely on certain data but do not specify the source often are viewed as de facto requirements to collect the information in the census when no other reliable or cost-effective source exists.

See also *Apportionment and districting; Census law; Content; Content determination.*

■ Terri Ann Lowenthal

Bibliography

Anderson, Margo J. *The American Census: A Social History.* New Haven, Conn.: Yale University, 1988.

U.S. General Accounting Office. *Decennial Census: Overview of Historical Census Issues.* GAO/GGD-98-103. Washington, D.C.: U.S. Government Printing Office, May 1998.

U.S. General Accounting Office. *Formula Grants: Effects of Adjusted Population Counts on Federal Funding to the States.* GAO/HEHS-99-69. Washington, D.C.: U.S. Government Printing Office, February 1999.

U.S. Superintendent of Documents. *United States Code.* Title 13—Census. Pittsburgh, Pa.: U.S. Government Printing Office.

Content

To fulfill the purposes of congressional apportionment specified by the U.S. Constitution, the decennial census of population need count only the number of persons (before 1870, the number of free and slave persons) in each state. From the beginning, however, members of Congress and others inside and outside the federal government recognized the value of having the census collect additional content to inform program administration, policy development, and general public understanding.

The first census in 1790 had very limited content. U.S. marshals in each judicial district obtained for each household a count of the number of free white males sixteen years of age or older, free white males under sixteen years, free white females, all other free persons, and slaves. The twenty-second census in 2000 had much more extensive content. All households were asked on the short form about the age, race, Hispanic origin, sex, and household relationship of each household member and whether the housing unit was owned or rented. In addition, about one-sixth of households were asked on the long form to answer another three dozen questions for each person (two-thirds of the questions pertained to people aged fifteen or older) and another two dozen questions for the housing unit.

In the decades between 1790 and 2000, the content of the census expanded and changed in response to changing needs for information about particular groups (for example, immigrants, farmers, veterans, people with disabilities) and for information relevant to particular issues (for example, education, transportation). Some topics have appeared in almost every census, and most censuses have covered a wide range of topics.

Statistical sampling, in which questions are asked of samples of households instead of all households, has been used in recent censuses to reduce the costs and public burden of providing all of the information that is needed from the census. (Sampling for content was begun on a small scale in the 1940 census and greatly expanded subsequently.) For the 1990 and 2000 censuses, concerted efforts were made to maintain and, if possible, scale back the number of questions, so that these censuses had somewhat fewer questions than were asked in 1980.

Listed below (in *italics*) are the short-form and long-form population items in the 2000 census, with a summary of their appearance in earlier censuses. Question wording and detail vary, often substantially, across censuses. (See *Long form*, Table 1, for an item-by-item comparison of population and housing census content in 1960 to 2000.)

2000 Census Short-Form Population Items

Age, race, and sex
Asked in every census from 1790 to 2000 (race question in 2000 permits respondent to mark one or more races).

Hispanic origin
Asked in 1930 (in the race question) and in 1970 to 2000.

Relationship to head of household
Asked in 1880 to 2000.

2000 Census Long-Form Population Items

Ancestry
Asked in 1980 to 2000.

Citizenship and year of immigration
Citizenship asked in 1820, 1830, 1870, 1890 to 2000; year of immigration asked in 1900 to 1930, 1970 to 2000; year of naturalization asked in 1920; eligibility to vote asked in 1870.

Disability (several questions)
Items related to physical or mental disabilities asked in 1830 to 1890, 1900 (supplemental schedules), 1910, 1920 to 1930 (supplemental schedules), 1970 to 2000.

Education (school attendance, including whether public or private, and highest grade completed)
School attendance asked in 1850 to 2000; public or private school asked in 1960 to 2000; educational attainment asked in 1940 to 2000; literacy asked in 1840 to 1930; vocational training asked in 1970.

Employment status last week
Asked in 1930 to 2000; duration of unemployment asked in 1880 to 1910, 1930 (supplemental schedule), 1940, 1950, 1980.

Hours usually worked per week last year
Asked in 1980 to 2000; hours worked last week asked in 1940 to 1990.

Income (total and by source, such as wages, Social Security)
Asked in 1940 to 2000; categories expanded over time.

Language (whether speak other than English at home, how well speak English)
Language asked in 1890 to 1940, 1960 to 2000; how well speak English asked in 1980 to 2000; language of parents asked in 1910, 1920.

Marital status
Asked in 1880 to 2000; other marriage-related questions asked in 1850 to 1910, 1930 to 1980; number of children living asked in 1890 to 1910; number of children ever born asked in 1890 to 1910, 1940 to 1990.

Occupation and industry of current employment, class of worker
Occupation asked in 1850 to 2000; industry asked in 1820, 1840, 1910 to 2000; class of worker asked in 1910 to 2000; occupation, industry, and class of worker five years ago asked in 1970; activity five years ago asked in 1970, 1980.

Place of birth
Asked in 1850 to 2000; place of birth of parents asked in 1870 to 1970.

Place of work and *transportation to work* (several questions)
Asked in 1960 to 2000.

Responsibility for grandchildren
New question in 2000.

Prior residence (five years ago) and *farm residence* (housing item)
Prior residence asked in 1940 to 2000; farm residence asked in 1890 to 2000; year moved into pre-

sent residence asked in 1960, 1970, 1980 to 2000 (housing item); whether previously a farm resident asked in 1940, 1950.

Veteran status (including period of service) and *years of military service*

Veteran status asked in 1840, 1890, 1910, 1930 to 2000; period of service asked in 1930, 1950 to 2000; years of military service asked in 1990, 2000; questions on dependents of veterans asked in 1890, 1940.

Weeks worked last year

Asked in 1940 to 2000.

Year last worked

Asked in 1960 to 2000.

The 2000 census includes one new question (responsibility for grandchildren) and significant changes to previous questions (for example, disability), but it does not include some questions that were asked in earlier censuses—for example, occupation five years ago and vocational training (asked in 1970), value of real estate (asked in 1850 to 1870), and value of personal property (asked in 1860 and 1870). Further, censuses from 1850 through 1930 included not only general population questions, but also one or more supplemental schedules (forms for interviewers to record answers). In 1850 to 1890, questions were asked on a supplemental schedule about people who died in the previous year. In 1880 to 1930, detailed questions were posed on one or more supplemental schedules for such groups as people with disabilities or people who were residents of institutions. (Recent censuses include residents of institutions, who are categorized by type of institution, but no special questions were formulated for them.) In 1880 to 1910, there were supplemental schedules for Native Americans. The 1930 census included a supplemental schedule on unemployment.

The population census has often been conducted in conjunction with other censuses. In 1810 the population census was augmented by a census of manufactures. In later decades, censuses of agriculture, mining, governments, business, and transportation were conducted at the same time as the population census, but economic and government censuses are now conducted in years that do not conflict with the census of population.

Since 1940, the population census has included a census of housing as an integral component (see list of housing items in the 1960 to 2000 censuses in *Long form*, Table 1). In every census since 1950, a survey of residential financing was conducted in conjunction with the population and housing census; and in 1960 and 1970, a survey of components of change in the housing stock (for example, new additions, demolitions) was conducted in conjunction with the population and housing census.

See also *Content determination; Housing; Long form; Related data sources; Sampling for content.*

■ Constance F. Citro

Bibliography

U.S. Bureau of the Census. "Population and Housing Inquiries in U.S. Decennial Censuses, 1790–1970." Working paper no. 39. Washington, D.C.: U.S. Department of Commerce, 1973.

Content determination

The process of determining the content of the decennial population census (the questions asked) involves many players. The U.S. Congress was largely responsible for setting the content of the first few censuses, under its constitutional mandate that a census be conducted every ten years "in such Manner as they [the members of Congress] shall by Law direct," and it continues to play a role in content determination today. However, other agencies and groups have increasingly assumed important roles in content determination as well. In recent censuses, extensive testing has also contributed to decisions about including items in the census and about the best ways to ask questions so as to obtain valid responses. The resulting information collected by each census reflects the balance of forces about which questions appeared most needed to support public policy, provide time series for analysis, and serve the general public understanding.

History

For the first census in 1790, members of Congress debated the merits of including additional questions beyond the minimal constitutional requirement to ascertain the number of free and slave persons (excluding Native Americans not taxed). James Madison argued for asking not only for basic demographic information, such as age and sex, but also for such information as occupation to help understand the economic makeup of the country. The final law stipulated more limited content; specifically, for each household, the numbers of free white males by age (over and under age sixteen), free white females, all other free persons, and slaves.

Groups such as the American Philosophical Society lobbied Congress to expand the number of questions for the 1800 census. However, the only new items comprised a finer breakdown of the white male and female populations by age, Congress having decided that additional questions were either unnecessary or unconstitutional. The 1820 census marked the first time that Congress agreed to a census inquiry about the economic composition of the population. The question asked the number of household members principally engaged in agriculture, manufacturing, or commerce.

President John Quincy Adams, who had directed the 1820 census when he was secretary of state, made several suggestions for the 1830 census that were adopted, including the addition of further detail on age. Congress also added questions on the numbers of people who were deaf, blind, or dumb.

The 1850 census saw an important development in how the form and content of the census were determined. A Census Board, consisting of the secretaries of state and interior and the postmaster general, was set up to draft legislation for the census. The board enlisted the aid of expert advisers, who recommended that the census schedules (forms) be expanded and restructured to collect data for each individual instead of collecting summaries for each household. They also recommended that different schedules be developed for different elements of the census, such as free persons, slaves, people who had died in the preceding year, agriculture, manufacturing, and other "social" statistics (for example, information on schools, libraries, crime, religion). After extensive debate, Congress adopted most of their recommended changes, which significantly added to the census content. (An exception was that southern senators blocked the inclusion of many of the proposed new questions for slaves.)

The 1850 census legislation governed the content of the 1860 census. For the 1870 census, a House select committee, headed by James Garfield, with advice from outside experts, recommended adding new questions on marital status, immigration, and other topics, but most of its recommendations were not adopted.

The 1880 census saw increased lobbying on the part of academics, businesses, and other groups, as well as members of Congress, to add, modify, or drop specific questions from the census. By the 1920 census, such requests had proliferated. A new player—a joint Census Advisory Committee of the American Statistical Association and American Economic Association—was formed in 1918. This committee helped the Census Bureau (established as a permanent agency in 1902) sort through and prioritize the myriad requests for new questions on the census. For the 1920 census, the Census Bureau recommended to Congress that the number of questions be reduced and the schedules made less complex.

The Census Act of 1929 authorized the director of the census to select the census items, subject to approval by the secretary of commerce. The Census Bureau then faced directly the tension between keeping the census content relatively simple and consistent over time and the interest of many groups and individuals in adding "their items" to the census. Beginning with the 1930 census the Census Bureau used the mechanism of public conferences to solicit input and involve interested parties in the development of census content.

The advent of modern statistical sampling methods made it possible to accommodate more questions in the census, without incurring the costs and public burden of asking everyone to respond. For the first time in the 1940 census, six new questions were asked of only 5 percent of the population instead of everyone. Subsequent censuses greatly expanded the use of sampling for content. Beginning in 1960, separate "short" and "long" forms were used for mail delivery to households. The short form contained the items asked of all households; one or more long forms included the short-form items plus sample items asked of only some households.

Content Determination Today

Congress remains an important player in the determination of census content for the modern census. By provisions of the Census Act of 1954, the Census Bureau is required to submit to Congress a list of topics to be included in the census three years before Census Day (April 1) and a list of specific questions two years before Census Day. Following the 1990 census, Congress expressed strong interest in simplifying the short form and even eliminating the long form, on grounds that the length and complexity of the forms contributed to undercoverage of the population. The Census Bureau conducted extensive testing on "user-friendly" short and long forms and also developed plans for a new American Community Survey, which, if fully implemented, could replace the long form in the 2010 census.

Congress has also occasionally intervened on specific questions. For example, Asian American groups turned to Congress to help reverse a Census Bureau decision about the format of the 1990 census race question. The Census Bureau wanted the question to ask Asian and Pacific Islander Americans to write in their specific country of origin instead of checking a box from a list of countries. Pressure from Congress and the Asian American community, which stemmed from concern about the likely poor quality of write-in entries, led the Census Bureau to adopt a check-off list for 1990 similar to that used in 1980.

Beginning with the 1960 census, a federal interagency council, organized by the U.S. Office of Management and Budget (OMB), has played a major role in determining census content. Because of the growth in federal programs that use census data to allocate funds to states and localities and other federally mandated uses of census data (for example, for civil rights enforcement), primacy has been given in recent censuses to questions that are needed for federal program purposes. The interagency councils and their subcommittees have provided forums for agencies to debate and establish priorities. One such interagency group pressed successfully in the 1970 census to have a question on Hispanic origin added at a very late date to one of the long forms used in that census (the 5 percent form).

OMB also has a formal role in the determination of census content because of the requirement that it clear all federal agency questionnaires intended for more than nine people. OMB reviews and approves the forms that are used in census tests, the dress rehearsals conducted in recent censuses, and the census itself. In 1987 OMB disapproved the 1990 census dress rehearsal questionnaire, citing public burden, and ordered a reduction in the planned sample size for the long form, the deletion of several questions, and the placement of some housing items on the long form instead of the short form. Opposition from Congress and the census data user community to these changes resulted in a compromise whereby only a few questions were deleted or moved from the short to the long form. Also, the overall long-form sample size was maintained, although a smaller sampling fraction was used in more densely settled areas.

Input on census content is also regularly obtained from a broad range of groups and individuals through such mechanisms as formal advisory committees, public meetings, conferences, and other contacts. However, recent censuses have given primacy to content items that fulfill federal data needs.

For the 2000 census, the decision was made to limit the census content almost entirely to items that were mandated in federal legislation for such purposes as fund allocation or required for federal purposes in that the census was the only source of needed data. Further, to be included on the short form, the item had to be needed at the smallest level of census geography, the census block. Federal agencies played a key role in determining which census items were mandated, required, or only loosely tied to federal programs. The Census Bureau also surveyed nonfederal groups about their uses of census items and commissioned case studies of data applications from the Association of Public Data Users. Input from these efforts was helpful in supporting the retention of some items in the 2000 census that were not specifically mandated or required for federal programs. Overall, the result was a significant reduction in the length of the short form, as well as some changes in the long form. (See *Long form*, Table 1, for the short-form and long-form population and housing items in the 1960 to 2000 censuses.)

The Census Bureau carried out extensive research and experimentation on the appearance and content of the forms for recent censuses. A mail survey of a large sample of housing units conducted several years before the census, the National Content Test, was used to test alternative question wording and the feasibility of including proposed new or modified questions. Other tests of question wording and questionnaire format were carried out through small-scale surveys, cognitive research in which small groups of respondents were walked through the questionnaire or in other ways probed to see how they interpreted questions, and experiments with alternative questionnaires during the census itself. These kinds of tests and research were important to increase the likelihood that respondents would interpret the questions as they were intended and provide valid answers.

See also *Advisory committees; American Community Survey; Congress and the census; Long form; Sampling for content; Statistical policy and oversight.*

■ Constance F. Citro

Bibliography

Anderson, Margo J. *The American Census: A Social History.* New Haven, Conn.: Yale University Press, 1988.

Magnuson, Diana L. "Who and What Determined the Content of the U.S. Population Schedule over Time." *Historical Methods* 28 (winter 1995): 11–26.

U.S. Bureau of the Census. "Planning the Census." In *1990 Census of Population and Housing History*, part B, chapter 2. Washington, D.C.: U.S. Department of Commerce, 1995.

Coverage evaluation

As was suspected by George Washington with respect to the first census in 1790 and to anyone who has considered the matter since then, the decennial census does not obtain a complete count. Although most people are included only once and at the proper address, many people (and households) are missed, and others are included more than once or are otherwise included erroneously (for example, those born after census day). In other words, the decennial census experiences an *undercount* and an *overcount*. There are also those who are included but at the wrong address, and depending on the level of geography used by the application and the distance between the two addresses, the result can be an undercount and an overcount in two different areas. For a given demographic group or region, the effect of undercoverage and overcoverage—almost always expressed as a percentage—is represented by the *net undercount*, the difference between the undercount and the overcount. (These do not ordinarily balance out, since people who are likely to be overcounted are not generally the same as those likely to be missed.) When the net undercount is uneven across groups or regions the census is subject to a *differential (net) undercount*. The differential undercount, typically expressed (for a group or region) in relation to the national level of undercoverage, is a useful summary of the effect of census undercoverage for an individual group or region.

The measurement of under- and overcoverage is an extremely important component of an overall assessment of census quality. As with all its data products, the Census Bureau feels an obligation both to inform users as to the quality of the estimates it provides and to improve the quality of the estimates over time. To support both of these purposes, the Census Bureau has used *coverage evaluation* programs to measure the degree of census undercoverage since at least as far back as the 1950 census. These programs make use of previous censuses, surveys, and administrative records to measure differential undercount at various levels of geographic and demographic aggregation as well as to understand the mechanism of census omission, double counting, and other errors. The important uses for which census counts are produced, and the success of these coverage evaluation programs in measuring census undercoverage, have raised the possibility of using the information from these programs to "adjust" the census for undercoverage, that is, to use the information from these programs to improve the accuracy of the census counts.

The Major Types of Coverage Evaluation Programs

Demographic Analysis. Demographic analysis makes use of the following equation to estimate census undercoverage for the current census for a particular demographic group (particular subgroups are ignored here): Current census count = Previous census count + Intercensal births + Intercensal immigration - Intercensal deaths - Intercensal emigration. As written, the completeness of the current census is then evaluated only in comparison with that of the preceding census. To reduce this dependence, one typically uses a census that is more distant than the one ten years ago, with the intercensal period then indicating multiple decades of separation. For age groups born since the base census, the previous census count is obviously not needed. In recent censuses, since birth records have been considered to be relatively complete only since 1935, the above equation was used only for people born after 1935. For the population age sixty-five and over, Medicare records have been used to measure census undercoverage. For those in between, various extrapolation methods involving use of information from multiple censuses and sex ratios have been used. Demographic analysis was the preferred method for assessing census completeness starting with the 1950 census and continuing at least through the 1970 census.

Post-Enumeration Survey and Dual-Systems Estimation. The method now suggested for use by the Census Bureau for coverage evaluation of the United States decennial census is the use of a post-enumeration survey (PES) coupled with dual-systems estimation (DSE). The original idea was to take a random sample of areas and conduct a second "census" in those areas with better enumerators. Then the ratio of the census count to the survey count would measure census completeness. This approach was considered to be unsatisfactory because it did not achieve uniformly superior coverage to the census. It was believed that the inferior coverage was because the survey did not enjoy the same imprimatur as the census. Therefore, this "do it again, better" idea was replaced by "do it again, independently," a method suggested first in 1949.

This method, improved and expanded by the Census Bureau for decennial census application, actually involves two sample survey operations. The first, the so-called *P-sample*, is a sample of blocks (or block clusters) for which an address list is created through a separate listing process. After nonresponse follow-up for the census is completed (therefore the term *post-enumeration*), enumerators obtain an interview at each of these addresses. These post-enumeration survey interviews are matched to the census enumerations for the PES blocks, with four types of individuals comprising the entire population: those in the census and in the PES, those in the census and not in the PES, those in the PES and not in the census, and those in neither the census nor the PES. These four types of individuals are represented as a 2×2 contingency table. In Table 1, "N" denotes the total population count. All but the n_{22} cell (sometimes referred to as the "fourth" cell) can be directly estimated. The estimation of N—equivalent to estimation of the n_{22} cell—is based on three separate assumptions. First, it is assumed that each individual has the same probability p_c of being included in the census and that each individual has the same probability p_p—possibly different from p_c—of being included in the post-enumeration survey, the so-called homogeneity assumption. Second, given the separate operations of the census and the PES, it is assumed that inclusion in the census is independent of inclusion in the PES. Third, it is assumed that the matching is accurate. If these assumptions are at least approximately true, then one can estimate N as follows. Since the probability of being included in the census overall is n_{1+}/N, and the probability of being included in the census for those included in the PES is n_{11}/n_{+1}, except for sample variation, given the assumption of independence of the census and PES inclusion processes, these probabilities should be equal. Equating these probabilities and reexpressing the resulting equation gives the following estimate for the total population count: $N = [n_{1+}n_{+1}] / n_{11}$.

Although the assumption of independence is generally considered to be sound, the Census Bureau has long recognized that the enumeration probabilities are not

constant (homogeneous). Therefore, post-enumeration strata are used to group individuals in an effort to have more homogeneous inclusion probabilities within these strata. The strata currently are based on age, race, sex, ethnicity, census region, and whether an individual owns or rents his or her residence.

A major complication is that erroneous enumerations and overcounts inflate the census count, and census imputations (responses for nonresponding households that are filled in using information for neighboring households of similar type) are not capable of being matched. To account for these, a second sample survey operation, the *E-sample*, takes place in parallel to the P-sample. The E-sample is a sample of census enumerations for the PES blocks. These enumerations are rechecked for validity and for whether they are represented on other responses (duplicates). Letting E_{cen} denote the number of valid census enumerations as measured for the PES blocks, letting II denote the number of census imputations, and letting EE denote the number of erroneous (and duplicate) enumerations in the PES blocks, we get the final dual-systems estimation as used by the Census Bureau (within post-enumeration strata):

$$DSE = \left[\frac{n_{1+} (n_{+1} - II)}{n_{11}} \right] \left[1 - \frac{EE}{E_{cen}} \right]$$

The final undercoverage percentage for a post-enumeration stratum is the ratio of the DSE count to the census count minus one. The estimate of the undercoverage percentage for a geographic area is then a weighted linear combination of these undercoverage percentages, weighted by the percentage that each post-enumeration stratum represents in the given area. The adjusted count is the census count multiplied by one plus the undercoverage percentage.

Reverse Record Check. The Canadian census, taken every five years, makes use of the following procedure to evaluate census undercoverage. A sample is put together, composed of the following four subsamples: (1) a sample of census enumerations from the previous census, (2) a sample of intercensal immigrants, (3) a sample of intercensal births, and (4) a sample of census omissions from the previous census. Sample (4) can never be a true sample; it is identified from a small matching operation based on information from the reverse record check of the previous census. The sample is then traced to present-day addresses and it is determined whether each individual is a resident of Canada as of census day and therefore should have

Table 1

	PES		
	In	Out	Total census count
Census In	n_{11}	n_{12}	n_{1+}
Out	n_{21}	n_{22}	
Total PES count	n_{+1}		N

been counted in the census. This alternative count is compared with the census count to measure (net) undercoverage. A small-scale matching then is only used to create the fourth sample component, needed to evaluate the subsequent census. With each subsequent application of a reverse record check, the fourth sample will become closer to a true sample, because the undercovered population not represented initially is gradually reduced by death and emigration.

Megalist, Super Census, Systematic Observation. Three additional ideas for coverage evaluation, some of which have been tested but none ever implemented on a national scale, are megalist (multilist and composite list), super census, and systematic observation. In the process called *composite list*, many administrative record lists are merged and duplicates are weeded out. Then, after the people are traced to current addresses if necessary, the merged list is matched to the census. The results of the matching operation are input into dual-systems estimation. The second possibility, referred to as *multilist*, is not to merge the lists, but to match them individually to the census and each other, and then use what is known as triple- or higher system estimation (based on a higher dimensional contingency table), which are generalizations of dual-systems estimation.

The *super census* process makes use of repeated enumeration attempts, and possibly administrative records, to obtain what is considered to be a complete count of a sample of areas, comparable in size to a sample for a post-enumeration survey. These counts are then weighted up to provide estimates of the total population count. There is no matching to the census, only a comparison of counts for areas as in a reverse record check.

Systematic observation is a coverage evaluation program in which a substantial number of census employees are each given several months to obtain a complete list (including only basic demographic information and addresses) of the residents of a small area, possibly comprising one or two census blocks. Once obtained, this list is matched to the census enumerations in those areas. Clearly, even if the number of areas was relatively small, this procedure would provide information, much of it anecdotal, on the causes of census undercoverage. One would then use ratio estimation for estimation strata (similar to post-enumeration strata) to develop estimates of census undercoverage for large areas and demographic groups.

A Quick History of Coverage Evaluation in the U.S. Census

Coverage evaluation was first made possible during the mid-point of the twentieth century as a result of the development of sample survey methodology and the improvement in the accuracy and completeness of vital statistics records. In 1950 the Census Bureau used a post-enumeration survey, made up of a list sample and an area sample, based on the "do it again, better" idea. The area sample was used to measure omissions of whole households, and the list sample was used to measure omissions within households and other errors. Enumerations from both the list and the area samples were matched to census records. Also, the 1950 census was evaluated for undercoverage using demographic analysis.

In 1960 the Census Bureau again used a post-enumeration survey, with a design similar to that used in 1950. In addition, record checks (comparisons with aggregate counts based on administrative records) of the number of college students and the elderly were also carried out. A small study of a reverse record check was also conducted in 1960. However, difficulty in tracing the sample to current addresses as a result of the ten-year gap between censuses made it clear that this method was not promising for evaluating the U.S. decennial census.

Given the discrepancy between demographic analysis estimates of undercoverage, considered to be reliable for 1960, and those from the PES based on the "do it again, better" methodology, coverage evaluation for the 1970 census relied primarily on demographic analysis. In addition, a match study between the Current Population Survey (CPS) and the census and some record checks provided additional information for targeted groups, namely the elderly and males age twenty to twenty-nine living in the District of Columbia.

In 1980 the Census Bureau first used a post-enumeration survey with the "do it again, independently" methodology. The PES used the April and August samples from the Current Population Survey. The entire process, the sample and the estimation, was referred to as the Post-Enumeration Program, or PEP. It was hoped that this program would provide details on census undercoverage for relatively small geographic areas and demographic groups. The 1980 census also was the first to use an E-sample. Unfortunately, data collection problems with PEP had the result that a match status between the CPS and the census could not be determined for about 8 percent of the individuals. In addition, difficulties in using the August CPS sample-based estimates arose because of people changing residences. As a result, different treatments for nonresponse caused relatively wide variations in estimates of undercoverage. Demographic analysis was again used in 1980. However, the relatively large amount of undocumented immigration (very roughly measured) was thought to reduce the utility of these estimates, especially for non-black populations.

In 1990 the Census Bureau again focused its efforts on coverage evaluation through use of a PES with dual-systems estimation, in addition to demographic analysis. (One of the tests leading up to the 1990 census, the Forward Trace Study, had again shown the difficulty in tracing addresses over a ten-year time frame, making it clear again that a reverse record check would be difficult to implement.) In 1990 the post-enumeration survey, instead of being based on the CPS, used a stand-alone sample survey of 165,000 housing units. Through use of a stand-alone survey some of the operational problems that occurred in 1980, especially with respect to nonresponse and unresolved matching, but also with respect to questionnaire design and timing, were reduced. After a substantial computer-programming error was eliminated and some additional fine-tuning was made in 1992, the report by the Census Bureau's Committee on Adjustment of Postcensal Estimates defended the reliability of the PES estimates for areas of 100,000 and higher but did not fully support their use for smaller areas. Demographic analysis was again used, mainly as a control total to help corroborate the PES results. The use of sex ratios from demographic analysis to help estimate the "fourth cell" of dual-systems estimation was discussed by the bureau before the 1990 census. However, this method was not implemented.

Finally, the plans for 2000 were very similar to those for 1990. A post-enumeration survey and dual-systems estimation provided the cornerstone of coverage evaluation. The sample size used was 300,000 housing units, again in a stand-alone survey. Demographic analysis was again used in the same role as it was in 1990.

Weaknesses (and Strengths) of PES and Other Methods of Coverage Evaluation

In this section the major weaknesses and strengths of these various approaches to coverage evaluation are presented. For some of the procedures that have never been implemented nationally, it is certainly possible that additional weaknesses will be discovered when attempts are made at a more complete implementation.

Demographic Analysis. Demographic analysis relies on information on documented immigration, emigration, and undocumented immigration. The latter two are measured very indirectly and with considerable error. Therefore, for groups that are likely to emigrate and immigrate (especially illegally), the resulting estimates can be strongly biased. Further, given the lack of historical use of ethnicity on birth and immigration records (although recently there have been efforts to change this), demographic analysis cannot provide useful estimates of undercoverage for the Hispanic population. Possibly the most important limitation for demographic analysis is that, given the lack of reliable information on interstate migration, it is not currently possible to provide useful estimates of undercoverage for subnational areas. Finally, only estimates of net undercoverage are available. Therefore, there are no estimates of gross omissions, or gross overcounts, which limits the information on how to reduce over- and undercounts in the next census.

Given the relative infrequency of immigration and emigration for blacks, demographic analysis is still widely believed to provide, at the national level, the best measurement of census net undercoverage for blacks. Also, the total population count from demographic analysis is still of interest in assessing overall census completeness, which is referred to as the "error of closure."

Reverse Record Check. The greatest worry when using a reverse record check in the United States is the difficulty in tracing addresses from the previous census to the current time period. This alone makes application of a reverse record check difficult to justify. In addition, the incompleteness of information on immigration, especially undocumented immigration, and the failure of the sample of census omissions to be a random sample from that population are two additional concerns. Also worthy of mention is that there is no separate measurement of census gross undercoverage or gross overcoverage, which limits the information on how to improve coverage for the subsequent census.

Still, assuming the tracing problem could be addressed, the relatively small amount of matching needed and the relative lack of statistical modeling give this method interesting advantages. Clearly, the tracing problem is less pronounced for the Canadian quinquennial census.

Composite List, Super Census, and Systematic Observation.

The composite list method relies on several difficult assumptions. The composite list approach assumes that the various lists contain identifiers that facilitate matching and that there is low nonresponse for the variables used for matching. In addition, it assumes that the addresses used are the addresses of residence and that the matching is accurate. Also, the merged list must not have much differential undercoverage. Finally, the composite list method makes use of dual-systems estimation, and so the assumptions discussed above also need to obtain to a reasonable extent if this technique is to be applied safely. The multilist approach has similar problems.

The super census method has a serious weakness, which is that a very large number of areas must be sampled so that the variance of the resulting estimate of undercoverage is low enough to be useful. This weakness could cause super census to be an extremely expensive approach to carry out. In addition, depending on the methods used, this procedure could suffer from the same problem of failing to exceed census coverage that is typical of the "do it again, better" approach.

The systematic observation method is obviously greatly dependent on finding a large number of individuals who are capable of gaining the trust of a small group of people in a relatively short amount of time. Also, it is possible that the same problem of failing to exceed census coverage could weaken this methodology in a large-scale application. Finally, the estimates from systematic observation also have a large variance because of the necessarily small size of the program.

Post-Enumeration Survey and Dual-Systems Estimation.

A post-enumeration survey making use of dual-systems estimation has several weaknesses. Of primary concern is whether the error rate for confirmed matches and nonmatches of the matching operation can be kept very low. Also, although the unresolved match rate was reduced from the 1980 to the 1990 census, given the relatively low amount of undercoverage, the treatment of unresolved matches also has to be of extremely high quality to provide reliable estimates of undercoverage. A second weakness, related to the first, is that it is very difficult to estimate undercoverage for people that move in or out of the PES blocks between the census and the PES interview. In dealing with this issue, the Census Bureau has made use of two methods of defining the universe that is being counted: (1) those present in the PES blocks on census day (PES-A), and (2) those present during the time of the PES interview (PES-B).

Besides errors in matching and the problem with people who move, the largest source of bias in dual-systems estimation is likely due to *correlation bias*. Recall that one of the assumptions underlying dual-systems estimation is that the probabilities of inclusion in the census and PES (within post-enumeration strata) are constant. Correlation bias is the correlation, generally expected to be positive, between the probabilities of individuals being included in the census and the PES. (The failure of the independence assumption is also sometimes said to cause correlation bias. The effect of this failure is the same as that from correlation bias and so it is difficult to distinguish between them in practice.) Except for unusual situations, correlation bias will result from heterogeneity in both sets of probabilities of inclusion. It can be shown that positive correlation bias will cause the adjusted census counts themselves to be underestimates of the true counts. This weakness is addressed mainly by using either more or different post-enumeration strata. However, the benefits of doing so are limited because the size of the PES limits the number of post-enumeration strata that can be used, and it would be difficult to define strongly different strata (using the same number of cells) because the information that is collected on the census short form is of somewhat limited use in modeling census undercoverage.

To address the problem of correlation bias, it is worth mentioning three alternative methodologies that avoid making either the independence assumption or the homogeneity assumption. One approach is to add a third measurement system, usually using administrative records, referred to as *triple-system estimation*. This is similar to the multilist approach, in which one of the lists is enumerations from the post-enumeration survey. A second approach is called *census plus*, which uses field reconciliation of discrepancies between the census count and the PES count to achieve a "true" count at the household level. This method was tested during the mid-1990s and was found to present some difficulties in implementation. Finally, J. M. Alho and his colleagues have attempted to model census undercoverage at the individual level, using generalizations of logistic regression.

Other difficulties with dual-systems estimation can only be touched on here. First, since the census counts have no sampling variability but the PES counts do, it is not uncommon in the smaller post-enumeration strata for n_{1+} to be smaller than n_{11}, which makes it difficult to interpret the n_{12} cell. A second weakness is that the amount of fieldwork and matching makes it difficult to complete the adjustment long enough before the December 31 deadline for delivery to the president of state counts for reapportionment of Congress to enable a careful review, if it could be finished at all. Finally, also in using dual-systems estimation for adjustment, there are questions concerning the methods used to "carry down" the estimates to low levels of geography, and there are also questions about the methods used to "smooth" the estimates for the post-enumeration strata using a regression-type model to help reduce the variance of these estimates.

Although such statements can be considered controversial, it seems widely acknowledged, at least for areas of more than 100,000 people and for large demographic groups, that a PES is informative about census undercoverage and overcoverage and that there is currently no other approach for the U.S. census that can provide this information.

Key Findings for Recent Censuses

The various programs, especially demographic analysis and dual-systems estimation, have provided a considerable amount of information on who is missed in the census. There is also information on who is double-counted and who is subject to erroneous enumeration, which will not be discussed here.

Trends in Census Undercoverage. In the 1950 census, the PES measured a net national undercount of 1.4 percent, whereas demographic analysis measured a net national undercount of 4.1 percent. The differential undercount of blacks compared with non-blacks was measured by demographic analysis to be 3.6 percent.

In the 1960 census the PES measured a net national undercount of 1.9 percent, the reverse record check measured a net national undercount of between 2.5 and 3.1 percent, and demographic analysis measured a net national undercount of 3.1 percent. The differential undercount between blacks and non-blacks was measured by demographic analysis to be 3.9 percent.

In the 1970 census there was no PES. Demographic analysis measured a net national undercount of 2.7 per-

cent. The differential undercount between blacks and non-blacks was measured by demographic analysis to be 4.3 percent.

In the 1980 census the PES, making use of dual-systems estimation for the first time, measured a net national undercount of between 0.8 and 1.4 percent, depending on the assumptions used. Demographic analysis measured a net national undercount of 1.2 percent. The differential undercount between blacks and non-blacks was measured by demographic analysis to be 3.7 percent.

Finally, in the 1990 census, the PES measured the differential undercount as 1.6 percent. Demographic analysis measured the differential undercount to be 1.8 percent. The differential undercount between blacks and non-blacks was measured by demographic analysis to be 4.4 percent.

Who Is Missed? Based on the results of dual-systems estimation and other sources, E. P. Ericksen and his colleagues have summarized the likely causes of census undercoverage. They mention illiteracy or households in which English is not the primary language, general unfamiliarity with surveys, housing units without a clear individual address, and households in high crime areas as plausible causes of being missed in the census. L. A. Brownrigg and M. de la Puente have listed the following characteristics as contributing to census undercoverage: mobility, language problems, concealment, irregular relationship to head of household, and resistance to government interaction. One of the best predictors of census undercoverage in 1990 for larger geographic areas was low census mail return rate. These are all reasonable findings and agree with basic intuitions about the census process. In demographic terms, the demographic groups that experience the greatest percentage of undercoverage are black males (and probably Hispanic males), with net undercoverage rates for the 1990 census for black males of 8.5 percent, compared with 0.6 percent for non-black females.

One important question is whether the majority of census misses are due to missed housing units or to missed individuals within otherwise enumerated housing units. Howard Hogan reports that there are actually four categories: (1) people missed in a housing unit in which other people were enumerated in the census, (2) people missed in a housing unit listed in the census address list, (3) people missed in a housing unit that was missed but in a building that was included in the census address list, and (4) people missed in a housing unit that was missed by the census address list. If one considers people missed in otherwise enumerated structures to be the first two categories, about two-thirds of census misses are for people living in listed housing units.

It is important to understand that census overcoverage is a real problem. Hogan reports that in the 1990 census, based on the E-sample, there were 14 million erroneous enumerations due to duplications, fictitious enumerations, geocoding errors, people enumerated at the wrong address, census enumerations without names, and other causes. (This is in comparison with 18 million estimated omissions.) Of these 14 million, approximately 4 million were duplicate enumerations.

See also *Capture-recapture methods; Errors in the census.*

■ Michael Cohen

Bibliography

Alho, J. M., M. H. Mulry, K. Wurdeman, and J. Kim. "Estimating Heterogeneity in the Probabilities of Enumeration for Dual-System Estimation. *Journal of the American Statistical Association* 88 (1993): 1130-1136.

Anderson, Margo J., and Stephen E. Fienberg. *Who Counts: The Politics of Census-Taking in Contemporary America.* New York: Russell Sage Foundation, 1999.

Brownrigg, L. A., and M. de la Puente. *Alternative Enumeration Methods and Results: Resolution and Resolved Populations by Site.* Washington, D.C.: U.S. Bureau of the Census, 1993.

Coale, Ansley. "The Population of the United States in 1950 Classified by Age, Sex, and Color—A Revision of Census Figures." *Journal of the American Statistical Association* 50 (1955): 16-54.

Committee on Adjustment of Postcensal Estimates. *Assessment of Accuracy of Adjusted versus Unadjusted 1990 Census Base for Use in Intercensal Estimates.* Report to the Bureau of the Census. Washington, D.C.: U.S. Bureau of the Census, 1992.

Ericksen, E. P., L. F. Estrada, J. W. Tukey, and K. M. Wolter. *Report on the 1990 Decennial Census and the Post-Enumeration Survey.* Report submitted by members of the Special Advisory Panel to the Secretary of the U.S. Department of Commerce. Washington, D.C.: U.S. Bureau of the Census, 1991.

Fein, David. "The Social Sources of Census Omission: Racial and Ethnic Differences in Omission Rates in Recent U.S. Censuses." Ph.D. diss., Princeton University, 1989.

Hogan, Howard. "The 1990 PES: Operations and Results." *Journal of the American Statistical Association* 88 (1993): 1047-1060.

National Research Council. *The Bicentennial Census: New Directions for Methodology in 1990.* Edited by Constance F. Citro and Michael L. Cohen. Washington, D.C.: National Academy Press, 1985.

Robinson, J. G., B. Ahmed, P. das Gupta, and K. A. Woodrow. "Estimation of Population Coverage in the 1990 United States Census Based on Demographic Analysis. *Journal of the American Statistical Association* 88 (1993): 1061-1071.

Coverage improvement procedures

Recent censuses have included special programs to improve the coverage of the population. These programs are in addition to efforts to obtain a more complete count through advertising and quality control of census field operations.

The U.S. Census Bureau first adopted special coverage improvement procedures for the 1970 census on the basis of three assumptions: (1) the need for greater accuracy in the population count than achieved in the past because of the use of the data for legislative redistricting under "one-person, one-vote" court requirements and for federal fund allocations; (2) the perception that it was becoming increasingly difficult to obtain a complete count in the absence of additional coverage efforts; and (3) the belief that new methods would be required to achieve improvements in coverage. By contrast, the 1950 and 1960 censuses were planned on the assumption that undercoverage was largely because enumerators failed to follow instructions. Consequently, stress was placed on simplifying procedures and increasing training and quality control. However, evaluation of the 1960 census results indicated that much undercoverage stemmed from reasons that would not likely be addressed by such approaches as better enumerator training. These reasons included that some people were fearful of being counted or that they were missed because they were not strongly attached to a particular household.

1970 Census

Programs to encourage public cooperation with the census, particularly among hard-to-count groups, were important components of the Census Bureau's strategy to obtain complete coverage in 1970. These programs included public information efforts and community education programs, assistance centers set up in twenty cities that the public could call or visit for help in filling out census forms, and instruction sheets and questionnaires in Spanish and Chinese where needed. Special efforts to improve enumerator performance in the twenty largest cities were also adopted.

The Census Bureau also implemented specific coverage improvement programs designed to add housing units and persons to the count. Several programs were carried out prior to Census Day (April 1) to correct the address list used for mailing questionnaires. A post-census check of the address list in selected areas was also carried out. Other coverage improvement programs in 1970 included a recheck of housing units originally classified as vacant to determine whether they were occupied; a cross-check of respondents' answers to a question on the number of living quarters at their address against the census address list; a check of persons who reported a change of address to the U.S. Postal Service during the census enumeration period; a "Missed Persons" campaign that placed cards in community centers, carry-outs, barbershops, and so on, to try to obtain minimal information from people with no fixed address; and a "Were You Counted?" campaign to encourage people not originally counted to come forward.

Many of the coverage improvement programs in the 1970 census were carried out selectively in areas in which they presumably would be most effective. Two programs, the National Vacancy Check and the Post-Enumeration Post Office Check of the address list in selected areas of sixteen southern states, were carried out for samples of addresses and the results used to add people and housing units to the census count. The 1970 census is the only census in which statistical sampling procedures have been used to add people to the count.

The special coverage improvement programs in 1970 added about 3 percent to the cost of the census and about 6 percent to the total population count. The most effective programs in adding people were the address checks carried out prior to Census Day. The National Vacancy Check also added (imputed) a significant number of people to the count.

1980 Census

The 1980 census coverage improvement strategy exhibited three differences from that of 1970. First, substantially more resources were put into coverage improvement in 1980 than in 1970. Programs aimed at increasing public cooperation—particularly among hard-to-count groups—such as special publicity efforts, assistance centers, and foreign-language questionnaires, were greatly expanded, as were the number and extent of programs designed specifically to add housing units and persons to the count. (The cost of specific coverage improvement programs in 1980 was about six times the cost of such programs in 1970 in constant dollars.)

Second, the Census Bureau made a deliberate decision to conduct most specific coverage improvement programs on a nationwide basis and to avoid the use of sampling and imputation. However, some programs were implemented selectively in areas specifically designated for the purpose. Third, new programs were adopted to tackle the problem of undercoverage of people in otherwise enumerated households.

Several coverage improvement programs in 1980, similar to those in 1970, were designed to improve the address list prior to Census Day. The address list was also rechecked in some areas after Census Day. A Vacant/Delete Check was carried out on a 100 percent basis to recheck the status of housing units that were originally thought to be vacant or not a residential address. In a new Local Review program, the Census Bureau provided the opportunity for local officials to assess preliminary housing unit and population counts.

Programs that were carried out during the census enumeration period to improve the count of persons included a casual count operation, in which Census Bureau staff visited places in central cities frequented by transients who might otherwise be missed; rechecks of responses to questions on the number of units in the building and the roster of people in the household; a "Were You Counted?" program similar to that of 1970; and a Nonhousehold Sources Program. The last program—an innovation in 1980—involved matching several administrative lists to census records for selected areas in urban district offices. Census field staff followed up people on the lists who were not found in the census to determine if they should be added to the count. The lists used were driver's license records, immigration records, and (in New York City only) public assistance records.

Overall, the specific coverage improvement programs that were implemented in 1980 added about 8 percent to the total population count—a somewhat higher percentage than in 1970. Most of the added people resulted from the improvements to the address list that were achieved by the pre–census day address checks. The Vacant/Delete Check also added a significant number of people to the count and helped reduce the differential undercount of minorities, although it appears to have overcounted some people as well. The other post–Census Day coverage improvement programs added very few people to the count.

1990 Census

Coverage improvement programs in the 1990 census were similar to those in the 1980 count, although some 1980 programs were dropped and some new programs were added. Specific coverage improvement programs in 1990 included address list checks prior to Census Day and, for the first time, a precensus local review, in which local governments in mailout-mailback areas reviewed census maps and counts of addresses by block to look for discrepancies with their own information.

Other specific coverage improvement programs in 1980 were:

- enumeration of shelters and street locations where the homeless might be found;
- 100 percent recheck of housing units originally classified as vacant or nonresidential (the Vacant/Delete Check);
- Parolee/Probationer Check, in which parole and probation officers were given census questionnaires to distribute to people under their jurisdiction, the responses cross-checked against the census records, and people added to the count if no match was found (administrative lists of parolees and probationers were also checked against census records);
- "Were You Counted?" campaign;
- recanvass of blocks containing about 15 percent of housing units that were thought to have new construction or other structures that might have been missed; and
- post-census Local Review program (more extensive than in 1980) in which local governments were sent preliminary housing unit counts by block to assess. The Census Bureau recanvassed blocks with significant differences between the census count and local information.

As in 1970 and 1980, most of the people added to the count from specific coverage improvement programs in 1990 were the result of the pre–Census Day address check programs. The Vacant/Delete Check also added two million people, but evidence exists that some of them had already been counted. The Parolee/Probationer Check had a very high rate of erroneous additions to the count.

2000 Census

As originally planned, the 2000 census would have scaled back the use of specific coverage improvement programs, while expanding such programs as foreign-language questionnaires, walk-in and telephone assistance, and targeted outreach and publicity to hard-to-count population groups and areas. Cutbacks would have involved programs for improving the address list as well as specific programs for improving the count after Census Day.

The original plan for the census master address list was to update the 1990 census list with information from the U.S. Postal Service and recheck the list in selected areas. Also, legislation was enacted to allow the Census Bureau to share the address list with local governments and obtain their input through a Local Update of Census Addresses (LUCA) program. Late in the decade it became clear that more checks were needed to obtain a high-quality address list, so a complete canvass of the address list was carried out by Census Bureau staff. In addition, addresses provided by localities through the LUCA program were added to the list and rechecked by Census Bureau staff.

Originally, the use of specific coverage improvement programs during the census enumeration period was to be limited on the assumption that an Integrated Coverage Measurement (ICM) program would result in corrected population counts by December 31, 2000. (The ICM corrections for census undercounts and overcounts would result from matching the responses of a coverage evaluation survey to the census responses.) However, the U.S. Supreme Court ruled that survey sampling procedures could not be used for the population counts for reapportionment of congressional seats. Hence, the Census Bureau planned to deliver unadjusted population counts by December 31, 2000, with adjusted counts to come later. (The adjustments would be based on matching an Accuracy and Coverage Evaluation survey— smaller than the originally planned ICM survey—with census records.)

Consequently, the Census Bureau expanded the planned recheck of units initially designated as vacant or nonresidential. Originally, this recheck was to be conducted of a 30 percent sample of vacant units;

instead, the recheck was carried out on a 100 percent basis. Other coverage improvement programs included telephone follow-up of certain types of households (for example, those that provided information for fewer than the total number of people reported to be living in the household); procedures to enumerate homeless and transient populations; and a "Be Counted" program in which questionnaires were made available at local sites.

See also *Accuracy and Coverage Evaluation; Editing and imputation; Enumeration: field procedures; Sampling in the census.*

■ Constance F. Citro

Bibliography

Ericksen, Eugene P., Leobardo F. Estrada, John W. Tukey, and Kirk M. Wolter. *Report on the 1990 Decennial Census and the Post-Enumeration Survey.* Washington, D.C.: U.S. Department of Commerce, 1991.

National Research Council, Committee on National Statistics, Panel on Decennial Census Methodology. *The Bicentennial Census: New Directions for Methodology in 1990,* edited by Constance F. Citro and Michael L. Cohen. Washington, D.C.: National Academy Press, 1985.

U.S. Bureau of the Census. *Census 2000 Operational Plan Using Traditional Census-Taking Methods.* Washington, D.C.: U.S. Department of Commerce, 1999.

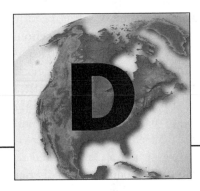

Data capture

Data capture is the transferring of data from census questionnaires into a format that is suitable for processing. It is that part of a census operation that lies in between the collection of data and the preparation of tabulations.

Prior to 1850

From the first census in 1790 until 1830, federal marshals charged with taking the census did not make use of standard census schedules, or forms, nor were there any uniform tallying instructions. The marshals and their assistants were required to submit aggregate counts to officials in Washington, D.C., not the actual census forms. Not until 1830 were uniform schedules distributed to marshals and returned and checked by clerks in Washington.

The population census schedules used prior to 1850 recorded information for an entire household on a single line, with individual columns providing specific information on characteristics, for example, the number of persons fifteen to twenty years of age in the household. All data were reported for the entire household, including aggregated information for the individuals contained within. Thus, clerks added together the data on the census schedules themselves, making the tallying process much like the construction of tabulations. The results of these tallies would then be further aggregated into summaries for various geographic areas.

1850 to 1890

Starting with the 1850 census, information was presented on the census schedule, line-by-line for each person in the household. Now, rather than adding together pre-aggregated data for households, the task changed to counting individual responses. Tallies were constructed in order to create the classifications that would later lead to finished tabulations; clerks tallied the number of occurrences of a characteristic (for example, males, persons ten to fifteen years old, farmers), sometimes by passing through the forms several times. Thus, there was little distinction between creating tallies and creating tabulations. What clerks tallied were essentially table cells that were then checked for inconsistency and printed as a final product. As the content of the census grew increasingly complex, tally systems became unwieldy and prone to duplication, as when tallies needed to be repeated many times in order to achieve consistency between tabulations.

A first rather modest advance came just after the 1870 census, when Charles W. Seaton created a device to make manual tallying faster. Seaton was chief clerk of the 1870 and 1880 censuses and became census superintendent between 1881 and 1885. The device consisted of a series of rollers on a wood frame, through which a lengthy tally sheet would pass. The objective of the "Seaton Device" was to make portions of the tally sheet that were physically distant appear close together for several different items on the schedule. This enabled the clerk to make physical tally marks at six or more spots on the tally sheet simultaneously, without physically moving around the tally sheet to find different items. Despite increases in productivity, this device still required manual tallying.

It wasn't until the 1880s that the first ideas regarding automated alternatives to manual tallying started to be seriously considered. The nation's population was growing dramatically in the nineteenth century and the number of items on the census schedules followed suit. More data were compiled for an increasingly large population. Charles Pidgin and William Hunt devised an idea to transcribe data for the 1885 census of Massachusetts in a way that presented all information for each person on a single card. These cards (or "chips," as they were sometimes referred to) could then be color-coded or flagged with other markers that permitted them to be sifted and sorted in a host of ways. Although the time needed to create these "cards" was more substantial than that embodied in the traditional tally system, the payoff in flexibility for later compilation and tabulation more than offset the initial investment. And, indeed, the rich level of detail found in the 1885 census of Massachusetts provides ample testimony that this idea had a future.

Consolidation of information for an individual on a single card meant that key sorts, such as those by age and sex, needed to be done only once and could be retained for later use. The traditional tallying system required that some sorts, even basic ones by age and sex, be done over and over again. Most important of all, however, this new mode of processing separated tallying from tabulation for the first time.

1890 to 1930

The removal of data from census schedules using an independent data capture process was first used in the 1890 census. Data for individuals from census schedules were coded onto cards that would later be mechanically processed to produce tabulations. The idea was to create perforations in cards, with each spot representing a questionnaire response. "Punched cards," as they came to be known, were then passed over a series of electronic contacts that would "count" or, in effect, "read" the responses; data could then be compiled in a variety of ways to produce aggregates that formed the cells of tabulations. This idea was the brainchild of Herman Hollerith, who later founded International Business Machines (IBM). Hollerith received guidance on the ultimate applications of his new ideas from John

Shaw Billings, a colleague who had a special interest in vital statistics data.

The schedules for the 1890 census were different from those used in earlier decades. A separate tally sheet was now provided for each family or household with questions running down the table stub and separate columns for each individual. "Punching clerks" recorded responses by creating perforations with a hand punch. In time, however, various punching machines were developed to make this task quicker and easier. The "gang punch" device made multiple perforations at the same time, as when a card needed to receive codes for a predetermined enumeration district or other geographic area. Innovations with each successive census permitted higher levels of output within the punching operation. Keypunch machines, on which operators hit keys to record responses as holes in cards, came into use. As keypunching became more efficient, operations involving different sets of cards became more common, as with the creation of "family cards" in the 1900 and 1910 censuses or "occupation cards" in 1920.

Although the tabulation of data had advanced significantly as a result of Hollerith's innovation, it is important to recognize that the job of data capture was more labor intensive than ever. More census questionnaire items needed to be coded onto cards for an increasingly larger population.

1940 to 1990

Science brought innovations into the 1940 census in many areas, such as the incorporation of sampling. So, too, with data capture methods. A new machine, "the reproducer," permitted mass transfer of information punched on one set of cards to another. A new IBM machine could not only accumulate information from consecutive cards but could now add across different fields on the same card, creating important totals and subtotals that earlier required separate punching operations. Special cards were created for many new items, such as labor force and migration, that were obtained on a sample basis.

The most significant period for innovation in data capture occurred in the 1950s, with the advent of machines that permitted more direct entry and compilation of data from the questionnaires. Card-to-tape machines were developed as part of the emerging technology associated with the electronic computer; the large-scale effort associated with punched cards, however, was still present in 1950, but that was soon to change. In 1951 the census of Canada used what was referred to as "mark-sense" schedules; cards were punched by mechanical means from questionnaires on which enumerators had made marks. This system was considered for the 1950 U.S. Census, but time constraints made its full adoption impractical. During the 1950s, however, the U.S. Census Bureau, in conjunction with the National Bureau of Standards, developed FOSDIC, the Film Optical Sensing Device for Input to Computers. FOSDIC is capable of "reading" information from a negative microfilm copy of census questionnaires and transferring responses to magnetic tape for processing. The data on the tape are then put into a computer for compilation and tabulation. Questionnaires make use of "index marks," solid black squares printed on the questionnaire, followed by a series of circles containing responses. After finding the black mark, a light beam scans the circles and determines which ones are filled in.

Since FOSDIC used microfilmed questionnaires, this meant that the actual questionnaires, once shot, could be stored away from the main processing operation. Microfilm was more compact and efficient, resulting in faster and more accurate data capture. By some estimates, data capture increased sixtyfold with the advent of FOSDIC. The development of this new capture mode may have overcome the huge burden of manual punching, but it put more pressure on field staff. Enumerators now had to make sure that responses were recorded in a way that FOSDIC could accept. In addition, a professional programming staff of specially trained people had to be maintained for processing, including groups of clerks that needed to manually edit input from "write-in" responses. Still, in the 1950s, advances in data capture had outpaced those of the previous seventy years.

The advent of computers meant that programs could be developed to compile, edit, and tabulate data. By 1970 innovations in FOSDIC efficiency and advances in computing permitted the bureau to handle an increasing number of questionnaires. Mail-out, mail-back was now the primary method of data collection, and the level of demographic and geographic detail available from the data was unprecedented. The Census Bureau's facility in Jeffersonville, Indiana, received questionnaires from some 399 district offices between May and September 1970—425 truckloads, with a gross weight of 6.1 million pounds. Questionnaires were checked in, sorted, and microfilmed. The microfilm was then developed on site by a private contractor and shipped to bureau headquarters in Suitland, Maryland, for FOSDIC processing. All told, about 77,000 rolls of microfilm were scanned in short-form questionnaire processing, with some 30 percent of the rolls requiring reprocessing, mostly because of poor markings made by respondents and bureau coders. "Diaries," control counts of population and housing and key operational items (for example, codes for rejected questionnaires), were created as processing evaluation tools. These diaries were especially handy for the evaluation of clerical coding operations that translated questionnaire write-in responses into marked circles for FOSDIC input.

In 1980 more accurate FOSDIC processing was developed. At the same time, the bureau started to use more efficient strategies for getting questionnaires to the processing centers. It wasn't until 1990, however, that the bureau fully implemented concurrent processing—the conversion of questionnaire data on an individual form-flow basis, with editing and correction being done in the field. Rather than wait for all questionnaires to be received before engaging in large-scale data capture efforts, 1990 saw capture take place on a flow basis, as questionnaires were received. Prior to this time, automated processing at the Census Bureau's Processing Centers (seven in 1990) usually did not occur until manual-collection offices had completed their work and were ready to close and ship questionnaires. The Processing Centers were then responsible for turning the questionnaire responses into machine-readable data using FOSDIC technology. This included the labor-intensive job of keying write-in entries; although word-recognition technology now permitted computers to code many responses, several hundred clerks were still needed to assign codes to responses that could not be directly coded via computer (500 clerks alone at the Jeffersonville Processing Center). A clerical staff of almost 1,100 was needed to code industry and occupation in the Kansas City Processing Office in 1990.

More powerful computer hardware and innovative software replaced earlier diaries with elaborate coverage, content, and consistency editing. Questionnaires with missing or multiple answers were more readily identified and, later on, programs were developed to check for gross inconsistencies between items, permitting bureau staffers to quickly gauge the quality of responses and initiate corrective measures.

2000

The 2000 census brought with it several important changes in data capture. Although the bureau had used private contractors for some aspects of its earlier capture efforts, private sector involvement in 2000 data capture was unprecedented. The days of home-grown innovations at the bureau had given way to more cost-efficient, commercially developed technologies. Three of the four data capture centers for Census 2000 were supported by private sector contractors, with the sole government site being the Census Bureau's National Processing Center in Jeffersonville. These centers made use of advanced optical scanning technologies, including optical character recognition (OCR). A suite of software extracted information from forms that contained a combination of machine printing, hand printing, optical marks, and bar codes. Images of each questionnaire were created and modern diaries were established, with pertinent management systems information that permitted an evaluation of operations and initial assessments of response quality.

The data capture system for 2000 (DCS-2000) captured information from more than 120 million census questionnaires, or close to 1.4 billion pages. The DCS-2000 scanned questionnaires and created digital images that served as input to further data processing. In effect, the system directly scanned forms and converted them into ASCII text. As in times past, images that could not be recognized by the OCR technology needed to be examined by census workers and manually entered into the system. Overall, however, the bureau's newest approach to data capture represented the logical next step in a history that has taken full advantage of innovations.

See also *Pre-computer tabulation systems.*

■ Joseph J. Salvo

Bibliography

Truesdell, Leon E. *The Development of Punch Card Tabulation in the Bureau of the Census: 1890–1940.* Washington, D.C.: U.S. Bureau of the Census, 1965.

U.S. Bureau of the Census. *1990 Census of Population and Housing: History, Part C.* CPH(R)-2C. Washington, D.C., 1995.

———. *United States Censuses of Population and Housing, 1970: Procedural History.* PHC(R)-1. Washington, D.C., 1976.

———. *United States Censuses of Population and Housing, 1960: Processing the Data.* Washington, D.C., 1962.

U.S. General Accounting Office. *2000 Census: New Data Capture System Progress and Risks.* GAO/AIMD-00-61. Washington, D.C., 2000.

Data dissemination and use

Data dissemination refers to the processes and products used to distribute the results of the census. In the early years of our nation, this consisted simply of a formal handing over of the official counts from the president or the secretary of state, who were responsible for conducting the census, to the Congress. The numbers were then used for reapportionment, the constitutional purpose of the census. The single printed report from the 1790 census consisted of fifty-six pages. With each census, the process became more complex and the dissemination broader. By the middle of the nineteenth century, the content of the census questionnaire had grown to include information beyond the basic population, age, and race counts, and reports were printed in large quantities and distributed to federal officials, state governors, congressmen, and colleges and universities. By the end of the twentieth century, census data had become a vast resource, integral to many societal institutions, including Congress, government agencies, universities, and commercial organizations.

Data Products

Printed reports were the only data products from 1790 through 1950, starting with the simple fifty-six-page report from the 1790 census, later including elaborate hand-drawn colored maps and graphics, and by 1990 growing to about 450,000 pages in multiple volumes with detailed characteristics for geographic areas, ranging from the nation to the city block. Computerized data were introduced with the 1960 census but it was not until the 1990 census that reductions in the number of printed reports occurred as more data were distributed through electronic means.

The technological developments of the mid-twentieth century resulted in many new forms of data dissemination. Tabulating machines, precursors of today's computers, were invented in the late nineteenth century for the purpose of processing census data. By 1960 computers had become integral to the census process and the Census Bureau began to distribute data on computer tape. About the same time, some data were distributed on microfiche. In more recent decades, the development of TIGER/Line files with geographic and cartographic information has spurred the growth of Geographic Information Systems (GIS) and mapping software. TIGER (Topologically Integrated Geographic Encoding and Referencing) files contain neither maps nor data, but a digital database of geographic features that can be used in mapping and GIS software.

Computerized data products developed for the 1960 through the 1990 censuses consisted primarily of Summary Tape Files (STFs) and Public Use Microdata Samples (PUMS) on magnetic tape for use with mainframe computers. STFs are computerized summaries of the data. They include predefined frequency counts or tabulations for all geographic entities recognized or defined by the Census Bureau. They are used most often to analyze characteristics of specific geographic areas. PUMS contain basic coded information about a sample of individuals and households. PUMS users can use statistical software to develop tabulations not available in the STFs. PUMS are used most often to analyze detailed characteristics of people and households for the nation, states, and other large geographic areas. Because PUMS contain information about individuals, the geographic identification was, until 1980, restricted to areas with 250,000 or more people to protect the confidentiality of the respondents. That limit was then dropped to areas of 100,000 or more in population. In addition to these standard data products, the Census Bureau produces special tabulations, paid for by the requester, for user-defined geographic areas or subject-matter tables. All special tabulations are subject to the Census Bureau's usual standards that ensure that confidential information is not revealed.

With the 1990 census, electronic data products were expanded to include CD-ROMs and online access. STFs and PUMS were released on CD-ROM shortly after the tape versions. The CD-ROMs were much smaller and less expensive than the tapes. At a time when use of personal computers was exploding in offices and homes, these CD-ROMs quickly supplanted the tape files as the medium of choice. Online access to selected data via the Census Bureau's Cendata system provided an early step in the direction of the anticipated large-scale Internet dissemination of the 2000 census. By 1999 the Census Bureau's World Wide Web site had evolved into a comprehensive source of key data products. With different formats for different products, the Web site provides access to or information about all of the Census Bureau's data products.

Microform products (microfilm and microfiche) are miniaturized photographs of the printed reports that must be read through a special viewer. Used primarily in dissemination of the 1980 and 1990 censuses, microform products benefited libraries and other users because they required much less space than printed reports and also included additional data from the STFs that were not in any printed report.

Microfilm is also used internally as the Census Bureau's storage medium for the original census schedules and questionnaires. Carefully guarded for seventy-two years after each census, these are then made available to the public through the National Archives. During the seventy-two years when the original census data are not public, the Census Bureau offers an Age Search Service, for a fee, whereby individuals can obtain transcripts of selected data from these records. Information is released only to the named person, his or her heirs, or legal representatives. These transcripts, which may contain information on a person's age, sex, race, state or country of birth, and relationship to the householder, can be used as evidence to qualify for social security or other retirement benefits, for passport applications, to prove relationship in settling estates, for genealogical research, and other uses when a birth certificate is not available.

Data Uses and Users

Beyond the constitutional purpose of reapportioning Congress, Census data are used for a variety of public and private purposes. Many federal, state, and local laws require that funds be distributed based on the census counts. Billions of federal and state dollars each year are transferred to local governments based on census data. Census data are also used for planning community, private, and public facilities and services, such as schools, shopping centers, health facilities, and residential developments. Many federal and state government agencies have units that analyze census data and publish special reports. The Census Bureau itself publishes a large variety of analytical reports. Local government agencies often distribute area profiles and maps. Larger cities often use census data to conduct detailed analyses of many aspects of their populations. Universities and private research organizations produce studies that use census data and related resources, particularly in the fields of demography, sociology, economics, and urban planning. In recent decades increasing numbers of commercial organizations use census data for assessing the markets for their products. A large industry of demographic data companies repackages census data and sells products such as area profiles for marketing, topical maps, specialized data books, and CD-ROMS.

Data products can be obtained directly from the Census Bureau or through other organizations. Libraries are perhaps the most common source of census data. The Federal Depository Library Program originated in the early nineteenth century and now consists of more than 1,400 libraries. These libraries maintain copies of selected census data products. In addition, the Census Bureau has established formal networks of data users to ensure widespread availability. The State Data Center program establishes a lead agency and affiliates in each state to maintain and distribute census data within the state. Often the State Data Centers are also depository libraries. National Census Information Centers are nonprofit organizations that focus on minority concerns. They facilitate data access for their constituencies. Business and Industry Data Centers, usually within chambers of commerce or small business development centers, are established to promote development by providing access to economic data. The National Clearinghouse for Census Data Services is a listing of organizations offering services and assistance related to census data.

Members of many associations share an interest in the quality of the census data that are critical to their organizations. The American Statistical Association has monitored census data and other federal statistical programs for more than 150 years. The Association of Public Data Users was founded in 1975 specifically to foster interaction among users of then newly available electronic data products. The Council of Professional Associations on Federal Statistics provides a forum for these and many other associations to learn about and exchange information on federal statistics and current developments in census data.

See also *Archival access to the census; Depository libraries; Dissemination of data: electronic products; Dissemination of data: printed publications; Pre-computer tabulation systems; PUMS; State data centers.*

■ Deirdre A. Gaquin

Bibliography

Anderson, Margo J. *The American Census: A Social History.* New Haven, Conn.: Yale University Press, 1988.

U.S. Bureau of the Census. *Census '80: Continuing the Factfinder Tradition.* Washington, D.C., 1980.

———. *1990 Census of Population and Housing: Guide, Part A. Text.* Washington, D.C., 1992.

———. *Census Catalog and Guide, 1997.* Washington, D.C., 1997.

Data products: evolution

Throughout the history of the United States the decennial census has reflected the changing social, political and economic interests of the country. The published reports have reflected the needs of government, academic, and public data users and the format has reflected the technology available at the time.

The Early Censuses

The law, passed on March 1, 1790, originally mandating the decennial census, was directed at the constitutional reapportionment of Congress, the redistricting of state and local territories, and the collection of taxes. The data collection forms were not standard and only a limited number of "questions" was asked in the early censuses. Neither privacy nor confidentiality was of concern. The law required no formal reports or publication of data. It demanded only the posting of the census schedules in "two of the most public places within *each jurisdiction*, there to remain for the inspection of all concerned..." and "that the aggregate amount of each description of persons" for every district be transmitted to the president. Nonetheless, even the 1790 census resulted in a single fifty-six-page report based on six inquiries.

In 1907–1908 the Bureau of the Census published twelve volumes titled *Heads of Families at the First Census of the United States taken in the Year 1790.* This volume also contains the names of heads of families from all states included in the census except for Delaware, Georgia, Kentucky, New Jersey, and Tennessee, the schedules for which were burned in 1812.

The 1800 census was similar in scope and method except that the marshals made their reports to the secretary of state rather than to the president. Data were collected for additional age groups and, until the creation of standardized forms in 1830, marshals included items on occupation or ethnic origin at will, and summarized the data as they thought appropriate. As a result published tables were not consistent for specific states or counties.

For the 1810 census, statisticians and members of Congress recognized the census as a potential source of information on the economic state of the nation. Voluntary efforts to collect such data had been largely unsuccessful and although the 1810 census of manufactures was hardly error-free, a two-volume report, one on demographics and one on industry, was published in 1811. Questions on citizenship were added in 1820 and a similar pair of volumes was published. In 1830 the manufacturing census was abandoned and efforts were concentrated on the collection of population data.

Once there were three data points to compare (1790, 1800, and 1810), unofficial but highly useful publications compared the condition of the country at each of them. This type of comparison became an ongoing part of the official census publications. It would be many years before a permanent Bureau of the Census would be established, but this type of analytic work eventually became an ongoing part of its responsibility.

Although standardized forms were initiated in 1830, errors and inconsistencies in the data were still apparent. Corrected editions of both volumes from 1830 were issued, but the issuing of corrected editions was not the general rule.

The Temporary Census Office

In 1850 a centralized census office was authorized for decennial data collection. It was established before each census was conducted and, until the end of the century, was disbanded once the results had been tabulated and published.

The number of census publications also increased with the 1850 census. Both a huge volume containing limited data for states, counties, and towns and a far briefer abstract of detailed national data appeared in 1853. A separate compendium, containing retrospective census data, was published in 1854. Mortality data were covered in a publication of 1855, and a digest of the statistics of manufacture based on the Seventh Census appeared in 1858. A similar group of publications followed the 1860 census with the addition of a separate volume on agriculture. The remainder of the publications from the eighth census appeared between 1864 and 1866. The 1870 census publications were organized similarly. Only in 1880 were separate volumes produced for special subjects with separate parts for individual states. The result was more than twenty-two volumes, each with numerous sections. Fifteen volumes and more than two hundred bulletins and reports were produced in 1890. More data were being collected and more tabulations published.

There was a growing emphasis on social statistics. Censuses just prior to the Civil War requested more information about slaves. As the century progressed, more data became available on people with physical and mental handicaps, on people in jails, and on occupations, marital status, and ethnic origin. Detailed questions on incarceration reached their peak numbers in 1880 and 1890. Throughout this period, efforts were made to standardize the data collection geography and hence the reporting geography.

Before the 1880 census, the authorizing legislation provided that the Census Office be placed within the Department of the Interior and that a superintendent be appointed for each census. Francis Walker was appointed superintendent for the 1880 census, and he was eager to make this tenth census a landmark effort. Accordingly, he produced over three hundred bulletins containing preliminary figures early in the decade; individual volumes for the population, manufactures, agriculture, and vital statistics of the nation; and additional volumes addressing industrial and economic growth. These latter volumes, written by special experts, combined statistics with explanatory text. These publications represented monumental efforts since the tabulations were all performed manually by clerks. With a growing population and a growing demand for detailed reports, it was 1888 before the final results of the 1880 census were published.

Efforts to automate the tabulation process were encouraged. Herman Hollerith, the developer of the punched card, easily won a competition among three alternate methods. Using Hollerith's equipment only for the population section, the Census Office in 1890 was able to complete most of its work in less than half the time it had taken in 1880.

With the Hollerith Electric Tabulating Machine, it was possible to perform more complex tabulations than in the past. In addition to an increased number of preliminary and special bulletins, detailed volumes contained both statistics and analyses on such subjects as population, "the insane, feeble-minded, deaf, dumb and blind," "crime, pauperism and benevolence," vital and social statistics, agriculture, manufacturing, mineral industries, churches, Indians, insurance, real estate mortgages, "farms and homes," transportation, and "wealth, debt and taxation."

A Permanent Census Office

The new Bureau of the Census was soon moved to the Department of Commerce and Labor, where it undertook a number of nontraditional projects. Among these were the compilation of immigration data; special censuses of Cuba, the Philippines, and Oklahoma (likely in preparation for Oklahoma's admission to the Union as the forty-sixth state in 1907); the completion of an official register of the United States; special reports on marriage and divorce; as well as several interpretive volumes on population growth. Business and economics became a main focus of the bureau, and surveys in this area became more frequent.

The 1910 census was the first completed under the auspices of a permanent Bureau of the Census. The data collected were similar to those of previous censuses, and the final publications were similar as well. However, the data that were ready first were made available initially as press releases and then as official bulletins. By 1914 the bureau had published eleven volumes plus numerous specialized population and economic bulletins and state supplements. Noteworthy was the fact that for the first time census data were provided for small subdivisions of cities or neighborhoods. In order to do this, census tracts were delineated in eight large cities, including New York, which had initially requested these small-area data.

It is worth noting that while items from earlier censuses are available in library catalogs under "U.S. Census Office," those from 1910, the thirteenth census, and after are organized under "U.S. Bureau of the Census."

The "Modern" Census

The 1940 census reflected dramatic changes in all areas of census operation. Reflecting the interests of the Depression years, the bureau expanded the number of questions on employment and unemployment, internal migration, and income. A census of housing was taken at the same time as the population census, and the combined effort has been known ever since as the Census of Population and Housing. The addition of housing questions provided more data on the quality of the nation's housing and on the need for a public housing program.

Advanced statistical techniques, such as sampling, were introduced as standard procedures. As a result, preliminary returns were published more than eight months before the complete tabulations and it was possible to publish more detailed tables and to review tabulations with greater efficiency. The wartime pressures on the Census Bureau resulted in an even greater number of publications than had been produced during the 1930s, and for the first time, tables for small-area socioeconomic data were produced for the sixty cities tracted at that time.

There was already some standardization of the publication program with the use of such titles as "Number of Inhabitants" and "Detailed Characteristics of the Population." There were also census tract reports, special subject reports, and procedural reports. The 1940 census thus resulted in an unprecedented number of printed reports.

Sampling was extended to the housing census in 1950. Subsequently, sampling design varied from census to census, with the common goal of producing accurate estimates of population and housing characteristics for areas as small as census tracts. The number of questions asked of the entire population was reduced to that necessary to identify the population and to avoid duplication. The resultant publications included a variety of working and technical reports in addition to the standard tabular reports and the procedural history.

Standard metropolitan statistical areas (SMSAs) were defined for the 1950 census and census county divisions for 1960. Census tract (CT) data were only published for SMSAs, which meant that until 1990, when the entire nation was covered by tracts or block numbering area (BNA) equivalents, there was more small-area data for the urbanized parts of the country than for the rural ones.

The use of census data for the allocation of government funds continued and the reapportionment issue re-emerged in the courts. As a result, census reports grew more detailed. The major innovation in 1950 was the initiation of a survey of residential financing. Similar surveys were conducted for the rest of the century. Surveys of components of housing change were included with the 1960 and 1970 censuses.

The Bureau as a Service Agency

Before 1960 the Census Bureau was first and foremost a production agency; its product was a set of printed volumes that summarized the results of each census. Relatively little attention was paid to issues of data access or use. In addition to the published volumes, special tabulations were available on a limited basis only. In response to a growing interest in census data by external users a service unit was created at the bureau to deal directly with user needs and to distribute standard data products.

After the 1960 census, the data existed in machine-readable form. Special extracts were created to meet the needs of both governmental and nongovernmental users. Since there was no program for the distribution of standard off-the-shelf tape products, data requests were costly and time-consuming. The first Public Use Samples (actual census form responses without personal identifiers), the 1/10,000 and the 1/1,000 samples, met the needs of those who wished to create their own tabulations or perform other types of data analysis. These were initially released on punched cards to a selected group of academic data users. They were subsequently released on magnetic tape. The bureau also released standard tapes with limited tabular data for census tracts.

The data on these tapes were not subject to the kind of checking and validating that is now a routine part of the bureau's operation; however, they met the needs of many users. Documentation was limited and data were difficult to use since no packaged software was yet available for statistical analysis. An additional problem, especially with the tract data, was that no plans had been made to preserve or archive these data. As a result, some of these data seem to have disappeared.

Based on input from both internal and external advisory groups, the bureau designed a series of data products to supplement the standard printed volumes. To introduce these products, they initiated a serial newsletter called *Small Area Data Notes* and issued a two-volume Census User's Guide to document the aggregate data products known as the "Counts."

Because the cost of both printing and paper had already skyrocketed, the computer tapes contained substantially more data than the printed reports. They were usually issued well before their printed equivalents. However, printed reports were more widely available and were easier and cheaper to use. Heavy data users found the tapes to be more efficient. The public-use sample data allowed users to create their own extracts and tabulations for larger geographic areas.

The First, Second, and Third Counts were based on 100-percent data: enumeration districts, census tracts, and blocks respectively. The Fourth, Fifth, and Sixth Counts were based on sample data. The Fourth Count was—and is—the most heavily used because it includes all of the socioeconomic and detailed housing items for almost all levels of geography. The Fifth Count provided limited sample data for three-digit and five-digit zip codes and for enumeration districts. The Sixth Count contained extremely complex and detailed tables for very large geographic areas such as states, metropolitan areas, and large cities. Anticipating a decline in the use of printed materials, the bureau cut the size of its print order for the 1970 census under Vincent

Barabba. However, the publicity associated with the tape products only increased the total use of printed as well as of machine-readable census data.

Prior to the 1970 census, the bureau also established the Data Access and Use Laboratory. Outside the bureau, Jack Beresford established the nonprofit Data Use and Access Laboratory (DUALabs) to make the tape data more accessible and more usable. Funded by the Ford Foundation, in cooperation with the Center for Research Libraries, DUALabs produced compressed versions of the 1970 count data; their MOD software was available through major research libraries and for internal use at several large corporations and municipal planning departments. Their compression algorithm reduced the tape required by 90 percent, and COBOL software made access to the data easy for experienced computer users. Use of data in this format declined with the demise of large IBM mainframes. Count data, which have been preserved, are available from the National Archives.

In addition to the count data, the bureau released a complex group of six 1/100 Public Use Samples: State; SMSA and County Group; and Neighborhood Characteristics, each for the 15 percent and the 5 percent samples. A 1/1,000 and a 1/10,000 file was made available for each of these samples. All of these data were distributed on either 800bpi or later 1600bpi magnetic tapes, and while each of the 1/100 samples required 33 reels of tape, each of the 1/1,000 required only three reels of tape and each of the 1/10,000 only one. The major problem with these data was their hierarchical format (household, family, and individual), but extracts were readily analyzed using the statistical packages that were by then widely available. A new sample of the 1960 census made these data more comparable to the 1970 state sample. Later, thanks to the efforts of Halliman Winsborough of the University of Wisconsin, public use samples from the 1940 and 1950 censuses were produced from microfilm records.

Several geographic products were also made available for use with the Count and Public Use Sample data. These included files for identifying SMSAs, counties, places, census tracts, and enumeration districts; a collection of printed maps for use in locating county groups, census tracts, and enumeration districts; and the Geographic Area Code Index (GACI) that provided quick access to codes for counties, places, and townships.

During the 1970s, an increasing awareness of the value of census data emerged for the comparative study of areas of all sizes and of rare populations. In 1980, efforts were made to eliminate several standard printed reports. Although the block statistics program was expanded substantially, the reports from it were made available only on tape and microfiche. Efforts to eliminate tract reports met with great objections from documents librarians and planners, and as a result were published as in the past. The "detailed characteristics" reports were not included in the original 1980 publication program but were subsequently published; these reports were finally eliminated in 1990. The number of printed special and subject reports was decreased in 1980 but made available on tapes and CDs as Subject Summary Tapes (SSTs) in 1990. The counts were renamed Summary Tape Files (STFs) and the Public Use Samples became Public Use Microdata Samples or PUMS. The age of microcomputers was only beginning and computer-readable data were still being released on magnetic tape. In response to strong user demands, the format of the STFs was changed so that each record began with a geographic segment. Medians were computed, and the data suppression codes were replaced with a different method of disclosure avoidance.

As a result of a change in the sampling design, the PUMS was less complicated in 1980. They used three samples instead of six and the County Group sample was released for 5 percent of the population. However, it was still not possible to identify places with populations of less than 100,000.

Census 2000 Products: New Media for Data Delivery

The initial plan for the 1990 census was to produce products that closely resembled those produced from the 1980 census. However, by the time the bureau started to prepare the 1990 products, it was obvious that most depository libraries and many individual users had access to microcomputers. As a result, CD-ROMS containing the PL94-171 data for reapportionment and redistricting, selected Summary Tape Files, and Subject Summary Tape Files, Public Use Microdata Samples, and geographic products were available for less money and were the media used for depository library distribution. Microfiche was eliminated, but the printed reports grew in size since they included more tables for both race and ethnic groups and for individual geographic areas. Economic census data and a limited amount of decennial data from 1980 were also made available on CDs.

As browsers such as Mosaic and later Netscape and Explorer provided data users with Internet access, the bureau experimented with various forms of online access. Among these FERRET, a system for creating data extracts which thus far has not been used for decennial census data (http://ferret.bls.census.gov/cgi-bin/ferret). The Data Extract System (DES) is another extract system developed for use with microdata including the 1990 PUMS (http://www.census.gov/des/d5). Selected 1990 summary data for STF1 and STF3 can be displayed for multiple geographic areas through 1990 census Lookup (http://venus.census.gov/cdrom/lookup). The American FactFinder is the newest database engine currently in use with 1990 census data (http://factfinder.census.gov/java_prod/dads.ui.home Page.HomePage). Although originally designed for use with the economic censuses, it does contain some 1990 data. Presumably, it will be further developed for use with the 2000 census.

As the Bureau prepares to tabulate data for 2000, it also looks back to make selected historical census data available online by searching on "historical" and on selected census years. Although the PUMS data are widely available on census and at other URL's, notably at IPUMS (http://www.hist.umn.edu/~ipums98/index.html) it is not possible to easily access pre-1990 summary tables online. Princeton University's Data and Statistical Service (*http://www.princeton.edu/~data/*) is exploring providing access to the 1970 aggregate or "count" data.

In retrospect, the technological development and growth of the Bureau of the Census, although not anticipated by the nation in 1790, have clearly met their desires. We can only look ahead to the continuing growth in the usefulness and the accessibility of the data provided.

■ Judith S. Rowe

Bibliography

Anderson, Margo J., and Stephen E. Fienberg. *Who Counts? The Politics of Census-taking in Contemporary America*. New York: Russell Sage Foundation, 1999.

Cassedy, James H. *Demography in Early America: Beginnings of the Statistical Mind, 1600–1800*. Cambridge, Mass.: Harvard University Press, 1969.

Dodd, Donald B. *Historical Statistics of the States of the United States: Two Centuries of the Census, 1790–1990*. Westport, Conn.: Greenwood Press, 1993.

Eckler, A. Ross. *The Bureau of the Census*. New York: Praeger, 1972.

Greene, Evarts Boutell, and Virginia D. Harrington. *American Population Before the Federal Census of 1790*. Baltimore: Genealogical Pub. Co., 1993.

Schmeckebier, Laurence Frederick. *The Statistical Work of the National Government.* Baltimore: Johns Hopkins Press, 1925.

Truesdell, Leon E. *The Development of Punch Card Tabulation in the Bureau of the Census, 1890–1940: With Outlines of Actual Tabulation Programs.* Washington, D.C.: U.S. Government Printing Office, 1965.

U.S. Bureau of the Census. *Historical Statistics of the United States, 1789–1945.* Washington, D.C.: U.S. Department of Commerce, 1949.

U.S. Bureau of the Census. *1970 Census Users' Guide.* Part I. Washington, D.C.: U.S. Department of Commerce, 1970.

U.S. Bureau of the Census. *1970 Census Users' Guide.* Part II. Washington, D.C.: U.S. Department of Commerce, 1970.

U.S. Bureau of the Census. *Population and Housing Inquiries in U.S. Decennial Censuses 1790–1970.* Working Paper 39. Washington, D.C.: U.S. Department of Commerce, 1973.

U.S. Bureau of the Census. *Public Use Samples of Basic Records from the 1970 Census: Description and Technical Documentation.* Washington, D.C.: U.S. Department of Commerce, 1972.

U.S. Congress. Office of Technology Assessment. *Federal Information Dissemination in an Electronic Age: Informing the Nation.* Washington, D.C.: U.S. Government Printing Office, 1988.

Wright, C. D., and W. C. Hunt. *The History and Growth of the United States Census, Prepared for the Senate Committee on the Census.* Washington, D.C.: U.S. Government Printing Office, 1900.

Decennial censuses

1790 census

The population of the United States, as reported in the 1790 census, was 3,929,625. This total was used to apportion 105 seats in the House of Representatives among the fifteen states. Although census-taking was familiar to many Americans from the colonial period, the 1790 census was the first time that the population of all the states was counted at the same time.

The census followed from the ratification of the Constitution in 1788. As part of a compromise over representation, the Constitution required that an "actual enumeration" be taken within three years of the first meeting of Congress, and within every ten years thereafter, for purposes of allocating seats in the House of Representatives, direct taxes, and votes in the elec-toral college. The relative proportions among the states were to be based on the size of the free population (white and black) and three-fifths of all slaves, with Indians not taxed being excluded.

The Constitution had assigned sixty-five seats in the House to the thirteen original states on the basis of population estimates. Because of concerns about the small size of the House and possible inequities in the original apportionment, Congress moved promptly to take the census. On May 18, 1789, the House of Representatives began work on a bill to take the census; the final version was signed into law by President George Washington on March 1, 1790. It stipulated that the count should begin on August 1, 1790, and should be completed within nine months. Although the Constitution required only that the population be divided into free, slave, and Indians not taxed, James Madison, then in the House, argued for greater detail as beneficial to the process of passing useful legislation. At minimum, he wanted to know the total of adult, white males, that part of the population most involved in the political life of the country. As a result, the census separated the free population into white males above and below the age

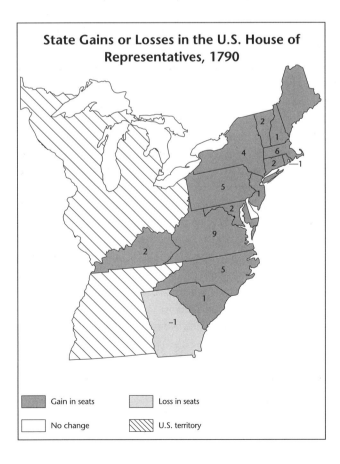

State Gains or Losses in the U.S. House of Representatives, 1790

of sixteen, white females, and free blacks. Slaves were counted with no distinctions by age or sex; Indians were excluded from the count by the law. Madison also urged that occupations be recorded because he believed that political interests were largely the reflection of economic divisions. Others disagreed, arguing that the people would be suspicious about too many questions about their economic status, that many individuals worked in a variety of occupations, and so would be hard to classify, and that collecting the extra data was unnecessary, useful only for "idle people to make a book." Local counts were made by household, with the head listed by name and the rest of the family counted under the appropriate headings. Although the final law required more information than the minimum specified in the Constitution, the first census contained less detail than many colonial censuses.

The census was taken under the supervision of local federal marshals, who were empowered to hire assistants as they needed. Most assistants were paid at the rate of $1 per 150 people counted. In towns of more than five thousand, the rate was reduced to $1 per 300, while in thinly settled areas the rate increased to $1 per 50. The assistants were not provided with printed forms. Total cost of the census was $44,377. Failure to provide information to the census-takers could lead to a $20 fine. To ensure accuracy, all assistants were required to post their tabulations in public places for inspection and correction. When the marshals were satisfied with the results, they forwarded them to Secretary of State Thomas Jefferson, who passed them on to President Washington. Washington presented a table of the population to Congress on October 27, 1791, though reports from South Carolina had not yet been received. Vermont and the Southwest Territory, neither part of the original area to be counted, both managed to get their totals to the government before South Carolina. A fifty-six-page book containing considerable detail was published in 1791. Partial results had appeared in the press before then. Preservation of some of the original manuscripts provided specific information about town and county populations as well as the size of families, which was useful to scholars who later returned to the local sources.

As the results arrived at the capital, Jefferson and others remarked that the total was probably too low, estimating the true number might approach 4.1 million—representing about a 5 percent undercount. Jefferson and Washington were among many who thought a larger number projected the strength of the country and a promising future among the nations of the world. They paid almost no attention to other facts, such as 17.8 percent of the total population being slave, 50.9 percent of all whites being male, or 49.0 percent of white males being under the age of sixteen. These proportions were familiar from the colonial period and so, presumably, did not merit comment.

■ Robert V. Wells

Bibliography

Anderson, Margo J. *The American Census: A Social History.* New Haven: Yale University Press, 1988.

Cohen, Patricia Cline. *A Calculating People: The Spread of Numeracy in Early America.* Chicago: University of Chicago Press, 1982.

U.S. Bureau of the Census. *A Century of Population Growth: From the First Census of the United States to the Twelfth, 1790–1900.* Washington, D.C.: U.S. Government Printing Office, 1909.

1800 census

The 1800 census counted 5,308,483 people in the United States. That total was used to apportion 141 seats in the House of Representatives to the sixteen states. (Ohio received one seat in 1803, upon its admission to the union.)

The 1800 census was similar to that of 1790 in many ways. The law authorizing the taking of the census in 1800 again relied on federal marshals and their assistants as enumerators. After the marshals had collected the data, checked for errors, and arrived at totals, they sent the final versions for each state to the secretary of state, who in turn presented them to the president for submission to Congress. The official version was published in a seventy-four-page volume, though newspapers provided summaries to their readers. An estimated 900 enumerators were involved in taking the census, about 250 more than in 1790; the total cost was $66,000, an increase of $22,000 from the first census. Because of the increase in population, the estimated cost per capita rose only from 1.1 to 1.2 cents.

As Congress prepared for the census, both the American Philosophical Society and the Connecticut Academy of Arts and Sciences urged expanding the number of questions to provide a more complex picture of the American people. In addition to reviving

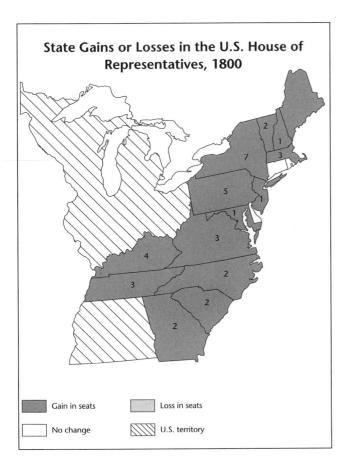

State Gains or Losses in the U.S. House of Representatives, 1800

Gain in seats

Loss in seats

No change

U.S. territory

James Madison's appeal for information on occupations, discarded in 1790, they suggested greater detail on age as well as recording nativity (place of birth) and marital status. Although Congress did agree to collect more information on age, it decided that additional questions were either unnecessary or unconstitutional. The white population, both male and female, was divided into the following categories by age: under ten, ten to under sixteen, sixteen to under twenty-six, twenty-six to under forty-five, and forty-five and up. The reasons for these particular divisions are unclear, as colonial censuses used ten and sixteen to set off children, but never both, and sixty was the most common maximum age used before 1775. Perhaps young men between sixteen and twenty-six were the prime choices for military service, but that does not explain the other divisions. Heads of families were included in the appropriate category by age and sex, in addition to being listed in the census schedule. Once again, no details were required for either free blacks or slaves.

The 1800 census was taken amidst one of the most controversial presidential elections in American history. As a result, much of the correspondence of the period is more concerned with the election and the subsequent decision in the House to select Thomas Jefferson as president over his running mate, Aaron Burr, than with the census. Three secretaries of state oversaw the 1800 count. Thomas Pickering served as secretary of state through mid-1800 and was the target of the Republicans in 1799 as Congress debated whether census legislation allowed the secretary too much freedom in establishing regulations for taking the census. President John Adams replaced Pickering with John Marshall, who served until President Jefferson and Secretary of State James Madison took office in the spring of 1801. After Madison replaced Marshall, he had to prod new marshals in several states to complete the work of their predecessors and to reassure them that the Treasury Department would pay them. In May 1801, Tench Coxe, a Jefferson supporter and writer on statistical matters, unsuccessfully urged Madison to have the president request that the public voluntarily report desired data on occupation and nativity. Madison also received requests for copies of the census from Treasury Secretary Albert Gallatin and the American ambassador to London, Rufus King.

Jefferson made reference to the census in his first State of the Union message in 1801, noting with pride that the population had doubled in just over twenty-two years. In the midst of diplomatic problems caused by the Anglo-French conflict that would ultimately give rise to the War of 1812, Jefferson observed that Americans did not take pleasure from their rapid growth because of "the injuries it may enable us to do to others," but because of what it meant for the settlement of "the extensive country still remaining vacant . . . [and] the multiplications of men susceptible of happiness, educated in the love of order, habituated to self-government, and valuing its blessings above all price."

In addition to rapid growth, Jefferson and others could have noted such national characteristics as 101 men for every 100 women, 49.5 percent under the age of sixteen, 12.2 percent age forty-five or older, 17.0 percent held in slavery, and 2.1 percent free blacks. Variations were readily apparent from one state to another, not only in size and racial composition, but also by age and sex. By and large, the New England states were whiter, older, and more female than other parts of the country.

■ Robert V. Wells

Bibliography

Anderson, Margo J. *The American Census: A Social History.* New Haven: Yale University Press, 1988.

Cassedy, James H. *Demography in Early America: Beginnings of the Statistical Mind, 1600–1800.* Cambridge, Mass.: Harvard University Press, 1969.

Cohen, Patricia Cline. *A Calculating People: The Spread of Numeracy in Early America.* Chicago: University of Chicago Press, 1982.

1810 census

The population of the United States according to the 1810 census was 7,239,881. By the end of the 1810s, 186 seats in the House of Representatives were allocated among the twenty-three states.

Under the direction of the secretary of state, the federal government instructed the marshals and their assistants to collect information about the population as of Monday, August 6, 1810. The five months originally set for the enumeration were extended until June

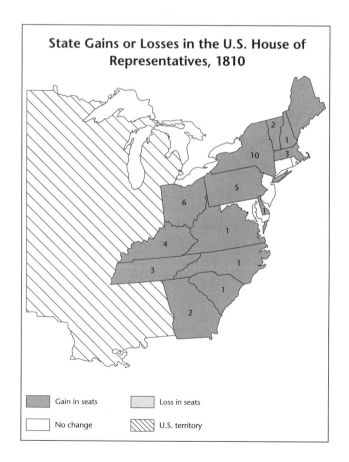

State Gains or Losses in the U.S. House of Representatives, 1810

Gain in seats · Loss in seats · No change · U.S. territory

3, 1811, for assistants to make their returns and until July 1, 1811, for the marshals to complete the work. Two publications were issued after the census: a 180-page folio volume devoted to population and a 233-page quarto volume on manufacturing, prepared and summarized by political economist and former high federal official Tench Coxe of Philadelphia. The total cost of the census, including printing, was $178,444.67 or two cents per person enumerated.

In the 1810 census, only the names of heads of families were recorded. For the first time, the law required that an inquiry be made at every dwelling house or to the head of every household. The categories of information collected were identical to that of the preceding census. Free white males and females were separately tallied into the five age groups of under ten years, ten to fifteen, sixteen to twenty-five, twenty-six to forty-four, and forty-five and older. The numbers of slaves and other free persons—blacks and taxed Native Americans—were recorded with no distinction made as to sex or age.

Since 1800, the population had grown by 36 percent. The United States remained a rural society in 1810. The share of the urban population, places with twenty-five hundred or more people, crept forward from 6.1 to 7.2 percent of the total population. There were forty-six such towns and cities in 1810 compared with thirty-three in 1800. Because of Thomas Jefferson's purchase of the Louisiana Territory from France in 1803, which nearly doubled the area of North America under the control of the United States, population density declined from 6.1 to 4.3 enumerated persons per square mile between 1800 and 1810. All segments of the population increased rapidly. The size of the enslaved population expanded by 33 percent during the first decade of the nineteenth century, and one-sixth of Americans were held in slavery in 1810. The percentage of free blacks in the total population of color increased from 10.8 to 13.5 between 1800 and 1810. During the decade, Congress approved the first law limiting immigration to the United States. The forced importation of blacks in the slave trade, which the Constitution had allowed to continue legally for twenty years, was finally ended in 1808.

In his introduction to the volume on industrial statistics, Coxe pointed to numerous imperfections and omissions but eschewed any attempt to estimate the correct figures. Information was collected on more than two hundred products and production facilities such as mills and tanneries and was tabulated for states and smaller civil divisions. The tables effectively conveyed an impression of the diversity and widespread nature of industrial production in the country. Overall, however, Coxe admitted and later commentators concur that the effort was unsuccessful in documenting the aggregate of industrial activity in the United States.

The constitutionally pertinent population, based on counting slaves as three-fifths of free persons, of the average congressional district increased slightly from thirty-three thousand to thirty-five thousand, but no state lost a representative. Gaining ten seats, New York replaced Virginia as the state with the most members of Congress, a rank it would hold for 160 years until California emerged after 1970 as the most populous state. Pennsylvania and Ohio both gained five seats and Kentucky added four. The share of House seats held by the South declined for the first time, from 46 to 44 percent, but the regions still had equal numbers of senators. Politicians and commentators began to take note of what was to become a trend toward northern population dominance. A major aspect of the Missouri Compromise of 1820 was the paired admission of Missouri as a slave state and Maine, previously a noncontiguous district of Massachusetts, as a free state.

The results of the 1810 and other early censuses of the United States were most important in shaping a vision of growth and progress in the country and in providing the demographic framework for the conflict between the North and South.

■ Daniel Scott Smith

Bibliography

Anderson, Margo J. *The American Census: A Social History.* New Haven: Yale University Press, 1988.

Coxe, Tench. *A Statement of the Arts and Manufactures of the United States of America, for the Year 1810.* New York: Norman Ross Publishing, 1990; orig. pub. Philadelphia, 1814.

Inter-University Consortium for Political and Social Research (ICPSR). *Historical, Demographic, Economic, and Social Data: The United States, 1790–1970.* Part No. 3. Ann Arbor, Mich.: ICPSR, 1984. County-level computer file available to persons at ICPSR-affiliated institutions. Information at http://www.icpsr.umich.edu/cgi/archive1.html.

U.S. Bureau of the Census. *Historical Statistics of the United States, Colonial Times to 1970, Bicentennial Edition.* Washington, D.C.: U.S. Government Printing Office, 1975.

U.S. Secretary of State. *Aggregate Amount of Persons within the United States in the Year 1810.* New York: Norman Ross Publishing, 1990; orig. pub. Washington, D.C., 1811.

Wright, Carroll D. *The History and Growth of the United States Census.* Washington, D.C.: U.S. Government Printing Office, 1900.

1820 census

The population of the United States was 9,638,453 at the time of the 1820 census. Two hundred and thirteen seats in the House of Representatives were apportioned among the twenty-four states.

Under the supervision of Secretary of State John Quincy Adams, the federal government instructed the marshals and assistants to record the facts about the population located in their customary residencies as of Monday, August 7, 1820. The enumerators were given six months to complete their interviews, whether done at each dwelling or with a household head elsewhere. Because of delays, Congress in March 1821 had to extend the deadline until September 1 of that year. The total cost of the census, including printing, was $208,525.99 or just over two cents per person enumerated. Published were a 160-page folio volume of population data and a 100-page volume of information on manufacturing. Neither the process of counting nor the publication of the results generated controversy or even much commentary.

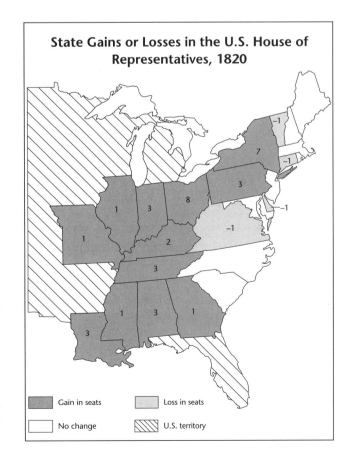

State Gains or Losses in the U.S. House of Representatives, 1820

Gain in seats
Loss in seats
No change
U.S. territory

Although the House of Representatives grew by twenty-seven seats, the constitutionally pertinent population of the average congressional district, based on counting slaves as three-fifths of free persons, grew as well—from thirty-five thousand after the 1810 census to forty thousand after the 1820 census. Four states—Connecticut, Delaware, Vermont, and Virginia—lost one representative from their delegations. Consequent to rapid growth in the Middle Atlantic region, the delegations from New York and Pennsylvania, the two largest, grew from fifty to sixty, and Ohio in the West expanded its number of representatives from six to fourteen. The trend toward more rapid population growth in the North than in the slave states continued. State legislatures were not required to use the results from the census in laying out the boundaries of congressional districts. On average, nevertheless, districts varied only 11 percent from the state average in those states having two or more districts.

As was the case until the 1850 census, only the names of heads of families were recorded. The instructions asked the enumerators to delineate the white population into five age groups for females (under ten, ten to fifteen, sixteen to twenty-five, twenty-six to forty-four, and forty-five and older) and six for males (sixteen- and seventeen-year-olds separately recorded). Aliens who had not been naturalized were included both in the age categories and in a separate tally. They numbered more than fifty-three thousand nationally. For the first time, the numbers of slaves and free colored persons were recorded by sex and age. Only four age categories (under fourteen, fourteen to twenty-five, twenty-six to forty-four, and forty-five and older) were used for these segments of the population. Finally, some 4,631 Native Americans who paid taxes were separately recorded.

Since 1810, the population had grown by 33 percent and the size of the House of Representatives by 14 percent. The United States remained an overwhelmingly rural, agricultural society. The population in towns and cities expanded at virtually the same rate as that in the countryside. Only 7.2 percent resided in the sixty-one places that had twenty-five hundred or more in population. Because of a high birth rate, the population remained youthful. The median age of the entire population was only 16.6 years, an increase of 0.6 years since 1810. The enslaved population expanded by 29 percent over the course of the 1810s. Some 16 percent of enumerated Americans were slaves at the time of the fourth census, while 13 percent of African Americans were legally free.

Congress had rejected the respective requests of James Madison and Thomas Jefferson that a question about occupation be included in the first and second census. The 1820 census for the first time tallied the principal activities of persons, including those of slaves, into three broad and exclusive categories. In his instructions, Adams recognized that many in the relatively unspecialized American economy were engaged in more than one sector. Some 83 percent were in agriculture; 14 percent in manufacturing, including such hand labor carried out in households; and 3 percent in commerce. In a separate folio volume of one hundred pages, fourteen categories of information on each separately enumerated manufacturing establishment were detailed. Among these inquiries were the numbers of men, women, and children employed, the amount of capital invested, and the total wages paid. These returns were, however, incomplete, and economic historians have found them of limited use.

The 1820 census represented another increment in the gradual expansion of the decennial count's scope and documented the continuing rapid growth of the American population during the first half of the nineteenth century.

■ Daniel Scott Smith

Bibliography

Anderson, Margo J. *The American Census: A Social History.* New Haven: Yale University Press, 1988.

Parsons, Stanley D., William W. Beach, and Dan Hermann. *United States Congressional Districts 1788–1841.* Westport, Conn.: Greenwood Press, 1978.

U.S. Secretary of State. *Census for 1820.* Washington, D.C.: Gales & Seaton, 1821.

U.S. Secretary of State. *Digest of Accounts of Manufacturing Establishments in the United States, and of their Manufactures.* Washington, D.C.: Gales & Seaton, 1823.

Wright, Carroll D. *The History and Growth of the United States Census.* Washington, D.C.: U.S. Government Printing Office, 1900.

1830 census

According to the 1830 census, the population of the United States was 12,866,020 (including 5,318 persons on ships and thus not in any state or territory). Two hundred forty seats in the House of Representatives were apportioned among the twenty-four states.

An enumeration bill establishing the census of 1830

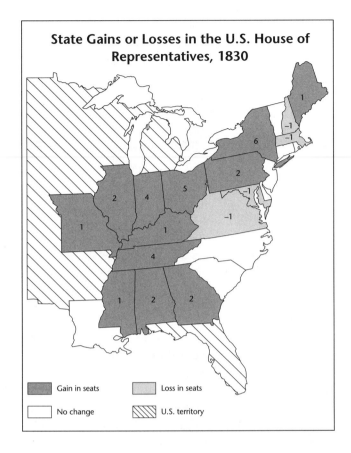

State Gains or Losses in the U.S. House of Representatives, 1830

Gain in seats

Loss in seats

No change

U.S. territory

five, and one hundred) did not easily allow longevity by race to be compared. The undifferentiated grouping of all blacks between fifty-five and one hundred particularly hampered potential study of life expectation for blacks.

Congress added one new inquiry to the 1830 census. Assistant marshals were asked to gather data on the numbers of deaf, dumb, and blind, sorted by race, and, except for the blind, by three age categories (under fourteen, fourteen to twenty-four, twenty-five and up). As in 1820, a column identified foreigners not naturalized. Congress also moved the date of the census ahead two months, to June 1 instead of August 1 as in 1820, on President Adams's suggestion that this would permit a longer stretch of good weather for the house-to-house enumeration. Congress allowed six months for the process to be completed. An amended act passed February 3, 1831, extended the terminal date for aggregating returns until August 1, 1831. The amendment also directed the secretary of state "to note all the clerical errors in the returns" and publish the corrections along with the aggregate returns of the marshals.

President Andrew Jackson's secretary of state, Martin Van Buren, directed the census. For the first time, the State Department provided a printed schedule for the enumerators. The uniform schedule measured 18-1/2 by 16 inches, with columns printed on both the front and back. As before, marshals and assistant marshals in the field were to conduct the census, and they were directed by Congress to obtain information "by actual inquiry at every dwelling house." A penalty of $20 was charged to anyone over sixteen who refused to answer census questions. The assistant marshals prepared two copies of the returns and posted them in public places for inspection and verification. One copy was then deposited with the local district court and the other sent to the State Department, along with the marshal's aggregation of the district's returns.

In 1830 the U.S. population was 8.8 percent urban; 18 percent African American; and 15.6 percent slave.

In 1832, Washington, D.C., printer Duff Green published the population returns. Three thousand books were produced, with copies distributed to colleges and historical societies. The aggregation by county and state was followed by a long "errata" section containing the corrections made by temporary clerks hired by the State Department to double-check the calculations of the marshals.

■ Patricia Cline Cohen

was passed on March 23, 1830. As in previous censuses, this one called for the enumeration of households under the household head's name, with all residents classified by sex, age categories, race, and civil condition (free or slave). The broad three-part occupational categorization inaugurated in the 1820 census was dropped. On the suggestion of John Quincy Adams, who had directed the 1820 census when he was secretary of state, the 1830 census further refined age classifications. Adams, as president, argued for ten-year intervals up to one hundred and over in his fourth annual message to Congress in December 1828, on the grounds that this would allow for highly interesting "comparative tables of longevity." Congress enacted this suggestion, but for white males and females only. Thirteen age columns for whites replaced the five from 1820, bounded by the ages five, ten, fifteen, twenty, thirty, forty, fifty, sixty, seventy, eighty, ninety, and one hundred. Slightly altered age categories were also established for blacks, both slave and free, dividing them into six groups instead of the four used in 1820 and including a column for those over one hundred. The broad boundaries (ten, twenty-four, thirty-six, fifty-

Bibliography

Bohme, Frederick G. *200 Years of U.S. Census Taking: Population and Housing Questions, 1790–1990.* Washington, D.C.: U.S. Government Printing Office, 1989.

Wright, Carroll D. *The History and Growth of the United States Census, Prepared for the Senate Committee on the Census.* Washington, D.C.: U.S. Government Printing Office, 1900.

1840 census

The 1840 census tallied the U.S. population at 17,069,453, leading to an apportionment of 223 seats in the House of Representatives among the twenty-six states. The American population was 10.8 percent urban, 16.8 percent African American, and 14.6 percent slave.

An enumeration bill establishing the census of 1840 was passed in the closing days of the Twenty-fifth Congress, in February 1839. With strong bipartisan support, lawmakers duplicated the language of the 1830 census act, providing for the enumeration of households under the household head's name, with all resi-

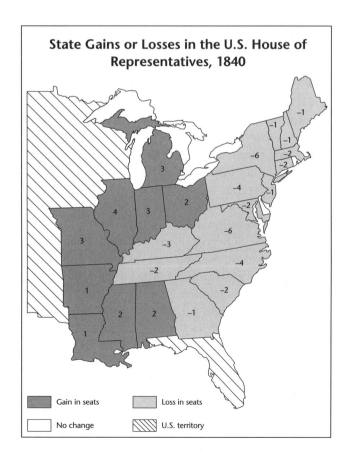

State Gains or Losses in the U.S. House of Representatives, 1840

Gain in seats   Loss in seats

No change   U.S. territory

dents classified by sex, age categories, race, and civil condition (free or slave). For whites, the age categories were bounded by the ages five, ten, fifteen, twenty, thirty, forty, fifty, sixty, seventy, eighty, ninety, and one hundred; for blacks, both slave and free, the category boundaries remained as they had been in 1830, at ages ten, twenty-four, thirty-six, fifty-five, and one hundred. (A proposal by Rep. William Slade, a Vermont Whig, to count the black population by age categories comparable to whites failed even to come to a vote.) The enumeration bill continued the practice, started in 1830, of gathering information on the numbers of deaf, dumb, and blind, sorted by race.

Congress added three new inquiries to the 1840 census. One stipulated a count of the numbers of insane and idiots, distinguished by race and mode of support (at public or private charge). A second called for a list, by name and age, of all pensioners still drawing government support for Revolutionary War service, information vital for forecasting future pension payments and for checking the accuracy of the pension rolls. A third amendment, at once ambitious, unprecedented, and unspecified, directed that "statistical tables" should be returned, containing "all such information in relation to mines, agriculture, commerce, manufacturers, and schools, as will exhibit a full view of the pursuits, industry, education, and resources of the country."

Previous federal censuses had been directly supervised by the secretary of state, but this time Secretary John Forsyth hired William A. Weaver to superintend the entire job, from preparing the schedule to publishing the results. For the population schedule, Weaver devised an oversized, two-sided form with seventy-four columns, including the question on pensioners and the notation of deaf, dumb, blind, insane, and idiot persons. Weaver designated seven occupational categories (mining, agriculture, commerce, manufacturing, learned professions, ocean navigators, and navigators on internal waters), and he added seven columns for tallying schools and scholars (in colleges, academies, common schools). A final column recorded persons over the age of twenty who could not read or write. These inquiries went to satisfy the desire for fuller economic and educational statistics. To answer thoroughly the congressional call for a "full view" of the country's resources, Weaver prepared a second schedule consisting of 214 inquiries about production and investment in economic enterprises including mining, agriculture, horticulture, commerce, fisheries, forestry, and manufacturing. The resulting compilation yielded figures for the number of swine, retail stores, bushels of potatoes, and employees in cotton manufacturing, among another two hundred economic statistics, for every census district in the country.

The census began on June 1, 1840; returns came in slowly, and aggregation in Washington, D.C., proceeded even more slowly. In February 1841 the Senate requested a progress report, a call repeated by the House in summer 1841. In October the state tallies of population were made public, both in an official government publication and in privately published statistical almanacs. In 1842 the economic statistics were printed by two printing firms, Blair & Rives and Thomas Allen.

Two controversies quickly engulfed the 1840 census. One, relatively minor, concerned the two rival firms that had printed the volume of economic statistics. One firm had held exclusive government printing contracts for a decade under Democratic rule, but the 1841 inauguration of a Whig presidential administration led a new secretary of state (Daniel Webster) to promise the lucrative job to a Whig printer. Congressional hearings to sort out the contract dispute generated a significant byproduct: exceptional documentation about methods used to process the census at the Department of State.

A second controversy of national proportions arose over the detection of peculiar patterns of rates of insanity and idiocy by race. Close inspection of the published data by insanity expert Dr. Edward Jarvis of Massachusetts revealed an apparent precipitous rise in black insanity neatly correlated with geography. The ratio of insane blacks to all blacks in Maine was 1 in 14; in Louisiana, the ratio was 1 in 5,650. Ratios for each state, arrayed from far north to far south, exhibited an amazingly uniform gradient. Overall, the North's ratio was 1 in 162.4, while the South's was 1 in 1,558. The corresponding ratio for whites showed almost no North/South difference. Charges of fraud, data tampering, and incompetence greeted this finding in publications in the North. But some Southern essayists defended the data, linking it to other data on poverty and crime to support their view that freedom was very harmful to blacks.

That the data were clearly in error could be easily shown in 1842: Insane blacks were tallied in northern towns where no black population existed. Yet William Weaver defended the integrity of his procedures; the data tallies had been made by assistant marshals working independently across the country, ruling out conspiracy. Southern politicians such as John C. Calhoun, the new secretary of state in 1842, found it too useful

a piece of ammunition in slavery debates to repudiate. The errors likely resulted from the complex layout of the manuscript population schedule, with its three-tiered headings obscuring the racial sort in the insanity and idiocy columns. But the data were never officially disavowed or corrected.

■ Patricia Cline Cohen

Bibliography

Cohen, Patricia Cline. *A Calculating People: The Spread of Numeracy in Early America.* New York: Routledge, 1999.

Deutsch, Albert. "The First U.S. Census of the Insane (1840) and Its Use as Pro-Slavery Propaganda." *Bulletin of the History of Medicine* 15 (1944): 469–482.

Grob, Gerald. *Edward Jarvis and the Medical World of Nineteenth-Century America.* Knoxville: University of Tennessee Press, 1978.

1850 census

The population of the United States in 1850 was 23,191,876. Two hundred thirty-four House seats were apportioned among the thirty-one states. In the ten years since the preceding census, the American population increased 35.9 percent, equivalent to an average annual growth rate of 3.1 percent and a doubling of the population every 22.6 years. The rapid population growth of the 1840s abetted and was stimulated by one of the most dramatic periods of territorial expansion in the nation's history. Florida, Iowa, Texas, and Wisconsin were admitted to the union, and new territories were established in California, Minnesota, New Mexico, Oregon, and Utah. The new territories in the West increased the area of the United States to 2,991,655 square miles, an increase of 67 percent from 1840. Although the addition of new territories caused the nation's overall population density to fall from 9.8 inhabitants per square mile in 1840 to 7.9 in 1850, states east of the Mississippi River experienced increased population densities and rapid urbanization. The total population living in urban places—defined as incorporated places of twenty-five hundred or more inhabitants—increased from 10.8 to 15.3 percent.

Of the 23.2 million inhabitants of the United States in 1850, 19.6 million (84.3 percent) were classified by census enumerators as "White" and 3.6 million (15.7 percent) as "Black" or "Mulatto." Approximately 88.5 percent of the white population in 1850 was native-

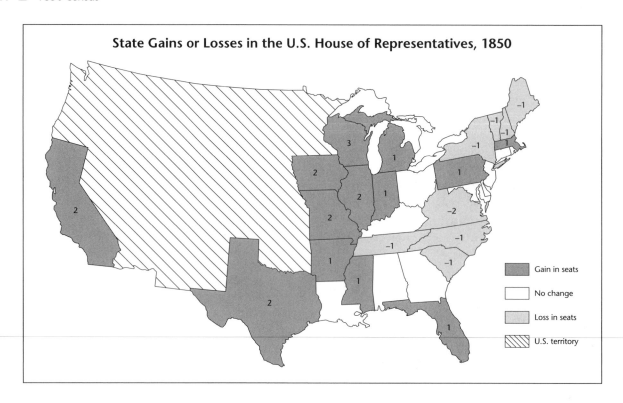

State Gains or Losses in the U.S. House of Representatives, 1850

Gain in seats

No change

Loss in seats

U.S. territory

born. Among the foreign-born population, immigrants from Ireland predominated (43 percent of all foreign-born whites), followed by Germany (26 percent), England (12 percent), Scotland (3 percent), France (2 percent), and Wales (1 percent). The vast majority of the black and mulatto population lived in servitude: 3.2 million (89.0 percent) were enumerated as slaves and just 0.4 million (11.0 percent) were enumerated as "free coloreds." Despite the high percentage of the black population held in bondage and the virtual absence of immigration, the black population increased by 26.6 percent in the 1840s, an average annual rate of 2.4 percent.

The 1850 census marked a major turning point in American census-taking. It was the first census to use the individual as the basic unit of enumeration and the first census to be tabulated and analyzed exclusively in Washington, D.C. Previous censuses, in contrast, had been conducted on the household level and relied on field enumerators to make initial tabulations. The 1850 census was also the first census to have a Census Board overseeing pre-enumeration issues, the first to include a question on place of birth, and the first to ask detailed information on age and occupation. As a result, the 1850 census serves as a baseline from which to evaluate the immense social and economic transformations of the late nineteenth and early twentieth centuries,

including the impact of immigration, internal migration, industrialization, and urbanization on the American population.

The creation of the Census Board in 1849 and the appointment of Joseph C. G. Kennedy as its secretary profoundly shaped the 1850 census. Kennedy and members of the Census Board solicited outside advice on what should be asked on the census, how it should be conducted, and how the results should be reported. Many of the nation's statisticians were convinced that the cumbersome eighty-column form used in the 1840 census resulted in a significant number of errors, and they suggested the need for radical change. Late in 1849, Lemuel Shattuck of the American Statistical Association and Archibald Russell of the American Geographical and Statistical Society were invited to Washington to help Kennedy design the 1850 schedules. The result, modeled after Shattuck's 1845 census of Boston, was a dramatic expansion in the scope and design of the census. Each individual in the population—free and slave—was to be given his or her own line on the new forms. The number of questions grew; to be recorded was every individual's name, age, sex, color, and occupation (if male and over fifteen years of age), value of real estate owned, state or country of birth, whether married within previous year, whether attended school in previous year, literacy (if over twenty years of age), and whether deaf, dumb, blind, insane, idiotic, pauper, or convict. The slave schedule initially was conceived as including most of the questions on the schedule for free inhabitants. It also was to include a question on the number of children each woman had borne, whether the children were still living, and the name of the owner. Unfortunately, southern senators, fearing detailed analyses of slavery, were able to delete many of the proposed questions from the schedule when the census bill came up for debate. The final slave schedule approved by the Senate identified each slave by number only. In addition, it included questions on the age, sex, and color of each slave, whether the slave was deaf, dumb, blind, insane, idiotic, or a fugitive from the state, the name of the owner, and the number of slaves manumitted.

The 1850 census was conducted in the field by forty-five marshals and 3,231 assistant marshals. Marshals were responsible for subdividing their districts into "known civil divisions" and ensuring that assistant marshals accurately completed the schedules. Assistant marshals were responsible for the enumeration, traveling door to door to complete the six different census schedules (free population, slave inhabitants, mortality, agriculture, manufacturing, and social statistics). Under the new census act, the raw completed schedules were returned to Washington for tallying. It soon became apparent that condensing the new schedules for publication was a formidable task. Kennedy eventually increased the size of the Census Office staff from 70 to more than 170 to process the returns. Even so, publication of the results was delayed and Congress was soon accusing Kennedy of "incompetence" and "extravagance." In retrospect, difficulties in processing the 1850 census are understandable in light of the dramatic changes in census content and procedure and the rudimentary processing capabilities of the mid-nineteenth century. Kennedy, however, lost his job after Franklin Pierce won the presidency in 1852. He was replaced by James D. B. DeBow, a southern Democrat, statistician, and renowned editor. DeBow oversaw the publication of a one-thousand-page volume on population statistics in 1853, a condensed edition called the *Compendium* in 1854, and a volume on the statistics of mortality in 1855, after which the Census Office was officially disbanded. Joseph Kennedy was reappointed three years later to publish the results of the manufacturing census.

See also *Decennial censuses, 1840 census, 1860 census, 1870 census.*

■ J. David Hacker

Bibliography

Anderson, Margo J. *The American Census: A Social History.* New Haven: Yale University Press, 1988.

Magnuson, Diana Lynn. "The Making of a Modern Census: The United States Census of Population, 1790–1940." Ph.D. dissertation, University of Minnesota, 1995.

U.S. Bureau of the Census. *Historical Statistics of the United States, Colonial Times to 1970: Bicentennial Edition.* Washington, D.C.: U.S. Government Printing Office, 1975.

U.S. Census Office. *Mortality Statistics of the Seventh Census of the United States.* Washington, D.C.: A. O. P. Nicholson, 1855.

U.S. Census Office. *Statistical View of the United States, Being a Compendium of the Seventh Census.* Washington, D.C.: A. O. P. Nicholson, 1854.

U.S. Census Office. *The Seventh Census of the United States: 1850. Embracing a Statistical View of Each of the States and Territories, Arranged by Counties, Towns, Etc.* Washington, D.C.: Robert Armstrong, 1853.

U.S. Department of the Interior. *Abstract of the Statistics of Manufactures, According to the Returns of the Seventh Census.* Washington, D.C., 1859.

Wright, Carroll, and William C. Hunt. *History and Growth of the United States Census.* Washington, D.C.: U.S. Government Printing Office, 1900.

1860 census

According to the 1860 census, the population of the United States was 31,443,321. Two hundred forty-one seats in the House of Representatives were apportioned among the thirty-three states. The census revealed that the American population continued to grow rapidly. Between 1850 and 1860 the population increased 35.6 percent, equivalent to an average annual growth rate of 3.0 percent. Minnesota and Oregon were admitted as new states, and territories were established in Colorado, the Dakotas, Kansas, Nebraska, Nevada, and Washington. (Kansas was admitted to the union on January 29, 1861, bringing the total number of states to thirty-four.) The area of the United States increased to 3,021,295 square miles, resulting in a population density of 10.6 inhabitants per square mile. Although most Americans continued to reside in rural areas, an increasing percentage chose to live in incorporated towns and cities. The total population living in urban places increased from 15.3 percent in 1850 to 19.8 percent in 1860.

Of the 31.4 million inhabitants of the United States in 1860, 26.9 million (85.6 percent) were classified by

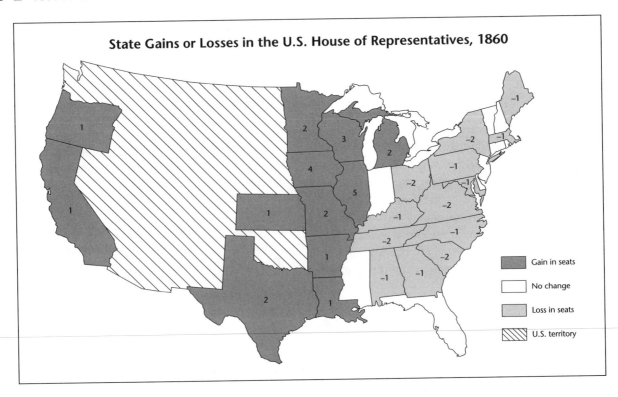

State Gains or Losses in the U.S. House of Representatives, 1860

census enumerators as "White," 4.4 million (14.1 percent) as "Black" or "Mulatto," thirty-five thousand (0.1 percent) as "Chinese," and forty-four thousand (0.1 percent) as "Indians"—indicating only those Native Americans living off reservations and no longer maintaining tribal affiliations. Heavy immigration in the previous decade, especially from Ireland, Great Britain, and northwestern Europe, increased the percentage of the white population that was foreign-born from 11.5 percent in 1850 to 15.2 percent in 1860. The vast majority of the black and mulatto population continued to live in servitude: 3.95 million (89.0 percent) were enumerated as slaves and just 0.49 million (11.0 percent) were enumerated as "free coloreds." The total black population increased by 22.1 percent in the 1850s, an average annual rate of 2.0 percent, down from the 2.4 percent average annual increase in the previous decade.

The 1860 census was taken in the year preceding the outbreak of the American Civil War. In part, the war was the result of demographic forces evident in the census. Rapid population growth, western migration, and the territorial expansion of the United States in the early nineteenth century routinely raised the divisive issue of whether to allow slavery in newly acquired territories. Less rapid growth in the South helped under-

mine the precarious balance of power achieved in the antebellum period. Between 1790 and 1860 the South's share of seats in the House of Representatives fell from 46 percent to 35 percent. The relative decline of southern population allowed Abraham Lincoln to win the presidential election in 1860 even though he was not on the ballot in the South. The census data also reveal that the North and South were becoming more demographically distinct. Although the northern and southern white populations were similar in ethnic composition in 1830, seven out of every eight immigrants in the intervening period settled in the free states. As a result, the South's white population in 1860 was ethnically more homogeneous than the North's. The North also underwent more rapid urbanization and industrialization: Twenty-six percent of northerners lived in urban areas, and 40 percent had nonfarm occupations. In the South, only 10 percent lived in urban areas and 84 percent worked in agriculture. Most important, the North and South differed in their racial composition. Ninety-five percent of the nation's black population in 1860 lived in the South, where they composed 34 percent of the population. In contrast, blacks composed only 1 percent of the population of the free states. The 1860 census data also reveal the immense political problem of slavery and its abolition. The nearly four million slaves in the United States were "worth" approximately $1.2 billion, almost twenty times the size of the federal budget.

The late 1850s were replete with acrimonious attacks on and defenses of slavery. Although little information on the South's "peculiar institution" could be obtained from the 1850 census, abolitionists and proslavery pundits alike used census data to bolster their arguments. Both sides misused the few data that were available. Despite the heightened interest in the use of census data for social and economic analysis, no significant changes were made in the administration, content, or processing of the 1860 census. Congress did not pass any new legislation, and the 1860 census was taken under the 1850 census act. Joseph C. G. Kennedy was again appointed as census superintendent, and though he made a few modest changes to the schedules and instructions to assistant marshals to remedy misunderstandings in the 1850 census, there appears to have been little or no debate on the changes in Congress. The inquiry "profession, occupation, or trade" of males over fifteen years of age was extended to females over fifteen years of age, and a new question on personal wealth—"value of personal estate"—was added to the existing question "value of real estate."

The 1860 census was conducted in the field by 4,417 assistant marshals. From his experience processing the 1850 census returns, Kennedy was prepared for the large task of condensing the 1860 returns for publication. When the completed schedules began to arrive in the fall of 1860, he quickly increased the size of the clerical staff. At its maximum, the size of the office force reached 184, a small increase from 1850. In addition to cross-tabulating the returns and publishing the results, the Census Office assisted in the northern war effort. Kennedy prepared a report for President Lincoln on the number of men age eighteen to forty-five in the free, slave, and "border" states to compare the potential military strength of the Union and Confederacy. The 1860 census was also used to assess direct taxes to finance the war. Finally, the 1860 census was used to reallocate the House of Representatives after the abolition of slavery and the end of the three-fifths compromise.

The cost of the 1860 census was $3.47 million, or eight cents per capita. Kennedy oversaw the publication of three census volumes: a preliminary report published in 1862, the official population report in 1864, and a volume on agriculture also published in 1864. Additional volumes on manufactures and the statistics

of mortality and property were published under the direction of the secretary of the interior in 1865 and 1866, respectively. The combined published reports totaled 1,969 pages, up from 1,423 pages in 1850.

See also *Civil War and the census; Decennial censuses, 1850 census, 1870 census.*

■ J. David Hacker

Bibliography

Anderson, Margo J. *The American Census: A Social History.* New Haven: Yale University Press, 1988.
McPherson, James M. "Antebellum Southern Exceptionalism: A New Look at an Old Question." *Civil War History* 29 (1983): 230–244.
Magnuson, Diana Lynn. "The Making of a Modern Census: The United States Census of Population, 1790–1940." Ph.D. dissertation, University of Minnesota, 1995.
U.S. Bureau of the Census. *Historical Statistics of the United States, Colonial Times to 1970: Bicentennial Edition.* Washington, D.C.: U.S. Government Printing Office, 1975.
U.S. Census Office. *Agriculture of the United States in 1860; Compiled from the Original Returns of the Eighth Census.* Washington, D.C.: U.S. Government Printing Office, 1864.
U.S. Census Office. *Manufactures of the United States in 1860; Compiled from the Original Returns of the Eighth Census.* Washington, D.C., 1865.
U.S. Census Office. *Population of the United States in 1860; Compiled from the Original Returns of the Eighth Census.* Washington, D.C.: U.S. Government Printing Office, 1864.
U.S. Census Office. *Preliminary Report on the Eighth Census.* Washington, D.C.: U.S. Government Printing Office, 1862.
U.S. Census Office. *Statistics of the United States, (Including Mortality, Property, &c.,) in 1860; Compiled from the Original Returns and Being the Final Exhibit of the Eighth Census.* Washington, D.C.: A. O. P. Nicholson, 1866.
Wright, Carroll, and William C. Hunt. *History and Growth of the United States Census.* Washington, D.C.: U.S. Government Printing Office, 1900.

1870 census

The 1870 count put the U.S. population at 38,558,371. The total was revised later to 39,818,449 to adjust for a suspected undercount in thirteen southern states. Two hundred ninety-two seats in the House of Representatives were apportioned among the thirty-seven states. Between 1860 and 1870 the population increased 22.6

percent (26.6 percent after adjustment for the southern undercount), at that time the lowest decennial growth rate in the nation's history. Kansas, Nebraska, Nevada, and West Virginia were admitted as new states, and new territories were established in Arizona, Idaho, Montana, and Wyoming. The area of the United States remained at 3,021,295 square miles, resulting in a population density of 13.0 inhabitants per square mile. The total population living in urban places increased from 19.8 percent in 1860 to 25.7 percent in 1870.

Of the 38.6 million inhabitants of the United States originally enumerated in 1870, 33.6 million (87.1 percent) were classified by census enumerators as "White," 4.9 million (12.7 percent) as "Black" or "Mulatto," sixty-three thousand (0.2 percent) as "Chinese," and twenty-six thousand (0.1 percent) as "Indians Taxed"—meaning only those Native Americans living off reservations and no longer maintaining tribal affiliations. Continued immigration increased the percentage of the white population that was foreign-born from 15.2 percent in 1860 to 16.4 percent in 1870. Only the 1890 census recorded a higher percentage of foreign-born whites (16.6 percent). The 1870 census was the first census to record complete information for the newly freed black population. The total black population increased by 9.9 percent in the 1860s, down dramatically from the 22.1 percent increase in the previous decade.

The 1870 census was also the first census to apportion Congress after the passage of the Thirteenth Amendment, which abolished slavery and ended the three-fifths compromise. Ironically, Confederate defeat in the Civil War and the abolition of slavery resulted in the South receiving a bonus of about fifteen seats in the House of Representatives. The expected southern windfall explains in part northern Republican support for black suffrage and the Fourteenth Amendment, Section 2 of which reduced each state's apportionment by the percentage of males age twenty-one and older who were denied the right to vote on grounds other than rebellion or other crime.

Although Section 2 of the Fourteenth Amendment was never implemented, a House Select Committee was formed to investigate using the census to administer its political penalties. The committee, headed by James A. Garfield of Ohio, went further—calling on statistical experts for advice and proposing a major revision of the legislation governing the census. Garfield and the committee hoped that the elimination of Schedule No. 2 (Slave Inhabitants) would free up space to add new questions and refine existing ones. In addition to new questions mandated by the Fourteenth Amendment regarding the abridgment of citizenship rights, the committee proposed including a question on the relationship of each person to the head of the fam-

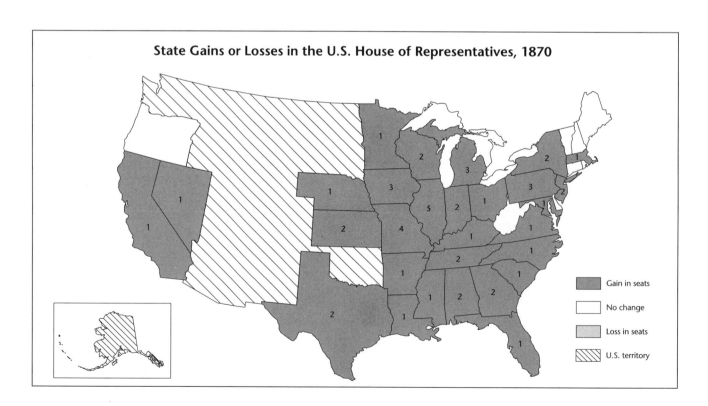

State Gains or Losses in the U.S. House of Representatives, 1870

Gain in seats

No change

Loss in seats

U.S. territory

ily, a question on each person's marital status, and a number of other questions regarding language spoken, religion professed, and whether parents were of foreign birth. Garfield also proposed changing the compensation system for enumerators, shortening the time allowed for the enumeration from months to days, and shifting the responsibility for the field enumeration from the U.S. marshals to field supervisors appointed for each congressional district. Passage of the Fifteenth Amendment, which nullified state laws restricting black suffrage, however, eliminated the ostensible reason for the census reforms, and the proposed legislation failed. In the end, a few additions were made to the population schedule. The category "Chinese" was added to the question on "Color"; literacy was divided into two questions intended to distinguish reading and writing capabilities; and new questions were added on month of birth (for individuals born within the year), month of marriage (for individuals married within the year), whether father was of foreign birth, whether mother was of foreign birth, whether a male citizen of the United States twenty-one years of age and upward, and whether a male citizen of the United States twenty-one years of age and upward whose right to vote was denied or abridged on grounds other than rebellion or other crime. The new schedules no longer inquired as to whether the individual was a pauper or convict. The census was administered under the 1850 law.

The 1870 census was taken under the supervision of Francis Amasa Walker, a twenty-nine-year-old relative newcomer to Washington, D.C., and a distinguished veteran of the Civil War. Walker's prior experience with the census was limited to a few months helping to draft a new census bill as a member of Garfield's staff. Despite his relative inexperience, Walker was the first superintendent to bring a modern, statistical approach to the census. Walker complained about his lack of control over the sixty-two marshals and 6,530 assistant marshals, but he was able to eliminate the practice of "farming out" subdivisions and "taking the census" at election and court days, practices believed to have been prevalent in the South in previous censuses. Walker believed that marshals were poorly trained for their duties as enumerators and that assistant marshals were often appointed for reasons of patronage with no regard to their qualifications. In Washington, where he was able to assert control, Walker tripled the size of the office staff to 450 in an effort to publish more detailed tabulations and shorten the time to publication. Although Walker exceeded his budget and had to return to Congress for more funds, the main volume on the statistics of population was published in 1872, one to two years earlier than in previous censuses. Three more volumes were published in 1872 and a statistical atlas was published in 1874. The combined published reports totaled 3,421 pages, up from 1,969 pages in 1860.

The 1870 count seemed to confirm Walker's dim view of the census field staff. Complaints of excessive undercounts in New York and Philadelphia resulted in the unusual step of the president ordering a recount. City boosters in Philadelphia believed that as much as a third of its population had not been enumerated. The recount, taken in the winter when the population was more likely to be indoors and with rigorous efforts on the part of city officials to ensure full enumeration, resulted in an increase of only 2.5 percent. New York's recount found only 2 percent more people. Ten years later, when the 1880 census was conducted, a more serious deficiency was discovered in the 1870 census's enumeration of the South. The population of most southern states had grown so dramatically that several observers charged the census with fraud in the form of overcounting. An investigation conducted by census geographer Henry Gannett, however, concluded that the 1870 count was too low, a result of the unsettled conditions in the Reconstruction South and the appointment of poorly trained enumerators, some of whom were said to be poorly educated blacks or "carpetbaggers" unfamiliar with the local terrain. The 1890 Census Office later estimated the 1870 undercount in the South at 1.26 million, or 10.1 percent of the southern population. Although no modern investigation has been conducted to verify the undercount estimates—which ignored the potential demographic impact of the Civil War and assumed linear population growth between 1860 and 1880—the 1890 census office's adjusted total for the 1870 population (39.8 million) is preferred by most historians and is typically cited in official census publications.

See also *Civil War and the census; Decennial censuses, 1850 census, 1860 census, 1880 census.*

■ J. David Hacker

Bibliography

Anderson, Margo J. *The American Census: A Social History.* New Haven: Yale University Press, 1988.

Hacker, J. David. "The Human Cost of War: White Population in the United States, 1850–1880." Ph.D. dissertation, University of Minnesota, 1999.

Magnuson, Diana Lynn. "The Making of a Modern Census: The United States Census of Population, 1790–1940." Ph.D. dissertation, University of Minnesota, 1995.

U.S. Bureau of the Census. *Historical Statistics of the United States, Colonial Times to 1970: Bicentennial Edition.* Washington, D.C.: U.S. Government Printing Office, 1975.

U.S. Census Office. *A Compendium of the Ninth Census.* Washington, D.C.: U.S. Government Printing Office, 1872.

U.S. Census Office. *Ninth Census,* Volume I: *The Statistics of the Population of the United States.* Washington, D.C.: U.S. Government Printing Office, 1872.

U.S. Census Office. *Ninth Census,* Volume II: *The Vital Statistics of the United States.* Washington, D.C.: U.S. Government Printing Office, 1872.

U.S. Census Office. *Ninth Census,* Volume III: *The Statistics of the Wealth and Industry of the United States.* Washington, D.C.: U.S. Government Printing Office, 1872.

U.S. Census Office. *Statistical Atlas of the United States Based on the Results of the Ninth Census.* New York: J. Bien, 1874.

Wright, Carroll, and William C. Hunt. *History and Growth of the United States Census.* Washington, D.C.: U.S. Government Printing Office, 1900.

1880 census

The population of the United States in 1880 was 50,155,783. Three hundred and thirty-two House seats were apportioned among the thirty-eight states. The area of the country was 3,021,295 square miles. One hundred fifty supervisors and 31,382 enumerators conducted fieldwork for the census. The tenth census was administrated by the Department of the Interior from Washington, D.C. Francis Amasa Walker served as superintendent of census from 1879 to 1881; Charles W. Seaton, from 1881 to 1885. The total cost of the census was $5,790,000.

The content of the census, dictated by the Census Act of March 3, 1879, required enumerators to return responses to twenty-six questions. The schedule contained eight questions on home and personal qualities; four on marital status; two on occupation; six on health; three on education; and three on nativity. Of particular significance were the questions regarding the relationship of each person to the head of the household and the civil condition of each person (single, married, widowed, or divorced). Walker and others concerned with the census of population had lobbied for these queries since before 1870.

The Census Act of 1879 and the April 20, 1880, amendment ushered in a new era of administrating the census and marked a high point in census innovation and experimentation. First, the 1879 legislation eliminated the marshals who fulfilled decennial canvassing duties and replaced them with a much larger field force appointed exclusively and tem-

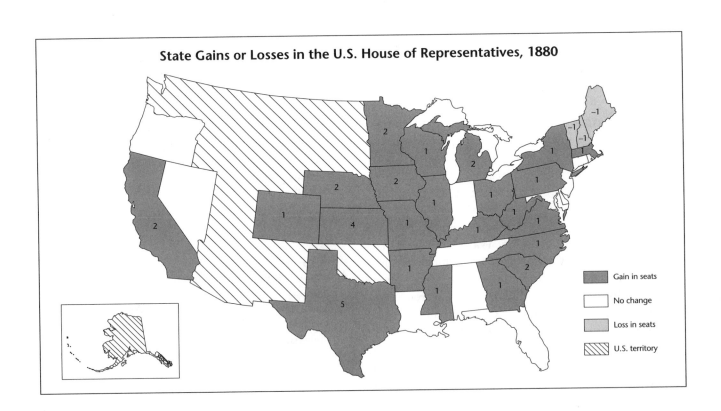

State Gains or Losses in the U.S. House of Representatives, 1880

porarily for the task of enumerating the population.

The new law divided the country into specially drawn supervisors' districts, instead of judicial districts, as administrative units for overseeing census-taking. Responsibility for dividing the country into 150 census districts, each with its own resident supervisor, lay with the census superintendent, contingent upon the approval of the secretary of the interior. Supervisors' districts did not cross state or territorial lines. Supervisors were nominated by the president, in consultation with the superintendent, and were confirmed by the Senate. The secretary of the interior designated the number of supervisors to be appointed for each state and territory, but each state was to have at least one. Under the new census law, supervisors were required to be residents of the state or territory of their appointment.

In addition to supervisors' districts, the 1879 census law required the use of smaller and more clearly defined enumeration districts (in 1870 enumeration districts were limited to twenty thousand people; in 1880 they were cut to four thousand). The task of defining enumeration districts fell upon census supervisors who followed specific rules defined by the Census Office. One of the most important tasks of the census supervisors was the selection of enumerators. The census law and Superintendent Walker set general guidelines for supervisors to follow in choosing canvassers. Simply, supervisors were required to solicit and encourage qualified applicants and to make appointments based on each applicant's merit.

Second, the 1879 law bolstered the administrative position of the superintendent of the census within the Department of the Interior. Prior to 1879, the position of superintendent of the census had only the sanction of appropriation acts. According to the new census law, the superintendent was to be appointed by the president, with the advice and consent of the Senate, and the post terminated when the census returns were compiled and published. Almost immediately after his appointment, Walker began the task of assembling his clerical staff in Washington. One of Walker's first appointments was Charles W. Seaton as chief clerk. The 1880 census machinery, which reached a peak of 1,495 employees, was more than triple the size of the 1870 census clerical staff.

Additional changes in census law included shortening the enumeration period to the first two weeks in June, significantly increasing the penalty for noncompliance with the census from $30 to $100, and issuing preliminary results of the census. Beginning with the 1880 census, the Census Office experimented with issuing periodic bulletins containing preliminary results of the population count. The experiment was so successful that the Census Office continued its use in successive censuses and expanded it to include other principal results.

Superintendent Walker exerted considerable influence over the development and implementation of procedures governing training and overseeing his field staff. Many of Walker's procedural innovations in 1880 would be used and refined in succeeding censuses. A decade before, Walker had experienced great frustration over his inability to adequately train and supervise his vast field staff for enumerating the census. Walker rectified this situation for the 1880 census. Supervisors and enumerators received instructions regarding responsibilities, pay rates, commissions and oaths, and details outlining completing a census schedule prior to the enumeration period. All enumerators were required to report each day, via a standard form on postal cards, to the central office in Washington and their district supervisor. These daily reports indicated the number of hours and minutes engaged in the service as well as the number of persons, farms, manufacturing establishments, and deaths enumerated that day. Given the widespread efforts to check the quality of the first few days' fieldwork, Walker likely dictated this step to the supervisors.

The Census Office produced a record number of publications at the close of the 1880 census: twenty-two quarto volumes, a compendium in two parts, and a monograph. The total number of pages in published reports was 21,458.

■ Diana L. Magnuson

Bibliography

Anderson, Margo J. *The American Census: A Social History*. New Haven: Yale University Press, 1988.

Holt, W. Stull. *The Bureau of the Census: Its History, Activities, and Organization*. Washington, D.C.: Brookings Institution, 1929.

Magnuson, Diana L. "The Making of a Modern Census: The United States Census of Population, 1790–1940." Ph.D. dissertation, University of Minnesota, 1995.

Wright, Carroll D., and William C. Hunt. *The History and Growth of the United States Census*. Washington, D.C.: U.S. Government Printing Office, 1900.

1890 census

According to the 1890 census, the population of the United States was 62,947,714. Included in the enumeration were the territories of Idaho, Oklahoma, and Wyoming. Three hundred and fifty-seven seats in the House of Representatives were apportioned among the forty-two states. The area of the country was 3,021,295 square miles. One hundred seventy-five supervisors and 46,804 enumerators conducted fieldwork for the census. The eleventh census was administered by the Department of the Interior from Washington, D.C., and was overseen by Robert P. Porter, who served as superintendent of census from 1889 to 1893, and Carroll D. Wright, who served from 1893 to 1897. The total cost of the census was $11,547,000.

The content of the census of population, as stipulated by the Census Act of March 1, 1889, required enumerators to return responses to thirty household questions. The schedule contained five questions regarding personal description; two each regarding marital status, occupation, and health; three regarding education; six regarding nativity; five regarding home and farm ownership; and one question each regarding veteran status, ability to speak English, female fertility, whether a prisoner, convict, homeless child, or pauper, and the supplemental schedule. Five groups of inquiries

made their first appearance on the 1890 population schedule: fertility, citizenship, ability to speak English, and ownership of homes and farms. The fertility and citizenship queries had been lobbied for in past census debates. The "mother of how many children" and "number of these children living" were used in the Massachusetts and Rhode Island state censuses in 1885 with relative success. The inclusion of the queries regarding citizenship, "number of years in the United States," "whether naturalized," and "whether naturalization papers have been taken out" had been urged upon Congress in past decades. National concern with the enormous number of immigrants entering the United States from southern and eastern Europe during this period likely contributed to the inclusion of these questions, as well as the question on ability to speak English. The scope of the 1890 enumeration was greater than any previous census.

Administratively speaking, the structure of the census machinery began what would be a trend of institutional expansion. The Census Act of 1889 provided that the secretary of the interior could appoint a chief clerk, a disbursing clerk, two stenographers, ten chiefs of division, ninety clerks of classes one through four (clerks were classified according to job description and pay scale), and as many clerk, copyist, and computers as deemed necessary. In addition, the secretary of the

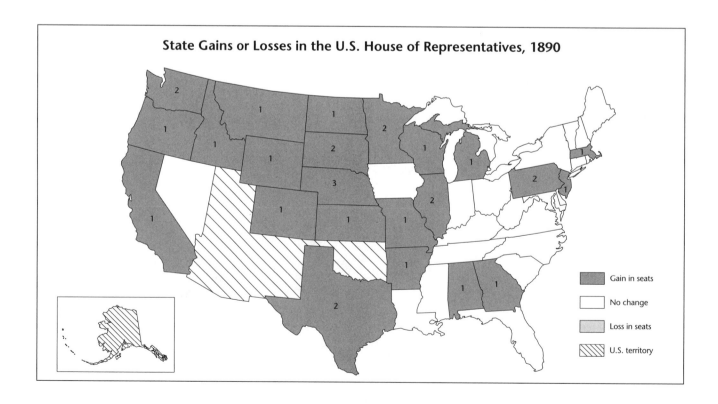

State Gains or Losses in the U.S. House of Representatives, 1890

interior was authorized to appoint watchmen, messengers, and charwomen. The maximum number of census office employees for the 1890 census was 3,143.

The adoption of the family schedule in 1890 permitted experimentation with its use as a prior schedule. The schedules were distributed to all known households prior to the official date of enumeration and on enumeration day an enumerator retrieved the completed schedule and answered any questions. Despite initial praise for this innovation, the use of separate forms for each household was cumbersome, and the 1900 census of population schedule returned to the familiar format.

The 1890 census was taken under the model of training and oversight instituted by Francis A. Walker for the tenth census. The only discernible differences in the training and oversight of field staff in 1890 from the 1880 enumeration were the creation of a "supervisors correspondence" position within the Census Office (held by a single special agent) and an increase in the detail of supervisor and enumerator instructions.

For the first time in census history, the work of tabulating census results was carried out by automatic tabulating machinery. Herman Hollerith invented the "Hollerith system," which utilized a single punched card for each person enumerated. Details from the population schedule were transferred to cards via a punched hole. The cards were then run through an electric tabulating machine that counted the data entered on them. The Hollerith system afforded the Census Office not only greater accuracy and speed in compiling the results, but also the opportunity to manipulate various combinations of population statistics heretofore impossible. Thus the published results of the 1890 census of population are much more detailed than those of previous censuses.

The Census Office produced a record number of publications at the close of the 1890 census of population: twenty-four volumes, a compendium in three parts, an abstract, and a statistical atlas. The total number of pages in published reports was 26,408.

■ Diana L. Magnuson

Bibliography

Anderson, Margo J. *The American Census: A Social History.* New Haven: Yale University Press, 1988.

Holt, W. Stull. *The Bureau of the Census: Its History, Activities, and Organization.* Washington, D.C.: Brookings Institution, 1929.

Magnuson, Diana L. "The Making of a Modern Census: The United States Census of Population, 1790–1940." Ph.D. dissertation, University of Minnesota, 1995.

Wright, Carroll D., and William C. Hunt. *The History and Growth of the United States Census.* Washington, D.C.: U.S. Government Printing Office, 1900.

1900 census

The 1900 census put the U.S. population at 75,994,575. Included in the enumeration were the territories of Hawaii and Oklahoma. Three hundred and ninety-one seats in the House of Representatives were apportioned among the forty-five states. The area of the country was 3,021,295 square miles. Three hundred supervisors and 52,871 enumerators conducted the fieldwork for the census. The twelfth census was administered by the Department of the Interior from Washington, D.C. William R. Merriam was director of the census from 1899 to 1903; Simon N. D. North, from 1903 to 1909. The total cost of the census was $11,854,000.

The content of the census of population, provided for by the Census Act of March 3, 1899, required enumerators to return responses to twenty-eight questions. The schedule contained twelve questions regarding home and personal characteristics; three each regarding nativity, citizenship, and ownership of home; two regarding occupation; four regarding education; and one regarding the number on the farm schedule. Three of these queries were new to the 1900 census: date of birth, number of years married, and year of immigration to the United States. Questions about the health status of Americans were moved from the population schedule to a separate schedule. In addition, the economic censuses, which became more elaborate in the late nineteenth century, were shifted to a different year so as not to compete in terms of resources with the population census.

The administrative machinery of the 1900 census remained relatively constant with that of the preceding two censuses. Several legislated changes should be noted, however. First, the title of the head of the Census Office was renamed from superintendent to director of the census. Second, a new position, assistant director of the census, was created with the stipulation that it be filled by "an experienced practical statistician." The assistant director was to serve only during the three-year decennial census period (beginning the year before the census). Third, power to appoint and remove Census Office

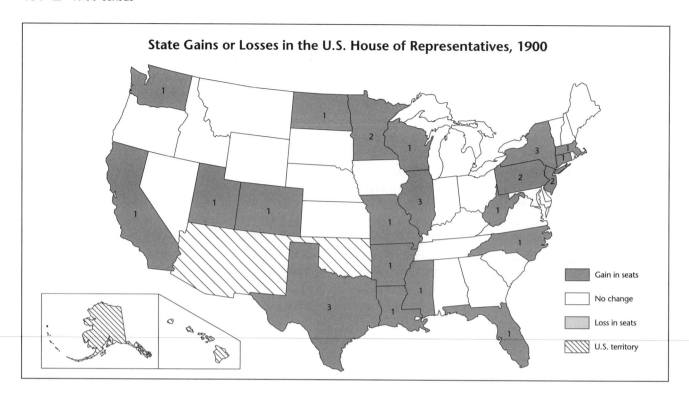

State Gains or Losses in the U.S. House of Representatives, 1900

Gain in seats

No change

Loss in seats

U.S. territory

employees was shifted from the secretary of the interior to the director of the census, significantly strengthening the administrative position of the director of the census. All the director's appointees, with the exception of enumerators, special agents, and the lowest paid laborers, were required to pass noncompetitive examinations to assume their posts. The maximum size of the 1900 census office force was 3,447.

The 1900 census was taken under the model of training and oversight instituted by Francis A. Walker for the 1880 census with two notable innovations, the enumerator examination and the street book. Prior to 1900, supervisors made enumerator appointments based upon their own judgment of the character and competency of each applicant. For the 1900 census, enumerator applicants were required to submit to a written, nonproctored examination. The street book remained part of the enumerator's portfolio for succeeding censuses. The Census Office used the street book to aid in the enumeration of larger municipalities and to counter any complaints against the accuracy of the returns. The street book facilitated organization and completeness of the canvass on the part of the enumerator; canvassers used it to account for every house, building, or place of abode in their enumeration district. Supervisors in turn used the street book to verify the completeness of each enumerator's canvass. Just as in 1890, the 1900 decen-nial census of population saw an increase in the volume of instructions for facilitating training and oversight of supervisors and enumerators.

Electrical tabulating machines, first introduced at the 1890 census, were again employed in the compilation of the 1900 results. The practicality the machines demonstrated a decade earlier convinced census officials to employ their use on a large scale in 1900, and the innovations of the automatic feeder and sorting machine increased their effectiveness.

In 1902 Congress enacted the Permanent Census Act, which made the census bureau a permanent agency within the Department of the Interior. One year later the Census Office became part of the newly created Department of Commerce and Labor. It was generally appreciated that the enormity of the task assigned to the Census Office warranted an intercensal period, to both complete the previous census and prepare for the next. The Census Office produced ten volumes and an abstract of the 1900 census. The total number of pages in published reports was 10,925.

■ Diana L. Magnuson

Bibliography

Anderson, Margo J. *The American Census: A Social History*. New Haven: Yale University Press, 1988.

Holt, W. Stull. *The Bureau of the Census: Its History, Activities, and Organization*. Washington, D.C.: Brookings Institution, 1929.

Magnuson, Diana L. "The Making of a Modern Census: The United States Census of Population, 1790–1940." Ph.D. dissertation, University of Minnesota, 1995.

1910 census

The population of the United States in 1910 was 91,972,266. Included in the enumeration were the territories of Hawaii and Puerto Rico. Four hundred and thirty-five House seats were apportioned among the forty-six states. The area of the country was 3,021,295 square miles. For the first time in eighty years, the date of enumeration was changed from June 1 to April 15. Three hundred thirty-five supervisors and 70,286 enumerators conducted fieldwork for the census. The thirteenth census was administered by the Department of Commerce and Labor from Washington, D.C. Edward Dana Durand was director of the census from 1909 to 1913; William J. Harris, from 1913 to 1914; and Samuel L. Rogers, from 1915 to 1921. The total cost of the census was $15,968,000.

The Census Act of July 2, 1909, required enumerators to return responses to thirty-two questions. The schedule contained eleven questions on home and personal characteristics; three on nativity; two on citizenship; one on language; five on occupation; three on education; four on home ownership; two on health; and one on service in the Civil War. An amendment to the 1909 census act, passed on March 24, 1910, required the enumeration of the mother tongue of each respondent's mother and father, thus bringing the total number of questions on the 1910 schedule to thirty-four.

The establishment of a permanent Census Bureau—first within the Department of the Interior in 1902 and then as part of the Department of Commerce and Labor in 1903—affected the 1910 census of population in several important ways. First, having a permanent bureau facilitated an unusually early start on the 1910 decennial census. Second, after 1903 the secretary of commerce and labor appointed a special advisory commission on the recommendation of the director of the census. Responsibilities of the special advisory commission included evaluating the conditions surrounding census work and preparing a report to educate Congress before it enacted legislation for the 1910 census. Third, a permanent census office afforded the bureau intercensal periods to become more sophisti-

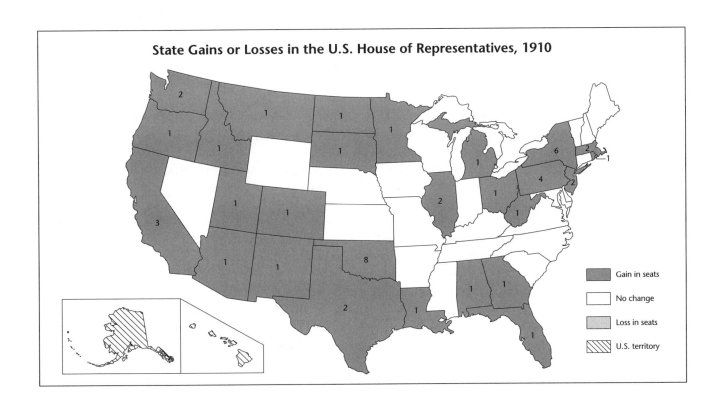

State Gains or Losses in the U.S. House of Representatives, 1910

cated in its administrative structure, interpret the results of the enumeration, and prepare for the next census.

The structure of the 1910 census closely resembled that of its immediate predecessor. A few refinements dictated by the new census law are noteworthy. First, the director was empowered to appoint by recommendation a geographer, a chief statistician, an appointment clerk, a private secretary, two stenographers, and eight expert chiefs of division, all without examination by the secretary of commerce and labor. Only the assistant director was appointed by the president with the advice and consent of the Senate. Breaking from the tradition of previous censuses, the remaining positions of two hundred clerks of classes one through four, clerks, copyists, skilled and unskilled laborers, and charwomen were appointed by the director of the census in the order of their rating on eligibility lists and in accordance with civil service rules. This change in the method of appointing lower level office employees was considered a vast improvement over the old practices that were largely based upon patronage. The maximum size of the census office force was 3,738.

Creation of the permanent Census Bureau did not significantly alter enumeration procedure. Refinements in the selection process and in training and oversight of field staff, however, continued to be the trend. Supervisors were required to apply for the positions and were theoretically chosen based upon their qualifications. Once appointed to their positions, supervisors received copious written instructions and were required to attend training conventions held in major cities across the United States. At these conventions the director or assistant director of the census, accompanied by the chief statistician for population or the chief statistician for agriculture, gave oral instructions to the supervisors and answered their questions. Beginning in 1910, persons seeking enumerator posts were required to submit an application to their respective supervisors and take a competitive proctored exam. Enumerators received a carefully revised instruction manual, oral instructions from their supervisors, and continuous supervision and instruction over the course of the enumeration period. A new member of the field staff, the inspector, became an extension of the supervisor. Inspectors were hired to help supervisors maintain constant contact with enumerators and provide information and oversight.

The Census Bureau published eleven volumes as well as *Abstract of the Census, Statistical Atlas of the United States, The Blind in the United States (1910), Deaf Mutes in the United States (1910), and Indian Population in the United States and Alaska.* The total number of pages in published reports was 11,456.

■ Diana L. Magnuson

Bibliography

Anderson, Margo J. *The American Census: A Social History.* New Haven: Yale University Press, 1988.

Holt, W. Stull. *The Bureau of the Census: Its History, Activities, and Organization.* Washington, D.C.: Brookings Institution, 1929.

Magnuson, Diana L. "The Making of a Modern Census: The United States Census of Population, 1790–1940." Ph.D. dissertation, University of Minnesota, 1995.

1920 census

The 1920 census put the U.S. population at 105,710,620. Included in the enumeration were the territories of Guam, Hawaii, the Panama Canal Zone, Puerto Rico, and Samoa. House seats were not reapportioned following the 1920 census. The area of the country was 3,021,295 square miles. For only the second time in ninety years, the enumeration date of the census was changed; the canvass was moved up from April 15 to January 1. Three hundred seventy-two supervisors and 87,234 enumerators conducted fieldwork for the census. Women were employed as supervisors for the first time; three received original appointments and two were appointed to fill vacancies. The census was administered by the Department of Commerce from Washington, D.C. Samuel L. Rogers (1915–1921) and William Mott Steuart (1921–1933) served as director of the census. The total cost of the census was $25,117,000.

The Census Act of March 3, 1919, required enumerators to return responses to twenty-nine questions. The schedule contained ten questions on home and personal characteristics; two on home ownership; three each on citizenship and education; seven on nativity and mother tongue; and four on occupation.

Administratively the 1920 census machinery closely followed that of the 1910 census. Two changes affecting the organization of the Census Bureau are noteworthy. First, the 1919 law authorized the director of the census to appoint as many temporary clerks in classes one through nine as necessary, provided that they had passed an examination guided by Civil Service Commission rules. Second, the 372 supervisors provided for under the new census law were to be appointed by the secretary of commerce upon the recommendation of the director. Since the Census Act of 1879 supervisors were appointed by the president with the advice and consent of the Senate. The maximum size of the census office force in Washington was 6,301.

The administration of the 1920 census, the fourteenth decennial census, continued the process of refining the training and oversight of census field staff. The Census Bureau carefully revised all schedules, forms, and instructions for field staff. In an effort to facilitate greater accuracy of the enumeration, the trend toward greater contact between the director of the census and his supervisors continued. The innovation of supervisors conferences directed by census administrators, begun in 1910, was continued. Greater personal contact was also built into the training and oversight of enumerators by their respective supervisors. Supervisors in large cities were authorized to employ one or two inspectors to provide daily support in overseeing enumerators.

Probably the most significant result of the 1920 tabulation was the Census Bureau report that a majority of Americans, for the first time in U.S. history, lived in "urban" places (defined as having populations of twenty-five hundred or more). The statistic raised controversy among the American public. Three concerns emerged as "old stock" American statistical analysts contemplated this momentous demographic change. First, a decline in the rural population and a gain in the urban population were perceived as a harbinger of the end of political liberty. Jeffersonian republican political theory had relied on the virtue of independent yeoman farmers and artisans to sustain political liberty and institutions, and these population groups were a declining proportion of the national population. Second, the constitutionally mandated reapportionment mechanism automatically shifted political power from those areas of the country with declining populations to those with growing populations. Until the last quarter of the nineteenth century, this power had shifted westward. After the 1920 census, states with large urban populations (located primarily in the northeast) clearly would be the apportionment winners. Third, urban growth was being fueled by immigration, not natural reproduction of native-born Americans. Nativists feared the impact of urban immigrant working-class political power on the national scene.

Nonapportionment of the 1920s

The 1920s was the only decade in American history in which the House and electoral college were not reapportioned according to population changes. The reasons for this are numerous and complex. The size of the House increased at every apportionment since the beginning of Congress, except in 1840. There were physical limitations of the House chamber to hold even the 435 seats allotted in 1910. However, the apportionment debate centered not only on practical gains and losses of congressional seats and power but also on serious social and political feelings and demographic questions that cut to the heart of a changing America.

The apportionment debate began as usual after the report of the 1920 census data. The basic controversy centered on two propositions: (1) expand the House once more to accommodate all states and ensure no losses of seats; or (2) fix the House size at 435 and reapportion accordingly. The debate began in 1921 and lasted virtually the entire decade. Many of the arguments used were as old as the Republic with respect to the size of the House and political representation.

Those arguing for an increased size of the House put forth the following rationale:

1. The recent enfranchisement of women meant an increase in the size of the average constituency and the need for more representatives.
2. More representatives would better serve democracy since they could be located closer to their constituents.
3. More representatives would keep power from being concentrated in the hands of a few.
4. The mathematical formula was generally unfair.
5. The census figures were inaccurate, especially in rural areas.
6. The nation was disrupted by World War I and an accurate count was not made.[1]

Those arguing for keeping the size of the House at 435 and for passing an apportionment bill immediately put forth the following rationale:

1. More representatives would lessen the efficiency of the House operation.
2. More representatives would decrease the amount of debate time for all.

continued

Nonapportionment of the 1920s *continued*

3. More representatives would incur additional cost.
4. There should be fair redistribution of representatives and districts.
5. The American people and media supported reapportionment.
6. The Constitution mandated action on reapportionment every ten years.

One argument to increase the size of the House or to delay apportionment was new to the debate or at least was brought up in a consistent and vitriolic way as never before in American history. This argument concerned the growth of the city and its influence on American politics and culture. In the floor debate, the urban-rural conflict was brought out, usually by fearful rural representatives, as one significant theme. City values were corrupting fundamental native "American" religious and moral life. City bosses were corrupting American political life. Cites were filled with immigrants wishing to repeal prohibition. Cities were filled with immigrants wishing to repeal the new restrictive immigration laws. The hostility toward the city brought out the fear of changing economic, cultural, social, demographic, and technological realities of twentieth-century America.

An analysis of roll-call voting on the various apportionment bills suggests that the representatives from states likely to lose seats wanted an increased House size or no apportionment at all. These states were usually rural agricultural states (see maps showing state gains or losses in 1910 and 1930). Representatives from states

likely to increase in seats favored fixing the size of the House and passing an apportionment bill. These states usually had urban industrial areas and other growing areas. The states that had no change in seats were critical. Rural "no change" states seemed to vote against reapportionment, especially from the Democratic rural South. Urban "no changers" tended to support reapportionment, many from the Republican Northeast.[2]

In spite of the constitutional and legal questions involved, Congress did not pass an apportionment bill after the census. The 1922 elections were held with the same numbers given to each state in 1910. Throughout the 1920s apportionment was debated on and off with the same forces in the House and Senate aligning and blocking passage of a bill. As the time for a new census came near sentiment arose to once again make apportionment automatic with the census as in 1850 and 1860. With President Herbert Hoover's support, a bill was passed in 1929 to incorporate apportionment in the census with automatic calculations based on a House fixed at 435 seats. This system of automatic reapportionment has been in effect since that time.

1. Charles W. Eagles, *Democracy Delayed: Congressional Reapportionment and the Urban-Rural Conflict in the 1920s* (Athens, Ga.: University of Georgia Press, 1990), 33-62; Lawrence F. Schmeckebier, *Congressional Apportionment* (Washington, D.C.: Brookings Institution, 1941), 120-124.
2. Eagles, *Democracy*, 85-115.

Source: Kenneth C. Martis and Gregory A. Elmes, *The Historical Atlas of State Power in Congress, 1790-1990* (Washington, D.C.: Congressional Quarterly, 1993), 163-165.

Within this milieu, a debate over the method of apportionment postponed the passage of the fifteenth census bill, providing for the 1930 census, until June 1929 (*see box, "Nonapportionment of the 1920s"*). The bill that passed required an automatic apportionment if Congress took no action (as it had done in the 1920s). The language of the bill directed that a present Congress could not bind a future Congress, but apportionment would not be delayed.

The Census Bureau published a number of volumes by the end of the 1920 census period: eleven major volumes, *Abstract of the Fourteenth Census, Statistical Atlas of the United States, Children in Gainful Occupations, Deaf-Mute Population of the United States, Blind Popula-*

tion of the United States, and seven monographs. The total number of pages in published reports was 14,550.

■ Diana L. Magnuson

Bibliography

Anderson, Margo J. *The American Census: A Social History.* New Haven: Yale University Press, 1988.

Holt, W. Stull. *The Bureau of the Census: Its History, Activities, and Organization.* Washington, D.C.: Brookings Institution, 1929.

Magnuson, Diana L. "The Making of a Modern Census: The United States Census of Population, 1790–1940." Ph.D. dissertation, University of Minnesota, 1995.

1930 census

The population of the United States in 1930 was 122,775,046. Included in the enumeration were the territories of Guam, Hawaii, the Panama Canal Zone, Puerto Rico, Samoa, and the Virgin Islands. Four hundred and thirty-five seats in the House of Representatives were apportioned among the forty-eight states. The area of the country was 3,021,295 square miles. The enumeration date was moved back to April 1, 1930, from the January 1 date of the 1920 census. Five hundred seventy-five supervisors and 87,756 enumerators conducted fieldwork for the census. The census was administered by the Department of Commerce from Washington, D.C., and under the supervision of Director of the Census William Mott Steuart (1921–1933). The total cost of the census was $40,156,000.

The content of the census of population, provided for by the Census Act of June 18, 1929, required enumerators to return responses to thirty-two questions. The schedule contained fifteen questions regarding home and personal qualities; two each regarding education, veteran status, and employment; three each regarding nativity, citizenship, and occupation and industry; and one each regarding mother tongue and the number on the farm schedule. While the majority of the queries were "standard" and represented merely an amplification of past questions or categories, two questions—on homemaker status and radio set ownership—reflected Congress's growing interest in the changing status of women and the new "consumer economy" in the first quarter of the twentieth century.

The 1930 census was administered much like its immediate predecessor. However, the 1929 census law did make a few significant changes. First, two assistant directors, appointed by the secretary of commerce upon the recommendation of the director of the census, were provided for in the new legislation. Since 1899, census legislation had required the appointment of a single assistant director by the president, with the advice and

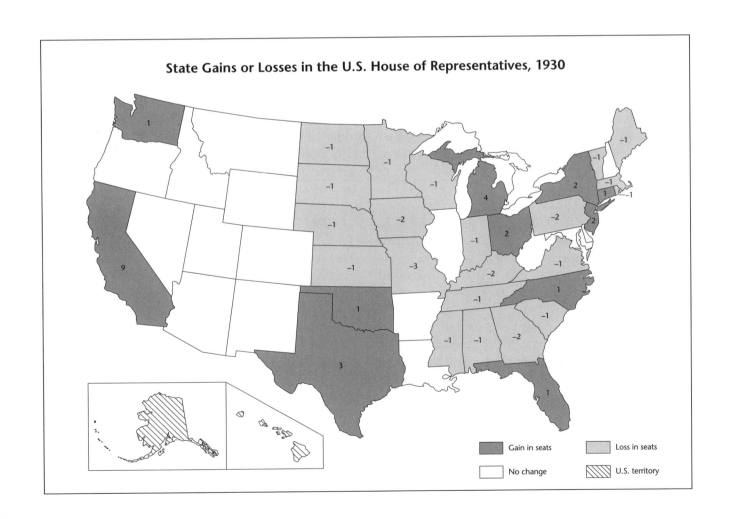

State Gains or Losses in the U.S. House of Representatives, 1930

Gain in seats

Loss in seats

No change

U.S. territory

consent of the Senate. For the fifteenth decennial census, one assistant director acted as the executive assistant to the director and performed the duties previously assigned to the chief clerk. The other assistant director served as the technical and statistical adviser to the director and was required to possess experience in statistical work. Second, the 1929 census legislation empowered the director of the census to hire as many temporary employees as deemed necessary for the work during the decennial census period. In addition, the director fixed the rates of compensation for all temporary clerical employees. Third, civil service rules were applied to the appointment process of special agents; supervisors, supervisors' clerks, enumerators, and interpreters were exempt from civil service examination.

An alteration in the 1929 census law regarding the apportionment process had important ramifications for the 1930 and future censuses. A protracted and contentious debate over the issue held up passage of the census bill until June 1929. The final compromise bill required an automatic apportionment if, as in the 1920s, Congress took no action. The bill stipulated that a present Congress could not bind a future Congress. However, apportionment could not be delayed.

In an effort to increase the accuracy of the canvass, as well as expedite training and oversight of enumerators' work, the Census Bureau increased the total number of supervisors from 372 to 575. As in previous twentieth-century censuses, supervisors received advance instructions for carrying out the details of the enumeration. These instructions were again in the form of pamphlets, supplemental written instructions in the form of letters, and oral instructions given at conferences. The Census Bureau facilitated constant communication between the bureau in Washington and the supervisors. Enumerators received a revised pamphlet of instructions as well as oral instructions from their respective supervisors and field assistants. In 1930 inspectors were called field assistants but served the same purpose of instructing and advising enumerators.

The Census Bureau published a total of thirty-two volumes by the end of the 1930 decennial census period, including six volumes on the population, two on unemployment, and an abstract. The total number of pages in published reports was 35,700.

■ Diana L. Magnuson

Bibliography

Anderson, Margo J. *The American Census: A Social History.* New Haven: Yale University Press, 1988.

Holt, W. Stull. *The Bureau of the Census: Its History, Activities, and Organization.* Washington, D.C.: Brookings Institution, 1929.

Magnuson, Diana L. "The Making of a Modern Census: The United States Census of Population, 1790–1940." Ph.D. dissertation, University of Minnesota, 1995.

1940 census

The population of the continental United States in 1940 was 131,669,275. Four hundred thirty-five seats in the House of Representatives were apportioned among the forty-eight states.

Developments in the 1930s

The Census Bureau faced drastic staff reductions after completion of the 1930 census. But the election of Franklin D. Roosevelt in 1932 brought new government programs and expanded demand for statistical information. The Roosevelt administration worked closely with professional organizations to create a plan for improved collection of statistical data.

The Committee on Government Statistics and Information Services (COGSIS) was created in 1933 under the sponsorship of the American Statistical Association (ASA) and the Social Science Research Council (SSRC), with funding from the Rockefeller Foundation. COGSIS operated from June 1934 to December 1935, providing statistical advisory services to the secretaries of agriculture, commerce, interior, and labor and offering an opportunity for reorganization and coordination of federal statistical services.

COGSIS influenced the Census Bureau in two ways. First, the committee responded to a request from Director of the Census William Lane Austin to survey the bureau's work in the field of population. COGSIS solicited confidential comments from users of population data, reviewed the population schedule and tabulation procedures, and made various recommendations. Second, vital Census Bureau personnel came from COGSIS. Stuart A. Rice, president of ASA and chair of COGSIS in the summer of 1933, served as assistant director of the bureau from 1933 to 1935. He was instrumental in the hiring of Calvert L. Dedrick, a former researcher at SSRC and staff member of COGSIS, who was named assistant chief statistician in 1937. Dedrick played a central role in Morris H. Hansen beginning work in the area of sampling.

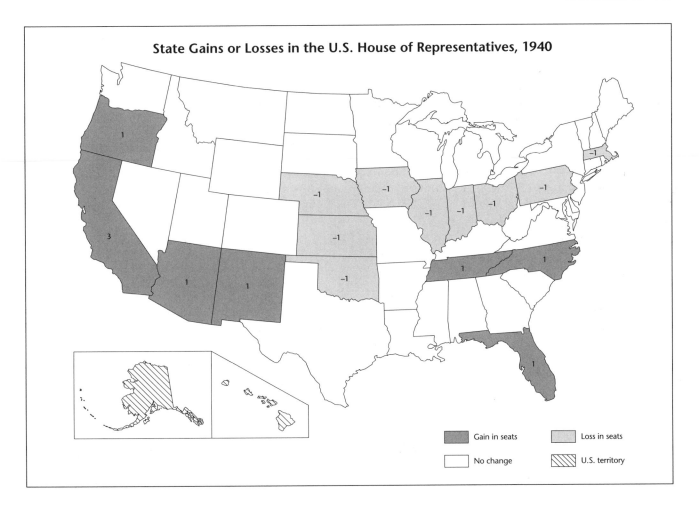

State Gains or Losses in the U.S. House of Representatives, 1940

Gain in seats • Loss in seats • No change • U.S. territory

Congress approved a national unemployment census in 1937, on the basis of a voluntary registration of unemployed and partially employed persons. A temporary agency was established under the direction of John D. Biggers to carry out the unemployment census. Biggers requested that Director Austin provide the personnel for the operation. He assigned Dedrick and several other bureau staff to the project.

Along with many other statisticians, Dedrick had opposed voluntary registration for conducting the census, arguing that it would bias the results. He convinced Biggers that a check census was necessary, and a 2 percent sample representing the 80 percent of the population served by postal delivery routes was designed. The household enumeration of this sample was the first nationwide use of probability and area sampling to canvass a population from which no lists were available. Results from the probability sample were used to estimate error rates in the voluntary figures. The bureau was also involved in editing and tabulating the results, offering valuable experience for the 1940 census.

Preparations for the 1940 Census

In the Census Act of 1929, the director of the Census Bureau gained responsibility for developing specific census questions, subject to approval by the secretary of commerce. In early 1939 Austin requested the chief statisticians of the various bureau divisions to develop a schedule for the 1940 census. A tentative schedule was presented for public discussion at conferences in March and April. These also covered the use of sampling techniques for inclusion of questions not appearing on the main population schedule. In addition, a technical advisory committee held meetings on the proposed schedule in the late spring of 1939. On the basis of these efforts, preliminary schedules, instructions, and other forms were tested in a special census in Indiana in August 1939.

Reflecting the economic problems of the era, the 1940 census brought added emphasis to questions of the national labor force. The first complete classification of work status for all persons fourteen years and over in a specific week (March 24–30, 1940) was introduced to replace the concept of "gainful worker" used in 1930. Number of weeks worked in 1939 was added to further measure unemployment. A new, eleven-category scheme of occupational classification developed by Alba M. Edwards was introduced, and a new industrial classification based upon the Standard Industrial Classification was used.

Two questions on income in 1939 were recommended for inclusion on the 1940 population schedule: (1) the amount of wages or salary received and (2) whether or not more than $50 was from sources other than wages or salary. These questions generated some public criticism and adverse publicity. Senator Charles W. Tobey of New Hampshire called on the secretary of commerce to delete the questions but was refused. He then introduced a Senate resolution requiring deletion of the questions. However, Senate leadership did not allow the resolution to get out of committee. In response to the controversy, the bureau developed a confidential reporting form for income questions but only two hundred thousand were used. The 1940 census also introduced new questions on children born to ever-married women, highest grade of school completed, and place of residence five years earlier. These were among the recommendations made by COGSIS.

A major innovation of the 1940 census was incorporation of sampling as an integral component of enumeration. Sampling procedures were used to gather supplementary information from one out of every twenty persons. Two lines on the forty-line population schedules were designated for the asking of supplementary questions appearing at the bottom of the form. Five different styles of schedule were used to reduce possible effects of line bias.

Austin and Leon Truesdell, chief of the Population Division, opposed use of sampling, while Assistant Director Vergil D. Reed and Dedrick favored the procedure. With his chief economic adviser in favor of sampling, Secretary of Commerce Harry Hopkins decided to allow its use. Philip M. Hauser, assistant chief statistician in the Population Division, and Dedrick planned the implementation of sampling in consultations with Hansen and sampling expert Fredrick F. Stephan, then secretary-treasurer of the ASA. The bureau also used the services of W. Edwards Deming of the Department of Agriculture.

By approval of Congress on August 11, 1939, the sixteenth decennial census included a housing census, the first nationwide inventory of housing. The housing census was conducted in conjunction with the population census and gathered information on the number, characteristics, and geographical distribution of dwelling structures and units in the continental United States, Alaska, Hawaii, Puerto Rico, and the Virgin Islands.

Enumeration, Processing, and Reporting

Enumeration of the population began on April 2, 1940, and was designed for completion within two weeks in any incorporated place of at least twenty-five hundred persons in 1930 and within thirty days in all other places. Inhabitants were enumerated at their usual place of residence. On April 8, 1940, field staff went to all hotels, tourist facilities, and one-night lodging houses and left forms for self-enumeration of guests. These were collected the following day. A staff of approximately 120,000 enumerators, 529 district supervisors, and 104 area managers was responsible for conducting the enumeration.

After district supervisors issued preliminary population counts for every county and each city of ten thousand persons or more, completed enumeration forms were shipped by registered mail to the bureau. Hand counts of the population and housing schedules were then compared with field counts.

Coding and verification of the population and housing schedules were done in phases, with a separate step for treatment of the occupation, industry, and class of worker data. As part of coding in 1940, the bureau developed and implemented a method for allocating unknown ages. Under the direction of Deming, sampling was also incorporated into the verification of coding and card punching. Based upon error records, sample verification was used for coders and punchers who achieved certain accuracy standards.

Tabulation procedures involved a number of counts made from a variety of punched cards: individual, supplementary (sample) individual, fertility (ever-married women), sample family, dwelling, household, and mortgage. Results from counts were published as series of state and U.S. summary preliminary bulletins, which were later bound together as volumes.

Entry into World War II had an impact on the operation of the bureau and work on preparation of final reports. The Second War Powers Act of 1942 authorized the secretary of commerce to make information on census schedules available to war agencies. The bureau became chiefly involved in preparing statistics for defense and war agencies. Advance releases were provided on foreign-born Germans and Italians in the United States and on Japanese in the United States and Hawaii. Special releases were also prepared on a number of labor force-related issues. A planned program of special reports and publication of a statistical atlas had to be abandoned. Designs for widespread distribution of 1940 census publications were curtailed. Instead, about sixteen hundred libraries throughout the nation were designated as depository centers for Census Bureau publications.

■ Robert M. Jenkins

Bibliography

Deming, W. Edwards, and Leon Geoffrey. "On Sample Inspection in the Processing of Census Returns." *Journal of the American Statistical Association* 36 (September 1941): 351–360.

Eckler, A. Ross. "Employment and Income Statistics." *Journal of the American Statistical Association* 36 (September 1941): 381–386.

Eckler, A. Ross. *The Bureau of the Census.* New York: Praeger Publishers, 1972.

Jenkins, Robert M. *Procedural History of the 1940 Census of Housing and Population.* Madison: University of Wisconsin Press, 1985.

1950 census

The 1950 census revealed that the population of the United States, comprising the forty-eight states and the District of Columbia, was 150,697,361. This census also covered the territories of Alaska, American Samoa, Guam, Hawaii, the Panama Canal Zone, the Trust Territory of the Pacific Islands (enumerated by the U.S. Navy), and the U.S. Virgin Islands, as well as the Commonwealth of Puerto Rico. Following the census, 435 seats in the House of Representatives were reapportioned among the forty-eight states.

General Background

For many decades, most of the censuses, including the censuses of agriculture, manufactures, mineral industries, business, and, since 1940, housing, were taken in the same year and were considered to comprise the decennial census. By 1950, the manufactures, mineral industries, and business censuses had been moved to other years and were no longer part of the decennial census. The census of agriculture remained part of the 1950 decennial census but was shifted to a different cycle in 1954. This article focuses on the censuses of population and housing.

The 1950 census was taken as the nation was recovering from the dislocations of World War II, while continuing some trends that were launched or accelerated by the war, for example, the increase in labor force participation of women. The latter part of the 1940–1950 decade was marked by an upsurge in population growth, fed by increasing birth rates and immigration. The 1950 census aimed to measure the effects of these and other social and economic developments.

The 1950 census was taken in accordance with the constitutional requirement (Article I, Section 2) that a census be conducted within every ten-year period. The manner in which the census of population was taken was prescribed by the Act of June 18, 1929. Congress authorized the periodic taking of a decennial census of housing in the Act of July 15, 1949. (The legislation authorizing the first housing census in 1940 did not provide for subsequent censuses.)

Planning the Census

While Congress appropriated $200,000 for census planning in July 1947, preparations had begun the previous year. Bureau employees reviewed the uses of data from previous censuses, consulted with data users, considered requests for new information, prepared budget estimates, and, in a series of experiments with supplements to the Current Population Survey and other surveys and special censuses, tested question wording, schedule design, enumerator instructions, and revisions of such concepts as dwelling unit and usual residence. Test censuses were conducted in two counties in Missouri in April and May 1948, in several counties in Kentucky and Illinois and in Minneapolis, Minnesota, in October 1948, and in South Carolina, rural areas throughout the country, and Atlanta, Georgia, in May 1949. The Bureau of the Budget (now the Office of Management and Budget) coordinated federal government input on proposed census plans and procedures.

One trend that influenced the planning for the 1950 census was the growing suburbanization of the population. A new designation of "urbanized area" was adopted, to apply to cities of fifty thousand or more together with their closely built-up adjacent territory. These fringes were classified as urban. In a related development, recognizing that large unincorporated places were becoming increasingly important in the

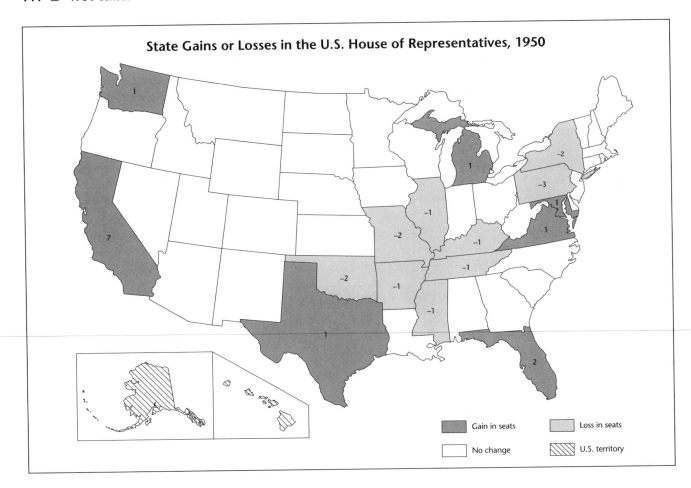

State Gains or Losses in the U.S. House of Representatives, 1950

Gain in seats Loss in seats No change U.S. territory

population distribution, the Census Bureau decided to identify those not within the boundaries of urbanized areas and to compile separate statistics for them. The newly developed concepts and measurements affected the definitions of urban and rural, converting some areas from rural to urban. The urban population for 1950 under the old definition was 59 percent of the total population; under the new definition, it was 64 percent.

During the 1940s, the Census Bureau cooperated with the Bureau of the Budget and other federal agencies in establishing a set of standard metropolitan areas to replace the variety of definitions of big-city areas that had been used in various government programs. The new definitions were to be used for all statistical purposes by all agencies. Unlike the Census Bureau's metropolitan districts and urbanized areas, which required detailed census geography, the standard metropolitan areas were made up of whole counties (towns in New England) so that any data available by counties could be compiled for standard metropolitan areas. These new

areas were used in the publications of the 1950 census.

The 1950 census was the first to use a more refined set of definitions of household, family, and individual, each subdivided into various types. The new definitions were adopted by the Census Bureau in 1947 and used since then in censuses and surveys.

The instructions to enumerators continued to allow anyone to be designated as head of the household for relationship classification purposes, that is, to determine the status of other household members in terms of "relationship to head." However, if a woman was listed as head and her husband was present, he was reclassified as the head when the completed schedule was reviewed in the census office. At the time, the number of such cases was small.

The Questionnaire

The basic schedule for the 1950 census, form P1, was a white, 10" by 22" sheet printed in green ink on both sides. The front included space for population information for thirty persons, with a separate line for each person. The reverse side, the housing schedule, contained spaces for information for twelve dwelling units that housed the persons enumerated on the population side of the form.

Population questions asked of all respondents were age, sex, race, relationship to head of the household, marital status, birthplace, citizenship, farm residence, and, for those over fourteen years of age, occupation, industry, class of worker, employment status, and the number of hours worked the previous week.

The rising costs of data collection, additional demands for information, and improved techniques led to the increased use of sampling in 1950. The sample size was increased and more questions were put on a sample basis. Questions at the bottom of the population schedule were asked for the one person in five whose name fell on a sample line that was indicated in black. There were five printings to vary the sample lines. The person whose name fell on the last sample line was also asked additional questions.

Among the inquiries on the population schedule shifted from 100 percent coverage in 1940 to the sample in 1950 were school attendance and educational attainment, place of residence the previous year, duration of unemployment, and the number of weeks worked the previous year. New questions on the duration of marriage and the number of years widowed, divorced, or separated were added to the sample. The questions on income were also moved to the sample in 1950, but respondents were asked to provide more detail on specific amounts of income received in several different categories. It thus became possible to tabulate total income for individuals instead of just wage or salary income and to tabulate family income. The income data related to the calendar year 1949.

As in 1940, a separate form was available for use by a respondent who did not wish to divulge the income information to the local enumerator. This confidential income report form was handled somewhat differently than the 1940 version. It was a self-mailing piece that the householder was asked to complete and send to the census office.

The housing census of 1940 had posed all questions on a 100 percent basis. In 1950, eighteen items were asked on a 100 percent basis, but many others were moved to the sample. These included inquiries on electric lighting, heating equipment, fuels used for cooking and heating, refrigeration, and ownership of radios. New questions on the presence of television sets and a kitchen sink were added to the sample. A sample survey, the Survey of Residential Financing, was conducted as a supplement to the housing census.

The housing sample was somewhat different from the 20 percent population sample. A 20 percent sample was obtained for certain items, but instead of asking one household in every five to answer all the sample items, the sample questions were divided into five groups. Each household responded to one of the five groups of questions.

Data Collection

To take the decennial census, the Census Bureau added six area offices and 391 district offices to the eight area offices and sixty-seven district offices the agency used for current surveys. Eighteen more district offices were opened in the territories and possessions.

Each area office covered three or four states (or parts of states) and was responsible for between thirteen and forty-one district offices. Area office managers and their assistants were career civil servants. The rest of the decennial field staff consisted of temporary personnel. Area managers and their assistants selected district office supervisory staff from lists provided by the local member of Congress or by state and local organizations.

The boundaries of most district offices coincided with those of congressional districts and contained an average population of 350,000. District offices had to be open and staffed by March 1, 1950, and were expected to complete their work by June 30.

Crew leaders and enumerators had to pass a written test, be U.S. citizens, have a high school education or its equivalent, and be able to perform the duties assigned. Veterans received a special preference. Most of the 133,000 enumerators employed as of March 31, 1950, in the continental United States were homemakers. Enumerators were paid at a fixed rate of $1 per hour or at a piece rate designed to yield about $1 per hour.

Each enumerator collected census information from the inhabitants of an area called an enumeration district. For the 1950 census, about 230,000 enumeration districts were defined for the United States and its territories. Enumeration districts were delineated in a manner that permitted enumerators to complete their work in the time allotted and allowed the data from enumeration districts to be aggregated into all the legal, political, and administrative areas for which census statistics were to be published.

The bureau established special enumeration procedures and questionnaires (individual and military census reports, which contained only the population questions) to include people who were traveling during the census, had no fixed residence, or were members of the armed forces or merchant marine.

Repeating a special feature of the 1940 census, enumerators were required to fill out an "infant card" for every infant born in the first quarter of 1950. It was used in a post-census evaluation of the completeness of the count of infants, who were considered especially liable to be overlooked in the enumeration of "persons," and also for the evaluation of the completeness of birth registration. In addition to their use for evaluation, the infant cards served as a coverage improvement device because they reminded the enumerator to ask about infants and provided an extra-pay incentive for enumerating them.

For most previous censuses, the instructions to enumerators told them to enumerate college students at their parental homes, even if they lived most of the year in or near the college. Beginning in 1950, such college students were to be counted as residing in the college area. This change, in the interest of getting a more complete and geographically accurate count, also had the effect of being beneficial to college towns by increasing their population counts.

As the enumeration was completed, district office supervisors announced the population of each city of ten thousand or more and of each county. Supervisors emphasized that these preliminary counts would not be final until those enumerated away from home could be added. By law, the bureau had to provide final figures to the president by December 1, 1950, eight months after the start of the census.

Data Products

The 1950 census of population and housing resulted in the publication of nearly seventy-three thousand pages of printed reports. The first population reports to appear were the preliminary counts released by district offices for the cities and counties within each district. Appearing as early as June 1950, the preliminary data were superseded beginning in the fall of 1950 by the advance reports, which were the first to provide final population totals. The first advance reports gave population figures for the continental United States by regions, divisions, and states. The state population totals were those reported to the president on November 2, 1950, together with the number of representatives to which each state was entitled in the Eighty-third and subsequent Congresses. Later advance reports provided final population figures for various legal, political, and administrative areas.

Detailed information from the population census was published in four series: *Number of Inhabitants, Characteristics of the Population, Census Tract Statistics,* and *Special Reports.* The *Number of Inhabitants* volumes presented population figures for each state, for its constituent counties, for minor civil divisions within each county, and for all towns.

Characteristics of the Population gave general characteristics of the population (for example, age, sex, race, nativity, citizenship, educational attainment, marital status, country of birth, income, and so on) for counties, places of twenty-five hundred or more inhabitants, urbanized and metropolitan areas, and other geographic units. Detailed characteristics were presented for large areas of each state, such as cities and standard metropolitan areas of one hundred thousand or more inhabitants.

Census Tract Statistics reports were published separately for each area and included a variety of population and housing data for each census tract. *Special Reports* presented data that were too detailed to report in the regular volumes. They generally referred to the country as a whole or to large regions and covered such topics as employment and personal characteristics, occupational and industrial characteristics, family characteristics, the institutional population, and nativity and parentage.

The publications of the census of housing also included preliminary and advance reports. District offices released preliminary housing unit counts beginning in July 1950. Final figures for housing characteristics first appeared in the advance reports, beginning in August 1951.

The Census Bureau published detailed data from the housing census in five series. The *General Characteristics* volumes provided data on occupancy and tenure of housing units, type of structure, race and number of occupants, condition and plumbing facilities, number of rooms and persons per room, rent, and value of owner-occupied units. *Nonfarm Housing Characteristics* contained cross-tabulations of housing characteristics by monthly rent, value, sex and age of household head, type of household, and family income. For occupied housing units in 119 farming areas, *Farm Housing Characteristics* presented cross-tabulations of housing characteristics with such variables as year built, heating equipment, plumbing facilities, number of occupants, and sex and age of household head. The statistics in *Residential Financing* described the financial characteristics of mortgages and the characteristics of property owners.

The Census Bureau increased the number of cities for which it tabulated and published statistics for city blocks from 191 in 1940 to 209 in 1950. Begun on an experimental basis a decade earlier, block statistics became a regular part of the decennial publication program with the 1950 census.

For the first time since the 1920 census, the Census Bureau published monographs. The publishing program was sponsored by the Census Bureau and the Social Science Research Council, and it produced thirteen books, written by specialists on such subjects as the changing population, immigration, families, children, labor force, income, and housing.

Evaluating the Census

The 1950 census included the first post-enumeration survey (PES). It consisted of two samples, one of areas to measure completeness of coverage of housing units and the other of households to measure completeness of coverage of persons within enumerated units and to evaluate the quality of the content of the census returns. The PES estimated the gross census undercount to be 3.4 million persons and the net undercount to be 2.1 million or 1.4 percent of the enumerated total. This first evaluation attempt, based on a small sample and estimation techniques that would be improved for later censuses, was deemed to be an inadequate appraisal. Demographic analytical studies indicated that a more valid estimate of the net undercount in the 1950 census might have been 5 million to 5.5 million. Some years after the census, the Census Bureau made public an estimate of the national net undercount based on a more thorough study. The estimate was 4.1 percent, compared with a retroactive estimate of 5.4 percent for 1940.

Another evaluation matched the 1950 census returns with corresponding returns from the April 1950 Current Population Survey (CPS), a monthly large sample survey conducted by the Census Bureau, that asked many of the same questions as the population census. Among the findings of the matching study were that response variability and response bias were greater for the census than for the CPS and that labor force participation estimates were significantly higher in the

CPS. The CPS enumerators were considerably more experienced than the temporary workers hired for the census field work. The CPS-census match was repeated in succeeding censuses.

Selected Findings from the 1950 Census

The population of the United States according to the 1950 census increased by 14.5 percent over the 1940 figure. This was twice as great a percentage increase as that for the 1930–1940 decade, when the economic depression held down population growth. During the depression some demographers had predicted that the U.S. population would level off at about 150 million. Had they been correct, the 1950 total would have become the ceiling. However, they were wrong.

The resident population totals as of April 1 in the census of 1950 (as well as 1940 and 1960) included the armed forces within the country but excluded the armed forces and others outside it. This exclusion was not consistent among all the decennial censuses.

The increase in population growth in the decade of the 1940s was fed by a resurgence in birth rates in the latter part of the decade, as well as a resurgence in net immigration. Of the increase in population of about nineteen million, 90 percent was attributed to natural increase and 10 percent to net immigration. Despite some rebound in immigration, the percentage of the U.S. population that was foreign-born continued its long-term decline, to 6.9 percent in 1950.

The influence of depression, war, and post-war recovery was reflected in changes in the age distribution of the population. Measured from about the beginning of the depression in 1930 to the time of the 1950 census, the population age five to nineteen declined, despite the increase in the total population. The number under age five increased by 42 percent, reflecting the early years of the post-war baby boom. The long-term increase in the older population continued, with substantial increases in the age group forty-five to sixty-four and especially the age group sixty-five and over.

The average size of households continued its long-term decline, from 5.7 persons in 1790 to 3.4 persons in 1950.

The 1950 census showed a continuing trend toward population concentration in metropolitan areas, reaching a level of 57 percent metropolitan. The most rapid increase was in the coastal areas. The percentage increase in metropolitan-residing population was more than twice as great for blacks as for whites. The fastest growing states in order according to the size of percentage of growth in the decade ending in 1950 were California, Arizona, Florida, and Nevada. The fastest growing region, by far, was the West, at a rate three to four times as great as the other regions.

In general, housing improved during the decade of the 1940s. More homes were equipped with essential plumbing facilities and household conveniences. A booming economy, favorable tax laws, a rejuvenated home building industry, and easier financing encouraged a great increase in home ownership. For the first time, more than half of the occupied homes were owner-occupied. The proportion of units with electric lighting increased from 79 percent in 1940 to 94 percent in 1950. Fewer units were crowded. Yet, 1950 still saw a nation in which more than one-third of the housing lacked complete plumbing.

See also *Data capture*.

■ Edwin D. Goldfield and David M. Pemberton

Bibliography

Goldfield, Edwin D. "Innovations in the Decennial Census of Population and Housing: 1940–1990." Commissioned paper prepared for the Year 2000 Census Panel Studies. Washington, D.C.: National Research Council, Committee on National Statistics, August 1992.

"The Minnesota Historical Census Projects." *Historical Methods* 28 (Winter 1995).

Taeuber, Conrad, and Irene B. Taeuber. *The Changing Population of the United States.* New York: John Wiley & Sons, 1958.

Taeuber, Irene B., and Conrad Taeuber. *People of the United States in the 20th Century.* Washington, D.C.: U.S. Government Printing Office, 1971.

U.S. Bureau of the Census. *Population and Housing Inquiries in the U.S. Decennial Censuses, 1790–1970.* Working paper 39. Washington, D.C.: U.S. Government Printing Office, 1973.

———. *The 1950 Censuses—How They Were Taken.* Procedural studies of the 1950 censuses, no. 2. Washington, D.C.: U.S. Government Printing Office, 1955.

———. *200 Years of U.S. Census Taking: Population and Housing Questions, 1790–1990.* Washington, D.C.: U.S. Government Printing Office, 1989.

1960 census

According to the 1960 census, the population of the United States, including the contiguous forty-eight states, the District of Columbia, and the newly admitted states of Alaska and Hawaii, was 179,323,175. This census also covered the Commonwealth of Puerto Rico and the territories of American Samoa, Guam, the Panama Canal Zone, the U.S. Virgin Islands, and a number of smaller islands. The high commissioner of the Trust Territory of the Pacific Islands conducted a census in 1958; the Census Bureau tabulated its results and released the data together with the rest of the information from the 1960 census. Following the census, all 435 seats in the U.S. House of Representatives were reapportioned among the fifty states.

General Background

The demographic situation of the nation at the time of the 1960 census was marked by a continuation of the recovery in the population growth rate following the end of World War II, but with the beginning of a slackening in the rate of growth. The unemployment rate was relatively low, and the employment rate for women was climbing upward, already higher than the temporary peak during World War II.

The growth of the United States (defined as the contiguous forty-eight states and the District of Columbia) was augmented by the admission to statehood of Alaska and Hawaii in 1959. In this article, numbers for 1960 are for the United States including Alaska and Hawaii; comparisons of 1960 with 1950 or earlier dates are for the conterminous United States, excluding Alaska and Hawaii.

The 1960 census was taken in accordance with the constitutional requirement (Article I, Section 2) that a census be conducted within every ten-year period. The statute that authorizes the Census Bureau to take the population and housing census is Title 13 of the United States Code. Legislated in 1954, Title 13 consolidated a number of laws authorizing various Census Bureau activities into a single statute.

Planning the Census

While congressional appropriations earmarked for the 1960 decennial census began in fiscal year 1958, the bureau had begun planning for the census as early as 1955. Bureau staff consulted with the agency's advisory committees and representatives of business, professional, and civic organizations, evaluated requests for new information, and tested elements of census-taking such as question wording, questionnaire design and content, and enumeration and sampling procedures in

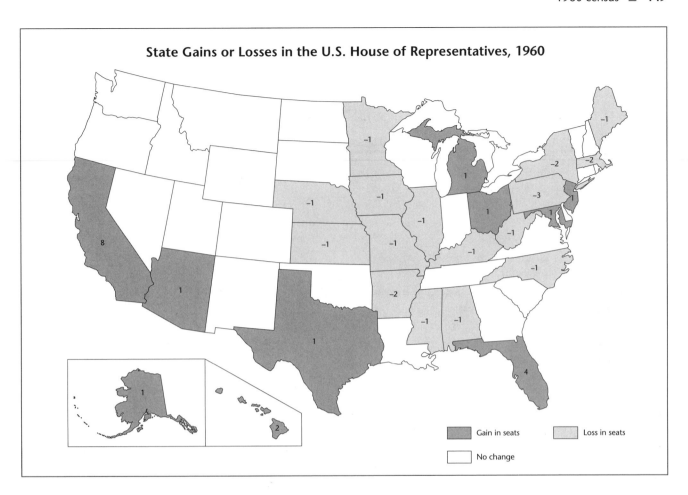

State Gains or Losses in the U.S. House of Representatives, 1960

a series of supplements to ongoing surveys and special censuses. The Bureau of the Budget (now the Office of Management and Budget) coordinated federal governmental input on proposed census plans and procedures.

Experimentation with self-enumeration in the decennial census, to replace the conventional door-to-door canvass and interviewing by enumerators, continued during the 1950s and resulted in considerable use of mail and self-enumeration in the 1960 census. However, a heavy reliance still remained on door-to-door canvassing and enumerator follow-up, especially in rural areas.

In the research that led to the introduction of mail and self-enumeration, measures of enumerator variability when enumerators were used were contrasted with the variability found when self-enumeration was used. High rates of enumerator error, often consistent through the enumerator's work area, characterized all but the simplest questions. This suggested that the census could be more accurate if self-enumeration could be used as much as feasible. Nonsampling errors, such as those made by enumerators, were typically greater than sampling errors. Thus more accurate statistics could be obtained on a sampling basis than on a 100 percent basis for many questions if the nonsampling errors made by enumerators could be sufficiently reduced by using self-enumeration.

In the 1960 census, the definition of "head of household" continued to display a gender bias. The head of a household was the person reported as such, except that in the case of a married couple, the husband was always considered the head.

With the substantial changes for the 1950 census in geographical concepts and measurements and in residential rules (for example, where to count college students), the preparation for the 1960 census in these matters consisted mainly of updating, refinement, and expansion of coverage. A considerable increase was evident in the number of census tracts, to more cities and to the outlying portions of metropolitan areas. There were 23,365 tracts delineated for 1960, almost twice as many as for 1950.

The Questionnaire

For 1960, the 100 percent and sample questions were placed on two separate questionnaires (the "short form" and the "long form"). The main reason was to allow for more rapid processing and publication of the 100 percent statistics.

Previous censuses had used a line schedule as the main data-collection form. For example, the 1950 form was a large sheet with thirty lines for persons on one side and space for housing information for twelve units on the reverse. The 1960 census used a separate questionnaire for each household and its housing unit. The use of mail and self-enumeration necessitated a separate form for each household.

The changes in questionnaire content were more numerous in 1960 than in 1950. New population questions included commuting (place of work and means of transportation to work), length of residence, whether school enrolled in was public or private, for whom worked (for example, company name—to be coded by industry classification in the data-processing procedure), date of first marriage, and more specific household relationship information. The question on age in previous censuses was replaced by a question on month and year of birth to reduce the biases, such as a tendency to round, in age reporting. With self-enumeration for most of the population, the question on race became largely one of self-identification rather than observation by the enumerator. Only the questions on relationship, sex, race, month and year of birth, and marital status were asked of all persons. All other population items were collected on a 25 percent basis (every fourth household). The housing unit or group quarters was the sampling unit; everyone living in that unit became a member of the sample.

New housing questions were access to housing unit, presence of cooking equipment, water heating fuel, clothes washing machine, clothes dryer, air conditioning, home food freezer, number of bathrooms, source of water, sewage disposal, telephone, automobiles, number of bedrooms, basement, elevator, mobility of trailers, and duration of vacancy for vacant units. Added to the Survey of Residential Financing, which had been introduced in 1950, was a Survey of Components of Change, which measured the quantitative and qualitative impact of basic changes that occurred in the housing inventory during the decade 1950–1960. The two inquiries constituted a large-scale sample survey conducted in the fall of 1959 and early 1960 as a part of the housing census. In the basic housing census, fourteen questions were asked for all housing units and thirty questions were asked on a sample basis, either 25 percent, 20 percent, or 5 percent. The 20 percent and 5 percent samples were subdivisions of the 25 percent sample (every fourth housing unit—the same sample as for the population inquiry).

Data Collection

During the late 1950s, the Census Bureau maintained seventeen permanent regional offices to support data collection for special censuses and current surveys. To collect the information for the 1960 decennial census, the bureau set up 399 temporary district offices throughout the fifty states and the District of Columbia. (Six additional district offices were established in Puerto Rico and one each in American Samoa, Guam, the Panama Canal Zone, and the U.S. Virgin Islands.) District office managers reported to one of the seventeen regional offices. The main factor in determining the number of district offices in each region was population density.

The area for which each district office was responsible was divided into crew leader districts, and the latter were subdivided into enumeration districts. Each crew leader supervised an average of fifteen or sixteen enumerators. The population of enumeration districts ranged from one hundred to two thousand people. Peak employment for enumerators came to 156,966 on April 7, 1960; the largest number of crew leaders employed on a given day was 10,271, also on April 7.

In the 1960 census, the Census Bureau used a two-stage procedure in areas comprising 82 percent of the population. Advance forms containing the 100 percent questions were delivered by mail. Enumerators visited all households and transcribed the 100 percent items to a FOSDIC (film optical sensing device for input to computers) machine-readable form. If the advance form had not been completed, the enumerator obtained the information and filled out the FOSDIC form. About 60 percent of the advance forms had been filled out before the enumerator's visit. At every fourth household the enumerator left a sample long form to be completed by the household and mailed back to the census district office. The mail response rate for the sample questions was 77 percent. Follow-up enumerators visited households that had not mailed back the forms. In the 18 percent remainder of the country, mainly rural, where the two-stage procedure was not used, a single-stage procedure was employed. Advance forms were mailed out and then were followed by enumerators' visits to all households to fill out the short forms and the sample long forms.

In 1960 a major formal program of quality control was instituted for the field work. It provided supervisors with definite procedures for detecting and, when necessary, rejecting unacceptable work.

For tabulation and publication, some of the population statistics were based on a subsample of one-fifth of the collected 25 percent sample questionnaires. Sampling yielded economies in cost and tabulation time. Sampling rates depended on the size of the geographic areas or population and housing categories being tabulated and on the degree of reliability needed.

The use of household questionnaires and households as the sampling units made possible the collection and compilation of better and more extensive household and family statistics.

Data Products

The 1960 decennial census produced approximately 138,000 pages of census reports. Most were released between 1961 and 1963, but specialized volumes continued to come out until well into the decade.

The first reports to be published were the preliminary counts of states, counties, and incorporated places of one thousand or more inhabitants. Appearing between May and September of 1961, these preliminary reports were superseded beginning in August by the advance reports, which contained final population counts for each state and a number of geographic units within each state. Later advance reports provided final figures for personal characteristics such as age, sex, race, and marital status and for some economic and social characteristics, by state and other geographic areas.

Detailed information from the population census was published in four series of volumes. The first series, with the overall title of *Characteristics of the Population*, was divided into four subseries. The first subseries, *Number of Inhabitants*, contained final population counts from the 100 percent questionnaires for states, counties, standard metropolitan statistical areas, urbanized areas, incorporated places, minor civil divisions, and unincorporated places with at least one thousand inhabitants.

The second subseries, *Characteristics of the Population*, provided final 100 percent data for age, sex, marital status, race, and relationship to household head for states, counties, standard metropolitan statistical areas, urbanized areas, places with one thousand or more inhabitants, and minor civil divisions.

The third subseries, *General Social and Economic Characteristics*, presented data taken from the sample questionnaire on such variables as nativity, mother tongue, school enrollment and years of school completed, family composition, veteran status, employment status, occupational and industry group, and income. These data were given for states, counties, standard metropolitan statistical areas, urbanized areas, and urban places. The fourth subseries, *Detailed Characteristics*, provided cross-tabulations for 100 percent and sample data for many of the topics treated in *General Social and Economic Characteristics* for larger geographic areas such as states, large counties, and cities.

The second series of reports from the population census, *Subject Reports*, consisted of detailed cross-tabulations for the United States and its regions for such variables as race, fertility, marital status, families, education, employment, occupation, industry, and income. The third series, *Selected Area Reports*, presented selected characteristics for specialized geographic areas and for Americans overseas. *Supplementary Reports* presented population data for a variety of geographic areas, miscellaneous types of data, and selected tables from earlier publications.

The 1960 census of housing produced a series of preliminary and advance reports, followed by several series of final reports. The preliminary reports contained preliminary housing-unit counts on a state-by-state basis for many urban places. Advance reports presented final data on housing units by tenure, race of occupants, number of rooms, rent, and other variables for standard metropolitan statistical areas and some places.

Final reports from the census of housing were published in seven series. The first, *States and Small Areas*, presented occupancy and structural characteristics, equipment and facilities, and financial characteristics of housing units or their occupants for states, counties, standard metropolitan statistical areas, and other geographic areas. The *Metropolitan Housing* series of reports provided cross-tabulations of housing and household characteristics for the United States and most standard metropolitan statistical areas. The *City Blocks* series contained a limited amount of housing data for each block in cities with fifty thousand or more inhabitants and for 172 other urban places.

The fourth series, *Components of Inventory Change*, was released in two parts and described changes in the nation's housing stock. *Residential Finance* also had two parts and presented information on home finance and characteristics of some types of owner-occupied housing and on rental and vacant properties. *Housing of Senior Citizens* contained cross-tabulations of household and housing characteristics for housing units having one or more household members age sixty years or older. *Special Reports for Local Housing Authorities* focused on the social and economic characteristics of respondents living in substandard housing and on the characteristics of the housing.

A joint population and housing series, *Census Tract Reports*, was part of a new series that combined data from both censuses. A new methodological series described some census operations, evaluated census procedures, and presented results from experiments.

An innovation for the 1960 census was the production of public-use samples from the census returns. These were samples of the basic records for individual persons, households, and housing units, with the identifying information, such as name, address, and detailed geography, removed to preserve confidentiality. The bureau made these data available to the public on computer tapes, so that researchers could make their own special tabulations. The first samples were released on tape, and also on punch cards, in 1963. The series has been extended forward and backward, to succeeding and preceding censuses.

A related innovation for the 1960 census was the production of summary tapes for public use, containing more subject and geographic detail than the printed reports. They fall under the same confidentiality rules as the printed report data. They were made available on a small scale for the 1960 census and greatly expanded for succeeding censuses.

Following the example of the 1950 census, a program was established for a series of monographs to follow the 1960 census, again with the cooperation of the Social Science Research Council. It produced five books, a considerably smaller number than the 1950 program. The 1960 monograph series was published by the U.S. Government Printing Office.

Evaluating the Census

The 1960 census operation featured many evaluations and research projects looking toward improvements for future censuses as well as evaluations of the quality of the 1960 census. From the many studies proposed, twenty-two were selected for implementation. This emphasis on researching, experimenting, and analyzing enabled the Census Bureau to learn, and share with the public, more technical knowledge about the workings of censuses than had been accomplished in earlier censuses and to get an early start on planning for the 1970 census.

Litigation

The issue of privacy was raised in the case of the *United States v. William Rickenbacker* in 1961–1963. The defendant argued that his refusal to respond in the 1960 census, and his advocacy of a boycott of the census, was justified because the census, for which answers are required under penalty of law, was an unreasonable invasion of privacy. The U.S. District Court reached a decision in favor of the government and found Rickenbacker guilty of violating the census law. He received a suspended sentence of sixty days' imprisonment and a fine of $100 and was placed on probation for one day. The Court of Appeals upheld the action, stating: "The authority to gather reliable statistical data reasonably relating to governmental purposes and functions is a necessity if modern government is to legislate intelligently and effectively." This was the final judgment in the case, because the Supreme Court declined to review it.

Selected Findings from the 1960 Census

The population of the United States (including the new states of Alaska and Hawaii) according to the 1960 census increased by 18.5 percent over the 1950 figure of 151,325,798 with states-to-be Alaska and Hawaii added in. This was the greatest percentage increase since the 1900–1910 decade and is higher than any increase for decades subsequent to 1960, at least to date. In absolute terms, the increase of nearly twenty-eight million people is the greatest for any decade in the history of the United States. Credit for the record goes mainly to the post-World War II baby boom, plus the resumption of immigration. In the 1950–1960 decade, as in the preceding decade, natural increase accounted for 90 percent of the total increase and net immigration for 10 percent.

The percentage of the population that was foreign-born continued its decline, to 5.4 percent in 1960. State-to-state migration continued to increase. In 1960,

16.9 percent of the U.S.-native population of California had been born in other states, a far higher proportion than that of any other state of the conterminous United States.

Population growth continued to be concentrated in urban, especially metropolitan, areas. The percentage urban increased from 64.0 percent in 1950 to 69.9 percent in 1960. In that period the percentage urban for the black population increased from 62.4 percent in 1950 to 73.2 percent in 1960. After a long history of the black population being concentrated in the rural South, blacks had finally become more urban than whites.

Although women's rate of participation in the labor force continued to increase, it still was far below that for men. In 1960 the proportion of men fourteen years of age and over in the labor force was 77.4 percent; for women, it was 34.5 percent.

The fastest growing states in order according to the size of percentage of growth in the decade ending in 1960 were Florida, Nevada, Alaska, and Arizona. The West continued to far outstrip the other regions in rate of population growth.

The housing census showed that the rate of residential construction in the 1950–1960 decade continued almost unabated from the previous decade. Home ownership gained impressively; the proportion of homeowners was higher than at any other date for which data on tenure were collected. Quality of housing improved. The percentage of housing units lacking plumbing decreased significantly in the decade from slightly over 35 percent to about 17 percent. The percentage of "crowded" (based on persons per room) housing units continued to decrease. Television sets became a staple of the American home, with 87 percent of the occupied units having at last one set, an increase from 12 percent in 1950.

See also *Data capture*.

■ Edwin D. Goldfield and David M. Pemberton

Bibliography

Goldfield, Edwin D. "Innovations in the Decennial Census of Population and Housing: 1940–1990." Commissioned paper prepared for the Year 2000 Census Panel Studies. Washington, D.C.: National Research Council, Committee on National Statistics, August 1992.

"The Minnesota Historical Census Projects." *Historical Methods* 28 (Winter 1995).

Taeuber, Irene B., and Conrad Taeuber. *People of the United States in the 20th Century*. Washington, D.C.: U.S. Government Printing Office, 1971.

U.S. Bureau of the Census. *1960 Censuses of Population and Housing: Procedural History*. Washington, D.C.: U.S. Government Printing Office, 1966.

———. *Population and Housing Inquiries in the U.S. Decennial Censuses, 1790–1970*. Working paper 39. Washington, D.C.: U.S. Government Printing Office, 1973.

———. *200 Years of U.S. Census Taking: Population and Housing Questions, 1790–1990*. Washington, D.C.: U.S. Government Printing Office, 1989.

1970 census

Shortly before the 1970 census, the population of the United States passed the 200 million mark. The 1970 count of 203,302,031 represented an increase of more than 13 percent, or almost 24 million people since 1960. This level of growth could not match the 18.5 percent increase recorded between 1950 and 1960, and was indicative of what would become a pattern of slower growth in the nation's population in the last few decades of the twentieth century.

Two factors lay behind the decline in the growth rate. First, the baby boom was over. Demographers define this period of high birth rates as 1946 to 1964, with its peak in 1957. By 1970, the nation was well into a "baby bust." This meant that far fewer children were being born than in previous decades. At the same time, the oldest baby boomers were growing up and moving out of their parental homes. Unlike their parents, however, many were deferring marriage and childbirth to later ages.

Second, the immigration rate, while slightly higher than in the immediately previous decades, was still low (1.7 immigrants per 1,000 U.S. population). In later decades, the immigration rate would rise sharply. Immigrants, and their children born in the United States, contribute significantly to overall population growth.

The large number of children born in the baby-boom years lowered the population's median age to twenty-eight years—that is, half the people in the United States were younger and half were older. This was the lowest median age figure since 1930 (in 2000, the median age was almost thirty-six years). The strength of the young population, particularly of children under age eighteen, meant that the nation's resources were concentrating on education, including building schools. The 2000 picture was significantly different.

The 1970 census was most remarkable for two innovations: the mailout-mailback census and the routine

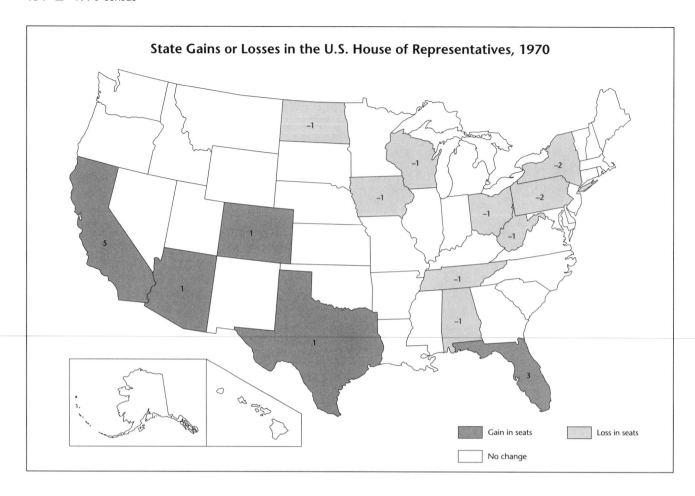

State Gains or Losses in the U.S. House of Representatives, 1970

Gain in seats | Loss in seats | No change

dissemination of data in electronic form. The mailout-mailback method was used for the first time in a population and housing census. Covering major urban areas and some adjacent counties, pre-addressed census questionnaires were delivered to about 60 percent of the nation's housing units on March 28, 1970. Householders were asked to fill in the questionnaires and mail them back to the local census office on census day (April 1).

The mailing list for the pre-addressed questionnaires was assembled from commercial sources, augmented by checks both by postal carriers and by census field staff. The addresses were then processed through an address coding guide (ACG), which coded them to census tract, block, and other geographic identifiers. The ACG was the forerunner of the Topologically Integrated Geographic Encoding and Referencing System (TIGER).

Because commercial lists were available only in major urban areas, the remainder of the country was enumerated through the conventional methods used in earlier censuses, where the address list was constructed and geographically coded by enumerators as they conducted the census on a door-to-door basis.

As in 1960, the census questions were divided between a "short form" and a "long form." The short-form population items, asked in every household, were name, relationship to head of household, color or race, age, month and year of birth, and marital status. Short-form housing items were living quarters at address (subsequently referred to as "units in structure"), telephone, direct entrance, complete kitchen facilities, number of rooms, a set of plumbing questions (piped hot water, toilet, bathtub or shower), basement, tenure (own or rent), housing value, and rent. The plumbing items, which became the subject of great controversy before the 1980 and 1990 censuses, were critical to measuring housing quality. In 1970 many Americans still lived in housing that lacked these basic amenities.

The long form went to 20 percent of the households (the other 80 percent received only the short form). The long form was split into two questionnaires. The majority of items were included on both, but a special subset of questions was asked only in 15 percent of the households, while another subset went to only 5 percent.

The 1970 census continued use of a 1960s innovation: the FOSDIC (film optical sensing device for input to computers) system for capturing the data from the paper questionnaire for processing. FOSDIC was much more efficient than the older method, keypunching IBM cards for every questionnaire and reading the punched cards into the computer. However, the FOSDIC questionnaire required respondents to fill in circles for most of the responses. The questions were laid out in two columns on oversized pages in a booklet. They could be intimidating for those with lower education or literacy levels as well as for older persons with sight problems. These considerations were much more critical in a mailout-mailback census than they were in a census where paid enumerators filled out the questionnaires.

The second major innovation of 1970, Summary Tape Files, represented the first routine delivery of data in electronic format. The STFs were used on mainframe computer systems, which were the standard of the time. The STFs contained far more data than could be or would be included in printed reports. Users could use the computer to aggregate data across different geographic areas (such as a group of census tracts), create new statistics from the existing tables, and calculate percentages and other statistical presentations of the data for publication. The data could be arranged in a variety of ways to suit the needs of the user. The concept of "data intermediaries" was born, as some demographers and planners became expert.

Using the STFs required programming. Most users, even intermediaries, were not in a position to create their own software. The most important person to facilitate addressing this problem was John C. "Jack" Beresford, an innovative and far-thinking young Census Bureau employee who advanced the concept of data delivery in this electronic format. After observing that the bureau had no plans to create software to accompany the data files, he formed a company known as DUALabs (Data Use and Access Laboratories) to ensure that methods for using summary tapes would be created. Initially supported by a group of public and private sector clients who planned to use the STFs, DUALabs later received a grant from the Ford Foundation to spread these techniques to the nation's colleges and universities. The MOD series, as the software was named, became the prototype method for handling summary data. In addition, the documentation prepared by DUALabs became the standard for describing the structure and content of the 1970 summary files.

The 1970 summary files should be viewed as experimental. Many of the lessons learned were incorporated into the 1980 STFs and continue into the twenty-first century. They were controversial, as many Census Bureau staff members feared release of the data in this form would lead to breaches of confidentiality. These fears proved to be unfounded. Summary files have made the transition from the mainframe to the personal computer. They remain the prime method for comprehensive data dissemination from the decennial census.

Public Use Microdata Sample files had been produced for the 1960 census, but they were small samples with limited geographic identification. In 1970 six 1 percent samples were released on computer tape—three that were drawn from the census records for households that returned the 15 percent long form and three that were drawn from the census records for households that received the 5 percent long form. Three different geographic identification schemes were used. For the first time, users could prepare their own tabulations for such areas as states and Standard Metropolitan Statistical Areas and counties or groups of counties. However, no area was identified in the files unless it had a population of at least 250,000.

■ Patricia C. Becker

Bibliography

U.S. Bureau of the Census. *Data Collection Forms and Procedures,* 1970 Census Report PHC(R)-2. Washington, D.C.: U.S. Government Printing Office, 1971.

U.S. Bureau of the Census. *Statistical Abstract of the United States, 1998.* Washington, D.C.: U.S. Government Printing Office, 1998.

1980 census

The population of the United States in 1980 was 226,545,805. This represented an increase of some 23 million people, or more than 11 percent since 1970. The demographic picture of the nation was dominated by the emergence of the baby-boom generation as adults, forming their own households and participating in the labor force. Female labor force participation, especially among women with young children, increased dramatically in the 1970s. At the same time, women were having fewer children, with more than 1 million fewer births in 1975 compared with 1957, the peak year of the baby-boom.

Average household size had dropped significantly, as a result of three major factors: (1) the low birth rate, (2) an increase in single-person households caused by deferred marriage and a growing divorce rate, and (3) a growing elderly population. Almost 24 percent of households contained only one person, compared with 17 percent in 1970.

Other notable changes in the nation's socioeconomic and demographic patterns during the 1970s included a significant increase in the proportion of children living with only one parent, a marked decrease in the number of school-aged children, and a great decline in population growth in the nation's Northeast and Midwest regions (the "Rust Belt"). By 1980, the nation had a new demographic pattern, different from 1970 and earlier, which was to persist for at least the next twenty years.

The 1980 census continued and expanded upon the innovative methods introduced in 1970 and established several new procedures. Mailout-mailback census methods were extended to areas containing more than 95 percent of the nation's housing units. A new procedure, called Local Review, enabled local officials to examine census housing unit counts. The Summary Tape Files (STFs) and the Public Use Microdata Sample (PUMS) continued as the major form of data delivery in electronic format. The issue of census undercount, and possible adjustment, moved from the academic domain into the political arena. A new file, the PL 94-171 Reapportionment/Redistricting File, was mandated by law to provide data at the census block level for the entire nation. For this reason, census block numbering became universal.

The census questionnaire continued to be divided into a "short form" and a "long form," but the split long-form sample used in 1960 and 1970 was eliminated. Cost considerations led to a smaller sample size; only one in six households received the long form, instead of the 20 percent in the 1970 sample and 25

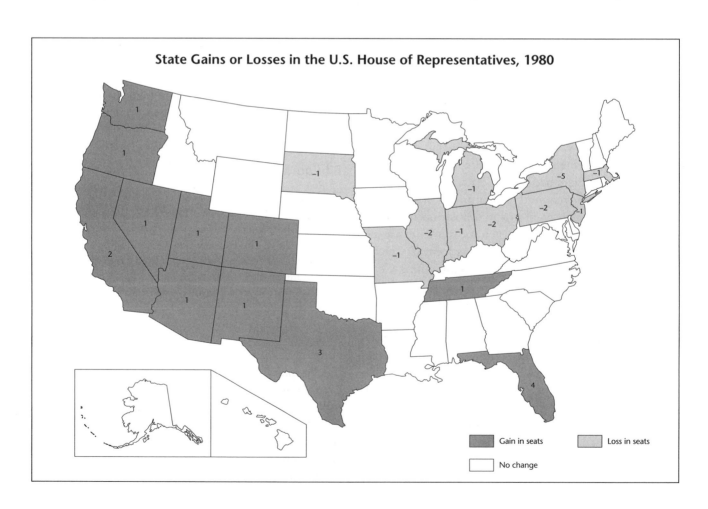

State Gains or Losses in the U.S. House of Representatives, 1980

Gain in seats   Loss in seats   No change

percent in 1960. Special provisions were made for small communities (under twenty-five hundred population), where a 50 percent sampling fraction was used to improve the quality of income and poverty data utilized in revenue sharing and other government programs.

In 1978 a bill was introduced in Congress that would have separated the long-form questions from the census, instead calling for a separate survey of a sample of households later in the year. Both the Census Bureau and the professional community opposed this idea. It would have generated extra costs for poorer quality data, because census promotional activity and the sense of a legal mandate to respond would be absent at the time of the later survey. The bill did not survive a committee vote.

After the 1980 census was completed, President Ronald Reagan in 1981 mandated an across-the-board budget cut of 12 percent. As a consequence, the Census Bureau was forced to delay coding of long-form information and to cut by half coding of the journey to work and migration questionnaire items. The result was poorer data for use in transportation planning, in defining metropolitan areas, and in analyzing migration patterns within smaller metropolitan areas.

The 1980 census was the first that was required to produce data by race and Hispanic origin to conform with Directive 15, issued by the Office of Management and Budget (OMB) in 1977. The data requirements for the PL 94-171 file included a count of the total population and the population eighteen and older by each of five race groups (White, Negro or Black, Asian and Pacific Islander, American Indian, and Other) in total and for persons who also reported a Hispanic origin. These items were required to meet the data needs of the Voting Rights Act. Thus, for the first time, Hispanic origin and race categories other than Negro or Black received prominent attention on the questionnaire and in the early tabulations.

Another reason for heightened concern over the population distribution by race was the growing understanding that the population missed by the census, the undercount, was disproportionately comprised of minority group members. Many interest groups argued that the census should be adjusted to compensate for the undercount. However, in the opinion of professionals at the bureau, the methods to achieve fair and equitable adjustment were not yet available, and so Census Director Vincent Barabba announced shortly before census day that no census adjustment would be made in 1980. This announcement spurred numerous

lawsuits, which occupied Census Bureau staff in court well into the 1980s. In the end, however, there was no 1980 census adjustment.

The 1980 Census Products program included most of the reports that had traditionally been published as books, as well as four major Summary Tape Files, three Public Use Microdata Sample files, and a large number of special products designed for specific governmental needs. One of the PUMS files provided a very large 5 percent sample of the population; also, the population size cutoff for identifying areas in the PUMS files was lowered from 250,000 in 1970 to 100,000 in 1980. Learning from the lessons of the 1970 tape products, bureau staff worked hard, and with significant success, to standardize the files and improve their documentation.

The special products included the Equal Employment Opportunity File created for the U.S. Office of Civil Rights to assist in setting goals for affirmative action plans and validating discrimination claims. Another important file was the Census Transportation Planning Package, designed for the Department of Transportation and distributed to metropolitan and state planning agencies. An STF3 ZIP Code file was produced as a special product funded by a consortium of private sector data vendors; under the agreement, the files were released to the public after eighteen months. A School District Data Base provided tabulations for use by the education community.

Microfiche was used extensively to provide information that was not formally printed, including a data set for every residential block in the nation. Microfiche was also the vehicle used to make the tables available from two of the summary files, STF1 and STF3, readable and printable. These were widely distributed to libraries and to agencies affiliated with the State Data Center (SDC) program.

The State Data Centers were created under joint statistical agreements between the Census Bureau and the states. Each state was permitted to name a number of affiliates, based on their population size. Both the core agencies and the affiliates received complimentary copies of all census publications on tape and in print. In exchange, they were expected to provide census data service to local users and to document the level of service in annual reports. The SDC participants around the country elected a Coordinating Council, whose members traveled periodically, at bureau expense, to meet at bureau headquarters in Washington, D.C.

In tandem with the SDC program, the bureau decided to create its own software package, CENSPAC, for use in processing the STFs. The decision generated substantial controversy and, in the end, did not work out well. The software's full potential was never realized, and after some time the bureau decided to discontinue further work on it. STF users either created their own software, used packages such as SPSS or SAS to access the data, or used an upgraded version of the MOD series software created by DUALabs (Data Use and Access Laboratories) for the 1970 census.

■ Patricia C. Becker

Bibliography

Anderson, Margo J. *The American Census: A Social History.* New Haven: Yale University Press, 1988.

Choldin, Harvey. *Looking for the Last Percent.* New Brunswick, N.J.: Rutgers University Press, 1994.

U.S. Bureau of the Census. *Changes in American Family Life.* Report P-23, No. 163. Washington, D.C.: U.S. Government Printing Office, August 1989.

———. *History, Part A.* Census report PHC80(R)-2A. Washington, D.C.: U.S. Government Printing Office, 1986.

———. *Statistical Abstract of the United States, 1998.* Washington, D.C.: U.S. Government Printing Office, 1998.

———. *The Coverage of Housing in the 1980 Census.* Census report PHC80-E1. Washington, D.C.: U.S. Government Printing Office, 1984.

1990 census

By the 1990 decennial count, the U.S. population was 249,632,692. Four hundred thirty-five House seats were apportioned among the fifty states.

The 1990 U.S. census was a statistical triumph and a public relations disaster. This may be the fate of all modern censuses in a litigious society in which all the rewards at the state and local level go to getting a count for each constituency as large as possible, instead of one as accurate as possible. The decennial census moves too much power (in terms of seats in Congress, state legislatures, and local governing bodies) and too much money (in terms of billions of dollars in federal programs) not to be controversial and its results hotly contested. Thus, no constituency is completely satisfied with its census count.

The 1990 census was a mix of technological breakthroughs and innovations coupled with reuse of the basic procedures of the 1970 and 1980 censuses. Those procedures were the mailing of questionnaires to all households with street addresses plus multiple, in-person, follow-up calls on households that did not return their questionnaires. Special procedures were devised for counting those with rural, non-street addresses, those living in shelters or on the street, transients, prisoners and parolees, and other special groups. Some procedures proved no longer adequate given the changes in society. More racial and ethnic diversity, new immigrants, less sense of the need for "civic" participation, and more varied household structures were evident than in prior decades. Whereas 78 percent and 75 percent of households returned the mailed questionnaires in 1970 and 1980, respectively, only 63 percent in 1990 did by the deadline for follow-up calls (although another 2 percent came in later). The Census Bureau had anticipated a drop to 70 percent, but the remainder of the shortfall meant more than six million additional households had to be contacted in person.

Litigation and Controversy

Hanging like a black cloud over the 1990 census was litigation demanding that census counts be adjusted for undercount. The first lawsuit was filed in 1988, two years before census-taking began, by New York City; the state of New York; Chicago; the state of California; Los Angeles; Dade County, Florida; and a number of organizations and individuals that joined in as plaintiffs. The lawsuit (*The City of New York et al. v. U.S. Department of Commerce et al.*) created a negative media environment for both census-taking and the final results of the census. Reporters, cartoonists, and comedians alike took up a litany that the Census Bureau could not count. In all, twenty-one suits were filed contesting the 1990 census, most of them over undercount. The last was settled in 1996. None changed the 1990 results, although research by the Census Bureau after the count identified a net undercount, first estimated in 1991 as 2.1 percent and revised in early 1992 to 1.6 percent, of four million persons after subtracting missed persons from people counted twice or otherwise erroneously enumerated.

The decision whether or not to adjust the census count—as called for by the *New York et al.* plaintiffs—was the biggest controversy of the 1990 census. The deadline for decision was July 15, 1991, seven and one-half months after the counts for the nation and each of the fifty states and the District of Columbia were delivered to President George Bush. Until the adjustment decision was made, every count delivered was marked as being subject to correction.

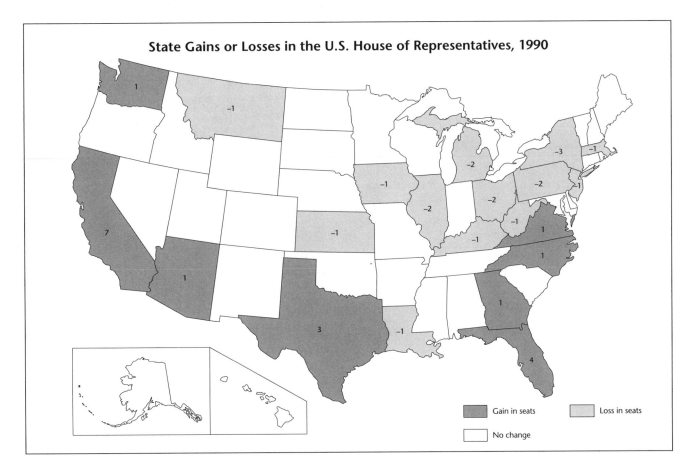

State Gains or Losses in the U.S. House of Representatives, 1990

The census director, Barbara Everitt Bryant, felt the undercount research accurate enough to recommend adjustment to the secretary of commerce. By law, the secretary of commerce had ultimate decision power for the census. A Census Bureau study committee of statisticians and demographers split seven to two in favor of the position that adjustment would improve the accuracy of the census. An advisory panel to the secretary (the appointment of which was required under a stipulation agreement of the New York City lawsuit) split four to four. The undersecretary for economic affairs recommended against adjustment. With advisers divided and unconvinced by the research, Secretary of Commerce Robert A. Mosbacher decided not to adjust the count. Clearly, this was a decision about which reasonable men and women disagreed. After moving up through the courts, the Supreme Court handed down the decision in March 1996 that the secretary had not made an arbitrary or capricious decision when he decided not to statistically adjust the census for the undercount. The count as enumerated stood.

The accurate job the Census Bureau did in counting a net of more than 98 percent of a highly mobile population got little media attention compared with that given the undercount. However, the data were well received and were used more extensively than any previous census data.

The 1990 Count

Of the 249,632,692 people counted in the 1990 census, 248,709,873 were resident in the United States; the remaining 922,819 were overseas military and federal employees and their dependents. The total was shy of the one-quarter of a billion the Census Bureau had estimated as the current population just prior to census start. The count showed a growth in the national population of 9.8 percent over the decade since the 1980 census.

Population growth was unevenly distributed, as it had been during the prior decade. Three states (Iowa, West Virginia, and Wyoming) plus the District of Columbia lost population while four states (Alaska, Arizona, Florida, and Nevada) had gains of more than 30 percent. By region, the West grew 22.3 percent; the South, 13.4 percent; the Northeast, 3.4 percent; and the Midwest, 1.4 percent.

The U.S. Constitution provides for the census as the basis for reapportionment of seats in the House of Representatives among the states every ten years. Reapportionment is like dividing a cherry pie with 435 cherries into fifty pieces in which none of the cherries can be split and every piece gets at least one cherry. The uneven population growth resulted in the shifting of a net of fifteen seats out of the Midwest and Northeast to the South and West. The big gainer was California, with its number of representatives increasing from forty-five to fifty-two. California thus became the first state to hold more than 12 percent of the House of Representatives since New York in 1840. The shift of representatives to the South and West continued a trend. After the 1980 census, seventeen seats had moved in the same direction.

The Census Bureau conducts many ongoing demographic surveys and produces population estimates over the course of the decade. The results of the census, therefore, produced few surprises—with two exceptions. Both the Hispanic and Asian populations had increased far more than had been estimated. Hispanics (who can be of any race according to federal government definitions) zoomed from 6.4 to 9.0 percent, a growth of 53 percent in the decade; Asian/Pacific Islanders from 1.5 to 2.9 percent, a growth of 108 percent.

The Undercount

The Census Bureau used two types of research to estimate the size and characteristics of undercount in the census: (1) demographic analysis (DA) and (2) a post-enumeration survey (PES) coupled with dual-systems estimation (using matches of survey enumerations to census enumerations in sampled areas). Demographic analysis uses noncensus data such as births, deaths, immigration, and migration records. DA is usable for national estimates, or estimates for blacks and nonblacks, but cannot provide detail on geographic changes and other demographic characteristics. The demographic analysis estimate of the undercount was 1.8 percent, slightly larger than the estimate of 1.2 percent for 1980. Between 1940 (when demographic analysis was first used) and 1980, both the total undercount and the difference in undercount between blacks and nonblacks were steadily reduced. It was a setback that both the undercount and the racial difference in it increased for 1990 despite substantially

more efforts to count hard-to-enumerate groups.

The post-enumeration survey produced estimates of the population by age, race and ethnic groups, geographic areas, and types of areas. A PES can determine what types of people have been overcounted (that is, counted twice) as well as those not counted. The initial estimate made by June 1991 was a net undercount of 2.1 percent. This was refined after further research, plus the discovery of a computer coding error, and finalized in August 1992 as a net undercount of 1.6 percent.

The undercount varied by demographic groups. The different geographical distribution of these demographic groups meant that the undercount varied for geographic areas. The 1990 PES coupled with dual-systems estimation produced the most thorough analysis ever of census undercount (see Table 1).

Cost of the Census

Cost for the ten-year cycle from 1984 to 1993—for planning, testing, census rehearsals, taking of the census, data processing, tabulating and distributing results—was $2.6 billion. The sum displeased some congressional appropriators because the cost was more than that for which population growth plus inflation could account. Most of the additional money was spent trying to reduce the undercount. Looked at another way, the cost of the 1990 census was $10.40 per person, or about $1 per year for data that would be used for a decade.

Technological Triumphs

The 1990 census had some big wins: creation of a computerized mapping system for all seven million blocks in the nation, creation of a computerized Master Address File, and delivery of the data in a form that anyone with a personal computer (PC) could use. The census also had some smaller wins: bar coding of questionnaires and distributed data processing. No data processing glitches occurred in taking the 1990 census even though more than 100 million questionnaires were processed within a few months.

Creation of the mapping system called TIGER (Topologically Integrated Geographic Encoding and Referencing) was a rare example of federal agency cooperation under a tight deadline. The Census Bureau and the U.S. Geological Survey (USGS) produced a geographic information system (GIS) with every point along every street, highway, stream, river, railroad, and local

Table 1. Undercount in the 1990 Census

Population Segment	Net Undercount (Percent)
Residents of	
Owner occupied housing	0.07
Renter occupied housing	4.31
Race	
Whites (nonblacks)	1.18
Males	1.52
Females	0.85
Blacks	4.43
Males	4.90
Females	4.01
Asian/Pacific Islanders	2.33
Males	3.44
Females	1.25
American Indians	4.52
Males	5.18
Females	3.86
Ethnicity	
Hispanic (of any race)	4.96
Males	5.51
Females	4.39
Age	
0–17	3.28
18–29	2.99
30–49	1.36
55+	-0.92
Total	1.58

eration of personal computers. The 1990 census was made available on CD-ROMs, usable by any group or individual with a PC and CD-ROM reader. Thus census data became accessible to the taxpayers who paid for these data. Although delivery of 1990 data on CD-ROMs in 1991 was a technological breakthrough, by 1995 that census data moved to the Internet at www.census.gov. This could not have been envisioned at the time the census was taken.

■ Barbara Everitt Bryant

Bibliography

Anderson, Margo J., and Stephen E. Fienberg. *Who Counts? Census Taking in Contemporary America.* New York: Russell Sage Foundation, 1999.

Bryant, Barbara Everitt, and William Dunn. *Moving Power and Money: The Politics of Census Taking* Ithaca, N.Y.: New Strategist Publications, 1995.

Choldin, Harvey. *Looking for the Last Percent.* New Brunswick, N.J.: Rutgers University Press, 1994.

Steffey, Duane L., and Norman Bradburn, eds. *Counting People in the Information Age.* Washington, D.C.: National Academy Press, 1994.

U.S. Bureau of the Census. *TIGER: The Coast-to-Coast Digital Map Data Base.* Washington, D.C.: U.S. Department of Commerce, U.S. Bureau of the Census, November 1989.

U.S. Superintendent of Documents. *United States Code.* Title 13—Census. Pittsburgh, Pa.: U.S. Government Printing Office.

boundary in the country computer digitized by latitude and longitude. Enumerators in prior censuses set off with local maps of varying quality, but a national system now was in place that could print maps on demand. Because neither the Census Bureau nor USGS can patent or copyright its work, TIGER became a public asset. It spawned a multibillion-dollar GIS industry as the mapping system underlying every computer product that produces maps of the United States—including those used by 911 emergency services.

The 1990 Master Address File was the first census address list ever computerized. While people move, most buildings do not. With updating, it becomes a permanent tool for Census Bureau use for censuses and surveys.

The 1970 and 1980 censuses were available to data users on tapes. These data tapes required large mainframe computer systems, systems available only to those in large corporate, academic, or government environments. The decade of the 1980s saw the prolif-

2000 census

The 2000 census measured a U.S. population of approximately 275,000,000. Four hundred and thirty-five seats were apportioned in the House of Representatives among the fifty states.

Census 2000 found key changes in the American population, each of which required new, sometimes controversial, changes in census-taking. New directions in the population made it harder for census-takers to reach people by mail or in person. Demands to restrain the federal budget set limits on the census workforce during the planning phase for 2000 that were unprecedented, at least in modern times. And new developments in census-taking techniques and technology offered both promise and peril in meeting the diverse demands of an increasingly diverse population, including the fundamental goal of ensuring representation in government for everyone.

In short, the results of Census 2000 can be summed up by a single word: diversity. And that very diversity forced census-taking into new territory because the census counts people where they live—that is, where their political representation is apportioned. Population diversity makes it hard to both find people and connect them to a single address.

Household Diversity

Probably the most historic demographic change measured by Census 2000 is a new and seemingly permanent diversity in American households. This diversity has many social and economic causes, but the demographic cause is represented by a single number: the increasing average age of Americans, nearly thirty-seven in 2000.

Census 2000 thus reported the effects of perhaps the most notable achievement of the twentieth century, the health care revolution. By 2000 the death of a child was a tragedy, no longer routine as it was at the beginning of the century. Virtually all children reached adulthood, and ongoing changes in health permitted most adults to survive into what used to be considered old age. As a result of the extraordinary increase in life expectancy over the century, the 2000 census found roughly equal numbers of Americans in each broad age group up to the oldest. This revolutionary change was erasing the traditional graphic portrait of the nation's population—the shape of a pyramid, marked by large numbers of children, fewer adults, and still fewer old people. It was turning instead into a pillar.

One historic demographic change usually leads to another. In 2000 the majority of households consisted of adults only, not of adults and children, as they have throughout history. A longer life expectancy means that most people live the bulk of their adult lives not raising children, if only because by the time they reach midlife, their children are grown. So the 2000 census found that married couples without children (under age eighteen in the home) were the nation's new "traditional" family. And households with only one person in them, most often older people alone after the death of a spouse, also outnumbered by a thin margin the old "traditional" family. Married couples represented only slightly more than half of the nation's households.

In census-taking terms, the variety of American households presented several challenges for counting them. Probably the most acute was the increasing difficulty of finding people at home. In 2000 a record high

share of the population was in the workforce, partly because women's labor force participation continued to climb over the decade, particularly among women whose children were grown, and partly because the mammoth baby-boom generation was in the midst of the prime working ages.

Another difficulty was assigning people to a particular home. The growing numbers of children living in nontraditional families challenged the census process because these children often live in more than one place. The growing numbers of older people also challenged the process because they, too, often live in more than one place. In short, traditional households were not only more likely to be home, but they were also more likely to have only one home for all of their members.

Because the single largest cost of the census is its giant temporary workforce, keeping census costs in bounds made it crucial to get the maximum number of Americans to answer the census by mail. Going door to door to get census information from the record high proportion of Americans who did not mail back their census form drove 1990 costs to record levels. The outlook for 2000 was even more bleak, and not just because more households than ever might have no one at home when the census-taker called.

Over the decade Americans' willingness to respond to surveys diminished. The growth of marketing by mail filled their mailboxes with appeals, and the growth of the Internet and computerized databases heightened their concerns about maintaining privacy. Many Americans were also expressing renewed mistrust in government. On top of all this, the president and Congress had committed themselves to reducing both the size and cost of government, and they initially requested a less costly census with no sacrifice in accuracy.

So Census 2000 gave every household an unprecedented set of opportunities to answer the census voluntarily—using multiple mailings, placing extra forms in places people go, taking responses by telephone, and designing user-friendly forms. In another first, a paid advertising campaign targeted the nation's diverse audiences, telling them the census was coming and why they should answer it.

More Diversity

While increasing household diversity made the average American harder to find, other kinds of diversity worsened the perennial census problem of finding all Americans. The 1990 census was the first since the Census Bureau began measuring the undercount—the gap between the total population as measured by birth, death, and immigration records and the census count—to reverse the trend of reducing it. In the decade leading to 2000, demographic trends continued to increase the numbers and proportion of people with characteristics that make them particularly hard to count.

Minority populations are especially hard to count, partly because they tend to feel excluded from or even threatened by government, but mostly because their living arrangements often do not fit the classic door-to-door census pattern. So the growth of the nation's minority population was another manifestation of increasing diversity and increasingly diverse demands on the census.

Blacks continued to be the nation's largest minority group; American Indians, its smallest. Continued high immigration made growth especially large among Hispanics, putting them on track to become the largest minority group early in the twenty-first century. Immigration also made Asians the nation's fastest growing minority. As a result, the census measured the nation's majority non-Hispanic white population at its lowest level in modern times—less than three-fourths of the total. Nevertheless, this majority was much larger than it was at the nation's founding.

The diverse living arrangements the census found were also a major challenge to census-takers. On the one hand, the census found a very high rate of home ownership. It also found a lessening of Americans' migration from the North and East to the South and West, compared with the 1970s and 1980s. Both home ownership and geographic stability make traditional census-taking techniques work better.

On the other hand, increased immigration and growth of minority populations also created more of the kinds of households that traditional techniques tend to miss. "Colonias" (unofficial communities with no public services) proliferated along the nation's border with Mexico; immigrant families or groups crowded into single-family units in cities where housing is costly. And many young adults, particularly men, found it hard to put down roots in an economy transforming under the impact of technology.

In 1990 the census missed a net 1.8 percent of the population, compared with 1.2 percent in 1980. Yet the increased costs of both censuses—beyond simple growth in the number of households—resulted almost entirely from efforts to extend traditional census-taking methods to untraditional living arrangements. Both the General Accounting Office (GAO) and the National Academy of Sciences concluded early in the planning for Census 2000 that, even if improved, those methods could contribute only marginally to overall census accuracy and efficiency in 2000. The academy and GAO independently recommended statistical sampling as the tool that could fill a gap that was growing larger.

This change proved politically controversial, and in a new way. Previous controversies over the undercount were primarily geographic, pitting the growth states of the Sun Belt against states in the Northeast and Midwest where population was growing slowly if at all. In 2000 the political issue was still based on geographic differences, but was focused on cities versus suburbs. For the first time in decades, the Congress was led by the Republicans. They attributed their success to voters from the suburbs, where traditional census-taking techniques work well. Eliminating the undercount would give more representation to cities, whose inhabitants were more likely to vote for the Democrats. With a slowdown in migration, particularly from cities to suburbs, the strategists from each party became fixated on maximizing the count in the areas that were most important to them. The political controversy thus pitted Republicans against Democrats, not region against region.

Controversy over using statistical sampling thus became the defining characteristic of Census 2000. The Supreme Court decided before the census that the sampling techniques could not be used to apportion the House of Representatives. But it left the door open to using them for other purposes. So the final innovation of Census 2000 was the provision of two sets of numbers, one showing the results of the traditional techniques, the other the results adjusted by statistical quality control procedures.

■ Martha Farnsworth Riche

Bibliography

Riche, Martha Farnsworth. "Cultural and Political Dimensions of the U.S. Census: Past and Present." *American Behavioral Scientist*, vol. 42, no. 6 (March 1999): 933–945.

Riche, Martha Farnsworth. "U.S. Population, 1900–1999." *Population Bulletin* 55 (2000).

Riche, Martha Farnsworth, and Judith Waldrop. "America's Changing Demographic Tapestry." In James W. Hughes and Joseph Seneca, eds., *America's Demographic Tapestry*. New Brunswick, N.J.: Rutgers University Press, 1999.

Demographic analysis

In the United States, methods of demographic analysis have become the standard for measuring coverage trends between censuses and differences in coverage by age, sex, and race at the national level. Demographic analysis (DA) has documented the long-term reduction in the census net undercount rate over the last fifty years; yet demographic analysis also reveals the persistent and disproportionate undercount of certain demographic groups (such as black men). A goal of Census 2000 is to reduce these differential undercounts.

Demographic analysis represents a macro-level approach to measuring coverage, where analytic estimates of net undercount are derived by comparing aggregate sets of data or counts. In general, DA population estimates are developed for the census date by analysis of various types of demographic data essentially independent of the census, such as administrative statistics on births, deaths, and immigration; estimates of emigration and undocumented immigration; and Medicare data. The difference between the DA estimated population and the census count provides an estimate of the net census undercount.

Data collected in post-enumeration surveys and dual system estimation are components of another methodology used by the Census Bureau to measure undercount. In Census 2000, this program is called the Accuracy and Coverage Evaluation (A.C.E.). In the A.C.E., a stratified sample of census blocks are reinterviewed independently of the census enumeration. The results of these interviews are checked against the census records on an individual basis to see who was missed and who was counted in error. The A.C.E. represents a micro-level approach and differs fundamentally from the demographic analysis method. The A.C.E. program is described elsewhere in this volume; DA is the focus of this article.

Description of the Demographic Analysis Method

The particular analytic procedure used to estimate coverage nationally for the various demographic subgroups depends primarily on the nature and availability of the required demographic data. Two principal demographic techniques will be used to produce the demographic analysis estimates for 2000, one for the population under age 65 and another for the population 65 and over. Essentially the same methodology was used for the 1990 census. In this section we describe the age group components, the development of historical estimates, and the limitations of the estimates.

Age Group Components. Ages under sixty-five. The demographic analysis estimates for the population below age sixty-five are based on the compilation of historical estimates of the components of population change: births (B), deaths (D), immigration (I), and emigration (E). Presuming that the components are measured accurately, the population estimates (P0-64) are derived by the basic demographic accounting equation applied to each birth cohort:

$$P0\text{-}64 = B - D + I - E \qquad (1)$$

The actual calculations are carried out for single-year birth cohorts. For example, the estimate of the population age forty on April 1, 2000, is based on births from April 1959 to March 1960 (adjusted for underregistration), reduced by deaths to the cohort in each year between 1960 and 2000, and incremented by estimated immigration and emigration of the cohort over the forty-year period.

The historical data on births come from the vital registration system. These data have been available for all states since about 1933. The extent of underregistration has been empirically quantified and correction factors are available. Births represent by far the largest component in equation 1. The component of deaths is based on administrative records. These records are relatively complete. Data on legal immigration come from the Immigration and Naturalization Service. The number of emigrants and undocumented immigrants are estimated using analytic methods; these two components are subject to the greatest uncertainty.

Age sixty-five and over. Administrative data on aggregate Medicare enrollments are used to estimate the population age sixty-five and over (P65+):

$$P65+ = M + m, \qquad (2)$$

where M is the aggregate Medicare enrollment and m is the estimate of underenrollment. Although Medicare enrollment data are generally presumed to be quite accurate, adjustments are made to the basic data to account for groups who are omitted.

Development of Historical Estimates for Multiple Censuses. The foundation of the demographic method is the logical consistency and relation of the underlying demographic data. With the use of components of change (births, deaths, net immigration), the estimated population for a birth cohort can be carried forward through time to derive estimates of net undercount in a series of censuses as the cohort ages (for example, age 0–4 in 1950, 10–14 in 1960, 20–24 in 1970, 30–34 in 1980, 40–44 in 1990, and 50–54 in 2000). Similarly, an older cohort in 1990 based on Medicare data can be carried backward in time to derive estimates for the cohort at younger ages (for example, 65–69 in 2000, 55–59 in 1990, 45–49 in 1980, 35–39 in 1970, and so on). In this way, consistent estimates of net undercount for 1940 to 2000 based on demographic analysis are produced.

These multiple series of net undercount estimates for cohorts across censuses are linked through the components of population change. This linkage of the estimates provides a consistent basis to judge changes in patterns of coverage over time and to assess the plausibility of the demographic estimates themselves.

Limitations of the Demographic Estimates. The aggregate administrative data and estimates that are incorporated in equations 1 and 2 are corrected for various types of errors. Many assumptions go into this estimation process, some of which can be validated and some of which are based on quite limited information.

Births are by far the largest component of population change involved in the DA system; thus even relatively small errors in the estimates of births and the assumptions used to correct for underregistration can have significant effects. The adjustments for birth underregistration are based on three tests of registration completeness (1940, 1950, and 1964–1968). The estimated level of completeness was 92.5 in 1940 (81.9 percent for black births), 97.9 in 1950 (93.7 for black births), and 99.2 by 1964–1968. Factors for other years are derived by interpolation and extrapolation. In particular, the estimated number of black births depends on the quality of the correction factors. An investigation and subsequent revision of the 1940 birth registration results led to a downward adjustment to the time series of black births (1935–1950) and lowered the estimated net undercount for those black cohorts.

With the exception of a correction for infant deaths occurring in years prior to 1960, death statistics are used without any adjustments for misreporting of age, sex, or race or for underregistration. Immigration and emigration, while smaller overall components than births or deaths, are subject to more relative error because of the greater uncertainty of some specific estimated elements (especially emigration and undocumented immigration).

The overall accuracy of the demographic estimates depends on the quality of the demographic data and corrections. The internal consistency of the demographic estimates permits trends and changes in coverage patterns over time to be estimated more precisely than the exact level of net coverage in any given census.

Finally, note that the principal demographic estimates for age, sex, and race groups measure net undercount in the census. They do not tell us about the separate components of net coverage error (omissions, erroneous inclusions) or net content error.

Historical Trends, 1940–1990

Table 1 presents historically consistent estimates of percent net undercount for the decennial censuses from 1940 to 1990. The demographic estimates document the long-term decline in net census undercounts over the last fifty years. The net undercount in the 1990 census is estimated to have been under 2 percent, well below the estimated 5.4 percent in 1940. The estimated undercount has declined both for blacks (from 8.4 percent in 1940 to 5.7 percent in 1990) and nonblacks (5.0 percent to 1.3 percent). For all groups, the net undercount in 1990 was higher than in 1980, but below 1970 levels.

Despite the overall declines in net undercount, the undercount rate for blacks has remained persistently

Table 1. Demographic Analysis Estimates of Percentage Net Undercount, by Race: 1940-1990

	1940	1950	1960	1970	1980	1990
Percent:						
Total	5.4	4.1	3.1	2.7	1.2	1.8
Black	8.4	7.5	6.6	6.5	4.5	5.7
Nonblack	5.0	3.8	2.7	2.2	0.8	1.3
Percentage Point Difference:						
Black-Nonblack	3.4	3.6	3.9	4.3	3.7	4.4

Table 2. Demographic Analysis Estimates of Percentage Net Undercount for Blacks: 1960–1990

	1960	1970	1980	1990
Percent:				
Total	3.1	2.7	1.2	1.8
Black	6.6	6.5	4.5	5.7
Black men				
20–64	13.4	13.1	11.3	11.2
Black 0–9				
(male and female)	5.4	8.1	7.0	8.0
Other Black	4.4	2.9	0.4	2.0

higher than the rate for nonblacks in each census between 1940 and 1990. In fact, the excess of the net undercount rate for blacks has hovered in the range of 3.4 to 4.4 percentage points over the last six censuses (see last row of Table 1). The differential undercount is most pronounced for black men and black children.

Table 2 gives a perspective of how the relatively high net undercounts for black men and black children contribute disproportionately to the well-known differential undercount for all blacks.

The pattern of relatively high undercounts among black subgroups in 1990 repeats the pattern from 1960 to 1980. Indeed, crude historical demographic estimates of percentage net undercount that extend back to 1880 demonstrate the intractable nature of the undercount for certain groups, especially black men.

History of Demographic Analysis

Demographic analysis has a long history in the Census Bureau. The first demographic-based estimates of net undercount focused on the 1940 census and specific demographic subgroups. One study by the Bureau of the Census in 1944 looked at the completeness of enumeration of children under age five and found significant differences in the coverage of black and nonblack children. Another study, by Daniel O. Price, examined the completeness of the 1940 census for young men age twenty-one through thirty-five. Price used figures from the first compulsory draft registration which started on October 16, 1940. He created comparable census figures by using demographic analysis to age the census count on April 1 to October 16, 1940. Black men were found to be undercounted by 13 percent, compared to 3.1 percent for all men in this age group.

In the 1950s, Ansley Coale used the balancing equation of demography (combining birth, death, and migration statistics) to create an estimate of the true population against which the 1950 census could be evaluated. Coale used different analytic procedures for different age groups and assumed age misstatements and errors of omission to form similar patterns from one census to the next. He was the first to identify age-sex patterns of coverage as well as race differences.

In 1966, Jacob S. Siegel and Melvin Zelnik evaluated the completeness of the 1960 census using the DA method. Again, different analytical procedures were applied to different age-sex groups. The age, sex, and race patterns of estimated undercount for 1960 were found to be similar to those in the 1950 census. Up to age fifty, the enumeration was less complete for men than for women. Up to age sixty or sixty-five, the enumeration of nonwhites was less complete than the enumeration of whites.

By the 1970 census, the DA results had become the standard for measuring trends and differentials in coverage. Other developments occurred around this time. Data from the Medicare system became available for improving the DA estimates of the population sixty-five and over. Finally, by using state-of-birth data, subnational DA estimates were developed for the first time.

The DA methodology continued to be developed, new data sources were incorporated, and estimated components of change were improved for the coverage evaluations of the 1980 and 1990 censuses. In 1980, an explicit estimate of the number of undocumented residents was included as a demographic component for the first time. In 1990, explicit measures of uncertainty in the DA net undercount estimates were developed.

Research on methodological improvements and refinements to the DA estimates continues as we approach Census 2000. In recent years, plans have evolved for expansion of the demographic evaluation program. The vision is to produce coverage estimates on a timely basis (during the census process) and to extend the scope of demographic coverage indicators below the national level. More recently, the vision also includes the use of demographic benchmarks, such as housing unit estimates, as a tool to provide assessment of coverage early in the census process. This goal has become more attainable as the automation of data collection and processing ensure earlier availability and accessibility of the data. The 1995 Census Test in Paterson, New Jersey; Oakland, California, and six parishes in northwest Louisiana provided the first opportunity to demonstrate the utility of an evaluation program expanded to the subnational level. The Census 2000 Dress Rehearsal in Sacramento, California; Menominee County, Wisconsin; and eleven counties in South Carolina offered the opportunity to focus on housing unit estimates as well. In sum, the DA program for Census 2000 is more comprehensive in its scope and timeliness than previous evaluations.

The demographic indicators of coverage for subnational areas are subject to the same limitations as the national estimates and more. Their error distribution is unknown, and will always be difficult to estimate. Systematic series of consistency checks are used to assess the plausibility of the estimates. As with the national estimates, the intention is to use the new indicators only for broadly assessing patterns of coverage across geographic areas and changes in coverage between censuses.

See also *Accuracy and Coverage Evaluation; Population estimates and projections.*

■ J. Gregory Robinson and Kirsten K. West

Bibliography

Coale, Ansley J. "The Population of the United States in 1950 Classified by Age, Sex and Color—A Revision of Census Figures." *Journal of the American Statistical Association* 50, no. 269 (1955): 16–54.

Das Gupta, Prithwis. "Demographic Evaluation Project D10: Models for Assessing Errors in Undercount Rates Based on Demographic Analysis." *Preliminary Research and Evaluation Memorandum* 84. Washington, D.C.: U.S. Bureau of the Census, 1991.

Fernandez, Edward W. *Using Analytical Techniques to Evaluate the 1990 Census of Coverage of Young Hispanics.* Technical Working Paper No. 11, Population Division. Washington, D.C.: U.S. Bureau of the Census, 1995.

Himes, Christine L., and Clifford C. Clogg. "An Overview of Demographic Analysis as a Method for Evaluating Census Coverage in the United States." *Population Index* 58, no. 4 (1992): 587–607. Princeton, N.J.: Office of Population Research.

Hogan, Howard R., and J. Gregory Robinson. *What the Census Bureau's Coverage Evaluation Programs Tell Us About Differential Undercount.* Richmond, Va.: Bureau of the Census: Research Conference on Undercounted Ethnic Populations, 1993.

Kohn, Felipe. "Evaluation of Reduction in Differential Undercount Based on the Analysis of Sex Ratios." *Integrated Coverage Measurement (ICM) Evaluation Project 13.* Washington, D.C.: U.S. Bureau of the Census, 1996.

Passel, Jeffrey. S. "Age-Period-Cohort Analysis of Census Undercount Rates for Race-Sex Groups, 1940–1980: Implications for the Method of Demographic Analysis." *Proceedings of the Social Statistics Section of the American Statistical Association* (1991): 326–331. Washington, D.C.: American Statistical Association.

Passel, Jeffrey. S. *Demographic Analysis: A Report on Its Utility for Adjusting the 1990 Census.* Washington, D.C.: The Urban Institute, 1990.

Price, Daniel O. "A Check on Underenumeration in the 1940 Census." *American Sociological Review* 12 (1947): 44–49.

Robinson, J. Gregory, Kirsten K. West and Arjun Adlakha. "Assessment of Consistency of Census Results with Demographic Benchmarks." *Census 2000 Dress Rehearsal Evaluation Memorandum C7.* Washington, D.C.: U.S. Bureau of the Census, 1999.

Robinson, J. Gregory. "Evaluation of CensusPlus and Dual System Estimates Results with Independent Demographic Benchmarks." *Integrated Coverage Measurement (ICM) Evaluation Project 15.* Washington, D.C.: U.S. Bureau of the Census, 1996.

———. "Demographic Review of the Housing and Population Results of the 1995 Test Censuses." *Memorandum to Arthur J. Norton, Chief, Population Division, U.S. Bureau of the Census.* Washington, D.C.: U.S. Bureau of the Census, 1996.

———. "Use of Analytical Methods for Coverage Evaluation in the 2000 Census." Paper presented at the Annual Meeting of the Population Association of America, Miami, May 5–7, 1994.

Robinson, J. Gregory, B. Ahmed, P. Das Gupta, and K. A. Woodrow. "Estimation of Population Coverage in the 1990 United States Census Based on Demographic Analysis." *Journal of the American Statistical Association* 88, no. 423 (1993): 1061-1071.

Robinson, J. Gregory, B. Ahmed, and E. Fernandez. "Demographic Analysis as an Expanded Program for Early Coverage Evaluation of the 2000 Census." *Proceedings of the 1993 Annual Research Conference* (1993): 166-200. Arlington, Va.: U.S. Bureau of the Census.

Robinson, J. Gregory. "Demographic Analysis Evaluation Project D1: Error in the Birth Registration Completeness Estimates." *Preliminary Research and Evaluation Memorandum* no. 74 (1991). Washington, D.C.: U.S. Bureau of the Census.

Robinson, J. Gregory and Howard Hogan. "Differential Coverage in the United States Census of Population: An Historical Review." *Proceedings of Statistics Canada Symposium* 90 (1990): 67-78.

Robinson, J. Gregory, P. Das Gupta, and B. Ahmed. "A Case Study in the Investigation of Errors in Estimates of Coverage Based on Demographic Analysis: Black Adults Aged 35 to 54 in 1980." *Proceedings of the Social Statistics Section of the Annual Meeting of The American Statistical Association* (1990): 187-192.

Siegel, Jacob S., and Melvin Zelnik. "An Evaluation of Coverage in the 1960 Census of Population by Techniques of Demographic Analysis and by Composite Methods." In *Proceedings of the Social Statistics Section of the American Statistical Association* (1966): 71-85. Washington, D.C.: American Statistical Association.

U.S. Bureau of the Census. "The Coverage of Population in the 1980 Census," by Robert Fay, Jeffrey S. Passel and J. Gregory Robinson. *Evaluation and Research Reports, PHC80-E4.* Washington, D.C.: U.S. Government Printing Office, 1988.

———. "Developmental Estimates of the Coverage of the Population of States in the 1970 Census: Demographic Analysis." *Current Population Reports.* Series P-23, No. 65. Washington, D.C.: U.S. Government Printing Office, 1977.

———. "Estimates of Coverage of Population by Sex, Race, and Age: Demographic Analysis." *Census of Population and Housing: 1970 Evaluation and Research Program, No. PHC(E)-4.* Washington, D.C.: U.S. Government Printing Office, 1974.

———. "Standardized Fertility Rates and Reproduction Rates."*Population. Differential Fertility, 1940 and 1910. Sixteenth Census of the United States: 1940.* U.S. Department of Commerce, U.S. Bureau of the Census. Washington, D.C.

West, Kirsten, and J. Gregory Robinson. "An Assessment of Census 2000 Dress Rehearsal Results: Consistency of Housing Unit Data with Demographic Benchmarks."*Proceedings of the Social Statistics Section of the American Statistical Association.* Washington, D.C.: American Statistical Association, forthcoming.

Depository libraries

One of the best ways to locate and use current or historical census data is to visit a depository library. The Federal Depository Library Program (FDLP) is a cooperative venture between the United States Government Printing Office (GPO) and America's library community. Authorized by Title 44, Chapter 19, of the U.S. Code, the purpose of the FDLP is to make government information readily accessible to the general public at no cost to the user. Under the provisions of the program, the GPO provides participating libraries with publications and databases at no charge; in turn, the libraries agree to provide access to materials and help the public use them. Slightly more than 1,400 depository libraries currently operate in the United States and its territories.

History of the FDLP

As far back as 1813 Congress recognized the fundamental importance of distributing government information to as wide an audience as possible. The American Antiquarian Society's Philadelphia library became the country's first depository library. A truly national network for distributing government publications began to take shape in the 1850s, when a series of resolutions and laws established the necessary components, including the transfer of pertinent responsibility from the Department of the Interior to the newly established Government Printing Office in 1861. Landmark legislation in 1895 further centralized printing and distribution activities, increased the scope and number of depository libraries, established an ongoing publications catalog, and reduced duplication and waste in the system. The Depository Library Program as it exists today took shape through the passage of the Depository Library Act of 1962. Changes in the 1970s further expanded the types of libraries eligible for depository status and incorporated microfiche as a significant means of distributing publications. Throughout the 1990s, Congress, the Government Printing Office, and the library community have worked toward establishing a coherent policy of handling electronic information, including the passage of major legislation in 1993.

Depository Basics

A library can obtain depository status in one of two ways. By law, certain types of libraries are eligible to become a depository on request; these include state libraries, federal and state appellate court libraries, federal agency libraries, and accredited law school libraries. The second method is to be nominated by the institution's congressional delegation. Each congressional district is entitled to two depository libraries created in this way, and the state is entitled to two additional depositories nominated by its senators. In practice, not all congressional districts have two such depositories—some have three, others have only one. This situation results from a combination of local needs and the history of congressional redistricting in the area.

The law specifies two types of depository libraries: regional and selective. Regional Depositories are required to receive all depository materials published by the GPO and to keep them in perpetuity. Each state is entitled to two Regional Depositories, but because of the high cost of maintaining regional status, most states have only one. At present, there are fifty-three Regional Depositories in the United States.

Selective Depositories, as the name suggests, may choose which categories of publications they wish to receive, in keeping with the local library's collecting policies and needs. Selective Depositories may also discard older publications deemed no longer useful, although the library must follow GPO guidelines for doing so. All Selective Depositories are encouraged to accept a small "core collection" of important designated publications, such as the *Budget of the U.S. Government*. At present, decennial census publications for the library's home state are included on the core list, as are the bureau's *County and City Data Book* and *Statistical Abstract*.

FDLP law specifies that the Government Printing Office must provide depository libraries with designated documents free of charge. In turn, depositories agree to process and shelve the materials in a manner and timeliness similar to other library materials; to provide the requisite computers, microform readers, photocopiers, and other equipment necessary to use the materials; and to provide the general public with assistance in locating and using the publications.

Technically, depository materials are owned by the government, not by individual libraries. The law requires depository libraries to provide all members of the public access to those materials, even if an individual is not otherwise entitled to use that library. For example, regular access to a university library might be restricted to students, faculty, and alumni of the school, but anyone who wishes to do so has the right to use that library's depository publications.

Individual libraries may determine local circulation policies for their depository collections. Some libraries allow depository materials to be borrowed, others limit access to in-library use only. The GPO also allows depositories to organize their collections according to local policies. Some libraries intershelve depository publications with all other books, magazines, and library materials. Many libraries keep their depository collections separate, typically in a "government documents" department. GPO inspectors visit every depository library at least once every seven years to ensure that the institution is following FDLP policies and guidelines.

It is important to remember that depository libraries, even regional ones, are not comprehensive repositories for every government document. Many government publications are "non-depository" titles. The law requires the Government Printing Office to assign depository status only to publications of "public interest or educational value." (Researchers can use the Internet to determine the depository status of GPO publications by consulting the *Monthly Catalog of U.S. Government Publications* at http://www.access.gpo.gov/su_docs/dpos/adpos400.html. This version of the *Monthly Catalog* contains entries for all GPO publications listed from 1994 to the present.) For smaller print runs, individual agencies can arrange their own printing, bypassing the GPO completely, and most of these items never find their way to libraries.

A second limitation is that some materials designated as depository publications fall through the cracks somehow and never get distributed to libraries. It should be noted that the Census Bureau has a strong tradition of cooperating with the GPO, and nearly all of the bureau's important publications are distributed through the depository program.

Benefits of Using Depository Libraries

Depository libraries offer several major benefits to people looking for census data: depositories are conveniently located across the United State; access to them is free and open to everyone; and depository librarians are familiar with census publications, terminology, and concepts and are happy to share that knowledge with anyone, from casual user to serious researcher. In addition, a typical depository library will receive related statistical data from a host of other federal agencies, such as the Bureau of Economic Analysis or the Bureau of Labor Statistics. Most depository libraries also purchase commercially produced databases, printed indexes, and other resources to enhance the usefulness of their census materials.

Larger depository collections offer several advantages beyond what might be found through the Census Bureau's regional offices or its State Data Centers. First, major depositories collect census information for the entire country, whereas other organizations might limit coverage to their home state. Second, many libraries have maintained depository status for a century or more, creating a rich collection of retrospective census materials unavailable elsewhere.

An obvious question that comes to mind is, Why do we need depository libraries if everything from the government is now on the Internet? The short, but perhaps not obvious, answer is, "Everything is not on the Internet." Although the government's official policy, promulgated in the U.S. Office of Management and Budget's circular A-130 (February 1996), encourages government agencies to distribute public information electronically, a large number of important publications have not yet made the transition from a paper environment. For example, although the Census Bureau stands at the forefront of Internet publishing, a great deal of retrospective census data may never find its way to the World Wide Web.

A second answer is that the continued existence of depository libraries provides a safeguard against the ever-increasing pressures on federal agencies to charge fees for electronic data. Finally, depository librarians are expert at organizing information in all its forms, and some of the best Web-based guides and directories of government information sources have been created by depository librarians or the GPO itself.

Locating the Nearest Depository Library

As of 1999, 66 percent of America's 1,400 depository libraries were housed in colleges, universities, or community colleges, and 20 percent could be found in public libraries. The remaining 14 percent were located in federal agency libraries, official state libraries, court libraries, and other specialized organizations.

Census users can locate their nearest depository by consulting the *Federal Depository Library Directory* on the Internet (http://www.access.gpo.gov/su_docs/dpos/ldirect.html). This interactive search service is part of the Government Printing Office's *GPO Access* database. The Web-based directory is searchable by state, city, ZIP code, telephone area code, or congressional district. Users can also search by library, institution, or librarian name. Search results can be limited by library type, depository type (regional or selective), library size, or the year the library was first designated as a depository. Directory listings include each depository library's address, telephone and fax numbers, names of key staff members, and links to the library's Web site.

Depository Libraries Today and Tomorrow

The biggest challenges facing the Federal Depository Library Program are the Internet and electronic publishing. As of 1999, traditional printed products represented a small percentage of the information for which the GPO was responsible. In addition to the agency's own *GPO Access* Web site, most federal orga-

nizations maintain their own extensive Internet resources. Many publications formerly available as tangible paper products now exist only in electronic form. In one sense, the advent of the Internet makes government publications more accessible than ever before. Still, the decentralized, ever-changing nature of the Internet, together with its enormous size, can make it difficult for users to locate needed information from the government. Recognizing these concerns, Congress passed the Government Printing Office Electronic Information Access Enhancement Act of 1993. The law recognizes the GPO's responsibility for cataloging and keeping track of the government's electronic publications, a task that the GPO is addressing via *GPO Access*, the *Monthly Catalog*, and other means.

A related concern is that some government-produced electronic publications, such as the Commerce Department's *STAT-USA* database, are not free to the general public. Whether because of legislative mandate or agency budget constraints, such fee-based products are likely to proliferate in the coming years. This is a particular concern for census users because the bureau has clearly stated that the Internet will become its primary means of data dissemination for the future. Much of this electronic information will be free, but some portions will most likely not be. The Government Printing Office and the library community will continue working with Congress and with agencies like the Census Bureau to ensure that important fee-based electronic products will be available to visitors of depository libraries at no cost, and that historical archives of electronic publications will be preserved for future generations.

See also *Archival access to the census; Dissemination of data: printed publications.*

■ Michael Lavin

Bibliography

Note: All of the Government Printing Office publications listed below can also be found in electronic form on the "FDl Administration Publications" page of *GPO Access*, <http://www.access.gpo.gov/su_docs/dpos/fdlppubs.html#4>.

Brown, Wendy R. "Federal Initiatives to Promote Access to Electronic Government Information: The Impact on the Federal Depository Library Program."*Law Library Journal* 91 (Spring 1999): 291–303.
Herman, Edward. *Locating United States Government Information: A Guide to Sources.* 2d ed. Buffalo, N.Y.: William S. Hein, 1997.
Morehead, Joe. *Introduction to United States Government Infor-*

mation Sources. 5th ed. Englewood, Colo.: Libraries Unlimited, 1996.

O'Mahony, Daniel P. "The Federal Depository Library Program in Transition: A Perspective at the Turn of the Century." *Government Information Quarterly* 15 (1998): 13–26.

Robinson, Judith Schiek. *Tapping the Government Grapevine: The User-Friendly Guide to U.S. Government Information Sources.* 3d ed. Phoenix. Ariz.: Oryx Press, 1998.

U.S. Government Printing Office. *Study to Identify Measures for a Successful Transition to a More Electronic Federal Depository Library Program: Final Report to Congress.* Washington, D.C., 1996.

U.S. Library Programs Service, Government Printing Office. *Federal Depository Library Manual.* Washington, D.C., 1993.

———. *Keeping America Informed: The Federal Depository Library Program.* Washington, D.C., 1999.

U.S. Office of the Assistant Printer, Government Printing Office. *List of Classes of U.S. Government Publications Available for Selection by Depository Libraries.* Washington, 1999.

Disability

Since 1830, the decennial census has asked a variety of different questions on the disability status of the population. The data are not uniform over the years, nor were questions asked consistently from 1830 forward. Reporting of the results of questions on disability also varies widely from census to census. Data users thus need to take particular care in examining the format of particular questions and understanding their intent, since concepts of disability, as well as the legislative responsibilities of the federal government with regard to disabled Americans, have changed over the years. Current federal policy is defined by the Americans with Disabilities Act (1990). The act defines disability as a "physical or mental impairment that substantially limits one or more of the major life activities."

The 2000 census long form contains two areas of questions on an individual's disability status. The first asks for yes or no answers to whether the person has "any of the following long-lasting conditions: Blindness, deafness, or a severe vision or hearing impairment" and whether the individual has "a condition that substantially limits one or more basic physical activities such as walking, climbing stairs, reaching, lifting, or carrying." The second asks if a "physical, mental, or emotional condition lasting 6 months or more" causes the individual to have "any difficulty" in "learning, remembering, or con-

centrating" or in "dressing, bathing, or getting around inside the home." For persons sixteen years of age or more, the questions ask if the person has difficulty "going outside the home alone to shop or visit a doctor's office" or "working at a job or business."

The questions identify the number of persons of working age who could be limited from working by a long-lasting condition. They also identify the number of individuals who could need help or care in managing daily activities because of a "long-lasting condition."

Prior census questions addressed similar concerns, albeit at different levels of detail. The 1830 census, which collected data by household only, asked for the number of individuals in the household who were "deaf and dumb" in three age cohorts: under fourteen, from fourteen to twenty-four, and twenty-five and up. The information was gathered for whites and separately for slaves and the free colored. The 1830 census also asked for the numbers of blind whites and blind free coloreds and slaves but did not ask for age breakdowns. The 1840 census added questions on the number of "insane and idiots," by race, and whether they were "at public charge" or "at private charge," that is, cared for privately or in public institutions. In the parlance of the day, an "insane" person was mentally ill; an "idiot" was "feeble-minded" or mentally retarded. By 1880, disability questions on the main population questionnaire had increased to six, and the enumerator was asked to record for each individual counted whether the person was, "on the day of the enumerator's visit, sick or temporarily disabled, so as to be unable to attend to ordinary business or duties"; "blind"; "deaf and dumb"; "idiotic"; "insane"; or "maimed, crippled, bedridden, or otherwise disabled." From 1880 to 1930 the decennial census also used "supplemental schedules" on the disabled, which collected a wide variety of additional data. Questions on disability were not asked on the main population census form for the census of 1900 and for the counts from 1920 to 1960; they were resumed in 1970 on the long form.

The questions used to gauge disability have been the subject of much debate in modern census taking. After the 1970 census, a post-census disability survey tested the reliability of data collected in the 1970 count. The survey re-asked a sample of census respondents about their disability status as of census day 1970. A sizable number of respondents who earlier reported disabilities no longer did so in the survey, leading many to question the reliability of responses. Some researchers proposed dropping the questions for 1980. Organizations serving the disabled community pointed out that the decennial census was the only source of small-area data on disability and put pressure on the bureau to retain the items. They were continued in 1980.

During the 1980s, content specialists sought to create a question that went beyond the 1970 item that focused exclusively on disabilities related to work. An item was needed that could encompass the entire population and not just those who were in the working ages. As a result, an item was added that asked about health conditions lasting six or more months that made it difficult or impossible to use public transportation. Post-censal studies showed, however, that the responses to the new public transportation disability item were difficult to interpret. Planners, for example, viewed the data from this item as too general, especially in light of the wide differences among communities in the types of public transportation that were referred to in the question. Ultimately, the Health and Disability Interagency Working Group recommended that the public transportation disability item be dropped from the 1990 census, and the transportation planners concurred.

In addition to the questions on work disability, two items were added in 1990: health conditions lasting six months or more that affected mobility and self-care. These items were regarded as more useful as a measure of disability for the overall population, including those who have low levels of labor force participation, such as the elderly.

About 10 percent of Americans of working age (ages sixteen to sixty-four), and 20 percent of Americans sixty-five and over reported a disability in the 1990 census that limited their ability to work, get around, or perform personal care. Data on the number and characteristics of disabled Americans are also collected in periodic surveys such as the Survey of Income and Program Participation (SIPP) and the Current Population Survey and through administrative records of agencies charged with caring for the disabled. SIPP provides the most detailed federal survey data. For persons fifteen years old and over, the SIPP disability questions cover limitations in functional activities (seeing, hearing, speaking, lifting and carrying, using stairs, and walking), in activities of daily living, or ADLs (getting around inside the home, getting in or out of a bed or chair, bathing, dressing, eating, and toileting), and in instrumental activities of daily living, or IADLs (going outside the home, keeping track of money or bills, preparing meals, doing light housework, and using the telephone). SIPP also obtains information on the use of wheelchairs and crutches, canes, and walkers; the presence of certain conditions related to mental functioning; the presence of a work disability; and the disability status of children. According to the SIPP from 1991–1992, 49 million noninstitutionalized Americans (about 20 percent of the population) have a disability; 34 percent of those with disabilities were age sixty-five or older.

In the past a much smaller proportion of the population reported the particular mental and physical categories of disability asked on the census. Between 1850 and 1880 the total deaf, dumb, blind, insane, and idiotic population ranged from 0.2 to 0.5 percent of the total population. The 1880 census counted 0.68 percent of the population, about 341,000 people, as "maimed, crippled, bedridden, or otherwise disabled."

■ Margo Anderson

Bibliography

Integrated Public Use Microdata Samples. www.ipums.umn.edu.
U.S. Bureau of the Census. *Americans with Disabilities.* Statistical Brief. SB/94-1. Washington, D.C.: U.S. Government Printing Office, 1994.
———. *1990 Census of Population and Housing: History, Part D,* chap. 14. CPH-R-2D. Washington, D.C.: U.S. Government Post Office, 1996.
———. *Population and Housing Inquiries in U.S. Decennial Censuses, 1790–1970.* Working paper no. 39. Washington, D.C.: U.S. Government Printing Office, 1973.

Dissemination of data: electronic products

The advances in computation, communication, and information technology over the past forty years have had a dramatic impact on the dissemination and use of census data. Until the 1960 census, printed reports issued by the Bureau of the Census were the primary source of information from the decennial censuses. These reports presented tabulations and summary statistics for a variety of geographic and census-defined areas as well as selected sub-populations. For the 1960 census, the Census Bureau released to the public for the first time tabulated data and microdata on punched card and magnetic tape media. These files were precursors to the Summary Tape Files (STF) and Public Use Microdata Sample (PUMS) files that were disseminated for the 1970 and subsequent censuses.

The tabular data for 1960 were distributed in electronic formats similar to those used in subsequent censuses. Documentation and support were minimal. Data Use and Access Laboratories (DUALabs), created as a private organization by Jack Beresford, former chief of the Census Bureau's Data Access and Use Laboratory (DAUL), distributed and supported the summary tape data from the 1970 census.

The microdata released for 1960 differed significantly from those released for 1970 and subsequent censuses. Two samples were released, 1/1,000 and 1/10,000, each as flat (or rectangular) files that included in each data record a subset of housing-level and person-level data.

In the early 1970s, the Bureau of the Census re-released the 1960 microdata (the documentation from DUALabs is dated January 1973). The intent was to provide a 1/100 sample for 1960 structured similarly to the 1970 public use sample that was forthcoming. DUALabs documented, disseminated, and supported this 1960 Public Use Sample (PUS), as it was referred to in their documentation. The 1960 PUS was structured hierarchically (person-level records nested within housing-level records) with larger numbers of items and more detailed geography than were included in the original 1960 releases from the Bureau of the Census. Although copies of the original 1960 microdata files from the Bureau of the Census still exist, most users of 1960 microdata use the 1/100 PUS released by DUALabs in 1973 (or the IPUMS version of the data).

Mainframe computing technology evolved through the 1970s and 1980s with the capability to handle increasingly larger data sets at increasingly faster speeds. Software for managing and analyzing data was also developed during this period. Then, in the 1990s came desktop computers with processing and data storage capabilities that exceeded those of earlier mainframes, client-server networks, parallel processors, read-only compact disks (CD-ROM), the Internet, browsers, and the World Wide Web (WWW). The consequences of these recent developments have filtered into the dissemination of 1990 census data in the last years of the decade, and will be more fully apparent when the 2000 census data become available.

Initial releases of public machine-readable files were made possible by the installation at the Census Bureau of a tape-based Remington-Rand Univac processing system for handling the 1960 census. The Univac (UNIVersal Automatic Calculator), delivered to the Census Bureau in 1951, was one of the first computers available for non-military and non-defense applications. The machine-readable files allowed users with access to advanced computing facilities to produce custom analyses, which had not been possible from printed reports.

The printed reports were often sufficient for persons seeking specific demographic information about a geographical or political area. However, printed reports have two major shortcomings. (1) They may not have precisely the information a user desires. The Census Bureau attempts with each census to foresee information that will be most needed by the public and to provide that information in the printed reports. Even with the production of hundreds of printed volumes containing tens of thousands of tables, the Census Bureau cannot fully anticipate and meet all needs. (2) The printed reports cannot be easily used for analyses and comparisons across large numbers of areas or characteristics. Researchers, for example, who wish to compare metropolitan areas across the nation need to work with hundreds of printed tabulations. The release of these data on machine-readable media offers users the opportunity to manipulate census data better to meet their particular needs.

Census data have proven to be relevant to a broad range of concerns of interest to researchers, policy-makers, decision-makers, planners, and the commercial community. While the primary constitutional purpose of the decennial census is to provide population counts required for the allocation of seats in the House of Representatives to the states, the uses of the data now extend far beyond that initial purpose. Much of the content of the census questionnaire is linked to the requirements of federal agencies for planning, monitoring, and evaluating programs. For example, items on income and other economic data are used by a number of federal agencies. Information on motor vehicles, time leaving for work, travel time, and place of work are of special interest to the Department of Transportation. In 1970, an item on battery-powered radios provided information relevant to civil defense and emergency planning should mass failures occur in the national electric power grid.

State and local agencies have similar needs for census data. The Census Bureau has established regional offices to provide support services to users. State data centers have been organized in all states to assist state, local, and other public agencies with the use of census data, including with intercensal estimates of the population at various sub-state geographies. While the data alone as distributed by the Census Bureau are frequently of interest, agencies often wish to link other data to census data. The geographic detail provided in the published and STF files allows linking of local data to the demographic characteristics of those local areas. The availability of the STF files has also allowed local users to aggregate small-area data for census-defined entities such as block, block group, and tract into areas more meaningful to their specific concerns.

Of the commercial users of census data, marketing is among the largest. Census data offer a basis for defining potential market areas for almost any product or service. From studies of the relationships between consumer behavior and demographic characteristics, marketers can project sales for specific areas based on the demographic character of the areas. The availability of summary and microdata in machine-readable formats greatly facilitates the linking of the demographic detail to other data sets.

The machine-readable files present users with problems they do not face in retrieving information from the published reports. Users often need a fuller understanding of census data concepts than is required to interpret the published tables. They need to understand data structures and data management and may need access to programming assistance. They also require computing equipment capable of handling the media. An overall consequence is that users need dollars and time to extract information from the machine-readable files.

The PUMS files present unique problems to users. An understanding of census data concepts can be essential. Even items that appear to be unambiguous may need careful interpretation when accessed in the PUMS. For example, the PUMS contains persons who report no hours worked and yet report earnings. Novice users will find this confusing until they realize that the hours worked item is "hours worked last week" while the earnings items refer to last year. Similarly, a user might be puzzled by a tabulation that shows no pre-teen births, unless one is aware that "children ever born" is only asked of women fifteen and older.

Because files are based on sample data, the likelihood of sampling error must be considered, especially when working with small sub-populations. Users must also be aware that responses to the census are self-reported and thus subject to inaccuracies and inconsistencies. While the Census Bureau applies editing procedures to minimize inconsistencies in the data, some remain and can be perplexing when encountered.

Technology, Dissemination, and Users

The Census Bureau has a strong history of innovation in information processing. The 1890 census was tabulated using punched cards and counting hardware designed by Herman Hollerith, a Census Bureau employee. The technology later became the foundation for International Business Machines Corporation (IBM). Stored program digital computing technology was first described in the late 1930s. Morris Hansen and others at the Census Bureau realized the substantial reductions in tabulating time that could be gained by using electronic pulses rather than mechanical holes to sense data. The Census Bureau contracted with the Eckert-Mauchly Computer Corporation to design a machine for statistical purposes. When the Univac computer was delivered to the Census Bureau in March 1951, it was too late to help with much of the 1950 census processing. However, having a computer on hand for the planning and processing of the 1960 census put the Census Bureau in the lead on data processing when compared with other federal agencies and, in fact, large corporations. Other improvements in technology, such as magnetic tape as a storage medium and Film Optical Sensing Device for Input to Computers (FOSDIC) processing as a means to transfer data to machine readable form, also contributed to the move to electronic processing and dissemination of data.

The 1960s

The 1960 census data were the first to be released in summary and microdata files for analysis outside the Census Bureau. This represented a drastic change in policy for the Census Bureau. Users would be allowed to produce their own tabulations and statistics, although the Census Bureau would still produce printed reports for those without access to electronic computing facilities. Allowing access to microdata files raised the issue of respondent disclosure or confidentiality. Initially, the data were released with the understanding that they would not be redistributed, but by the end of the decade the Census Bureau was willing to enlarge the sampling fraction for the microdata files tenfold and treated the files as publicly accessible.

The 1960 microdata files were precursors to the PUMS released for the 1970 and subsequent censuses. While a major innovation, they were not that widely used. This was primarily due to technological constraints, although the required familiarity with census concepts and data structures tended to limit use to those who had prior experience with census data.

The microdata files were released in 1960 as one-in-one-thousand (1/1,000) and one-in-ten-thousand (1/10,000) samples. The card files comprised 180,000 and 18,000 cards, respectively. Only the 1/1,000 was released on tape, thirteen reels in Univac format and seven reels in IBM format. Standards for storing data on magnetic tape were not yet defined. Use of the tapes typically required custom programming to handle the physical and logical layout of the data on the tapes. No software was available for managing or analyzing data. Consequently, users also needed access to programmers who could write routines to tabulate data and perform similar manipulations.

The common practice was to create more manageable extract or work files from the tapes, usually limited to one reel in size to permit convenient handling on the mainframe systems available at that time. Set-ups for computer runs often required job control language (JCL) statements to link input and output (I/O) devices logically to the computing hardware. Processing performance for simple tasks was limited primarily by the maximum rates of data transfer from the storage media to the computer (I/O bound). More extensive processing, such as might be required for data recodes and transformations, could result in performance being limited by the processing power of the computer (compute bound). Even in the simple case, several hours could be required to process the 1/1,000 file.

The machine-readable files presented users with problems they had not faced in retrieving information from the published reports. While most users of census data at this time had some familiarity with census data and data concepts, they now needed to understand data structures and data management and have access to programming assistance. They also needed access to computing equipment capable of handling the media. An overall consequence was that significant planning was required to extract information from the machine-readable files. Generating a simple extract from the seven tape reels of the 1960 1/1,000 file, for example, could require several days of programming time and thousands of dollars of computing costs (in current dollars). Most computer processing was done in batch mode, a single task being executed at a time, although multi-tasking and time-sharing systems appeared toward the end of the decade. Consequently, special arrangements with computing services were likely necessary to have the dedicated computing time available for managing and processing multiple-reel tape files. Runs were commonly scheduled for night or weekend hours. To conserve money in a university research environment, several users would often pool resources to generate a single extract that could serve multiple needs. The result could be several weeks of programming time and a computer run costing thousands of dollars. The computer run might need to be repeated once or twice to handle programming errors and to accommodate new needs on the part of the researchers that became identified during the turn-around period, which on occasion could extend to months.

Storage requirements were an important consideration when distributing data on media such as cards and magnetic tape. To reduce the number of cards or tapes required, steps were usually taken to limit the number of characters, bytes, or columns. In 1960 these included restricting the number of items made available, coding two or more items into one character position, and using over-punches (+ or -), multiple punches, and non-numeric codes to allow larger numbers of responses to be coded into one character position. Each of these presented difficulties to the users of the files. Custom programming was typically required to handle non-numeric codes. At some user sites, the original files were expanded to eliminate the non-numeric data. Some attempts were made at using data compression techniques to reduce the storage requirements, but the operating systems available in the 1960s typically required that data be uncompressed and stored back on magnetic media prior to use, negating the major virtue of compression.

The 1960 data introduced users to sample weights. Housing data were gathered from 25-percent, 20-percent, or 5-percent samples of the housing units. Users performing their own analyses on the microdata needed to weight properly any given housing item to produce the correct population estimate.

The 1970s

The response of users to the release of the 1960 data in machine-readable formats and the evolving computer technology encouraged the Census Bureau to increase the number of summary and microdata files to be made available from the 1970 census. A series of summary tapes covering the First, Second, and Third Counts (100-percent items), and the Fourth through Sixth counts (sample items), were created. Each count was subdivided into sub-files with varying degrees of geographic detail. Population and housing tabulations were released in separate files for some counts. The tapes were generally released by state. In total, more than two thousand summary tapes were available from the 1970 census. The Fourth Count files, for example, were distributed on approximately one thousand tapes. Separate population and housing data sets were released as Files A, B, and C for tracts, minor civil divisions, and selected census areas, respectively. The sheer quantity of data available presented problems to users. A former Census Bureau employee, Jack Beresford, created a company, DUALabs, with the express purpose of releasing compressed versions of the census files. This reduced the count of tapes by a factor of ten, but still left users with multiple reel data sets to handle and the additional need of uncompressing the data before they could be accessed and analyzed. DUALabs distributed routines that could be embedded in user-written programs to expand the data. Some programmers developed sophisticated extraction routines to increase the efficiency and versatility of the retrieval process from the compressed tapes.

Users faced other problems. Tabulations in the STF were typically defined for specified populations with as many as five-way tabulations presented. Extracting specific numbers desired from specific tabulations was challenging. With the release of so much data with such fine geographic detail, maintaining user confidentiality became a concern in 1970. The policy adopted for the 1970 STF files was to suppress either complete tables or portions of them if counts were sufficiently small to risk a breach of confidentiality. Custom programming was required to handle the suppression codes properly.

Magnetic tape technology improved rapidly in the late 1960s and early 1970s. Tape was commonly available in 7-track at 556 and 800 bytes per inch (bpi) densities and 9-track at 800 bpi. Standards for the logical structure of data on tape were beginning to emerge, but users had no guarantee that a tape they acquired could be read by the computer system to which they had access.

Public Use Microdata Sample (PUMS) files were also released in 1970. Six 1/100 files were created. The 1970 long form was distributed in two versions, one to 5 percent and the other to 15 percent samples of hous-

ing units. Three levels of geographic detail were also created: state; county group, and neighborhood characteristics. Thus, 5-percent and 15-percent PUMS files were made available for each geographic level.

The 1970 PUMS differed in structure from the 1960 microdata file in that the housing and person data were ordered hierarchically—a housing record was followed by records for each of the persons living in the housing unit. The neighborhood characteristics files added a third, higher-level hierarchy that summarized neighborhood-level characteristics as percentages, means, or medians. These provided contextual information for the housing units and persons within the neighborhood. Thus, a neighborhood record would be followed by a series of housing records with the persons in a given housing unit nested under the corresponding housing record.

The hierarchical structure of the data posed a significant challenge to users. Statistical packages were becoming available, but data management capabilities were limited and, in general, they could not directly handle hierarchical file structures. Each of the 1/100 files was a multiple-reel file with the consequent problems associated with handling on the available computing systems.

Use of both the STF and the PUMS data from 1970 was restricted largely to persons with access to significant technical support and computing resources. As in 1960, users also needed to have a sound understanding of census-data concepts.

The 1980s

The changes in computing technology in the 1970s, while significant, had primarily quantitative rather than qualitative effects on the ability of users to work with census data. This tended to be true in the 1980s as well. More tabulations were released in the STF series and larger samples were available from the PUMS. The 1/1,000 sample from 1960 that increased to six 1/100 samples from the 1970 census became 1/100 and 5/100 PUMS in 1980 with a total of more than 15 million person and housing records included in the 1980 5-percent (5/100) PUMS. Higher tape densities (6250 bpi) allowed significantly larger quantities of data to be stored per reel, approximately 160 MB. Fewer reels of tape were required for the distribution of the STF files and the five and twenty-two reels required for the 1-percent and 5-percent PUMS, respectively, were more manageable than the dozens of reels required for the 1970 PUMS.

Tape standards were well defined. Multiple-reel data sets could be handled more easily and reliably than before. The data were distributed as uncompressed text files. Statistical packages were incorporating data management capabilities that could handle the hierarchical data structure of the PUMS. Users still needed to understand census-data concepts to work effectively with the data and usually needed access to programming assistance and related technical assistance. Users continued to rely on work files in the form of extracts from the full data sets, and rarely created their own extracts, depending upon programmers to write custom and efficient routines to generate the needed files. Mainframes were too costly for the inefficient, error-prone routines that a typical user might write. Documenting and cataloging work files became an important activity in research centers where extensive use of the census data was made.

Throughout the 1970s and 1980s, most processing of machine-readable census data was done in tape-based mainframe computing environments. The advent of time-shared computing in the late 1960s allowed some interactive handling of census data, but most users were limited to batch processing of tape-based data. A large university mainframe might have two megabytes (MB) of random access memory (RAM), increasing to eight MB in the late 1980s. When large quantities of hard disk storage became available on mainframes, the cost could range to more than $120 per year per MB. Storing the equivalent of a tape of data online was costly.

By the end of the 1980s and into the 1990s, computing environments underwent significant changes as the consequences of the revolution in microprocessor and network technologies became apparent.

The 1990s

The changes in computing, networking, and information technology during the 1990 decade have had both quantitative and qualitative ramifications for users. Computing power and data storage capacities have increased dramatically to the point that a data set such as the 5-percent PUMS with 18 million housing and person records can be stored on the disk of a desktop personal computer (PC) and processed at speeds greater than those of the mainframes of a few years earlier. Users can work directly from the full data set with less need for creating and maintaining extracts and work files. Two gigabyte (GB) of RAM and tens of GB

of hard disk storage can be installed on a PC running at 550 MHz and higher speeds at a cost of less than $10,000. Highly optimized analytic software running on parallel systems has been demonstrated that can process full national censuses at effective rates on the order of 20 million records per processor per second. Analyses that once required access to technical personnel and resources, thousands of dollars, and days-even months-of time can now be done in a fraction of the time by relatively naïve users. Constraints on the use of information imposed by limited technological expertise and resources have been largely removed. Once a machine is purchased, the costs of making another run is nil. In effect, users can now afford to make errors.

The Census Bureau used record swapping techniques rather than suppression to protect confidentiality in the STF files. Users who had succeeded in handling the 1980 files generally found it easier to work with the 1990 data. The development of read-only compact disk (CD-ROM) technology has provided a medium for the low-cost distribution of massive amounts of data. A single CD-ROM can store 640 MB of data, approximately the capacity of four high-density open reel tapes. Digital Versatile Disks (DVD) will extend those capacities tenfold in the immediate future.

Many of the 1990 census data sets and reports that were released on magnetic tape have also been made available on CD-ROM. Now STF1, STF3, and the Public Law 94-171 files as well as the 1-percent and 5-percent PUMS are available on disk. The Census Bureau has developed software to facilitate extracting data from the disks. GO is a basic information retrieval program included on the STF CD-ROMs. It allows easy access to individual tables in STF files. Extract is a more general program designed to allow multiple tables sharing some common traits to be extracted in a single operation. QuickTab, distributed on the PUMS disks, allows users to create data extracts subject to record and item selection criteria and to generate frequency counts and cross-tabulations.

However, the Internet and the World Wide Web were the most dramatic developments of the 1990s. They have made massive amounts of information and data readily accessible to millions of people. At the beginning of the decade, the Internet allowed computers worldwide to establish computer-to-computer links. File transfer protocol (FTP) provided a mechanism for moving large amounts of data from one computer to another, significantly reducing the need to transfer data by tape or other media. The evolution of standard communication protocols made possible the development of Mosaic, the first of the network browsers, which the National Center for Supercomputer Applications (NCSA) at the University of Illinois demonstrated in 1993. Netscape, Internet Explorer, and similar commercial products soon followed.

Other developments have taken advantage of the technological revolution. Early in the decade, William P. Butz and J. Michael Fortier of the Census Bureau proposed the development of a system that could store the full national census online within a computing environment that had the capability to analyze data and generate reports upon demand. These concepts simmered for a few years until 1996, when the Census Bureau proposed the development of the Data Access and Dissemination System (DADS). This system, which has evolved into the American Factfinder (accessible from the Census Bureau home page-www.census.gov), provides easy access to much of the 1990 census data that were published or distributed as STF files. Custom reports and maps can be created from the Web. The technical capabilities exist to allow custom tabulations and analyses to be generated in real time from either the sample data or complete data files. The feasibility of doing so has been demonstrated by several projects around the country that allow users to work interactively with PUMS, Current Population Survey (CPS), and similar microdata files.

Perhaps the most significant consequence of the technology of the 1990s was what has been termed the democratization of census data. Access to and use of census data is no longer restricted to those who possess the expertise and resources to acquire, manage, and analyze data from STF and PUMS files. The Web and the resources accessible via the Web have opened access to the information in census data to any person familiar with browsers. Thus, millions of Americans now possess the basic skills to find information from the census. However, removal of the technical barriers to acquiring information has not eliminated the need to understand the census and the data concepts that underlie the reports and tables that can be so readily accessed.

2000 and Beyond

The revolution in information technology over the past forty years has had a significant impact on who uses census data and how the data are used. For the first thirty years of that period, the primary effect was to allow those using machine-readable files to accomplish more. More data were available, the data could be managed and analyzed more rapidly, and more complex and sophisticated analyses could be performed. Over the past ten years, many of the obstacles to accessing and using decennial census data have been removed or diminished to the point that novice users can accomplish tasks that once required access to costly mainframe computing resources and extensive technical knowledge and skills.

Most of this recent change has come with the advent of the Internet and the Word Wide Web. Information can now be located from the desktop. Data can be drawn from CD-ROMs, from the Census Bureau's homepage on the WWW, or from other public, private, and commercial sites that make census data available.

Certain needs and directions for the future are apparent. Large numbers of persons will have access to information from the census. Intelligent and meaningful use of this information still requires users to have a sound understanding of the census and data concepts. A massive educational, training, and support program seems necessary if that understanding is to be developed in the mass public.

Many Web services are based on client/server technology. These have important advantages over approaches that disseminate data for use on local computing systems. In a manner somewhat analogous to the mainframe, the client/server model allows the costs of technical expertise and state-of-the-art resources to be shared by a large number of users. Thus, remote users can take advantage of the capabilities of much larger and more complex computing, data storage, and analytic resources than they may be able to afford as individual users. High-performance parallel systems will allow users to generate instantaneous custom reports based on analyses of the full census and sample files, if needed. Responsibility for the control, management, and updating of information is also tightly focused. Correcting and updating information at a single or limited number of sources is much easier than updating thousands of tapes or CD-ROMs that have been widely distributed to individual users.

The ability to generate custom reports on demand from the full census files will require renewed efforts to guarantee the confidentiality of individuals. The risks of deductive and complementary disclosure of individual identity have increased markedly as ease of access to information has increased. For example, one can readily generate tables with cells containing single individuals from the PUMS files. The high cost of doing so in the past provided significant protection against breaches of confidentiality. Now the costs of doing so are trivial for many users and could become so for all users in the near future. Considerable attention will need to be given to the issue of confidentiality in the coming years. The coming decade will see a marked increase in the use of census data and products. While improving technology will continue to ease access to information, the likely movement to the American Community Survey (ACS) may present new challenges to the census user community.

■ Albert F. Anderson and Lisa Neidert

Bibliography

Anderson, Margo J. *The American Census: A Social History*. New Haven: Yale University Press, 1988.

Lavin, Michael R. *Understanding the Census: A Guide for Marketers, Planners, Grant Writers and Other Data Users*. Kenmore, N.Y.: Epoch Books, Inc., 1996.

Dissemination of data: printed publications

Beginning with the first census in 1790 and continuing until the present, the results of census enumerations have been published in printed products. Early on, James Madison, Thomas Jefferson, and others recognized that information about the labor force, manufacturing, and agriculture would be useful not only to their contemporaries but also to future generations. The form and content of subsequent printed publications have reflected their farsightedness as each succeeding census has included more statistics on economic and social issues. Following the establishment of a permanent Census Bureau in 1902, printed reports have been issued with greater frequency and on far more diverse topics than was envisioned in the nineteenth century. Advances in technology and the more complex needs of a larger and expanding population have combined to increase the Census Bureau's statistics-gathering activities and capabilities, resulting in a burgeoning quantity of printed reports during the twentieth century. Paradoxically, at the beginning of the twenty-first century the role of printed reports is being eclipsed by CD-ROMs and the Internet.

The Earliest Census Reports

The first printed census publication, the report of the first census, taken in 1790 by the federal marshals, consisted of a fifty-six-page octavo pamphlet. Statistics in the report included the number of persons in the judicial districts, the number of free white males aged sixteen and up, the number of free white males under sixteen, free white females, all other free individuals, and slaves. It was delivered to President George Washington in 1791, and one copy was forwarded to each of the clerks of the district courts. Printing was contracted out to a private firm, as were all the census printed products until the eighth census (1860), when the Government Printing Office was assigned the responsibility for printing census publications.

Nineteenth-Century Census Reports

Beginning with the census of 1800, the marshals reported the results of the census to the secretary of state, instead of the president; the secretary of state then forwarded the reports to Congress and the president. The second census printed report was published as a 70-page folio volume in 1801. The population reports of the third census, in 1810, were still relatively brief, consisting of a 180-page volume, published in 1811. The 1810 census contained the first statistics on manufactures. Although the threat of war at the time prompted the report, it led Congress to want to know more about the industrial capacity of the American manufacturing sector. Published in 1813 the relatively brief report (233 pages) included the kind, quantity, and value of goods manufactured, number of establishments, and the number of machines used under certain circumstances. The data were not consistent from area to area, but this report represents a first attempt at gathering industrial statistics. The collection of this data was supervised by the secretary of the treasury.

The fourth census (1820) also included industrial statistics but was hampered, like the third census, by the incompleteness of the returns from the various districts. For the first time, legislation authorizing the census of 1820 included a provision that one copy of the report be provided to each of the colleges and universities in the United States as well as to members of

Congress, officers of the government, and judges of the United States courts. The inclusion of colleges and universities in the dissemination scheme ensured that the data would reach beyond government officials and set a precedent that would continue through the establishment of the Federal Depository Library Program. The cost of printing these reports was $11,014; postage to disseminate them came to $1,229.

The printed results of the fifth census (1830) were presented in a large folio of 163 pages. It was so poorly printed that Congress mandated its reprinting under the direct supervision of the secretary of state. The defective printing and the reprinted edition were then bound together for dissemination along with population figures from the censuses of 1790, 1800, 1810, and 1820 by counties as well as statistics by districts. This time the cost of printing rose to $18,473 and postage to $7,098.

The four-volume census of 1840 was the last census to be limited in scope to information about population only. Although the earlier attempts at collecting and publishing statistics about manufacturing had not been totally successful, lawmakers and scholars recognized the importance of broadening the scope of the data collected and disseminated in the reports.

With each succeeding decennial census taken between 1850 and 1900, the size and number of printed reports increased, reflecting the expanding subject coverage of the census, the growth of the population, the expansion of the economic sector, and the more widespread interest in statistical data on the part of public officials, scholars, and others. The format of printed reports was inconsistent from census to census, primarily because activities ceased at the completion of each census for the lack of permanent staff. Thus, there was little or no advanced planning for the next census; record keeping was haphazard; and the data included many errors, especially in the sixth census (1840). However, the results of the eighth census, taken in 1860, were published in a four-volume format in which the first volume was devoted to population, the second to statistics on agriculture, the third to statistics on manufacturers, and one on miscellaneous statistics. This publication pattern would continue into the twentieth century.

Throughout the nineteenth century, the content of the reports increased with each census. The first information on manufactures was included in the census of 1810; information about agriculture, mining, and fisheries first appeared in the census of 1840; and information on social issues such as taxation, churches, pauperism, and crime was included in the census of 1850. With each succeeding decennial census, the scope of the data that were collected and disseminated in the printed reports expanded. Maps first appeared in the ninth census, in 1870. The number of reports dramatically increased with the censuses of 1880 and 1890. This is exemplified by the fact that the number of volumes in the 1880 census ballooned to twenty-two, more than in all eight censuses that preceded it. Almost from the beginning, complaints had been made that the publication of the reports was delayed beyond all reasonable expectations. These delays culminated with the tenth census in 1880, when the earliest reports were not published until 1883 and the last report was published in 1888. Some of these problems had been addressed in legislation of 1879 and 1880, which established a Census Office in the Department of the Interior, provided for a superintendent of the census to be appointed by the president, and transferred responsibility for taking the census from the marshals to 150 supervisors. Not addressed was the problem of the lack of a permanent staff; the terms of the supervisors ended with the completion of each census. New technological developments in the form of punched cards and electric tabulating machines began to address the problem of tardy reporting of the results with the 1890 census. Statistics that were tabulated and compiled first could be published as they were ready, in the form of press releases and preliminary reports. This was especially important for high-demand products such as total population counts of cities, counties, states, and the nation as a whole. These machines were primitive by today's standards, but they were improved and used to tabulate and compile census data until the introduction of the computer in the mid-twentieth century.

Printed Census Reports in the First Half of the Twentieth Century

As the new century dawned, Congress finally passed legislation in 1902 that established the Bureau of the Census as a permanent unit within the Department of the Interior. (With reorganizations in 1903 and 1913, the bureau moved to the Department of Commerce and Labor.) The most important aspect of this legislation, which would have a far-reaching effect on the printed reports, was that the Census Bureau was now an ongoing organization with a permanent staff. This change enabled the staff to engage in long-term planning and to respond much more quickly to new demands and needs for data products. A permanent Census Bureau also allowed for more flexibility in the intervals at which data could be collected and published. For example, data on agriculture had been included in the decennial census as far back as the census of 1840, and printed reports dealing with agricultural information were included in each of the decennial censuses through 1920. Following the census of 1910, it was recognized that the data would be more useful if it were collected and published more frequently than every ten years, so plans were made for a quinquennial census of agriculture beginning in 1915. The outbreak of World War I, however, postponed the beginning of the five-year census until 1925.

By the turn of the twentieth century, statisticians, political leaders, and scholars also recognized that statistical data from other sectors of the economy should be collected and disseminated in printed reports that were independent of the decennial census of population. The first economic census, the census of business, was conducted in 1929. The results of this census included printed reports with data on retail and wholesale trade, service industries, and construction. Data on these subjects were also collected and disseminated in censuses for 1933, 1935, and 1939. After an interruption for World War II, the census of business was taken in 1948, 1954, 1958, 1963, and 1967.

With the publication of the 1940 census, the presentation of the data collected in the decennial census was reorganized for the first time since the census of 1850. The statistics collected on population were presented in the census of population, which was structured into four volumes similar to those used today: *Number of Inhabitants; Characteristics of the Population; The Labor Force;* and *Characteristics by Age, Marital Status, Relationship, Education, and Citizenship.* Housing data were separated from population data and published in a separate census of housing report. Statistics on economic activity were published in printed reports on agriculture, manufactures, mineral industries, business (including one volume on retail trade, one on wholesale trade, and one on service establishments). These would later evolve into six of the separate quinquennial economic censuses. The 1940 census was also notable because it was the first census to include printed reports containing demographic and socioeconomic statistics for census tracts in the sixty cities that had been subdivided into tracts.

A key concept that was greatly expanded upon during the twentieth century is that of census geography.

Early censuses mainly included reports of data by political units: states, counties, townships, cities, and so forth. But collecting data just within political boundaries is not always precise enough to provide an accurate and useful count, especially in rural areas close to cities. Therefore, the Census Bureau developed geographic units that are defined independently of political boundaries. Printed reports now contained tables of statistics for metropolitan statistical areas, census tracts, urbanized areas, and other geographical subdivisions created by the bureau in cooperation with local leaders. Another outcome of this concern with geography is that the Census Bureau has compiled thousands of maps of detailed urban and rural areas.

In order to achieve consistency between and within census reports, it became necessary to provide standardized definitions of terms, concepts, and geographic units. Almost every census printed report now contains an appendix in which detailed explanations and definitions are provided for *housing unit, central business district, ancestry,* and other important terms.

The use of sample data enabled the bureau to publish reports on a wider variety of subjects than had been possible or practical before. In the 1940 census, for the first time, several questions were asked of a sample of people instead of everyone. Building on this experience with sampling, the 1950 census included collection and dissemination of sample data from 20 percent of the population and 3.3 percent of the population. There are four numbered volumes in the 1950 census, as there were for the 1940 census, but with different titles and organization. Volume 1, *Number of Inhabitants,* consists of fifty-four reports, including a United States summary, and reports for each state, the District of Columbia, and the territories and possessions. Volume 2, *Characteristics of the Population,* provides additional data for the same geographical areas as volume 1. Volume 3, *Census Tracts,* contains the reports for the sixty-four areas that had been divided into tracts. Volume 4, *Special Reports,* contains nineteen reports on economic and family characteristics, national origin and race, mobility of the population, and other subjects.

The 1960 census included more data, presented in more reports than any census that preceded it. Volume 1, *Characteristics of the Population,* consists of fifty-nine parts, including a United States summary and fifty-five reports for states and outlying areas. Volume 2, *Subject Reports* is made up of thirty-three reports on social and economic characteristics by nativity, parentage, and country of origin. Volume 3, the *Selected Area Reports*, consists of five reports of statistical data for places, including state economic areas, size of place, Americans overseas, standard metropolitan statistical areas, and type of place. A fourth and unnumbered volume contains the census tract reports for 180 standard metropolitan statistical areas. Data on housing are contained in the reports of a companion but separate *Census of Housing*.

The publication of printed reports of the census of population and housing reached its zenith with the censuses of 1970 and 1980. Following the four-volume pattern established during the previous thirty years, each had a volume on Characteristics of the Population, a volume of Subject Reports, Census Tract Reports, and a volume of Supplementary Reports in addition to numerous other reports in print as well as microfiche format. By 1990 budget constraints within the federal government resulted in a drastic reduction in the number of printed reports. They included four volumes: *General Population Characteristics*, which includes complete count data on race, Hispanic origin, age, marital status, and so forth for states, counties, places, and county subdivisions; *Summary Social, Economic, and Housing Characteristics*, which contains data derived entirely from sample counts ranging from 12 to 50 percent for states, counties, places, and subcounty divisions; *General Housing Characteristics*, which contains complete count data on such topics as unit value or rent, number of rooms, tenure, vacancy for states, counties, places, and subcounty divisions; and *Detailed Housing Characteristics*, which contains more extensive data than *General Housing Characteristics* based on sample data.

Technology and the Modern Census

Arguably the most important technological development in the history of the census occurred with the incorporation of the computer into the collection, tabulation, and production of census reports. The 1950 census of population and housing and the 1954 economic censuses marked the first of the computer to process data. During the 1950s, the bureau's attention remained on the production of the census reports in a timely manner, and the use of the computer was seen as a way to accomplish this goal. Not only could computers be used to tabulate the data but they were also used to produce the printed reports. The 1960 census of population and housing was the first decennial census in which the computer took the place of the old punched card system for tabulating the data.

Besides increasing the speed at which the data could be tabulated and published in the printed reports, the use of the computer also made it possible for reports to be generated on topics of a much higher degree of specificity. As the Census Bureau became more user oriented, this enabled it to provide special reports on demand to particular user groups.

Up to and including the 1960 census most census reports were published as printed reports either as ink on paper or, later in the twentieth century, on microfiche. During the transition era starting in 1970, census publications have been issued in a variety of formats, including print, microfiche, CD-ROM, computer tape, floppy disk, and on the Internet. Publication in electronic formats has been shrinking the central role formerly occupied by printed reports. There are several reasons for this. Publications in print format are static: pages can be copied, but the data cannot be manipulated. Data published electronically on CD-ROM, magnetic tape, or on the Internet, can be manipulated to fit the specific needs of the user by means of specialized programs. Data products that are published on the Internet can be used conveniently in one's office, home, or other location without taking up the storage space necessary for printed reports. Similarly, electronic data products on the Internet are often cheaper for the individual to use. All these factors are compelling reasons for the dramatic reduction of availability of printed reports of data collected in the 1990 and later censuses of population, the economic censuses, and other report series. Reflective of this, the results of the 2000 census will include three volumes for each state and the following national volumes in print format: *Census 2000: Summary Population and Housing Characteristics*; *Census 2000: Summary Social, Economic, and Housing Characteristics*; and *Census 2000: Population and Housing Unit Counts*. Most of the other data gathered in the 2000 census will be distributed in electronic format. Still, the community of users of census data includes individuals who, as yet, do not have ready access to computers. Therefore, at least for a while, *Statistical Abstract of the United States, County and City Data Book*, and other reports of general interest will continue to be available in multiple formats.

Resources on Printed Products

For more comprehensive information on the printed reports in all the censuses through 1980, the user should consult Suzanne Schulze's three-volume work:

Population Information in Nineteenth Century Census Volumes; Population Information in Twentieth Century Census Volumes, 1900–1940; and *Population Information in Twentieth Century Census Volumes, 1950–1980.* The most complete listing of census publications from the first through the sixteenth censuses remains *Catalog of United States Census Publications, 1790–1945,* by Henry J. Dubester. It has been reprinted several times; the most recent edition, *Dubester's U.S. Census Bibliography with SuDocs Class Numbers and Indexes,* by Kevin L. Cook, also includes supplemental entries, a title index, a series index, and a Superintendent of Documents Classification Number index. Between 1945 and 1984 the Bureau of the Census published the *Bureau of the Census Catalog* in which were listed all the publications, in all formats, issued by the bureau. This publication was followed by the *Census Catalog and Guide,* which is still published annually and, like its predecessor, lists all the publications of the bureau. Some important statistical publications were originally published by other government agencies and later transferred to the Census Bureau.

Perhaps the most widely used census report, the *Statistical Abstract of the United States,* was first published in 1878 by the Department of the Treasury. The early editions of this report reflected data gathered primarily by that agency. Between 1903 and 1937 various statistics-gathering agencies expanded the scope of its coverage; in 1938, the Census Bureau began issuing the publication. It is a compendium census report in which data from many different agencies on a wide variety of topics are assembled in one recurring source. It and other compendia like it are particularly useful to students and others who want an easy-to-use source of comparative statistical information.

■ Janice S. Fryer

Bibliography

Cook, Kevin L. *Dubester's U.S. Census Bibliography with SuDocs Class Numbers and Indexes.* Englewood, Colo.: Libraries Unlimited, 1996.

Dubester, Henry J. *Catalog of United States Census Publications, 1790–1945.* Washington, D.C.: U.S. Government Printing Office, 1950.

Kaplan, Charles P., and Thomas L. Van Valey. *Census '80: Continuing the Factfinder Tradition.* Washington, D.C.: U.S. Government Printing Office, 1980.

Schulze, Suzanne. *Population Information in Nineteenth Century Census Volumes.* Phoenix, Ariz.: Oryx Press, 1983.

———. *Population Information in Twentieth Century Census Volumes, 1900–1940.* Phoenix, Ariz.: Oryx Press, 1985.

———. *Population Information in Twentieth Century Census Volumes, 1950–1980.* Phoenix, Ariz.: Oryx Press, 1985.

U.S. Bureau of the Census. *Bureau of the Census Catalog of Publications, 1790–1972.* Washington, D.C.: U.S. Government Printing Office, 1974.

———. *Bureau of the Census Catalog, 1973–1984.* Washington, D.C.: U.S. Government Printing Office, 1973–1984.

———. *Census Catalog and Guide, 1985–.* Washington, D.C.: U.S. Government Printing Office, 1985–.

Wright, Carroll D. *History and Growth of the United States Census.* Prepared for the Senate Committee on the Census. Washington, D.C.: U.S. Government Printing Office, 1900.

Dissemination of data: secondary products

Secondary data products of the decennial censuses are produced for special purposes outside the scope of the primary decennial census report series and summary files, to the extent that there *are* primary products since that concept is not recognized nor used by the Census Bureau. The reports and products that are declared and funded prior to the census can be regarded as planned, or primary, products. In general, primary products supply basic counts and summary data for all aspects of the census and include what are termed *statistical summary data files* and *subject reports.* Because the content of the census varies over time in response to social needs and political pressures, primary and secondary products cannot be differentiated on the basis of content or subject matter. Furthermore, what may be a special topic in one census year may be part of the primary reports in the next. The difference between secondary products and primary products is determined according to how the products are defined by the Census Bureau. Secondary products can be defined as being products that are not part of the primary series and are created to meet special needs of nongovernmental bodies, the internal requirements of the Census Bureau, or the needs of other government agencies. The creation and production of these tabulations are often requested by and funded by other agencies to support mandated programs or for research within the agencies.

Today, metropolitan, state, and federal governments

use secondary data products to meet the requirements of many federal programs and to supply data needed for federal grants. In some cases, state and local funding may require census data found in these products, and some products are necessary to the private sector in meeting statutory requirements. The best known of these are the Equal Employment Opportunity data, but financial institutions also use census products to meet the reporting requirements of the Home Mortgage Disclosure Act. For agencies that need data as presented by the Census Bureau, these products may supply the required numbers. Statistical data are needed in formula-based grant programs, and population statistics influence a vast amount of targeted dollar outlays. Income and housing data are also important in the distribution of federal funds. Secondary products also facilitate academic research and provide additional materials to both for-profit businesses and not-for-profit organizations.

History

The ability to create secondary products was realized in 1850 when the census began to collect individual-level data. This made post-census tabulations possible, although difficulties in performing tabulations meant that few special reports were created in the nineteenth century. The first large-scale special uses of the census began during the Civil War when the Census Office supplied special tabulations and reports directly to the War Department. From that time through the 1950s secondary reports were frequently prepared in response to pressing social and economic issues. Beginning with the 1900 census, secondary products became commonplace. Among the many reports from the 1900 census were *Child Labor in the United States* and a compendium titled *Supplementary Analysis and Derivative Tables, Twelfth Census of the United States*, which included "The Negro Farmer," by W. E. Burghardt Du Bois. Following the 1910 census came reports such as *Deaf-mutes in the United States* as well as a similar report dealing with the blind. Many special reports of this time were prepared by Joseph A. Hill, chief statistician in the Division of Revision and Results, Bureau of the Census. For example, his *Occupations of the First and Second Generations of Immigrants in the United States and Fecundity of Immigrant Women* were published in 1911 as reports of the Immigration Commission. Immigration would also be an important issue surrounding the 1920 census, as would the growth of cities and child

labor. Included here are the reports *Immigrants and Their Children, Children in Gainful Occupations at the Fourteenth Census of the United States* and *Farm Population of the United States: An Analysis of the 1920 Farm Population Figures, Especially in Comparison with Urban Data*, which are examples that reflect the concerns of the day. Following the 1930 census was a series of reports dealing with unemployment based on a special unemployment schedule used in that enumeration. Other reports published in the early part of the twentieth century were *Women in Gainful Occupations, 1870-1920* (1929), *The Negro Population, 1790-1915* (1918), *Paupers in Almshouses, 1910* (1915), and *Prisoners and Juvenile Delinquents in the United States, 1910* (1918).

In the 1940s, secondary products focused on housing, the labor force, and internal migration. Reports from the 1940 census included *The Labor Force (Sample Statistics) Employment and Family Characteristics of Women, Housing Special Reports Series H-46* and *Internal Migration: Color and Sex of Migrants*. Also from 1940 was a special report dealing with education, *Educational Attainment by Economic Characteristics and Marital Status*. In 1950 there was continued interest in housing issues, including *Special Tabulation for Local Housing Authorities. Series HC-6*. The 1960 census products included the first special transportation planning product, *Transportation Planning Data for Urbanized Areas Based on 1960 Census*, as well as reports dealing with poverty and aging. The Housing and Home Finance Agency published *Senior Citizens and How They Live: An Analysis of 1960 Census Data*. Following the 1960 census, primary publications dealing with racial minorities were produced. Thus what had been a special or secondary topic became a primary one.

Since 1970 many of these supplemental or special reports have been issued both in print and as data files. In 1980 many of the data products were included as part of the Summary Tape Files only, but the print reports were issued under separate titles. In 1990 there was a large increase in the number of secondary products and programs or series under which these products can be found. With the release of public-use versions of the microdata files and geographical cross-referencing facilities, it is possible to create tabulations for many special populations on many topics or to create the standard tables for nonstandard geographic areas. Still, secondary data products remain a valued source for business, government, and research.

Finding the special subject report files from any but the latest census is problematic, and many older pub-

In its first century, 1790 to 1890, the census was a manual enterprise, unaided by machinery. Apart from the use of printing presses to disseminate statistical summaries, the entire operation was documented in longhand. Pictured here is an enlargement of the page below from the 1790 census ledger, preserved at the National Archives. Fourth from the top is the name of Paul Revere. *Source: AP/Wide World*

The complete ledger page from Boston, Massachusetts, illustrates the method of the day. Paul Revere's name is in the second column, eleventh from the bottom. The column headings are: Names of Heads of Families; Free white Males of 16 years old, and upwards; Free white Males, under 16 years; Free white Females; All other free Persons; Slaves. *Source: National Archives*

DISTICTS	Free white Males of 16 years and upwards, including heads of families.	Free white Males under sixteen years.	Free white Females, including heads of families.	All other free persons.	Slaves.	Total.
Vermont	22435	22328	40505	255	16	85539
N. Hampshire	36086	34851	70160	630	158	141885
Maine	24384	24748	46870	538	NONE	96540
Massachusetts	95453	87289	190582	5463	NONE	378787
Rhode Island	16019	15799	32652	3407	948	68825
Connecticut	60523	54403	117448	2808	2764	237946
New York	83700	78122	152320	4654	21324	340120
New Jersey	45251	41416	83287	2762	11423	184139
Pennsylvania	110788	106948	206363	6537	3737	434373
Delaware	11783	12143	22384	3899	8887	59094
Maryland	55915	51339	101395	8043	103036	319728
Virginia	110936	116135	215046	12866	292627	747610
Kentucky	15154	17057	28922	114	12430	73677
N. Carolina	69988	77506	140710	4975	100572	393751
S. Carolina	35576	37722	66880	1801	107094	249073
Georgia	13103	14044	25739	398	29264	82548
	807094	791850	1541263	59150	694280	3893635

Total number of Inhabitants of the United States exclutive of S. Weftern and N. Territory.	Free white Males of 21 years and upwards.	Free Males under 21 years of age.	Free white Female.	All other Persons.	Slaves.	Total
S.W. territory	6271	10277	15365	361	3417	35691
N. Ditto	—	—	—	—	—	—

After all enumerators had reported their results to their U.S. marshal, and all U.S. marshals had reported back to Washington, the results were summed and printed for dissemination to Congress, the administration, and the public. Above is a printed summary of results for the 1790 census. *Source:* National Archives

The machinery for tabulating census results began to change dramatically around 1890, when the predecessors of modern computers began to appear. Shown here is the first complete tabulating system of Herman Hollerith, with the "counting" mechanism to the left, the "contact" mechanism in the center, and the "sorting box" to the right. *Source:* National Archives

In a photo dated 1930, Census Bureau draftsmen in the Geographers Bureau draw census tracts. *Source:* National Archives

For fifty years the Census Bureau made incremental improvements to Hollerith's punchcard technology. *Source:* left, right: National Archives

As late as the 1940 census, punchcards were still in use. *Source:* National Archives

After World War II, tabulating machines gave way to true computers. The Census Bureau was the first civilian government agency to acquire a computer, taking receipt of a Universal Automatic Computer (UNIVAC) on March 31, 1951. J. Presper Eckert, one of the designers of the UNIVAC, sits at the controls of the computer on June 14, 1951. It has a clock speed of about 2.25 MHz and five thousand vacuum tubes. *Source:* Corbis/Bettmann

The UNIVAC was first utilized in October 1955, to compile results from the 1954 Census of Business. *Source:* National Archives

A technician replaces a vacuum tube of a UNIVAC on October 19, 1955. *Source:* Corbis/Bettmann

Data processing today utilizes the latest technology. *Source:* top, bottom: U.S. Bureau of the Census

Although advances in technology from 1890 onward dramatically changed the nature of data processing and analysis, enumerators through the twentieth century continued to visit many people in person, as they did in the nineteenth. Here, a census taker interviews a group of men, women, and children, in a sketch published in *Harper's Weekly* on November 19, 1870. *Source:* Library of Congress

Harper's takes a humorous look at the census of 1890; the old woman thinks the enumerator wants to take her senses. *Source:* Library of Congress

An enumerator on horseback
makes his rounds in Puerto Rico.
Source: National Archives

In the 1930 census an
enumerator walks into the
fields to visit a farmer.
Source: National Archives

Albert Einstein chats with a census employee canvassing during the 1950 count. *Source:* Robert K. Cromwell

In two photos from the 2000 census, an enumerator in Hawaii knocks on a door, while one in Alaska takes Census Bureau director Kenneth Prewitt for a ride on his snowmobile in Unalakleet, Alaska. Unalakleet is located some four hundred miles northwest of Anchorage, on the Bering Sea, and is home to about eight hundred people. *Source:* left: U.S. Bureau of the Census; right: AP/Wide World

Enumerators are only one class of Census Bureau employees. At the apex stands the director. Nominated by President Bill Clinton and unanimously confirmed by the Senate, Kenneth Prewitt became director of the Census Bureau on October 21, 1998. He came to government service after a career in higher education and private philanthropy, having served as president of the Social Science Research Council, senior vice president of the Rockefeller Foundation, and director of the National Opinion Research Center, based at the University of Chicago. He taught for fifteen years at the University of Chicago. *Source:* U.S. Bureau of the Census

Below the Census Bureau director are a cadre of full-time employees and, during the actual enumeration, a large staff of temporary workers. Here, workers in Washington, D.C., transfer data to punch cards, for use with mechanical statistical machines, circa March 1939. *Source:* Corbis/Bettmann

In two undated photos, workers in warehouse-like conditions tabulate data. *Source:* top, bottom: National Archives

In Suitland, Maryland, employees in 1949 comb through card catalogs that contain a card for every person in the nation. *Source:* Corbis/Bettmann

To process the estimated 150 million census forms returned by American households in the 2000 census, the Census Bureau and its private-sector partners created four data capture centers: in Pomona, California; Phoenix, Arizona; Jeffersonville, Indiana; and Baltimore County, Maryland. The government agency contracted with TRW, National Computer Systems, Lockheed Martin, and other corporations to help turn the individual census answers into summary statistical data. The sites were chosen based in part on labor availability; each center hired roughly two thousand temporary employees. *Source:* top, bottom: U.S. Bureau of the Census

The U.S. Census Bureau has long relied on advertising to boost the participation rate. Like all good advertising, Census Bureau advertising is tailored to the audience. The 1944 agricultural census poster featured Uncle Sam and appealed to patriotism. *Source:* National Archives

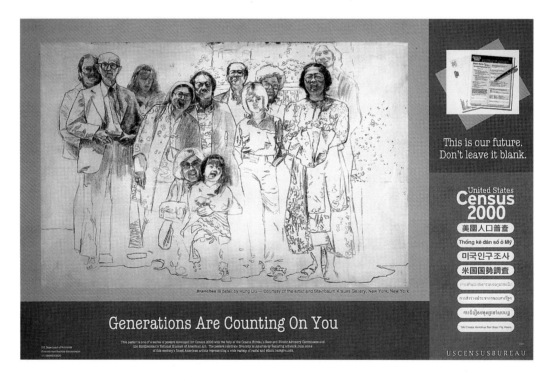

For the 2000 census, the bureau established committees to advise on the design of advertising materials tailored to specific groups. The poster on the top was vetted by the Census Advisory Committee on the African American Population; that on the bottom, tailored to Americans of Asian descent, was approved by the full Race and Ethnic Advisory Committee. All Census 2000 posters incorporated a variation of the catchphrase, "This is your future. Don't leave it blank"— an appeal to self-interest rather than to patriotism. *Source:* top, bottom: U.S. Bureau of the Census

"It's OK Boys. You can tell him everything...
He's the Census Man!"

You're right, Rafe! The Census-Taker hasn't got any connection with the "Revenooers." Anything anybody tells him is strictly confidential. By law, Census facts and figures can't be shown to the tax people, the police, or anybody else.

Everything the Census-Taker asks is important to you and your family. Your answers will help leaders in industry, business, labor and civic groups to plan such things as better schools, better roads, better housing; better distribution of such services as telephones, gas, water, and electricity.

What's more, if you want to have a voice in the government you have to be counted in the Census. According to the Constitution, the number of Representatives your state is entitled to send to Congress is determined by the Census taken every ten years.

The Census man will come around to your house some time after April 1. Be ready to answer all his questions accurately, and honestly, and *quickly*. (Remember, it's a big job to count upwards of a hundred and fifty million noses!)

WHAT TO DO WHEN THE CENSUS-TAKER COMES

1. Ask him to show his official card. This identifies him as an employee of the Census Bureau.

2. Be friendly. Invite him in. He will stay only a few minutes.

3. In non-English-speaking homes, have an adult or older child ready to translate.

4. Answer all questions accurately and honestly. Remember—the information you give is strictly confidential. Under law, it is not available to any individual or any other Government agency.

Radio and newspapers will do their best to tell you beforehand what most of the questions are. Watch for them and have your answers ready.

Like other American business firms, we believe that business has a responsibility to contribute to the public welfare. This advertisement is therefore sponsored by

The modern U.S. census is largely the product of two contemporaneous processes: rapid population growth, fueled in part by immigration; and rapid technological advance. Below is an image of Herman Hollerith (1860–1929), American statistician and inventor of punch cards and the electrical tabulating machines to read them. His machines were used for the censuses of 1890 and 1900. The company that he founded would become International Business Machines (IBM). *Source:* National Archives

Mistrust of government runs deep in American culture. Congress, through the statutes that govern the collection and use of census data, guarantee the American people confidentiality. The Census Bureau works hard to maintain confidentiality and to advertise respondents' rights as well as responsibilities under the law. *Source:* U.S. Bureau of the Census, *The 1950 Censuses: How They Were Taken* (Washington, D.C.: U.S. Government Printing Office, 1955), iv.

Hollerith's invention greatly simplified enumeration of the rapidly growing population; immigrants en route to the United States stand shoulder-to-shoulder on the deck of the S.S. *Patricia*, December 10, 1906. *Source:* Library of Congress

The census is responsible for documenting the ethnic and racial composition of the population. Hispanic men in Madera, California, wait to be chosen for basketball teams beside a census poster that says answers given on census forms are confidential, on March 18, 2000. The Census Bureau went to great lengths in 2000 to convince migrant workers, indigenous people, and undocumented immigrants to fill out census forms. Distrustful of the government and fearful of the Immigration and Naturalization Service, migrant workers and undocumented immigrants are chronically undercounted in the census. *Source:* AP/Wide World lications are out of print. Print reports from the past are still available in many libraries. The *Census Catalog and Guide* for the years 1985 through 1998 provides a fairly comprehensive list of secondary data products produced since 1980. For products from the 1970 census, a *Directory of Data Files* was first issued in 1979 with loose-leaf updates running through 1984.

Current Subject Areas

From 1970 through 1990 the subject areas covered by secondary products have remained more or less the same, with a few exceptions. Many population studies closely parallel those of the Current Population Survey modules and involve the same agencies. These include the subject areas found in the 1990 Subject Summary Tape Files (SSTFs) that were made available on CD-ROM. These subject areas include aging, educational attainment, commuting or journey to work, fertility, minorities and ethnic groups, poverty, work disabilities, employment status, occupation and industry, and work experience. A number of special reports deal with housing: housing of the elderly, housing characteristics of new units, mobile homes, condominium housing, and metropolitan housing. The SSTF series provides detailed population items such as age, citizenship, educational attainment, employment status, and other relevant attributes for the subject population. Housing studies include some demographic data about the householder as well as detailed housing characteristics.

Subject-based secondary products covering items such as migration, marriage and living arrangements, foreign born, citizens living abroad, and income and earnings are used by various Census Bureau divisions and programs. The population estimates and projections programs use many census items. Among them are details about the demographics of the population at the time of the census and data on household structure, family relationships, child bearing, women of child-bearing age, migration, and persons in institutions or group quarters. Since 1970 the Census Bureau has produced modified counts of age, race, and sex that provide adjustments to compensate for errors in the census tabulations, especially for the very young, very old, and persons of nonspecified races. These modified counts also included adjustments made to counties or other areas that may have challenged Census Bureau numbers and were able to have their population counts revised.

Other Products

The 1990 Special Tabulation Program (STP) provides small-area data dealing with veterans, aging, and housing. These tabulations were funded by the Veterans Administration, the Administration on Aging, and the Department of Housing and Urban Development. There were over 100 other special tabulations, some providing unique detail and cross-tabulations. Most of these were announced in Census Bureau publications of the time but were never available from Customer Services and become more difficult to locate as time passes. For example, *STP 89, Characteristics of Displaced Homemakers and Single Parents File*, was released on diskette in 1993 and was available from the Decennial Programs Coordination Branch. That branch no longer exists. Computer printouts were available from the Population Division and from the Housing and Household Economic Statistics Division (HHES). HHES repackaged a set of listings for sale as a group. This set, called *The Historical Poverty Tables*, contains comparisons of poverty characteristics from the 1970, 1980, and 1990 censuses.

Mandated programs dealing with equal employment have led to the creation of special products to meet the needs of employers. The *Equal Employment Opportunity (EEO) Special File* (1980 and 1990) provides detailed occupation, race, sex, and Hispanic origin counts for states, counties, metropolitan areas, and large cities. There is a separate table for educational attainment, age, and sex. In 1990 two supplemental EEO files were funded by external sources, and the data from that work are available to the public.

Secondary data products dealing with transportation, journey to work, place of work, and vehicle availability have been created ever since the questions relating to these subjects were first asked in 1960. These files and reports find many uses at the national, state, and local levels. For example, they are used to define labor markets and to meet mandated programs, many dealing with the Clean Air Act. The Bureau of Transportation Statistics distributed special census tabulations in their *Census Transportation Planning Package* of 1990 and the *Urban Transportation Planning Packages* of 1970 and 1980. The 1970 and 1980 products were released and distributed by the Census Bureau.

Data on education, funded by the National Center for Education Statistics (NCES), have been made available by both the Census Bureau and the private sector. Since 1940 the Census Bureau has prepared special data products dealing with educational attainment. Similar data are found in the Current Population Survey supplemental questions on that topic and the Current Population Report Series. In 1970, NCES funded tabulations by school district for 1st Count and 5th Count data files but contracted with Applied Urbanetics to compile some tables from the 1970 4th Count at the school district level. The Census Bureau produced a block group to school district geographic reference for districts with at least 300 students. For each block group or enumeration district, Office of Education school district codes were given. In 1980 the Census Bureau was the contracting agent for school district-level summaries and a geographic reference file, but in 1990 NCES turned to the private sector to deliver 1990 census data at the school district level.

Geographic Coverage

Geographic coverage for secondary products varies. The data may be summarized for the nation, for states, or for metropolitan areas. For many subject areas, the state is the smallest area for which tabulations are produced, but many products deal only with metropolitan or urban areas. Some products deal with special types of areas, such as school districts or congressional districts, but cover the same tabulations as the regular report series.

■ Ann S. Gray

Bibliography

U.S. Bureau of the Census. *Census Catalog and Guide.* Washington, D.C.: U.S. Department of Commerce, Bureau of the Census. Available for 1980-1998. For sale by the Superintendent of Documents, U.S. Government Printing Office. Also available at http://www.census.gov/prod/www/abs/catalogs.html.

U.S. Bureau of the Census. *Directory of Data Files.* Washington, D.C.: U.S. Department of Commerce, Bureau of the Census, 1979. With updates through 1984.

Dress rehearsal

The dress rehearsal is the last major test of census procedures before the decennial census and is therefore the culmination of all the planned innovations for that census. The Census Bureau chooses several sites around the country and mounts a full-scale census in each of these local areas. The 1998 dress rehearsal for the 2000 census took place at three sites: Columbia, South Carolina; Sacramento, California; and the Menominee Indian Reservation, in Wisconsin.

Throughout the decade the bureau conducts small-scale tests of changes in census procedures planned for future censuses. It also conducts such tests during the enumeration itself. They include tests of instructions, question wording, question order, employment and training procedures, and other census elements. Once a census plan is designed, all these elements are tested again in the dress rehearsal. The bureau evaluates the operational plan in the dress rehearsal to anticipate and identify problems with the enumeration and to make final changes to the plan before the full April enumeration. The dress rehearsal takes place about two years before the enumeration to allow for a full evaluation.

The bureau began to include tests of census procedures, including the dress rehearsals, before the 1940 census. In August 1939 it took a special census of St. Joseph and Marshall Counties, Indiana, which it used to finalize plans for the April 1940 count. In later years the dress rehearsal became the culmination of a decade or more of smaller procedural tests.

See also *Census testing.*

■ Margo Anderson

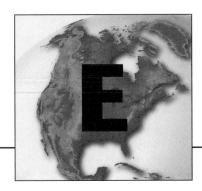

Economic Census

The Economic Census is an enumeration of business establishments in the United States. It provides a detailed portrait of the nation's economy once every five years, for years ending in "2" and "7."

Data from the Economic Census serve as the foundation for the nation's system of statistics about the functioning of the American economy. While many monthly, quarterly, and annual surveys provide the numbers most closely watched by private and government economists for the latest in economic trends, the once-every-five-years Economic Census provides the statistical controls and sampling frames that make many of those surveys possible. Further, the census yields rich data products of its own, providing far greater precision and geographic detail than are possible from the more frequent surveys and making possible many applications ranging from economic research to business-to-business marketing.

Data Collection

Most of the data in the Economic Census are collected by mail. Forms were mailed to five million businesses at the end of 1997, and companies were asked to report their activity during all of that calendar year. Nearly five hundred variations of the census form were sent, each customized to particular industries, so that companies could respond in terms meaningful to their own kind of business.

Some very small businesses were not sent census forms to complete, particularly businesses without paid employees. Instead of sending out sixteen million forms to nonemployers in the 1997 census, the Census Bureau adapted information to the extent possible from the administrative records of other federal agencies.

The Economic Census is mandated by law under Title 13 of the United States Code (sections 131, 191, and 224). The law requires firms to respond and specifies penalties for firms that fail to report. The law also requires the Census Bureau to maintain confidentiality. Individual responses may be seen only by sworn Census Bureau employees. No data are published that could reveal the identity or activity of any business.

The Economic Census traces its beginnings to the 1810 decennial census, when questions on manufacturing were included with those for population. Coverage of economic activities was expanded in subsequent censuses to include mining and some commercial activities. The 1905 Manufactures Census was the first time a census was taken separately from the regular decennial population census. Censuses covering retail and wholesale trade and construction industries were added in 1930, as were some service trades in 1933. The 1954 Economic Census was the first time the various censuses were integrated: providing comparable census data across economic sectors, using consistent time periods, concepts, definitions, classifications, and reporting units. Censuses were taken for 1958 and 1963, and, starting in 1967, have continued at five-year intervals.

Basic Concepts

The core data from the Economic Census are summarized in terms of business establishments; for example, the number and aggregate employment of establishments in a certain kind of business located in a certain area. An establishment, as defined for census and survey purposes, is a business or industrial unit at a single geographic location that produces or distributes goods or performs services, such as a single store or factory.

Classifying economic activity establishment by establishment is only one of three alternatives. Some census results are classified by company or firm (an entity owning or controlling any number of establishments, including those of subsidiary firms). But because different establishments within the same company can be located in different areas or be engaged in different kinds of business, the establishment basis of reporting yields more precise information than data reported in terms of companies.

Users frequently want data in terms of particular products produced or sold, a third way to classify economic activity. Census forms ask for dollar volume of sales for key products appropriate to each industry, but these data are limited to avoid placing an unreasonable record-keeping burden on businesses. Further, many of the statistics collected in the Economic Census, such as employment or capital expenditures, are associated with particular establishments but cannot generally be reported separately for individual product lines. Thus, only a few specialized data series, such as retail Merchandise Line Sales or product tables in manufacturing census reports, present statistics by product line. Most of the basic census statistics reflect the classification of establishments, not companies or products.

Classifying Industries

Most data from Economic Censuses are classified by industry, and, since the 1930s, that grouping has been based on the Standard Industrial Classification (SIC) system. For 1997, most census reports switched to the new North American Industry Classification System (NAICS). Only a few reports from the 1997 Economic Census classify data by SIC.

NAICS, developed in cooperation with Canada and Mexico, classifies North America's economic activities at two-, three-, four-, and five-digit levels of detail, and the U.S. version of NAICS further defines industries to a sixth digit (see Table 1).

Table 1. NAICS Hierarchic Structure

NAICS level	Example	
---	NAICS code	Description
Sector	51	Information
Subsector	513	Broadcasting and telecommunications
Industry group	5133	Telecommunications
Industry	51332	Wireless telecommunications carriers, except satellite
U.S. Industry	513321	Paging

Note: NAICS = North American Industry Classification System.

The Census Bureau also classifies products, and, in the case of manufacturing and mining, products are classified in a manner consistent with the industry structure. For 1997, the first six digits of the ten-digit product code are the same as the NAICS code for the industry with which the product is most frequently associated. Broad product or service lines also are provided for retail and wholesale trade and other service industries, although their numbering is independent of the industry code.

Both NAICS and SIC categorize each establishment by the principal activity in which it is engaged. Some establishments engage in more than one kind of activity and, thus, may not fit neatly into a single industry category. Nonetheless, each establishment is classified into only one NAICS or SIC on the basis of its primary activity. Its secondary activities are still counted, for example, toward total sales, but they do not affect the classification. For instance, the total sales of furniture retailers (SIC 5712 or NAICS 44211) in a given area should not be interpreted as the total sales of furniture. Stores in that industry may sell other items in addition to furniture, and other kinds of businesses, such as department stores (SIC 5311 or NAICS 45211), also sell furniture. This is an inevitable limitation of the establishment basis of classification.

Despite their limitations, standard industry classification systems have major advantages. Their widespread use, inside and outside the government, promotes uniformity and comparability in the presentation of statistics collected by various federal and state agencies, trade associations, and private research organizations.

Coverage of the Census

Economic Censuses have never covered all of the economy. The program expanded steadily up to 1992, when the 1992 Economic Census, together with the censuses of agriculture and governments conducted separately, covered roughly 98 percent of economic activity. Coverage was roughly the same for 1997, although with the regrouping of industries in NAICS, the exclusions were shifted around. For example, landscaping and veterinary services—classified as agricultural services under the SIC system—seemed logically excluded from the Economic Census. Those industries were moved into professional, administrative, and other service categories, and, because census funding did not expand to allow their coverage, they seemed to make more awkward holes in the coverage of the economy.

The 1997 Economic Census covers 1,057 of the 1,170 industries in NAICS. Specific exclusions are noted in Table 2.

Another limitation to the coverage of the Economic Census is that most of the statistics apply only to establishments with payroll; that is, they omit small, single-establishment companies with no paid employees—what are sometimes called "mom and pop" businesses. This limitation is a practical one, because the census is conducted by mail and the best records for developing the mailing list of businesses come from the federal payroll tax (Social Security) system. To gauge the number and sales of nonemployer businesses—those not covered by payroll tax records—the Census Bureau obtains some statistics from the Internal Revenue Service derived from business income tax returns. Statistics about nonemployers are confined to specialized reports, and most Economic Census reports summarize statistics about only those establishments with paid employees.

On the one hand, statistics on manufactures are not much affected by the exclusion of establishments without employees. On the other hand, in retailing, services, and construction, establishments without paid employees—for instance, door-to-door sales people, consultants, independent contractors—are relatively common. In 1992 nonemployer establishments accounted for about 2.8 percent of retail sales nationwide, 10.6 percent of service receipts, and 7.3 percent of construction receipts. Certain small industries, such as barber shops, are dominated by nonemployers, and in a number of others—such as real estate operators and agents, tax return preparers, child day care providers, used car dealers—nonemployers account for more than a quarter of all receipts.

Table 2. NAICS Sectors and Their Coverage in the 1997 Economic Census

NAICS code	Economic sector[a]
11	Agriculture, Forestry, Fishing, and Hunting (Separate census of agriculture, conducted by the Department of Agriculture, covers farming but excludes agricultural services, forestry, and fisheries)
21	Mining
22	Utilities
23	Construction
31–33	Manufacturing
42	Wholesale Trade
44–45	Retail Trade
48–49	Transportation and Warehousing (Census excludes U.S. Postal Service, large certificated passenger air transportation, and all rail transportation)
51	Information
52	Finance and Insurance (Census excludes funds and trusts)
53	Real Estate and Rental and Leasing
54	Professional, Scientific, and Technical Services (Census excludes landscape architecture and veterinary services)
55	Management of Companies and Enterprises
56	Administrative and Support, Waste Management, and Remediation Services (Census excludes landscaping services)
61	Educational Services (Census excludes elementary and secondary schools, colleges, and professional schools)
62	Health Care and Social Assistance
71	Arts, Entertainment, and Recreation
72	Accommodation and Foodservices
81	Other Services (Except Public Administration) (Census excludes pet care; labor, political, and religious organizations; and private households)
92	Public Administration (Separate census of governments does not present data according to NAICS or SIC systems)

Note: NAICS = North American Industry Classification System; SIC = Standard Industrial Classification.

[a]The Economic Census covers all industries except where noted. For a complete list of industries, see www.census.gov.naics.

Geographic Areas

The most detailed Economic Census data are provided for the United States as a whole. Key statistics, albeit progressively fewer, are available for states, metropolitan areas (MAs), counties, and places with twenty-five hundred or more inhabitants. Only limited data are provided for zip codes. The level of geographic detail varies by sector, as shown in Table 3.

Within a given area, the more economic activity there is, the more detail is available. Thus, a county with many factories is likely to have more industry detail in a manufacturing census report than a county with fewer manufacturers. All of the data are scrutinized closely to avoid possible disclosure of information about particular firms. This can be frustrating for a user who finds that a desired number has been replaced with a (D) for "disclosure" and therefore must rely on data at a higher level of aggregation.

Because of cost of preparation and the potential for statistical disclosure, no incorporated places with fewer than twenty-five hundred inhabitants, unincorporated places, or census tracts are reported separately in the Economic Census.

Economic Census Products

Economic Census results are published in a variety of printed and electronic products.

Types of Reports

Most data from the Economic Census look something like those illustrated in Table 4. Each table presents statistics for a set of industries or geographic areas or both. The focus is on economic activity during a particular census year. (Statistics from previous censuses are presented in only a few specialized tables.) The statistics are complemented by narrative material—basic concepts, methodology, reliability, and detailed explanations of terms—included in the same printed report, CD-ROM, or other system.

Table 3. Geographic Areas in the 1997 Economic Census

Sector	States	Metropolitan areas	Counties	Places 2500+	Zip codes
Mining	X				
Utilities	X	X			
Construction	X				
Manufacturing	X	X	X	X	X
Wholesale Trade	X	X	X	X	
Retail Trade	X	X	X	X	X
Transportation and Warehousing	X	X			
Information	X	X	X	X	
Finance and Insurance	X	X	X	X	
Real Estate and Rental and Leasing	X	X	X	X	
Professional, Scientific, and Technical Services	X	X	X	X	X
Management of Companies and Enterprises	X				
Administrative and Support, Waste Management, and Remediation Services	X	X	X	X	X
Educational Services	X	X	t	t	t
Health Care and Social Assistance	X	X	t	t	t
Arts, Entertainment, and Recreation	X	X	t	t	t
Accommodation and Foodservices	X	X	X	X	X
Other Services (Except Public Administration)	X	X	t	t	t

Note: t = data are not available for tax-exempt firms at this level.

Detailed Reports. Detailed reports are issued sector by sector. With the exception of zip code statistics, these reports were issued in print up through the 1992 census; starting in 1997, their data were available only on CD-ROM and on the Census Bureau's Internet site:

- *Geographic Area Series* (published for all sectors) provides detail for establishments with employees as illustrated in Table 4. They include data for the nation, states, and substate areas listed in Table 3, except zip codes.
- *Zip Code Statistics* (selected sectors, see Table 3) include primarily counts of establishments by employment- or sales-size by industry or both.
- *Industry Series* (manufacturing, mining, and construction) provides national totals on individual industries, their products, and materials consumed, plus limited data for states.
- *Subject Series* (all sectors) provides national and limited state and metropolitan area data on special topics including Merchandise Line Sales, Concentration Ratios, and Establishment and Firm Size.

Summary Reports by Sector. Summary reports by sector provide highlights of the data in print for 1997. They feature primarily national data and general statistics by state, and they are similar in many respects to "General Summary" or "U.S. Summary" reports published in 1992 and prior years. Given that few reports now appear in print, the summary reports for 1997 also include illustrations of some of the more detailed data available in electronic media.

Core Business Statistics. Core Business Statistics was new for 1997. The series provides data for most or all industries, economy-wide. An *Advance Report* gave the first data for broad NAICS and SIC categories. The *Bridge between NAICS and SIC* shows the relationships between NAICS and SIC categories in detail. *Comparative Statistics* shows national and state totals classified by SIC for both 1992 and 1997—comparisons not possible with other, NAICS-based reports. *Nonemployer Statistics* also is the only source for information about sixteen million small businesses not included in other census reports.

Table 4. Sample Data in a Geographic Area Series

NAICS code	Geographic area and kind of business	Establishments (number)	Sales ($1,000)	Annual payroll ($1,000)	Paid employees for pay period including March 12 (number)
	COLORADO				
44–45	*Retail trade*	22,921	28,532,646	283,457	3,488,242
441	*Motor vehicle and parts dealers*	1,340	6,018,542	18,932	484,044
4411	Automobile dealers	546	5,305,849	13,631	384,357
44111	New car dealers	262	5,024,487	12,503	363,316
44112	Used car dealers	284	281,362	1,128	21,041
4412	Other motor vehicle dealers	173	272,136	1,171	26,057
44121	Recreational vehicle dealers	60	142,413	432	11,438
44122	Motorcycle, boat, and other motor vehicle dealers	113	129,723	739	14,619
441221	Motorcycle dealers	71	86,493	486	9,799
441222	Boat dealers	27	31,333	172	3,303
441229	All other motor vehicle dealers	15	11,897	81	1,517
4413	Automotive parts, accessories, and tire stores	605	434,640	4,089	72,952
442	*Furniture and home furnishings stores*	1,749	1,543,869	10,380	187,582
4421	Furniture stores	449	447,968	2,899	61,219

Note: NAICS = North American Industry Classification System.

Other Reports. The *Survey of Minority-Owned Business Enterprises*, conducted in conjunction with the Economic Census, measures the extent of business ownership by specific minority groups in the United States: blacks, persons of Hispanic origin, Asians and Pacific Islanders, and American Indians and Alaska Natives. A report is issued on each of these groups. There is also a report on firms owned by women, and each report gives corresponding characteristics for all businesses.

Business Expenses documents various types of operating expenses including supplemental labor costs, energy costs, taxes, and a variety of purchased services including advertising, legal and accounting services, and repairs. It covers these items for broad categories of retailers, merchant wholesalers, and service firms as classified under SIC.

All of the foregoing reports provide data for the United States. Reports from complementary censuses cover some but not all sectors of the economies in Puerto Rico, the Virgin Islands, Guam, and the Commonwealth of the Northern Mariana Islands, under the title *Censuses of Outlying Areas.*

Timing of Reports

Most final 1997 Economic Census reports were published in 1999 and 2000. This may not appear to be very timely, but 1997 was only the reference year. Most data were not obtained from companies until 1998, so that the respondent could provide information reflecting all activity, such as sales or capital expenditures, during the entire calendar year of reference.

Table 5 lists key dates in the publication of 1997 census data.

Printed Reports, CD-ROMs, and the Internet

Economic Census data are now published primarily in electronic formats, although some reports are also published in print.

Printed Reports. Printed reports were the only method of publication of Economic Census data up until 1972, but they continued as the most popular format until CD-ROMs and the Internet became widely used. Starting in 1997, only a few of the reports, all of which were published in electronic media, also appeared in print.

Page-Image Files on the Internet. Starting with the 1992 Economic Census, all printed reports were also made available as portable document format (PDF) files on the Internet, readable with the free Adobe Acrobat reader. For 1997, the corresponding reports were published on the Web in the same format but were not printed. Users wishing hard copy of PDF reports can easily print them at a local printer with Acrobat or can pay the Census Bureau to print a report with a rudimentary binding at a cost of $25 or more depending on the size of the report.

American FactFinder Database on the Internet. Starting with 1997, all Economic Census data are accessible via the American FactFinder system at the Census Bureau Web site. Custom reports can be retrieved through a "Build a Query" mode, or "Quick Reports" can be generated for any industry or area. Reports can be printed or downloaded to the user's computer in a variety of formats. The FactFinder database is updated with new releases every week, of particular importance during time periods when the data are first being published.

CD-ROMs. CD-ROM is the most efficient mechanism for transferring large census databases in their entirety. Software on each compact disc provides the capability to select, reformat, merge, and rank the numbers, and then to export the data to a spreadsheet or other application for further manipulation. From 1999 to early 2001, new CD-ROMs with progressively more data were issued quarterly.

Table 5. Key Dates in the Publication of the 1997 Economic Census

Date	Publication
Early 1999	Advance report (in print)
1999	Industry Series
Mid-1999– early 2000	Geographic Area Series
Mid-2000	Bridge between NAICS and SIC (in print)
Mid-2000	Comparative Statistics
Mid-2000– late 2000	Minority- and Women-Owned Business (in print)
Mid-2000– early 2001	Subject Series
Early 2001	Summary reports (in print)
Mid-2001	ZIP Code Statistics

Note: For details, see www.census.gov/econ97.

Access to Microdata: Special Tabulations and Studies

One of the most popular forms of data release for users of demographic data from the Census Bureau is the public-use microdata file. Samples from the bureau's various household surveys, including the Census of Population and Housing, are made available to data users after detailed geographic information has been removed and other modifications are made to reduce the potential that any respondent could be identified. Public-use microdata files allow users to retabulate the data in a variety of ways to examine different relationships that may not be highlighted in published tables.

Unfortunately, the typical business establishment is far more identifiable than the typical household. Government agencies that regulate or tax businesses, as well as trade associations, publishers of business information, and other private entities, frequently maintain large amounts of information about many specific businesses. Some of this information is made publicly available by the subject business itself (for example, in classified telephone directories or in reports to shareholders). Thus, any file of microdata about unidentified business establishments from a census would have some potential for being matched to information from other sources to indirectly identify, and thus disclose confidential information about, at least some specific businesses. In the absence of methods to keep such records anonymous, there can be no public-use microdata files about firms or establishments.

When users need the census data reanalyzed in a special way, they can contract with the Census Bureau to make a "special tabulation" of its confidential records. The microdata records are handled only by sworn Census Bureau personnel, and the resulting data are screened for possible disclosure prior to release—in the same manner as regular census publications. The bureau's costs in preparing a special tabulation, typically in the thousands of dollars, must be reimbursed by the customer or group of customers.

One special project has led to the development of a Longitudinal Research Database (LRD) of manufacturing plants, with data assembled to cover a series of census and intervening survey years. These and other microdata files are not available for public use, but the bureau has a special staff (the Center for Economic Studies) with its own dedicated computers to work with economic microdata. Appropriately funded outside researchers can be sworn in as Census Bureau staff to work with the data at Census Bureau centers in Berkeley, Boston, Los Angeles, Pittsburgh, and Washington, D.C., but data publication requires the same kind of scrutiny to avoid disclosure of confidential information that applies to all other Census Bureau products.

Assembling Time Series Data

One of the preeminent virtues of the Economic Census program is that comparable data have been collected at fixed intervals and with consistent definitions across decades, even though these data were previously published under separate census titles, such as the Census of Manufactures or the Census of Retail Trade, or collectively as the plural Economic Censuses.

Nonetheless, all of these reports were designed in the context of limited budgets for printing, and census reports typically include little historical data. Comparative statistics, covering the current and most recent previous census, have generally been included for the United States and for states. Left to the user is the assembly of time series—such as the growth of retailing in a particular area or trends in a particular manufacturing industry.

Acquiring Reports from Previous Censuses

While printed reports are typically available for sale for only a few years after their issuance, the Census Bureau archived all printed material on microfiche from 1968 until publication began on PDF. Users may purchase from the Census Bureau copies of the microfiche or paper copy generated from the microfiche for any title from the 1967 through 1987 censuses. Collections of older reports are maintained at certain major libraries; individual reports may be borrowed through interlibrary loan.

Volume 1j of the 1992 CD-ROM series includes a national time series from the Annual Survey of Manufactures from 1958 to 1995 and monthly retail sales from 1967 to 1994. Volume 4 of the 1992 CD-ROM series, entitled "Nonemployer Statistics," includes Geographic Area Series files for 1987 for retail trade, wholesale trade, service industries, and manufacturing in a format that mirrors their 1992 counterparts. More comprehensive data for 1987, and a few data sets for 1982 and 1977, are included on the final 1987 Economic Census CD-ROM (1e).

Selected tape files from Economic Censuses 1972 to 1982 may be obtained from the National Archives and Records Administration.

Industry Comparability

The implementation of NAICS causes major disruptions in the availability of comparable information across time periods. In the last thirty years, the SIC system was updated three times (in 1967, 1972, and 1987), and each time a significant number of new industries was introduced into the existing framework. What was different for 1997 was that the whole framework changed.

While data for nearly half of the SICs in use in 1992 can be derived from 1997 NAICS industries, a substantial number of industries cannot be much more than approximated under NAICS. That makes the 1997 Economic Census particularly important, because census questionnaires identified industry components finely enough that data could be categorized under either NAICS or SIC; and as a result certain key data could be published according to the old system as well as the new. The Comparative Statistics report presented the number of establishments, sales, employment, and payroll for each SIC for the nation and each state, for both 1997 and 1992. Thus, basic SIC-by-state time series can be carried backward from 1997 to 1987 and farther to the extent that particular industries were not affected by SIC changes in 1987, 1972, and 1967.

NAICS time series can go forward from 1997, but they cannot generally go backward to earlier years, because many NAICS categories require information that was not collected in 1992 and earlier censuses. For instance, NAICS 45321, Office Supplies and Stationery Stores, differs from SIC 5943, Stationery Stores, primarily by the addition of certain office supply stores that were previously classified in wholesale trade. Census questionnaires prior to 1997 did not separately differentiate office supply stores from other kinds of office supply wholesalers, so NAICS 45321 cannot be estimated for prior periods.

Users have access to correspondence tables between the old and new systems in the formal NAICS Manual (available both in print and on the Web). These tables show for each NAICS industry the SIC categories or parts thereof that comprise them and for each SIC industry the NAICS industries or parts thereof to which their establishments are likely to be reclassified. The 1997 Economic Census *Bridge between NAICS and SIC* report takes that correspondence a significant step further by showing the number of establishments, sales, employment, and payroll at the national level for each of those intersections between the old and new

systems. For example, the Bridge report shows the number and sales of those office supply stores that were transferred out of wholesale trade, along with other components of the new retail Office Supply and Stationery Stores category.

At broader levels of classification, the changes between SIC and NAICS were further confounded by the rearrangement of the hierarchy. The Service Industries division of the SIC was subdivided into five new sectors and parts of four others. Less noticeable, but perhaps more troublesome, were shifts affecting sectors—such as manufacturing, wholesale trade, and retail trade—that retained their status as sector titles in NAICS but were affected by changes in scope. Retail trade was roughly 10 percent smaller under NAICS than under SIC just because eating and drinking places were transferred to the new Accommodation and Food-services sector, not to mention smaller changes resulting from transfers between retail and wholesale trade such as the office supply stores. Manufacturing also lost more than 10 percent of its employment just because significant components were reclassified elsewhere.

Some further changes to NAICS will be implemented for the 2002 Economic Census, including redefinition of industries in Construction and Wholesale Trade and separate identification of Electronic Shopping and Electronic Auctions within the Electronic Shopping and Mail-Order Houses industry group.

Scope of Economic Census Programs

Prior to 1992, the Economic Census program covered less of the American economy. In 1987 and earlier years, the census did not include Finance, Insurance, and Real Estate; and it included only selected transportation industries within the Transportation, Communication, and Utilities sector. The addition of those components boosted census coverage from roughly 76 percent of the gross domestic product in 1987 to about 98 percent in 1992. The coverage of service industries expanded in 1967, 1977, and 1987. Thus, time series available for some industries are relatively short.

Geographic Comparability

Most students of economic trends confine themselves to looking at the nation, states, and counties. County boundary changes are few and far between, while many places, metropolitan areas, and zip codes change boundaries over time. Geographic comparability of substate areas could be a moot issue between 1992 and 1997, because no 1997 data were published for counties, places, and metropolitan areas on a basis allowing for comparison with 1992 data (that is, SIC). Questions as seemingly routine as "Did manufacturing employment in my area go up or down?" remained unanswered for 1997.

Sources For More Information

The definitive publication about industry classification is the NAICS Manual, available in print, on CD-ROM, and at the Web site www.census.gov/naics. The manual, in whatever medium, includes definitions for each industry, an alphabetic index, and detailed tables illustrating the correspondence between NAICS and SIC categories, and vice versa.

The free Web site is generally the preferred form of the manual. It incorporates a search system that allows the user to enter a search term or SIC code and receive a list of candidate NAICS codes, link from there to NAICS definitions, and in turn traverse to the NAICS-to-SIC correspondence tables. The Web site includes details not available in print or on CD-ROM.

Another important reference is the *Bridge between NAICS and SIC*. Fortunately for data users, the 1997 Economic Census collected enough information from each establishment to classify data according to both NAICS and SIC. The Bridge report shows 1997 Economic Census data cross-tabulated by both NAICS and SIC, so that it is possible to see how much of each SIC went to particular NAICS codes—and vice versa—thereby defining comparability much more thoroughly than any other source.

The Web site www.census.gov/naics provides access to all of the major references—the NAICS manual, the Bridge report, background papers, and brochures.

Various informational and promotional brochures have been published about the 1997 Economic Census and are available from the Customer Services Center, U.S. Bureau of the Census, Washington, D.C. 20233 (301) 457-4100.

The most comprehensive reference is the Guide to the Economic Census, maintained on the Web at www.census.gov/econguide. The coverage of the guide is much broader than the Economic Census, including cross-references to related data as well as to other reference material already on the Web.

The guide is also accessible from the more general Economic Census Web site, which is linked from the Census Bureau's home page, www.census.gov. That cite provides direct access to all available economic census data, to copies of the hundreds of forms used in the census, answers to frequently asked questions, media resources, and all other available materials.

■ Paul T. Zeisset

Bibliography

Ambler, Carole A., and James E. Kristoff. "Introducing the North American Industry Classification System." *Government Information Quarterly* 15 (1998).

Zeisset, Paul T., and Mark E. Wallace. *How NAICS Will Affect Data Users.* Lanham, Md.: Bernan Press, 1997; also available at www.census.gov/epcd/www/naicsusr.html.

Editing and imputation

Two related steps in processing census questionnaires are editing to reconcile inconsistent or anomalous answers for a person or household, and imputation to supply values for missing responses by using information obtained from other persons or households. Throughout the history of the census, the volume of responses has spurred technological innovation to automate as much of the data processing as possible. Computerization has taken over much of the editing that was formerly carried out by clerical review (although some clerical editing is still performed). Computerization has also made it possible to develop sophisticated imputation techniques.

Terms and Techniques

Editing in the census refers to review and modification of responses provided by a person or household from other information in the household. For example, if the marital status of the person listed as the spouse of the first person in the household is reported as "divorced," the entry will be changed to "now married." Editing is also performed by applying the logic of the questionnaire. For example, if an entry is provided for a person under age fifteen for an item that pertains to people fifteen years of age and older (for example, occupation), the entry will be changed to an appropriate "not applicable" code.

Imputation in the census refers to providing responses for missing items by using not only other information for the person or household, but also information from other, similar persons or households. Imputation is sometimes distinguished in the census as "allocation" versus "substitution": *allocation* is the imputation of values (answers) for missing data items when some of the person's characteristics are known; *substitution* is the imputation of values for all items when the only information known is that a person or housing unit is present.

Two imputation techniques that have been used in computerized processing of census data are the "cold deck" method and the "hot deck" method. Cold decks were originally sets of punched cards that contained numeric values representing known distributions of the answers to questions from earlier censuses or surveys. The term *deck* continued to be used even after the distributions were provided to computers in other forms. The distribution of values in a cold deck does not change. Each value is used in sequence to allocate missing data, and the sequence is repeated as often as necessary. For example, if other data show that 40 percent of married men have served in the military, then a cold deck might contain the following random sequence of ten values to impute veteran status for married men in the census: 1, 2, 1, 1, 2, 2, 2, 2, 1, 2 (four 1's representing yes, served in the military, and six 2's representing no, did not serve). If twenty-one married men did not respond to the item, then the cold deck values would be assigned in order. The first man would receive a value of 1, the second man a value of 2, and so on. The tenth man in this example would receive a value of 2, and the eleventh man would be assigned a 1, which is the first value in the sequence. Consequently, to assign values for military service for all twenty-one married men, the first value in the sequence would be used three times (for the first, eleventh, and twenty-first man), and the other nine values would be used twice.

Hot decks are distributions of values that are constantly altered as questionnaires are processed and data for the latest person or housing unit are substituted for the values already in the hot deck matrix. Imputation (allocation) of a missing entry is made from the latest value stored in the matrix that fits other known characteristics of the person or housing unit. For example, a person reported as a twenty-year-old male relative for whom marital status was not reported would be allocated the same marital status as the latest such person processed. When no information is available about the persons in a housing unit, people in a previously processed housing unit are selected as a substitute, and

all their basic (short-form) characteristics are duplicated. (When it is not known whether a housing unit is occupied or vacant, an imputation is first performed to assign occupancy status.)

Compared with cold decks, hot decks have the advantage of using data from the current census that is being processed rather than a previous census or survey; also, hot decks preserve more of the variability that characterizes the population. Further, hot decks, by using information for similar, recently processed people or housing units take advantage of commonalities of characteristics among small geographic areas. Today, cold decks are not used in census processing except to determine the starting values for distributions.

Editing and imputation are designed to make census data more complete and accurate. However, the procedures used may introduce error. Although rates of allocation and substitution are published for each census, there have been no systematic studies of error from editing or imputation. Analysis of allocation rates for the 1990 census found that they were higher for questionnaires obtained by enumerator follow-up than for questionnaires returned by households in the mail and that they were higher for long-form items, such as income and place of work, than for short-form items, such as age and sex.

History

For the censuses of 1790–1820, U.S. marshals and their assistants tallied (added up) the responses to census questions from households in their districts without further review of their work in Washington, D.C. For the 1830 and 1840 censuses, temporary clerks were hired in Washington to examine the marshals' returns and note errors. Clerks took over the job of tallying the returns and organizing the data for publication beginning with the 1850 census. Electromechanical punched card tabulating machines were used as early as the census of 1890 to automate the process of tallying people in various response categories. However, armies of clerks still had the job of recording the census responses on punched cards for input to the tabulating equipment.

Over the decades, more and more editing was performed by clerks in the process of encoding census responses for punching onto cards. For example, elaborate rules were developed for coding occupation, which provided for editing (modifying) some responses on the basis of other information about the person.

Thus, in some censuses, occupation entries believed to be inappropriate for the gender or race of the respondent, and therefore believed to be erroneously reported, could be changed during editing to other categories believed to be appropriate and more likely correct (for example, "tailor" for a woman respondent might be changed to "seamstress").

For the first 150 years of census taking, there was no imputation for missing data. (In place of imputation, census publications carried counts of "not reported" for specific items.) The first use of imputation occurred in the 1940 census, when a method was devised to impute age for persons for whom age was not reported on the schedule. (W. Edwards Deming, who subsequently became a world-renowned industrial adviser on quality control, originated the method.) The procedure—similar to a cold deck—involved randomly selecting a value for age from an appropriate deck of cards, selected according to what other information was known about the person for whom age was missing.

For the 1950 census new multicolumn punched card sorting machines were used to automate the editing and coding of employment status, which depended on often inconsistent or incomplete responses to multiple questions. A "decision table" was devised that specified an employment status code (for example, "employed," "unemployed," "not in the labor force") for each of the possible combinations of answers and missing values to the relevant questions. This table was wired into the multicolumn sorters. Clerks punched the actual responses onto cards, and the employment status code was produced automatically by running the cards through the sorters.

The advent of high-speed computing technology significantly expanded the opportunities for sophisticated editing and imputation of census data. The UNIVAC I computer, developed under contract to the Census Bureau, was delivered in time for some of the last tabulation work on the 1950 census. Improved UNIVAC models were used to perform the majority of the data processing for the 1960 census, and the sophistication of computerized data processing has increased for each subsequent census.

The 1960 census used computers for data editing and to impute values for missing responses from cold and hot decks. The 1970 census used editing and imputation techniques similar to those used in the 1960 census but made much fuller use of hot decks. The 1980 census saw the development of statistical matching techniques, which made hot deck imputation proce-dures even more sophisticated. The computer searched for the "best match" for a person or household missing one or more related data items on the basis of a large number of known characteristics instead of the one or two characteristics that were used in the past.

Even after the introduction of computers for census data processing, there has still been an initial clerical editing stage prior to data entry. In the 1990 census, clerks reviewed the questionnaires and made changes in specified instances (for example, if a write-in response was provided instead of a filled-in answer box, the clerk would fill in the appropriate box whenever possible). For missing or inconsistent data, clerks telephoned households to obtain more complete information. Finally, when a questionnaire "failed edit" and the household could not be reached by telephone, the questionnaire was included in the workload for enumerators to follow up in person. (A questionnaire could "fail edit" if it contained incomplete or inconsistent information about the number of people residing at the household or if too many content items were blank.) Only after these steps were completed were the data recorded and put through further editing and imputation by computer.

In the 2000 census, clerical review was limited to a coverage edit; that is, to checking that each household was completely counted with regard to the number of persons. For households for which coverage problems were detected (for example, the household reported five persons but only provided information for two of them), clerks telephoned the households to obtain more information. Content edits, for missing or incomplete responses to specific items, were handled solely by computer.

See also *Data capture; Data dissemination and use; Precomputer tabulation systems; Sampling for content.*

■ Constance F. Citro

Bibliography

Goldfield, Edwin D. "Innovations in the Decennial Census of Population and Housing: 1940–1990." Paper delivered to the Panel on Census Requirements in the Year 2000 and Beyond, Committee on National Statistics, National Research Council, Washington, D.C., October 1992.

U.S. Bureau of the Census. *1970 Census of Population and Housing Procedural History.* Washington, D.C.: U.S. Department of Commerce, 1976.

Education: changing questions and classifications

Without interruption, one or more questions about education have been asked in every decennial census since 1840. Despite a certain amount of change that has occurred in the questions over time, there is a remarkable degree of consistency in their basic format. Most of the changes that have taken place reflect responses to what might be considered critical changes occurring in the U.S. society at large.

School Enrollment and Literacy, 1840–1930

The first questions about education appear in the 1840 census. Enumerators were asked to record the number of persons attending "universities and colleges," "academies and grammar schools," and "primary and common schools." Included in this enumeration was the "number of students at public charge." The focus of these questions was not persons in households but, rather, the number of persons in *schools*. Immediately following these questions was another item intended to identify "Persons over the age of 20 who could not read and write."

In 1850 a major change was made to the counting procedure, one that would remain in place in roughly the same form for the next nine censuses. In this census, a question about school enrollment was asked for the persons in each household. The yes or no question, "Attended school within the last year," was accompanied with instructions that it was to be asked of all persons, and should not include Sunday schools.

From 1850 to 1930, these two concepts—school enrollment and literacy—constituted the scope of measurement regarding education in the decennial census. The choice of these questions reflects a nation undergoing major changes in public education and literacy efforts, as well as national concern about a growing immigrant population. In some years ability to read and write was determined by separate questions (1870–1920); in other years by a single item (1840–1860, 1930). In some years school enrollment was asked as the number of months in school (1890–1900), whereas in others it was simply enrollment at any time since the start of the school year—September 1 (1910–1930) or during the "census year" (1880–1890). In several of these censuses, a question about the ability to speak English immediately followed the reading and writing questions.

Enrollment and Attainment—1940–1980

The next major change in census education questions occurred in the 1940 census. An entirely new aspect of education—attainment, or completed education—was queried for the first time. The question concerning the "highest grade of school attended," allowed for responses ranging from "none" to the "5th or higher year" of college. Other changes were incorporated as well. In 1940 the reference date for school enrollment was shortened from anytime in the previous school year to March 1, just one month prior to census enumeration day; in 1950 the date was changed to February 1 and has remained there since then. Finally, the focus of all schooling was designated as "regular school," defined as schooling that would lead to a high school or college degree.

In 1950 the new attainment question was improved so that the current grade of enrollment response could be used to determine whether the highest grade attended had been completed or was still in process (because the person was still enrolled). At this point the school enrollment and educational attainment questions became to some degree "linked," since estimating attainment clearly required one to use some of the information from the enrollment item.

Over the next several censuses these combined enrollment and attainment questions were modified to continue to capture and reflect emerging social changes. In 1960 the school enrollment categories were expanded to include a separate category for "private or parochial" schools. In 1970 "parochial" was a separate category; in 1980 it became "private, church-related"; and in 1990 (and 2000) the independent category for church-related schooling had disappeared altogether, subsumed into the category "private school, private college."

Another source of change since the major revision in 1940 relates to the categories of educational attainment. In 1970 the category "nursery school" was added to the questionnaire, reflecting the increased use of nursery schools for young children. In 1980 the upper bound was expanded, including categories for single years of college up through the eighth year.

The 1970 census included an attempt to measure "vocational schooling," which by the Census Bureau definition was presumed to be outside the designation of "regular schooling." This two-part question assessed whether the person had "ever completed a vocational training program" and the "main field" of the vocational training. Evaluation of the responses to this question after the census was completed revealed very high rates of inconsistency in response to the questions, and the item was dropped from future censuses.

Questionnaire Changes in 1990–2000

The most recent major change to the education items was implemented in 1990; it switched the focus of educational attainment from "years of school" to "highest degree or level" completed. Research conducted after the 1980 census had concluded that the "years of school" concept was too vague at the college level, with many people reporting not a completed level of schooling, but rather, the amount of time—number of calendar years—spent in schooling. The research showed that individuals could much more reliably report a completed earned degree than they could the usual or required amount of time it took to get the degree. The 1990 census thus switched to a redesigned attainment question with grades below the high school completion level, and degree categories (for example, bachelor's, master's, doctorate) above the high school completion level.

Since the enrollment and attainment questions from 1940 to 1980 were designed to be somewhat interdependent, the creation of the new attainment question based on degrees required redesign of the school enrollment item as well. In part because of the lack of a federally mandated need for individual grades of school enrollment, and a more practical need of physical space on the form, the resulting enrollment question restricts the ability to measure school enrollment at specific single grades, resulting in a loss of some information from the item used from 1940 to 1980.

The 150-year history of education questions in the census clearly illustrates their role as an instrument of social measurement. As the social definition of education continues to evolve, it is likely that so too will the measurement recording tool.

■ Robert Kominski

Bibliography

Kominsky, Robert. *Evaluation of the 1980 Decennial Census Education Questions*. 1980 Census Preliminary Evaluation Results Memorandum No. 104. Washington, D.C.: U.S. Census Bureau, 1985.

Kominsky, Robert, and Paul Siegel. *Measuring Educational Attainment in the 1990 Census*. Paper presented at the annual meeting of the American Sociological Association, Washington, D.C., 1987.

U.S. Bureau of the Census. *200 Years of U.S. Census Taking: Population and Housing Questions, 1790–1990*. Washington, D.C.: Government Printing Office, 1989.

Woltman, Henry. *Accuracy of Responses for Vocational Training*. 1970 Census Preliminary Evaluation Results Memorandum No. 42. Washington, D.C.: U.S. Census Bureau, 1974.

Electronic publications

See *Dissemination of data: electronic products.*

Enumeration: field procedures

The process of collecting data in the field is at the heart of the decennial census. Almost all of the population is enumerated at the location where each person lives. Field procedures are created and designed to accomplish this task.

1960 Census

The 1960 census was a transitional census in terms of the procedures used for the enumeration. It was the last census conducted with what has since become known as the "conventional" method, one that had been in place for over 150 years. The most important feature of this method was the absence of a list of addresses, or housing units, prior to the census-taking. Instead, enumerators created an address list at the same time that they enumerated the population. The 1960 census also was the first census to use the post office to assist in the enumeration and to use separate short and long forms for individual households. A major innovation in 1960 was the use of FOSDIC (Film Optical Sensing Device for Input to Computers). FOSDIC allowed the data collected for each person and household to be read directly into a computer, avoiding the time-consuming intermediate step of keypunching the information onto IBM cards.

The 1960 procedures called for census crew leaders (enumerators who were in charge of several lower-level enumerators) to travel over the enumeration districts to which he or she had been assigned. An enumeration district was comprised of blocks or otherwise-defined geographical territories that were considered an appropriate assignment area for a single enumerator. The crew leaders verified the accuracy of their enumerators' maps, marked their routes, pre-listed the first twenty-five housing units for the purpose of checking later on the enumerators' work, and identified "special places," such as hotels and hospitals, that would require a different type of enumeration procedure.

During the last ten days in March 1960, the post office delivered two documents to each occupied housing unit in the country. These were not identified by address, but simply dropped at each unit's mailbox. One document, the Advance Census Report, was a brief questionnaire containing the short-form, or "100-percent," questions. The other document was a statement requesting that householders fill out the questionnaire and retain it for the enumerator's visit.

Beginning on April 1 in most parts of the country, enumerators visited each housing unit. If the questionnaire had been filled in, the enumerator transferred the information contained on it to the "FOSDIC Schedule," which was designed to be used with the Census Bureau's computerized tabulation equipment. If the questionnaire had not been filled in, the enumerator obtained the information directly from the respondent; in addition, he or she collected information on housing through direct observation.

Enumerators also carried listing books in which they recorded the address or description of each place visited, the name of the head of the household, and the total number of persons enumerated. Where necessary, they recorded the fact that a unit was vacant or indicated that a specific location required another visit.

Twenty-five percent of households were selected for inclusion in the long-form, or "25-percent," sample. In the enumerators' listing books, households were listed on a repeating series of lines labeled A, B, C, and D. All households that appeared on the lines labeled "A" were included in the long-form sample. In 82 percent of the country, the long-form sample data were collected in a two-stage enumeration process. Geographically, most of the two-stage areas were in the Northeast and Midwest, the upper South, eastern Texas, and along the West Coast. The remaining 18 percent, located in low-density areas primarily in the deep South and Rocky Mountain areas of the country, were covered in one stage in which both short- and long-form data were collected in the same visit. In the two-stage households that had been selected into the sample, the enumerator left a questionnaire with the sample questions. Respondents were asked to fill it in and mail it back to the local district office.

A variety of procedures were used in special situations. Individuals in group quarters were enumerated on a special form; 25 percent of these respondents were asked to fill in the sample questionnaire for the enumerator to pick up. Other procedures covered transients in hotels and motels and in missions, flophouses, and similar places with very low rent. Military and maritime personnel were enumerated through their military installations. Data on Americans abroad were collected through the Departments of Defense and State. Finally, "Were You Counted?" forms were made widely available. The 1960 census was the first to count students living away at college as part of the college community's population rather than assigning them back to their parental addresses. Younger children in boarding schools were counted at their parental homes.

Close-out procedures were employed after three visits to a housing unit failed to yield an interview. In single-stage households, information was obtained from neighbors, hired help, or an apartment house manager. Similar procedures were used when interviews could not be completed in two-stage households. In either case, questionnaires and pre-addressed postage-free envelopes were left at the unit so that respondents could provide the information by mail.

The 1960 census was conducted through 399 district offices spread among 17 permanent regional field offices. The total number of job positions exceeded 170,000.

The 1970 Census

The 1970 census brought a major procedural innovation: introduction of the mailout-mailback method of census enumeration. This new procedure was used in major metropolitan areas, which, while accounting for only a small proportion of U.S. geography, covered 60 percent of the nation's 70 million housing units. The remainder of the country was enumerated using procedures similar to those used in 1960, except that the long-form sample data questions were administered at the same time as the short-form data items.

The address list of 42 million mailout-mailback housing units was compiled in advance of the census. It began with commercial mailing lists and was updated by postal carriers on their individual routes. All computer processing was done using computer tapes on a

Census Bureau mainframe. An Address Coding Guide (ACG) was developed independently and used to assign census geographic information (census tract and block, city, county, and congressional district) to each address. Individual serial numbers and codes for district office and enumeration district were added. Twenty percent of households were randomly assigned to receive long-form questionnaires. Finally, address labels and address registers (ARs) were generated. The census forms were mailed on March 28, 1970.

In mailout-mailback areas where commercial lists were not available or where there was no city-style delivery system, census workers conducted a special listing operation prior to the census-taking to create the address list. The subsequent compilation and addressing work was accomplished manually in the district offices.

Two additional post office checks were performed on the address lists; after each, missing address information was forwarded to the district offices for AR updates and manual questionnaire addressing. In twenty-one inner-city areas, district office personnel conducted a pre-canvass operation to double-check the master AR once more.

The sampling fraction for long-form data was reduced from 1 in 4 for the 1960 census to 1 in 5 for the 1970 census. In addition, this "20-percent" sample was split further into two groups. Three out of four of the 20-percent sample households (or 15 percent of all households) received one questionnaire, while one in four (or 5 percent) received a somewhat different questionnaire. Thus, the census delivered four data sets: a 100-percent sample, a 20-percent sample, a 15-percent sample, and a 5-percent sample.

After sufficient time had passed for most mailed questionnaires to be logged in at the district offices or at the bureau's central processing office in Jeffersonville, Indiana, the first follow-up stage began with enumerators visiting addresses from which no mail response had been recorded. A second follow-up stage commenced when the first was completed, with close-out procedures used after that.

Data collection procedures in special situations were, generally, a continuation of the 1960 census methods. Special coverage procedures, however, were new in 1970. The bureau had released coverage information after the 1960 census, and the concept of "undercount" was just emerging as a public issue. Special public information materials were prepared for minority and selected ethnic groups. Intensive efforts were made to work with representatives of community organizations, social agencies, and civil rights groups who interacted with hard-to-count populations. Another first was creation of a staff of outreach workers, recruited from and targeted to inner-city communities. Questionnaires and some instructional materials were translated into Spanish and Chinese to assist in enumerating non-English-speaking residents. Local communities formed Complete Count Committees, which assisted in outreach and promotion and in distribution of the "Were You Counted?" forms designed to enumerate people who were otherwise missed.

Post-census evaluation indicated that these methods did improve coverage. The housing-unit missed rates declined from 3.1 percent in 1960 to 2.2 percent in 1970. Most of this improvement was due to better coverage of occupied units. The research also showed that coverage was significantly better among the commercial mailing list units (0.9 percent missed) than among those units listed by census workers in pre-list or conventional census operations (2.6 percent missed).

The 1970 census was conducted through 393 district offices managed through 12 permanent regional offices. The total staffing level was about 185,000.

The 1980 Census

Census officials deemed the 1970 mailout-mailback method successful. It was extended to more than 95 percent of the country's housing in 1980, with conventional methods used only in the northern sections of New England and the Midwest, and in most sections of the Rocky Mountain states. As in 1970, addresses were compiled through two different means. In urban areas with city-style postal delivery, commercial lists comprised the TAR (Tape Address Register), which was then checked by the post office and geo-coded using the GBF-DIME, a file that had been created during the intervening decade as a replacement for the 1970 census's ACG. An additional post office check and a pre-canvass operation provided further updates.

The sampling fraction for 1980 long forms was again reduced, this time to an overall 1 in 6. However, small governmental units (estimated to have a population count of under 2,500) were sampled at 1 in 2 in order to improve the quality of income and poverty data used in revenue-sharing formulas.

A 1980 innovation was implementation of the Local Review program, which provided local officials an opportunity to check the housing counts at the enumeration district level. Problems in geo-coding precluded the pre-census stage of the program from being carried out. In the post-census phase, local communities received a printout showing population, housing unit, and group quarters counts in each enumeration district (rather than census block, as originally planned) within their boundaries.

Each local community had ten working days to submit responses to the local district office, suggesting areas that appeared to be undercovered and providing detailed "hard evidence" in the form of address information to support its claims. The program's logistics were difficult, as the post-census responses often arrived just as the local district office was in close-out mode. Census evaluations noted that the program provided questionable benefits, though many local community evaluations indicated otherwise. About 32 percent of the eligible governments participated, with half of those reporting potential problems requiring investigation

The remaining mailout-mailback area was pre-listed, as it had been in 1970. These addresses were keyed into the computer in 1979. In both TAR and pre-list enumeration districts, address registers and mailing labels were generated by computer. Methods in the conventional census areas followed the pattern established in earlier censuses.

Follow-up procedures were generally the same as in 1970. The task was more difficult, however, because in a much larger proportion of households no one was at home during the day. This necessitated a greater number of calls in the evening and on weekends. The local review materials were created at the end of the first follow-up stage.

Special places and other types of non-housing- unit living situations were enumerated as in previous census operations. Some special attention was paid to achieve earlier enumeration in places where there was significant population turnover in April, such as in college dormitories. Military personnel were generally counted in the community where they were stationed or based, except for two Navy fleets, whose personnel were included in the overseas population.

Coverage improvement activities were again expanded over the previous census. A total of fourteen different programs were executed, eleven of which took place during the data collection time frame. (A description of each activity, along with an evaluation of its effectiveness, may be found in Census Report PHC80-E3, listed in the bibliography.) Programs such as the Spanish language questionnaire, the establishment of assistance centers, the "Were You Counted?" campaign,

and the vacant/delete check, in which enumerators revisited each housing unit categorized as vacant or nonresidential to double-check its status, were judged successful and carried forward to the 1990 census.

Regional census centers were established in each of the twelve regional office cities for the express purpose of carrying out decennial census activities. These centers coordinated and supervised a total of 409 district offices. An estimated 460,000 people were employed during some stage of the field operation, with 270,000 working during the peak follow-up weeks in April and May.

1990 Census

The overall 1990 field enumeration design was much the same as that used in 1980. Of the five field enumerations discussed in this article, the 1990 enumeration saw the least amount of change in method from the preceding census.

The master address list used for the mailout-mailback operation (now called the Address Control File, or ACF) included about 86.2 million housing units comprising over 85 percent of the national total. Of these, 55 million came from the TAR obtained from commercial mailing lists. This address list was improved through the Advance Post Office Check (APOC) and a pre-canvass operation.

The remaining mailout-mailback addresses were obtained through a pre-list operation. Originally planned to include 32 million housing units, it was reduced to 27.8 million. The remaining addresses were designated for the update/leave operation, in which census enumerators checked the address list and delivered the questionnaires at census time. Respondents were asked to mail these questionnaires back. This list, too, was improved through APOC activities. The number of addresses added through APOC and field work totaled nearly 1.2 million.

Finally, about 5.7 million housing units were covered through the list/enumerate procedure, similar to the pre-1970 conventional census method. Postal carriers delivered unaddressed short form questionnaires called ACRs (advance census reports). Enumerators collected them and asked additional questions in those households selected randomly to receive the long form.

As in 1980, the long-form questions were asked, overall, in 1 in 6 households. Oversampling (at a rate of 1 in 2) was used in very small communities, while very large census tracts were reduced to 1 in 8. Follow-up procedures were similar to previous censuses, as were methods for enumerating special places.

The Local Review program was again implemented to provide an opportunity for local input into the quality of the address list. The geographic coding systems worked properly, so that participating local governments were able to evaluate the housing counts at the block level both before and after the census. About 30 percent of local governments participated. Upon evaluation the program was deemed a success both in terms of improvement to the address lists (units added and deleted and geographic corrections) and in terms of the opportunity it offered to local government officials.

The 1990 census was conducted in 13 regional census centers supervising 463 district offices. More than 550,000 temporary workers were hired to conduct the field enumeration work.

Census 2000

Over the three-census period since the inception of the mailout-mailback method in 1970, there was a continuing decline in the final mail return rate, which represents the proportion of occupied households that return the form. The first use of mailout-mailback techniques in the 1970 census produced a final mail return rate from occupied households of 87 percent; that is, about seven out of eight households returned the form by mail and did not require a follow-up visit in the field. The comparable figures were 81 percent in 1980 and 74 percent in 1990.

The initial mail response rate for all units on the address list, including those found to be vacant or non-residential and those that could not receive their mail at a city-style address, was even lower. For example, the rate calculated on this basis was 78 percent in 1970, 75 percent in 1980, and 65 percent in 1990. Reversing this decline, or at least holding level at the 1990 rate, was a major concern in Census 2000 planning. As a result, there was considerable sentiment to re-engineer census methods. Significant Census Bureau, federal agency, and advisory resources were devoted to these efforts in the early 1990s. The result was significant change in the census design. Much of this change was facilitated by an extraordinary growth in technology that permitted entirely new ways of conducting census activities.

The first major change involved the replacement of the FOSDIC system, first implemented in 1960. The system's technical requirements forced creation of census forms that were not considered user-friendly. After much experimentation, the Census Bureau developed a form that could be read into a computer via optical scanning. This made it possible to read letter characters and numbers rather than just filled-in circles, greatly improving form design options.

A second change involved the passage in 1994 of the Census Address List Improvement Act. This legislation drastically altered the method by which the Master Address File (MAF) was created. The law permitted address-sharing in two different ways. First, it authorized the U.S. Postal Service to share its Delivery Sequence File (DSF) with the Census Bureau. Improvements in technology had also meant a more efficient delivery system at the Postal Service, which now maintained its own master file complete with nine-digit ZIP coding to facilitate efficient mail delivery. The law made it possible for the Census Bureau to create its initial MAF from a combination of the 1990 ACR and the DSF.

The 1994 law also permitted the Census Bureau, with confidentiality restrictions, to share its MAF with local governments. This program, designated LUCA (Local Update of Census Addresses), was much more extensive than the Local Review program it replaced. Local governments, if they chose to participate, could actually check each MAF entry by address against local files. The program was slow in getting out to the governments, however, and was plagued by missed deadlines and extremely tight schedules.

Another technological change affecting Census 2000 was connected to the emergence of the 911 emergency services system during the period 1985–95. These systems, heavy users of GIS (Geographic Information Systems) techniques, require city-style addresses. Consequently, thousands of communities had converted from rural route/box number postal delivery to house numbers and street names. Initial MAF planning assumed that these systems would become nearly universal in time for Census 2000 use. However, many rural households opted to keep their post office boxes for mail delivery even though they were identified with house numbers for 911 purposes.

These problems notwithstanding, the 2000 MAF was the most complete address list ever to be used in a mailout-mailback census. The Census Bureau plans to maintain the file on a permanent basis and to use it as a sampling frame for the American Community Survey and perhaps other current survey programs.

Field enumeration procedures for 2000 were similar to those used in 1990. The number of list/enumerate housing units was reduced to fewer than 1 million.

Update/leave techniques were employed in areas where city-style addressing was not consistently in place; concerns over the completeness of this list led the bureau to conduct a complete review and update at the time of census form delivery in March 2000. The older pre-list activity, where address lists were built by census enumerators for use in mailout-mailback, was generally eliminated.

The response rate decline led to another major change: a paid advertising campaign. In 1990 and earlier, the Census Bureau had relied on public service announcements that were not well targeted. Beginning in late 1999, a $167 million professionally created campaign got under way. Its initial goal was to acquaint Americans with the upcoming census and with the reasons why they should participate. A later phase, beginning in April, was designed to promote cooperation in the non-response follow-up stage. Another aspect of the campaign focused on privacy and confidentiality issues. In addition to the paid campaign, the bureau also worked hard to promote Census 2000 coverage in the media.

Several years will elapse before Census 2000's innovative changes can be evaluated and reported. As of this writing, the Census Bureau has achieved an initial response rate equal to that in the 1990 census, and an army of enumerators—both larger and significantly better paid than in years past—is now in the field following up on non-respondents.

See also *Address list development; Coverage improvement procedures; Enumeration: special populations; Housing.*

■ Patricia C. Becker

Bibliography

National Research Council, Committee on National Statistics, Panel on Census Requirements in the Year 2000 and Beyond. *Modernizing the U.S. Census.* Ed. Barry Edmonston and Charles Schultze. Washington, D.C.: National Academy Press, 1995.

U.S. Bureau of the Census. *Census 2000 Operational Plan Using Traditional Census-Taking Methods.* Washington, D.C.: Government Printing Office, January 1999.

———. *Procedural Report on the 1960 Censuses of Population and Housing,* Working Paper No. 16. Washington, D.C.: Government Printing Office, 1963.

U.S. Bureau of the Census, Census of Population and Housing: 1970. *Data Collection Forms and Procedures* (PHC(R)-2). Washington, D.C.: Government Printing Office, 1971.

———. *The Coverage of Housing in the 1970 Census* (PHC(E)-5. Washington, D.C.: Government Printing Office, 1973.

U.S. Bureau of the Census, Census of Population and Housing (1980). *History, Part A* (PHC80-R-2A). Washington, D.C.: Government Printing Office, September 1986.

———. *Programs to Improve Coverage in the 1980 Census* (PHC80-E3). Washington, D.C.: Government Printing Office, January 1987.

U.S. Bureau of the Census, 1990 Census of Population and Housing. *History* (2990 CPH-R 2A-D) Parts A-D. Washington, D.C.: Government Printing Office, October 1993 (Part A), October 1995 (Parts B and C), March 1996 (Part D).

———. *Programs to Improve Coverage in the 1990 Census* (1990 CPH-E-3). Washington, D.C.: Government Printing Office, November 1993.

Author's note: A similar series of reports will be produced for Census 2000.

Enumeration: special populations

The decennial census enumerates people who live in housing units, such as single-family homes, town homes, apartments, condominiums, and mobile homes, each of which is a separate living quarters. In addition, and unlike household surveys, the census enumerates people living in other kinds of situations. In the 2000 census, special populations included people living in nonmilitary group quarters (for example, nursing homes, college dormitories), people living on military installations and ships, people in transient locations at the time of the census (for example, staying at recreational vehicle campgrounds, traveling with fairs and carnivals), people living in migrant and seasonal farmworker camps, and the homeless.

In 1990 the "group quarters population" of those living in special places, including military installations, amounted to 6.7 million people, or 2.7 percent of the population enumerated in that census. Of the 1990 group quarters population, 49 percent lived in such institutions as nursing homes, long-term-care facilities for people with physical or mental disabilities, and prisons; 29 percent were college students in dormitories; and the rest lived in military barracks, rooming houses, and other types of group quarters. In contrast to household surveys, college students in dorms are counted at the dormitory location and not at the location of their parents' residence.

Special Places

Group quarters, or special places, include college dormitories, nursing homes, long-term-stay hospitals, convents, monasteries, orphanages, boarding and rooming houses, jails, prisons, institutions for people with mental and physical disabilities, and others. To enumerate people in such places, the Census Bureau first builds a list of special places. For the 2000 census the bureau updated its inventory of special places through a Special Place Facility Questionnaire Operation conducted in 1999. In this operation, computer-assisted telephone interviewing, supplemented by some personal visits, was used to update existing information from the special place inventory, identify additional group quarters, identify contact persons at each location, assign a group quarters type code, determine availability of administrative records, and identify any housing units at the special place. A special place may include either or both institutionalized group quarters and noninstitutionalized group quarters (for example, a nurses' dormitory at a residential care facility). It may also include one or more housing units or separate living quarters (for example, a separate unit for a resident manager).

Starting in January 2000 local census office staff made advance visits to meet with special place facility staff to discuss the upcoming enumeration. In April 2000 census staff visited each place, listed the residents, and distributed questionnaire packets. The enumerators returned a few days later to pick up the forms and provide assistance in completing the questionnaires when needed. In some instances in which residents could not enumerate themselves (for example, some nursing home residents), administrative records were used to complete the enumeration. Counts for each place were verified by comparing them with the Special Place Facility Questionnaire results and with facility administrative records. Enumerators rechecked the counts by telephone for places that failed the verification and places with more than 100 residents. At a small number of facilities, such as jails and prisons, the facility staff conducted the enumeration. They were sworn in as special census employees for this purpose to protect the confidentiality of the census information. No housing information was collected for people living in special places, unless they were living in a separate housing unit. Also, people staying only temporarily at some types of group quarters (for example, a group home or halfway house) were given the opportunity to indicate a usual residence at another location.

A similar special places operation has been carried out in previous recent censuses. In the nineteenth and early twentieth centuries, censuses included supplemental schedules, or forms, that ascertained detailed information about residents of certain kinds of institutions, such as prisons, institutions for people with disabilities, and almshouses.

Military and Maritime Enumeration

For the 2000 census, the Census Bureau worked with the U.S. Department of Defense and U.S. Coast Guard to identify both housing units and group quarters on military installations and ships assigned to a home port in the United States. Questionnaires were mailed to housing units on military installations; other methods, such as visiting installations and ships to enumerate people at their work stations, were used to count the military population in group quarters. The bureau also worked with the U.S. Maritime Administration to identify maritime vessels in operation at the time of the census and arrange to mail questionnaires to those ships.

In addition, the Department of Defense and other federal agencies were asked to provide counts of their employees assigned overseas and their dependents by home state from personnel records of the agencies. Such counts, which included people on board military ships assigned to a foreign home port, were included in the 2000 census population totals for states for reapportionment of the U.S. House of Representatives.

Transient Night Operation and Migrant Workers

Transient night (T-Night) for the 2000 census took place on Friday, March 31, 2000. T-Night enumerators interviewed people occupying commercial and public campgrounds, recreational vehicle campgrounds or parks, fairs and carnivals, campgrounds at racetracks, and marinas. Each person enumerated during T-Night was given the opportunity to report a usual residence at some other location. To enumerate migrant workers in the 2000 census, the Census Bureau worked with local officials and community-based organizations to identify camps and other locations at which migrant and seasonal farmworkers were expected to be found at census time.

Transient night has been included in previous recent censuses. Prior to the 1990 census, hotels and motels were among the locations visited, but such places were dropped in 1990 and 2000 because tests showed that visiting them added very few uncounted persons. Censuses prior to 1990 also included missions and flophouses in T-night operations.

The Homeless

The 2000 census used a procedure called Service-Based Enumeration (SBE) to count people with no usual residence who might otherwise be missed. SBE was conducted at selected service locations, such as shelters and soup kitchens, and at specifically identified nonsheltered outdoor locations. There was no attempt through SBE to provide a total count of the homeless or of users of the service facilities visited.

During 1999 the Census Bureau worked with local governments and community-based organizations to identify lists of service locations open at census time. Census staff then made an advance visit to SBE locations two to six weeks prior to enumeration to update information about the location and explain the process. Using simplified enumeration procedures and questionnaires, bureau staff conducted a one-time enumeration at shelters on the evening of March 27, 2000. They did the same during the day, March 28, at soup kitchens and at stops made by mobile food vans with regular schedules. Enumerators also visited outdoor locations where people live and eat, as identified by local officials and community groups, in the early morning of March 29. In addition, people with no usual residence could pick up "Be Counted" questionnaires at non-SBE locations, such as travelers' aid centers, health care clinics, and libraries.

The 1990 census was the first to include special procedures to try to count homeless people: the operation used in 1990 was called Shelter and Street Night (S-Night). Local governments were asked to identify locations at which homeless people stayed, such as shelters, bus and train stations, abandoned buildings, hotels and motels used to house homeless people, other very inexpensive hotels and motels, and street locations at which homeless people congregated. "Phase 1" enumeration was conducted in the evening hours of March 20 at shelters and low-cost hotels and motels. "Phase 2" enumeration was conducted between 2 A.M. and 4 A.M., March 21, at pre-identified street locations, abandoned buildings, and commerce places. In selected cities, enumerators stayed outside selected abandoned buildings until 8 A.M. to enumerate people as they left the buildings.

The S-Night operation attracted considerable media attention and was controversial because the results were viewed as an undercount of the homeless. In some large cities, media hindered the operation by converging on large shelters and commerce places, such as New York's Grand Central Station. Some coverage problems were identified, which were apparently due largely to incomplete location lists provided by local governments. Some additional locations were identified and enumerated on March 21 and 22, 1990. In all, 34,000 sites were canvassed. The total count of people enumerated at shelters was 178,000; those enumerated at street locations totaled 49,000.

See also *Americans overseas; Content; Enumeration: field procedures.*

■ Constance F. Citro

Bibliography

U.S. Bureau of the Census. *Census 2000 Operational Plan Using Traditional Census-Taking Methods.* Washington, D.C.: U.S. Department of Commerce, 1999.

———. "Field Enumeration." Chap. 6 in *1990 Census of Population and Housing: History.* Washington, D.C.: U.S. Department of Commerce, 1993.

———. *Population and Housing Inquiries in U.S. Decennial Censuses, 1790–1970.* Working paper no. 39. Washington, D.C.: U.S. Department of Commerce, 1973.

Errors in the census

Just as no book is free of typographical errors and no highway free of cracks, every census has errors. Although the large majority of American households return census forms that are complete and correct, errors can and do occur. For example, some people don't receive census forms because their addresses were inadvertently left off the Census Bureau's mailing list. Elsewhere, the person filling out the form omits some people while counting others. Still others get counted twice. The problems of "hard to find" addresses, ambiguous rules for defining "usual residence," and a mobile population combine to make a perfect census count an impossible ideal.

In general, two types of error occur within the census. *Omissions* refer to people who should have been counted but were not. *Erroneous enumerations* refer to those who were counted but should not have been included.

The *net undercount* is the difference between omissions and erroneous enumerations. In recent censuses, the net undercount has been positive, because omissions outnumber erroneous enumerations. Should the numbers of omissions and erroneous enumerations be exactly the same, the net undercount for the nation would equal zero, but there would still be serious problems in many local areas. Omissions and erroneous enumerations tend to occur in different types of places.

Omissions are especially likely to occur among low-income racial minorities living in urban areas. Rates of erroneous enumeration, although high among low-income racial minorities, are also high in vacation home areas and among other families maintaining a second residence, perhaps for a commuter marriage.

In 1990 the net undercount was about 5 million, based on demographic analysis, or 1.8 percent. Erroneous enumerations are conservatively estimated at 6 million and omissions at 11 million—a total of 17 million errors. For whites the net undercount was about 1 percent; for blacks and Hispanics, about 5 percent each.

How Omissions Occur

There are two general types of omission—whole household and partial household. A whole household omission occurs when the entire housing unit is left off the mailing list used by the Census Bureau. Some housing units are missed because no one finds the building. Others are missed because they are located in structures that appear to contain only one residence but actually contain several. For example, a three-story house, originally built for one family, is converted into apartments. From the outside, the census-taker sees only one door and one mailbox, and he or she does not search for nor find the extra housing units to update the mailing list.

Housing units for the very poor can be hard to find. Old apartment buildings, often located in high-crime areas, may not have separate mailboxes or identifiable numbers for the individual apartments. Many very poor people, frequently undocumented aliens, live in places like garages and tents located in the backyards of friends or relatives. Their addresses are not listed and they are not counted. Of course, homeless people, attached to no specific housing unit, cannot be included in the Census Bureau's mailing list. There are other procedures, admittedly imperfect, to try to count the homeless.

Partial household omissions occur when the census form arrives at a household but not everyone is counted. Some people are omitted because they are temporary residents. For example, a recently arrived immigrant from Mexico stays with a relative while looking for a job. Others are omitted because they spend time at more than one address. For example, a child with only one parent may live with a grandparent during the week while the parent works. The grandparent, thinking that the "usual" residence is at the parent's house, does not count the child. The parent, thinking that "usual" means "most of the time," does not count the child either.

The 1990 census form asked people to count themselves at their "usual residence," that is, the place where they live and eat most of the time. For nuclear family members—parents and their children—this was easy. For more distant relatives, and unrelated boarders, the rules were harder to apply. In 1990 the omission rates for such persons were about three times the rate for nuclear family members.

How Erroneous Enumerations Occur

Ambiguities about the term *usual residence* cause some people to be omitted, but others are counted twice, or at the wrong location. Just as rates of omission are higher for persons not in the nuclear family of the household head, so too are rates of erroneous enumeration.

When the Census Bureau prepares its mailing list, it has no way of knowing which addresses are second homes for a particular family. It mails the census forms to every address on its mailing list and waits for the returns. Census forms are frequently returned from "second homes," in spite of the "usual residence" instruction. Thus, "second count" erroneous enumerations take place in a vacation home or in an apartment used by one spouse in a commuter marriage. They also occur for retirees who spend the winter in Florida and the summer in the North. Similarly, the family moving around the April 1 census day may dutifully return its form at the original address. When the family arrives at the new address and finds a new census form, it might send that one in, too.

Erroneous enumerations also take place in rural areas where houses do not have street addresses. Census takers must rely on descriptions of houses, and they sometimes confuse houses that have and have not already been counted, causing double counting.

Erroneous Enumerations and the Census-Taking Process

The Census Bureau makes every effort to reduce the undercount by making repeated attempts to count people. Unfortunately, these attempts often create erroneous enumerations rather than eliminating omissions. The problem becomes more extreme as time passes beyond the April 1 census day.

In 1990 Non-Response Follow-up (NRFU) began on April 26 and continued through the spring and summer. The extended time period permitted repeat visits to all addresses not returning census forms by mail. In some cases, though, the person the census taker found and counted may have moved in after April 1. In others, the census taker found no one at the address and got the information from a neighbor or building supervisor. In many cases, this informant was not in fact knowledgeable. In this manner, erroneous counts were added to the census.

In 1990, after the conclusion of NRFU, millions of people still had not yet been counted. To reach these people, the Census Bureau mounted special "coverage improvement" programs such as the National Vacancy Check. This program involved a return to every address originally listed as vacant to count persons found there. Unfortunately, many people found at these addresses moved in after April 1 and their counts were erroneous. Other coverage improvement programs encountered similar problems.

In 1990 the Census Bureau estimated erroneous enumeration rates of 3 percent for mail-out, mail-back forms, 11 percent for Non-Response Follow-up, and 19 percent for Coverage Improvement. The increasing percentage of errors was largely due to the greater difficulty of later counting: 3 percent errors in April, 7 percent in May, doubling in June to 14 percent and growing to 19 percent in July; August and later saw errors of 28 percent.

Census Errors and the Mail-back Rate

Errors are more likely to occur when census taking is difficult. Omissions and erroneous enumerations partially offset each other in some areas, typically low-income minority neighborhoods in cities. But errors do not balance in all locations, and erroneous enumerations are a special problem in vacation home areas and rural areas without street addresses.

The mail-back rate is a good indicator of census-taking difficulty. Areas with low mail-back rates require more of the energy and financial resources of the Census Bureau, and the census process takes longer there. By comparing areas with high and low mailback rates in the 1990 census, we get a good picture of how the incidences of omissions and erroneous enumerations combine to produce a differential net undercount across areas.

As shown in Figure 1, the mail-back rates for most geographic areas varied from 55 to 85 percent. Rates of omission were strongly, and negatively, correlated with the mail-back rate. Where the mail-back rate was lower, fewer people were eventually found. The differences in omission rate were substantial, ranging from 3 to 18 percent.

Rates of erroneous enumeration were also negatively correlated with the mail-back rate, again reflect-

Figure 1. Where the Mailback Rate Is Lower, Census Problems Are Greater

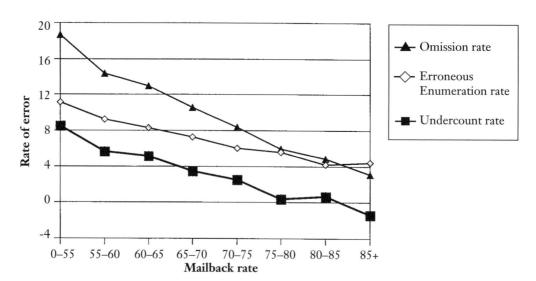

ing the greater difficulty of census taking when the mail-back rate was low. The differences in the erroneous enumeration rate were not as extreme as for the omission rate. They ranged from 4 to 10 percent.

Combining omissions and erroneous enumerations, the net undercount was largest in low mail-back areas and declined as the mail-back rate increased. Indeed, those areas with the highest mail-back rates showed a slight overcount.

In sum, both omissions and erroneous enumerations result from census-taking problems. They combine to create a greater net undercount in those areas where census taking is hardest. The problem is more complex than saying that the Census Bureau "misses people." Indeed, a small national net undercount is a misleading statistic. It ignores large numbers of omissions and erroneous enumerations, as well as their geographic variations. The people living in difficult census-taking areas are disproportionately low-income minorities, accounting for the greater net undercount of blacks and Hispanics compared with whites.

See also *Accuracy and Coverage Evaluation; Census testing; Coverage evaluation; Coverage improvement procedures.*

■ Eugene P. Ericksen

Bibliography

Hogan, Howard. "The 1990 Post-Enumeration Survey: Operations and Results." *Journal of the American Statistical Association* 88 (September 1993): 1047–1060.

Robinson, J. Gregory, Bashir Ahmed, Prithwas DasGupta, and Karen A. Woodrow. "Estimation of Population Coverage in the 1990 United States Census Based on Demographic Analysis." *Journal of the American Statistical Association* 88 (September 1993): 1061–1073.

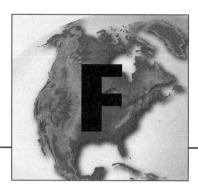

Family and household composition of the population

Basic demographic information collected about household members, including the number of members, their relationship to each other, and each person's sex, age, and marital status, is used to describe the composition of families and households. Their "composition" describes the *structure* of families and households—the set of statuses and associated roles that are important for the functioning of society. American families and households have diverse and complex structures. For example, households can contain married couples, unmarried couples, single mothers, children, grandparents, other relatives (such as brothers, sisters, or in-laws), roommates, or simply one person living alone. Family and household composition is the result of demographic *processes* or family-related events such as marriage, divorce, and childbearing. Changes in the timing, number, or sequences of these events transform family and household composition. Examining the composition of households allows us to monitor how families and households are changing.

The household-based census is primarily designed to obtain social, demographic, and economic information about all the people living at a residence. Consequently, it can be used only to examine the family relationships of people living together at a given point in time. For example, census data can tell us how many families contain grandchildren living with their grandparents, but not the total number of grandparents in the United States, because most grandparents do not live with their grandchildren.

Some Useful Definitions

U.S. households and families are made up of a wide variety of living arrangements: to discuss them, some definitions of key concepts are needed. A *household* can contain one or more people—everyone living in a housing unit makes up a household. In most cases, the person who owns or rents the residence is known as the *householder*. For the purposes of examining family and household composition using census data, the U.S. Census Bureau has defined two types of households: family and nonfamily. A *family household* has at least two members related by blood, marriage, or adoption, one of whom is the householder. *Families* consist of all related people in a family household. A *nonfamily household* can either be a person living alone or a householder living only with nonrelatives.

Families can be maintained by married couples or by a man or woman with no spouse at home and may or may not contain children. In contrast, nonfamily households can only be maintained by a man or woman with no relatives at home. In censuses conducted through 1990, *children* included sons and daughters by birth, stepchildren, and adopted children of the householder regardless of the child's age or marital status. *Own children* differ from *children* in that they are never married and are under the age of eighteen. Note that according to these definitions, nonfamily households cannot contain children or own children of the householder; all individuals under eighteen years in nonfamily households are simply unrelated individuals.

When we want to know about the different types of families and households and how they have changed, we look at the composition of households and families. When we want to know about the relationships and characteristics of people in households, we examine the living arrangements of the individual. For example, if we wanted to know about children and families, we could ask the question, "How many families have children?" But we could also ask, "How many children live in families?" In the first case, we are interested in family composition; in the second, we are interested in the living arrangements.

Recent Trends in Family and Household Composition

Changes in the number and types of households depend on population growth, shifts in the age composition of the population, and decisions individuals make about their living arrangements. Demographic trends in marriage, cohabitation, divorce, fertility, and mortality also influence family and household composition. Changes in the economy and improvements in the health of the elderly over time can also have an effect.

According to the 1990 census, there were 91.9 million households in the United States, up from 63.6 million in 1970. Traditionally, families have accounted for a large majority of all households—as recently as 1940 nine out of ten households were family households. This proportion decreased steadily to 80 percent in 1970, and by 1990 family households made up only 70 percent of all households. Part of the increase in nonfamily households was due to the growth in one-person households—people living alone. The proportion of households containing one person increased from 18 percent in 1970 to 25 percent in 1990.

Why did nonfamily households increase over this period? The postponement of marriage that took place after 1960 led to a substantial increase in the percentage of young, never-married adults. In 1970 census data indicated that about 7 percent of women and 11 percent of men age thirty to thirty-four had never married. By 1990 these figures increased to 18 percent and 26 percent, respectively. The delay of marriage means that young adults in 1990 were less likely than in the past to

be living with their spouses and more likely to be living alone, in a parent's home, or with roommates. For example, in 1970, 15 percent of households maintained by people under twenty-five contained one person, compared with 24 percent in 1990. In contrast 66 percent of households maintained by those under twenty-five were married-couple family households in 1970, compared with only 31 percent in 1990.

The delay in marriage coincided with an increase in cohabitation and divorce. The number of unmarried-couple households grew more than fivefold, from 523,000, or less than 1 percent of all households in 1970, to 2.9 million, or over 4 percent of households in 1990. Meanwhile, the proportion of divorced people more than doubled from 3 percent to 7 percent for men and from 4 percent to 10 percent for women from 1970 to 1990. These trends also decreased the proportion of married-couple families and increased the proportion of nonfamily households.

Significant improvements in the health and economic well-being of the elderly over the period increased the life expectancy and the quality of life of both men and women. This meant that the elderly were increasingly able to maintain their own homes. Not only has this augmented the number of households, but the fact that women continued to outlive men by a significant number of years led to a greater number and proportion of one-person nonfamily households. The proportion of women sixty-five years and over who lived alone grew from 32 percent in 1970 to 37 percent in 1990.

Households and families have become smaller over time. Between 1970 and 1990 the share of households with five or more people decreased from 20 percent to 11 percent. During the same period, the share of households with only one or two people increased from 47 percent to 57 percent. Another measure of household size is the average number of members in the household. Between 1970 and 1990 the average number of people per household declined from 3.2 to 2.6. The average family size also fell over this period, from 3.6 people in 1970 to 3.2 people in 1990.

Changes in fertility, marriage, divorce, and mortality all contributed to the declines in the size of American families and households. Between 1970 and 1990, births to married women declined sharply, whereas births to unmarried women increased. These two trends decreased the proportion of two-parent families and increased the proportion of one-parent families, which also tend to have fewer children. The cumulative effect of these trends was to shrink family and household size. Increases in divorce also reduced the size of households and families; divorce generally separates one household into two smaller households. As already discussed, the delay in marriage and improvements in the mortality and health of the elderly increased one-person households, thereby decreasing the average family and household size.

Other aspects of the composition of families changed as well. In 1990 there were 64.5 million families in the United States, up from 51.0 million in 1970. The number of families maintained by people with no spouse at home increased rapidly from 1970 to 1990. The number of families maintained by a female householder with no spouse at home grew by 94 percent, from 5.5 million in 1970 to 10.6 million in 1990. The percentage increase for families maintained by a male householder with no spouse at home was even larger at 124 percent, from 1.4 million in 1970 to 3.1 million in 1990. In contrast, married-couple families grew from 44.1 million to 50.7 million over the same period—only a 15 percent increase. These trends shifted the composition of family households more toward female- and male-householder families. In 1970 married couples maintained 86 percent of family households, but by 1990 this proportion had declined to 79 percent.

Families were less likely to contain own children under eighteen in 1990 than in 1970—48 percent compared with 55 percent. These changes reflect several demographic trends, including the delay of childbearing, the decline in the number of children people have, the delay of marriage, and the aging of the population. Because of the trend toward delayed marriage and childbearing, younger families were more likely to be childless in 1990 than in 1970. For example, in 1970, 90 percent of young women age twenty-five to thirty-four had been married at least once; of them, only 12 percent were childless. In 1990 only 76 percent of women age twenty-five to thirty-four had ever been married; of them, 23 percent were childless. Thus, fewer women in these prime childbearing ages had ever been married in 1990 (reflecting a delay of marriage), and nearly twice as many of them were childless (reflecting primarily a delay in childbearing, but also a delay in marriage).

One-parent families were more common by 1990. In 1970, 88 percent of families with own children had both parents in the household; 11 percent had mothers only; and 1 percent had fathers only. By 1990 the proportions of one-parent families had risen significantly—to 20 percent for mother-only families and 4 percent for father-only families, a sizable change given the short time period during which it occurred. Several demographic trends have affected the shift from two-parent to one-parent families. A larger proportion of births occurred to unmarried women in 1990 compared with 1970, which increased the proportion of never-married parents. The delays in marriage also augmented the risk of a nonmarital birth, because adults were single for more years. In addition, the growth in divorce among couples with children increased the proportion of unmarried parents.

Future Trends in Family and Household Composition

Using the 1990 census as a base, projections can be made about the family and household composition of the population in the future. The proportion of nonfamily households is projected to continue increasing from 30 percent in 1990, to 31 percent in 2000, and to 32 percent by 2010. The growth over this twenty-year period (2 percentage points) is expected to be substantially less than the growth that occurred from 1970 to 1990 (10 percentage points). Meanwhile, the proportion of one-person households is expected to remain at 25 percent in 2000 but increase to 27 percent in 2010. Two-parent families will continue to drop from 76 percent in 1990 to 75 percent in 2000, and are expected to reach 72 percent in 2010. This projected decline of 4 percentage points from 1990 to 2010 is also much less than the 12 percentage point reduction that occurred from 1970 to 1990. Meanwhile, mother-only families are expected to stabilize at 20 percent in 2000 before increasing again to 22 percent in 2010. Father-only families are projected to increase from 4 percent in 1990, to 5 percent in 2000, and, by 2010, to 6 percent of all families with own children. These projections indicate a substantial deceleration of the dramatic changes in family and household composition that characterized the 1970s and 1980s. Thus, the first decade of the new millennium is expected to be one of relative stability in the composition of American families and households.

Limitations of Census Data for Studying Family Composition

Census data provide a snapshot of the population at one point in time. They are excellent for describing changes in the *structure* of households and families because they are comparable across time and are large enough to allow analysis of extremely small groups in very small areas. However, census data are not adequate for describing the *processes* or events that change these structures. Standard measures of process include marriage, remarriage, divorce, fertility, and mortality rates; these measures are not currently available in the census. Administrative data collected by the National Center for Health Statistics are used to construct these vital statistics rates. Recently, family demographers have begun exploring the linkages between social and economic factors and these demographic processes. For these types of analysis, both census and administrative data are limited. The National Survey of Families and Households, the National Survey of Family Growth, the Survey of Income and Program Participation, and the National Longitudinal Surveys are more appropriate data sources for investigating these complex issues.

See also *Federal household surveys*.

■ Lynne M. Casper and Martin O'Connell

Bibliography

McLanahan, Sara, and Lynne Casper. "Growing Diversity and Inequality in the American Family." In *State of the Union: America in the 1990s*, volume 2, edited by Reynolds Farley. New York: Russell Sage Foundation, 1995.

Sweet, James A., and Larry L. Bumpass. *American Families and Households*. New York: Russell Sage Foundation, 1987.

Teachman, Jay D., Karen A. Polonko, and John Scanzoni. "Household and Family Demography: An Overview." In *Readings in Population Research Methodology*, volume 4, edited by Donald Bogue, Eduardo Arriaga, and Douglas Anderton. New York: United Nations Population Fund, 1993.

Federal administrative records

Records collected and maintained by federal agencies for the purpose of administering programs that affect broad segments of the population include some of the same kinds of information captured in the decennial census. The Census Bureau considered several potential uses of administrative records in conducting the 2000 census, and although none was adopted, research to evaluate prospective applications to future censuses will continue. This article discusses the strengths and limitations of federal administrative records as an alternative or supplement to the information collected on a census form, reviews the Census Bureau's unsuccessful effort to use administrative records in the 2000 census, and lays out several issues that must be addressed if administrative records are to play a role in the conduct of future censuses.

Major Federal Administrative Records

Each year the Internal Revenue Service (IRS) receives more than 100 million tax returns and more than a billion "information documents." Filers of tax returns and their dependents represent an estimated 85 percent or more of the entire U.S. population. Information documents—which include the statements that employers, financial institutions, and government agencies file to document wages, investment income, retirement income, and other benefits—cover an additional 10 percent or more of the population. With respect to items requested on the census short form, both tax returns and information documents provide a current address, and tax returns also provide each dependent's relationship to the tax filer. Both sets of documents also include Social Security numbers for nearly all persons represented, making it easy to link the tax information to demographic data maintained by the Social Security Administration (SSA). With these additional data, tax returns would approximate the content of the census short form. With respect to long form data, both the tax returns and information documents provide annual data on personal income by source and the marital status of the filer.

The SSA Numident file contains data collected from applications for Social Security numbers and replacement cards as well as applications to change the name associated with a previously issued number. Data recorded on the Numident include the Social Security number, date of birth, sex, race, Hispanic origin, country of birth, and all names associated with that number. The number of persons covered by the Numident file received a boost following the Tax Reform Act of 1986, which mandated the reporting of Social Security numbers for all dependents age five and older—a requirement that was expanded within a few years to age one and older. Most children now receive Social Security numbers shortly after birth, through an application process that is coordinated with the registering of births.

The SSA Master Beneficiary Record contains benefit payment data for the 44 million persons who receive old age, survivors, or disability insurance benefits. These data include current mailing addresses and benefit amounts. Because these data are used to issue payments, they are updated continuously as changes are reported.

The SSA Master Earnings File contains histories of annual earnings from jobs covered by Social Security—including self-employment. This file, which is updated from employers' annual reports of covered earnings, includes data for about 180 million persons. The employer submissions provide the SSA with a source of current address for persons who are not yet beneficiaries.

The Health Insurance Master Record, maintained by the Health Care Financing Administration (HCFA), is the primary administrative database for the Medicare program, which provides health insurance coverage to all persons age sixty-five and older and to younger persons with qualifying disabilities. The file covers the 33 million aged beneficiaries and 5 million younger but disabled beneficiaries and contains name, mailing address, sex, a limited race classification, age, and disability (for those under sixty-five).

Some federal agencies compile administrative records that are collected by the states and transmitted to Washington, D.C., to fulfill a legal obligation or as part of a federal-state cooperative effort. For example, the Medicaid program provides health insurance coverage to more than 40 million Americans through individual state programs, which receive federal reimbursements. As part of their reporting requirements, all states must now submit quarterly files of individual case record data directly to the HCFA. Another example is the vital statistics system. Following federal guidelines, each state compiles records of births and deaths and submits these data to the National Center for Health Statistics, which constructs and publishes national statistics on the number and characteristics of births and deaths. The Food Stamp Program, administered nationally by the Food and Nutrition Service of the U.S. Department of Agriculture, serves more than 20 million low-income households throughout the nation. Food stamp records are often cited as a potentially important resource for census use because they provide extensive data on households that often fall below the tax-filing threshold, but the states and localities that operate the program do not ordinarily share their administrative records with the federal government.

Limitations of Administrative Records

Despite the broad population coverage and census-relevant content of federal administrative records, these data have important limitations—particularly in the areas of data quality and timeliness. The addresses reported on tax returns are not always residential or consistent with the census concept of usual place of residence. An estimated 10 to 20 percent represent post office boxes, business addresses, or tax preparers. An unknown fraction of the remainder represent locations other than the census residence. In addition, children who are away at college may be reported on tax returns as living at home (that is, claimed as dependents), whereas the census would count them at their college addresses.

The tax-filing unit does not correspond, exactly, to a census household. Although most households contain a single filing unit, households with multiple filing units or with both filers and nonfilers are not uncommon. By sorting tax returns by address, filing units can be aggregated into households—subject to the completeness of the address information. Apartment unit numbers missing from some of the returns filed from multi-unit residences, for example, would result in separate households being combined erroneously. Furthermore, when filing units are aggregated in this manner, it may not be evident which unit contains the householder or how the members of one unit are related to a householder in another unit. Filing units may also include persons who reside in different households—as in the college student example cited above or when married couples live apart but file joint returns. In addition, filing unit composition is based on the preceding calendar year (the tax year) rather than the filing date. Marital status is defined as of December 31, whereas dependents can satisfy the residency test in the first half of the tax year. Furthermore, dependents who died at any time during the tax year are still counted in the filing unit, and filers themselves may have died during the year, leaving a filing obligation for their surviving spouses or estates.

Perhaps the most important limitation of federal administrative records involves the race and Hispanic origin data on the Numident. The infrequency with which these data are collected—just once in a lifetime for most individuals—precludes a consistent and current measure of racial and ethnic identity across the population. The Office of Management and Budget (OMB) revises its racial classification periodically, and the Census Bureau follows the OMB directives, but the Numident data generally reflect the classification used by the SSA at the time each individual applied for a Social Security number. Prior to 1980 the racial classification included only three categories: black, white, and other. Hispanic origin was not identified. In 1980 the SSA adopted the five-category classification mandated by OMB, replacing the "other" category with Hispanic origin (intended to take precedence over black or white), Asian or Pacific Islander, and North American Indian or Alaskan Native. To update the classification for persons who completed applications prior to 1980, the SSA staff has developed algorithms for identifying persons of Hispanic origin and Asian ancestry from surname and country of birth. These algorithms can identify very high percentages of both groups, but there is no comparable algorithm for identifying American Indians or Alaskan Natives.

An even more serious limitation of the Numident race data arises from the enumeration-at-birth program, initiated in 1990 to allow parents to obtain Social Security numbers for their newborn infants in conjunction with registering their births. Although the race of both biological parents (but not the newborn) is collected for the birth certificate, these data are requested in a confidential portion of the birth registration questionnaire and, for this reason, are not shared with the SSA. By the year 2010 nearly a quarter of the records in the Numident will lack a race classification.

The lag in data availability due to agency processing schedules is another important limitation of administrative records. Each year the IRS provides the Census Bureau with a file containing data extracted from all tax returns processed through late September. (The Census Bureau uses these data to estimate internal migration.) The file is received too late to be used in a census conducted in that year. Barring a change in what the IRS provides to the Census Bureau, and when, the Census Bureau would have to substitute the previous year's file in its census application. With about 16 percent of the population moving in a given year, a comparable fraction of the tax return addresses could be expected to be out of date and, therefore, inappropriate for use in a census. Furthermore, the relationship data would be at least fifteen months rather than three months out of date; close to 2 percent of the filers and dependents would be deceased; and all of the children born in the fifteen months before an April 1 census day would be missing.

Yet another limitation of administrative records, at least potentially, is that their contents are controlled by the agencies that maintain the files and, therefore, are subject to change without regard to their census use. Just as tax reform added children's Social Security numbers to the tax return, another tax law change could remove them—or, as happened in Canada, eliminate the reporting of dependents altogether.

With the addition of state records from federal programs that focus on the low-income population, it is possible that the coverage of administrative records could approach or even surpass that of a traditional census. Nevertheless, certain segments of the population may be systematically excluded. Recent immigrants, who are precluded from participation in some of the major state and federal programs, are the most prominent example. Homeless persons are another. If administrative records were intended to replace either the traditional census or a sample-based adjustment, the attainment of complete or at least unbiased coverage would be very important. With a more limited role, complete and unbiased coverage would be less critical.

Census 2000 and Beyond

In its April 1996 "Plan for Census 2000," the Census Bureau announced that administrative records would contribute to the 2000 census in several ways. These applications included updating the Master Address File (MAF); assisting with the enumeration of special population groups (such as American Indians, Alaskan Natives, people in group quarters, and people in remote areas); providing an alternative to in-person follow-up for about 5 percent of the households that do not return their census forms; augmenting the household rosters used in the coverage evaluation interviews; and filling in missing items on the long form. Ultimately, however, all of these applications were eliminated from the census plan, and except for address listings from the U.S. Postal Service, administrative records were not used in census 2000. The other applications were abandoned following discouraging research results from the 1995 and 1996 census tests. To support potential uses in 2010, the Census Bureau is focusing its near-term research on records from a small number of primarily federal sources.

Several issues must be addressed if administrative records are to play an important role in the 2010 census. First, the use of administrative records for purposes other than those for which they were collected raises legal questions; census applications may require legislation giving official recognition to statistical uses of such data and ensuring that the Census Bureau has continued access to key records and specific content. Second, in light of growing threats to the privacy and confidentiality of commercial and government records, the public attitude toward prospective census uses must be taken into consideration. Third, the processing cycles for key administrative records may have to be altered to meet the census schedule whenever the substitution of earlier data would seriously reduce data quality. Fourth, effective strategies for identifying duplicate records across systems and resolving conflicting data—particularly addresses—from multiple sources must be developed. Fifth, a vehicle for obtaining a contemporary measure of racial and ethnic identification across the population must be defined.

See also *Population estimates and projections; Related data sources.*

■ John Czajka

Bibliography

National Research Council. *Counting People in the Information Age.* Edited by Duane L. Steffey and Norman M. Bradburn. Washington, D.C.: National Academy Press, 1994.
———. *Modernizing the U.S. Census.* Edited by Barry Edmonston and Charles Schultze. Washington, D.C.: National Academy Press, 1995.
———. *Preparing for the 2000 Census: Interim Report II.* Edited by Andrew A. White and Keith F. Rust. Washington, D.C.: National Academy Press, 1997.
Sailer, Peter, and Michael Weber. "The IRS Population Count: An Update." *Proceedings of the Section on Survey Research Methods.* Alexandria, Va.: American Statistical Association, 1998.
Social Security Administration. *Social Security Bulletin. Annual Statistical Supplement.* Washington, D.C., 1998.

Federal agency uses of census data

Agencies of the U.S. government use the data from each decennial census for a wide range of purposes, including distribution of funds to states and localities, enforcement of civil rights laws, and program administration, planning, and evaluation. Federal statistical agencies, such as the Bureau of Labor Statistics and the National Center for Health Statistics, also use census data to support their programs throughout the decade. Some federal uses of census data involve the head count and such basic characteristics as age and sex that are obtained for all households on the census short form; other uses involve additional characteristics (for example, income) that are obtained for a sample of households on the census long form.

Many federal agency uses are mandated in law, either directly or indirectly in that the census is the only feasible data source to satisfy a mandate. A criterion for including an item in the census (short form or long form) is that it serves an important federal purpose. No item is included because it serves exclusively the interest of some other community (for example, business or academia), although many other organizations and individuals in addition to federal agencies use census data.

Government Allocation Programs

Each year, billions of dollars of federal funds (about $180 billion in fiscal year (FY) 1998) are allocated (distributed) to state and local governments or are used to reimburse state expenditures by means of formulas that include census population counts, population estimates based on the previous census, or other characteristics from the census (for example, income). The largest such program is Medicaid ($104 billion in federal spending in FY 1998), in which the federal government reimburses a percentage of each state's expenditures for medical care services for low-income elderly and disabled people and families with dependent children. The percentage of expenditures reimbursed for each state is determined by a formula that uses per capita income estimates from the U.S. Bureau of Economic Analysis (BEA). BEA develops personal income estimates for regions, states, and counties by using a wide range of administrative records, data from the decennial census and other censuses and surveys, and census-based population estimates.

Another large formula allocation program is Title I of the Elementary and Secondary Education Act, which supports compensatory education programs to meet the needs of educationally disadvantaged children. Title I funds (more than $7 billion in FY 1998) are provided to school districts on the basis of estimates of poor school-age children. The estimates used to derive from the most recent census long form; currently, the estimates are obtained from statistical models developed by the U.S. Bureau of the Census, which include census poverty data as one input. Yet another formula allocation program is the Community Development Block Grant program, which seeks to improve urban communities in terms of housing and economic opportunities for low-income people. This program allocates funds to states ($1.2 billion in FY 1998) on the basis of the larger amount computed under two formulas. Both formulas use decennial census data—total population, poverty population, and overcrowded housing units in the first formula, and total population, poverty population, and housing units built before 1940 in the second formula. The Community Development Block Grant program also allocates funds directly to localities ($2.9 billion in FY 1998) on the basis of formulas that use census data.

Other Uses of Census Data

Census data are widely used for civil rights enforcement. The 1965 Voting Rights Act and subsequent amendments require the U.S. Department of Justice to review redistricting plans in certain states and localities to ensure that they do not abridge voting rights for African Americans or language minorities, defined as people of Spanish heritage, American Indians, Asian Americans, and Alaskan Natives. This review requires small-area census data on age, race, and ethnicity. In addition, the 1975 and later amendments to the Voting Rights Act require the director of the Census Bureau to determine counties, cities, towns, and townships that must implement procedures for bilingual voting to protect the rights of language minorities. These determinations are currently made by using census long-form data on mother tongue, citizenship, educational attainment, and English-language ability, together with age, race, and ethnicity data. The U.S. Equal Employment Opportunity Commission regularly uses census long-form labor force data for zip codes and other geographic areas to analyze statistical evidence in class action charges of employment discrimination.

Federal agency uses of census data for program operation are numerous. For example, the U.S. Immigration and Naturalization Service uses census data for cities and towns on place of birth, citizenship, year of entry, and other long-form characteristics for planning and evaluation and for preparing congressionally required reports. As another example, the U.S. Department of Transportation uses census long-form data on disability for traffic analysis zones to monitor compliance with the Federal Transit Act and the Americans with Disabilities Act.

The census likewise serves several important functions for statistics compiled by federal statistical agencies. Census-based estimates of the population by age, sex, race, and ethnicity are used as denominators for vital rates, such as birth rates and death rates by age. These estimates are also used to adjust the weighting factors for interviewed households in sample surveys (for example, the Current Population Survey) to more accurately reflect the distribution of the population. This procedure is necessary because household surveys invariably have higher net undercoverage of the population than the census itself.

Census data from the short and long forms have many other federal statistical agency uses. The Bureau of Economic Analysis uses census data on income and other characteristics to develop regional, state, and county personal income estimates. In turn, BEA state estimates are used in several federal fund allocation and reimbursement programs (Medicaid, Child Care and Development Block Grant, Home Investment Partnerships Program, and others). As another example, the U.S. Office of Management and Budget has used decennial census data to define metropolitan statistical areas (MSAs); data on place of work are used to determine the linkages between central cities and their surrounding contiguous territory. In turn, there are many federal agency applications of MSAs, such as determining eligibility for fund allocations.

See also *Apportionment and districting; Content determination; Long form; Population estimates and projections; Small Area Income and Poverty Estimates; Statistical policy and oversight.*

■ Constance F. Citro

Bibliography

U.S. General Accounting Office. *Formula Grants—Effects of Adjusted Population Counts on Federal Funding to States.* GAO/HEHS-99-69. Washington, D.C.: U.S. Government Printing Office, 1999.

Federal household surveys

The census provides sufficient information on the population of the United States to satisfy the requirements of enumeration and apportionment as well as to support demographic and economic research. However, this information is updated only every ten years and thus is insufficient to answer all of the questions posed by Congress, policy makers, and researchers about the population, its characteristics, behaviors, and well-being. To acquire more timely information and to answer more in-depth questions, the Census Bureau relies on surveys that (in relation to the census) collect more information but on considerably fewer people. These people are chosen to allow the results to be generalized to the full population.

The trade-off between a census and a survey is typically the loss of geographic detail in exchange for increased information about the population of interest. For example, decennial census data can provide city and county planners with information on population size and demographic characteristics so they can meet the demand for schools, roads, and other services. However, the survey that supports the official estimates of poverty in the United States (the March Current Population Survey) can provide information only on the number and characteristics of the poor population among people at the state level. Even then, the precision of the estimates varies by the number of people in the sample from each state.

Both types of information are crucial; the census and surveys complement each other. The decennial census often provides the primary lists of households that will be sampled in a survey, and surveys often provide important intercensal estimates needed to update the decennial results throughout the decade.

What Is a Survey, and How Is It Different from a Census?

A survey is typically a collection of information about a group of people (or other units) obtained by asking questions of a subset (or sample) of the full population, much like the long-form component of the census. A survey can be taken of virtually any population, provided that a list of objects or units in that population (that is, universe) and a way to find them are available. For example, households, businesses, trees, or widgets can be surveyed. Federal surveys of the U.S. population tend to sample households or other organizations that provide services to that population, such as schools and school districts, and then ask specific questions about people. The universe for many federal surveys is the civilian noninstitutionalized population in the United States instead of the total population, although some federal surveys are targeted to populations outside that universe.

Ideally, the subset of the in-universe population selected for a sample resembles the full in-universe population for the characteristics of interest to the survey so that conclusions drawn from a survey can be applied to the entire population. Asking questions of a subset of the population instead of the full population allows the collector to ask more questions, given a fixed budget, than could be asked of every unit.

The long-form component of the census and the American Community Survey represent examples of federal surveys. They are exceptional because of their extremely large sample size (for example, in the 1990 census, the long form was distributed to nearly eighteen million households). The surveys discussed in this article are more modest in their size but are more ambitious in the amount of information collected.

Why Use a Survey Instead of a Census?

The official census is limited in its content and thus cannot be used to address many important political, economic, and social issues beyond enumeration and apportionment. Some issues require more in-depth sets of questions than those included in the decennial census to measure all facets of the problem. Consider, for example, an assessment of the impact of a change in taxes across the population at different income levels. Such a study of tax issues requires detailed information on income and population characteristics along with all the information included on federal income tax forms used to calculate tax liabilities before and after a proposed or actual change in the law.

Data collection efforts have fixed budgets and often do not have sufficient funds to collect much information on all people. Furthermore, the Paperwork Reduction Act directs the government to minimize the burden of data collection on the population as a whole, which can be done by questioning the minimum number of people as needed to accurately address an issue. Trade-offs exist between the accuracy of the results, the cost, the sample size, and the design. However, modern sampling and estimation techniques are employed to yield precise estimates needed to address many important issues, even with small to modest sample sizes. For example, the Consumer Expenditure Survey relies on a sample of fewer than twenty thousand addresses to describe the spending patterns of nearly 275 million people in the United States.

Survey results produced by the Census Bureau as well as other government agencies and private firms are used in many ways by researchers, the media, nonprofit organizations, marketing firms, and all levels of government. Researchers often use survey data to assess the impact of policy changes implemented in the past, such as the major changes to the welfare programs that were introduced in 1996. The media, the federal government, and other institutions routinely use survey data to describe the population and its characteristics, such as the number of people and families living below the poverty level or the proportion of the total population receiving benefits through mechanisms such as the unemployment insurance program. Researchers rely on analyses of underlying trends in the population covered by federal surveys to predict future patterns or to base decisions about future operations. Users of the data also simulate answers to "What if" questions, such as "What would happen to the Social Security trust fund if the age requirement for receiving Social Security retirement benefits was increased?"

To support this statistical research, the Census Bureau releases the results of federal surveys it conducts to the public or, in some cases, to the survey sponsor. The Census Bureau is required by law to strictly protect the confidentiality of individuals responding to the questions asked in the census and in surveys. Therefore, the data released can be in aggregate form (tables) or in the form of anonymous microdata (a file having one record per sample member where identifying information is suppressed). Survey results, such as the monthly estimates of unemployment and employment, are often quoted in the media and are frequently cited in publications or scholarly journals, working paper series, and other periodicals. The Census Bureau provides access to publicly available data from the federal surveys included in Table 1 through the Internet and through direct purchase arrangements.

How Does the Decennial Census Affect Federal Surveys?

Federal surveys of the U.S. population often yield estimates of people and their characteristics, such as the number of people with insurance coverage or the unemployment rate among different population groups. However, the underlying sampling method does not directly sample people in the country. Instead, the survey samples housing units, school districts, or other institutions providing services to the population. For many of the federal surveys in Table 1, the sample is based on addresses (such as 123 Main Street) obtained from the decennial census, and questions are asked of some or all of the people who reside at each of the chosen addresses. Other federal surveys may use the decennial information indirectly, such as the Medical Expenditure Panel Survey conducted by the private sector, which selects household units from the National Health Interview Survey (NHIS).

The samples in Table 1, drawn from addresses in the decennial census, typically use the most recent decennial census supplemented with information on new housing construction subsequent to the census. The master list of addresses from which the sample is drawn is referred to as the frame. To minimize the cost of data collection while maximizing the precision of the survey estimates, the selection of addresses from the frame is not based on a simple random sample. Instead, addresses are clustered based on geography and size. The sample selection process involves several stages of selection at successively lower levels of geography (referred to as multistage sampling).

The decennial census also plays a key role in preparing estimates from survey results.

How Long Has the Federal Government Been Conducting Surveys?

Federally sponsored surveys of the U.S. population date back to the nineteenth century. Early measures of trends in the cost of living were derived from annual surveys of income and expenditures conducted by the U.S. Department of Labor between 1888 and 1891. Periodic surveys of income and expenditures continued through the twentieth century leading up to the Consumer Expenditure Survey, which was formalized in the early 1970s. Until the formal survey was introduced, the expenditure surveys did not rely on the decennial census as the frame. The early expenditure surveys also did not rely on the same multistage probability sampling techniques currently in use.

The sampling methods now in use routinely by the federal government date back to the 1930s. The Financial Survey of Urban Housing began in 1934 using a sample of housing units drawn by randomly selecting blocks from large and small cities and then interviewing people in all units in the selected blocks. The Study of Consumer Purchases, conducted in 1935–1936, relied on a multistage design (then called double sampling). At the same time, the federal government conducted the National Health Survey using a sample of housing units selected from eighty-three cities and twenty-three rural counties.

In 1943 the Census Bureau conducted the Monthly Report on the Labor Force (the precursor to the Current Population Survey) using the more sophisticated form of multistage sampling currently in use for the surveys in Table 1. This report was developed as a

Table 1. Federal Surveys of the United States Population Using Decennial Census Results and Conducted by the Census Bureau

Characteristic	American Housing Survey (AHS)		Consumer Expenditure Survey (CE)	
	National Survey	Metropolitan Survey	Quarterly Interview Survey	Diary Survey
Purpose	Inform housing policy and housing program design and evaluation		Update Consumer Price Index and analyze consumer expenditures	
Frame	Decennial census + new construction		Decennial census + new construction	
Current Size	54,000 addresses, 53,000 interviewed households	72,000 addresses, 65,000 interviewed households	15,000 addresses	12,400 addresses
Frequency	Biennially (odd years)	Biennially with exceptions (even years)	Quarterly (continuous monthly interviewing)	Annual (although the two-week reference period is designated throughout the year so all weeks are covered)
Interviewing Mode	Personal visit and telephone, automated instrument		Personal visit, paper survey	Combination of personal visit and self-administered paper survey
Respondent	One adult resident (occupied unit) or owner or proxy (unoccupied unit)		One adult respondent for the household	
Sponsor	U.S. Department of Housing and Urban Development		Bureau of Labor Statistics	
History	National survey began as annual survey in 1973 based on 1970 census; originally named Annual Housing Surveys; biennial surveys began in 1982 (national survey) and 1996 (metropolitan survey); frame updated to 1980 census in 1985; sample size fluctuated with available funds; automation introduced in 1997		Began in 1979 based on 1970 decennial; updated base to 1980 decennial in 1985 and to 1990 decennial in 1995–1996; development of automated instruments began in 1998	
Weighting Controls	Housing unit controls derived from the decennial census, adjusted for undercount, and changes in the housing stock within a decade		Decennial census population adjusted for undercount and for births, deaths, immigration, and emigration within a decade	

continued

Table 1. (*cont.*)

Characteristic	Current Population Survey (CPS)		
	Basic	March Supplement	Other Supplements
Purpose	Provide monthly estimates on employment, unemployment, and labor force characteristics; annual estimate of income, poverty, and work experience; and periodic estimates of other topics		
Frame	Decennial census + new construction		
Current Size	59,500 addresses; 50,000 interviewed households covering 95,000 adults per month		
Frequency	Monthly (week of the 19th)	Annually in March	Annually with exceptions
Interviewing Mode	Personal visit and telephone, automated instrument		
Respondent	One adult responds for the unit and for each person in the unit (with some exceptions)		
Sponsor	Bureau of Labor Statistics and Census Bureau		Various agencies
History	Monthly survey began in 1942 based on the 1940 decennial census; the underlying frame was updated every ten years with most recent samples based on 1990 census; early samples were drawn from an area frame with address sampling introduced with the 1960 decennial frame; sample size fluctuated over the years with maximum of 85,000 households per month in 1980; the survey began with a national sample design and switched to a state-based sample in 1984		
Weighting Controls	Decennial census adjusted for undercount and for births, deaths, relocation, immigration, and emigration within a decade		

Characteristic	National Crime Victimization Survey (NCVS)		
	Basic	Police Public Contact Survey (PPCS)	School Crime Supplement (SCS)
Purpose	Provide estimates of crime victimization	Provide estimates of interaction with police and police use of excessive force	Provide information on school-related victimization
Frame	Decennial census + new construction		
Current Size	56,000 addresses, 104,000 people aged 12+	56,000 addresses, 96,000 people aged 16+	10,000 households, 14,000 students
Frequency	Semiannually (with interviewing spread evenly over six-month period)	Triennially	Biennially (with some exceptions)
Interviewing Mode	Personal and telephone interviews, automated and paper instruments		
Respondent	Each person aged 12+ in interviewed unit	Designated sample member	Students aged 12 to 18 enrolled in primary or secondary schools
Sponsor	Bureau of Justice Statistics		National Center for Education Statistics
History	Began in 1972 based on 1970 decennial census; base of the sample updated every ten years with most recent survey based on 1990 decennial census; sample size fluctuated over the years in response to available funds; PPCS supplement began in 1996; predecessors to SCS occurred in 1989 and 1995		
Weighting Controls	Decennial census population adjusted for undercount and for births, deaths, immigration, and emigration within a decade		

continued

Table 1. *(cont.)*

Characteristic	National Health Interview Survey (NHIS)	Survey of Women (SW) Component of the National Longitudinal Surveys (NLS)	National Survey of College Graduates (NSCG)
Purpose	Provide estimates of the amount and distribution of illness and utilization of health care services	Provide estimates of the work experience and characteristics of women ages 30-44 in 1968 and ages 14-24 in 1967	Estimate size and characteristics of U.S. scientists and engineers
Frame	Sample areas selected based on 1990 population	1960 decennial census	1990 decennial census long-form sample of adults
Current Size	41,000 completed interviews	5,700 women interviewed	42,500 adults
Frequency	Annually (with interviewing spread evenly over the year)	Biennially	Biennially
Interviewing Mode	Personal interviews, automated instrument	Personal interviews, automated instrument	Mail survey
Respondent	One adult responds for family and household questions, selected other adults respond to additional questions on adults and children	Designated sample person	Designated sample members
Sponsor	National Center for Health Statistics	Bureau of Labor Statistics	National Science Foundation
History	Began in 1957 based on 1950 decennial census; frame was updated in 1972, 1985, and 1995; various topical modules have been incorporated over the years to focus questions on topics of import for health services research	Began as two of four components of the National Longitudinal Surveys in late 1960s; Survey of Mature Women and Survey of Young Women were merged in 1995 to form the Survey of Women; the other two surveys were the Survey of Mature Men and the Survey of Young Men; automation was introduced to the SW in 1995	Predecessor was the National Survey of Natural and Social Scientists and Engineers conducted in 1970s and 1980s based on the 1970 and 1980 decennial census long-form samples
Weighting Controls	Decennial census population adjusted for undercount and for births, deaths, immigration, and emigration within a decade	Decennial census and CPS population estimates	1990 census long-form estimates

continued

continuation of a series of surveys designed to study unemployment in the United States. It was renamed in conjunction with the transfer of the project to the Census Bureau and the redesign of the sample. The name was changed to the Current Population Survey in 1947 with an expansion of its scope beyond labor force issues.

What Do Federal Surveys Measure?

Most surveys have a specific focus (such as the trends in the housing market in the United States) guiding the content determination and the selection of the sample. As such, the content of a federal survey is always unique.

Table 1. *(cont.)*

Characteristic	National Survey of Fishing, Hunting, and Wildlife-Associated Recreation (FHWAR)	New York City Housing Vacancy Survey (NYCHVS)
Purpose	Provide estimates of fishing, hunting, and wildlife-related activities to aid in managing fish and wildlife resources	Estimate the vacancy rate for New York City's rental stock and the characteristics of housing and residents in the city
Frame	1980 decennial census	Decennial census, new construction lists, and other local information on the formation of rental units
Current Size	77,000 households for screener interview, 28,000 and 14,000 adults selected for each of two follow-up surveys	18,000 units
Frequency	Household screener with three follow-up interviews, once every four months; two follow-up surveys (Fishing and Hunting, Wildlife Watching); entire survey repeated approximately every five years	Triennially (with some exceptions)
Interviewing Mode	Personal and telephone interviews, automated instrument	Personal interview, paper instrument
Respondent	Adult household member for the screener, designated sample adult for follow-up	Adult resident (occupied units) owner, manager, or proxy (vacant units)
Sponsor	Fish and Wildlife Service of the U.S. Department of the Interior	New York City Department of Housing Preservation and Development
History	Began in 1955 and repeated at approximately five-year intervals; prior to 1996, the follow-up survey was administered once with recall period of five to sixteen months; wildlife-watching survey introduced in 1980	Began in 1962 based on 1960 decennial census and repeated approximately every three years; updated frame in 1970s, 1980s, and 1990s with new decennial census results
Weighting Controls	Decennial census population adjusted for undercount and for births, deaths, immigration, and emigration within a decade	Housing unit controls derived from the decennial census, adjusted for undercount, and changes in the rental housing stock within a decade

continued

There are features common to the process of collecting these data. Typically, the government collects basic demographic and economic characteristics of people such as age, race, sex, marital status, familial relationships, educational attainment, income, and labor force activity. The level of detail varies depending on the objectives. For example, often surveys will contain some measure of income of the household or of the people in the unit. This topic could be addressed using a single question (for example, "What is the total income you received from all sources last year?") or using a series of highly detailed questions of each per-son on the specific sources of income, the amounts, and the distribution within the year (as is true for the Survey of Income and Program Participation (SIPP)). The objectives of the more detailed questions are to increase the accuracy of the estimate of total income or to provide details needed for analysis or both.

Most surveys query people on topics that the respondents know firsthand. Occasionally, and with permission from the respondent, data collectors supplement this personal information with information obtained directly from establishments that serve the respondents, such as school districts. The surveys in

Table 1. *(cont.)*

| Characteristic | Survey of Income and Program Participation (SIPP) | | |
	1984–1996 Panels	Survey of Program Dynamics	SIPP Methods Panel
Purpose	Describe patterns of income and benefit receipt and amounts in the United States and other special topics	Estimate the impact of the welfare reform legislation of 1996	Test improvements to SIPP instrument
Frame	1990 decennial census + new construction	1992 and 1993 SIPP samples	1990 decennial census + new construction
Current Size	34,000 households in Wave 1	18,000 households	2,000 interviewed households per experiment
Frequency	Every four months for four years	Once per year for six years	Periodic
Interviewing Mode	Telephone and personal interviews, automated instrument		
Respondent	People age 15 + in interviewed units		
Sponsor	Census Bureau		
History	Predecessor surveys took place in 1978, 1979 based on 1970 decennial census frame; first SIPP panel introduced in 1984 based on 1980 decennial frame and following sample adults for up to 2.5 years; subsequent panels of varying sizes and lengths introduced in 1985–1993 based on 1980 decennial frame	Sample members from 1992 and 1993 panels of SIPP are being followed and interviewed once per year between 1997 and 2002	Being introduced in 2000 to study alternative methods to improve quality of SIPP data
Weighting Controls	Decennial census adjusted for undercount and for births, deaths, relocation, immigration, and emigration within a decade		

Source: U.S. Bureau of the Census, Demographic Surveys Division, *Survey Abstracts* (Washington, D.C., June 1999).

Table 1 generally rely on self-reported information asked directly of respondents or information provided by another knowledgeable person serving as the sample member's proxy.

The sample selection process generally restricts units to residential addresses that are occupied and whose occupants are in the civilian population. Thus, the resulting sample estimates apply to the civilian noninstitutionalized population of the United States. There are exceptions, however. For example, the New York City Housing Vacancy Survey covers unoccupied units and covers the targeted geographic area of New York City.

How Are the Data Collected?

The questions posed to respondents in federal surveys are contained within a questionnaire or instrument. The questions could be administered like the decennial census where the questionnaire is mailed to the respondent who fills out the answers and mails it back. By their nature, these mail surveys are "self-administered"; that is, there is no interviewer to read the questions, and the questions are printed on paper. The National Survey of College Graduates is an example of a mail survey, although it also uses telephone interviews to follow up with sample members who do not respond initially.

Other surveys can be administered by an interviewer who reads each question and records the results. The interviewer can come in person to the respondent's home or contact the respondent by telephone. The telephone interviewers could be centrally located at one of three phone centers maintained by the Census Bureau or dispersed throughout the community. The SIPP represents a survey conducted by interviewers either in person or by telephone. When conducting the SIPP interview by phone, the interviewers are dispersed throughout the community, most likely calling from their homes instead of calling from a central location.

The questions administered in surveys can be recorded on paper, as noted for mail surveys, or automated on a computer. The latter is referred to as computer assisted interviewing (CAI). CAI surveys are becoming increasingly common among the federal surveys in Table 1 (seven out of ten surveys are automated and one more, the Consumer Expenditure Survey, soon will be).

CAI surveys could be interviewer-administered, representing surveys conducted in person using a laptop computer or by telephone using a shared computer such as those at the central telephone centers. CAI surveys could also be self-administered using instruments disseminated to respondents by telephone, by the Internet, or on a computer disk. The federal surveys discussed in Table 1 currently do not have a component administered through the Internet, although that option is under consideration by the Census Bureau.

Respondents to federal surveys are typically people age fifteen years and older residing at selected addresses who meet the selection criteria unique to each survey. Depending on the objectives of the survey, the respondents may include just one person from the household reporting for the entire unit, all people meeting the age cutoff, or a sample of people from the household. Occasionally, and only when it is important to improve the accuracy of the responses, questions are directed to children under age fifteen. For example, the National Crime Victimization Survey (NCVS) administers questions to crime victims age twelve and older. The National Health Interview Survey allows any person age eighteen or older to provide demographic characteristics for all household members and to provide characteristics of the family. The Census Bureau then selects one adult at random from each NHIS household to be administered a sample adult section of the instrument, and proxies for that respondent are not allowed. Finally, the Census Bureau selects a sample child at random from the NHIS household for information collected in the sample child section of the instrument, but, in this case, adults are allowed to provide the information on the selected child.

How Often Are Surveys Repeated?

As surveys can vary in their content and focus, they can vary in the number of repetitions and the interim time between repetitions. Surveys can occur one time and provide a single picture of a cross section of the population (cross-sectional). They can be repeated over time yielding a series of estimates that can be used to analyze trends (time series).

There are two types of repeated surveys: surveys that follow and reinterview the same unit over time (longitudinal) or surveys that rely on newly selected samples of the full population each time they are administered (repeated cross-sectional). A number of federal surveys, such as the NCVS, reflect a hybrid approach. In the NCVS, addresses selected for interview are visited for one month, retired for five months, and then revisited for one month, potentially being surveyed seven times over a three-year period. Although this sounds like a longitudinal survey, it is not because it does not follow people when they move. The SIPP, meanwhile, is purely a longitudinal study. It selects a sample of people for its first round of interviewing and then attempts to follow those people over time (as long as they remain alive and within the universe of the survey). In addition to being a longitudinal survey, the SIPP is refreshed every few years when the Census Bureau selects a new sample of people to follow.

How Good Are the Survey Data?

Statistical theory says that basing a study on a sample instead of a full population will provide accurate but not perfect results. The error associated with the use of a sample instead of a census is referred to as sampling error, and the level of sampling error varies depending on how the sample is selected and the sample size.

Formulas determining variation of the sample estimates from the population estimates quantify the amount of sampling error in a given survey. With each survey, the Census Bureau publishes a Source and Accuracy Statement that documents the level of sampling error and its impact on survey-based estimates. Typically, estimates are provided with a variety of statistics that indicates the degree of uncertainty of the estimates, such as confidence intervals or standard errors, and are suppressed from publication if deemed unreliable based on these measures. For example, a 1997 U.S. Department of the Interior and Department of Commerce report includes the number of elderly women (that is, women over sixty-five) who hunted or fished but does not record the number of elderly women who only hunted because the sample size is too small to support a reliable estimate.

The quality of the data collection process is crucial to the reliability of the estimates ultimately produced from each survey. Aside from sampling error, surveys will reflect some amount of nonsampling error. Nonsampling error refers to the deviation of the results from the truth for reasons other than the use of a sample to collect the data. Some examples follow.

First, a question must be phrased so that a respondent understands it; otherwise, the meaning of the response is uncertain. Second, the frame from which a sample is drawn may not be complete, such as the case with the decennial census as a result of an undercount. Third, the interviewer could fail to correctly record the respondent's answer. Fourth, the respondent may not use perfect recall in answering the questions or he or she may refuse to respond to some or all items. Fifth, errors could arise in the flow of the instrument, that is, in determining the appropriate question to pose during the interview. Finally, data processing errors could inadvertently change the answers after data collection.

Some of these forms of nonsampling error introduce bias into the survey estimates. Bias is a measure of the persistent deviation of the estimate from the true value and can be measured by the comparison of the survey estimates with reliable independent estimates. A form of bias that is typical in surveys is underreporting of income relative to an independently derived benchmark. For example, Marc Roemer reports that the 1999 March Current Population Survey estimate of the amount of Social Security income received by the U.S. civilian noninstitutionalized population is about 92 percent of an independently derived benchmark.

The Census Bureau and other data collection institutions employ a large number of quality assurance techniques to minimize errors in the survey results and to ensure that high-quality data are produced.

How Are Estimates Derived from a Survey?

Regardless of the focus, the federal surveys employ complex sampling algorithms; that is, the government does not simply select every tenth person in a row. Specifically, sample members are clustered in a way that minimizes the cost of data collection while maximizing the precision of the estimates. Thus, certain special techniques of estimation (primarily weighting) are required to use these data. Federal survey data will typically contain weights for people, weights for the units sampled (that is, addresses), and weights for one or more groupings of people within the units sampled. Population estimates are derived by totaling these weights over the sample members. Following is some important information on weights.

(1) In a simple random sample, if the sampling process selects one out of every five units from the full universe, then each selected sample unit represents five members of the universe (the selected unit and four others). Hence, the unit can be said to have a weight of five (which is the inverse of the rate of selection), and whenever that sample member is counted in an analysis, it is counted five times. In the case of complex sample designs, the weight still represents the inverse of the rate of selection. However, the rate of selection—and hence the weight—varies across sample members.

(2) Weights are used to compensate for noninterviewed units. If all people eligible for an interview at a selected address either cannot or will not be interviewed, the result is a unit noninterview. If left uncorrected, the weighted estimates likely will be biased. To minimize the impact of unit noninterviews on estimates derived from federal surveys, the Census Bureau adjusts the weights of interviewed units to compensate for the missing noninterviewed units.

(3) Counting people in interviewed units based on the unit weight does not always result in unbiased estimates of people because of noninterview, undercoverage, and the luck of the draw. Therefore, the Census Bureau constructs person weights, derived from unit weights but adjusted so that, when totaled over all people in the universe, they equal the numbers in the census population estimates. These estimates are derived from the decennial census but are corrected for the census undercount, thus minimizing the impact of that form of nonsampling error on the survey-based estimates. The control counts are also adjusted to account for births, deaths, immigration, and emigration between the decennial censuses.

Aside from creating weights to support estimation, the Census Bureau employs other processes to minimize nonsampling error in survey estimates. All new questions to be added to a survey are subjected to the census pretest policy stipulating that unless already proven successful in another survey, questions must be successfully tested before conducting the survey. Pretesting research is intended to address the issue of whether respondents interpret questions as intended and can provide appropriate answers. Additional techniques employed by the Census Bureau to test the validity of the questionnaire wording include cognitive techniques, focus groups, and expert review.

Some forms of nonsampling error can be minimized after the data are collected, such as the error associated with missing responses because of refusals, lack of knowledge, or instrument flow problems. As the assignment of weights includes a correction for non-interview and errors in the original frame, assignment of data to questions with missing responses reduces the impact of missing data on the resulting estimates. This assignment of answers to questions with missing responses is referred to as imputation. The success of imputation in reducing nonsampling error is a function of the approach used to impute the missing data, the amount of missing data to be imputed, and the extent to which and the way in which people with missing data differ from people with reported data.

In addition to imputing information not originally reported, the Census Bureau and other data collection agencies will edit information if good reason exists to suspect it was reported or recorded in error. For example, if a respondent reported not being enrolled in school and then reported attending college, the answers are inconsistent and one is likely to be incorrect. Data collectors often rely on experts in subject areas (such as an expert in education in this case) to make an assessment of which answer is the most likely to be correct and then edit the data accordingly.

Summary

Many federally sponsored surveys of the U.S. population rely on the decennial census either directly or indirectly. The surveys in Table 1 are those that rely directly on the decennial census for selecting the sample and controlling the estimates produced from the surveys. Although Table 1 focuses on surveys administered by the Census Bureau, numerous other federally sponsored surveys are administered by private firms. These firms rely at least indirectly on published estimates from the decennial census to control their estimates and establish their sample frames.

See also *American Community Survey; Long form.*

■ Pat Doyle

Bibliography

Bohme, Frederick G. "The Census Bureau's Current Programs: A History." Unpublished draft manuscript. U.S. Bureau of the Census, 1979–1981.

Duncan, Joseph W., and William C. Shelton. *Revolution in United States Government Statistics: 1926–1976.* Washington, D.C.: U.S. Department of Commerce, Office of Federal Statistical Policy and Standards, 1978.

Roemer, Marc., *Reconciling March CPS Money Income with the National Income and Product Accounts: An Evaluation of CPS Quality.* Proceedings of the American Statistical Association. Alexandria, Va.: American Statistical Association, 1999.

U.S. Bureau of the Census, Demographic Surveys Division. *Survey Abstracts.* Washington, D.C., June 1999.

U.S. Department of the Interior, Fish and Wildlife Service, and U.S. Department of Commerce, Census Bureau. *1996 Survey of Fishing, Hunting, and Wildlife-Associated Recreation.* Washington, D.C., 1997.

Foreign-born population of the United States

The foreign-born population includes U.S. residents born outside the United States of foreign parents. Excluded from the foreign-born population are persons born abroad of American parents. A larger category, the foreign stock, combines the foreign born and those with at least one parent of foreign birth. The foreign-born population comprises people in a variety of immigration categories who fulfill the residency rules of the census, including permanent resident aliens, naturalized citizens, and some temporary migrants, such as foreign students and exchange visitors.

A question on birthplace has been asked in each census since 1850 and has been used to distinguish U.S. natives from people of foreign birth. A question on parentage, which refers to the birthplace of an individual's parents, was asked in censuses between 1870 and 1970. Information on parentage and birthplace can be combined to identify the foreign-stock population.

Trends in Birthplace and Parentage

In 1850 the foreign-born numbered 2.2 million, accounting for just under 10 percent of the total population (see Table 1). The share of the foreign-born increased during subsequent decades, reaching nearly 15 percent in 1890. The huge immigrant flows from southern and eastern Europe, which started in the 1880s and continued into the 1920s, dramatically swelled the foreign-born population. By 1930 that population had peaked at 14.2 million but constituted under 12 percent of the total population. Restrictive immigration laws of the 1920s and the economic hardships of the Great Depression caused immigration to slow to a trickle until about 1935. In fact, between 1930 and 1934 more people departed than entered the country. The total foreign-born population declined for the next four decades, falling to 9.6 million in 1970, or under 5 percent of the population. The 1965 amendments to the Immigration and Nationality Act (INA), which opened up immigration to non-European countries, caused a resurgence in flows in the 1970s and 1980s. As a result, the foreign-born population climbed to 14.1 million in 1980; by 1990 it numbered 19.8 million, an all-time high, though it made up under 8 percent of the U.S. population.

Table 2 provides data on the foreign-stock population for the census years in which these data are available. Between 1890 and 1930 that population nearly doubled from 20.8 million to 40.3 million, and it accounted for approximately one-third of the U.S. population at both the start and end of the period. The decline in immigration after 1930 resulted in a corresponding drop in the foreign-stock population, which fell to 33.6 million by 1970, or just 17 percent of the total population.

The foreign-stock population is composed of first- and second-generation immigrants—that is, the foreign-born and their children. Children of the foreign-born include native-born people with both parents foreign-born and those with only one immigrant parent. During the early decades of the twentieth century, between 35 and 45 percent of the foreign-stock population was foreign-born, and around 40 percent con-

Table 1. U.S. Foreign-born Population: 1850–1990

Year	Total population	Foreign-born	Foreign-born (%)
1850	23,191,876	2,244,602	9.7
1860	31,443,321	4,138,697	13.2
1870	38,558,371	5,567,229	14.4
1880	50,155,783	6,679,943	13.3
1890	62,622,250	9,249,547	14.8
1900	75,994,575	10,341,276	13.6
1910	91,972,266	13,515,886	14.7
1920	105,710,620	13,920,692	13.2
1930	122,775,046	14,204,149	11.6
1940	131,669,275	11,594,896	8.8
1950	150,216,110	10,347,395	6.9
1960	179,325,671	9,738,091	5.4
1970	203,210,158	9,619,302	4.7
1980	226,545,805	14,079,906	6.2
1990	248,709,873	19,767,316	7.9

Source: Campbell Gibson and Emily Lennon, *Historical Census Statistics on the Foreign-Born Population of the United States: 1850 to 1990*. Working Paper 29 (Washington, D.C.: U.S. Bureau of the Census, 1999).

sisted of native-born individuals with both parents born abroad. The balance included the native-born with only one foreign-born parent—and the immigrant parent was much more likely to be the father than the mother. As immigration declined after 1930, the proportion of foreign-born people in the foreign stock also fell. By 1970 it had dipped to just 29 percent, with the second generation making up the difference.

Continent of Birth

The geographic origin of the foreign-born population is available for the 1850–1930 and 1960–1990 censuses (see Table 3). In the 1800s, a period of generally open-door immigration to the United States, Europe accounted for the overwhelming share of the foreign-born. In 1850, for example, 92 percent of the foreign-born population was from Europe, while only 7 percent came from North America (essentially Canada). For the next five decades Europe and Canada contributed over 97 percent of the foreign-born population. The domi-

Table 2. Foreign-stock Population: 1890–1930 and 1960–1970

Year	Total population	Foreign stock	Foreign stock (%)	"Native-born," both parents foreign-born	"Native-born," foreign-born father	"Native-born," foreign-born mother	Foreign-born
1890	62,622,250	20,781,945	33.2	39.0	11.4	5.0	44.5
1900	75,994,575	26,038,397	34.3	40.9	12.9	6.4	39.7
1910	91,972,266	32,480,839	35.3	39.9	12.2	6.4	41.6
1920	105,710,620	36,715,938	34.7	42.9	12.4	6.7	37.9
1930	122,775,046	40,286,278	32.8	43.5	13.9	7.4	35.3
1960	179,325,675	34,050,442	19.0	41.4	18.9	11.0	28.6
1970	203,210,158	33,575,232	16.5	NA	NA	NA	28.6

Note: NA = Not available.

Source: Campbell Gibson and Emily Lennon, *Historical Census Statistics on the Foreign-Born Population of the United States: 1850 to 1990.* Working Paper 29 (Washington, D.C.: U.S. Bureau of the Census, 1999).

nance of these two areas was assured when the United States banned the entry of Chinese and Japanese labor in 1882 and 1907, respectively, and virtually barred all Asian immigration in 1917. At the end of World War II these restrictions were slightly eased, but national origin immigration quotas continued to favor Europe and, specifically, countries in northern and western Europe. The 1965 amendments to the INA were a watershed in that they eliminated the quota system and created opportunities for immigration from all countries. As a result, the proportion of Asians and Latin Americans in the immigration stream to the United States soared, while both the number and share of European immigrants declined. By 1990 Latin Americans and Asians composed 44 percent and 26 percent, respectively, of the total U.S. foreign-born population, whereas Europeans made up just 23 percent. Thus the dominance of European birthplace evident among the foreign-born in the mid-nineteenth century waned at the close of the twentieth.

Changes also occurred in the geographic origin of the foreign-born population (see Table 4). In 1850 the most frequently reported country of birth among the 2.2 million foreign-born was Ireland, with 962,000 people, followed by Germany (584,000), Great Britain (379,000), and Canada (148,000). Eight of the top ten source countries were European. By 1920 the major source countries of the foreign-born reflected the growing presence of immigrants from southern and eastern Europe. Germany was the top source country, with 1.7 million people, followed by Italy, the Soviet Union,

Poland, and Canada. By 1990 Europe accounted for only three of the ten major source countries, and the ascendance of Latin America and Asia was evident in the rankings. Mexico, with 4.3 million people, was by far the most frequently reported country of birth, followed by China, the Philippines, Canada, and Cuba.

Demographic Characteristics

Table 5 shows the age and gender characteristics of the foreign-born population for censuses since 1870. The median age of the foreign-born population stood at thirty-eight in 1880, before massive immigration from southern and eastern Europe. In 1910, by which time these flows had peaked, the median age had declined to thirty-seven. Immigrants disproportionately enter the United States in their prime working ages and tend to be younger than the general population. But their median age climbs as their length of stay in a country increases. The median age of the foreign-born population is thus heavily influenced by the level of immigration to the United States. With the precipitous drop in immigration in the 1930s and 1940s, the foreign-born population declined because it was not being replenished by younger immigrants. By 1960 people age sixty-five and over composed nearly one-third of the total foreign-born population, and the median age reached a high of fifty-seven. With passage of the 1965 INA amendments, immigration once again increased, and the median age declined. By 1990 foreign-born people age sixty-five and over

Table 3. Continent of Birth of the Foreign-born Population: 1850–1930 and 1960–1990

Year	Total foreign-born*	Distribution of continent of birth (%)					
		Europe	Asia	Africa	Oceania	Latin America	North America
1850	2,202,625	92.2	0.1	0.0	0.0	0.9	6.7
1860	4,134,809	92.1	0.9	0.0	0.1	0.9	6.0
1870	5,563,637	88.8	1.2	0.0	0.1	1.0	8.9
1880	6,675,875	86.2	1.6	0.0	0.1	1.3	10.7
1890	9,243,535	86.9	1.2	0.0	0.1	1.2	10.6
1900	10,330,534	86.0	1.2	0.0	0.1	1.3	11.4
1910	13,506,272	87.4	1.4	0.0	0.1	2.1	9.0
1920	13,911,767	85.7	1.7	0.1	0.1	4.2	8.2
1930	14,197,553	83.0	1.9	0.1	0.1	5.6	9.2
1960	9,678,201	75.0	5.1	0.4	0.4	9.4	9.8
1970	9,303,570	61.7	8.9	0.9	0.4	19.4	8.7
1980	13,192,563	39.0	19.3	1.5	0.6	33.1	6.5
1990	18,959,158	22.9	26.3	1.9	0.5	44.3	4.0

Note: *With a stated continent of birth.

Source: Campbell Gibson and Emily Lennon, *Historical Census Statistics on the Foreign-Born Population of the United States: 1850 to 1990.* Working Paper 29 (Washington, D.C.: U.S. Bureau of the Census, 1999).

Table 4. Top Ten Source Countries of the Foreign-born: 1850, 1920, and 1990

1850		1920		1990	
1. Ireland	961,719	1. Germany	1,686,108	1. Mexico	4,298,014
2. Germany	583,774	2. Italy	1,610,113	2. China*	921,070
3. Great Britain	379,093	3. Soviet Union	1,400,495	3. Philippines	912,674
4. Canada	147,711	4. Poland	1,139,979	4. Canada	744,830
5. France	54,069	5. Canada	1,138,174	5. Cuba	736,971
6. Switzerland	13,358	6. Great Britain	1,135,489	6. Germany	711,929
7. Mexico	13,317	7. Ireland	1,037,234	7. United Kingdom	640,145
8. Norway	12,678	8. Sweden	625,585	8. Italy	580,592
9. Netherlands	9,848	9. Austria	575,627	9. Korea	568,397
10. Italy	3,679	10. Mexico	486,418	10. Vietnam	543,262
Total	2,244,602	Total	13,920,692	Total	19,767,316

Notes: *Includes the mainland, Taiwan, and Hong Kong.

Data are based on political boundaries existing at the time of the specified decennial census.

Source: Campbell Gibson and Emily Lennon, *Historical Census Statistics on the Foreign-Born Population of the United States: 1850 to 1990.* Working Paper 29 (Washington, D.C.: U.S. Bureau of the Census, 1999).

Table 5. Age Distribution and Sex Ratios of the Foreign-born Population: 1870–1990

Year	Total	Age distribution (%)				Median age(years)	Sex ratio*
		Under 15	15 to 44	45 to 64	65 and over		
1870	5,567,229	8.4	65.8	21.8	4.0	34.6	117.4
1880	6,679,943	6.5	58.6	28.8	6.1	38.3	119.1
1890	9,249,547	8.0	57.0	27.5	7.5	37.1	121.2
1900	10,341,276	5.0	58.0	27.8	9.2	38.5	119.5
1910	13,515,886	5.7	59.9	25.5	8.9	37.2	131.1
1920	13,920,692	4.0	56.4	29.9	9.7	40.0	122.9
1930	14,204,149	2.5	50.2	35.3	12.0	43.9	116.6
1940	11,594,896	0.7	33.4	47.8	18.0	51.0	111.8
1950	10,347,395	1.9	23.1	48.6	26.3	55.9	103.3
1960	9,738,091	5.2	24.7	37.5	32.6	57.2	95.6
1970	9,619,302	6.3	34.7	27.0	32.0	52.0	84.4
1980	14,079,906	8.8	48.4	21.6	21.2	39.9	87.8
1990	19,767,316	7.5	56.8	22.0	13.6	37.3	95.8

Note: *Males per 100 females.

Source: Campbell Gibson and Emily Lennon, *Historical Census Statistics on the Foreign-Born Population of the United States: 1850 to 1990.* Working Paper 29 (Washington, D.C.: U.S. Bureau of the Census, 1999).

made up 14 percent of the population, and the median age had dropped to thirty-seven. Although the foreign-born population has become increasingly youthful in the past few decades, it remains older than that of the United States as a whole: in 1990 the median age of the total population was thirty-three, with 13 percent sixty-five and over.

Historically, males have accounted for a disproportionate share of the immigrants to the United States, and this disparity has skewed the sex ratio of the foreign-born population. In the 1880 foreign-born population, for example, males outnumbered females 119 to 100. This sex ratio became even more skewed as southern and eastern European immigrants entered the country. Their sex ratios were among the most lopsided of any period, and by 1910 the sex ratio for the foreign-born population had increased to 131. While immigration dipped in the 1930s and early 1940s, for the first time women outnumbered men in the immigration flow, and for a few years after World War II, war brides entering the country made the immigrant stream even more disproportionately female. By 1950 the sex ratio of the total foreign-born population had dropped to 103, and by 1970 it had reached a low of 84, partly because of differences in the mortality rates of the sexes. The 1965 INA amendments, which made family reunification the main path of entry to the

United States, witnessed the continued, though reduced, dominance of the immigrant stream by women. In 1980 the sex ratio of the foreign-born population stood at 88, increasing to 96 in 1990.

Region and State of Residence

Table 6 provides census information on the foreign-born population's regional patterns of residence, as documented in censuses between 1850 and 1990. For the four major U.S. regions—the Northeast, Midwest, South, and West—population counts for the total and foreign-born populations are shown, as is the percentage of each region that is foreign-born.

Historically, the South has had the smallest proportion of foreign-born. It was just 3 percent in 1850 and declined for most of the early decades of the twentieth century, reaching a low of under 2 percent in 1940. In contrast, a large proportion of the population of the Northeast and West has been foreign-born. For example, in 1850 15 percent of the population of each of these regions was foreign-born. The absolute sizes of these foreign-born populations, of course, were quite different: in 1850 1.3 million people of foreign birth lived in the Northeast, compared with just 27,000 in the western states. The proportion of foreign-born increased dramatically in both regions in the following

Table 6. Number and Percentage of Foreign-born for U.S. Regions: 1850–1990

Year	Northeast			Midwest			South			West		
	Total population	Foreign-born	Foreign-born (%)	Total population	Foreign-born	Foreign-born (%)	Total population	Foreign-born	Foreign-born (%)	Total population	Foreign-born	Foreign-born (%)
1850	8,626,851	1,325,543	15.4	5,403,595	650,375	12.0	8,982,612	241,665	2.7	178,818	27,019	15.1
1860	10,594,268	2,023,905	19.1	9,096,716	1,543,358	17.0	11,133,361	392,432	3.5	618,976	179,002	28.9
1870	12,298,730	2,520,606	20.5	12,981,111	2,333,285	18.0	12,288,020	399,975	3.3	990,510	313,363	31.6
1880	14,507,407	2,814,520	19.4	17,364,111	2,916,829	16.8	16,516,568	448,532	2.7	1,767,697	500,062	28.3
1890	17,401,545	3,888,177	22.3	22,362,279	40,60,114	18.2	19,830,813	530,346	2.7	3,027,613	770,910	25.5
1900	21,046,695	4,762,796	22.6	26,333,004	4,158,474	15.8	24,523,527	573,685	2.3	40,91,349	846,321	20.7
1910	25,868,573	6,676,283	25.8	29,888,542	4,690,461	15.7	29,389,330	740,011	2.5	6,825,821	1,409,131	20.6
1920	29,662,053	6,846,363	23.1	34,019,792	4,607,794	13.5	33,125,803	868,354	2.6	8,902,972	1,598,181	18.0
1930	34,427,091	7,201,674	20.9	38,594,100	4,359,876	11.3	37,857,633	818,614	2.2	11,896,222	1,823,985	15.3
1940	35,976,777	6,102,546	17.0	40,143,332	3,358,966	8.4	41,665,901	639,788	1.5	13,883,265	1,493,596	10.8
1950	39,341,610	5,287,165	13.4	44,281,175	2,707,390	6.1	47,085,880	767,320	1.6	19,507,445	1,585,520	8.1
1960	44,681,702	4,574,743	10.2	51,623,773	2,276,959	4.4	54,963,470	962,920	1.8	28,056,726	1,923,521	6.9
1970	49,044,015	4,119,681	8.4	56,564,917	1,873,561	3.3	62,792,882	1,316,205	2.1	34,808,344	2,309,855	6.6
1980	49,135,283	4,505,923	9.2	58,865,670	2,114,190	3.6	75,372,362	2,894,757	3.8	43,172,490	4,565,036	10.6
1990	50,809,229	5,231,024	10.3	59,668,632	2,131,293	3.6	85,445,930	4,582,293	5.4	52,786,082	7,822,706	14.8

Source: Campbell Gibson and Emily Lennon, *Historical Census Statistics on the Foreign-Born Population of the United States: 1850 to 1990*. Working
Paper 29 (Washington, D.C.: U.S. Bureau of the Census, 1999).

decades. In the Northeast the huge flows from southern and eastern Europe boosted the foreign-born share to a high of 26 percent in 1910. In the West high levels of immigration, primarily recruited foreign workers, caused a dramatic increase in the proportion of foreign-born, which rose to 32 percent in 1870. Restricted Asian immigration precipitated a decline in the share of the foreign-born population in the following decades. Like the Northeast and West, the Midwest has historically had a high foreign-born component. The proportion of foreign-born in the population of the Midwest increased during the last decades of the nineteenth century—reaching a high of 18 percent in 1890—and largely fell in subsequent decades.

The drop-off in immigration in the 1930s and 1940s brought large decreases in the proportion of foreign-born. By 1970 the percentages of foreign-born in the Northeast (8 percent), Midwest (3 percent), and West (7 percent) had reached all-time lows. As immigration bounced back after the 1965 INA amendments, the proportion of foreign-born began to rise again. In 1990 the West had the highest percentage of foreign-born (15 percent), followed by the Northeast (10 percent), the South (5 percent), and the Midwest (4 percent).

The past 140 years of census data also show shifts in the geographic distribution of the foreign-born population, shifts that reflect changes in the settlement patterns of immigrants and in the distribution of the national population. In 1850 59 percent of the foreign-born population lived in the Northeast, 29 percent in the Midwest, 11 percent in the South, and just 1 percent in the West (see Figure 1). By 1920 the share of the foreign-born population living in the Northeast had declined to 49 percent, with both the Midwest and the West increasing their share of the population to 33 percent and 12 percent, respectively. Changes in immigrant sources brought about by the 1965 INA amendments—specifically, the rising number of immigrants from Asia and Mexico—have resulted in a dramatic redistribution of the foreign-born population. Asians settle disproportionately in the western states, and Mexicans primarily immigrate to those in the West and South. By 1990 the West had accounted for 40 percent of the foreign-born, and the Northeast's share had fallen to 27 percent. Nearly one-quarter (23 percent) of the foreign-born population lived in the South, a fraction comparable to that observed in the Northeast, while 11 percent lived in the Midwest.

These shifts in the regional distribution of the foreign-born population are further illustrated by data on the states with the largest share of that population in 1850, 1920, and 1990 (see Figure 2). In 1850 most of

Figure 1. Foreign-born Population by Region of Residence: 1850, 1920, and 1990

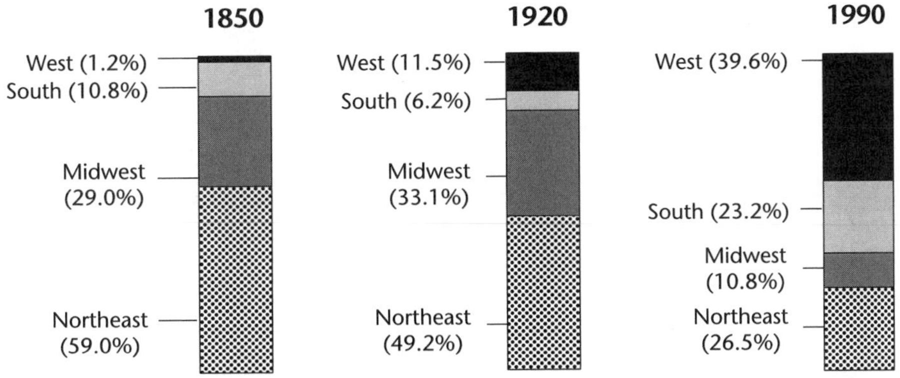

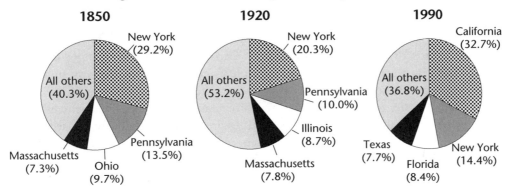

Source: Campbell Gibson and Emily Lennon, *Historical Census Statistics on the Foreign-born Population of the United States: 1850 to 1990*, Working Paper 29 (Washington, D.C.: U.S. Bureau of the Census, 1999).

Figure 2. States with the Highest Share of the Foreign-born Population: 1850, 1920, and 1990

Source: Campbell Gibson and Emily Lennon, *Historical Census Statistics on the Foreign-born Population of the United States: 1850 to 1990*, Working Paper 29 (Washington, D.C.: U.S. Bureau of the Census, 1999).

the foreign-born population lived in the Northeast and Midwest: 29 percent in New York, 14 percent in Pennsylvania, 10 percent in Ohio, and 7 percent in Massachusetts. In 1920 the four top states included New York, with one-fifth of the foreign-born population, as well as Pennsylvania and Massachusetts. Illinois (9 percent) also was among the top states, reflecting the importance of Chicago to immigration settlement. In 1990 the list was remarkably different. Although New York remained on the list, its share of the foreign-born population had dropped to 14 percent, while nearly one-third lived in California. The increasing presence of immigrants in the South pushed Florida and Texas into the list of top four states, both with about 8 percent of the foreign-born population.

See also *Center of population.*

■ Arun Peter Lobo and Ellen Percy Kraly

Bibliography

Gibson, Campbell, and Emily Lennon. *Historical Census Statistics on the Foreign-Born Population of the United States: 1850 to 1990.* Working Paper 29. Washington, D.C.: U.S. Bureau of the Census, 1999.

Lobo, Arun Peter, and Joseph J. Salvo. "Changing U.S. Immigration Law and the Occupational Selectivity of Asian Immigrants." *International Migration Review* 32, no. 3 (1998): 737-760.

Lobo, Arun Peter, and Joseph J. Salvo. "Resurgent Irish Immigration to the U.S. in the 1980s and Early 1990s: A Sociodemographic Profile." *International Migration* 36, no. 2 (1998): 257-280.

Warren, Robert, and Ellen Percy Kraly. *The Elusive Exodus: Emigration from the United States.* Population Trends in Public Policy 8. Washington, D.C.: Population Reference Bureau, 1985.

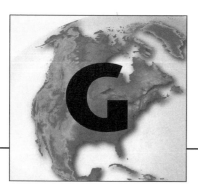

Genealogy

The census generates records of great genealogical value by attaching names to its records of the population. Each census provides a snapshot of one's ancestors who lived in the United States on the census day. Taken collectively, census records allow the researcher to trace family movements across the country and to piece together many aspects of individual lives that may otherwise have escaped the public record.

Genealogical research depends on the survival of the original census schedules. Also called returns, these are the questionnaires, listing individuals by name, that were filled out by census-takers. The vast majority of the census schedules from 1790 to the present have survived, either in their original form or on microfilm. Major exceptions are several states' records from 1790 (including Virginia, which was then the most populous state); all New Jersey records prior to 1840; and the 1890 census, which was almost completely destroyed by fire in 1921. In general, the earliest census records for a territory or state are the most likely to be missing.

The National Archives serves as repository for the census schedules and is responsible for microfilming them for research use. Entire sets of census microfilms are available to researchers at the Archives and its branches, as well as at major genealogical research libraries. State libraries typically have census microfilms for their own and adjoining states, as do many large public libraries. In addition, microfilms can be accessed via interlibrary loan or may be purchased, either directly from the Archives or from commercial vendors. Users can print individual pages from microfilm.

Census schedules are arranged by local jurisdiction, first by county or city, then by smaller civil division (sometimes the divisions were devised by the Census Bureau and its predecessor agencies). Where populations are small, particularly in early censuses, several counties may be grouped together on a single roll of microfilm. Within the schedule, records are arranged by household, usually in the order visited by the census-taker. In occasional instances households are listed alphabetically.

The arrangement of census schedules creates a need for indexes, so that researchers can quickly pinpoint households by county, city, and manuscript page. Print indexes have been published commercially for all states through 1850 and for many states in subsequent years. These books are usually available in any library or archive that owns census microfilms. A different type of index, the Soundex, covers the census schedules for 1880, 1900, 1910, and 1920. Devised in the 1930s to help federal agencies locate households by the sound instead of the spelling of surnames, the Soundex creates an alphanumeric code based on four key letters in each surname. Like the schedules themselves, the Soundex was handwritten and is most accessible to researchers via microfilm.

Some census schedules have been transcribed and published in book form. Most significantly, all surviving census schedules from 1790 were published by the National Archives beginning in 1907; these volumes have been reprinted often. Some census indexes for the period 1800–1840 transcribe the tallies of people by sex and age in each household. Many transcriptions of the schedules for specific counties have been produced by individuals, historical societies, and genealogical publishers, with a heavy emphasis on 1850. The quality, price, and long-term availability of these transcriptions vary widely. Alternatively, books for some census schedules provide images of each microfilm page.

An important restriction on genealogical use of the census is that schedules do not become publicly available until seventy-two years after an enumeration. This is intended to guard the privacy of living persons for the duration of an average lifetime.

What Kinds of Genealogical Data Are Present in the Census?

The census has asked increasingly detailed questions over time, so that more recent census schedules tend to offer more information for genealogists.

From 1790 to 1840, the census tracked names for heads of household only. Hence women and free African Americans are named in the schedule only if they headed a household. Other free persons are listed only by the number of each sex in each age group; these age categories became narrower by 1830 and 1840. Slaves were also tallied, by number and sex, on the main schedule.

Beginning with 1850, all whites and free African Americans in each household are listed by name, with their age and state or country of birth. Other questions, from 1850 on, identify persons who attended school within the previous year, adults who could not read or write, and the profession and value of real estate for each individual (often blank for all but heads of household). In 1850 and 1860, slaves were enumerated on a separate schedule, where they are listed only by sex and age under their owner's name. Hence only with the 1870 census are names listed of all persons from all racial groups—the categories then being white, black, mulatto, Chinese, and Indian.

From 1850 on, the censuses also began to include vital records for individuals and more details about family relationships. As a result, indicators are found of births within the year prior to the census day (1870–1880); marriages within the year (1850–1880); number of years married (1900–1910); number of children born to each woman and number still living (1900–1910); foreign-born parents (1870); and parents' birthplaces (1880–1920). In 1900 only, the census includes the month and year of birth for each person. Deaths within the year were recorded in separate "mortality" schedules from 1850 to 1880 and for 1885. An important caveat to note is that prior to 1880 the census did not ask for each person's relationship to the head of household.

How Does the Census Compare with Other Sources of Genealogical Data?

The census has greatest genealogical value when used in conjunction with other records, such as tax lists, wills, deeds, marriage registers, family Bibles, and other years of the census itself. Even using the pre-1850 schedules one can track family movements and gather clues to ages and number of children. Examining schedules instead of relying on indexes lets one identify a household's neighbors, some of whom may be part of an extended family.

The census records have many potential sources of error. Census-takers could mishear or misspell information, and they might overlook or double-count individuals and neighborhoods. Occasionally a census-taker recorded more or less information than was required. A household's information was typically gathered from one person, who might substitute guesswork for ages and birthplaces—or choose to lie. Rarely should a census record be discounted by a genealogist; but rarely should it be taken as fully accurate if not corroborated by other records.

Any errors in the schedules themselves are compounded by transcriptions, including indexes. A compiler may misread handwriting, make typographical errors, or overlook some of the data. Researchers should refer to the actual schedules whenever possible. Anything but the original handwriting is a step farther removed from one's ancestors.

In cases where the census does not survive, or is somehow insufficient, alternative records of comparable value may exist. Tax lists have been published as substitutes for lost censuses, notably Virginia/West Virginia in 1790 and Kentucky in 1790 and 1800. The lists generally include all taxpayers, not just the heads of household who appear in the census. Where they survive, lists cover each year, allowing one to pinpoint the date a person died or left the community. In some states, they also predate the 1790 census. Tax lists are typically found in state archives and, like the census, are accessible via microfilm. Some have been published or indexed.

How Is New Technology Changing the Use of Census Schedules?

New electronic media make indexes and transcriptions of census records easier to search and more cost-effective to disseminate, via the Internet and CD-ROMs. A CD-ROM, for example, can include transcriptions of schedules for an entire state in a census year—the equivalent, for a year such as 1850, of dozens of rolls of microfilm. The Internet, in particular, has spurred volunteer efforts on the part of genealogists, notably the USGenWeb Census Project, which aims to transcribe all federal census schedules and makes data available for free. More commonly, however, census indexes are included with other genealogical databases in fee-based Web sites. New technology poses at least one danger: older print sources might be scanned into electronic form, which is a far less accurate method than traditional keying if records are not carefully proofread.

Commercial vendors have also begun to digitize the photographic images of the schedules themselves. Whereas most electronic products and Web sites still rely on transcriptions, this new method of census imaging allows users to view the original record on a computer screen and transcribe it for themselves. The computer interface also eases the navigation among the various pages of the record and makes the printing of images far less cumbersome than from microfilm machines. Although this technology is a commercial development, it presents the greatest advance for genealogists since microfilm itself—if it can be made as broadly available via libraries and archives.

■ Paul McClure

Bibliography

Greenwood, Val D. *The Researcher's Guide to American Genealogy*, 2nd ed. Baltimore: Genealogical Publishing Co., 1990.

Luebking, Sandra H., ed. *The Source: A Guidebook of American Genealogy*. Orem, Utah: Ancestry, Inc., 1997.

National Archives and Records Administration. *National Archives Microfilm Resources for Research: A Comprehensive Catalog*. Washington, D.C.: U.S. Government Printing Office, 1996.

Geography: distribution of the population

Analyzing the spatial distribution of population entails identifying *where* people live so as to gain insight into *how* they live. Coordinates of latitude and longitude for each dwelling unit show exactly where people live, but making sense of such information requires condensing it into meaningful categories. Concerns over urban and rural shares of the population and the size, shape, and form of settlements have been recurring issues.

When the first census was conducted in 1790, the U.S. population was concentrated along the Atlantic coast. About 5 percent of the population was urban (lived in cities and towns with twenty-five hundred or more people), and the biggest city was New York City, home to 33,131 people. As the twentieth century drew to a close, the urban share of the total population was close to 80 percent, and New York City (in expanded boundaries) was home to nearly 7.5 million people. Like other parts of the Northeast, New York City's growth was strongly influenced by immigration, especially the surges early and late in the twentieth century, and by migration from Puerto Rico, especially after World War II.

1890–1929

One hundred years after the first census was conducted, the superintendent of the census declared that the frontier could no longer be detected by the traditional measure: a line of counties with fewer than two people per square mile. To many, this change in population geography marked a milestone—a new era of American history, with new forces shaping American values, character, and institutions.

Low-density counties and small towns continued to grow rapidly early in the twentieth century. Big cities, especially in the Northeast and Midwest, were also growing as their expanding factories attracted the "new immigrants," whose southern and eastern European origins distinguished them from earlier immigrants from northern and western Europe. Improved transportation and communication enabled some cities to become service centers for expanding "hinterlands." In 1890 Chicago replaced Philadelphia as America's "second city," a moniker that Chicago clung to even after it lost this position to Los Angeles in 1990.

Immigration to the Northeast and Midwest in the late nineteenth and early twentieth centuries supplied needed labor and may have slowed movement of African Americans from the South, a region then dependent on low-wage labor to harvest crops. After World War II, agricultural mechanization and other changes in the South resulted in many African Americans moving to other regions just as demand for factory labor was falling in the North.

In 1920 a second major milestone was passed: The census showed the United States to be more urban than rural. Moreover, some large cities presented a stark image of unforeseen density and greater heterogeneity in the melting pot. Partly for these reasons, Congress was reluctant to use the 1920 census for its central purpose, the reapportionment of the House of Representatives. Reapportionment remained a contentious issue throughout the decade and did not occur until the 1930 census.

1930–2000

Early in the twentieth century some cities began to spill over their boundaries as new technology, in the form of streetcars and automobiles, encouraged the growth of suburbs. The Great Depression of the 1930s slowed suburbanization and metropolitanization in much of the country and changed how the migrants who redistribute population are seen. Past views of migrants as heroic pioneers or individuals taking advantage of new opportunities gave way to images of people forced off the land by conditions in the Dust Bowl and seeking too few jobs in California and the West. In the end, most of the migrants stayed in the West, many finding defense-related jobs during World War II.

After World War II, policies to foster economic growth seemed necessary to keep the country from slipping back into depression. Investing in roads might encourage automobile production and new housing construction on open land just beyond city boundaries. Such public investment appealed to veterans who needed housing for the baby boom they were creating. Programs that seemed to favor suburban growth also facilitated the exodus of whites from cities, just as growing numbers of African Americans were arriving from the rural South. The causes and consequences of suburbanization and segregation of the races continue to be key issues in population geography.

The new settlement pattern—cities surrounded by suburban rings—renewed efforts made earlier in the twentieth century to identify metropolitan areas in a standard way throughout the country. When metropolitan-area standards were implemented after the 1950 census, another milestone was evident in the United States: a majority of the population lived in metropolitan areas of fifty thousand or more people. The 1970 census recorded still another milestone: Suburbanites outnumbered residents of central cities. Cities and suburbs were growing apart, as cities became increasingly poor and home to a rising share of the nation's older housing and minority populations.

In the 1950s and 1960s many core cities that had earlier boomed as their factories grew started to lose population rapidly, and by the 1970s many had lost one-half of their peak population (usually reached around World War II). By now, the metaphor for many metropolitan areas was a doughnut—a core losing population and a suburban fringe growing rapidly. In many areas, the hole in the doughnut grew larger as older, inner suburbs started to lose population.

The 1970s witnessed a new twist in population redistribution: a shift of growth toward smaller cities, towns, and even unincorporated territory (but not farms) outside metropolitan areas. This "rural renaissance" faded in the 1980s but returned in the mid-1990s as a more muted "rural rebound." By the close of the twentieth century, overall population redistribution was seen to be an increasingly dynamic process, subject to new, external forces that included the effects of trade agreements, globalization of production processes, and technological changes that alter workplace-residence relationships. The most consistent redistributive trend since World War II has been the growth of population on the fringes of metropolitan areas, creating "edge cities" where urban sprawls into rural and metropolitan areas fuse.

See also *Tabulation geography*.

■ Larry Long

Bibliography

Frey, William H. "The New Geography of Population Shifts." In Reynolds Farley, ed., *State of the Union: America in the 1990s*, pp. 271–336. New York: Russell Sage Foundation, 1995.

Nucci, Alfred, and Larry Long. "Spatial and Demographic Dynamics of Metropolitan and Nonmetropolitan Territory in the United States." *International Journal of Population Geography* 1 (1995): 165–181.

Plane, David, and Peter Rogerson. *The Geographical Analysis of Population*. New York: John Wiley and Sons, 1994.

Grassroots groups

Grassroots groups and institutions are playing increasingly significant roles in shaping the content and operations of decennial censuses—raising awareness of group-specific interests, needs, and opportunities as well as promoting and mobilizing locally for the count. By their very nature, increased numbers, and stake in the outcomes, though, they also have stepped up the intensity of the demands, issues, and debates associated with the census.

For all of the national planning and processing that goes into the decennial census, its success still hangs on the prospect that, locally, people will be found, respond, and become part of the official count and data bank. The ease and effectiveness with which that has happened in recent censuses, especially given the increasingly varied and hard-to-reach populations in the United States, depended upon many factors.

Particularly since the 1970 census and with growing frequency and urgency heading into the 2000 count, the message from advocacy and other groups to the Bureau of the Census has been that effective planning and working relationships with community organizations and engagement of local groups in the enumeration process are critical to a successful count. Ignore or underuse this infrastructure familiar with the people, languages, and neighborhoods, they argue, and the potential for inaccuracy, mistrust, and undercounts increases. The message from the groups to their constituencies has been that their political representation, civil rights, and share of population-dependent government dollars weigh in the balance. If members are not counted, the loss is substantial.

Thousands of such groups exist across the country, defined not only by geographic and political boundaries, but also by shared issues, interests, loyalties, and characteristics—race, nativity, age, gender, socioeconomic status, disability, veteran status, and others. All of these have come to factor in one way or another into the conduct and applications of the decennial census.

The groups range in size and level of influence from "true" grassroots, citizen-based organizations and small political and governmental units to larger "conglomerates," the high-profile institutions with a broader, often national, reach that implement and thrive through their local affiliates and chapters. Their ability to speak with authority on the national platform (in the case of the census, in congressional hearings and on national advisory committees) comes in part because of the significant need they can identify and the numbers they can muster.

The growing savvy and tenacity of these grassroots groups and their national advocates have made them formidable supporters and defiers of proposals and policies regarding the content, operations, and applications of recent censuses, and they have brought a new dynamic into the decennial planning. However, the same qualities that give them an edge in advising on and tending to local details of census preparations, promotion, and operations also promote narrower perspectives, making national-level compromise among their competing interests much trickier. Moreover, their effective, face-to-face, quick-response manner of moving through tasks runs against the grain of the bureaucratic framework that gives order to the massive census operations.

Growing Relationship between Grassroots Groups and the Census Bureau

The New Deal, post–World War II, and Great Society programs—reliant on decennial data for allocations and implementation—helped to fuel interest in and demands on the census. The train of events from revenue sharing, the dramatic demographic changes of the 1980s, the census undercounts, and the rekindling of "decentralization" as the way to attend to the "people's business" fired up community-based organizations, minority organizations, and national and regional coalitions of these groups. Organizational representatives were provided several occasions to vocalize group concerns and enumerate the missed opportunities and missteps in the counts of 1970, 1980, and 1990.

Congressional testimony presented in hearings on the censuses of the past thirty years repeated many of the same themes—the traditional approach to counting the population was not in sync with the growth and transformation of society; the decennial was not employing methods that would reach the people who were the hardest to enumerate; effective systems were not in place to work with the smaller units of government that could serve as resources; and ethnic and other civic organizations were not effectively utilized to ensure that enumerators spoke the languages of the residents in the neighborhoods.

In response to critiques about the extent of its reach

into localities, the Bureau of the Census cited the enormity of census awareness programs involving community-based organizations and advocacy groups in supporting the census and encouraging member and client participation—more than fifty thousand organizations as part of the census effort in 1990 alone.

But grassroots organizations and national confederations of these organizations pointed out that an effective reach called for a deeper understanding of the social and political infrastructures in place within communities, of what it takes to connect with specific populations, and of how to fashion productive relationships.

Cities that had appealed to a variety of community organizations and other grassroots groupings, for example, had more successful census count campaigns, according to municipal leagues. They cited, in particular, the role of neighborhood associations, increasing in number and likely to be even more influential in future censuses.

Minority community organizations, too, argued many racial and ethnic advocacy groups, were uniquely situated to promote their constituents' participation because of their community base and the perception that they would focus on important group issues. With this credibility, the groups would be better able to convince their communities that the census was a legitimate government effort to gather data and that confidentiality would be maintained. At the same time, the grassroots organizations could provide direct assistance on census operations—helping to answer constituent questions, distributing materials in appropriate languages, and recommending techniques that might elicit stronger response rates.

Other groups and networks cited the benefits of solidifying long-term relationships and trust between the Bureau of the Census and communities, arguing that census outreach to the grassroots level should be ongoing, not comprised of isolated, independent campaign activities taking place in the years just prior to the count. To have the grassroots fully engaged in the count, they noted, interactions between the Bureau of the Census and the communities should be continuous and deal with many aspects of census outreach and operations—from the policies and courtesies associated with retaining census workers and enumerators locally to the development of census questionnaires that reflect a sensitivity to and understanding of the varied populations and their circumstances.

Over the years, many national advocacy groups with grassroots cores or otherwise strong links to community-based organizations have moved out in front on the issues of census outreach and operations and of promoting grassroots opportunities for improving awareness and, ultimately, the count itself.

After the 1990 census experience, the National Association for the Advancement of Colored People, which through its network of state and local affiliates had informally engaged in joint efforts with the Bureau of the Census since the 1970s, coupled an offer of assistance with its recommendation that the Bureau's National Services Program mount an extensive campaign to identify and engage a range of national- and community-based public or private organizations. These organizations provide direct assistance not only to ethnic and racial minorities but also to the homeless, disabled, documented and undocumented aliens, public assistance recipients, and other demographic groups.

The Mexican American Legal and Defense Education Fund, which also had partnered with the bureau and conducted census awareness campaigns since the 1970 census, announced plans to expand those efforts going into the 2000 census, seeking to reach about three million parents through schools and churches and three million young adults through community organizations, youth centers, sporting events, and concerts.

Active, inclusive representation on the census advisory committees for 2000 from these and other grassroots-dependent organizations as varied as the American Legion, American Civil Liberties Union, American-Arab Anti-Discrimination Committee, Association of MultiEthnic Americans, League of United Latin American Citizens, National Association of Community Action Agencies, National Association of Towns and Townships, National Association of Counties, National Coalition for the Homeless, National Congress of American Indians, National Federation of Filipino-American Associations, National League of Cities, National Urban League, and many others once again turned attention to the most effective methods for reaching the hardest-to-enumerate populations and forging solid working relationships with the bureau.

The Census 2000 plan and, particularly, the Partnership Program reflected the sense that a solid foundation for broad-based participation in and implementation of the decennial had to be built at the grassroots level. By census day 2000, partnership agreements had been finalized between the Bureau of the Census and more than 260 national organizations, many of which reach deeply into communities via local affiliations.

Grassroots Groups Using the Decennial Data

Although the spotlight has been on the roles they have played or could play in planning, in education and awareness programs, and in the enumeration process, grassroots groups and many of their national advocates have been highly visible in the debates over census content and the uses of decennial data to further their causes.

In just one example of congressional testimony on the questions that would be included in the 2000 census, a representative of a coalition of ethnic organizations argued that it was imperative for the groups, run mostly by volunteers, to be able to know who or where their communities are, how to mobilize them, and, in this instance, how to help them in the process of becoming citizens or increasingly involved in civic life. The ancestry data generated in the census were invaluable to their efforts.

Following the 1990 count, the Bureau of the Census initiated a program to get the decennial data and data from other programs back into the minority communities. The Census Information Center Program, a cooperative effort between the bureau and five national nonprofit organizations representing the interests of racial and ethnic communities, makes census information and data available to the participating organizations for analysis and policy planning and further dissemination through a network of regional and local affiliates. Among the participants are the Asian and Pacific Islander Center for Census Information and Services, IndianNet Information Center, National Council of La Raza, National Urban League, William C. Velazquez Institute, and dozens of affiliate agencies, centers, and projects.

See also *Local involvement in census taking; Not-for-profit organizations; State and local governments: legislatures.*

■ Deborah A. Gona

Bibliography

Ehrenhalt, Alan. *Democracy in the Mirror: Politics, Reform, and Reality in Grassroots America.* Washington, D.C.: Congressional Quarterly, 1998.

U.S. Congress. House. Committee on Government Operations and Committee on Post Office and Civil Service. *Problems with the 1980 Census Count. Joint Hearing before the Commerce, Consumer, and Monetary Affairs Subcommittee of the Committee on Government Operations and the Census and Population Subcommittee of the Committee on Post Office and Civil Service.* 96th Cong., 2nd sess., July 31, 1980.

U.S. Congress. House. Committee on Government Reform and Oversight. *Oversight of the 2000 Census: Reviewing the Long and Short Form Questionnaires. Hearing before the Subcommittee on the Census of the Committee on Government Reform and Oversight.* 105th Cong., 2nd sess., May 21, 1998. Serial 105-180.

U.S. Congress. House. Committee on Government Reform and Oversight. *Oversight of the 2000 Census: Revisiting the 1990 Census. Hearing before the Subcommittee on the Census of the Committee on Government Reform and Oversight.* 105th Cong., 2nd sess., May 5, 1998. Serial 105-159.

U.S. Congress. House. Committee on Post Office and Civil Service. *The Role of Community and Advocacy Organizations during the 1990 Census and in Planning for the 2000 Census. Hearings before the Subcommittee on Census and Population of the Committee on Post Office and Civil Service.* 102nd Cong., 1st sess., October 29 and 20, 1991. Serial 102-32.

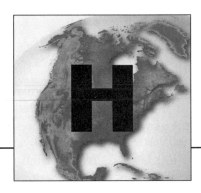

Hispanic population

In 1998 about 44 percent of all U.S. Hispanics were immigrants. The Hispanic population numbers about 30.4 million and is growing rapidly. It grew by more than 35 percent between 1990 and 1998 (compared with an 8 percent increase for the total U.S. population). Half of the Hispanic population growth from 1980 to 1990 was due to immigration and half to Hispanic births in the United States. Immigration remains a significant source of Hispanic population growth in the early twenty-first century.

By all projections the Hispanic population will continue to grow much faster than the U.S. population well into this century. By 2050 Hispanics will compose about 25 percent of the U.S. population. In 1998 school-age Hispanics outnumbered school-age African Americans, and by 2005 the total Hispanic population will exceed the total population of African Americans. In sharp contrast to the Hispanic population, the white non-Hispanic group is projected to grow slowly for the next fifty years.

Population Distribution

Hispanics, like the group "Asian & Other Races," is an aggregation of several distinct national origin subgroups: Central and South American, Cuban, Mexican, Puerto Rican, and other Hispanics. The Mexican-origin population is by far the largest, constituting 63 percent of the total Hispanic population in 1997. Hispanics with origins in Central or South America accounted for more than 14 percent of the Hispanics living in the fifty states, Puerto Ricans for almost 11 percent, other Hispanics for more than 7 percent, and Cuban-origin Hispanics for little more than 4 percent.

The 2000 census will likely reveal two new and striking aspects of Hispanic population growth. First, the *number* of Hispanics has increased in metropolitan areas that previously had few Hispanics. For example, in 1998 it was estimated that Georgia had more than 200,000 Hispanic residents, almost twice as many as it had in 1990. Second, the *proportion* of Hispanics in small rural towns, especially those associated with agricultural and food processing operations, has risen. In Siler City, North Carolina, the 1990 census found that 184 Hispanics composed 4 percent of the town's population. In 1998, after a rapid increase in hog farming, half of Siler City's residents were Hispanics.

Despite the trend towards geographic dispersion, much of the Hispanic population is concentrated in just a few states. More than a third of the nation's Hispanics live in California. That state and Texas are home to more than half of the national Hispanic population.

Hispanics are more highly urbanized than non-Hispanics. In 1990 two-thirds of all U.S. Hispanics lived in one of sixteen metropolitan areas: Chicago-Gary; Dallas-Fort Worth; Denver-Boulder; El Paso; Fresno; Houston-Galveston; Los Angeles-Anaheim-Riverside; McAllen-Edinburg-Mission; Miami-Ft. Lauderdale; New York-New Jersey; Philadelphia-Wilmington-Trenton; Phoenix; San Antonio; San Diego; San Francisco-Oakland-San José; and Washington, D.C.

The high concentration of Hispanics in a few states and cities facilitates both population research and policy making. The focus and geographic scope of some projects or policies may be appropriately limited to states or cities with high concentrations of Hispanics.

Age Distribution

Hispanics are a relatively young population. More than a third are under age eighteen, compared with about a quarter of non-Hispanics. Data from the 1997 Current Population Survey (CPS) show that Hispanics have much younger age distributions (median age of twenty-six) than do non-Hispanics (median age of almost thirty-six). The data also highlight the age differences among Hispanic subgroups. For example, whereas the median age of Mexican-origin Hispanics is twenty-four, it is almost 41 for Cuban-origin Hispanics.

Population researchers believe that Hispanics will make up a large part of the young population in the near future. They base their conclusion on two recent trends. First, many Hispanic adults are relatively young and have relatively more child-bearing years ahead of them than do members of other groups with older median ages. Second, Hispanic fertility has decreased but is still high compared with that of most other groups in the United States.

Employment and Earnings

Although the labor force participation rate (calculated for males sixteen years and over) is higher for Hispanics than for non-Hispanics (79 percent and 73 percent, respectively), unemployment rates for Hispanics are considerably higher than those for non-Hispanics (9.2 percent and 5.2 percent). Median earnings are considerably lower for Hispanic males and females ($16,284 and $11,830, respectively) than they are for non-Hispanic males and females ($26,943 and $16,459). Among Hispanics, Mexican-origin males and females have the lowest median earnings, while Cuban males and females have the highest.

Poverty Level

On poverty measurements, Hispanics fare much worse than non-Hispanics. About three in ten Hispanics live below the poverty level, compared with just a little more than one out of ten non-Hispanics. Further, more than four in ten Hispanics under age eighteen live below the poverty line. Among Hispanic groups, Puerto Ricans and those of Mexican origin have the highest percentage of people living in poverty, while Cubans have the lowest.

Families

The demise of the traditional family—a married father and mother with one or more children—has been widely reported among the general population. Fewer people marry and have children today than in the past. However, Hispanics are more likely to live in a family household (that is, to live with relatives) than are non-Hispanics. Moreover, thirty-eight percent of Hispanic households are traditional families consisting of a married couple living with their own children under age eighteen. In comparision, only twenty-six percent of all households are traditional families. Also more prevalent among Hispanics than non-Hispanics are female-headed families. Twenty-two percent of Hispanic families fall into this category, as opposed to 18 percent of all families. Within Hispanic subgroups, 39 percent of Puerto Rican families are led by females, compared with 17 percent of Cuban-origin families.

Immigration

Immigration has long been at the top of the nation's agenda, and many of the most strongly expressed opinions about immigration have opposed it. The number, variety, and visibility of immigrant groups in general and of immigrant Hispanics in particular have been increasing. Because immigration rates are up and expected to stay high, immigration will continue to shape the composition of Hispanic communities in the United States. Current laws and programs admit about 800,000 to 1,000,000 immigrants a year. This figure represents a 33 percent increase over the immigration numbers reported in the 1980s.

From 1970 to 1990 the Hispanic proportion of all immigrants counted in the census increased from 19 percent to 40 percent. Census counts include documented and undocumented immigrants as well as temporary residents of the United States. During this period the number of immigrants to the United States increased from 9.6 million to 19.8 million. In 1997 more immigrants listed Mexico as their birthplace than any other country. The Census Bureau and the Immigration and Naturalization Service estimated that undocumented residents of the United States totaled 5 million in 1996, with a margin of error of plus or minus 400,000. Hispanics accounted for more than two-thirds of that total.

Most undocumented immigrants come to the United States from Mexico to seek relatively well-paying jobs. Even though they take jobs that pay little by U.S. standards, immigrants can typically make at least ten times as much in the United States as in Mexico. The wages that immigrants send back to Mexico amount to several billion dollars every year. In Mexico these "migradollars" have a major positive impact on the Mexican economy. Recent research suggests that interest rate increases accelerate undocumented migration. When interest rates are high in Mexico, immigrants view a sojourn to the United States as an alternative means of financing purchases and investments.

See also *Immigration*.

■ Jorge Chapa

Hispanic/Latino ethnicity and identifiers

The census concept of Hispanic ethnicity and the various identifiers by which the conceptualization was made concrete have changed many times since the first crude effort in the 1930 census to conceptualize and identify Hispanics who were not immigrants or the children of immigrants. These changes reflect the substantial changes in the composition of this population that occurred during the twentieth century. They also reflect the increase in the size and status of the population and in the Census Bureau's and the nation's awareness and knowledge of this group. During the early part of the twentieth century, almost all of the population now identified as Hispanic were people of Mexican origin who were largely concentrated in a few southwestern states. In contrast, Census 2000 will report data on more than twenty categories of Hispanics who are to be found in increasingly large numbers in all fifty states. Because the composition of this population and its conceptualization have changed tremendously, this article uses the term *Hispanic* in its contemporary sense and notes how earlier identifiers and conceptualizations differed from the contemporary meaning.

1850–1930: Conflating Immigrants, Race, and National Origin

The census has counted the population by race since its inception and has used a nativity question to keep track of immigrants since 1850 and a parentage question to keep track of the children of immigrants from 1880 to 1970. Censuses from 1910 through 1970 (excluding 1950) included questions about the language that respondents spoke at home as a child, also known as their mother tongue. The mother tongue questions were typically coded and tabulated only for immigrants and the children of immigrants. Thus the enduring census concerns with race and immigration were not a fully appropriate precedent for enumerating Hispanics. The first significant population of Hispanics in the United States was found among the residents of Texas when it became a state in 1845. The lands annexed in 1848 as a result of the Mexican War added substantially to the total Hispanic population. The history of the Southwest shows that the descendants of the original Hispanic residents of the annexed areas and those of the Mexican nationals who continued to migrate there were typically relegated to a subordinate status in a largely segregated social world. As a result, the typical immigrant notion did not apply. The census concept of race did not fit well either. In varying degrees, the populations of Central and South America are largely *mestizos*—the result of the racial mixture of European colonizers and the indigenous residents. Motivated by the generally xenophobic concerns of the time, the 1930 census attempted to enumerate these Hispanics by using the concept of a Mexican race.

There were many serious problems with this approach. Many of these Hispanics were U.S. citizens and the U.S.-born children of U.S.-born parents. The Mexican identifier appropriately applies to citizens of Mexico. Additionally, many of these Hispanics did not want to be identified as members of a socially subordinate group commonly referred to as Mexicans, regardless of their nativity or how many generations their ancestors had resided in the United States. The preferred and polite term used as an alternative at the time was *Latin*. For example, consider the name of the organization known as LULAC, the League of Latin American Citizens, founded in Texas in 1929. The organization's name also emphasizes the U.S. citizenship of many Hispanics. Unfortunately, LULAC's name did not send its message as clearly as it could because *Latin American Citizens* can also be understood to refer to citizens of Latin America, a name used at least since the 1890s in the same sense it is today. One of the clear indications of the inadequacy of the Mexican race approach is that many people were identified as being of Mexican birth or parentage but not of Mexican race. This highlights another problem with the approach. This identifier depended on the judgment of the enumerators, which apparently was neither consistent nor always reliable. Finally and perhaps most important, being racially designated as Mexican excluded the possibility of being classified as white. At the time many rights and privileges, including the right to become a U.S. citizen, were explicitly available to whites only. Because of these problems and in response to protest and litigation, the Census Bureau dropped the use of the Mexican race identifier after 1930. This experience also set the precedent for the current practice of separating race and Hispanic ethnicity into two items on the census questionnaire.

1940–1970: Objective Identifiers and Post-enumeration Attribution

Another specific effort to identify and enumerate the Hispanic population was not made until the 1950 census. Puerto Ricans started to migrate to the United States in large numbers after World War II. Even though all Puerto Ricans were made U.S. citizens by the Jones Act passed in 1917, the 1950 census was the first to include Puerto Rico as a response to the place of birth question typically used to determine foreign places of birth or parentage.

Also for the first time in 1950, the last names of respondents in the five southwestern states that had originally been part of Mexico (Arizona, California, Colorado, New Mexico, and Texas) were also compared to a list of Spanish surnames. The main reason for restricting the use of the Spanish surname identifier to the Southwest points to one of the identifier's major limitations. Many Spanish surnames are also found among people whose ancestors were from European countries where one of the Latin-based Romance languages was spoken, such as Italy and Portugal. Given their migration and settlement history, people from these European countries were more likely to be found outside the Southwest, and Hispanics with Spanish surnames were more likely to be found in that region.

Even if all Hispanics did at one time have Spanish surnames at birth, intermarriage would tend to make this identifier less precise and useful because the marriage of a Spanish-surnamed woman to a non-Spanish-surnamed man would typically result in the woman using the man's surname as her family name. Any children of such a union would also typically be given the non-Spanish surname. The Hispanic mother and her partly Hispanic children would not be detected by the use of the Spanish surname list. The marriage of a Hispanic Spanish-surnamed man to a non-Hispanic woman would typically result in the woman being mistakenly identified as Hispanic; however, the children of this union would usually have the father's Spanish surname.

Despite these problems, a continuously improved Spanish surname list was used as a Hispanic identifier from 1950 to 1980. This same procedure was also used to identify Hispanics in research based on birth and death certificates and other records and files. One of the appealing aspects of the surname identifier derives from the fact that it could be used retrospectively on information collected without any other means of identifying Hispanics.

The 1970 census collected and analyzed six different Hispanic identifiers on two different long forms in an effort to determine how to best count the Hispanic population. One of the long forms was distributed to a 15 percent sample, the other to a 5 percent sample. The identifiers included country of foreign birth or parentage, Spanish language, Spanish mother tongue, Spanish surname, Spanish heritage, and, for the first time, self-identification. The number and diversity of Hispanic identifiers found in the 1970 census mirrors the growth in the size and diversity of the Hispanic population and the strength of the Census Bureau's urge to get a good grasp on this population. By this time, the exodus from Cuba had resulted in a large increase in the populations of Cubans; the number of Puerto Ricans living in the United States continued to grow; and the number of recent Mexican immigrants swelled—all on top of the growing number of U.S.-born children with Hispanic ancestry.

In 1970 the Spanish language and Spanish mother tongue variable were determined for all respondents in the 15 percent sample, including respondents who were U.S.-born children of U.S.-born parents. Spanish language was made a household rather than an individual attribute. The responses were tabulated so that all of the persons in a household in which either the head of the household or the spouse had spoken Spanish as a child were counted as having a Spanish language background.

Spanish heritage was a new composite identifier created during post-enumeration data processing with different operational definitions in different parts of the country. In the five southwestern states the identifier referred to the combination of people who either had a Spanish surname or had lived in a Spanish language household. In the three Middle Atlantic states of New York, New Jersey, and Pennsylvania, anyone who was born in Puerto Rico or who was of Puerto Rican parentage was deemed as being of Spanish heritage. Finally, in the rest of the states, the identifier was equated with the expanded concept of Spanish language.

1970–2000: Standardizing Subjective Self-identification as Spanish/Hispanic Origin

In the 1970 census, respondents in the 5 percent sample were asked, "Is this person of Spanish/Hispanic origin?" The possible responses were "Mexican," "Puerto Rican," "Cuban," Central or South American," "Other Spanish," and "No. None of these." The extensive analysis of all of the Spanish identifiers used in 1970 showed that this identifier was the best because it was the most consistent; it distinguished among Mexicans, Puerto Ricans, Cubans, and the like; and it worked for respondents who were neither foreign born nor of foreign parentage. The demographic advantages of this identifier coincided with political and legal considerations. In 1976, Congress passed the Roybal Resolution (P.L. 93-311), requiring the use of a self-identified Hispanic question on federal censuses and surveys. The use of this identifier was further promulgated in the Office of Management and Budget Directive 15, first released in 1977. However, Directive 15 permits the use of a combined race and Spanish origin question. The data collected from a combined question are significantly different than data collected using separate race and Hispanic questions. Self-identification has now become the accepted standard for determining Hispanic origins. Slightly modified and improved versions of the question have been part of the short form in the 1980, 1990, and 2000 censuses. One modification in these subsequent censuses was to make the "Mexican" origin response category more inclusive by changing it to "Mexican, Mexican American, Chicano."

Despite its advantages, this 1970 question had several problems. First, there was a large rate of nonresponse. Based on the analysis of other characteristics, many of the nonrespondents were non-Hispanics. In subsequent censuses, this problem was addressed by placing the negative response "No, not Spanish/Hispanic origin" first because it applied to most of the population. In 2000, nonresponse was addressed further by asking the Hispanic question before the race question. Testing showed that many non-Hispanics did not answer the Hispanic question when it was asked after the race question because they felt that their response to the race question also responded to the Hispanic question.

Another problem with the 1970 question was that many of the non-Hispanic residents of Alabama, Arkansas, Georgia, Mississippi, North Carolina, South Carolina, and Tennessee identified themselves as being of Central or South American origin because they were Americans (U.S. citizens) living in the southern or central part of the United States. Subsequent censuses dropped this specific response.

A third problem was that it was unclear who the "Other Spanish/Hispanic" respondents were. This problem has been solved in 1990 and 2000 by allowing those who identified themselves as "Other Hispanic" to write in a more specific group.

In order to reflect the growing popularity of the term *Latino*, all residents of the United States were asked in Census 2000 if they were "Spanish/Hispanic/Latino." Many writers claim that the census has always preferred to use objective rather than subjective measures. The history of the Hispanic identifiers that preceded self-identification can be seen as steps toward an objective measure. The fact that the best solution was the subjective Spanish/Hispanic/Latino identifier suggests that this identifier will become a central aspect of the census and of American society in a manner similar to the other major subjective census question—race.

See also *Census of Puerto Rico*.

■ Jorge Chapa

Bibliography

Anderson, Margo, and Stephen E. Fienberg. *Who Counts? The Politics of Census-Taking in Contemporary America.* New York: Russell Sage Foundation, 1999.

Bean, Frank, and Martha Tienda. *The Hispanic Population of the United States.* New York: Russell Sage Foundation, 1987.

del Pinal, Jorge. "Treatment and Counting of Latinos in the Census." In *The Latino Encyclopedia*, edited by R. Chabrash and R. Chabrash. New York: Marshall Cavendish, 1996.

del Pinal, Jorge, and Audrey Singer. "Generations of Diversity: Latinos in the United States." *Population Bulletin* 52 (October 1997).

Hayes-Bautista, David, and Jorge Chapa. 1987. "Latino Terminology: Conceptual Basis for Standardized Terminology." *Journal of the American Public Health Association* 77 (January 1987): 61–68.

Hernandez, Jose, Leo Estrada, and David Alivirez. "Census Data and the Problem of Conceptually Defining the Mexican American Population." *Social Science Quarterly* 53 (winter 1973): 671–687.

Siegel, Jacob S., and Jeffrey S. Passel. *Coverage of the Hispanic Population in the 1970 Census: A Methodological Analysis.* Current Population Reports. Special Studies, Series P-23, No. 82. Washington, D.C.: U.S. Government Printing Office, 1979.

Teller, Charles H., Jose Hernandez, Leo Estrada, and David Alivirez. *Cuantos Somos: A Demographic Study of the Mexican-American Population.* Monograph No. 2. Center for Mexican American Studies, The University of Texas at Austin, 1977.

Homelessness

See *Enumeration: special populations*.

Housing

Housing is complementary to population in the Decennial Census of Population and Housing. It is both the framework for collecting information about people and a subject of interest in its own right.

While a few items regarding housing were collected on censuses going back to 1890, the first official Census of Housing was conducted in 1940. During the Great Depression of the 1930s, new construction had virtually come to a halt, existing structures were deteriorating, and many families were living doubled-up. The poor conditions and need for corrective action were voiced by President Franklin D. Roosevelt when, in his second inaugural address in 1937, he said, "I see a third of the nation ill-housed."

The requirement to assess the condition of housing stock and to judge the effect of New Deal legislation led Congress to authorize the Census of Housing. The law stated, in part:

Be it enacted by the Senate and House of Representatives of the United States of America in Congress assembled; that to provide information concerning the number, characteristics (including utilities and equipment), and geographical distribution of dwelling structures and dwelling units in the United States, the Director of the Census shall take a census of housing in each State . . . at the same time, and as part of the population inquiry of the sixteenth decennial census.

A committee composed principally of federal government agency representatives developed a set of questions. This first Census of Housing laid a comprehensive foundation for the content of future censuses, and many of the same inquiries continued into the 2000 census. The 1940 questionnaire items may be classified into three broad groups. First, facilities and equipment items included toilet facilities, bathtub or shower, electric light, refrigeration, radio, heating equipment, and cooking fuel. Second, physical characteristics included size and type of structure, exterior material, need of major repairs, year built, rooms, and water supply. Third, financial characteristics items included value, rent, utility cost, mortgage status, present debt, mortgage payments, taxes included, interest rate, and type of mortgage holder.

Over time, some questions were dropped for lack of use or because the information could not be collected accurately, while others were added as the data needs of the nation changed. The content of the Census of Housing reflects changing technology and housing standards. For example, as electric lighting became nearly universal, including questions about it was no longer important. The item on television sets was added in 1950, but then dropped in 1980 when TV, too, had become nearly universal. Condominium, cooperative, and congregate housing categories were identified and tabulated as these alternative housing forms became more common and important to the understanding of the total housing stock.

A major procedural change, beginning in 1970, had a significant impact on the collection of housing data. Questionnaires delivered by mail and designed for self-enumeration could not capture information on housing condition. Other housing concepts had to be translated to question language and levels of detail that could be handled by the public. Applying the definition of a housing unit to individual structures became more dependent on how addresses were recorded on mailing lists and less subject to determination by an enumerator. In general, the impact of this change from field enumeration to mailout-mailback questionnaires was more serious for housing data items than for population items.

The mailout-mailback censuses of 1980 and 1990 included housing items on both the short (full count) and the long (sample count) forms. Respondents were asked whether they owned or rented their units (tenure), the monthly rent in rental units and the market value of the property in owner units, the type of structure, and other items. Questions on plumbing facilities were moved from the 1980 short form to the 1990 long form.

Another major change took place in 2000. Because of congressional pressure to shorten the questionnaire, housing content on the short form was reduced to one item: tenure (rent/own). This item remained because it is required for calculation of the census undercount. All other housing items were moved to the long-form questionnaire.

The Housing Unit Definition

The concept of "housing unit" has an official definition that has changed over the past several decades. Whatever official definition is in place for a particular census, however, its implementation in address list development makes a significant difference in the data that are later tabulated and published.

The Census Concept: 1960 to 2000. The housing unit concept, defining the units within which the population is enumerated, is crucial to the conduct of the census as well as to using the data it produces. The definition establishes the control unit for census sample surveys as well as the standard to be applied in local surveys and other research. At its heart, the definition establishes the criteria for what constitutes living together and living separately among people living under one roof, for what is housing and what is something else (now called group quarters), and for what is part of the housing stock and what is not.

The definition of a housing unit has changed in small but significant ways over time. In 1960 it was: "A housing unit is a group of rooms or a single room occupied as separate living quarters by a family. However, a housing unit might also be occupied by a group of unrelated persons living together or by a person living alone. Vacant living quarters intended for occupancy as separate living quarters are also housing units. A housing unit is separate when *its occupants did not live and eat with any other household and when there was either . . .* direct access from the outside or through a common hall, or a kitchen or cooking equipment for the exclusive use of the occupants" (italics added).

There were two exceptions. If the unit was occupied by five or more persons unrelated to the head of the household or to each other, the unit was a group quarters. Unusual structures such as trailers, boats, and railroad cars were not classified as living quarters unless they were occupied.

The 1960 census was conducted by trained enumerators who could observe the arrangement of housing units in structures. However, a number of questions designed to provide proper classification were included on the questionnaire, to ensure more accurate application of the definition to individual units than had been the case in 1950 and earlier. Thus, question H3 determined whether the unit was a regular structure or a trailer; H4 identified whether there was direct access from the outside or through a common hall, or only through another unit; and H5 recorded the presence of a kitchen or cooking equipment for exclusive use of the occupants.

The definition of a housing unit changed only slightly between 1960 and 1970. Units were required to have either direct access (defined as above) or "complete kitchen facilities," now defined as a sink with piped water, a range or cook stove, and a refrigerator, for the exclusive use of the occupants. Units that had only cooking equipment such as a hotplate and that lacked direct access were not separate housing units.

Two small, but significant, changes were made in the definition for the 1980 census. First, the population criterion for distinguishing between housing units and group quarters was raised from five (in addition to the householder or person in charge) to nine. This had the effect of defining slightly more housing units and meant that small group homes and communes (with between six and ten people) would be enumerated as housing units. Second, cooking equipment was removed from the definition. This meant that, to qualify as a separate housing unit, the living quarters had to have direct access from the outside or through a common hall.

The housing unit definition established in 1980 continued in force for 1990. The 1980 question on number of units at an address was dropped in favor of moving an item on units in structure to the 100 percent or short form. The item on direct access was also dropped. Thus, no questions on the 1990 census form checked directly for features that identify the criteria for the housing unit definition.

Three changes were made to the definition for the 2000 census. First, the concept of "eating separately" was effectively eliminated; no items on the questionnaire asked about eating arrangements. Second, the number of nonrelatives criterion for conversion of housing units to group quarters was eliminated, which meant that larger buildings used as group homes, fraternity houses, and the like may be enumerated as housing units. Third, vacant rooms in permanent resident hotels were no longer counted as housing units.

Restated, the 2000 definition was:

> a house, an apartment, a mobile home or trailer, a group of rooms or a single room occupied as separate living quarters or, if vacant, intended for occupancy as separate living quarters. Separate living quarters are those in which the occupants live separately from any other persons in the building and which have direct access from the outside or through a common hall. For vacant units, the criteria of separateness and direct access are applied to the intended occupants wherever possible. If that information cannot be obtained, the criteria are applied to the previous occupants.

Address List Development

Address list development is an integral part of the census, because the population is enumerated at the addresses, representing housing units, on the list. Before the widespread use of mailout-mailback procedures in 1970, enumerators created the address list in the process of conducting the census. From 1970 to 1990, most of the mailout-mailback address list (called the Master Address Register, or MAR) was constructed initially from commercial lists purchased from mailing companies. Several procedures served to update this list, including a block canvass conducted by census enumerators and an address check by postal carriers.

A completely new procedure was created for the 2000 census. In geographic areas with city-style addresses (house numbers, street names, apartment numbers), the Master Address File (MAF) was created through a combination of the 1990 census MAR and the U.S. Postal Service's Postal Delivery Sequence File. The Census Bureau plans to maintain the MAF on a continuing basis, so that it can serve as the sampling frame for the American Community Survey and will not need to be created anew for the 2010 census.

In geographic areas where residents receive their mail through post office boxes or rural route delivery, a different procedure is required. Most housing of this type has been listed by enumerators prior to the census. This permits census questionnaires to be delivered by address or by location or description at the time of the census, and then to be completed and mailed back in the same fashion as those mailed out in city-style areas.

In remote, difficult-to-reach areas, a procedure called list/enumerate requires that enumerators visit each housing unit, create the list, and complete the enumeration. This procedure, used for the entire census in 1960, applied to less than 1 percent of the nation's housing in 2000.

Special Places. A census procedure called special places enumeration is used to enumerate people who do not live in traditional housing units. Most of this population lives in a type of housing called group quarters, which includes college dormitories, nursing homes, prisons, homeless and domestic abuse shelters, and long-term care hospitals. Census staff visit these places in advance to identify their characteristics and return at census time to distribute questionnaire packets. Other persons, who have no place of residence (the homeless), are enumerated at street locations or at service facilities such as soup kitchens and medical clinics.

Data Tabulations

The housing unit definition is inherent in all tabulation of housing data in the census. Housing units are either occupied or vacant. People live either in households (occupied housing units) or in group quarters. Tabulations have not changed much over time; the changes in applications of the definition are the most important consideration.

The housing unit definition is crucial to all tabulation of data for housing units and households in the census. The changes over time are relatively minor, in that they affect a small part, less than 5 percent, of the nation's housing stock. Most occupied and vacant units are either single-family homes (attached or detached or manufactured housing in mobile home parks), apartment buildings being occupied as they were built, or small multiple structures with separate addresses for each unit. These units are easy to define and record properly in a listing of the inventory, whether the work is done by a commercial vendor, a unit of government, or census enumerators.

Some units are located in problem structures. Buildings that look like single-family homes but have two housing units are one example. Other problems occur where single-family homes are broken into apartments or where large stately apartment buildings are broken into smaller apartments. Rooming houses are another example of structure re-use, as are apartments built (perhaps illegally) in the basements or attics of single-family homes or in nonresidential buildings such as warehouses. Hotels being used as housing for permanent residents present another problem; this is the category of housing often called SRO, or single room occupancy.

When comparing the census count of the housing stock with a locally developed inventory, it is important to note the problems in structures of the type described above. Some people may not be missed, but the structure may be enumerated as a special place and classified as group quarters even though the units meet the technical definition of separate housing units. The census process simply finds it easier to enumerate the population in this manner.

Another problem concerns the application of the definition to determine whether or not a structure, and its vacant unit(s), is in or out of the housing stock. The traditional definition (found only in instructions to enumerators) says that a housing unit exists if it is "protected from the elements." In new housing construction, this means that there is a roof and windows to keep the rain out. In the case of deteriorating housing that is on its way out of the inventory, application of these criteria is less clear. In any event, the determination is made by an enumerator and, in census activities, may be subject to high variability.

The trend over time in the census has been to focus less on the types of problems outlined above, as they become a smaller proportion of the total housing stock. However, these units are disproportionately located in large cities with older housing stock and disproportionately occupied by households with low income. Failure to identify and enumerate these units properly is one component of the undercount.

The definition of a housing unit and the resulting census count of housing units may be used in many different local activities. Three important ones are (1) in creating a sampling frame in an area sampling design for local surveys, (2) in the building permit method for intercensal population estimates, and (3) in preparing for and conducting the local review process at the time of the decennial census. The problems described above must be understood and their impact must be incorporated into the design for these activities.

Housing Data Items

Some housing data items that are tabulated and published in census products come directly from the questions themselves, while others are new variables calculated from the response to two or more questions.

Tenure. Tenure is the formal name for the question that asks householders if their home is owned with a mortgage, owned free and clear, rented for cash rent, or occupied without payment of cash rent. It measures the concept called home ownership, one of the most important benchmarks of prosperity in American society. The item remained on the short form for 2000, permitting tabulation at the census block level. It is highly accurate and not subject to change from one census to another.

Condominiums and Cooperatives. Condominiums and cooperatives are types of home ownership that are variations from the usual "own free and clear" or "own with a mortgage" situations. Most homes are "fee simple," which means that the title to the property includes a defined parcel of land and all of its improvements (house, garage, barn, and so on). In a condominium, each owner owns his own living space (from the walls in) and a share of the common space defined in the condominium agreement. However, home values for condominiums can be considered in the same category as home values for "fee simple" properties.

Cooperatives are buildings or parcels of buildings that are entirely jointly owned. Each member, when purchasing his living quarters, is buying a share of the cooperative. Co-ops, as they are called, often require two payments. One goes to the cooperative association so that it can pay its mortgage and other bills. The other is for the lender from whom the co-op buyer borrowed the money required to purchase a share of the cooperative association. This payment reflects both the growing equity held by the cooperative and the appreciated market value of the property. Census items about value and rent costs do not work well for co-op occupant shareholders.

Type of Structure/Units in Structure.

Structure type refers to the kind of building in which a housing unit is located. The census cannot describe every variety of building, but instead concentrates on the major categories into which most housing may be classified. Most structure type categories in the census are defined by the number of units in the building. The questions that define type of structure have been on either the short form or the long form in different censuses.

Value and Contract Rent.

The value of owner-occupied single-family homes and contract rent for renter-occupied units are the only socioeconomic indicators available for housing. Collected as complete count items through 1990, they were tabulated at the census block level and for communities of every size. Combined with other housing cost items and household income, they provide important information on housing affordability. As with several other housing items, value and contract rent were on the long form in the 2000 census.

Value is the respondent's estimate of what the owner-occupied unit would bring in a sale on the open market (that is, the current market value). (The value of vacant for-sale homes was estimated by census enumerators.) The statement of value is not tested or confirmed in any way by independent estimates, such as a survey of homes sold or the value established by the tax assessor.

Contract rent information is based on a fact well known to the respondent and thus is reasonably reliable. The major problem comes in variability in the items included in rent (some of which are taken into account when considering gross rent). In small areas (such as census tracts or small communities) where the rental housing stock is a mixture of single-family and apartment units, some furnished and some not, a mean or median figure is not particularly useful. In these instances, cross-tabulations by structure type and calculations of gross rent provide a more accurate statement of housing cost.

With the growth in senior citizen population, a wider variety of housing options is being created to meet their needs. Congregate housing, collected and reported in 1990 for the first time, is one variation. Subsidized housing with group services is another; no census data are available to distinguish such units from ordinary apartments. The American Housing Survey provides greater detail on these alternative forms of housing tenure and more opportunity for analysis.

Contract rent is the amount of money a tenant, or renter, has agreed to pay the landlord each month. (For vacant units, it is the asking rent.) The rent may or may not include such items as water, heat and other utilities, or furniture.

Value and contract rent are relatively straightforward variables that have changed little in concept over time. The most important change is related to inflation; the range of estimated value and of contract rents has grown substantially over the thirty-year period in question. The value item is subject to significant error because the accuracy of the respondent's estimate of his home's value varies, based on many factors. Comparison with more objective statements of value, such as the tax assessor's valuation or a list of comparable sale prices, would usually yield large differences. Nonetheless, the value variable is useful because it provides a comparative measure across small geographic areas.

Analysis of median value at the census tract level, at least in one city (Detroit), has shown a consistent pattern when compared with assessors' figures. The rent item, which is much more accurate on its face, is combined with household income to determine the proportion of households that is paying a large share of their income for housing. This variable is used in determination of the use of federal housing funding for such activities as rent subsidies.

Year Built.

This question asks: "About when was this building first built?" Choices range from the year prior to and including the census, two five-year time periods in the preceding decade, and then decades (for example, 1960 to 1969, 1950 to 1959) back to the oldest building category: 1939 or earlier. This oldest building category has remained unchanged for several censuses.

The accuracy of year built responses varies widely. First, homeowners are much more likely to know the answer than are renters. Second, accuracy declines with the age of the house; that is, a response of "1999 or 2000" is much more likely to be correct than a response of "1940 to 1949." Thus, data users should not interpret these responses as absolute. Local property tax or building department records are much more likely to provide accurate data on the age of housing in the community. However, as with the value item, comparisons between different geographic areas will likely be reasonable.

Length of Residence. The length of time since a household moved into its current quarters is measured through a question that asks: "When did [you] move into this house, apartment or mobile home?" As with year built, several time-period choices are offered. The 2000 list ended with "1969 or earlier."

This item works well in one-person households and in others where all the members of the household moved in at the same time (other than children born later). It poses problems for the respondent, and becomes less accurate, when the two householders in a household moved in at different times. For example, a single woman lives in a house with her children; upon marriage, her husband moves in. His length of residence in the house is different from hers. From an analytic perspective, the response should reflect her move-in date, but often the husband's move-in date will have been reported. The aggregate distribution of this item provides useful information about small areas such as census tracts. It is of less interest at state and higher levels.

Rooms and Bedrooms. A question on rooms has been in the census since 1940, while a separate item on bedrooms has been asked since 1960. In the number of rooms item, respondents are instructed not to count bathrooms, porches, halls, foyers, balconies, or half-rooms. The result is a reasonable report of number of rooms, yielding data tabulations that closely match local records. The bedrooms item clearly tells respondents to count the number that they would list if the house or apartment were on the market for sale and rent. Again, this yields reasonable data.

Housing Facilities. The plumbing facilities questions are among the most controversial items on the census questionnaire, leading to accusations that "the census is in our bathroom" and the like. From 1940 to 1970, the items were broken up—separate questions asked about toilets, bathing facilities, and hot and cold piped water. In 1980 the questions were combined into a single short-form question on "complete plumbing facilities," instructing respondents to mark "yes" if all three items were included. Largely because of the controversial nature of the item, it was moved to the long form in 1990 and continued there in 2000.

Complete kitchen facilities, defined as a sink with piped water, a range or stove, and a refrigerator, were part of the housing unit definition through 1970.

When the concept was removed from the definition in 1980, the question was moved to the long form, where it has remained ever since. The item on telephone service has been on the census since 1960, usually on the long form.

All of these inquiries about facilities are measures of housing quality—of the degree to which the standard (having all of them) is met in various parts of the country and in rural as compared with urban areas.

Heating Fuel. This long-form item provides critical information for determining the need for infrastructure to support access to heating fuel and has been asked in each census since 1940. Understandably, the responses vary widely both by section of the country and by the degree of urbanization. It is of less interest in cities and suburbs in the Northeast and Midwest, where almost all homes are heated by natural gas. It is very important in rural areas, which may not have access to a utility system, and in areas of the South where these utilities are unevenly available.

Number of Automobiles. This is a question about the household, not the housing unit, but has been included in the housing section of the questionnaire since 1960. It is of critical use in transportation planning, as well as in planning social services for households that neither have cars nor good access to public transportation. The 2000 form of the question was: "How many automobiles, vans, or trucks are kept at home for use by members of your household?" This means that vehicles that are not owned by the household, such as company cars, are still included in the total if a household member drives them home each night.

Housing Costs. Most of these items were first asked in 1940. On the 2000 long form, they included the annual cost of electricity, gas, water and sewer, and other heating fuels. Since 1980, homeowners have also been asked about their mortgage payment and whether it includes taxes or insurance, a second mortgage or home equity loan and its monthly payments, and the cost of real estate taxes and insurance. Since 1990, condominium owners are also asked to provide their monthly fee, an item that also serves to identify condominium status. Similar questions are aimed at mobile home owners. The product of all these items is the total housing cost sustained by the household; that is, what it costs per month, or per year, to live in their home.

The information is critical for analysis and support of federal and other housing programs.

See also *Content determination; Local involvement in census taking; Long form.*

■ Patricia C. Becker

Bibliography

U.S. Census Bureau. *Housing: Financial Characteristics.* CDR-13. Washington, D.C.: U.S. Department of Commerce, May 1990.

U.S. Census Bureau. *Housing: Occupancy and Structural Characteristics.* 1990 Census of Population and Housing, Content Determination Reports, CDR-11. Washington, D.C.: U.S. Department of Commerce, April 1990.

U.S. Census Bureau. *Housing: Plumbing, Equipment, and Fuels.* CDR-12. Washington, D.C.: U.S. Department of Commerce, January 1989.

U.S. Census Bureau. *1980 Census of Population and Housing.* Users Guide (PHC80-R1-), issued in three parts. Washington, D.C., 1982–1983.

U.S. Census Bureau. *1990 Census Questionnaire Content* series. Washington, D.C.: U.S. Department of Commerce: 1990-CQC-8 (Type of Housing and Tenure), December 1992; 1990-CQC-9 (Number of Rooms and Bedrooms), April 1993; 1990-CQC-10 (Year Moved in and Year Structure Built), June 1993; 1990-CQC-11 (Value of Home and Monthly Rent), April 1992; 1990-CQC-25 (Complete Plumbing and Kitchen Facilities), December 1993; 1990-CQC-26 (Telephone and Vehicle Availability), January 1994; 1990-CQC-27 (Home Heating Fuels); 1990-CQC-28 (Source of wager and Sewage Disposal); 1990-CQC-29 (Condominium Status and Farm Residence); 1990-CQC-30 (Housing Costs), November 1994.

U.S. Census Bureau. *Procedural Report on the 1960 Censuses of Population and Housing.* Working paper no. 16. Washington, D.C., 1963.

U.S. Census Bureau. "Revised Housing Unit Definition for Census 2000." Decision memorandum no. 8, February 1997.

U.S. Census Bureau. *U.S. Census of Population and Housing: 1970.* The Coverage of Housing in the 1970 Census (PHC(E)-5). Washington, D.C., 1973.

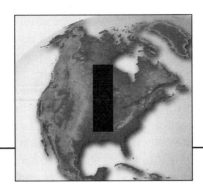

Immigration

The role of immigration in the formation and development of the United States can hardly be overstated. From colonial times to the present, the population of the country has been shaped and reshaped, both in size and racial/ethnic composition, by expanding and contracting waves of immigrants. By one measure, for example, more than 40 percent of U.S. population growth between 1900 and 1990 is attributable to post-1900 immigration.

The nation's continuing interest in immigration is reflected directly in the decennial census. Despite the ebbs and flows of immigration, a question on country of birth has appeared in every census since 1850, a continuous run as long as any question other than the basic demographic categories of age, sex, and race. Information needed to assess the impacts of immigrants has been provided by other, related census questions.

U.S. citizenship, perhaps the major difference between natives and immigrants, is now collected by legal mandate, but the topic was not always covered in previous censuses. A citizenship question appeared very early, in 1820 and 1830, but was omitted in 1850, 1860, and 1880 even though country of birth was asked. (A related question on year of naturalization appeared in 1920.) The ability to speak a language other than English was a question topic (in various forms) from 1890 to 2000, with the exception of 1950.

The pace of immigration is one of the key factors affecting not only the size of the foreign-born population, but also its impact on the United States. More recent immigrants tend to be less well integrated—less likely to be citizens or speak English and more likely to have lower incomes, for example. Data on year of immigration permit measurement and assessment of such factors. This question appeared in the censuses of 1890 to 1930 and since 1970. For Census 2000, the wording of this question has been altered to permit collection of better (that is, more accurate) data.

Immigration Policy

The broad outlines of contending forces in U.S. immigration policy have been apparent from early times—providing sanctuary for political and economic refugees versus admitting only those who will benefit the U.S. economically and socially while excluding those likely to become public burdens. Notwithstanding these common themes, the bases for admission and, especially, exclusion have been defined differently throughout the country's history. Until the 1870s, the United States had virtually open immigration. The first broad controls were *qualitative* in nature, excluding criminals and prostitutes (1876), physically and mentally ill (1891, 1907), and those likely to become paupers (1907). A distinctive feature of the increasing exclusionary bent over the period from 1882 until 1924 was its racially based character; the Chinese Exclusion Act of 1882 barred Chinese, the Gentlemen's Agreement in 1907 expanded exclusions to Japanese, and, in 1917, all Asians and illiterates were barred.

In 1921 and 1924, the first *quantitative* restrictions

on immigration were imposed, ultimately leading to a ceiling of 150,000 per year on European immigration. The ethnically based nature of restrictions was reinforced as admission was determined by the proportion of a national origin group present in the United States according to the census of 1890. This provision had the effect of limiting severely immigration from southern and eastern Europe, the origins of most immigrants after 1890, but relatively few before then.

The restrictions on immigration, reinforced in 1952, lasted until the passage of the Immigration and Nationality Act Amendments of 1965, which marked the beginning of a new, more inclusionary era in immigration policy. The new law repealed the discriminatory national origins quota system and replaced it with a uniform limit of twenty thousand immigrants per country for all countries outside the Western Hemisphere. The law established a preference system based on family unification and skills and, for the first time, imposed a limit on Western Hemisphere (and especially Mexican) immigration. Further amendments in 1976 brought the Western Hemisphere under the twenty thousand per country limit (with somewhat larger, special quotas for the neighboring countries of Mexico and Canada). The new laws set the stage for massive shifts in the origins of legal immigrants and for large-scale illegal immigration.

The period from 1980 to 1990 saw a complete restructuring of U.S. immigration policy beginning with the Refugee Act of 1980. This act set up a permanent and systematic procedure for admitting refugees and asylees. It committed the country to receiving a substantial number of refugees while bringing the legal definition of refugees in line with international standards, instead of more narrow ideological standards. The Refugee Act reinforced the shift in origins away from Europe. The Immigration Reform and Control Act of 1986 (IRCA) focused on illegal immigration. IRCA contained the first penalties for employers who knowingly hire illegal immigrants. At the same time, it created two large programs to grant legal status to certain illegal immigrants who had worked or lived in the United States for significant periods of time. Ultimately, about 2.7 million formerly illegal immigrants, mostly Mexican, became legal through IRCA's amnesty programs, further reinforcing the shifting origins of immigration. The Immigration Act of 1990 was the culmination of the decade of reform. The act represented a major liberalization of legal immigration policy, increasing total admissions by 40 percent (includ-

ing a tripling of employment-based immigration, emphasizing skills).

Notwithstanding the decade of reform in the 1980s, immigration remained a focus of congressional attention in the 1990s. Three laws passed in 1996 had significant implications for immigration and immigrant policy—Antiterrorism and Effective Death Penalty Act, Personal Responsibility and Work Opportunity Reconciliation Act, and Illegal Immigration Reform and Immigrant Responsibility Act. Despite widespread calls for reductions in the level of legal immigration, Congress did not alter admission levels with these new laws, but instead placed restrictions on immigrants' rights. Requirements for sponsoring immigrants were tightened and made enforceable; penalties affecting subsequent legal admission could now be enforced against illegal immigrants. However, the most noteworthy provisions of the laws affected immigrants' rights and responsibilities. For the first time, eligibility for a broad range of social programs, which had been open to most legal residents of the country, was limited to citizens. Further, the federal government, while barring some immigrants from all programs, ceded to states the right to determine eligibility standards affecting other immigrants. While these new laws may ultimately affect the mix of immigrants coming to the country, in terms of both origins and characteristics, they have not been in place long enough to affect immigration flows.

Immigration Numbers and Patterns

The impacts of immigration can be assessed with two complementary demographic concepts—stocks and flows. Immigration flows are the numbers of immigrants coming into (and going out of) a country. As a result of the flows (and through mortality), the number of immigrants living in a country changes; this foreign-born population represents the stock of immigrants in the country. Immigration flows are measured with data and estimates on admissions, arrivals, and exits; immigrant stocks are measured with census or survey data.

Immigration flows increased steadily from the 1820s until the Civil War, with mass immigration beginning in the late 1840s as 1.7 million immigrants arrived during the decade, fleeing political turmoil and famines in northern Europe and Ireland (see Table 1). Through World War I, immigration continued with steady increases being interrupted by economic and political conditions on both sides of the Atlantic. Thus, immigration decreased during the Civil War (to 2.3 million for the 1860s from 2.6 million for the 1850s) and increased only slightly during Reconstruction (2.8 million in the 1870s). Immigration surged to 5.2 million during the 1880s but fell to 3.7 million in the 1890s, with further increases being interrupted by several economic panics in the United States. With economic prosperity in the 1900s, immigration again increased to 9.0 million; during the 1905–1914 decade, immigration averaged more than 1 million per year, a level not to be seen again until the 1990s. However, for the entire decade of the 1910s, immigration decreased to 6.0 million because of the effects of World War I in Europe.

Two major sources of immigrants were evident during the long period of mass immigration from the 1840s through the 1910s. Through the 1880s, by far the largest numbers of immigrants came from Germany, Ireland, and the United Kingdom (including northern Ireland). During this era, smaller, but significant, numbers also came from Scandinavia and other countries of northern and western Europe. A shift in origins began during the 1880s but was occurring on a large scale by the 1890s. During the 1890–1920 period, the principal sources of immigration were countries of southern and eastern Europe—including, but not limited to, Italy, Russia (mainly Jewish immigrants), Poland, and Austria-Hungary. Concerns about the United States' ability to integrate immigrants from these new source regions led to the ethnically based restrictions embodied in legislation of 1921 and 1924. With the imposition of the national origin quotas that favored northern and western Europe came severe limits on immigration from other parts of Europe and the rest of the world. As a result, immigration flows began to drop in the late 1920s so that only 4.1 million immigrants arrived in the 1920s with the majority coming by 1924.

By the 1930s, the Great Depression led to a lack of economic opportunities in the United States and to reduction of the resources available to potential migrants abroad. As a result, immigration levels plummeted. For the entire decade of the 1930s, only about half a million persons moved to the United States—less than any decade since the 1820s and less than one normal year's worth of immigration circa 1980. More people emigrated from the country than immigrated during the 1930s, yielding the only decade in the nation's history with net out-migration. The very low levels of immigration continued during World War II, with only about 1 million immigrants coming during the 1940s.

Table 1. Immigration to the United States, 1821–1830 to 1991–2000

(In millions)

| Decade | All Immigration | Legal Immigration | | | |
		Total	Europe and Canada	All Other	Other[a]
1821–1830	0.1	0.1	0.1	0.0	—
1831–1840	0.6	0.6	0.5	0.1	—
1841–1850	1.7	1.7	1.6	0.1	—
1851–1860	2.6	2.6	2.5	0.1	—
1861–1870	2.3	2.3	2.2	0.1	—
1871–1880	2.8	2.9	2.7	0.2	—
1881–1890	5.2	5.2	5.1	0.1	—
1891–1900	3.7	3.7	3.6	0.1	—
1901–1910	9.0	8.8	8.2	0.6	0.2
1911–1920	6.0	5.8	5.1	0.7	0.3
1921–1930	4.1	4.1	3.4	0.7	—
1931–1940	0.5	0.6	0.5	0.1	—
1941–1950	1.0	1.0	0.8	0.2	—
1951–1960	2.5	2.5	1.7	0.8	—
1961–1970	3.8	3.3	1.5	1.8	0.5
1971–1980	7.0	4.5	1.0	3.5	2.5
1981–1990	10.0	6.0	0.9	5.1	4.0
1991–2000[b]	11.0	8.0	1.7	6.3	3.0

Source: U.S. Immigration and Naturalization Service, *Statistical Yearbook of the Immigration and Naturalization Service: 1996* (Washington, D.C.: U.S. Government Printing Office, 1997); and author's estimates.

— = Not applicable.

[a] Mainly undocumented immigration, estimated by author.

[b] Estimated by author.

After the war, more normal patterns of immigration resumed, but in the context of the 1924 Immigration and Naturalization Act and the McCarran-Walter Act of 1952 with numerical limits, national origins quotas favoring northern and western Europe, and the effective bar to immigration from Asia. Legal immigration during the 1950s averaged about 250,000 per year with roughly two-thirds of the immigrants coming from Europe and Canada (see Table 2).

The Immigration and Nationality Act Amendments of 1965 changed the nature of immigration to the United States, ushering in the current era of high immigration. The repeal of the national origins quota system and the dropping of the ban on Asian immigration opened U.S. immigration to more of the world. As a result, immigration levels increased even though the numerical ceilings were kept in place. Under the previous immigration regime, not all slots were filled

Table 2. Origins of Legal Immigrants, 1951–1960 to 1991–2000

Decade	Total	Europe and Canada	Asia	Mexico	Other Latin America	All Other
Number of Immigrants (In Thousands)						
1951–1960	2,520	1,700	150	300	320	40
1961–1970	3,320	1,540	430	450	850	50
1971–1980	4,490	970	1,590	640	1,170	120
1981–1990[a]	5,980	890	2,670	690	1,530	200
1991–2000[a]	8,190	1,670	3,300	990	1,920	310
Percentage of Immigrants						
1951–1960	100	67	6	12	13	2
1961–1970	100	46	13	14	26	2
1971–1980	100	22	35	14	26	3
1981–1990[a]	100	15	45	12	26	3
1991–2000[a]	100	20	40	12	23	4

Source: U.S. Immigration and Naturalization Service, *Statistical Yearbook of the Immigration and Naturalization Service: 1996* (Washington, D.C.: U.S. Government Printing Office, 1997); and author's estimates for 1997–2000.

[a]Excludes Immigration Reform and Control Act of 1986 legalizations.

because the demand to enter from northern and western Europe was not great. However, a sizable demand was evident in the newly opened areas so that the proportion of immigrants from Asia and Latin America increased.

By the 1960s, average annual immigration increased to more than 300,000 per year; in the 1970s, it reached 450,000 per year. By the 1970s, immigration from Europe had dropped numerically to roughly half the level of the 1950s and accounted for only about one-fifth of total legal immigration. Asia now accounted for 35 percent of legal immigrants and Latin America, 40 percent.

What is striking about the changes engendered by the 1965 immigration amendments is the generally unanticipated consequences. The rationale for the elimination of national origin quotas and the opening of Asian migration was largely based on the civil rights' notion of nondiscrimination, rather than immigration-specific justifications. Few politicians or commentators envisioned the subsequent shift of origins from Europe to Asia. Moreover, the increases in immigration levels were generally not anticipated either.

These trends continued into the 1980s and 1990s, but other policy changes contributed to further increases in immigration and to more changes in the origins of immigration flows to the United States. The Refugee Act of 1980 placed refugees outside the pref-

erence system, leading to a slight increase as annual legal immigration reached 600,000 per year in the 1980s. The admission of large numbers of southeast Asian refugees beginning in the mid-1980s reinforced the trends set in motion in 1965. Many Asians came as refugees, but others came directly under the preference system, and some relatives of southeast Asian refugees filled preference slots. During the 1980s, about 45 percent of legal entrants, or almost 2.7 million immigrants, were from Asia. This figure is larger than total legal immigration during the 1950s.

The Immigration Act of 1990 expanded legal immigration by roughly 40 percent, from about 500,000 per year to 700,000. Much of the increase was allocated to employment-based immigration, which roughly tripled, with an emphasis on highly skilled immigrants. The impact of the immigration flows is very apparent as annual immigration in the 1990s averaged more than 800,000 per year, an increase of almost one-third over the already high levels of the 1980s.

Trends in the Foreign-Born Population

In the United States, the immigrant population consists only of the first generation; that is, foreign-born persons. The United States operates on the principle of birthright citizenship—the U.S.-born children of immigrants are part of the native population. Thus, the country's immigrant population represents the accumulation of immigrants who move to the country, less those who die or emigrate (move out of the country).

In response to dramatic increases and decreases in immigration levels, the foreign-born population has endured its own swings. With sustained, relatively high levels of immigration, the foreign-born population grew steadily from 1850 (the first year it was measured in the census) through 1920, increasing from 2.2 million to 13.5 million (see Table 3). At the same time, the percentage of immigrants in the population grew from 9.7 percent in 1850, stayed in a fairly narrow range of 13-15 percent from 1860 through 1920, and reached a maximum of 14.7 percent in 1910, following the decade of maximum immigration. For this long period, roughly one of every seven Americans was an immigrant.

With the reductions in immigration resulting from the restrictive legislation of the 1920s (plus accompanying fairly high levels of emigration), growth in the foreign-born population slowed through 1930 as it peaked at 14.2 million. Then, as a result of the virtual cessation of immigration during the Great Depression and World War II, the immigrant population began to decrease as more foreign-born persons died or left the country than entered.

This demographic history left a foreign-born population at the end of World War II that was fairly old, aging rapidly, and decreasing in size. Even the increasing levels of immigration during the 1950s and 1960s were not high enough to offset the demographic momentum of population aging, so that the immigrant population continued to decrease through the 1970 census. The percentage of the population that was foreign-born decreased even more rapidly than the absolute numbers because the native population was growing rapidly, fueled by the post-war baby boom of 1947–1964. From 13.1 percent foreign-born in 1920, the percentage dropped to only 4.7 percent in 1970, when less than one in twenty Americans was an immigrant.

The post-1965 surge in immigration reversed this decreasing trend. By 1980, the number of immigrants was 14.1 million, only slightly less than the previous maximum that had occurred in 1930. The numbers grew rapidly during the 1980s and 1990s, almost reaching 20 million in 1990 and exceeding 26 million by 1998. The percentage foreign-born also grew rapidly. By 1998, almost 10 percent of the population consisted of immigrants. Although the number of immigrants was at an all-time high, the percentage foreign-born still remained well below the peak levels of 1860–1930.

Table 3. Foreign-Born Population of the United States, 1850–1998

Date	Foreign-Born Population (In Thousands)	Percentage of Total Population
1850	2,245	9.7
1860	4,139	13.2
1870	5,567	14.4
1880	6,680	13.3
1890	9,250	14.8
1900	10,341	13.6
1910	13,516	14.7
1920	13,921	13.2
1930	14,204	11.6
1940	11,595	8.9
1950	10,347	6.9
1960	9,738	5.4
1970	9,619	4.7
1980	14,080	6.2
1990	19,768	7.9
1995	24,763	9.3
1998	26,281	9.8

Source: Decennial census data through 1990; author's tabulations of Current Population Survey (CPS) data for 1995 and 1998.

The pattern of numerical change does contain the roots of some of the social friction surrounding immigration in the 1990s. In less than a generation, the number of immigrants in the U.S. population almost tripled and the percentage foreign-born more than doubled. The situation facing most of the adult population at the end of the 1990s was different from what they knew as children or what their parents faced as adults. The rapid changes may be more significant than the absolute numbers.

Undocumented Immigration

Another source of concern over immigration and some confusion surrounding the meaning of the data relate to unauthorized (or illegal or undocumented) immigration; that is, the entry and settlement in the United States of persons not authorized by the legal admissions system. Although some references are found to concerns with illegal immigration in the first half of the twentieth century, these mainly involve the movement of farm labor from Mexico to the United States. Contemporary concern dates from the mid-to-late 1970s, when serious political discussion of the size of the undocumented alien population began. The number of undocumented immigrants living in the United States appears to have been severely overstated, however. One of the earliest recorded conjectures was by Immigration and Naturalization Service (INS) Commissioner Raymond Farrell, who testified in 1972 that 1 million illegal aliens were in the country. Although this figure was apparently just a guess, unsupported by empirical work, subsequent research suggests he may have been reasonably close. However, this estimate was not accepted at all. By 1976, the next INS commissioner placed the number at 4 million to 12 million, again without empirical support. While the actual undocumented population has never even approached the upper part of this range, the numbers were large and growing.

Undocumented migration streams had two principal roots. The first, accounting for a large majority of these early undocumented migrants, was the long-standing demand for labor, especially in agriculture, in the southwestern United States. Mexicans, mostly men, gladly met this demand. The second stream of undocumented migrants is related to increasing international flows of migrants and travelers. As more people moved to the United States, more of their friends and relatives came to visit. More tourists came to the United States, too. With these greatly increased international flows, some people simply decided to stay in the United States to live. By the mid-1980s, the undocumented population reached a peak of roughly 4 million to 5 million. In the late 1980s, IRCA's legalization programs granted legal status to about 2.7 million formerly undocumented migrants. As a result, the size of the undocumented population decreased substantially.

IRCA also introduced measures intended to control illegal immigration. Specifically, it increased enforcement along the U.S.-Mexico border and made the knowing hire of undocumented immigrants illegal for the first time. IRCA was notably unsuccessful in controlling growth in the illegal population, however. After a short hiatus, the undocumented population began to increase again, at levels roughly the same or even higher than in the pre-IRCA period—200,000-300,000 per year. By the late 1990s, the undocumented population reached 5 million to 6 million, a level considerably higher than when IRCA was passed.

By 1998, undocumented aliens represented more than 20 percent of the foreign-born population living in the United States. They included clandestine entrants who sneaked into the country, usually across the Mexican border, and visa abusers, or persons who entered legally with a document permitting them to be in the United States for a specific period of time but who then failed to leave. Visa overstayers could account for 40 percent or so of the undocumented population. By far the largest group of undocumented immigrants was the more than 50 percent who came from Mexico. Other parts of Central and Latin America (mainly El Salvador, Guatemala, Honduras, the Dominican Republic, and Colombia) accounted for another one-quarter of the undocumented population.

The Mexican-born population, including both legal and unauthorized residents, reached more than 7 million in 1998; it represented more than one-quarter of the immigrants in the country. While most migration from Mexico over the last three decades of the twentieth century was undocumented at the time it occurred, most of the Mexicans living in the United States are *legally* in the country. This seeming inconsistency arises because IRCA's legalization programs gave legal status to about 2 million Mexicans and because most Mexicans who become legal immigrants each year are already in the United States illegally. It is very important to note that Mexico, in addition to being the source of most illegal migrants, is the largest single source of legal migrants to the United States.

Legal Status of the Immigrant Population

The legal status of the immigrant population in U.S. censuses and surveys continues to be a source of confusion and controversy. While the census classifies immigrants as naturalized citizens or aliens, it makes no further distinctions with regard to legal status. Yet myriad categories are of interest to analysts and policy makers. The five main immigrant populations of interest to most observers, in roughly decreasing order of size, are:

- Legal permanent residents or LPRs (roughly 9 million to 10 million in 1998);
- Naturalized citizens who were formerly LPRs (8 million to 9 million);
- Undocumented aliens (5 million to 6 million);
- Refugees, asylees, and parolees (2 million); and
- Nonimmigrant residents (1 million to 1.5 million).

These groups have substantially different characteristics, are affected by different laws and policies, and are changing at different rates.

The largest group in the foreign-born population is legal aliens, or aliens admitted for permanent residence. As defined here, LPRs are those persons who are not U.S. citizens and are regular family-based and employment-based immigrants; they also include aliens who acquired legal status under IRCA. In the late 1990s, roughly 700,000 LPR aliens were added to this population annually by legal immigration. However, 100,000-200,000 LPRs emigrated annually; roughly the same number died; and almost 1 million left the alien population by naturalizing. As a result, the LPR population was decreasing in the late 1990s. Humanitarian immigrants who entered the United States since 1980 account for about 2 million foreign-born or 8 percent of the immigrant population. This group includes refugees, asylees, Amerasians, Cuban-Haitian entrants, and certain parolees. Approximately one-third of the humanitarian entrants have become naturalized citizens.

"Nonimmigrants" are aliens admitted to the United States for specific, temporary periods and for specific purposes. There are solid data on annual admissions for nonimmigrants, but virtually no population estimates because no agency keeps track of how many nonimmigrants depart or change to other immigration statuses. More than 90 percent of nonimmigrant admissions are temporary visitors for business or pleasure (that is, tourists), with more than 75 percent of the total being tourists. These temporary visitors are not entitled to take up residence in the United States; if they do so, they fall into the unauthorized immigrant category. The largest group of nonimmigrants entitled to live in the country is foreign students and visiting faculty; temporary workers constitute another large group. Smaller groups of nonimmigrants include diplomatic personnel, treaty traders, au pairs, and the like. Because these nonimmigrants are considered residents of the United States, albeit temporary, they are included in decennial census counts. According to Jeffrey S. Passel and Rebecca L. Clark, about 1 million to 1.5 million nonimmigrants are living in the United States at any given time, but only about three-quarters appear in the census and survey data.

Undocumented aliens were a problematic feature of decennial enumerations in 1980 and 1990. Because the census counts are used to apportion seats in Congress, lawsuits have been filed to exclude undocumented aliens from the apportionment counts (*F.A.I.R. et al. v. Klutznick et al.* for the 1980 census and *Ridge et al. v. Verity et al.* for 1990). In both lawsuits, the plaintiffs argued that the presence of undocumented aliens increased representation in states with concentrations of undocumented aliens and diluted the representation of citizens in states with few undocumented aliens. They further argued that this dilution violated the constitutional provisions for representation and the "one man, one vote" Supreme Court decisions of the 1960s. The defendants countered with several arguments: One argument addressed the impracticality of identifying and excluding undocumented aliens. (In the suit surrounding the 1980 census, a related argument was also made that undocumented aliens would not appear in the census. This argument was based on the experience of 1970 but turned out to be false for both the 1980 and 1990 censuses, which included substantial numbers of undocumented aliens.) A more direct and substantive argument was that the Constitution's apportionment prescription was not restricted to citizens or potential voters but included the entire population (originally the entire free population plus three-fifths of the slave population but later changed to encompass the entire population). Thus, undocumented aliens, as part of the population of a state, should affect the number of representatives assigned to the state.

The Supreme Court decided both cases on narrow, technical grounds. Specifically, the plaintiffs were ruled not to have "standing" to even bring the suits because the damages alleged were both prospective and not specific. The Court seemed to address the substance of the cases through dicta by stating that the intent of the Constitution was to provide representation to persons other than the potential voting population. However, because this reasoning was not the basis for the ultimate decisions, issues surrounding the constitutionality of enumerating undocumented aliens in the decennial census have not been finally resolved. Census 2000 included undocumented aliens in the enumeration and the apportionment population.

■ Jeffrey S. Passel

Bibliography

Bean, Frank D., Barry Edmonston, and Jeffrey S. Passel. *Undocumented Migration to the United States: IRCA and the Experience of the 1980s.* Washington, D.C.: Urban Institute Press, 1990.

Edmonston, Barry, and Jeffrey S. Passel. *Immigration and Ethnicity: The Integration of America's Newest Arrivals.* Washington, D.C.: Urban Institute Press, 1994.

Fix, Michael, and Jeffrey S. Passel. *Immigration and Immigrants: Setting the Record Straight.* Washington, D.C.: Urban Institute, 1994.

Kaplan, Charles P., and Thomas L. Van Valey. *Census '80: Continuing the Factfinder Tradition.* Washington, D.C.: U.S. Bureau of the Census, 1980.

Passel, Jeffrey S. "The Number of Undocumented Immigrants in the United States: A Review and New Estimates." In David W. Haines and Karen E. Rosenblum, eds., *Illegal Immigration in America: A Reference Handbook*, pp. 27–111. Westport, Conn.: Greenwood Publishing, 1999.

Passel, Jeffrey S., and Rebecca L. Clark. *Immigrants in New York: Their Legal Status, Incomes, and Taxes.* Washington, D.C.: Urban Institute, 1998.

U.S. Bureau of the Census. *Questions Planned for Census 2000: Federal Legislative and Program Uses.* Washington, D.C., 1998.

U.S. Immigration and Naturalization Service. *Statistical Yearbook of the Immigration and Naturalization Service: 1996.* Washington, D.C.: U.S. Government Printing Office, 1997.

Income and poverty measures

Questions on annual income were first included in the 1940 census and have been asked in every subsequent census, with increasing detail requested. Since 1970 the census has also provided estimates of numbers of people in families with incomes below the official poverty thresholds. The concept underlying the census income questions is that of regular, before-tax money income.

Income in the 1940 Census

The decennial population census has obtained measures of socioeconomic status for at least 150 years: for example, the 1850 census asked about occupation of employment and value of real estate owned. However, no questions on income were asked in the census until 1940. To help understand the effects of the Great Depression, two questions about people's income were included in the 1940 population schedule used by enumerators. The two questions, asked of all people age fourteen and older, were the amount of wage and salary income earned in 1939 and a yes-no indicator of whether the person had more than $50 of other income in that year.

The Census Bureau anticipated public objection to the questions and adopted the following tactics to minimize burden and maximize response: (1) the questionnaire asked a specific dollar amount only for wage and salary income, which many workers knew was already reported to the government for Social Security purposes; (2) the questionnaire did not require people with more than $5,000 of wages and salaries to specify the amount; (3) people who did not want to let the enumerator (who might be a neighbor) know their income could ask for a confidential income form to fill out to mail back; and (4) the income items were the last ones asked.

The inclusion of income questions in the census generated some adverse publicity and congressional hearings. However, public cooperation was excellent. The nonresponse rate to the wage and salary income item was only 2 percent, and only 0.5 percent of the forty million people who reported such income used the confidential form.

Income Questions between 1950 and 2000

The 1950 census used sampling to reduce the burden of the census considerably. The income questions were obtained for a 20 percent sample of people age fourteen and older, who were asked for amounts of wages and salaries, net self-employment income, and income from other sources in 1949. Enumerators asked the sample questions of every fifth person by using "line schedules" that included a line for each household member. If a head of a family fell into the sample, that person was also asked about the income of other family members from wages and salaries, self-employment, and other sources.

In the 1960 census the format changed from line schedules to household questionnaires. Questions on wages and salaries, net self-employment income, and all other income in 1959 were asked on the long-form questionnaire of all household members age fourteen and up in a 25 percent sample of households.

In 1970 income questions were included on each of the two long-form questionnaires (15 percent and 5 percent) used in that census, making up a 20 percent sample of households. The income questions, asked of people fourteen years and older in sample households, were expanded to provide amounts for six types of income for 1969: wages and salaries, net nonfarm self-employment income, net farm self-employment income, Social Security or railroad retirement income, public assistance or welfare income, and all other income.

In 1980 about 19 percent of households received the long-form questionnaire. It included questions, asked of people age fifteen and older in sample households, on amounts for seven types of income for 1979: wages and salaries; net nonfarm self-employment income; net farm self-employment income; interest, dividends, royalties, and net rental income; Social Security or railroad retirement income; Supplemental Security Income, Aid to Families with Dependent Children (AFDC) or other public assistance or welfare income; and all other income. A separate question asked for total income.

The 1990 census treatment of income was very similar to that of 1980. About 17 percent of households received the long-form questionnaire, which asked each person age fifteen and older in sample households questions on total income in 1989 and amounts for eight sources. The categories were the same as in 1980, except that a separate category was provided for pension income; also, income from estates and trusts was included with interest, dividends, royalties, and net rental income instead of in the "other" category.

The 2000 census treatment of income was very similar to that of 1990. About 17 percent of households received the long-form questionnaire, which asked everyone age fifteen and older in sample households questions on total income in 1999 and amounts for eight sources. The categories were the same as in 1990, except that net farm and nonfarm self-employment income were combined into a single category, a separate category was provided for Supplemental Security Income, and the category for AFDC or other public assistance income was renamed as "any public assistance or welfare payments from the state or local welfare office" to reflect legislation from 1996 that replaced AFDC with a block grant program to the states ("welfare reform").

Poverty Measures

The U.S. Bureau of the Budget (now the Office of Management and Budget) adopted a measure of poverty for official use in 1969. The measure had first been developed for 1963 by Mollie Orshansky of the U.S. Social Security Administration. Poverty statistics were first tabulated from census data in 1970; annual poverty statistics are published each fall from the Current Population Survey (CPS) March Income Supplement.

Official poverty rates are based on comparing before-tax money income for a family or unrelated individual to the appropriate poverty threshold to determine if the family or individual falls below the threshold. Oversimplifying, the thresholds were developed as the cost of a minimum adequate diet times three, to allow for other needed consumption. They vary by the total number of persons and children in the family and (for one-person and two-person families) by whether the head is over or under age sixty-five. (Originally there were also separate thresholds for farm versus nonfarm families and single-parent families headed by women versus other families.) The thresholds assume that children and the elderly require less than working-age adults. Also, while the thresholds assume that larger families need more than smaller families, they recognize economies of scale—for example, larger families can make more efficient use of food purchases, with less waste; conversely, smaller families need such basic living spaces as kitchens just as much as larger families. Each year the thresholds are updated for inflation by the change in the Consumer Price Index for all urban consumers (CPI-U).

The poverty measure has been critiqued by a panel of the National Academy of Sciences/National Research Council and others. Work is ongoing at the Census Bureau to develop experimental poverty measures that revise the thresholds and income concept.

Concept and Quality Issues

The basic income concept in the 1940–2000 censuses, which also applies to the official poverty measure— namely regular, before-tax money income—has been stable across time. The concept excludes lump-sum money income (such as capital gains or inheritance). It also excludes any income amounts that could be attributed to the value of assets—for example, many economists argue that homeowners' incomes should include imputed amounts for the flow of services they receive from ownership.

More important for comparative analysis across time and population groups, the census income concept excludes in-kind benefits, which have grown substantially over the past few decades. For example, the Food Stamp, Medicare, and Medicaid programs did not exist in 1960 and were barely in place by 1970, but are now providing billions of dollars of benefits to substantial portions of the population. Privately provided fringe benefits, such as group health and life insurance, also have become much more common. There are difficult questions of how to value in-kind benefits, particularly for medical care, but there is no doubt that the money-only income concept underestimates available economic resources for families and individuals, particularly in censuses since 1970.

The census income concept is also a pre-tax concept. It thereby ignores changes in tax burdens that have occurred over the years and that affect population groups differently. For example, the recent expansion of the Earned Income Tax Credit, which helps low-income working families, is not captured in income and poverty statistics from the census or the March CPS.

Several sources of error affect the quality of responses to the census income questions. These sources include sampling error, which varies from census to census according to the sampling rates used (in the 1980–2000 censuses, rates vary by size of place); nonresponse to the income questions, which has increased over time; errors in the procedures the Census Bureau uses to impute missing responses; and respondent errors, such as underreporting and overreporting. By comparison with the March CPS, the census tends to obtain higher income estimates, perhaps because of more complete reporting by higher-income families.

In making decennial census income data available to users, the Census Bureau topcodes dollar amounts; that is, it reports dollar amounts up to a limit and then provides a broad top category. For example, in the 1980 census Public Use Microdata Sample (PUMS) files, income amounts were generally shown in dollars up to a top category of "$75,000 or more." In the 1990 census PUMS files, the top category varied by type of income and state of residence. The purpose of topcoding is to protect the confidentiality of individual responses.

See also *Confidentiality; Editing and imputation; Federal household surveys; Long form; Sampling for content.*

■ Constance F. Citro

Bibliography

Bureau of the Census

Citro, Constance F. *The Concept of Income in the U.S. Decennial Censuses: 1960–90.* Arlington, Va.: Association of Public Data Users, 1996.

Short, Kathleen, Thesia Garner, David Johnson, and Patricia Doyle. *Experimental Poverty Measures 1990 to 1997.* Current Population Reports, Consumer Income, Series P60-205. Washington, D.C.: U.S. Department of Commerce, 1999.

National Research Council

National Research Council. Committee on National Statistics, Panel on Poverty and Family Assistance: Concepts, Information Needs, and Measurement Methods. *Measuring Poverty: A New Approach*, edited by Constance F. Citro and Robert T. Michael. Washington, D.C.: National Academy Press, 1995.

International coordination in population censuses

If Ambrose Bierce had ever been asked to define international coordination in census-taking, his definition might have read something like the following: (1) An idealized arrangement, often advocated but never achieved, under which all countries would adopt the same census content, timing, and outputs, almost invariably those of the country of the proposer; (2) a misnomer for international cooperation in census-taking.

The primary obstacle to true international coordination in census-taking is that population censuses are basically national undertakings carried out for largely national purposes. Accordingly, while the notion of a unitary global census operation with a single set of questions, field and processing procedures, and outputs has been repeatedly proposed in one form or another over the decades, and has been repeatedly ignored, important more modest efforts are now well established. These efforts, better characterized today as international cooperation than international coordination, include the organized exchange of census data and census experience among national census authorities in different countries; the development, adoption, and dissemination of international recommendations for concepts, definitions, and classifications for use in population censuses; and different forms of technical assistance and training designed to help developing or other countries facing special challenges in carrying out their censuses.

The modern history of international cooperation in work on population censuses began in the middle of the nineteenth century initially in the context of a series of quasi-diplomatic international statistical congresses. When that system of congresses broke down around 1870, the work on collaboration was continued under the auspices of the newly established International Statistical Institute (ISI). Census-related work in this period covered such subjects as agreement on the meaning of the de jure–de facto concepts of census enumeration and the initial development of a standard occupational classification.

After World War I, the ISI continued to promote exchange of information and the development of new international standard statistical definitions and classifications. However, in the 1920s and thereafter the primary locus of work on developing and promoting standard international definitions and classifications for statistical use, including those relating to population censuses, shifted to international organizations such as the League of Nations, followed by the United Nations and the International Labour Organization.

Another vehicle for promoting coordination in work on censuses, particularly in the 1930s and 1940s, was the administrative systems of countries with large colonial empires. By its very nature a colonial regime might be seen as providing an ideal setting for comparatively rigorous coordination of statistical work as opposed to the simple fostering of cooperation and the exchange of information. Nevertheless, while considerable uniformity was achieved in the timing of census enumerations (for example, throughout the British empire censuses were generally taken in years ending in "1"), census methods and content varied widely depending on local conditions and needs.

Since the end of World War II, there have been four primary means through which international coordination and international cooperation in the population census field have operated: (1) United Nations resolutions and recommendations pertaining to population and housing censuses; (2) multilateral and bilateral exchanges and syntheses of information on census content, methods, and problems among national census authorities; (3) financial and technical assistance and related training provided to developing countries and other countries needing special assistance; and (4) overall, more knowledgeable and better-trained census users. Each of these means is reviewed, in turn, in the balance of this article.

United Nations Recommendations and Related Documentation on Population and Housing

On July 19, 1995, the United Nations Economic and Social Council, on the recommendation of its Statistical Commission (a body consisting of representatives, usually the chief governmental statisticians, from twenty-four member states of the United Nations which reports directly to the Economic and Social Council), inaugurated the 1995–2004 census decade by adopting a formal resolution urging "Member States to carry out population and housing censuses during the period 1995–2004, taking into account international and regional recommendations." This resolution, "E/1995/7 (2000 World Population and Housing Census Programme)," provided the framework for the global United Nations population and housing census

recommendations adopted in 1997 by the Statistical Commission. The recommendations, published as *Principles and Recommendations for Population and Housing Censuses* (United Nations, 1998), provided basic definitions of census terminology and concepts, as well as guidance on methodology, census content, and outputs, including tabulations.

Roughly comparable resolutions and global census recommendations have been initiated by the Statistical Commission every ten years since the 1950 census decade that ran from 1945 to 1954. (Prior to the 1980 census decade, separate recommendations were issued for population censuses and housing censuses.) Although these global United Nations recommendations potentially could provide considerable scope for international coordination in census content, timing, and methods, the growing awareness that national data needs and conditions of enumeration vary markedly among countries has resulted in the successive abandonment of a unitary model of a proper population census. For example, in earlier decades priority was granted to topics explicitly recommended for inclusion. Recent recommendations take a more pragmatic approach to the choice of content. Similarly, in the first several census decades an effort was made to encourage at least approximate simultaneity in the timing of enumeration. For example, the resolution adopted in connection with the 1970 census decade recommended that countries carry out their censuses "preferably around the year 1970." Beginning with the census decade of the 1980s, the emphasis shifted to the importance of fixed periodicity of census enumerations within each country. References to a desired year of enumeration were dropped.

Multilateral and Bilateral Exchanges of Information on Census Content, Methods, and Problems among National Census Authorities

An important and growing aspect of international cooperation in census-taking is the exchange of relevant information and experience among groups of countries facing the common challenge of conducting a timely, reliable, and cost-effective population census to satisfy a diverse body of user needs. At the global level this work has led to the production of handbooks and other technical studies by the United Nations Statistics Division and the statistical services of the specialized agencies. Since 1945 the exchange of census information and experience has been of particular importance at the regional level under the auspices first of the Conference of European Statisticians and the Economic Commission for Europe and the Organization of American States. Subsequently, the statistical services of other United Nations regional commissions and the European Union, as well as a wide variety of sub-regional groups of countries, also provided important focal points for the collection, distillation, and dissemination of census experience.

Financial and Technical Assistance and Related Training Provided to Developing Countries and Other Countries Needing Special Assistance

Other potential sources for promoting, at least indirectly, international coordination in census-taking come from the various programs of technical assistance provided to countries that have planned and carried out population censuses since 1945. Many of the components of this assistance (particularly training, advisory services, and the provision of data processing equipment and services) also have had a tendency to encourage the replication of the census methods and content of those providing the assistance. However, in terms of achieving a high degree of overall international coordination, the impact of this factor has been diminished by the philosophy of most multilateral technical cooperation programs that have recognized a degree of diversity as a matter of principle. On the other hand, these programs of assistance are a prime example of effective international cooperation in the population census field.

More Knowledgeable and Better-Trained Census Users

A factor that can be expected to have a growing impact on census outputs and content, and eventually census methods, is the growing body of reasonably knowledgeable census users in all parts of the world. Such users, while recognizing that a unitary census model of census operations may be irrelevant for their needs, have a growing interest in similar data, including internationally comparable data, which are aggregated or analyzed in similar ways, often for similar purposes. Thus, in the long run, these users may well be the most powerful advocates for the improved international coordination of the concepts, classifications, and definitions used in population censuses.

See also *Censuses in other countries; U.S. insular areas.*

■ William Seltzer

Bibliography

Bierce, Ambrose. *The Devil's Dictionary*. Oxford: Oxford University Press, 1999. Originally published in 1911.

Seltzer, William. "Statistical Standards and National, Regional and Global Requirements and Capabilities." *1996 Proceedings of the Government Statistics Section of the American Statistical Association*. Washington, D.C.: American Statistical Association, 1996.

United Nations. *Statistical Commission. Report of the Thirteenth Session (20 April–7 May 1965)*. E/4045. Economic and Social Council, Official Records: 39th session. New York: United Nations, 1965.

———. *Principles and Recommendations for Population and Housing Censuses*. Series M, No. 67, United Nations publication sales no. E.80.XVII.8. New York: United Nations, 1980.

———. *Principles and Recommendations for Population and Housing Censuses, Revision 1*. Series M, No. 67/Rev. 1, United Nations publication sales no. E.98.XVII.8. New York: United Nations, 1998.

Westergaad, Harald. *Contributions to the History of Statistics*. London: P. S. King and Son, 1932.

IPUMS

IPUMS is an acronym for Integrated Public Use Microdata Series, a coherent individual-level national database that describes the characteristics of 55 million Americans in thirteen census years spanning the period from 1850 through 1990. It combines nationally representative probability samples produced by the Census Bureau for the period since 1940 with new high-precision historical samples produced at the University of Minnesota and elsewhere. By putting all samples in a common format, imposing consistent variable coding, and carefully documenting changes in variables over time, the IPUMS facilitates the use of the census samples as a time series.

The IPUMS includes information about both individuals and households in a hierarchical structure, so researchers can construct new variables based on information from multiple household members. Because it is microdata as opposed to summary aggregate data, the IPUMS allows researchers to create tabulations tailored to particular research questions and to carry out individual-level multivariate analyses. Among key research areas are economic development, poverty and inequality, industrial and occupational structures, household and family compositions, the household economy, female labor force participation, employment patterns, population growth, urbanization, internal migration, immigration, nuptiality, fertility, and education.

The database includes comprehensive documentation amounting to some 3,000 pages of text, including detailed analyses of the comparability of every variable across every census year. Both the database and the documentation are distributed through an online data access system at http://www.ipums.umn.edu, which provides powerful extraction and search capabilities to allow easy access to both metadata and microdata. The project is funded by the National Science Foundation and the National Institutes of Health, so all data and documentation are available without cost.

Characteristics

The characteristics of the IPUMS samples are detailed in Table 1. The only census years missing from the series are 1890, because the census manuscripts were destroyed by fire; 1930, which is still subject to 72-year census confidentiality rules; and 2000, which is not yet available. In 2002, it will be possible to add the censuses from 1930 and 2000 to the series. For years prior to 1970, the samples generally include 1 percent of the population. In several cases—1860, 1870, 1900, and 1910—the preliminary versions of the samples currently available are smaller, but each will eventually contain at least 1 percent of the population. Thus by 2007, the IPUMS should include samples of at least 1-in-100 density for every possible census year since 1850.

The pre-1940 samples are smaller than the recent ones, partly because the population was smaller. Moreover, the sample density available for the period since 1970 is much higher than in earlier census years: for each of the past three censuses, microdata are available for at least 6 percent of the population, allowing analysis of very small population subgroups. The census also tended to ask more questions over time, as is indirectly

Table 1. Characteristics of IPUMS National Census Microdata Samples

Census Year	Year Completed	Completed Sample Densities	Number of Variables	Currently Available (9/99) Cases (000)	Currently Available (9/99) File size (Mb)	Final Versions Cases (000)	Final Versions File size (Mb)
Historical Samples							
1850	1994	1%	92	198	79	198	79
1860	2001	1%	94	177	70	354	141
1870	2001	1%	94	214	85	428	170
1880	2002	100%	123	503	204	50,300	20,435
1900	2003	1%	115	100[e]	41	870	361
1910	2004	1.16%	125	366[e]	152	1,281	504
1920	1999	1%	122	1,037	433	1,037	433
1930[a]	2007	1%	122			1,172	487
Census Bureau Samples							
1940	1984	1%	174	1,351	584	1,351	584
1950	1984	1%	170	1,922	798	1,922	798
1960	1973	1%	141	1,780	790	1,780	790
1970	1972	6%[b]	206	12,180	5,576	12,180	5,576
1980	1983	8%[c]	276	15,871	7,526	18,138	8,601
1990	1992	6%[d]	252	15,000	7,247	15,000	7,247
2000[a]	2002	5%	251			14,000	6,764
Total				50,699	23,587	120,011	52,970

Notes:

a. Planned; release date and sample densities subject to change.

b. The 1970 census has six independent 1% samples.

c. The 1980 census has a 5% sample and three 1% samples.

d. The 1990 census has a 5% sample and a 1% sample.

e. The preliminary versions of the 1900 and 1910 samples were created by Prof. Samuel Preston.

Table 2. Availability of Select IPUMS Subject Areas, 1850–1990

	1850	1860	1870	1880	1900	1910	1920	1940	1950	1960	1970	1980	1990
Household record													
State	X	X	X	X	X	X	X	X	X	X	X	X	X
County	X	X	X	X	X	X	X	.	.	.	.	.	.
County group/microdata area	.	.	.	.	.	.	.	.	.	.	X	X	X
State economic area	X	X	X	X	X	X	X	X	X	.	.	.	.
Metropolitan area	X	X	X	X	X	X	X	X	X	.	X	X	X
City	X	X	X	X	X	X	X	X	X	.	.	X	X
Size of place	X	X	X	X	X	X	X	X	X	.	.	X	X
Urban/rural status	X	X	X	X	X	X	X	.	.	X	X	X	X
Farm	X	X	X	X	X	X	X	X	X	X	X	X	X
Ownership of dwelling	.	.	.	.	X	X	X	X	.	X	X	X	X
Mortgage status	.	.	.	.	X	X	X	.	.	.	.	X	X
Value of house or property	.	.	.	.	.	.	.	X	.	X	X	X	X
Monthly rent	.	.	.	.	.	.	.	X	.	X	X	X	X
Total family income	.	.	.	.	.	.	.	.	X	X	X	X	X
Person record													
Relationship to household head	.	.	.	X	X	X	X	X	X	X	X	X	X
Age	X	X	X	X	X	X	X	X	X	X	X	X	X
Sex	X	X	X	X	X	X	X	X	X	X	X	X	X
Race	X	X	X	X	X	X	X	X	X	X	X	X	X
Marital status	.	.	.	X	X	X	X	X	X	X	X	X	X
Age at first marriage	.	.	.	.	.	.	.	X	.	X	X	X	.
Duration of marriage	.	.	.	.	.	X	X	.	X	.	.	.	.
Times married	.	.	.	.	.	X	.	X	X	X	X	.	.
Children ever born	.	.	.	.	X	X	.	X	X	X	X	.	X
Birthplace	X	X	X	X	X	X	X	X	X	X	X	X	X
Parents' birthplaces	.	.	.	X	X	X	X	X	X	X	X	.	.
Ancestry	.	.	.	.	.	.	.	.	.	.	.	X	X
Years in the United States	.	.	.	.	X	X	X	.	.	.	X	X	X
Mother tongue	.	.	.	.	.	X	X	X	.	X	X	.	.
Language spoken	.	.	.	.	.	X	.	.	.	.	.	X	X
School attendance	X	X	X	X	X	X	X	X	X	X	X	X	X
Educational attainment	..	.	.	.	.	.	.	X	X	X	X	X	X
Literacy	X	X	X	X	X	X	X	.	.	.	.	.	.
Employment status	.	.	.	.	.	X	.	X	X	X	X	X	X
Occupation	X	X	X	X	X	X	X	X	X	X	X	X	X
Industry	.	.	.	.	.	X	X	X	X	X	X	X	X
Class of worker	.	.	.	.	.	X	X	X	X	X	X	X	X
Weeks worked last year	.	.	.	.	.	.	.	X	X	X	X	X	X
Weeks unemployed	.	.	.	X	X	X	.	X	X	.	.	X	.
Total personal income	.	.	.	.	.	.	.	.	X	X	X	X	X
Wage and salary income	.	.	.	.	.	.	.	X	X	X	X	X	X
Value of personal or real estate	X	X	X	.	.	.	.	.	.	.	.	.	.
Migration status	.	.	.	.	.	.	.	X	X	X	X	X	X
Veteran status	.	.	.	.	.	X	.	X	X	X	X	X	X
Surname similarity code	X	X	X	X	X	X	X	X	X				
Name	X	X	X	X	X	X	X	.	.	.	.	.	.

Note: X = available in that census year.

shown by the column for the number of variables in Table 1. Although the early samples are smaller and less detailed than their modern counterparts, they are at present the largest samples available for quantitative historical research in that period, and are capable of supporting research on topics ranging from marriage and fertility to social stratification and household structure.

The IPUMS will soon incorporate a much larger sample for the census of 1880. Volunteers working with the Church of Jesus Christ of Latter-day Saints (LDS) have invested approximately two million hours transcribing information from the 1880 U.S. Census of Population. This database—which covers the entire U.S. population of 50 million persons—has the potential to become our most important resource for the study of the economic and social organization of late-nineteenth century American society. The LDS holds the copyright to these data, but has agreed to make them freely available for inclusion in the IPUMS in exchange for assistance in cleaning the data. The project should be complete by 2002. The new data from 1880 will allow the construction of cross-tabulations on a wide range of topics that were not covered by census publications or that were incompletely tabulated, and will fill a gap in aggregate data series for counties and cities. Perhaps even more important is the potential for longitudinal and multilevel analyses opened up by the availability of the 1880 data.

The IPUMS is designed to encourage analyses that incorporate multiple census years for the study of change over time. The census has always contained certain core questions that are generally comparable over the time span of the database. Other questions have come and gone. Table 2 describes many subject areas covered by the census since 1850 (many of these topics correspond to multiple variables in the database). In general, the IPUMS samples include all the census questions available in each year, but for the period from 1940 on, some detail is suppressed in order to preserve respondent confidentiality. In particular, geographic detail is far superior in the pre-1940 samples. In fact,

the samples for the period prior to 1940 generally include the names and addresses of the respondents. By contrast, topics such as income, educational attainment, and migration have only been covered by the census for the past fifty years. All IPUMS samples also include a common set of constructed variables to allow easy data manipulation. Most important among these is a set of family interrelationship variables that have proven broadly useful in the construction of consistent family composition and own-child fertility measures.

Future Plans

Future plans for the IPUMS call for extension of the paradigm to twenty-one countries. For most of these countries, the new database will include multiple samples spanning the period from 1960 to 2000. For some countries, the chronological depth is far greater, stretching back into the nineteenth century. The inclusion of international data will allow investigations of social change across space as well as through time.

The IPUMS project will also incorporate additional U.S. data. The present IPUMS incorporates only material from the decennial census, and this is a significant weakness. A new project is planned to add data from the monthly Current Population Surveys from 1964 onwards, Census 2000, and annual samples from the American Community Survey for the period after 2000.

See also *PUMS*.

■ Steven Ruggles

Bibliography

Ruggles, Steven, ed. "The Minnesota Historical Census Projects." Special Issue. *Historical Methods* 28 (winter 1995).

Ruggles, Steven, and Patricia Kelly Hall, eds. "IPUMS: The Integrated Public Use Microdata Series." Special Issue. *Historical Methods* 32 (summer 1999).

Ruggles, Steven, and Matthew Sobek. *Integrated Public Use Microdata Series: Version 2.0.5* volumes. Minneapolis: University of Minnesota, 1998–1999.

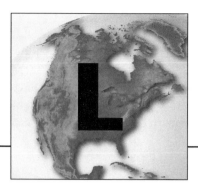

Litigation and the census

Litigation related to census-taking methods and procedures has generally fallen into five categories: (1) prosecutions of householders for refusing to respond to census questions; (2) prosecutions of enumerators or census employees for failing to do their jobs; (3) challenges to or defenses of the confidentiality of information on the individual census forms; (4) challenges to the Census Bureau to remedy the differential undercount of subgroups of the population; and (5) challenges to the sampling procedures proposed for taking the census. The suits, which span censuses conducted from 1790, the year of the first count, to 2000, illustrate the complexities and ambiguities in census taking. They also provide an evolving set of standards for determining the count's accuracy and precision and for assessing the relative responsibilities of the public and the government for conducting the census.

Taking the census has always required residents to cooperate with the census taker and provide the requested information. Today, the federal government relies on households to respond voluntarily and to return the census form they receive in the mail. But Congress determined at the outset of the Republic that responding would be mandatory for all residents and that individuals who refused to comply would be subject to legal penalties. The first census law, written in 1790, contained such a penalty, permitting the assistant U.S. marshal to sue a household head in federal court for $20 if the individual refused to provide information.

Several suits were filed in South Carolina under this provision. Such prosecutions have been extremely rare over the centuries, but they do occur. The penalty in 2000 for willfully refusing to fill out the census form was $100; the penalty for giving false information was $500.

Similarly, census enumerators who violated their oaths and failed to do their jobs properly could also be legally prosecuted. In 1790 assistant marshals were fined $200 for not completing their work competently and on time. The current census statutory language (Title 13) levies a fine of up to $2,000 and a sentence of five years in jail on enumerators who neglect their duties or submit false information. Among those who have been prosecuted and convicted under these provisions are the enumerators who in 1910 systematically padded the population of Tacoma, Washington, by over 35 percent.

Another major area of litigation affecting the census focuses on the confidentiality of the answers reported on census forms. In the nineteenth century census forms were considered open records. They were either posted at county courthouses for correction or provided, in whole or in part, to local governments for reference and preservation. Beginning in the late nineteenth century, as census officials became increasingly concerned about privacy, they sought to clarify and define census confidentiality. They did so by prosecuting enumerators or employees who revealed information on the forms. By 1929 they also had inserted in the statutory language statements specifying that census information be used "for statistical purposes" and barring publication of any data that might reveal information on "any particular establishment or individual." By the 1950s these provisions had been expanded to prevent courts from subpoenaing copies of individual census forms.

Lawsuits over Counting Procedures

A new type of challenge to the census emerged with the count of 1970, when the Census Bureau itself was sued. Local officials claimed that the bureau's procedures, particularly those affecting the mail census, would prevent some groups from being accurately counted. These suits did not fare well in federal court. District court judges decided that the bureau, in implementing its responsibilities under Title 13, had the authority to determine count procedures and methods. But the court also ruled that the bureau had a new responsibility—that those procedures and methods be fair to all of society's constituencies. After 1970 such suits proliferated as the courts became involved in determining counting procedures that previously had been considered only in legislative or administrative venues.

Several suits, for example, have challenged the bureau's rules for determining who is included in the population counts. The bureau faced district court challenges in 1980 and 1990 from plaintiffs who wanted it to exclude undocumented aliens from the apportionment population counts (*FAIR v. Klutznick*, 486 F. Supp. 564 (1980); *Ridge v. Verity*, 715 F. Supp. 1308 (1989)). In 1990 the state of Massachusetts, seeking a Supreme Court ruling, challenged the inclusion of overseas military personnel in the state counts for congressional apportionment (*Franklin v. Massachusetts*, 505 U.S. 788 (1992)). The decisions in these cases upheld the authority of the bureau to determine counting procedures.

The most serious of the suits challenging census procedures involved the census undercount. In the 1960s and 1970s Census Bureau evaluation studies demonstrated that the census counted whites, suburban areas, and the middle class more accurately than it did minorities, urban areas, and the poor. In 1980 the bureau faced over fifty lawsuits filed by state and local governments seeking to correct the differential undercount. The plaintiffs sought to ensure that undercounted constituencies retained political representation and economic resources. The most serious of the challenges were brought in district court by the city of Detroit (*Young v. Klutznick*, 497 F. Supp. 1318 (1980)) and the city and state of New York (*Carey v. Klutznick*, 508 F. Supp. 420 (1980)). Both suits tried to stop the bureau from reporting the official census results on schedule, in December 1980, and to force it to adjust the counts in light of the known undercount. Although in both cases the courts initially sided with the plaintiffs, the decisions were later stayed, and the 1980 census results were released to the president on time.

The suits did not die with the release of the 1980 results. Most were withdrawn or dismissed after the census, but the New York litigants continued to press their case, claiming that census procedures had not been properly implemented and that, even if they had been, the undercount should be corrected. They asked for a trial to determine if the bureau could adjust the 1980 census results to correct for errors in the count. If it could, they argued, the bureau should issue a second or revised set of data.

That trial took place in 1984. Three years later Judge John Sprizzo ruled in *Cuomo v. Baldrige* (674 F. Supp. 1089 (1987)) that the procedures used by the bureau were not "arbitrary and capricious" as defined in the Administrative Procedure Act (APA) of 1946. The judge accepted the testimony of high-level bureau officials and outside experts that the methods used to measure error in the 1980 census were not accurate enough to be used to adjust the count. The ruling upheld the authority of the bureau to determine the procedures for taking the census but implicitly left open the door to further litigation if plaintiffs could demonstrate that bureau procedures were arbitrary and capricious.

In the 1980s the bureau conducted a major research project to improve the adjustment methods so that they could be used to adjust the 1990 census if the differential undercount recurred. In 1987 the bureau announced its intention to implement the new adjustment procedures by adding a recently designed post-enumeration survey to the 1990 operational plan. The Commerce Department, the bureau's parent agency, overruled this plan, and in 1988 New York City and a coalition of other local governments and interest groups sued the bureau and the Commerce Department, asking the court to reinstate the new adjustment procedures, including the post-enumeration survey. The plaintiffs and the Commerce Department in 1989 reached a stipulation agreement to continue with the plans for the survey and a possible adjustment of the 1990 census. The parties also created a special panel to monitor census procedures and make recommendations to the commerce secretary, who was to recommend by July 1991 whether the 1990 census results should be adjusted.

In July 1991 Commerce Secretary Robert A. Mosbacher declined to adjust the 1990 census. The secretary admitted that a differential net undercount of minorities and some jurisdictions had existed in the 1990 census, but he also claimed that the proposed adjustment methods were not sufficiently accurate to improve the unadjusted counts. In response, the New York City plaintiffs returned to court, asserting that Mosbacher's decision had been arbitrary and capricious under the APA. After hearing arguments in May 1992, the district court in 1993 held that the decision of the commerce secretary had not been arbitrary and capricious. The judge also noted that if he had been asked to decide the case *de novo*—that is, from the beginning—he would have ordered the census adjusted. The New York City plaintiffs appealed the decision to a circuit court, which in summer 1994 reversed the ruling. In 1995 the Justice Department and the states of Pennsylvania, Wisconsin, and Oklahoma appealed the circuit court's ruling to the Supreme Court. The Court in March 1996 decided in favor of the commerce secretary (*Wisconsin v. City of New York*, 517 U.S. 1 (1996)).

Sampling Methods Challenged

By the second half of the 1990s, a substantial body of litigation had upheld the authority of the bureau and the Commerce Department to make decisions about census procedures. In 1997 Congress issued a new challenge to that authority. That year the Clinton administration and the Republican Congress disagreed on procedures for taking the 2000 census. They wrote language into the census appropriations bill allowing members of Congress and aggrieved individuals to sue the administration and the bureau and granting them expedited hearings if they felt that the proposed census plans would result in an inaccurate, invalid, or unconstitutional census. Early in 1998 House Speaker Newt Gingrich, R-Ga., and the Southeastern Legal Foundation filed separate district court suits under these provisions, charging that the plans for using statistical sampling in the nonresponse follow-up phase and the post-enumeration survey of the 2000 census violated the Constitution and the current provisions of Title 13 (*House v. U.S. Department of Commerce*, 11 F. Supp. 2d 76 (1998); *Glavin v. Clinton*, 19 F. Supp. 2d 543 (1998)).

In summer 1998 the courts decided these "sampling suits" in favor of the plaintiffs. The defendants appealed to the Supreme Court (*Department of Commerce v. U.S. House*, 525 U.S. 316 (1999)), which in January 1999 in-terpreted Title 13 to prevent sampling for determining the population counts for apportionment. The Court thus struck down the use of statistical sampling in the nonresponse follow-up phase of the count. The Court acknowledged that other provisions of Title 13 required the bureau to use sampling as the preferred counting method. The bureau interpreted the ruling to require unadjusted counts for apportioning seats in the House of Representatives among the fifty states and to mandate the Accuracy and Coverage Evaluation component of the census 2000 plan. If the evaluation, begun in summer 2000 and scheduled to be completed by early spring 2001, concludes that the adjusted counts are more accurate than the unadjusted counts, the bureau will issue adjusted counts that spring. Congress, states, and local governments could then use adjusted counts for determining legislative districts, allocating funds, and evaluating programs. As of mid-2000 further litigation was expected, after the 2000 census results were released, to clarify the legality and constitutionality of adjusted census data.

See also *Apportionment and districting; Capture-recapture methods; Census law; Confidentiality; Demographic analysis; Post-enumeration Survey.*

■ Margo Anderson

Bibliography

Anderson, Margo, and Stephen E. Fienberg. *Who Counts? The Politics of Census Taking in Contemporary America.* New York: Russell Sage Foundation, 1999.

Brown, Lawrence, et al. "Statistical Controversies in Census 2000." *Jurimetrics* 39 (summer 1999): 347–375.

Choldin, Harvey. *Looking for the Last Percent: The Controversy over Census Undercounts.* New Brunswick, N.J.: Rutgers University Press, 1994.

Local involvement in census taking

The decennial census is a federal enterprise, the result of an extraordinary consensus among the Framers of the Constitution that the distribution of political representation should be based on a census that employs uniform standards to enumerate the nation's population. Yet, there is an essential paradox in census taking: the federal government conducts the decennial census, but it is inherently a local enterprise that is closely dependent on cooperation between federal and local entities.

The more than one hundred years of experience in local census taking in the colonies provided those who met to form the laws of the new republic in the 1780s with a wealth of experience in the practices and outcomes of locally conducted censuses. The British had mandated colonial censuses, and forty-six were conducted in nine of the original thirteen states. At no time during the colonial period was a census of *all* colonies attempted, however, and no uniformity existed in the questions asked or methods used in these censuses. By 1787 it became obvious in the Continental Congress that sharing obligations (for example, taxes) and rights (for example, political representation) based on population was the path of choice, but absent fair counts of population for all colonies, such a path would prove useless. Also obvious were the diverse interests that localities had in particular outcomes, as evidenced by the debate over the definition of a "person" for census purposes and the status of slaves. All recognized that a federal-level coordinating body was necessary to conduct a uniform census at regular intervals. This federal coordination, however, would not remove the inherent tension among localities that, over the next 200 years, would vie for the influence and power connected to the census.

A big part of census history involves how local governments have tested their relationships with federal authorities since 1790. Although numerous issues have permeated the dialogue between the federal government and local organizations, most of these can be encompassed under two broad headings: census accuracy and the advent of small-area data.

Census Accuracy

Even the earliest attempts to enumerate the population of the colonies were fraught with response problems as a result of religious superstitions, fear of government reprisals, and sheer physical access to the territory of the newly formed nation. In the nineteenth century each census brought with it tensions regarding allegations of procedural problems and undercounts by state and local governments, especially as the census field operation expanded. Although questions regarding undercounts occurred at earlier points, it is in 1870 that the census superintendent Francis Amasa Walker had to contend with major allegations by many cities that the decennial census did not count everyone. These complaints sometimes resulted in a re-check of the census enumeration, which did sometimes result in higher counts, as was the case in New York City, Philadelphia, and Indianapolis in 1870.

In other instances, however, these allegations not only proved false, but upon closer scrutiny, revealed large-scale fraud sponsored by local organizations attempting to boost their counts. In Minneapolis and St. Paul, for example, allegations that schedules were lost in the 1890 census resulted in a re-enumeration that revealed widespread fraud on the part of census enumerators who attempted to boost population counts; as a result both cities saw substantial reductions in their official population counts. Civic involvement in census taking became more formalized in the twentieth century, with the advent of local area census committees and increased awareness of the decennial census as a planning tool. Many of these committees were genuinely helpful in the census-taking effort, but some were sponsors of fraudulent practices that systematically padded counts, all in the name of locally inspired "civic chauvinism." Writing in 1911, after the Census Bureau became a permanent entity within the Department of Commerce and Labor, the bureau director Edward Dana Durand reported deliberate conspiracies to inflate the enumeration in some cities. One of the most notable examples, according to his report, was in Tacoma, Washington, where the original count of more than 116,000 was reduced to about 84,000 after a second enumeration was conducted.

Despite attempts by some local groups to manipulate returns, undercounts in many localities were increasingly apparent. In Durand's 1911 account to the secretary of commerce and labor, he went on record about the issue of undercount by alluding to the problem of achieving absolute accuracy, given the vast physical area and enormous population of the nation. Indeed, he reported that a re-check of the 1910 enumeration in some cities did yield evidence of undercount. It was not until 1940, however, when modern statistical methods were first used in census taking, that the Census Bureau began formally evaluating census accuracy, by attempting to quantify the magnitude of the undercount and its effect, especially by race. By doing this, the bureau began a period of increased awareness that led to several programs aimed at formally including local governments in the census process. This included campaigns aimed at gaining local support for full participation in the census, especially after 1960, when the mail-back method became the primary mode of response. Declines in mail response with each passing decade prompted the bureau to adopt strategies aimed at forming local committees, composed of influential government officials and community leaders, to plan and implement local publicity and outreach campaigns. According to the Census Bureau, about 9,800 of the 39,000 local governments responded to the call for Complete Count Committees in 1990, with some 5,600 actually participating in the program.

The most serious attempt to directly involve local governments in making the census more accurate was "local review." The local review program began in 1980, when local governments were permitted to review housing unit counts before they became final so that deficits in the enumeration could be identified. The idea was to incorporate local knowledge and data to make the address list used in the enumeration more accurate before the census itself was taken (pre-census local review), and to review the preliminary housing unit counts from the actual enumeration before they became final so that problems in the field could be identified and fixed (post-census local review). The local government was given a limited period (usually thirty to sixty days) to respond with "challenges" based on local data. Title 13 of the U.S. Code, which protects the confidentiality of census respondents, prohibited the disclosure of individual addresses on the list in both 1980 and 1990, so local governments were not able to sort out problems at the address level, nor was the Census Bureau required to provide detailed feedback on the final disposition of these challenges. According to the U.S. General Accounting Office (GAO), just 32 percent of eligible governments participated in pre-census local review in 1990. The GAO concluded that three-quarters of those eligible governments that did not participate lacked the required data and staff resources to do so. As a result, the local review program had, even by the most optimistic accounts, only spotty success.

In 1994 Congress passed the Address List Improvement Act, a law that permitted local governments to receive and review the actual address list used to mail questionnaires in advance of the 2000 census, provided that reviewers sign an agreement not to disclose any information and to use it solely for the purpose of making the census more accurate. Despite this new incentive, the resource limitations of local governments, once again, acted to inhibit uniform and effective participation in the Local Update of Census Addresses (LUCA) program in 2000. Unlike in 1980 and 1990, no post-census review of counts has been offered to local governments because earlier post-census review programs were not cost-effective, according to the Census Bureau.

Another by-product of this heightened awareness about census accuracy was a series of lawsuits by localities surrounding the 1980 and 1990 censuses. Such litigation was now possible given the existence of statistical and demographic methods documenting the persistence of differential undercount by race and the creation of statistical algorithms to address the problem. Localities entered into extensive litigation in an attempt to force the Census Bureau to "correct" the undercount through the use of statistical methods. By and large, localities were unsuccessful in their attempts to force a statistical adjustment of census numbers.

The Advent of Small-Area Data

As the twentieth century began, the nation's cities were entering a period of unprecedented growth, absorbing large numbers of migrants from the nation's rural areas and immigrants from southern and eastern Europe. This high level of growth posed a dilemma for many local governments that were concerned about controlling the spread of communicable diseases, providing shelter to many new arrivals, and maintaining order. Whereas the federal government focused on broad changes to the nation, such as the disappearance of the frontier, and to changes at the state level for reapportionment purposes, local organizations became increasingly concerned about the vast changes in their local communities.

Local governments became more aware of their vested interests in the census counts and began to request data for small areas. In some cities, such as New York and Cleveland, the demand for small area data translated into locally sponsored programs of data tabulation for new units of geography that came to be known as census tracts. For more than thirty years, tabulations of small area data from the decennial census were created as a direct result of the commitment to local data analysis on the part of local organizations. Groups such as the New York Federation of Churches and the New York City 1920 Census Committee designed the small area tabulations that later became the foundation for the census tract program, as adopted by the Census Bureau in 1940. Until that time, the program was funded by local entities in New York, Cleveland, and other cities that found the information essential for addressing problems in their rapidly growing communities.

The creation of small area data became synonymous with local involvement in census-taking efforts. When the bureau formally instituted the census tract program in 1940, it established a link between federal and local organizations that remains firm to this day. By accepting the responsibility to prepare data for locally defined units, the federal government created a program that was heavily dependent on local input. Changes in census tract designations are done jointly with localities, usually a local government or their designated representatives. When the new era of federal funding began in the 1960s and 1970s, involvement in this program peaked because small area data were now being used to allocate funds for a variety of purposes, including community development initiatives. Today, the Census Bureau actively incorporates local area geographic knowledge into census work. Local area census tract committees are responsible for designating tract boundary changes before each census, based on a series of ground rules established by the Census Bureau in an attempt to achieve standardization and comparability over time.

See also *Census tracts; Coverage evaluation; Grassroots groups; Litigation and the census; State and local censuses.*

■ Joseph J. Salvo

Bibliography

Alterman, Hyman. *Counting People: The Census in History.* New York: Harcourt, Brace and World, 1969.

Barrows, Robert G. "The Ninth Federal Census of Indianapolis: A Case Study in Civic Chauvinism." *Indiana Magazine of History* 73 (March 1977): 1–16.

Stevens, L. Nye. "Expanding the Role of Local Governments: An Important Element of Census Reform." Testimony before the Subcommittee on Census and Population, Committee on Post Office and Civil Service in the U.S. House of Representatives. Washington, D.C.: U.S. General Accounting Office, 1991.

Superintendent of the Census. *Report of the Superintendent of Census to the Secretary of the Interior for the Six Months Ending December 31, 1890.* Washington, D.C.: U.S. Government Printing Office, 1891.

U.S. Bureau of the Census. *1990 Census of Population and Housing: History.* Part A, chapter 6. Washington, D.C., 1993.

———. *1980 Census of Population and Housing: History.* Part B, chapter 5. Washington, D.C., 1986.

———. *Report of the Director to the Secretary of Commerce and Labor Concerning the Operations of the Bureau for the Year 1909–10.* Washington, D.C.: U.S. Government Printing Office, 1911.

Long form

The long form is a questionnaire that is sent to a sample of addresses in the census. Long forms typically contain the "short-form" person and housing items that all households are asked to provide, together with additional items that only the households in the long-form sample are asked to provide. (Short-form items are generally limited to basic demographic and housing items; long-form items cover such topics as income, employment, veteran status, transportation to work, education, and others—see Table 1.)

The long form provides a way to obtain more information from the census than is needed for the basic head count without requiring the entire population to respond to all items. Use of the long form also reduces the costs of the census by eliminating the need to ask all of the short-form and long-form items of every household.

The Long Form in Censuses between 1960 and 2000

The 1960 census first introduced the concept of "short" and "long" forms or questionnaires. In the 1940 and 1950 censuses, some items were obtained from a sample of households, but separate forms were not employed. The use of mail delivery to help conduct the 1960 census necessitated the development of separate forms.

In 1960 the U.S. Postal Service dropped off questionnaires at all households containing the short-form or 100-percent items. Enumerators then visited these households to obtain the short-form answers. At every fourth household (25 percent) in areas of the country that contained about 80 percent of the housing, the enumerator left a long-form questionnaire to be filled in and mailed back by the household. Different forms were used in large cities of 50,000 or more people and other areas: each contained several questions unique to the form. In the remaining more rural areas that contained about 20 percent of the housing, the enumerators asked the long-form questions on the spot. In these areas, enumerators asked 20 percent of households one set of housing items, and 5 percent of households another set. Some housing items and all population items were asked of both groups, producing a 25 percent sample for those items. (In the more urban areas, households receiving the long-form sample filled out all items for the type of

Table 1. Questions on the Decennial Census: 1960–2000

Questionnaire Item	1960	1970	1980	1990	2000
Population Items					
Age (and/or date of birth)	S	S	S	S	S
Sex	S	S	S	S	S
Race	S	S	S	S	S
Hispanic origin		L[b]	S	S	S
Relationship to household head	S	S	S	S	S
Marital status	S	S	S	S	L
Age at or date of first marriage	L	L[b]	L		
Married more than once	L	L[b]	L		
If remarried, was first marriage ended by death?		L[b]	L		
Number of children ever born to mother	L	L	L	L	
School attendance/educational attainment	L	L	L	L	L
Public or private school (for people currently enrolled)	L	L[a]	L	L	L
Vocational training		L[b]			
Place of birth (short-form item in New York State in 1960)	L	L	L	L	L
Place of birth of mother and father	L	L[a]			
Citizenship (short-form item in New York State in 1960 and not asked elsewhere in that year)		L[b]	L	L	L
Year of immigration		L[b]	L	L	L
Language spoken at home (before came to U.S. if born abroad in 1960, as a child in 1970)	L	L[a]	L	L	L
How well English spoken			L	L	L
Ancestry			L	L	L
Veteran status/period of service (for men in 1960 and 1970)	L	L[a]	L	L	L
Years of military service				L	L
Place of residence 5 years ago (state of residence 5 years ago only on 5 percent long form in 1970)	L	L[a, b]	L	L	L
Year moved to present residence (see housing item on year household head moved into unit)		L	L[a]		
Work disability		L[b]	L	L	L
Transportation disability			L		
Disabled for going outside the home alone				L	L
Disabled for taking care of personal needs				L	L
Other disabilities (involving eyes, ears, cognition, mobility)					L
Duration of disability		L[b]			
Whether and how long responsible for grandchildren in home					L
Employment status	L	L	L	L	L
Hours worked in preceding week	L	L	L	L	
Occupation	L	L	L	L	L
Industry	L	L	L	L	L
Class of worker	L	L	L	L	L
Place of work	L	L[a]	L	L	L
Means of transportation to work	L	L[a]	L	L	L
Commuting time (and when usually left for work in 1990, 2000)			L	L	L
Carpooling				L	L	L
Year last worked	L	L	L	L	L
Weeks worked in preceding year	L	L	L	L	L
Hours worked per week in preceding year			L	L	L

continued

Table 1. *(cont'd)*

Questionnaire Items	1960	1970	1980	1990	2000
Population items (cont'd)					
Weeks unemployed in preceding year			L		
Activity 5 years ago		L	L		
Occupation, industry, class of worker 5 years ago		L[b]			
Income from earnings	L	L	L	L	L
Income from nonfarm self-employment (nonfarm plus farm self-employment in 1960 and 2000)	L	L	L	L	L
Income from farm self-employment		L	L	L	
Income from Social Security		L	L	L	L
Income from Supplemental Security Income					L
Income from public assistance		L	L	L	L
Income from interest, dividends, rent			L	L	L
Income from pensions				L	L
All other income (also total income in 1980, 1990, 2000)	L	L	L	L	L
Housing items					
Tenure–owned or rented	S	S	S	S	S
Type of property (e.g., whether includes a business; short-form item in large cities, long-form item otherwise in 1960; single-family homes only in 1980, 1990, 2000)	S[c]	S	S	S	L
Value (short-form item in large cities, long-form item otherwise in 1960)	S	S	S	S	L
Contract rent (short-form item in large cities, long-form item otherwise in 1960)	S	S	S	S	L
Does the rent include any meals?				S	L
Number of rooms	S	S	S	S	L
Access to unit	S[c]	S	S		
Condition (sound, deteriorating, dilapidated)	S[c]				
Condominium status			S	L	L
Bathing facilities	S	S			
Toilet facilities	S	S			
Whether hot and/or cold piped water	S	S			
Complete plumbing facilities			S	L	L
Kitchen, cooking facilities; complete kitchen facilities	S	S	L	L	L
Telephone available	L	S	L	L	L
Basement	L[a]	S			
Number of units at address (1970, 1980) or in structure (1990)		S	S	S	
Number of units in structure	L[a,c]	L	L		L
Farm residence/sales of farm products (asked only outside large cities in 1960; for single-family homes only in 2000)	L	L	L	L	L
Number of stories		L[b]	L		
Elevator (asked only in large cities in 1960; combined with question on number of stories)	L[a]	L[b]	L		
Second home		L[b]			
Whether trailer home mobile or fixed	L				
Year household head moved into unit (replaced population item on year moved in)			L	L	L
Year structure built	L	L	L	L	L
Utilities (for renters only in 1960 and 1970)					
Electricity costs	L	L	L	L	L
Gas costs	L	L	L	L	L

continued

Table 1. (cont'd)

Questionnaire Items	1960	1970	1980	1990	2000
Housing items (cont'd)					
Water costs	L	L	L	L	L
Oil, coal, etc., costs	L	L	L	L	L
Does the rent include land used for farming (asked only outside large cities in 1960)?	L				
Mortgage payment (and whether includes taxes and insurance)			L	L	L
Homeowners insurance			L	L	L
Real estate taxes (for owners only)			L	L	L
Whether have second mortgage			L	L	L
Payment for second mortgage(s)/home equity loans				L	L
Condominium or mobile home fee				L	L
Number of bathrooms	L[a]	L[a]	L		
Number of bedrooms	L[b]	L[b]	L	L	L
Heating equipment	L	L	L		
Cooking fuel		L[b]	L		
Heating fuel	L[b]	L[b]	L	L	L
Water heating fuel		L[b]	L		
Sewage disposal (asked only outside large cities in 1960)	L[a]	L[a]	L	L	
Source of water (asked only outside large cities in 1960)	L[a]	L[a]	L	L	
Air conditioning	L[b]	L[a]	L		
Automobiles (20 percent item in large cities, 5 percent item outside large cities in 1960; includes vans and trucks in 1990 and 2000)	L[a, b]	L[a]	L	L	L
Vans or trucks			L		
Clothes washer; clothes dryer	L[b]	L[b]			
Dishwasher		L[b]			
Home food freezer	L[b]	L[b]			
Radio sets (battery-operated only in 1970)	L[b]	L[b]			
Television sets	L[b]	L[b]			
Whether television equipped for UHF		L[b]			

Note: S indicates short form; L indicates long form.

[a]Indicates the 15 percent long form in 1970 and items that were transcribed on a 20 percent basis in 1960.

[b]Indicates the 5 percent long form in 1970 and items that were transcribed on a 5 percent basis in 1960.

[c]Item obtained by enumerator observation.

Source: Updated from Table A.2 in National Research Council (1995).

place—large city or other. Enumerators then transcribed the answers to computer-readable forms, transcribing the answers for 25 percent, 20 percent, or 5 percent of households, depending on the item.)

In 1970 households were sent either a short form (80 percent of households) or one of two versions of the long form. Each long form contained the 100 percent population and housing items and a common set of items asked of 20 percent of households. One version, however, also included a set of questions asked of 15 percent of households and the other a set asked of 5 percent of households.

The use of more than one long form in the 1960 and 1970 censuses, with some questions in common and other questions unique to the form (what is termed "matrix sampling"), helped reduce the burden of filling out the questionnaire on individual households. However, multiple long forms complicated the data processing and made it more difficult to use census data products.

In 1980 only one long form was used, but different fractions of households received it depending on the population size of their place of residence. In places with an estimated population of 2,500 or more, one in every six households received the long form; in smaller places, one in every two households received it. The overall sampling rate was approximately 19 percent. The primary reason for changing from a uniform 20 percent sampling rate to rates of 50 percent for small places (about 5 percent of the population) and 16.7 percent for all other places was to provide reliable per capita income data for use in allocating federal funds to 39,000 state and local jurisdictions under the provisions of the 1972 State and Local Fiscal Assistance Act. (This act is often referred to as General Revenue Sharing, a program that distributed several billion dollars each year from 1973 through 1987.)

In 1990 about one in every six households (17 percent) received the long form. Three different sampling rates were used to provide somewhat more reliable estimates for small areas and to decrease respondent burden in more densely populated areas. The sampling rate was one-in-two housing units (50 percent) in governmental units such as counties and towns with an estimated 1988 population of less than 2,500. Outside these areas, the sampling rate was one-in-six housing units (17 percent) in census tracts and equivalent areas with a pre-census housing count of fewer than 2,000 housing units (fewer than about 5,200 people) and one-in-eight housing units (13 percent) in larger census tracts and equivalent areas.

In 2000 the overall sampling rate was once again about one-in-six housing units, but there were four different sampling rates to reflect the goal of smoothing the rates and, therefore, the reliability of the estimates from the sample data (more than was done in 1990). Specifically, in 2000 the sampling rate was one-in-two (50 percent) for governmental units with fewer than 800 housing units (fewer than about 2,100 people); one-in-four (25 percent) for governmental units with 800–1,200 housing units (about 2,100–3,100 people); one-in-eight (13 percent) for census tracts with 2,000 or more housing units (about 5,200 people or more); and one-in-six (17 percent) in all other areas. Governmental units considered for oversampling in 2000 included school districts in addition to counties, towns, and townships because of the need for reliable estimates of school-age children in poverty for allocating federal funds to school districts under Title I of the Elementary and Secondary Education Act.

Replacing the Long Form with the American Community Survey

The American Community Survey (ACS) is planned to be a large-scale, continuing monthly sample survey of U.S. households, conducted primarily by mail, that will collect information similar to that provided by the census long-form sample. The ACS is currently under development. Beginning in 2003, it is planned that the ACS will sample 250,000 housing units each month throughout the decade, for an annual sample size of about 3 million housing units spread across all counties in the nation. Over a five-year period, the ACS sample size is expected to cumulate to about 15 million housing units, somewhat smaller than the 2000 census long-form sample size of about 18 million housing units.

If the ACS is successful, there could be no long-form sample in the 2010 and later censuses. In that event, every household in 2010 would receive a short form. A reason for replacing the census long-form sample with the ACS is the interest of data users in more up-to-date estimates for states and smaller geographic areas on such topics as poverty, education, and employment. Also, it is expected that the ACS could contribute to a more cost-effective short-form census, by facilitating continual updating of the Master Address File and in other ways. Further, dropping the long-form sample from the census would likely simplify census processing and somewhat reduce census costs.

See also *American Community Survey; Content determination; Sampling for content.*

■ Constance F. Citro

Bibliography

National Research Council. Committee on National Statistics, Panel on Census Requirements in the Year 2000 and Beyond. *Modernizing the U.S. Census*, edited by Barry Edmonston and Charles Schultze. Washington, D.C.: National Academy Press, 1995.

Mailing the census

See *Address list development; Data capture.*

Media attention to the census

The media are both a purveyor of information about the census and a consumer of census data. But they largely ignore the census in years between counts.

The media are often the primary source of public information about census plans, controversies over census methods and results, and the progress of the count itself. Media reporting on the census can help build or undermine public confidence in the census process. However, the research and testing, planning, and early preparations receive little coverage except in publications geared toward sophisticated data users and scientific audiences. The lack of attention parallels, to some extent, the failure of Congress to conduct more than cursory oversight of the census until the Census Bureau has finalized its plans and begun to put in place the infrastructure needed to conduct the count.

From a media perspective, the census also suffers from an ever-longer planning horizon. (For example, planning for the 2000 census began in 1991, and planning for the 2010 census began in 1998.) The Census Bureau's career staff work largely out of public view for many years, researching and testing new methods, identifying data content requirements, consulting stakeholders, and compiling their findings to produce an overall plan for the next census. Once it develops a plan, the bureau continues to refine the proposed methods and operations, conducting still more tests and, finally, a dress rehearsal two years before the count to evaluate how components of the plan work in a census-like environment and in tandem with each other.

Despite its long-term significance, little of this preparatory work has an immediate or direct impact on the American people. The planning stages often involve decisions that are highly technical or are subject to frequent modification depending on funding availability as well as feedback from stakeholders. None of these factors—lack of immediacy, complex procedures, and fluctuating decision points—is attractive to journalists in today's fast-paced world of news coverage.

Extraordinary advances in communications technology in the closing decades of the twentieth century have brought instantaneous access to news as it happens, driving policy makers and the media that cover them to concentrate on issues they believe resonate with the public in the short term. Journalists covering broad, national policy events tend to focus attention on issues that dominate debate in the legislative and political arenas at any given time. Local newspapers, radio, and television programs primarily report on events that affect their audiences in the present or foreseeable future. Despite the ongoing work to prepare for each census, the decennial count does not become an issue of currency from a news perspective until the Census

Bureau starts to deploy resources throughout the country, setting up regional and local offices, hiring temporary workers, and distributing promotional materials.

The cyclical nature of the census, which keeps it largely out of the public eye for long periods of time, also discourages media outlets from assigning one or more reporters to cover census issues on a regular basis until late in the decade. The lack of dedicated coverage means that key decisions during the period of census planning and preparation receive little or no attention from the media. As news organizations recognize the need to report on final preparations and implementation, journalists assigned to cover the story often have little historical perspective or familiarity with the census process, making knowledgeable reporting difficult.

Variety of Coverage

Nevertheless, coverage of the census varies greatly by medium. Print journalists have shown more interest in recent years in policy debates over census methods and funding, particularly as those controversies have threatened to disrupt planning for the census as well as overall government operations. During the 1990s, a relatively small but committed group of reporters for national and major local newspapers, as well as the wire services, closely followed the substantively arcane but rhetorically explosive political debate over the Census Bureau's proposed use of statistical sampling methods in 2000. Their coverage resulted in a number of in-depth articles several years before the census on the problem of undercounting and the consequences for local communities and electoral politics.

But while the print media is more conducive to stories that require substantial background information and explanation, radio and television are not well suited to covering events that are distant in time, involve complicated technical debates, and do not have an immediate demonstrable effect on listening or viewing audiences. The complex scientific, political, and legal issues that increasingly surface in the years between each census do not translate easily into the brief, sound-bite stories carried on most television and most radio news programs. Instead, radio and television reporters look for issues that lend themselves to easy explanation and that are likely to strike a chord with the audience. Consequently, television and radio coverage during the years between each census have tended to focus on isolated components of the count, such as enumeration of the homeless and changes in the options for reporting race and ethnicity, instead of more fundamental decisions concerning census methods and costs.

As the census design became more sophisticated in 1990 and 2000, many journalists struggled to understand the difficult technical work underlying the choice of methods. The 1990 census was the first to use a large-scale post-enumeration survey to measure coverage that could have provided the basis for correcting undercounts and overcounts using statistical estimation procedures. The proposed design for the 2000 census included a far more extensive use of sampling and statistical estimation. Many reporters struggled to understand how the procedures worked and how to describe the complicated scientific principles to their lay audiences. Print reporters assigned to cover the census over a longer time period were most likely to grasp the fundamental principles involved and convey the information to their readers with a reasonable degree of accuracy. Reporters who wrote about the census only sporadically often described the census plans erroneously in their articles. Television and radio news reporters generally shied away from discussing census methods in any detail, in part because of the complexity of the procedures.

Journalists have also strained to understand the relatively arcane legal issues that have shaped census methods and results in the decades since enactment of the 1965 Voting Rights Act and the proliferation of federal grant-in-aid programs since the War on Poverty in the 1960s. Lawsuits challenging the proposed use of sampling in the 2000 census (one filed by the U.S. House of Representatives itself) were widely covered in the media, particularly as the cases reached the U.S. Supreme Court on an expedited basis. A large number of news organizations incorrectly reported that the Court found the use of sampling to be unconstitutional, even though the decision was based solely on federal law and did not reach the constitutional question. In subsequent stories describing pre-census controversies, the misinformation was repeated often.

Media attention to the census increases substantially as the Census Bureau becomes a visible presence in communities across the country, opening local offices, hiring hundreds of thousands of temporary workers, and launching its promotional campaign. Because technological advances now allow the Census Bureau to track census response by local office area on an almost daily basis, local media can follow and assess the progress of the count for their own audiences. And because the average person is no longer a bystander but is actively engaged in the event, news stories can focus on how "real people" are affected by the census.

Ironically, while media coverage of problems with the census and the accuracy of the results is often extensive, once the population numbers and characteristic data are released, journalists tend to accept the information at face value, reporting demographic and socioeconomic findings without regard to the reliability of the data. The breadth of information collected in the census provides a windfall for journalists, particularly in the print media. The Census Bureau releases data from the decennial count on a flow basis over a period of about three years, as the data are tabulated for various levels of geography. The data from each census form the core of numerous articles and stories on the demographic and socioeconomic characteristics of communities across the country; favorite topics include racial and ethnic composition of neighborhoods, family structure and living arrangements, educational levels, and comparisons of urban, suburban, and rural life. Many journalists examine data from prior censuses to report on changes in the composition, distribution, and well-being of the population over time, often reporting their findings before demographers and other researchers have completed more scientific analyses.

Post-census Coverage

Even as media attention shifts primarily to the census results after the count is completed, the increase in post-census litigation over the accuracy of the census counts provides ongoing opportunities for occasional media coverage, often for years as the cases drag on. (For example, lawsuits challenging the accuracy of the 1980 census were not completed until 1988, while a lawsuit challenging the accuracy of the 1990 census was not heard by the U.S. Supreme Court until 1996.) Nevertheless, as each census recedes from the collective public memory with the passage of time, media interest in the controversies over census methods and results wanes, and relatively few journalists continue to follow regularly the post-census legal disputes.

While the vast majority of news organizations pay little attention to the census planning process over much of each decade, they rely heavily on information from the census as well as from Census Bureau data products disseminated between decennial years. Much of the intercensal data is derived using the decennial census as a benchmark or as a tool for calibrating ongoing surveys, such as the Survey of Income and Program Participation. Census Bureau data are widely used to support articles and stories about demographic, social, and economic trends and events, among both national and local media. The media also report widely on the bureau's intercensal population estimates, as well as studies and analyses, that are disseminated throughout the decade. Topics popular with the press include the bureau's frequent publications on mobility, marriage and family structure, population growth and movement among regions and states, immigration, and regional changes in racial and ethnic composition.

As a federal agency steeped in scientific research and development related to data collection, the Census Bureau has struggled to communicate effectively with the media, policy makers, and community-based stakeholders who are not well versed in the technical work that dominates much of census planning and preparation.

In recent years, an associate director for communications has been assigned to coordinate the Census Bureau's outreach to the media and has been responsible for a broader marketing and promotional campaign to encourage census participation. The U.S. Department of Commerce (the Census Bureau's parent agency) frequently has selected an individual for this position from outside the ranks of the Census Bureau's career employees and the scientific community generally. Conversely, the bureau's professional scientific employees generally are unfamiliar with the principles of public relations and are uncomfortable conversing in the public arena. The gap between operations and communications often has left the bureau struggling to explain its plans and decisions in terms that the media can understand and convey to their audiences.

From a communications standpoint, the Census Bureau was unprepared for the unusually high level of media attention focused on plans for the 2000 census, as partisan political disputes over the census design escalated. The bureau had grown accustomed to conducting its research, testing, and planning for each census largely out of the glare of the media and public spotlight, emerging only as final preparations unfolded and public promotion for census began. But litigation filed prior to both the 1990 and 2000 censuses, challenging the choice of methods, forced the bureau to discuss its plans publicly before some fundamental design decisions had been made. Relying on communications specialists with little background in the census process and career scientific staff with little experience in the public arena, the bureau often floundered in its well-meaning efforts to convince the media that its decisions were sound. Senior Census Bureau officials, however, have recognized the agency's relative lack of experience in dealing with the media and have made improved communication with the media and the bureau's wide range of stakeholders a priority for the future.

See also *Congress and the census; Data dissemination and use; Data products: evolution.*

■ Terri Ann Lowenthal

Metropolitan areas

The term *metropolitan area* generally means a large city including its suburbs. As presented in census publications since 1950, it refers to a set of geographic areas defined under various labels by the Office of Management and Budget (OMB) as a standard for federal statistical agencies in their presentation of data. The term has developed mostly independently of the related term *metropolis,* meaning a city of major importance in its country or region; many officially defined metropolitan areas in the United States are not metropolises in that sense.

As defined by the OMB, the general concept of a metropolitan area (MA) is a functional one: a large population nucleus or core together with adjacent communities having a high degree of economic and social integration with that core. Integration is measured using census data on commuting to work. In general entire counties form the building blocks for the MA, so that besides a city and its suburbs most definitions include smaller satellite communities and some open country. Thus, metropolitan should not be confused with urban; an MA generally includes at least one urbanized area (UA) but also rural population as defined by the census, while many small cities and towns are urban but not metropolitan.

The population outside any MA is termed nonmetropolitan, and recent census publications contain extensive data on the total metropolitan and nonmetropolitan population of the United States and the states. Within each MA, data generally are presented for the central city or cities, based on corporate boundaries, and the MA remainder outside central cities.

Although the latter category often is interpreted as representing the suburbs, the census itself has avoided that term, probably reflecting the lack of public consensus on what constitutes a suburb.

MA definitions are reviewed after each census and in most cases revised. However, because detailed census commuting data do not become available until the second year after the enumeration, decennial census output since 1960 generally has presented MA definitions that do not yet reflect changes in commuting patterns of the preceding decade. This lag also has been reflected in the redesign of many census surveys.

Only a few countries defined metropolitan areas officially in 1950, but by 1999 most were doing so at least for their capital city, sometimes with criteria and terminology borrowed from U.S. practice.

Defining MAs

Although the term *metropolitan area* did not emerge until the early 1900s, the recognition of an urban area larger than the official city existed as early as 1790, when Philadelphia already had several large built-up suburbs. The 1905 Census of Manufactures presented data on thirteen "industrial districts" defined in terms of subcounty minor civil divisions (MCDs), such as townships, districts, and (in certain states) towns.

In the decennial census, MAs first were officially defined in 1910 as *metropolitan districts* (MDs). The definitions generally were in terms of MCDs and followed a functional approach, not limited to the continuously built-up area. Lacking comprehensive data on commuting between core city and suburbs, the MDs included outlying MCDs chiefly on the basis of a population density of at least 150 per square mile.

The MDs were updated and the list of qualifying areas expanded in the censuses from 1920 to 1940, but their definitions by subcounty units severely limited their usefulness for the compilation of non-decennial data. This, in parallel with continuing suburban expansion, prompted the Census Bureau and other federal agencies to develop various mutually inconsistent metropolitan definitions using whole counties. As a result, in 1949–1950 the then Bureau of the Budget established specific criteria to define standard metropolitan areas (SMAs) for presentation in 1950, advised by an interagency committee and with most of the technical support provided by the Bureau of the Census.

Establishing the criteria called for four fundamental decisions: on what geographic building-blocks to use, on how large an area had to be to qualify, on how to define the core, and on how to determine the inclusion of units beyond the core. Generally the SMAs were defined in terms of counties and included each city of at least 50,000, with its county constituting the core. In the New England states, however, the SMA and its core were defined in terms of MCDs (towns and cities), which were well known and often used for statistical tabulations, and where use of counties would have forced some sizable unrelated cities into single SMAs. Although county building blocks would lead to some inaccuracies in the definitions, this disadvantage was judged to be outweighed by the large amount of statistical data that could be made available by county and hence by SMA.

Daily commuting of at least 15 percent of resident workers was established as the main basis for determining whether additional counties should be added to the core county. This cutoff number was chosen after examination of available data for specific areas. Since there were no national commuting data, decisions were made on the basis of local surveys of varying methods and coverage.

Besides establishing commuting as a measure of integration, counties had to meet certain requirements of "metropolitan character," such as having less than one-third of their labor force in agriculture and at least half their population in contiguous MCDs with at least 150 persons per square mile. Other criteria provided rules for identifying central cities and for titling the SMA. In all, 169 SMAs were defined for 1950, comprising 265 counties and 208 New England MCDs; there also were 3 SMAs defined in Puerto Rico.

Developments to 1990

Some changes were made in these criteria in the 1950s, 1960s, and 1970s. After 1960, census commuting data provided an improved basis for measuring integration. Requirements concerning the agricultural workforce were dropped after that measure ceased to affect the definitions. The size requirement for the qualifying city was broadened to allow first for twin-city pairs, later for a city with many contiguous densely populated places provided the combination exceeded a population of 50,000. The result, in conjunction with national population increases and substantial migration to large and small cities, was a sizable increase in the number of official areas, to 214 in 1960 and 245 in 1970. The term

SMA was changed to SMSA, adding "statistical," in 1959.

As the MAs became better known, some local areas desired to achieve independent metropolitan status, although they did not qualify under either the official criteria or the underlying concept. However, in 1959 the New York area was reduced by splitting off its New Jersey portion as several separate SMSAs, with similar surgery for Chicago. The pre-1959 extents of these two areas were recognized as standard consolidated areas (SCAs), thereby establishing a two-level metropolitan hierarchy. Likewise, Orange County, California, seceded from the Los Angeles SMSA in 1963, though no Los Angeles SCA was established then. Finally, in 1972 the Nassau-Suffolk SMSA was established on Long Island, although it did not even contain a qualifying central city.

These conspicuous disparities between the MA concept and its official implementation were addressed during the pre-1980 review of the standards. The census-defined urban area was adopted as the basis for the MA core, to consist of all counties with at least half their population in the UA. This criterion would have caused the several split-off areas to be reabsorbed by their metropolitan parents. However, it soon became clear that once defined officially, MAs of the size of Nassau-Suffolk, Newark, and Orange County could not easily be abolished again without local concurrence.

The result was the full incorporation into the criteria of the two-level hierarchy concept, with rules, based mainly on commuting ties, for defining subareas termed primary metropolitan statistical areas (PMSAs); any area containing PMSAs was labeled a consolidated MSA (CMSA), and all other areas became metropolitan statistical areas (MSAs). Besides standardizing the recognition of Nassau-Suffolk and the other seceding areas, these criteria permitted certain SMSAs to continue to be recognized as PSMAs, when they could no longer qualify separately because of heavy commuting to large neighbors. Recognition of any PMSA required support from local opinion, which the OMB obtained through congressional offices, which were also consulted about some area titles and other issues.

The 1980 criteria also tightened the rules for including outlying counties, after comments that much "metropolitan" territory was really rural, although it had a high percentage of commuters. This issue reflected an actual widening of significant commuting around many smaller cities, especially as the interstate highway system was completed. For 1990, however, few changes were made in the criteria. There were 334 official areas reported in 1980 and 355 in 1990. The 1990 census population in MAs was 192.7 million or 77.5 percent of the national total, as compared with 84.9 million and 56.1 percent in 1950.

By the 1980s the MAs had achieved a high degree of recognition, which served to multiply the interests eager to achieve particular MA configurations. While this sometimes had statistical aspects, for example, when submetropolitan cities campaigned to be recognized as MAs, more often it resulted from federal agency adoption of the MA boundaries to determine eligibility under some nonstatistical program. After 1972 virtually all demands for ad hoc definition changes were denied by the OMB, but a few definitions were changed by congressional action. There also was pressure, more easily dealt with, to make a few exceptions in marginal aspects of the standards such as area titles.

Developments Since 1990

With the MA system in its fifth decade, many users saw room for improvement. Scholars could envision a different approach to defining MAs than that adopted in 1949, but only at the cost of a major break in continuity from the existing system. Many users felt that the standards should be less complicated, at the same time that they recognized metropolitan structure to have become more complex.

The extensive decentralization of population and employment experienced by U.S. metropolitan areas after 1950 had largely been accommodated by the criteria, since most new outlying job centers still were within the UA and hence within the core used to define the MA. The expansion of the outlying zone of significant commuting, however, added to MAs more counties that were locally perceived as rural. Moreover, commuting increasingly linked formerly separate metropolitan centers, including Washington-Baltimore and other pairs with large populations, underscoring the importance of the rules for determining when such neighbors should be made a single area.

During the 1990s the OMB and the Census Bureau undertook an extensive review of the MA standards preparatory to revising them for use after the 2000 census. The review commissioned proposals by some out-side scholars and solicited opinion at two conferences. There was consensus on the need for a functionally conceived set of official metropolitan definitions in terms of counties, and an endorsement of further research toward the development of definitions in terms of subcounty units, preferably census tracts. Commuting was accepted as the most useful available measure of integration, with varying views about what percentage levels should be required. It also was proposed that the New England subcounty definitions had largely outlived their usefulness, and could be provided simply as an alternative to official New England MA definitions by county.

There were many recommendations that the current nonmetropolitan category should have some standard official subdivisions, but little consensus on how these should be determined. There were proposals to reduce the category by recognizing a large number of submetropolitan areas, defined in county terms using the MA standards, around cores down to perhaps 10,000 population, but with no subdivision of the remaining residual territory.

A wider range of views was found on other issues, such as the extent to which requirements of metropolitan character should be retained for outlying counties, and whether metropolitan subareas like the current PMSAs should continue to be recognized. Proposals offered suggest that commuting will be made virtually the sole determinant for including counties (which would result in expanding many MAs), but that the cut-off of 15 percent may be raised (which would have the opposite effect). Commuting would remain the basis for determining whether adjacent MAs should be merged or combined, but a raised commuting cutoff, if adopted, would dissolve some existing combinations. Subareas are likely to be recognized within at least the largest MAs.

Also still under discussion at press time were the extent to which local opinion should be consulted about the definitions, and various matters of terminology, such as the labels for the different levels of metropolitan and submetropolitan areas. The final revised standards are scheduled to appear in the *Federal Register* by fall 2000.

See also *Urban areas.*

■ Richard L. Forstall

Bibliography

Dahmann, Donald C., and James D. Fitzsimmons, eds. *Metropolitan and Nonmetropolitan Areas: New Approaches to Geographical Definition.* Working Paper 12, Population Division, U.S. Bureau of the Census, 1995.

Federal Committee on Standard Metropolitan Statistical Areas. "Documents Relating to the Metropolitan Statistical Area Classification for the 1980's." *Statistical Reporter,* August 1980, 335-384; reprinted 1980 in Federal Committee on Standard Metropolitan Statistical Areas. *The Metropolitan Statistical Area Classification.*

Forstall, Richard L. "Metropolitan Areas: A Historical Perspective" American Statistical Association, *1991 Proceedings of the Government Statistics Section,* 65-69.

Office of Management and Budget. "Recommendations from the Metropolitan Area Standards Review Committee to the Office of Management and Budget Concerning Changes to the Standards for Defining Metropolitan Areas." *Federal Register* 64 (202), October 20, 1999, 56628-56644.

Thompson, Warren S. *The Growth of Metropolitan Districts in the United States: 1900-1940.* Washington: Government Printing Office, 1948.

U.S. Bureau of the Census. *Industrial Districts: 1905—Manufactures and Population.* Washington: Government Printing Office, 1909. (1905 Census of Manufactures, Bulletin 101)

Migration

See *Immigration.*

Mortality schedules

See *Vital registration and vital statistics.*

Mother tongue/language spoken

See *Composition of the population.*

National Archives and Records Administration (NARA)

The National Archives of the United States, established in 1934, holds in trust a vast information resource: the unique and irreplaceable records of the U.S. federal government. Dating from the first Continental Congress and the earliest period of our federal history, the records come in many forms. They include textual records on paper, microfilm/fiche, and electronic media; nontextual records: architectural drawings, maps and other cartographic records, motion pictures, sound recordings, still pictures, and videotape recordings; electronic data files; and publications.

NARA acquires, preserves in perpetuity, and makes available for research records of enduring value created or received by organizations of the executive, legislative, and judicial branches of the federal government. Researchers can review textual and nontextual archival holdings at NARA's buildings in the Washington, D.C. area. Microfilm copies of records, including decennial census schedules and regional textual and nontextual holdings, may be reviewed at thirteen of NARA's Regional Records Services facilities nationwide. Reproductions of NARA's holdings in all forms are available on a cost-recovery basis. Some archival holdings on microfilm, including federal census population schedules covering the years 1790–1920, and the Soundex indexes to these schedules for the 1880–1920 censuses, are also available through the Microfilm Rental Program. A selection of scanned images from NARA's textual and nontextual holdings are available online via the Internet. More information for researchers is available at http://www.nara.gov/research, or from NARA's General Information Leaflet Number 30, "Information About the National Archives for Researchers."

The Bureau of the Census and the National Archives

Among the reasons advanced for the establishment of a permanent census bureau, as well as for a national archives, was to prevent the loss of valuable records. During the nineteenth century, a census office was established for each decennial census and was disbanded when its work was completed. Given this factor, and in the absence of a national archives until well into the twentieth century, the preservation of records from the censuses was inconsistent. In fact, according to Donald R. McCoy (1985), the fire in January 1921 at the Commerce Department building, which destroyed most of the 1890 decennial census schedules, significantly influenced the movement to establish an archives.

By the time the census office became permanent in 1902, the organization of census-related documentation was made up of three main classes: records, consisting of all documentation other than schedules and published reports, including unpublished tabulations; schedules, the documents on which individual census data were recorded; and publications. In 1942, the

National Archives formally appraised records and schedules of the Bureau of the Census as having long-term value. This evaluation was in response to an offer by the Bureau to transfer to archival custody records of various censuses from 1800 to 1930, the population schedules from 1790 to 1870, and some non-population census schedules. The National Archives accepted these historical materials in March 1942, noting that the records documented the administrative and organizational history of the census agency, and that the schedules had well-established value to historians, sociologists, economists, genealogists, and the general public.

In the 1930s and 1940s, the Census Bureau microfilmed the original census schedules of 1840–1880, the few schedules that were extant from 1890, and then the 1900 to 1940 schedules. The 1942 appraisal only partially resolved issues of the Bureau's archives because it did not address the population schedules for 1880 and after, nor the duplication of the schedules on microfilm. Resolution of these issues came early in the next decade.

In 1951, the National Archives and Records Service concluded that the microfilm form was adequate as the archival record of the census schedules after 1870. Following this decision, the Bureau and the Archives agreed that the Bureau would transfer the positive microfilm copies of schedules for 1840–1880 and the paper schedules for 1880 to the National Archives. They also agreed that the Bureau would transfer the master negative set of microfilm of the schedules for 1840–1940 to the Federal Records Center. The microfilmed schedules would be preserved as the permanent records of the decennial population census schedules and the Bureau would transfer its positive microfilm copies for the 1890 to 1940 schedules to the National Archives in the coming years, as it no longer needed them. Similar decisions have applied to the schedules of later decennial censuses. Finally, the Bureau and the Archives agreed that the Federal Records Center would acquire the original paper schedules of the 1950 Census of Population and Housing and would microfilm them. The paper schedules would be destroyed after successful completion of the microfilming.

An essential aspect of the 1952 agreement was an exchange of letters between the archivist of the United States, Wayne C. Grover and Roy V. Peel, director of the Bureau. In 1950 Congress had passed the Federal Property and Administrative Services Act, imposing a fifty-year limit on public release of federal records, unless the archivist determined that records should be closed for a longer period. In his testimony when this law was under consideration, the archivist referred to population census schedules as an example of records that might be closed for more than fifty years, noting that eventually they would be made available to researchers. Subsequently, the director wrote to the archivist, proposing nondisclosure of information in the population census schedules for a period of seventy-two years following the enumeration of each decennial census. In his letter of October 10, 1952, the archivist agreed. Thus the "seventy-two year rule" on the confidentiality of the population census schedules was mutually accepted by the National Archives and the Bureau of the Census. It balanced public release of federal records with the tradition of confidentiality of the census schedules for an extended period. The confidential nature of contemporary census information had evolved gradually during the latter part of the nineteenth century and in the 1920s the Bureau ruled that schedules from censuses prior to 1880 were publicly releasable. In fact, population schedules for the first nine censuses had been deposited in public places to ensure their accuracy.

The 1952 agreement facilitated release of information from the 1880 census to researchers. The Bureau transferred to the National Archives the paper census schedules for the 1880 census, and the microfilmed schedules for the 1840 to 1940 censuses. Rather than retain the 1880 paper schedules, the National Archives donated them in 1956 to the Daughters of the American Revolution (DAR), which subsequently sent some of them to nonfederal depositories nationwide. As agreed, the paper schedules from the 1950 census were destroyed after microfilming. The Bureau has transferred microfilmed schedules for the 1960 and 1970 censuses more recently, and transfers of the records for subsequent censuses will follow. In 1978, responding to controversy and objections from the Bureau to the National Archives' 1972 opening of the 1900 census schedules to researchers, Congress codified the "seventy-two year rule" into law.

In the mid-1970s, the Bureau of the Census, working with staff from the National Archives Machine-Readable Records Division, inventoried and proposed the disposition of the data files (the machine-readable or electronic records) of its Demographic Fields programs. In response, the National Archives appraised these materials and agreed to permanent retention of the decennial Public Use Microdata Sample files and the final decennial Census Summary Tape Files (STFs), both publicly released files and some tabulations that would be subject to the seventy-two-year rule. The appraisal archivist noted that these electronic files were the versions of the decennial census that the Bureau and other federal agencies had used, just as they had earlier relied on published and unpublished tabulations that had been on paper. Also, the organization of the electronic files by geography enhanced their informational value.

Decennial Census Records and Schedules in the National Archives of the United States

NARA arranges its holdings according to the archival principle of provenance that provides that records be attributed to the agency that created or maintained them, arranged as they were filed when in active use. At NARA application of the principle of provenance takes the form of numbered record groups, each comprising the records of a major government entity. The records of the Bureau of the Census and its predecessors form Record Group 29 (R.G. 29) and span the history of the United States from 1790 to the present. The balance of this entry describes R.G. 29 archives related to the decennial censuses of population and housing. For more detail, please refer to the bibliography below.

Textual Records: Administrative. Census Office, 1820–1905; Bureau of the Census, 1860–1986. The records of the Census Office document the fourth through the twelfth censuses (1820–1900). Those of the Bureau of the Census include Records of the Office of the Director, 1882–1983; the Census Advisory Committee, 1919–1963; and the Administrative Services Division. The latter include records of the chief clerk, 1912–1950, relating to census machine equipment, wartime activities, and procedures for taking the 1920–1940 censuses, as well as correspondence, memorandums, and reports from 1900 to1980. The textual records also hold a microfilm copy of 1792–1917 census publications in the Records of the Publications Division. Records of the Geography Division include descriptions of enumeration districts, 1830–1950, as well as publications relating to census mapping activities and the origin and use of the census tract, 1947–1952. Other series of administrative records include Records of the Office of the Assistant Director for Statistical Standards, 1850–1975; Records of the Assistant Director for Demographic Fields, 1870–1982; and Records of the Director of Public Information, 1890–1980.

Textual Records: Census Schedules. NARA preserves 3,100 volumes of manuscript schedules of decennial population censuses, 1790–1870; typescript copies of the 1810 and 1820 population schedules from the Ohio and Michigan Territories; 1,150 volumes of photostatic copies of the 1800–1830 population schedules; manuscript schedules of the slave population, 1850 and 1860; four volumes of schedules of a special census of Indians, 1880; seven volumes of damaged schedules from the 1860 and 1880 censuses; fragments of manuscript population schedules of the eleventh census, 1890; and territorial population schedules for Minnesota, 1856–57, Arizona, n.d., and Seminole County, Oklahoma, 1907. There are no schedules for some states and territories for the first four censuses, and the returns of some enumerators for later censuses are also missing. NARA also holds 37,770 microfilm rolls with population schedules, 1790–1950; the microfilm rolls from more recent censuses are even more voluminous.

Nontextual Records: Maps. NARA preserves census enumeration district maps, 1880–1970. They consist of approximately 110,000 printed, photocopied, and manuscript maps of cities, counties, lesser political units, and unincorporated areas. Only a small number are extant for 1880 and 1890, but availability increases with each decade. These maps show the boundaries and the numbers of enumeration districts that were established to administer and control census data collection. Wards, precincts, incorporated areas, urban unincorporated areas, townships, census supervisors' districts, and congressional districts may also appear on some maps. The content of enumeration district maps varies greatly between states and over time. The base maps that were used to portray the enumeration districts were obtained locally and include postal maps; general land office maps; soil survey maps; and maps produced by city, county, and state government offices as well as commercial map companies. NARA also has an incomplete set of published and manuscript maps and atlases produced by the Bureau of the Census to illustrate cartographically the findings of the decennial censuses, 1860–1970. The earlier statistical atlases show population by race and nationality, vital statistics, wealth, employment, handicapped groups, agriculture, irrigation and drainage, congressional districts, slaves (1860), and types of forest trees. Later maps show the distribution or percentage of the general population, ethnic population, older Americans, income, poverty areas, owned and rented housing, migration, high school education, retail sales, mineral industries, and the value of farm products.

Nontextual Records: Motion Picture Films. NARA has forty-three moving image titles in R.G. 29. They include training films for enumerators for the sixteenth Census (1940); "Know Your U.S.A," a film relating to the 1940 Census; and a 1940 film about the punchcard and tabulating operations of the Census Bureau. "Counting the Jobless" explains the 1937 Census of Unemployment. NARA has a theatrical trailer on the 1950 population census; a film on the test of a mailed census (n.d.); a National Educational Television series concerning the 1960 census that illustrates the history and work of the Census Bureau; television public information films and spots for the 1960 and 1980 population censuses; and two other Bureau of the Census releases: "Age/Sex Distribution of the Population 1905 to 2025" and "We: The People."

Nontextual Records: Sound Recordings. R.G. 29 includes twenty-two sound recording titles. Among them are "Uncle Sam Calling—Story of the 1940 Census"; a three-part interview with Dr. Roy V. Peel, August 2, 1950; as well as the 1950s public-service piece by the Golden Gate Quartet singing "There's A Man Going 'Round Taking Names." Other audio records include public information sound recordings, 1959–1960; excerpts from the 1980 Census Users Conference in Little Rock, Arkansas; and the 1990s public service announcement "The 1990 Census Is You," which accompanies a slide presentation of the same title used to publicize and encourage participation in that year's census.

Nontextual Records: Still Picture Records. Series of still picture holdings in R.G. 29 includes 302 photographic prints and lantern slides showing tabulating machines used by the Bureau of Census from 1890 to 1950; recording activities relating to the enumeration of the Navajo, ca. 1939; and documenting the programs and activities of the Bureau of Census during the 1940 and 1980 population censuses. Also included in the holdings are the slide presentation "The 1990 Census Is You" and twenty filmstrips that were used to train enumerators for the 1950 and 1960 censuses. In addition, NARA preserves twenty-nine posters encouraging the participation, particularly of ethnic minorities, in the 1980 Census.

Data Files: Public Use Microdata Sample Files. The Bureau of the Census produced public-use microdata sample files from the "Long Form" census schedules of the 1960–1990 censuses, and they are included among NARA's R.G. 29 electronic records holdings. Since the records in the public use sample files do not include any names of persons or households or any other personal identifiers, and because the geographic identifiers are at a level of aggregation that was designed to ensure complete confidentiality, the public use microdata sample files are fully open. The Bureau also transferred to NARA the public use sample microdata files of the 1940 and 1950 censuses, created by a University of Wisconsin, Madison project; and the National Science Foundation transferred the public-use sample from the 1900 census, created by an NSF-funded University of Washington project. Finally, in R.G. 453, Records of the Commission on Civil Rights, NARA preserves the 1970 census public use sample microdata extract files for Puerto Rican and Southwestern Spanish surname persons and households that the Bureau of the Census provided for the Commission.

Data Files: Census Summary Statistic Files. Summary statistic files contain basic tabulations of census statistics for various legal, administrative, and geographic areas. The Bureau began distributing summary statistic files in electronic form with the 1970 census. It has transferred to NARA complete collections of the tabulations known as the first and fifth counts of the 1970 Census; Public Law 94-171 and Summary Tape Files 1 and 3 from the 1980 Census; and complete sets of all publicly released Summary Tape Files from the 1990 Census. In R.G. 381, Records of the Community Services Administration, NARA preserves two separate series of statistical tabulations from the 1970 Census. One has tabulations for Standard Metropolitan Statistical Area poverty neighborhoods in 107 large central cities; the other records a selection of socioeconomic data for states and counties, based upon Office of Economic Opportunity criteria. Similarly, in R.G. 419, Records of the National Institute of Education (NIE), NARA preserves a data file created for NIE's 1975 to 1978 Compensatory Education Study that consists of county-level poverty estimates based on 1970 census data. Another electronic version of summary statistics, some of which come from the 1940–1980 decennial censuses, are the County and City Data Book electronic files in R.G. 29. NARA also preserves a complementary series in R.G. 512, Records of the Health Resources and Services Administration, their

Bureau of Health Manpower Area Resources Files. NARA's holdings of these electronic records include data from the 1940s to the 1990s; they include some decennial census data. Finally, Dr. Donald Bogue, emeritus professor of Sociology, University of Chicago, has donated to NARA summary statistic files compiled largely from census paper publications with data for census tracts from the 1940–1970 censuses.

Data Files: Cartographic. NARA's electronic records also include data files that the Bureau of the Census created specifically for geographic analysis. They include the Master Enumeration District List files (with coordinates) for the 1970 census; the Geographic Base File/Dual Independent Map Encoding (GBF/DIME) files for the 1980 census; and the TIGER (Topologically Integrated Geographic Encoding and Referencing)/Line files from the 1990 census.

Publications. In addition to the Bureau of the Census publications held as part of R.G. 29, NARA preserves a major collection of Bureau of the Census publications in R.G. 287, the Record Group known as Publications of the U.S. Government. The core collection of Bureau of the Census publications came to the National Archives in 1972 when the U.S. Government Printing Office transferred its library collection, sometimes known as the Public Documents Library. It includes multi-volume sets of books and magazines, monographs, guides, manuals, circulars, bulletins, indexes, reports, regulations, maps, charts, and posters. The R.G. 287 publications serve as the nation's "record" copy of government publications that are widely distributed, including to federal depository libraries, and it also includes selected publications unavailable in the depository library system.

See also *Census law; Confidentiality; Litigation and the census.*

■ Prepared by Margaret O'Neill Adams from materials written by Thomas E. Brown, Barbara Lewis Burger, Charles DeArman, Theodore J. Hull, Constance Potter, Rodney A. Ross, Richard H. Smith, and Aloha Smith

Bibliography

Publications about the National Archives and Records Administration

McCoy, Donald R. *The National Archives: America's Ministry of Documents 1934–1968.* Chapel Hill: The University of North Carolina Press, 1978.

Walch, Timothy, ed. *Guardians of Heritage: Essays on the History of the National Archives.* Washington, D.C.: The National Archives and Records Administration, 1985.

Printed Finding Aids Describing Decennial Census Records in the National Archives

National Archives and Records Administration. *Guide to Federal Records in the National Archives of the United States.* Compiled by Robert B. Matchette et al. Washington, D.C.: National Archives and Records Administration, 1995, 3 volumes. See especially the chapter on Records of the Bureau of the Census (Record Group 29), pp. 29–1 to 29–7. Also available at http://www.nara.gov/guide/.

———. *Guide to Genealogical Research in the National Archives.* Washington, DC: National Archives and Records Administration, revised, 1985; new revision forthcoming, 2000.

National Archives and Records Administration. *Guide to Holdings of the Still Picture Branch of the National Archives.* Compiled by Barbara Lewis Burger. Washington, D.C.: National Archives and Records Administration, 1990. Also available online at http://webgopher.nara.gov/00/inform/dc/audvis/guide.txt.

———. *Records of the Bureau of the Census, Record Group 29: Preliminary Inventory 161.* Compiled by Katherine H. Davidson and Charlotte M. Ashby. Washington, D.C.: National Archives and Records Administration, 1964; reprinted 1997.

National Archives and Records Administration. *The 1790–1890 Federal Population Censuses: Catalog of National Archives Microfilm.* Washington, D.C.: National Archives Trust Fund Board, revised 1997. Additional microfilm catalogs include *The 1900 Federal Population Census* (revised 1996); *The 1910 Federal Population Census* (1982); and *The 1920 Federal Population Census* (revised 1992).

———. *Cartographic Records of the Bureau of the Census: Preliminary Inventory 103.* Compiled by James B. Rhoads and Charlotte M. Ashby. Washington, D.C.: National Archives and Records Service, 1958.

Online Finding Aids describing Decennial Census Records in the National Archives

The Genealogy Page at http://www.nara.gov/genealogy/

Information about [electronic] records in the custody of the Center for Electronic Records from the Era of World War II, version as of December 1998 at http://www.nara.gov/nara/electronic/wwii.html.

NARA Archival Information Locator (NAIL) at http://www.nara.gov/nara/nail.html.

Summary statistic files, public use samples, and special tabulations from the 1970 (1980) Census of Population and Housing in the holdings of the Center for Electronic Records, at http://www.nara.gov/nara/electronic/cen1970.html and http://www.nara.gov/nara/electronic/cen1980.html.

Title List: A Preliminary and Partial Listing of the Data Files in the National Archives and Records Administration. Records of

the Bureau of the Census, R.G. 029 at http://www.nara.gov/electronic/com.html#census

Articles related to Decennial Census Records in the National Archives

Adams, Margaret O., and Thomas E. Brown. "Myths and Realities About the 1960 Census." *APDU [Association of Public Data Users] Newsletter.* September 1997, 8–9, 16.

Blake, Kellee. "First in the Path of the Firemen: The Fate of the 1890 Population Census." *Prologue: Quarterly of the National Archives and Records Administration.* Spring 1996, Vol. 28, No. 1. Also available at http://www.nara.gov/publications/prologue/1890cen1.html; .../1890cen2.html; .../1890cen3.html.

Green, Kellee. "The Fourteenth Numbering of the People: The 1920 Federal Census." *Prologue: Quarterly of the National Archives and Records Administration.* Summer 1991, Vol. 23, No. 2.

Not-for-profit organizations

Not-for-profit organizations, in the realm between the profit-making private sector and the government public sector, collectively have been labeled as the "independent sector," the "third sector," the "voluntary sector," and even the "invisible sector." Overall, though, and especially in recent years, not-for-profits hardly have been invisible when it comes to their use of census data or their opinions about the conduct and content of the decennial census.

The not-for-profit world of American organizational life is huge and complex. The sector includes agencies, organizations, institutions, and projects with vastly varied roles, purposes, and efficiencies, from multi-billion-dollar umbrella agencies raising funds to advance specific causes, to storefront churches delivering services to neighborhoods. It is a sector that engages in service delivery, education, fundraising, and political lobbying, and it has experienced significant growth in the numbers of new organizations formed since the mid-1960s.

It is the world of entities that belong neither to the government nor to business in nature (social and human services agencies, churches, schools, colleges and universities, research institutes, hospitals, foundations, social action and civil rights movements, arts and cultural organizations, community development groups, associations and mutual benefit societies, and a host of others).

Not-for-profits have had a major impact on the history of this country, helping to shape social and cultural values, playing mediating roles between large bureaucratic institutions and individuals, and providing services to millions of citizens, as Michael O'Neill describes (in *The Third America: The Emergence of the Nonprofit Sector in the United States,* 1989).

In its vast work this sector consumes, analyzes, and applies the results of the decennial census and intercensal estimates. Some organizations within the sector even function as "non-profit extensions" of the for-profit world, playing important roles in the economic and political realms and distributing value-added, census-derived information pertinent to their members.

Particularly since the 1970s, though, the not-for-profits began laying their claim among the stakeholders to the decennial census, working their way to the "census decision table" to ensure the preservation and inclusion of aspects of the census important to their constituencies for service delivery. These groups examine and comment forcefully on census operations and conduct to ensure that those they represent are not unduly disadvantaged by the results, and call attention to the specific interests or changes in society demonstrated within the ranks of their members, constituencies, and clientele.

Stakeholders on the User and Recipient Ends of the Decennial Data Application Spectrum

Even with the broad range of organizational types and functions that comprise the sector, the "not-for-profit" label often is associated with charities and the delivery of social and human services. A broad network of not-for-profits functions in this capacity. United Ways, Catholic Charities, Jewish Federations, Salvation Armies, Red Crosses, Urban Leagues, YMCAs, YWCAs, Big Brothers/Big Sisters, community action and development groups, social change organizations, youth groups, senior citizen associations, and thousands of other organizations provide food, shelter, day care, residential care, health care, legal services, job training, and hundreds of other services. Some are part of national networks; others are single organizations in a specific city. Many are multipurpose agencies operating direct service, advocacy, and education programs.

These types of not-for-profits use demographic, socioeconomic, and other data from the decennial census and intercensal estimates programs, not only to target clientele, plan and implement appropriate programs and services, and measure performance in communities, but also to identify and make the case of their worth to donor populations and foundations, meet preconditions of grant support, and ensure their share of governmental dollars allocated on the basis of census data.

The smaller geographic area data from the decennial census often serve to draw comparisons within and between communities, and act as benchmarks to validate local surveys of need conducted by not-for-profit, community-based organizations.

The interest of the not-for-profits in the census, though, reaches beyond their own use of the data to the implications of how the decennial census is conducted and how the results are used on them and those they represent. It was in early stages of discussion on the form and content of the 1980 census, even before the 1970 census was completed, that a broad-based coalition of groups, including not-for-profits, demanded to be part of the formal planning process. That phenomenon continued and expanded through the planning for the 2000 census.

Representatives of social and human service-oriented not-for-profits, advocacy groups, and racial and ethnic civil rights groups with a national reach have argued on a variety of census-related issues in recent years. One prominent example is the census undercount in any given year and the likelihood that persons of color and the rural and urban poor will be disproportionately represented among those uncounted. That these and other segments of the population more heavily served by not-for-profit organizations are missed more often than others in the count, the groups argue, simply compounds the consequences of the undercount and decreases the abilities of the not-for-profits and communities to sustain service requests in the face of funding based on lower, "official" numbers.

Groups like the National Association for the Advancement of Colored People, the Mexican American Legal and Defense Education Fund, the National Council of La Raza, the National Urban League, the National American Indian Council, the National Indian Education Association, and the Coalition for an Accurate Count of Asian and Pacific Islanders, among many others, have been players in the undercount and other census-related debates.

But so have other not-for-profits and major public interest groups representing state and local governments and government officials, including the U.S. Conference of Mayors, the National League of Cities, the National Association of Counties, the National Conference of State Legislatures, and the National Black Caucus of State Legislators.

Through their policy conferences, resolution adoptions, and congressional testimonies, not-for-profits like these have taken alternate sides on the use of statistical sampling to augment the traditional census count; they have requested population adjustments to known undercounts; they have noted difficulties with pre-census and post-census review periods, and gauged members' satisfaction with the census process and results. Along with not-for-profits in other functional areas, they have encouraged stronger community-level partnerships between the Bureau of the Census in planning, promoting awareness of, and implementing the decennial census.

The bureau, in consultations with the Census Advisory Committees and other stakeholders about how it could improve the census for the year 2000, consistently surfaced the suggestion that it expand and formalize partnerships with the spectrum of organizations. By census day 2000, partnership agreements had been finalized with over 260 national organizations.

See also *Advisory committees; Grassroots groups.*

■ Deborah A. Gona

Bibliography

O'Neill, Michael. *The Third America: The Emergence of the Nonprofit Sector in the United States.* San Francisco: Jossey-Bass, Inc., Publishers, 1989.

Tobin, Gary A. *Social Planning and Human Service Delivery in the Voluntary Sector.* Westport, Conn.: Greenwood Press, 1985.

U.S. Congress. House Committee on Post Office and Civil Service. *The Role of Community and Advocacy Organizations During the 1990 Census and in Planning for the 2000 Census. Hearings before the Subcommittee on Census and Population of the Committee on Post Office and Civil Service.* 102nd Cong., 1st Sess., October 29 and 20, 1991. Serial No. 102-32.

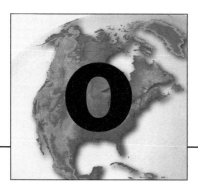

Occupation and education

Questions about occupation and education have been included in some form in every census for over 150 years. As long ago as the first census, in 1790, debates about content of the census reflected a view that knowledge about the social and economic composition of the population was needed in order to plan for the development of a new society. James Madison, a major supporter of this broader view of the census, proposed that information be collected about the different classes in the community, notably, manufacturing, agricultural, and commercial classes. His efforts to add such an item to the 1790 census failed. Thomas Jefferson made a similar proposal for the 1800 census, but again the proposals were not seriously considered by the Senate. Several more proposals were made before occupation became part of the information collected in the 1820 census.

Occupations

Three broad classes of occupation—agriculture, commerce, and manufactures—were the basis for the first official occupational count in 1820. Today we would view these as industrial classifications. That is, occupation, or what work one does, is separated from industry or where in the economy one performs the work. In 1820, although enumerators were given instructions to assign more specific occupations to each broad group, only the three broad categories can be identified in that census. Occupational categories used at each census date reflect the social and economic composition of the nation at that time. For example, the increasing division of labor in American society can be observed in the occupational classifications of each census.

No occupational information was collected in 1830, but in 1840, seven occupational categories were included (mining; agriculture; commerce; manufactures and traders; navigation of the ocean; navigation of canals, lakes, and rivers; and learned professions and engineers). Although these categories were more representative than the earlier three, they omitted servants, government officials, clerks, and others. Also, the census enumerated families rather than individuals in 1840 and listed the number of persons in each family that were in each broad occupational class.

A major change occurred in the 1850 census, when the enumeration shifted from the family to the individual. Separate schedules were provided for free persons and for slaves. Information on occupation was acquired only for free males over age fifteen years, but greater occupational detail was collected. In 1850, 323 specific occupations were classified under ten headings. In 1860, women as well as men over age fifteen years were asked their occupations, and the increasing complexity of the economy was reflected in the classification of 584 detailed occupations. Between 1870 and 1930, persons age ten years or older were included in the occupational inquiry, reflecting the prevalence of child labor in the United States. In 1940 and later the age limit was fourteen years and older, reflecting the effect of Child Labor Laws that prohibited or limited the paid work of children.

Other modifications reflected further changes in the American economy and labor force. Separate questions on occupation and industry were introduced in 1910, and the number of detailed categories shifted each decade. A major change occurred in 1870, when concern with the current work status of the person reporting an occupation was introduced. For example, was the individual "gainfully occupied" or, after 1930, "employed," "unemployed," or in another category such as "homemaker?" The person's actual activity during the census reference period was the basis for this classification.

These changes in coverage and in the census categories of occupations occurred because of an expanded economy, a greater division of labor, the emergence of new jobs, the disappearance of others, and some major shifts in broad occupational areas. The Census Bureau has made changes in the occupational classifications each decade, including two major changes since 1950. The 1950 and 1960 classifications are similar. A major reclassification and expansion of detailed occupation-industry-class of worker categories occurred in the 1970 census, from 466 categories in 1960 to 589 in 1970. In 1980 another major change occurred when the Census Bureau changed to a classification system designed to be consistent with the Standard Occupational Classification (SOC) developed by an interagency committee under a mandate from the Office of Management and Budget for use by all government agencies. The system was introduced in 1977 and revised several times, most recently in 1998. The 1980 and 1990 classifications are almost identical, and relatively few changes have been made for Census 2000.

In 1790 the nation was predominantly agricultural. By the mid-twentieth century, it had become predominately industrialized and commercial. Now it has become increasingly a service economy with continuing changes in job categories. By looking at the proportion of people in each occupational group, one can observe these broad social and economic changes. For example, the change from a largely rural to a largely urban population is evident in the declining percentage of gainful workers in agriculture from 86 percent in 1820 to below 60 percent by 1860 to 37 percent by 1900 and to 18 percent in 1940, when the gainful worker concept was last used in a census. From 1940 on, when employment was described in terms of labor force concepts, specifically employment, unemployment, and not in the labor force, the decline in agricultural workers continued to the point where it

reached only about 4 percent of the male civilian labor force in 1980. Other occupations were dropped from the classification scheme as technological advances made them obsolete.

The census occupational classifications revealed a number of other dramatic changes throughout the twentieth century. In addition to the movement from farm to nonfarm work, the composition of nonfarm work changed. Work in the service trades grew, as did the proportion of operatives, craftsmen, and related workers, whereas the number of laborers declined. The most significant rise in the twentieth century was observed in white-collar employment, from about 18 percent of workers in 1900 to over 40 percent in 1980. In particular, sales jobs increased somewhat and managerial and clerical jobs increased sharply.

Occupational trends were usually described in detail for men or for the total population until 1970, when the increasing involvement of women in the labor force required separate tabulations for men and women. The percent of women in the labor force increased from 18 percent in 1890 to 52 percent in 1980. Trends in the distribution of occupations for women differed somewhat from men. There was a notable drop in private household workers such as housekeepers from 1900 to 1980 and significant declines in the operative category as well. In contrast, trends among women were similar to those among men in the number of farm workers and other manual types of work as well as white-collar occupations. Some convergence in occupational distributions was evident by 1980, although many more women were still in clerical and service work whereas men were concentrated in managerial and craft occupations. This convergence continued through 1990 and undoubtedly will be even more evident in Census 2000.

Education

Information on literacy, the ability to read and write in any language, was first collected in 1840 and was collected in each census through 1930. The distinction between literate and illiterate persons, while not significant in recent years, differentiated a significant proportion of the population in earlier decades. In 1840, 22 percent of the population was illiterate. The illiteracy rate declined over the years to 11 percent by 1900 and to just over 4 percent in 1930. More recent interest in the census has been on school enrollment and educational attainment.

School enrollment statistics have been included in each census since 1850, primarily for younger persons. The proportion of the school-age population enrolled in school increased dramatically during the twentieth century. Between 1940 and 1990 the proportion of persons age five to twenty-four years who were enrolled in school increased from 58 percent in 1940 to 70 percent in 1990. In 1990, 96 percent of children age seven to fifteen years were enrolled in school. Recent trends have involved enrolling earlier and staying longer. In 1990, 30 percent of three and four year olds were enrolled in preschool, and 80 percent of five and six year olds were enrolled in school. At the other end of the age spectrum, over one third of persons age twenty to twenty-four years and 12 percent of those age twenty-five to thirty-four years were enrolled in school in 1990.

The principal measure of educational attainment, years of school completed, was not included in the census until 1940, but this measure has been collected ever since. Educational attainment is a good measure of socioeconomic achievement for adults who have passed the usual school completion age, generally defined as age twenty-five years and older. The educational attainment of persons in this age group increased dramatically throughout the twentieth century, particularly during the last half century. Three quarters of the adult population had completed high school in 1990, compared to only about 25 percent in 1940, 42 percent in 1960, and 67 percent in 1980. In addition, one fifth of the adult population had completed four years of college or more in 1990, compared to only 5 percent in 1940. Part of the increase in educational attainment is undoubtedly due to changing laws requiring that larger proportions of young people remain in school, first until age fifteen years and then, in most states, until age sixteen years. Thus persons born after 1930 were required to be in school long enough to complete at least a junior high level of education, if not high school. The results are evident in any breakdown of educational attainment by age. For example, among persons age twenty-five to thirty-four years, 84 percent have acquired at least a high school diploma, compared to only 45 percent of persons age seventy-five years or older.

In 1990 a significant change occurred in the way the educational attainment question was asked. In the censuses of 1940 through 1980, attainment was measured in terms of years of school completed. In 1990 the question was asked in terms of completion of specific degrees, so that, in 1990, one could say that 75 percent of the adult population had received a high school diploma, compared to 1940, when about 25 percent reported completion of four years of high school. This change was perceived as an improvement because some people complete four years of high school without receiving a degree. Also, the increased attainment levels required more detail on achievement at the upper end of the education measures.

For the first time, the 1990 census enabled identification of the number of adults who had received bachelor's, master's, doctorate, or professional degrees. In 1990, 20 percent of the population had received a bachelor's degree or higher, and about 7 percent of adults age twenty-five years or older reported that they had received master's, doctorates, or professional degrees. In general, the data show that the United States made major improvements in the education of its population in the last half of the twentieth century, in terms of both the proportion going to and staying in school and the proportion receiving high school and college diplomas and degrees.

That improvement is not the same for all population groups. As noted, there are age-related differences in educational attainment, but there have also been, and continue to be, differences by gender, race, and ethnicity. As of 1990, the differences in educational attainment between men and women were relatively small. For example, about 27 percent of men and 24 percent of women had a college degree. In contrast, although the educational attainment of major race and ethnic groups in the population has improved since 1960, some significant differences remained in 1990. The Asian and Pacific Islander groups had, for example, the largest proportion of college graduates of all groups, 37 percent compared to 20 percent of all persons age twenty-five years or older. This was largely due to the Asian part of the population, 38 percent of whom were college graduates, compared to 11 percent of the Pacific Islanders. Asian Indians had the largest proportion of college graduates, with 58 percent. Persons of Latino or Hispanic origin showed great variability in educational attainment, with those from Colombia or Spain having the largest proportion of high school graduates, 67 and 78 percent, respectively. In contrast only 34 percent of Salvadorans and 38 percent of Guatemalans had high school diplomas in 1990. Similar variations were found in college completion, with

20 percent of those from Spain completing college, compared to 5 percent of Salvadorans.

Differences also exist in terms of educational achievements of the populations of different regions and states within the United States. A good measure of disadvantage is the proportion of school dropouts, or of persons age fifteen to nineteen years who are not enrolled in school and who are not high school graduates. With increasing educational attainment, all states had lower dropout levels in 1990 than in previous decades. Considerable variation in the dropout rate exists, however, ranging from 15.2 percent in Nevada, to about 14 percent in Arizona, Florida, California, Georgia, and the District of Columbia, to only 4.6 percent in North Dakota. The states with the highest dropout rate were in the South and West generally. A similar trend is evident in the proportion of persons age twenty-five or over who have completed high school. High school completion is a basic measure of educational attainment and almost a necessity to obtain a job with any possibility for future advancement. Again, considerable variation exists by state, with many states in the South showing the lowest high school completion levels: 64 percent in Kentucky and Mississippi and 66–67 percent in West Virginia, Arkansas, Alabama, Tennessee, compared to 87 percent in Alaska, 85 percent in Utah, and 84 percent in Colorado and Washington state. Hence, there is still room for improvement in educational attainment.

Data on occupation and education were collected in Census 2000 and will continue to be valuable for social and economic planning for the twenty-first century.

■ Mary G. Powers

Bibliography

Kominski, Robert, and Andrea Adams. "Educational Attainment in the United States, 1993 and 1992." *Current Population Reports*, Series P-20, No. 476. U.S. Bureau of the Census. Washington, D.C.: U.S. Department of Commerce, 1993.

Kominski, Robert, and Andrea Adams. *We the Americans: Our Education*. U.S. Bureau of the Census. Washington, D.C.: U.S. Government Printing Office, 1993.

Nam, Charles B., and Mary G. Powers. *The Socioeconomic Approach to Status Measurement*. Houston, Texas: Cap & Gown Press, 1983.

U.S. Bureau of the Census. *Twelfth Census of the United States, 1900. Special Reports, Occupation*. Washington, D.C.: U.S. Government Printing Office, 1904.

Organization and administration of the census

Census 2000 was the largest peace-time mobilization in U.S. history. The Census Bureau hired more than 860,000 temporary employees to help identify 120 million housing units, count more than 275 million people, and process about 1.5 billion pieces of paper. The bureau accomplished this feat under intense political, social, and legal scrutiny, with decisions being made at the highest levels of government, for example, by the president, congressional leaders, and the U.S. Supreme Court. As if these challenges were not enough, the bureau faced an even greater one from the many changes that have taken place in U.S. society since the last census was taken in 1990, making census taking even more difficult.

The 1990 census was the most expensive census in American history, and, for the first time, it was less accurate than the preceding census. Much litigation followed, most of which challenged the results and called for an adjustment for coverage errors. In November 1990, the secretary of commerce, with congressional urging, directed the Census Bureau to establish a task force to consider both policy and technical issues in order to develop a design for Census 2000 and a demographic measurement system for related activities for 2000 through 2009.

The task force consisted of two interagency policy and technical committees and an advisory committee established by the secretary of commerce to represent the diverse interests of other census stakeholders. The advisory committee advised the secretary of commerce on the design and implementation of Census 2000. The task force's final recommendations, issued in June 1995, included suggestions that the post-enumeration survey be revised and that the Census Bureau use different and improved statistical procedures to reduce the differential undercount.

Concerned about the increasing costs and reduced accuracy of the census, Congress commissioned a National Academy of Sciences (NAS) panel to find a better way to meet the requirements of the census. The panel recommended incorporating sampling methods in a survey to follow-up known households that had not responded, in order to estimate those missed in the census. Based on recommendations from the NAS and others, the Census Bureau adopted the use of sampling. It also decided to contract with the private sector for a number of important census functions.

In 1997, Congress disagreed with the use of sampling methodology for all tabulations and directed the Census Bureau to plan for both a traditional census and one that incorporated sampling. Sites in the 1998 dress rehearsal census were assigned to one or the other method. In January 1999 the U.S. Supreme Court ruled that the reported counts for apportioning the House could not be based on sampling and estimation methods. The bureau then developed a third plan to conduct a traditional census, without sampling, to follow-up with nonrespondents to produce the counts for apportionment. The census was followed by an Accuracy and Coverage Evaluation survey to estimate those missed and to produce adjusted counts that could be used for all other purposes.

Management Structure

The Census Bureau is organized into eight directorates, each under an associate director. Seven of these directorates were involved in Census 2000. They include the decennial census, field operations, communications, information technology, demographic programs, methodology and standards, and finance and administration. Each associate director reports to the director through either the principal associate director for programs or the principal associate director and chief financial officer. Although the roles played by each directorate are crucial to the census, three positions are key: the director, a political appointee who is ultimately responsible to the president and Congress; the associate director for decennial census, who oversees all decisions for planning, budget, and operations; and the associate director for field operations, who oversees data collection by the Field Division, encompassing 12 Regional Offices (ROs), 12 Regional Census Centers (RCCs), 520 Local Census Offices (LCOs), and an army of temporary enumerators.

Because the decision-making process is so complex and covers a broad range of issues, an executive-level steering committee was established in 1997 to coordinate decisions on the census. The steering committee, which meets twice a week, includes the director, deputy director, the two principal associate directors, the associate and assistant directors for the decennial census and field operations, the associate director for communications, and the congressional affairs office chief.

The Office of the Associate Director for Decennial Census directs and provides planning and coordination of decennial censuses, assisted principally by the assistant director for decennial census, who serves as the chief operating officer. All funding for decennial-related operations is managed and coordinated by the decennial directorate. Under the associate director for decennial census are the Decennial Management Division (DMD), the Geography Division, the Decennial Statistical Studies Division (DSSD), and the Decennial Systems and Contracts Management Office (DSCMO). These divisions report to the associate director through the assistant director for decennial census.

The DMD provides overall direction for program planning and coordination of the decennial census; assigns functional responsibility to divisions; determines program priorities; and develops budget requirements, time schedules, and a progress reporting and control system. It monitors and documents program and budget status; serves as the primary point of contact on the decennial census program with the bureau's outside oversight groups, such as the General Accounting Office (GAO), the Office of the Inspector General, the Census Monitoring Board, congressional oversight committees, and the Department of Justice; develops census methodology plans; organizes test and research programs; and recommends policy for decennial program issues.

The Geography Division plans, coordinates, and administers all geographic and cartographic activities needed to facilitate the bureau's statistical programs throughout the United States and its territories. The DSSD develops and coordinates the application of statistical techniques in the design and conduct of decennial censuses. The DSCMO managed the development and implementation of major Census 2000 contracts, including development and implementation of a data capture system; acquisition of hardware, software, telecommunications, and integration services required to support the temporary offices; acquisition of other support such as printing of census forms; and conduct of telephone questionnaire assistance.

The Office of the Associate Director for Field Operations plans and conducts data collection for other censuses and surveys as well as the decennial census. Within this directorate are the Field Division, the National Processing Center (NPC), the Technologies Management Office (TMO), and the twelve ROs covering the United States, Puerto Rico, and the Island Areas. The Field Division plans, organizes, coordinates, and carries out the Census Bureau's data collection in the field. Through the twelve ROs it oversees the twelve RCCs, which operate a national network of temporary offices from which employees collected and processed Census 2000 data. The RCCs manage the 520 LCOs throughout the 50 states, Washington, D.C., and Puerto Rico. Census operations in American Samoa, the Commonwealth of the Northern Mariana Islands, Guam, and the U.S. Virgin Islands are conducted by the Census Bureau in partnership with the government of each Island Area.

The NPC, located in Jeffersonville, Indiana, conducts statistical processing operations for assigned current and special surveys or censuses and provides related administration and logistics services for assigned programs. The TMO develops and implements computer-assisted data collection and related support operations and oversees the development of automated questionnaires for computer-assisted interviewing and related systems and applications in support of critical data-collection programs.

Research

Prior to the census, research on census methodology is managed at headquarters under the associate director for decennial census and the associate director for methodology and standards. The major means for testing census methods and for obtaining operational information for the full deployment of the census is the dress rehearsal, which is managed by the associate director for decennial census.

The dress rehearsal for Census 2000 was conducted on April 18, 1998, in three sites—Columbia, South Carolina, and eleven surrounding counties, because this site had a mix of city-style, rural route, and box number address types and its population had a large proportion of African Americans; Menominee County, Wisconsin, because it contained the Menominee American Indian Reservation; and Sacramento, California, because of its population diversity. Because it was not decided at the time of the dress rehearsal which method would be used for the census—a traditional enumeration or an enumeration with sampling for nonresponse follow-up and for coverage improvement and adjustment—the dress rehearsal became a test of each method. Columbia was a traditional census site; Sacramento and Menominee were sampling sites. More than forty evaluation studies were conducted by the Planning, Research, and Evaluation Division (PRED), which comes under the associate director for methodology and standards.

Data Capture

Census 2000 was the first fully computerized census, from collecting data to releasing the final results on the Internet. Four high technology data capture centers processed more than 150 million census questionnaires, using state-of-the-art optical character recognition and optical mark recognition technology that can recognize and decipher handwritten responses in pen or pencil. Three of these centers, in facilities provided by contract with TRW and subcontractors, are each larger than 200,000 square feet in size and are valued at over $200 million. The data capture system and the staffing to operate the system at these sites was provided by Lockheed Martin. The centers are located in Baltimore County, Maryland; Pomona, California; and Phoenix, Arizona. The NPC, the Census Bureau's permanent facility in Jeffersonville, served as the fourth Census 2000 data capture center. The Census Bureau is responsible for the staffing and operation of the NPC. The DSCMO is responsible for managing the contractors of the data capture centers.

Major Census Operations

The plans for Census 2000 differed significantly from recent decennial censuses in a number of ways, including enumeration methodologies, promotion and outreach, automation, organization and management, and statistical methodologies.

Address list compilation. The Geography Division is responsible for the development of the Master Address File (MAF) that identifies all living quarters with a geographic location from the bureau's TIGER (Topologically Integrated Geographic Encoding and Referencing) database. TIGER links each living quarter to a spatial location and a specific geographic area. It provides the map products and geographic files for data collection. For city-style addresses, information is obtained from the U.S. Postal Service, which also conducts a check through its letter carriers to validate MAF addresses. In addition, Census Bureau ROs conduct a 100-percent block canvass to update and improve the MAF. For non-city-style addresses, census enumerators conduct a door-to-door canvass to update the MAF and TIGER databases.

Under its Local Update of Census Addresses (LUCA) partnership program, the Geography Division sends local or tribal government representatives the

MAF listings and maps for areas under their jurisdiction to obtain information to correct or further update the MAF. The Office of Management and Budget (OMB) manages an appeals process to resolve differences between the Census Bureau and localities regarding what should be included in the address list.

Questionnaire development, production, and mailing. Development of the census questionnaires is managed at headquarters by the DMD under the associate director for decennial census. Decisions on the content of the questionnaires are coordinated with the OMB and other federal agencies and are based on information obtained from many stakeholders. Congress reviews first the subjects and then the specific questions for the census forms.

The short form was mailed to 83 percent of the housing units and the long form to 17 percent. A variable rate sampling plan was used for the long form to achieve greater efficiency while maintaining accuracy at small geographic levels. The sample for the long form was drawn by the DSSD.

Mailing of the appropriate census forms is managed by the DSCMO and conducted by two contractors and the NPC. Forms are available in English and five other languages (Chinese, Korean, Spanish, Tagalog, and Vietnamese) when requested by returning the advance letter. In addition, questionnaire language guides are available in forty-nine languages.

Advertising and other census promotion. Census 2000 promotional efforts were managed by the associate director for communications. The efforts included paid advertising, partnerships, and media public relations programs. For the first time the Census Bureau used a paid advertising campaign for a decennial census. The campaign included a national media campaign, a targeted advertising effort, and special advertising messages and campaigns. This program was coordinated by the Census 2000 Promotional Office under the associate director for communications. The partnership component, managed by the Field Division, included over 30,000 partnership agreements with other federal agencies; state, local, and tribal governments; community organizations; and businesses. Over 600 partnership specialists and support staff work in the RCCs. The media and public relations component consisted of media specialists assigned to the RCCs to cultivate local press contacts and respond to local media inquiries. These specialists take guidance from the Public Information Office under the associate director for communications.

Recruitment and training. Recruitment and training of the hundreds of thousands of temporary employees is managed by the LCOs through the Field Division, which provides guidance on recruitment methods, selection, and pay rates that depend on local prevailing wage rates.

Data collection and enumeration. The major enumeration activities for Census 2000 occurred between March and August 2000. Throughout the data-collection period, information was entered into the computer and checked. These data-processing activities supported enumeration by identifying areas where information was missing or incomplete. The following activities were managed by the DMD and carried out by the Field Division, the DSSD, and other divisions as indicated:

- *Mailout-mailback and other distribution of census questionnaires.* The U.S. Postal Service delivered census questionnaires to more than 80 percent of all households. For a vast majority of the remaining households, a census worker left the questionnaires, while updating the list of addresses for the area. This procedure is known as *update/leave.* In the remaining areas, which were sparsely settled or remote, census workers collected information directly. Each address or location was listed, and census maps were updated with the location. This procedure is called *list/enumerate.*
- *Telephone and Internet assistance.* The Census Bureau operated a toll-free telephone questionnaire assistance system, run by a commercial phone center, and provided assistance in English, Spanish, and several other languages, in completing census questionnaires. Respondents also were able to access a census Internet Web site for assistance in completing their questionnaire and, in some cases, for providing their responses to the census short form.
- *Be Counted Program.* Just before census day, "Be Counted" forms in six languages were distributed at a variety of public locations. The forms allowed people to be included in the census if they believed they had not received a questionnaire or were not included on one.
- *Nonresponse follow-up.* Even with efforts to encourage everyone to provide information, some persons and households did not do so. About four weeks after census day, census workers were sent to follow-up all addresses for which a completed questionnaire was not received. Census staff also visited housing units potentially classified in error during nonre-

sponse follow-up to determine the status of the address on census day.

- *Coverage and content edits.* The Coverage Edit Follow-up Program obtained computer-assisted interviews by telephone to resolve two types of edit failures—population count discrepancy and large household follow-up to obtain missing data for households with more than six persons and for mailout-mailback, Be Counted, and Internet-collected data. For missing or incomplete responses to population or housing items, a content edit was made solely by computer through statistical imputation with no telephone or personal visit follow-up.

- *Unduplication of multiple responses.* The Census Bureau reviewed information when more than one questionnaire data set was captured for a census address, such as through a Be Counted form or a response on the Internet.

- *Other data collection.* Census 2000 had separate data-collection efforts for special places such as Puerto Rico, outlying areas, remote areas, reservations, and hard-to-enumerate areas; special residences such as institutions and group quarters; and special populations such as overseas federal civilian and military employees, transients, and people with no usual residence. As with the basic data collection, most of these efforts were conducted through the LCOs.

- *Accuracy and Coverage Evaluation Survey.* This separate, independent survey was used to measure and correct for differential coverage of the population. A sample of blocks containing about 300,000 households was drawn by the DSSD. An independent address list was prepared for these blocks and independent personal interviews conducted. Coverage factors were computed to adjust the initial census results by matching survey results to the census.

Data transmission. Using dedicated links and other secure lines, the Census 2000 telecommunications network linked all census offices, including census headquarters in Suitland, Maryland, the 520 LCOs, the 12 ROs, the 12 RCCs, the Puerto Rico Area Office, the Maryland Computer Center in Bowie, and the 4 DCCs. The Census Bureau also established communications links with planned commercial telephone centers to assist with telephone questionnaire assistance and the Coverage Edit Follow-up Program. Data transmission was managed by the TMO and DSCMO.

Research to improve future censuses. For the first time, a special sample of households, called the *master trace sample*, was selected from the census, and all census operational information was compiled for the sample, such as how and when each respondent replied and whether follow-ups were necessary and, if so, how many. The trace sample was managed by PRED. In addition, experiments were embedded in the 2000 census to test and evaluate census methods. These experiments were conducted by PRED and managed by the associate director for methodology and standards. Finally, the Census Bureau asked the NAS to begin research on evaluating methods for the 2010 census.

Data dissemination. The two most important products of the census are the state population counts for reapportionment of the House and the population counts within each state for redistricting. The Census Bureau director was required to deliver the former to the president by December 31, 2000. The latter were required by P.L. 94-171 to be delivered to the states within one year after census day. Individual states have their own timing requirements for the completion of redistricting.

Census 2000 data was disseminated by a new data retrieval system called the American Factfinder, developed under contract with IBM. This system enabled data users to access prepackaged data products, data documentation, and online help as well as build custom data products on- and offline.

Oversight. These census operations were under intense scrutiny by Congress, the GAO, the Census Monitoring Board, the U.S. Supreme Court, the media, and the National Academy of Sciences. Many offices at headquarters are responsible for providing information to these oversight groups, but responsibility lies ultimately with the Census Bureau director.

See also *Accuracy and Coverage Evaluation; Address list development; Advertising and the census; Advisory committees; Data dissemination and use; Enumeration: field procedures; Enumeration: special populations; Staffing.*

■ John H. Thompson

Bibliography

U.S. Bureau of the Census. *Updated Summary: Census 2000 Operational Plan.* Washington, D.C.: U.S. Department of Commerce, Economic and Statistics Administration, February 23, 1999.

U.S. Bureau of the Census. "Using Traditional Census-Taking Methods." *Census 2000 Operational Plan.* Washington, D.C.: U.S. Department of Commerce, Economic and Statistics Administration, January 1999.

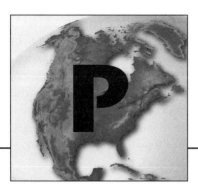

Population estimates and projections

The Census Bureau has an extensive and long-standing program to produce small-area population estimates by using the previous census updated with administrative records. The bureau began to produce national population estimates in the early 1900s; it began to produce state population estimates in the 1940s and substate estimates on a regular basis in the 1970s. Over the years, the scope of the estimates program has expanded in the geographic and demographic detail provided, often in response to mandates in federal legislation that have stimulated advances in estimation methods and access to data sources that are symptomatic of population change. In particular, the requirements of the State and Local Fiscal Assistance Act of 1972 for updated estimates of population for allocating funds to some 39,000 local governmental units (General Revenue Sharing) was a major factor in the development of the Census Bureau's estimates program for small areas. More recently, the Improving America's Schools Act of 1994 led to the development of population estimates for almost 15,000 school districts for use in allocating Title I Elementary and Secondary Education Act funds.

Currently, the Census Bureau produces estimates of total population by single years of age, sex, race, and Hispanic origin on a monthly basis for the United States and annually for states and counties as of July 1 of each year. The bureau also produces estimates of total population every two years for incorporated places and minor civil divisions of counties, in states that have such divisions. Recently, the bureau began producing biennial estimates of total population and of children age five through seventeen for school districts. The first such estimates for school districts were released in early 1999 for the 1996 estimation year.

Periodically the Census Bureau also issues population projections for the United States and individual states by single years of age, sex, race, and Hispanic origin. U.S. projections may be made for fifty or more years into the future; state projections may be made for twenty-five or more years into the future. The U.S. Social Security Administration (SSA) also produces population projections, covering seventy-five years, of the U.S. population by broad age group.

To produce substate population estimates, the Census Bureau works closely with state agencies that are members of the Federal-State Cooperative Program for Local Population Estimates (FSCPE). The FSCPE was initiated in the late 1960s to coordinate and improve state-prepared county population estimates and foster consistency between federal and state-prepared estimates. State FSCPE agencies provide data to the Census Bureau (on vital statistics such as births and deaths) for producing estimates. In turn, the state agencies review these estimates before they are released.

State FSCPE agencies also frequently prepare their own population estimates and projections. Local agencies have compared administrative records with census results to assess the quality and coverage of the census and to establish benchmarks that can be used later on in the decade to estimate population and housing. Estimates of housing unit undercoverage are frequently based on locally available tax assessment or utility data that can be used to estimate housing units. Information from the tax rolls or from water meters, electrical meters, and telephone hook-ups have all been used to evaluate the accuracy of the housing unit count (an important part of population estimation methods). Most recently, such data have been the foundation for counts of housing units used by jurisdictions to improve the Census Bureau's address list in the Local Update of Census Addresses (LUCA) program.

Uses

Census Bureau population estimates serve a variety of needs of federal, state, and local government agencies and academic and private-sector users. The Census Bureau uses national-level estimates by age, sex, race, and Hispanic origin as controls to weight the responses to national household surveys (for example, the Current Population Survey) so that they agree with the total population estimates by demographic characteristics. Without such weighting, the surveys would underestimate many demographic groups because coverage of the population is typically less complete in household surveys than in the decennial census. Beginning in 1994 the population controls for weighting survey results have included an adjustment for the undercount in the census itself, although such an adjustment is not part of the official estimates that are made publicly available.

Population estimates are also used as denominators for important national and subnational statistics, such as birth and death rates for the United States, states, and local areas, and per capita personal income estimates for the United States, states, and counties. In addition, population estimates are widely used in allocating federal funds to states and localities. Currently about $180 billion of federal dollars are allocated to states and other areas by formulas, many of which include population estimates as one of the factors in the formula.

At the local level, these estimates are used by planning agencies for the development of programs and their implementation and evaluation in a host of areas, such as day care, job training, elderly assistance, and transportation planning. Governments use population estimates together with administrative records to document need and to evaluate the reach and effectiveness of programs for compliance purposes. Such record keeping is an essential part of the program funding process that is the mainstay of service provision for many local governments.

Population projections are also used for a wide range of purposes. For example, state school officials may consult the Census Bureau's projections by state when seeking to project school building needs. Also, analysts for Social Security and retirement programs use SSA or Census Bureau long-range population projections in estimating the adequacy of funding to support pensions for retirees.

Methods for Estimates

In brief, the Census Bureau develops total population estimates for the United States by using the component method of demographic analysis, in which the population from the previous census is updated by adding numbers of births and international immigration and subtracting deaths and emigration. Methods for developing state and substate estimates have varied considerably over the years. Currently state estimates of total population are the sum of independently developed county estimates. The county and state totals are adjusted to sum to the national estimate.

The county estimates of total population are produced by the component method: (1) the numbers of births added to the previous census and the numbers of deaths subtracted from the previous census are based on reported vital statistics for each county; (2) reports of the Immigration and Naturalization Service are used to estimate net immigration from abroad; and (3) administrative records are used to estimate net migration among counties. Net migration of people under age sixty-five is estimated for each county from a year-to-year match of federal income tax returns; for people age sixty-five and over, net migration is estimated for each county from the change in Medicare enrollment. Estimates are developed separately for household and group quarters populations. For incorporated places and minor civil divisions, total population estimates are currently developed by a housing unit method. Information on changes in the housing stock obtained from building permits and other sources is combined with census-based estimates of vacancy rates and the numbers of people per housing unit to estimate the change in population for an area since the previous census. For school districts, total population estimates are developed by a shares method that uses previous census data. The share or proportion of the previous census county population for each school district (or school district part) in the county is applied to the county total population for the estimation year. For example, if three school districts in a county had 50 percent, 30 percent, and 20 percent of the county total population of 10,000 in the 1990 census, and the county is estimated (by the component method described previously) to have grown to 12,000 people in 1996, then the three school districts would be estimated in 1996 to have 6,000, 3,600, and 2,400 people, respectively. The shares method necessarily assumes that each school district in a county adds (or loses) population in the same proportion as the county as a whole. State estimates of the population by single years of age and sex, which are controlled to state total population estimates, are developed by a cohort-component method in which net migration rates for the school-age population are derived from school enrollment data. In turn, these rates are used to estimate migration rates for other age groups under age sixty-five. Medicare data are used to estimate migration rates for people age sixty-five and over. State estimates of the population by age, sex, race, and Hispanic origin are developed by a cohort-component method in which federal income tax return data are used to estimate net migration on the basis of estimates of gross in-migration and gross out-migration. This procedure is done for taxfilers and their dependents who are in a 20-percent sample of the Social Security Administration's Numident file (determined by matching Social Security Numbers). The 20-percent Numident file is made available to the Census Bureau for estimation purposes; it provides the demographic characteristics of the taxfilers. The resulting state age-sex-race-Hispanic origin estimates are then controlled to the state age-sex population estimates developed as described above.

County estimates of the population by age, sex, race, and Hispanic origin are developed by using a raking-ratio adjustment of the estimates from the previous census. In this approach, the counts for each county by age, sex, race, and Hispanic origin from the previous census are simultaneously adjusted to agree with the postcensal estimate of the total county population and the postcensal estimates for the applicable state by age, sex, race, and Hispanic origin. This ratio-raking procedure is applied separately for people in group quarters and people not in group quarters; it assumes that the demographic distribution of each county within a state changes in the same manner as that state's demographic distribution. School district estimates for children age five through seventeen are developed by using a shares

approach similar to that described for total population estimates for school districts. The population estimates are regularly evaluated by comparing estimates developed from the previous census for the current census year to the census counts for that year (for example, by comparing 1980 census-based estimates for 1990 to the 1990 census counts). Generally the estimates show proportionally larger differences from the census for smaller areas compared with larger areas and for demographic groups compared with the total population. The estimates also generally show proportionally larger differences from the census for areas in which the population is rapidly growing or declining compared with more stable areas. Finally, differences between the estimates and the census tend to be proportionately larger for estimates that are produced by synthetic methods (for example, the raking-ratio adjustment used to produce county demographic estimates and the shares method used to produce school district estimates of school-age children) compared with estimates that are produced by using components of population change. A special concern regarding these estimation methods is that the methods are only as good as the administrative statistics upon which they are built. The quality of data can vary substantially from jurisdiction to jurisdiction, as with building permit data reported to the Census Bureau. Field studies and other research surrounding the American Community Survey (ACS) have uncovered some of these problems. Permit data reporting has not always been complete and this can create shortfalls, especially in districts in which population growth is closely related to new housing construction. Even vital statistics data can be compromised by sometimes subtle differences in the way in which registry systems define and code such important characteristics as race and Hispanic origin.

Methods for Projections

The Census Bureau and SSA projections of the U.S. population by age begin with the bureau's latest population estimates. Projections are then developed by a cohort-component method in which rates of fertility, mortality, and immigration are applied to the base-year estimates and the population is moved forward in age over time. Typically, several series of projections or scenarios are produced that span a range of assumptions about each component. For example, the Census Bureau generally produces three series: one series assumes lower-than-expected mortality and higher-than-expected fertility, which gives an upper bound to expected population growth; another assumes higher-than-expected mortality and lower-than-expected fertility, which gives a lower bound to expected population growth; the third is in the middle. SSA produces several projection series as well. The SSA assumptions are not the same as the Census Bureau assumptions. Also, SSA combines assumptions in different ways to produce scenarios that help assess such factors as the old-age dependency ratio (the population sixty-five and older divided by the working-age population age twenty through sixty-four), which are critical to the financial health of the Social Security trust fund. Thus, SSA produces a series that assumes both low mortality and low fertility, which produces an upward bound on the old-age dependency ratio, and another series that assumes both high mortality and high fertility, which produces a lower bound on the old-age dependency ratio. Neither the Census Bureau nor the SSA projections allow for fluctuations in vital rates over the projection period. The Census Bureau's population projections by state incorporate further assumptions about internal migration. Four series of projections are produced, three of which assume that recent patterns of migration will continue with some variation. The fourth series assumes zero net internal migration.

See also *Address list development; Demographic analysis; Federal household surveys; Related data sources.*

■ Constance F. Citro, assisted by Meyer Zitter

Bibliography

Long, John F. *Post Censal Population Estimates: States, Counties, and Places.* Population Division Working Paper Series, No. 3. Bureau of the Census. Washington, D.C.: U.S. Department of Commerce, 1993.

Sink, Larry. *Estimates of the Population of Counties by Age, Sex, Race, and Hispanic Origin: 1990–1994.* Release 48 (Methodology). Bureau of the Census. Washington, D.C.: U.S. Department of Commerce, 1996.

Post-enumeration Survey

The Census Bureau conducts a Post-enumeration Survey (PES) after a census in order to measure how well the census covered the population. The PES measures two types of enumeration errors: omissions and erroneous inclusions. The Census Bureau staff studies these *gross errors* to understand the causes of census coverage error and to improve census-taking methods. To measure the overall accuracy of the census, the Census Bureau estimates the *net coverage error,* which describes the difference between the two types of gross error.

History

The Census Bureau conducted its first PES after the 1950 census. An evaluation of the 1940 census had demonstrated the need for an assessment of census coverage. A match of draft registration records to the 1940 census count of adult males of draft age showed, surprisingly, that more males were registered for the draft than were enumerated in the census.

The Census Bureau also conducted a PES after the 1960, 1980, and 1990 censuses and in test censuses in preparation for the 1980 and 1990 censuses. The PES consists of two sample surveys: a sample of census enumerations (the E sample) and an independent sample of the population (the P sample). The E sample measures erroneous enumerations, and the P sample measures omissions. The erroneous enumerations include duplications, inclusions of people in the wrong area, and enumerations of people who are not living in the United States. The P sample is independent of the census and selects blocks, clusters of blocks, or segments of blocks, including all the housing units in the selected areas. The PES requires that a list of those housing units be made because using the census address lists would violate the independence.

The implementation and estimation methodology of the PES has evolved over the years. The 1950 PES evaluated census content error in addition to census coverage error. The idea behind the PES was to perform a much higher quality census interview with highly trained interviewers; therefore, the PES interview was assumed to yield the truth. The true population size was taken to equal the census count multiplied by the ratio of the number of people in the PES housing units divided by the number of people the census found in those housing units.

The 1950 P and E samples each had about 25,000 housing units and were designed to overlap as much as possible. Sample selection occurred in two stages. First, the United States was divided into primary sampling units, of which 270 were selected. Within the primary sampling units, groups of six to ten housing units, called *segments,* were selected. The E samples consisted of all the census enumerations coded as residing in the selected segments.

Interviewers were instructed to interview an adult

resident at each housing unit in their assigned segments. The interviewers' materials contained the results of the original census interviews in their segments, concealed on a folded page. The interviewers were to refer to the original results only for comparison, after conducting the interview. The idea was that the comparison would help improve the results and resolve any discrepancies.

The results of the 1950 PES were disappointing. The survey did not find as large an undercount as demographic techniques showed to be present. Evidently the interviewers often merely confirmed the original interview and did not find missed housing units or missed people.

The same weaknesses appeared in the undercount estimates based on the 1960 PES. The methodological improvement of having the PES focus only on census coverage (content error was evaluated in a separate study) did not alleviate these problems.

The design of the 1960 PES again aimed to ascertain the truth. The P and E samples were selected independently, and there was no attempt to make them overlap. The P sample contained 25,000 dwellings and was an area sample of 2,500 segments. The selected segments were a subsample of the segments canvassed for the 1959 Survey of Change and Residential Finance (SCARF). The enumerators had information from the census and from the SCARF to aid in their re-enumeration and search for missed and erroneously included dwellings.

The E sample was a sample of 15,000 dwellings from the list of those in the census. On average, the sample had two clusters of three dwellings from each of the 2,400 census enumeration districts contained in the 335 primary sample units chosen for the Current Population Survey (CPS), which measures the unemployment rate. The interviewers were given the addresses but not the names of the occupants listed in the census.

Dual-Systems Estimation

The Census Bureau did not conduct a PES of the 1970 census; however, improvements in methodology led the Census Bureau to conduct one after the 1980 census. The improvements came from U.N.-sponsored developments, in which a dual-systems estimation method was used to estimate population size in other countries. Dual-systems estimation required only that the PES be a second enumeration of a sample of households rather than an improved enumeration

good enough to be considered the truth.

Respondents to the 1980 PES were matched to the original enumeration on a case-by-case basis. One complication arose over the issue of whether a person was considered correctly enumerated if he or she was counted at any address or only if there was one correct address where the person had to be counted. Another complication arose because some people moved between the time of the census and the PES interview.

Whether a person can be enumerated correctly at only one or multiple addresses is important because of the case-by-case matching. The matching operation has to know where to search for census enumerations. With Any-Address Matching, the PES interviewer asks the respondent to list all the addresses where he or she may have been enumerated. If the matching operation finds the respondent at one of these addresses or close to one of these addresses, the person is considered correctly enumerated. With Unique-Address Matching, the PES interviewer asks the respondent for a usual residence. In order to be enumerated correctly, the respondent has to be enumerated at that address. Unique-Address Matching is much easier to implement because only one address has to be considered.

The complication of how to handle movers is addressed in the three variations of the PES. In PES-A, the members of the P sample are the residents of a sampled housing unit on census day. In PES-B, the members of the P sample are the residents of the housing unit when the PES interview is conducted. A hybrid known as PES-C uses the number of movers into the sampled housing units (PES-B definition) to estimate the number of movers and the match rate for the people who have moved out (PES-A definition) to estimate the match rate for movers. All three variations have advantages and disadvantages. With PES-A, the movers have to be traced so that they can be interviewed, or the interviewers have to rely on neighbors. However, the matching is much easier because the enumeration is at the sampled housing unit if the movers were enumerated. With PES-B, the movers are easy to find because they now live at the sampled housing unit, but they must remember their former address well enough for census staff to find it in the census records. PES-C attempts to incorporate the best of the other two variations, but the interviewers have to collect much more information than they do with PES-A or PES-B.

The 1980 PES used Unique-Address Matching and the PES-B mover treatment. The matching operation was clerical and very time consuming. The P and E samples for the 1980 PES were selected in completely different ways. The P sample interviews were supplementary questions in the April and August waves of the CPS. As the CPS sample, the P sample included approximately 124,000 housing units with 62,000 from each wave. The CPS sample design is a two-stage design in which primary sampling units about the size of counties are selected at the first stage and segments of four housing units each are selected within each selected primary sampling unit.

The E sample for the 1980 PES was selected from every enumeration district in the United States. Ten enumerations were selected from each enumeration district, for a total sample size of about 110,000 households. Interviewers visited each household in the E sample. The interviewers checked that each person enumerated at the housing unit was a real person and that the address was each person's usual residence. The interviewers also checked that the geographic coding for the housing unit was correct. If the people who were enumerated in the census had moved, the interviewers inquired at other residences in the neighborhood and at the post office to determine who had lived at the address on census day.

The Census Bureau used data from the P and E samples and dual-systems estimation to estimate the population size. A comparison of the census to the estimated population size yielded the net undercount rate.

Controversy

After the 1980 census, New York City led the lawsuits by asking that the results of the 1980 PES be used to adjust the census for undercount. The Census Bureau took the position that the PES results were not of high enough quality to be used to adjust the census, and the courts did not order an adjustment.

Many people inside and outside the Census Bureau had concerns about the validity of the dual system estimates for the PES. A technical disadvantage of dual system estimates is that they may be subject to correlation bias because people missed by the census may also tend to be missed by the PES. Poststratification of the respondents by geography, sex, age, racial and ethnic groups, and population density reduces the bias by grouping together people with similar chances of being counted. However, the poststratification may not describe all the heterogeneity of enumeration probabilities and thereby may introduce correlation bias. Some variations of the estimation methodology have

been designed to reduce the correlation bias, but these have not been successfully implemented.

Another disadvantage of dual system estimation in a PES is that the matching between two independent lists, the PES and the census, requires a substantial amount of time. The matching requires that both the census enumeration files and the PES files be available. Further, matching people who move between the time of the census and the PES is a complicated, time-consuming process.

After the 1980 census, the Census Bureau launched a research program that made substantial improvements in PES methodology by taking advantage of advances in computer technology and implementing design adaptations. The case-by-case clerical matching was replaced by computerized matching with clerical review and matching of the difficult cases. For the computerized matching algorithms to be used efficiently, the P and E samples had to come from the same blocks, which was the basis of the sample design for the 1990 PES.

The 1990 PES was designed specifically for census coverage evaluation of the population living in housing units and noninstitutional group quarters and used Unique-Address Matching and PES-B treatment of movers. The sample selection used a single-stage sample design in which the United States was stratified by geographic area, percent minority population, percent renters, and urban versus rural areas. A sample of blocks was then selected within each stratum. The sample consisted of about 5,300 block clusters and 172,000 housing units. The design of the stratification complemented the poststratification used in the estimation of population size for small areas.

In July 1990, interviewers conducted P sample interviews in the sample blocks. The persons found in these interviews were matched to the census enumerations in these same blocks and one ring of surrounding blocks. A follow-up interview in November 1990 checked the status of anyone in the P sample who did not have a matching census enumeration. Follow-up interviewers also investigated any E sample enumerations in the sample block that did not have a matching P sample person.

PES estimates of the 1990 census undercount, produced in 1991, were not used to adjust the census. The Census Bureau evaluated the 1991 estimates extensively in preparation for the decision on whether to adjust the census. The evaluations were synthesized in the estimation of the total error in the estimates. In

1992 the PES estimates were revised and considered for use in the bureau's Postcensal Estimates Program. After careful evaluation, however, the Census Bureau decided not to use the PES estimates in this program.

The Census Bureau has a large amount of experience with the PES and knows that the estimates at the national level are comparable to those from demographic analysis. The PES is the only methodology that provides estimates of census coverage error for levels of geography below the national level and for all racial and ethnic groups. The PES methodology is part of Census 2000 in the form of the Accuracy and Coverage Evaluation Survey.

See also *Accuracy and Coverage Evaluation; Capture-recapture methods; Coverage evaluation; Demographic analysis; Errors in the census.*

■ Mary H. Mulry

Bibliography

Chandrasekar, C., and W. E. Deming. "On a Method of Estimating Birth and Death Rates and the Extent of Registration." *Journal of the American Statistical Association* 44 (March 1949): 101–115.

Citro, C. F., and M. L. Cohen. *The Bicentennial Census.* Washington, D. C.: National Academy Press, 1985.

Fay, R. E., J. S. Passel, and J. G. Robinson, with assistance from C. D. Cowan. *The Coverage of Population in the 1980 Census.* 1980 Census of Population and Housing, Evaluation and Research Reports PHC 80-E4. Washington, D.C.: U.S. Department of Commerce, 1988.

Hogan, H. "The 1990 Post Enumeration Survey: An Overview." *The American Statistician.* Alexandria, Va.: American Statistical Association, 1992, 261–269.

Marks, E. S., W. P. Mauldin, and H. Nisselson. "The Post-Enumeration Survey of the 1950 Census: A Case History in Survey Design." *Journal of the American Statistical Association* 48 (June 1953): 220–243.

Marks, E. S., and J. Waksberg. " Evaluation of Coverage in the 1960 Census Through Case-by-Case Checking." In *1966 Proceedings of the Social Statistics Section, American Statistical Association,* 62–70.

Marks, E. S., W. Seltzer, and K. Krotki. *Population Growth Estimation.* New York: The Population Council, 1974.

Mulry, M. H., and B. D. Spencer. "Accuracy of the 1990 Census and Adjustments." *Journal of the American Statistical Association* 88 (September 1993): 1080–1091.

Price, D. O. "A Check on Underenumeration in the 1940 Census." *American Sociological Review* 12 (February 1947): 44–49.

U.S. Bureau of the Census. *The Post-Enumeration Survey: 1950.* Bureau of the Census Technical Paper No. 4. Suitland, Md.: U.S. Bureau of the Census, 1960.

Pre-computer tabulation systems

The Census Bureau relied on hand tabulation for compilation and tabulation of census returns from the first census at 1790 until the introduction of machine tabulation late in 1872. The bureau continued to support experimentation and innovation with regard to tabulating census results well into the twentieth century and was among the first to recognize the usefulness of computers for data processing in the 1940s.

No clerical force was employed at the federal level for the compilation, verification, or correction of returns for the first three decennial censuses (1790–1810). The Census Act of March 1, 1790, which legislated the censuses of 1790, 1800, 1810, 1820, and 1830, simply required that assistant marshals provide "accurate returns of all persons, except Indians not taxed" and that each marshal would "transmit to the President of the United States the aggregate amount of each description of persons within their respective districts." Beginning in 1800, however, aggregate returns were turned over to the secretary of state. The Fourth Census (1820) employed an unidentified number of clerks (total remuneration, $925), whose specific tasks were also undisclosed.

New Tabulation Age

In several respects the Fifth Decennial Census (1830) represented the dawning of a new tabulating age. For the first time in decennial census-taking history, uniform printed schedules were distributed by the secretary of state, Martin Van Buren, to the marshals for the use of their assistants. Marshals were required to deliver one copy of each schedule filled out to the clerk of the district court and to the secretary of state, together with their compiled totals. Second, legislation passed on February 3, 1831, required the secretary of state "to note all the clerical errors in the returns of the marshals and assistants, whether in the additions, classification of inhabitants, or otherwise, and cause said notes to be printed, with the aggregate returns of the marshals, for the use of congress." In an effort to comply with this directive, Secretary of State Van Buren for the first time employed forty-three temporary clerks to carry out this task.

The ambitious scope of the Sixth Decennial Census schedule (1840), dictated by the census acts of March

3, 1830, and February 26, 1840, almost ensured the requirement of a clerical force to assist with compilation and tabulation of census returns. As before, the secretary of state, John Forsyth, was required to note "all the clerical errors in the returns of the marshals and assistants, whether in the additions, classification of inhabitants, or otherwise, and that he should direct to be printed the corrected aggregate returns only." To this effort the census legislation of February 1840 provided for a superintending clerk, a recording clerk, two assistant clerks and other such clerks necessary "to examine and correct the returns from the marshals and their assistants." The maximum size of the 1840 census office force was twenty-eight.

By 1850 there was a strong general appreciation among census pundits of the necessity for improving census machinery. An act approved March 3, 1849, established a Census Board, composed of the secretary of state, the attorney general, and the postmaster general. The act also provided for the appointment by the board of a secretary. This position was granted to Joseph C. G. Kennedy, who later assumed the title superintendent of the census (1850–1853). Further legislation, passed on May 23, 1850, significantly altered the scope of the canvass, necessitating among other things a larger office force in Washington. Compilation and tabulation of the results of the Seventh Census were begun under Superintendent Kennedy and completed under Superintendent James D. B. DeBow (1853–1854). The maximum size of the 1850 census office was 160. Clerks employed in the census office during the 1850 decennial census period held only temporary positions, and in the *Compendium of the Seventh Census* DeBow lamented the difficulties he faced in obtaining qualified personnel. DeBow complained that some clerks had "never compiled a table before, and are incapable of combining a column of figures correctly. Hundreds of thousands of pages of returns are placed in the hands of such persons to be digested. If any are qualified it is no merit of the system. In 1840 returns were given out by the job to whoever would take them. In 1850 such was the pressure of work, that almost anyone could at times have a desk."

The Eighth Decennial Census (1860) continued the practice of hiring a temporary clerical work force to carry out the task of hand compilation and tabulation of the enumeration. By an act of May 5, 1860, a classified clerical force was provided for the census office, including the superintendent and a chief clerk. The maximum office force reached 184 clerks.

Second Tabulation Age

Machine tabulation provided the second tabulation age (the first being the innovation of standardized printed schedules and provision of a clerical office force). The mechanization of tabulation had its beginning in late 1872 when the Census Office experimented with a tallying machine invented by Charles W. Seaton, the chief clerk of the Census Office. Seaton was paid $15,000 by the act of June 10, 1872, in full of all claims against the government for its use at the Ninth or any subsequent census. The Seaton Machine, as it was known, was used extensively in tabulating the 1880 census. Seaton's invention was simply a wooden box that contained parallel rollers that unwound at the bottom and then rewound at the top the paper tally sheets used by the clerks. The purpose of the machine was to condense a long tally sheet to a workable surface for the clerk. Hundreds of clerks still did the actual tallying by hand, but the Seaton Machine significantly sped up the tabulation process.

In 1890 the electric tabulating machine was used for the first time. Dr. Herman Hollerith, a Census Office employee, developed this "card" system, or the Hollerith machine, in the decade prior to the Eleventh Decennial Census. By the last quarter of the nineteenth century, the sheer scope of the decennial census and the broad demand for the statistics generated by the count challenged the Census Office to develop an efficient and accurate method of compilation and tabulation.

The system that Hollerith developed consisted of individual cards, the keyboard punch, and a series of automatic machines that verified, sorted, counted, and tabulated census data. Information gathered for each individual at the enumeration was first transferred to small cards measuring 6 5/8 by 3 1/4 inches by means of a mechanical keyboard punch. The position of the hole on the card indicated the particular fact to be recorded. Once punched, the cards were then run through a verification machine that threw out all inconsistencies and also provided a count for subsequent checking purposes. Next, the cards were separated into classes or groups by an automatic sorting machine, capable of handling up to 300 cards per minute. The cards were then run through a machine that counted them at the rate of 500 per minute. Finally, they were run through the electric tabulating machine capable of handling 375–425 cards per minute. The tabulating machine held a pin box that contained a needle, set on a fine spiral spring, for each possible hole in a card. The pin box was brought down over each card in turn; those needles meeting an unpunched surface were repressed, and those passing through the punched hole made an electric contact below, which in turn registered on a dial. At the conclusion of each "run" the counters were read and the result recorded. According to the Census Office, in the hands of an experienced and capable clerk the Hollerith machines could tabulate an average of 8,000–10,000 cards in a working day of six-and-a-half hours. In 1890 and 1900 the machines were run by hand.

At the Twelfth Census the Hollerith system was again used, with some refinements. Added to the machines used for the Eleventh Decennial tabulation were adding machine attachments used for preparing the statistics of agriculture. Automatic feeders and an improved automatic sorting machine were also used "to great advantage." The automatic sorting machine employed in 1900 was a 3-foot square and 5-feet-high frame, directly over a column of ten boxes. As with the tabulating machine, the cards in the 1900 sorter were fed downward one by one, before the pin box. The cards entered one of ten chutes determined by the electro-magnet, which in turn led to the ten boxes. Before a run, a clerk worked out the combinations of the pins in the pin box. An experienced clerk could operate the machine at a speed of 75,000 to 175,000 cards per day, depending upon the number of tabulations sought. Dials on the outside of the machine recorded the number of cards as they passed through, thus allowing the clerks to note their progress and to keep a record of daily productivity. Publicity for the Census Office championed the efficiency of the new machines and calculated that if the tallies of age, sex, nativity, and occupation had been made by hand, it would have taken one hundred clerks seven years, eleven months, and five days to complete the work.

The Census Bureau, made permanent in 1902, used its first intercensal period to refine tabulating machinery and to tackle new problems created by the solution of electric tabulation, namely, preparing the cards for tabulation (called "editing"). A congressional appropriation of $40,000 in February 1905 and the subsequent organization of its own machine shop in July 1905, allowed the bureau to begin developing its own tabulating machinery and thus to bypass the costly rental fees it had incurred at the previous decennial census. By late 1907 the bureau's machine shop declared that its tabulating and punching machines were far superior to those of its predecessors and ready for use at the Thirteenth Decennial Census.

The punching and tabulating machines developed by the Census Bureau were indeed different in a number of respects to their predecessors. Whereas the punching machine used in 1900 had only one key, that of 1910—which resembled a typewriter—had more than 250 keys corresponding to the various facts sought by the tabulation. The machine required an operating clerk to align the keys and the holes before punching, which theoretically allowed for the correction of errors before the actual punching began. The tabulating machines employed at the 1900 census recorded their count on dials that had to be transcribed by a clerk, the 1910 version automatically printed the results of the count. Automatic rather than hand feeding of the cards into the tabulator also sped up the process. The bureau employed three hundred keyboard punching machines and one hundred semiautomatic electric tabulating machines for the count of the Thirteenth Decennial Census.

Declarations of the superiority of the updated punching machine proved to be premature. The bureau's attempts to correct the problems concurrent with the tabulation of the Thirteenth Census were unsuccessful and the clerks were forced to use the old machines, thus slowing the entire process considerably. It is clear from the annual reports of the director of the census to the secretary of commerce from 1920 to the 1930s that the bureau focused considerable attention to the details of office work, particularly those of editing, punching, tabulating, and verifying the census returns. As the American population continued to grow in complexity and diversity in the twentieth century, the Census Bureau remained committed to refinement and innovation with regard to all aspects of tabulating the census returns.

■ Diana L. Magnuson

Bibliography

DeBow, J.D.B. *Compendium of the Seventh Census.* Washington, D.C.: Robert Armstrong, 1853.

Department of Commerce. *The Story of the Census, 1790–1916.* Washington, D.C.: Government Printing Office, 1916.

Merriam, William R. *American Census Taking.* Reprinted from *The Century Magazine* (April 1903).

Truesdell, Leon. *The Development of Punch Card Tabulation in the Bureau of the Census, 1890–1940.* Washington, D.C.: Government Printing Office, 1965.

Wright, Carroll D. and William C. Hunt. The History and Growth of the United States Census. Washington, D.C.: Government Printing Office, 1900.

Presidents and the census

See *Civil War and the census; Congress and the census; Decennial censuses; Statistical policy and oversight.*

Printed publications

See *Dissemination of data: printed publications*

Private sector

For many years the private sector has relied heavily on decennial census data for making decisions including selecting sites for plants and stores, target marketing, evaluating sales, and allocating advertising expenditures.

Census data have probably been used by businesses for well over a hundred years. In the nineteenth century, the census included questions on manufacturing, agriculture, mining, and fisheries. Companies likely made use of these data in their production planning. For example, companies manufacturing farm and mining equipment needed to know where the farms and mines were. In the twentieth century, companies started to make use of demographic and socioeconomic data to determine where to sell products. One of the first books to use census data was the annual *Survey of Buying Power*, published by Sales and Marketing Management Magazine (S&MM). The first edition of this book appeared in 1929, just before the crash on Wall Street. The *Survey of Buying Power* showed population, income, and sales data for every county and hundreds of cities. Each year throughout the decade, the data were updated to reflect changes in the population of the local areas. S&MM had tens of thousands of subscribers. The data were used for allocating sales and advertising dollars to sales territories, evaluating sales performance, and aiding in determining where to open new stores, among other things. The data were based upon decennial and economic census information. Most of this work was done by hand, and in some cases the data were put on punch cards for processing using IBM tabulating machines. Even though the 1960 census made some data available on tape, the use of computers to tabulate census and census-related information was minimal.

1970 Census Changes

For the 1970 census, the Census Bureau developed a new approach to tabulating data. Although the bureau continued to produce thousands of pages of printed information, the 1970 census was also available on computer tape. More information than ever before became available with the introduction of Summary Tape Files, including single- and cross-tabulations of data heavily used by the private sector. These data, including age, income, race, education, and occupation, were now available by metropolitan areas, counties, cities, census tracts, and minor and census civil divisions. Companies could easily compare their sales information to these demographic and socioeconomic characteristics. The data would then be summarized into sales territories or media market areas as defined by the Arbitron Company, which measures radio listening areas, and A. C. Nielsen, which measures television viewing areas. By comparing sales information with decennial census and economic data at local areas, companies could readily determine whether they were selling in the best markets, spending their promotion and advertising dollars the best way, and structuring sales territories that made sense.

The 1970 census also was the catalyst for the creation of a new type of firm: the data vendor. Most companies did not have the resources to extract and summarize decennial census data from the hundreds of tapes made available by the Census Bureau. Also, spending thousands of dollars for tapes that included unneeded information made little sense. This reality spawned a business for people who could perform these tasks. The first of these was National Planning Data Corporation (NPDC), which purchased the tapes from the Census Bureau and in turn extracted and summarized the data into summary files more easily used by the business community. Companies such as Market Statistics purchased these files from NPDC and in turn sold summary reports to businesses. Market Statistics also used the decennial census information in combination with other data to produce annual updates. At the same time, companies started to change the way they marketed their goods. Toward the latter part of the 1970s, new concepts such as market segmentation and target marketing became widespread. Companies wanted to target their products to those who best fit individual profiles that they developed for their goods. Also, they wanted to market and spend advertising dollars only in those areas where potential purchasers were concentrated. Census data available at the small-area level were the basis for targeted markets. One of the most popular means of marketing was through direct mail, using catalogues. Census data were tied to individual person record files developed by putting telephone directory and warrantee card information on tape. It was the beginning of a new era in marketing. All that was lacking was computing power.

Censuses, Computers, and Marketing

The Census Bureau made major advances in computer capabilities for the 1980 census. The file structures and delivery mechanisms, even though computing was still basically tape bound, were dramatic. The new files, coupled with much more powerful mainframes and—most important—the introduction of personal computers (PCs), again changed how census data would be used. Also, it became obvious that many more data files in the private sector could be linked to decennial census data. Market research findings from companies such as Simmons Market Research were merged with warrantee card information and census data. Factor and cluster analyses were used to reduce the number of variables and to develop clusters of neighborhood types. Clusters such as Blue Blood Estates and Shot Guns and Pick-Up Trucks were developed by the Claritas Corporation and became part of the terminology of marketing. These clusters were based upon the linkage of various mailing lists, decennial census data, and other demographic and market research data. None of this could have been possible without the availability of socioeconomic data available at local areas defined, for example, by block groups and ZIP Codes. The 1980s were a time when marketing moved from just the analysis of territories based upon county data to ZIP Code marketing based upon fifty thousand ZIP Codes, two hundred thousand block groups, and listings of tens of millions of households. The 1980s also saw the advent of new geographic information systems (GIS) based upon sophisticated mapping programs. Companies such as MapInfo and ESRI developed software that enabled analysts to see the results of their work on PCs. Sales territory data could be linked to decennial census information. Local markets could be viewed in terms of their cluster types. Market segments could be realigned to match the profile of the product and instantly viewed. Sales territories and the sales force could be easily kept up-to-date. GIS became an integral part of target marketing. These new clusters and

the associated data were put on PCs and sold as systems to marketers who wished, for example, to maximize the efficiency of direct marketing such as catalogue mailing to specific household types. Desktop computing systems would not have been possible without the development of the CD-ROM. Clients received from data vendors the entire system including the PC, data on CD-ROMs, software to compare summarized clusters of information with specific customer data, census data for further analysis, updated demographic and socioeconomic information, market research data, and GIS capability—all for one price. Only companies with the ability to make large investments in development costs could compete in this market.

In the decade of the 1990s, techniques such as cluster analysis along with linking technology were again pushed to the edge of technology. Marketers wanted to be able to target not just to ZIP Codes, but also to nine-digit ZIP Codes. Blocks were too big. Companies such as Donnelley Marketing and Acxiom Corporation had contracts with businesses throughout the United States and developed mammoth databases of households and individuals that for the most part reached every household in the nation that marketers wished to reach. Decennial census data and other databases were allocated to these households. At the same time, there was a consolidation of data firms. Both National Planning Data and Market Statistics, for example, no longer exist. They were absorbed by Claritas Corporation. Only a handful of very large data firms have survived. In the 1990s the big desktop systems were replaced by Internet systems.

The Internet will change how companies retrieve and use data. For the 2000 census, the Census Bureau will again play a major role in private sector uses of decennial census information. With the development of the American FactFinder system available from the Census Bureau's home page on the Internet, the bureau will not only enable users to retrieve data that used to be on CD-ROM or tape, but also enable users to develop their own tabulations. With this capability, analysts will be able to design tabulations that more closely meet targeted market socioeconomic segments for almost any type of geography. Such a capability may act as an impetus for new start-up demographic companies that wish to reach target markets. They will have the ability to design information systems based upon specific 2000 census data targeted to niche markets.

In summary, each decade has seen new uses of census data in the private sector. Much of this would have been either impossible, or at the least very difficult, without decennial census data and the continued technological advances developed by the Census Bureau. Ultimately, the benefactors of this progress have been those who market goods and services throughout the nation. These advanced techniques, along with the invaluable information from each decennial census, have helped shape the American economy.

See also *Uses of census data by the private sector.*

■ Edward J. Spar

PUMS

Public Use Microdata Samples (PUMS) are computerized data files produced by the Census Bureau for population research. PUMS files allow analysts to define their own tabulations and conduct detailed, multivariate analyses of population and housing issues. They provide analysts with greater freedom to extract information from census data than Summary Tape Files (STFs), which contain extensive, but finite, pretabulated data.

Contents

The information in the PUMS files, which is gathered from the long-form questionnaire, contains individual records for a sample of housing units, including the characteristics of each unit and the people residing in it. For example, in 1990, PUMS files contained 500 occupation categories, age by single years up to ninety, and wages in dollars up to $140,000. To protect the confidentiality of respondents, the Census Bureau excluded or restricted information that could lead to the identification of a housing unit or an individual. Although the PUMS files contain essentially all of the information collected, as well as some variables that were created by the Census Bureau by recoding the original information, response ranges on some variables were limited to further protect respondent confidentiality. PUMS files, which have been released for the 1960, 1970, 1980, and 1990 decennial censuses, are a planned product of Census 2000.

Groups outside of the Census Bureau have created Integrated Public Use Microdata Series (IPUMS) files from records of thirteen census years from 1850 through 1990. These files, created by a variety of individual researchers with funding from the National Institutes of Health and the National Science Foundation, are designed to facilitate the use of census data as a time series. They are available through the University of Minnesota Historical Census Projects (www.ipums.umn.edu). The IPUMS files are structured with a common format, impose consistent variable coding, and document changes in variables over time. More geographic detail is available in the pre-1940 samples because restrictions on the size of areas that could be identified arose with the 1940 census.

Each PUMS file contains all of the information collected from a subsample of the population given the long-form questionnaire. In contrast, the pretabulated data in STFs that the Census Bureau prepared from the census long form (for example, STFs 3 and 4 in the 1990 census) were based on the full sample of the population that received the long form. The PUMS samples were constructed by selecting housing units, including vacant units, as well as a sample of persons living in institutions and other group quarters.

The PUMS files were designed to be nationally representative. They contain statistical weights for each person and housing unit, which, when applied to the individual records, expand the sample to represent the total population. Nevertheless, tabulations from PUMS files produce only estimates of population characteristics and are subject to sampling variability.

File Types

In 1990, three PUMS files were produced for different types of samples. PUMS (A) contains a 5 percent sample of housing units and includes estimates for states and geographic subdivisions of states. PUMS (B) contains a 1 percent sample of housing units and estimates for metropolitan areas, including those that cross state boundaries. PUMS (O) contains a 3 percent sample of housing units with at least one person age 60 years or over. PUMS (O) has the same geographic composition as PUMS (A). Although decennial PUMS files contain a small percentage of records, they are still large, containing millions of records.

Unlike in the STFs, geographic detail in the PUMS files is limited and unique to the PUMS program. Tabulations from the STFs are available for a variety of political and statistical geographies, including counties, places, census tracts, and block groups, whereas the identification of geographic units from the PUMS files is limited to areas of 100,000 persons or more. The lowest level of geography available in the 1990 PUMS files was the Public Use Microdata Area (PUMA). PUMAs replaced the "county groups" used in the 1980 PUMS files and were defined by each state or local area according to Census Bureau specifications. Each PUMA must have at least 100,000 population and consists of a whole county or a subcounty area, such as a Minor Civil Division (MCD) in New England, a place, or a group of tracts. Counties or subcounty areas with less than 100,000 population were combined to produce PUMAs of at least 100,000 population in 1990. In the 1990 PUMS files, PUMAs were used to define (1) current residence in 1990, (2) residence in 1985, and (3) place of work. PUMA geography may not be comparable from census to census, because PUMA definitions change over time. Thus it may not be possible to recreate the 1980 PUMS "county groups" using 1990 PUMAs.

The 1990 PUMS files contain two types of records, arranged hierarchically, for each housing unit included in the sample. The first type is a housing unit record; the second is a record for a person. Housing unit and person records contain different information. Person records follow a housing unit record, one for each inhabitant of the housing unit. Each of the records contains a serial number linking persons to the proper housing unit. Persons selected into the sample who are living in group quarters have a dummy housing unit record as a place holder in the file, maintaining the file hierarchy. Person records do not follow records for vacant housing units. In 1990, serial numbers were used to link household records with person records. The structure of PUMS files was similar in 1980; however, serial numbers were not used to link household and person records. The relative position of these records (with person records nested under a single household record) was used in 1980 to link household characteristics to persons.

PUMS files allow data users to produce an infinite variety of tabulations from individual records. By comparison, STFs contain a finite amount of information in the form of fixed, pretabulated data. PUMS files are used by a variety of individuals and organizations, including federal, state, and local governments; academic researchers and students; the business sector, including marketing firms; and public service organizations. PUMS files are useful when information on small geographic areas is not required and when there is a need to study the relationships among census variables not presented in other Census Bureau products. Because PUMS files have been produced by the Census Bureau since the 1960 census, they may be used to study trends over time in some population characteristics. This type of application, however, is limited by the inconsistent definition of PUMAs over time, as well as by changes in the content of the decennial questionnaires.

Historically the Census Bureau has made PUMS files available as computer tapes and CD-ROMs. Files have been available for the nation as a whole and for states and the District of Columbia. PUMS files from the 2000 census will be available on CD-ROM.

See also *Confidentiality; Content; Geography: distribution of the population; IPUMS; Long form; Metropolitan areas; State data centers; Summary Tape Files.*

■ Nancy E. Dunton

Bibliography

Census of Population and Housing, 1990: Public Use Microdata Samples: U.S. Technical Documentation. Prepared by the Bureau of the Census. Washington, D.C.: Bureau of the Census, 1992.

Race: questions and classifications

Race is a fluid concept whose meaning has changed over time and across societies and geographic boundaries. Social scientists of the late nineteenth and early twentieth centuries saw the concept as a scientific one, rooted in biological and genetic differences among peoples. The Census Bureau's use of race does not reflect any biological or genetic reference. Rather, it reflects common usage by the general public as evidenced by the actions of the legislative and judicial bodies of the country. Policy concerns and changing social attitudes, as well as changes in the racial makeup of the population, have contributed to how people have classified themselves and others, how they have been categorized racially in official statistics, and how these data have been and are used by the federal government.

The Constitution required the collection of population data by race in the decennial census. Article 1, Section 2, contains the following language:

Representatives and direct Taxes shall be apportioned among the several States which may be included within this Union, according to their respective Numbers, which shall be determined by adding to the whole Number of free Persons, including those bound to Service for a Term of Years, and excluding Indians not taxed, three-fifths of all other Persons. The actual Enumeration shall be made within three years after the first Meeting of the Congress of the United States, and within every subsequent Term of ten Years, in such Manner as they shall by Law direct.

This ambiguous language was designed to identify the three racial groups defined in the United States at the outset of the Republic—"Whites," "Blacks or African Americans," and "American Indians." "Other persons" was the euphemism for "slaves" in the text of the Constitution. "Indians not taxed" were those American Indians who owed allegiance to their tribes, not to the United States.

Early Classifications

The 1790 census operationalized the language of the Constitution by asking for the name of the head of the family and the number of people in each household who were free white males sixteen years of age and over, free white males under sixteen years, free white females, all other free persons (that is, free people of color), and slaves. Since 1790 the categories and the methods for collecting data on race have changed many times. The number of racial classification categories expanded from three in 1790 to sixteen in 1990. The 1860 census was the first to identify Indians separately; "Chinese" was added as a race category in 1870. By the 1930 census, the number of racial categories had expanded to ten—"White," "Negro," "Indian," "Chinese," "Japanese," "Mexican," "Filipino," "Hindu," "Korean," and "Other." The Mexican category met opposition from both Mexican Americans and the

Mexican government and was not repeated in later censuses. The Hindu category was not repeated after 1940. The categories "Hawaiian," "Part Hawaiian," "Aleut," and "Eskimo" were added in 1960. Asians and Pacific Islanders have been classified as racial groups, and the nativity question on the census, asked of all residents from 1850 to 1950, also identified residents born in the countries of Asia or the Pacific islands.

Over the years, the census has attempted to quantify the amount of black or Indian blood among the inhabitants of the United States. Various definitions, such as "full-blooded" for Indians and "Black" or "Mulatto" for people of African descent, were used in different censuses to categorize people. Individuals were considered Indians if they were full blooded, if they were enrolled by a tribe or registered at an Indian agency, or, in the 1890 census, if those who knew them considered them to be Indians.

Prior to 1960, the observations of enumerators determined the designated race of respondents. Starting in 1960, Americans enumerated themselves on a mail questionnaire. As a result, the format of the question on race changed. The 1960 question asked, "Is this person White, Negro, American Indian, Japanese, Chinese, Filipino, Hawaiian, Part Hawaiian, Aleut, Eskimo (etc.)?"

For most of the nation's history, the United States was essentially a country of two major races: white and black. Until recently whites comprised about 80 percent of the population. Blacks represented from 12 to 19 percent of the total population. The proportion of the "Other race" population was very small and grew minimally, in part because citizenship law restricted naturalization to whites, and until the 1960s restrictive immigration quotas prevented nonwhites from coming to the United States.

Census 2000 and the New Classifications

For two hundred years inhabitants of the United States were classified in the decennial census in one and only one race group, despite the presence of people of mixed racial ancestry who did not fit in a single racial category. The racial identity of such individuals in the decennial censuses has changed along with legal mandates and societal perceptions. In some years the census dealt with multiracial respondents by including mixed-race categories (for example, "Mulatto," "Part Hawaiian") in the codes listed in the race question. If there was no appropriate multiracial race category, people of mixed

racial parentage were generally classified with the non-white parent. Over the years, the Census Bureau has identified these individuals by the race of the mother, the race of the father, or the first racial group mentioned by the respondent. For example, people of mixed white and other racial parentage were usually categorized in the "minority" race. For mixtures of Negro and Indian, individuals were generally categorized as Negro unless the Indian features were clearly predominant or unless the individual was accepted in the community as an Indian. In the 1950 census the Census Bureau attempted to categorize as separate groups some tri-racial mixtures of white, Negro, and Indian people living in certain compact communities in the eastern United States. These communities had existed for some time and were locally recognized by special names, such as Siouian or Croatan, Moor, and Tunica.

Along with greater self-reporting in the 1960 and later censuses came greater criticism of having to choose a single racial category. People of mixed race or their parents objected that it was unfair that they had to chose between the race of the mother and that of the father. For the question on race in the 1990 census, separate codes were assigned to a few predefined combinations (such as "White and Black," "White and Indian," and "White and Japanese") reported in the "Other race" response category to identify the size of such groups.

Much of the recent pressure for changing the race classification is a result of the growth in interracial unions and the number of children in such unions. The number of interracial couples grew from fewer than one-half million in 1960 to about 1.5 million in 1990, while the number of children in such marriages reached about 2 million in 1990. Although the multiracial issue is often thought of as involving primarily blacks and whites, children in such interracial unions have consistently represented only about 20 percent of all children in such interracial families. By contrast, in 1990 about 34 percent of all children in interracial families with at least one white partner were American Indian, and 45 percent were Asian.

The Office of Management and Budget (OMB) in the Executive Office of the President sets standards for statistical classifications. In response to legislative, programmatic, and administrative requirements by the federal government, OMB in 1977 issued its "Race and Ethnic Standards for Federal Statistics and Administrative Reporting." These standards specified four racial categories: "White," "Black," "American Indian and Alaskan Native," and "Asian and Pacific Islander." They also specified two ethnic categories: "Hispanic origin" and "Not of Hispanic origin." According to the standards, people of Hispanic origin could be of any race. After the 1990 census the standards came under criticism for no longer reflecting the increasing racial and ethnic diversity of the country. OMB solicited extensive public comment, undertook extensive consultation and public hearings, and issued revised standards in 1997. These new regulations defined the questions for Census 2000.

In Census 2000 survey respondents were asked to complete the following question on race for every household member: "What is this person's race? Mark [X] one or more races to indicate what this person considers himself/herself to be." There were fifteen response categories. Data from this question could be collapsed to comply with the five minimum racial categories—"White," "Black or African American," "American Indian or Alaska Native," "Asian," and "Native Hawaiian or Other Pacific Islander"—identified by OMB in its October 30, 1997, *Federal Register* notice, "Revisions to the Standards for the Classification of Federal Data on Race and Ethnicity" (see Table 1). The standards also stated that "respondents shall be offered the option of selecting one or more racial designations." The census question on race also permitted survey respondents to mark one or more race categories to allow indication of mixed racial parentage. Additionally,

the Census Bureau obtained permission from OMB to include a separate category, "Some Other Race."

Data Tabulation

Many federal agencies, including the Departments of Commerce, Education, Labor, and Justice, use decennial census information on race. All levels of government use information on race to implement and evaluate federal statutes such as the Equal Employment Opportunity Act, Civil Rights Act, Voting Rights Act, Public Health Act, and Fair Housing Act, among others. Public and private organizations use race data to identify areas where groups may require special services and to plan and implement programs that address specific educational, housing, and health needs. The private sector uses data on race and ethnicity to identify areas with a high concentration of a targeted racial population, allowing them to develop a marketing plan for the purpose of selling goods or providing services tailored to that population's needs.

Data on race from Census 2000 were tabulated using at least two different approaches. One, the "single race tabulation approach," presented data for the six single races, and for the "Two or More Races" category, as shown below. (Data for the specified Asian groups shown on the questionnaire were collapsed into the "Asian" race category, and data for the specified Pacific Islander groups were collapsed into the "Native Hawaiian and Other Pacific Islander" race category.)

Table 1. Office of Management and Budget's Categories and Definitions of Race Groups

Category	Definition
American Indian or Alaska Native	A person having origins in any of the original peoples of North and South America (including Central America), and who maintains tribal affiliation or community attachment.
Asian	A person having origins in any of the original peoples of the Far East, Southeast Asia, or the Indian subcontinent, including, for example, Cambodia, China, India, Japan, Korea, Malaysia, Pakistan, the Philippine Islands, Thailand, and Vietnam.
Black or African American	A person having origins in any of the black racial groups of Africa. Terms such as "Haitian" or "Negro" can be used in addition to "Black or African American."
Native Hawaiian or Other Pacific Islander	A person having origins in any of the original peoples of Hawaii, Guam, Samoa, or other Pacific Islands.
White	A person having origins in any of the original peoples of Europe, the Middle East, or North Africa.

Table 2. The Fifty-seven Combinations of Two or More Races

Two Races

White; Black or African American
White; American Indian and Alaska Native
White; Asian
White; Native Hawaiian and Other Pacific Islander
White; Some other race
Black; American Indian and Alaska Native
Black; Asian
Black; Native Hawaiian and Other Pacific Islander
Black; Some other race
American Indian and Alaska Native; Asian
American Indian and Alaska Native; Native Hawaiian or Other Pacific Islander
American Indian and Alaska Native; Some other race
Asian; Native Hawaiian and Other Pacific Islander
Asian; Some other race
Native Hawaiian and Other Pacific Islander; Some other race

Three Races

White; Black; American Indian and Alaska Native
White; Black; Asian
White; Black; Native Hawaiian and Other Pacific Islander
White; Black; Some other race
White; American Indian and Alaska Native; Asian
White; American Indian and Alaska Native; Native Hawaiian and Other Pacific Islander
White; American Indian and Alaska Native; Some other race
White; Asian; Native Hawaiian and Other Pacific Islander
White; Asian; Some other race
White; Native Hawaiian and Other Pacific Islander; Some other race
Black; American Indian and Alaska Native; Asian
Black; American Indian and Alaska Native; Native Hawaiian and Other Pacific Islander
Black; American Indian and Alaska Native; Some other race
Black; Asian; Native Hawaiian and Other Pacific Islander
Black; Asian; Some other race
Black; Native Hawaiian and Other Pacific Islander; Some other race
American Indian and Alaska Native; Asian; Native Hawaiian and Other Pacific Islander
American Indian and Alaska Native; Asian; Some other race
American Indian and Alaska Native; Native Hawaiian and Other Pacific Islander; Some other race
Asian; Native Hawaiian and Other Pacific Islander; Some other race

Four Races

White; Black; American Indian and Alaska Native; Asian
White; Black; American Indian and Alaska Native; Native Hawaiian and Other Pacific Islander
White; Black; American Indian and Alaska Native; Some other race
White; Black; Asian; Native Hawaiian and Other Pacific Islander
White; Black; Asian; Some other race
White; Black; Native Hawaiian and Other Pacific Islander; Some other race
White; American Indian and Alaska Native; Asian; Native Hawaiian and Other Pacific Islander
White; American Indian and Alaska Native; Asian; Some other race
White; American Indian and Alaska Native; Native Hawaiian and Other Pacific Islander; Some other race
White; Asian; Native Hawaiian and Other Pacific Islander; Some other race
Black; American Indian and Alaska Native; Asian; Native Hawaiian and Other Pacific Islander
Black; American Indian and Alaska Native; Asian; Some other race
Black; American Indian and Alaska Native; Native Hawaiian and Other Pacific Islander; Some other race
Black; Asian; Native Hawaiian and Other Pacific Islander; Some other race
American Indian and Alaska Native; Asian; Native Hawaiian and Other Pacific Islander; Some other race

Five Races

White; Black; American Indian and Alaska Native; Asian; Native Hawaiian and Other Pacific Islander
White; Black; American Indian and Alaska Native; Asian; Some other race
White; Black; American Indian and Alaska Native; Native Hawaiian and Other Pacific Islander; Some other race
White; Black; Asian; Native Hawaiian and Other Pacific Islander; Some other race
White; American Indian and Alaska Native; Asian; Native Hawaiian and Other Pacific Islander; Some other race
Black; American Indian and Alaska Native; Asian; Native Hawaiian and Other Pacific Islander; Some other race

Six Races

White; Black; American Indian and Alaska Native; Asian; Native Hawaiian and Other Pacific Islander; Some other race

White alone
Black or African American alone
American Indian and Alaska Native alone
Asian alone
Native Hawaiian and Other Pacific Islander alone
Some other race alone
Two or more races (reflected the number of
   respondents who reported two or more races)

For selected data products, such as the Public Law 94-171 file used for redistricting, data were shown in addition for fifty-seven possible combinations of more than one race. The fifty-seven possible combinations comprised fifteen categories of two races, twenty categories of three races, fifteen categories of four races, six categories of five races, and one category of six races (see Table 2). Also shown on this file were the six single-race categories, for a total of sixty-three categories.

For other purposes, a second approach showed data for the single race groups alone or in combination with one or more of the five OMB groups and the "Some Other Race" group used in the census; see list.

White alone or in combination with one or more
   other races
Black or African American alone or in combination
   with one or more other races
American Indian and Alaska Native alone or in
   combination with one or more other races
Asian alone or in combination with one or more
   other races
Native Hawaiian and Other Pacific Islander alone or
   in combination with one or more other races
Some other race alone or in combination with one
   or more other races

This was a tally of responses and not respondents, so the total for the six categories exceeded the total population. In selected data products, data for the Asian groups and the Native Hawaiian and Other Pacific Islander groups shown separately on the questionnaire, along with selected American Indian and Alaska Native tribes, were also shown. For Census 2000, less information on race and other characteristics were released in the form of printed reports and more data were available through the American FactFinder, the Census Bureau's electronic data dissemination system for Census 2000.

See *African-origin population; American Indians and Alaska Natives; Appendix, Standards for the Classification of Federal Data on Race and Ethnicity; Asian and Pacific Islander Americans; Hispanic/Latino ethnicity and identifiers; Three-fifths Compromise; White or European-origin population; White population of the United States.*

■ Claudette Bennett

Bibliography

Bennett, Claudette, Nampeo McKenney, and Roderick Harrison. "Racial Classification Issues concerning Children In Mixed -Race Households." Paper presented at the annual meeting of the Population Association of America, San Francisco, April 6–8, 1995.

Bennett, Claudette, Nampeo McKenney, and Roderick Harrison. "Reporting of One or More Races in the 1996 Race and Ethnic Targeted Test (RAETT): Implications for Census 2000." Paper presented at the annual meeting of the Population Association of America, Chicago, April 2–4, 1998.

Edmonston, Barry, Joshua Goldstein, and Juanita Tamayo Lott. *Spotlight on Heterogeneity: The Federal Standards for Racial and Ethnic Classification: Summary of a Workshop.* Washington, D.C.: National Academy Press, 1996.

U.S. Bureau of the Census. *Planning for Census 2000: Questions Planned for Census 2000, Federal Legislative and Program Uses.* Washington, D.C.: U.S. Government Printing Office, 1998.

———. *Twenty Censuses: Population and Housing Questions, 1790–1980.* Washington, D.C.: U.S. Government Printing Office, 1978.

———. *200 Years of U.S. Census Taking: Population and Housing Questions, 1790–1990.* Washington, D.C.: U.S. Government Printing Office, 1989.

U.S. Office of Management and Budget. "Revisions to the Standards for the Classification of Federal Data on Race and Ethnicity." *Federal Register* 62, no. 210 (October 30, 1997): 58782–58790.

Related data sources

Many data sources provide information about the population or relate to the decennial census. These sources include federal, state, and local administrative records; federally sponsored household surveys; population estimates and projections; small-area estimates of income and other characteristics; and other censuses. The decennial census is the largest and most costly of these data sources. Its benefits include the provision of data on a wide range of topics for small as well as large geographic areas and population groups. However, it is limited because the data are collected only once every ten years and provide little detail obtained on any one subject. Related data sources offer their own benefits and limitations. The decennial census both contributes to and benefits from other data sources.

Administrative Records

Administrative records contain data collected for the purpose of operating a program or providing a service. Major federal administrative records on the population include Social Security Administration files of wage earnings and benefits; Internal Revenue Service individual income tax returns; and Medicare records of payments and services maintained by the U.S. Health Care Financing Administration. Major state and local administrative records on the population include records for recipients of food stamps and cash welfare assistance, Medicaid records, unemployment insurance benefit records, state income tax records, and records of vital events (including births, deaths, marriages). Many state and local record systems receive federal funding and provide data for federal uses.

The Census Bureau uses administrative records, including IRS tax returns, Medicare records, and vital statistics, together with data from the previous census to develop population estimates. The estimates for a census year are used, in turn, to evaluate the completeness of coverage of the population in that census. There has been exploratory research with IRS tax returns and other administrative records to determine if they could provide an alternative to the census to obtain the head count and basic characteristics. Research is being conducted as part of the 2000 census to assess if administrative records could provide information equivalent to the short form or could augment the census by providing information for households that do not mail back a census questionnaire. Administrative records are also used to evaluate the quality of reporting in the census and household surveys (for example, for wage income) and to produce population, income, and other estimates for small areas in between censuses.

Advantages of administrative records are that they can be used at low additional cost for such statistical purposes as developing population estimates and evaluating survey quality, and that they are collected and recorded on a frequent basis. However, they typically have limited subject matter detail; the addresses in the records may be out of date or differ in other ways from people's actual place of residence; and their content, frequency of collection, and other features are subject to change to suit operational program needs and not statistical information needs.

Household Surveys

The federal government sponsors a large number of continuing and one-time household surveys, many of which use the master address list from the previous census, supplemented by information on new construction, as the frame from which to draw samples for interviews. Other federally sponsored surveys use summarized census data for geographic areas to develop a sample design that appropriately represents different areas of the country and different population groups. (Surveys that use the census master address list as a sampling frame are conducted by the Census Bureau because of the requirements in Title 13 of the U.S. Code for protecting the confidentiality of individually identifiable information obtained in the census.)

Household sample surveys typically include a very small fraction of households in comparison with those of the census, but they are usually conducted much more frequently than the census and obtain much greater detail on specific subjects. Examples of major federal household surveys are the following:

Current Population Survey. Personal and telephone interview survey of a sample of about 50,000 households; conducted monthly to obtain data for calculating the official monthly unemployment rate; supplemented in some months by special questionnaires (such as the March Income Supplement); sponsored by the Bureau of Labor Statistics.

National Health Interview Survey. Personal interview household survey conducted each week, with separate weekly samples cumulating to about 43,000 households for the year; questionnaire includes a core set of health and demographic items and questions on current health topics that change each year; sponsored by the National Center for Health Statistics.

National Survey of College Graduates. Mail survey with telephone and personal interview follow-up of about 50,000 people who reported in the 1990 census that they had a bachelor's degree and who in their first interview in 1993 reported a science or engineering degree or occupation; interviewed every two years; used with the National Survey of Recent College Graduates and the Survey of Doctorate Recipients to profile the nation's science and engineering work force; sponsored by the National Science Foundation.

Survey of Income and Program Participation (1996 Panel). Personal and telephone survey, which followed a sample of adults and children in about 37,000 households that were initially interviewed in spring 1996; interviews were conducted every four months for forty-eight months; extensive core questionnaire on demographic characteristics, work experience, earnings, program participation, and transfer income by month and asset income for the four-month period, together with one or more modules on special topics (such as child care, disability, net worth, pension plans); sponsored by the Census Bureau.

A new large-scale, continuing monthly sample survey of households, the American Community Survey (ACS), is currently under development. If it is implemented as planned, beginning in 2003, the ACS will sample 250,000 households each month (3 million households per year), using a mail questionnaire similar to the census long form. Over a five-year period, the ACS sample size will be almost as large as the long-form sample size.

Population Estimates and Projections

The Census Bureau has an extensive and long-standing program of population estimates and projections. Currently, it produces estimates of total population by age, sex, race, and Hispanic origin on a monthly basis for the United States and annually for states and counties. (Population projections for the next twenty-five or more years for the United States and states are issued periodically). The bureau also produces estimates of total population every two years for metropolitan areas, places, and, in selected states, county subdivisions. Recently, it began a program of biennial estimates of total population and people age five to seventeen for school districts.

Population estimates and projections are produced by using a variety of data sources. The estimates begin with the counts from the most recent census. Data sources that are used to update the census counts include birth and death records, information on immigrants, Medicare records, IRS tax return records (to estimate inter-area migration), state school enrollment data, and other sources. Some estimates are developed for smaller areas and summed to form estimates for larger areas (for example, county population estimates are summed to states); other estimates are developed by applying previous census information for smaller areas to the updated estimates for larger areas. The method of adjusting previous census information is used for county age estimates, which are developed by simultaneously adjusting census age data for counties to updated county total population estimates and updated state age estimates. This method is also used for school district estimates of total population and school-age children, which are developed by applying census school district data to updated county estimates.

To produce substate population estimates, the Census Bureau works closely with state agencies that are members of the Federal-State Cooperative Program for Local Population Estimates (FSCPE), established around 1970. State FSCPE agencies provide data to the Census Bureau (for example, vital statistics) for producing estimates, and they review the estimates before they are released. State FSCPE agencies also frequently prepare their own population estimates and projections.

Small-Area Income and Poverty Estimates

In 1993, the Census Bureau began a program of small-area income and poverty estimates (SAIPE). Previously, from 1971 to 1987, the bureau produced estimates of per capita income for governmental jurisdictions for use in allocating General Revenue Sharing funds.

Currently, the Census Bureau produces estimates every year for states and every other year for counties of median household income, people in poverty, children under age five in poverty (states only), children age five to seventeen in poverty, and people under age eighteen in poverty. The bureau also produces biennial estimates of children age five to seventeen in poverty for school districts.

The SAIPE estimates are produced using statistical models that incorporate data from such sources as the March Current Population Survey, the 1990 census, population estimates, food stamp records, IRS tax return records, and Bureau of Economic Analysis (BEA) personal income estimates. BEA produces total and per capita personal income estimates quarterly for states and annually for counties. The income estimates are based on a large number of data sources from administrative records, censuses, and surveys; the per capita income estimates are the result of dividing the income estimates by the Census Bureau's census-based population estimates.

Other Censuses

The federal government conducts periodic censuses of governments and economic entities. Such censuses were previously fielded in conjunction with the population census but are now conducted at different times. The U.S. Department of Agriculture conducts a census of agriculture every five years (responsibility for the agriculture census was recently transferred from the Census Bureau to the Department of Agriculture). The Census Bureau conducts a census of state and local governments and an economic census every five years. The scope of the economic census has expanded to where it now covers nearly all of the U.S. private economy, including manufacturing, minerals and mining, wholesale and retail trade, utilities, transportation, communication, construction, finance, insurance, and real estate.

See also *Agricultural censuses; American Community Survey; Confidentiality; Demographic analysis; Economic censuses; Federal administrative records; Federal household surveys; Population estimates and projections; Small Area Income and Poverty Estimates; State and local governments: uses of census data.*

■ Constance F. Citro

Bibliography

National Research Council, Committee on National Statistics, Panel on Estimates of Poverty for Small Geographic Areas. *Small-Area Income and Poverty Estimates: Priorities for 2000 and Beyond.* Ed. Constance F. Citro and Graham Kalton. Washington, D.C.: National Academy Press, 2000.

U.S. Bureau of the Census. *Guide to the Economic Census.* www.census.gov/econguide.

Rural areas

The U.S. census does not ask respondents whether they live in a rural or urban area. Rather, the extent of rural and urban populations is determined by the Census Bureau only after people and housing units are enumerated and assigned to governmental jurisdictions. Those jurisdictions (or in some instances partial jurisdictions) are then determined on the basis of population size and the nature of the jurisdiction to be rural or urban. To understand what *rural* means, one must first learn what *urban* means. The Census Bureau defines rural as comprising all territory, population, and housing units not classified as urban.

In census data products from the 100-percent count, *rural* is further divided into "places of less than 2,500" and "not in places." This division distinguishes those portions of the rural population living in densely settled, built-up areas from those living in more scattered, low-density locations. In data products based on the census long-form sample, another distinction is made that recognizes the increasing reality that the *occupational activity* of farming is no longer tightly identified with rural *residency*. Rural population and housing units are subdivided into "rural farm" and "rural nonfarm." In the 1990 census, "rural farm" comprised all rural housing units and people on farms (places from which $1,000 or more of agricultural products were sold in 1989). "Rural nonfarm" comprised the remaining rural housing units and people, approximately 94 percent of the total rural population. The urban and rural classifications cut across other hierarchies. For example, there generally is both urban and rural territory within both metropolitan and nonmetropolitan areas.

In censuses prior to 1950, a somewhat different definition of the urban population was used that excluded many large, densely settled unincorporated areas. In 1950, formally recognizing patterns of increasingly decentralized settlement, the Census Bureau adopted the concept of the "urbanized area" and delineated boundaries for many unincorporated places (today called "census designated places"). The effect of this change was to include more territory in the urban definition beginning in 1950. This definition of urban and rural territory has been maintained substantially unchanged, although modest exceptions have occurred in each of the succeeding censuses. For exact definitions, data users must consult the appendix materials in virtually all census data products.

All recent censuses include tables showing various characteristics of rural territory and populations. The concept of urbanization, generally defined as the processes that generate a rising proportion of the total population living in urban communities, is a common feature in such tables. Urbanization results both from an increase in the size of existing places and through additions of new places to the urban category. The obverse of these processes, resulting in a declining proportion of the population living in rural territory, is reflected in Figure 1. The U. S. population declined from 95 percent rural to 25 percent rural between the censuses of 1790 and 1990 (note that the censuses of

Figure 1. Percentage of U.S. Population in Rural Areas: 1790–1990

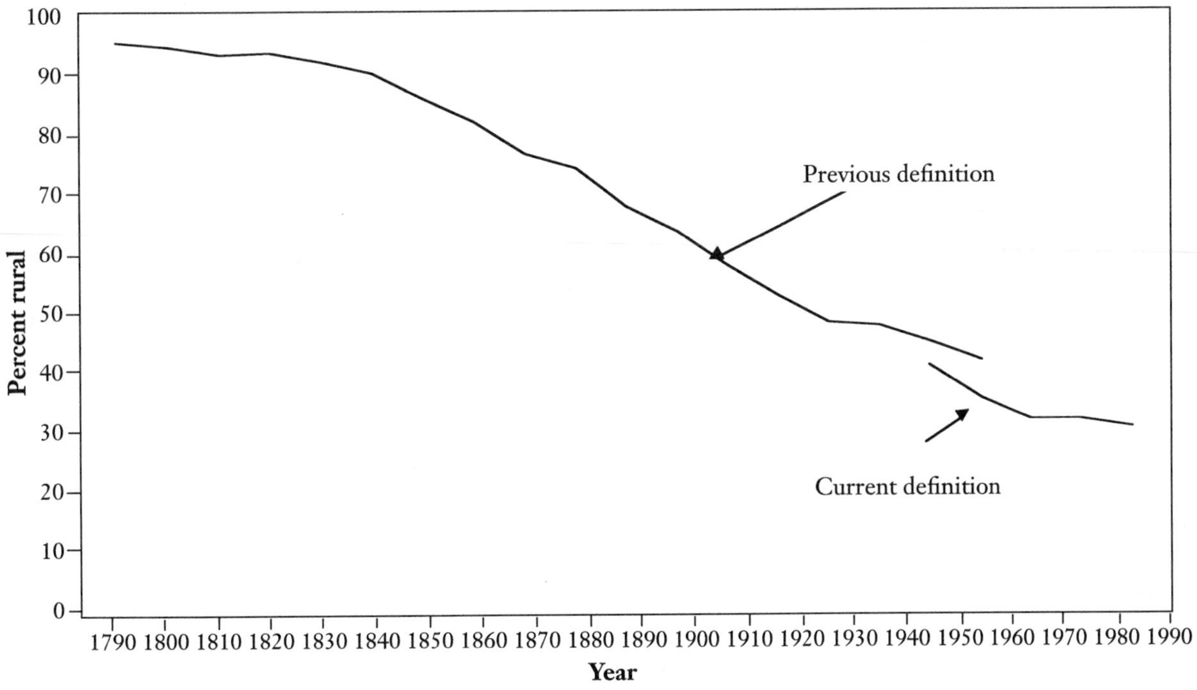

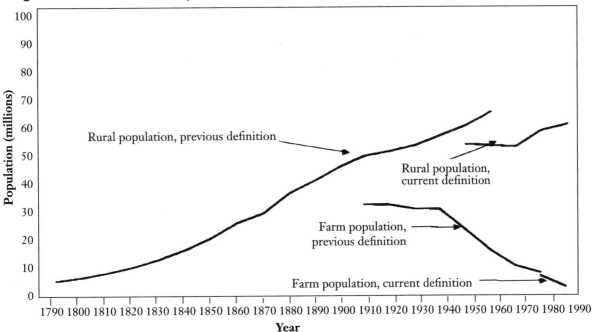

Source: U.S. Bureau of the Census, *1990 Census of Population and Housing: Population and Housing Unit Counts* (CPH-2-1) (Washington, D.C.: U.S. Government Printing Office, 1993), Table 4.

Figure 2. U.S. Total Rural Population and Farm Population: 1790–1990

Sources: Rural population counts: U.S. Bureau of the Census, *1990 Census of Population and Housing: Population and Housing Unit Counts* (CPH-2-1) (Washington, D.C.: U.S. Government Printing Office, 1993), Table 4. Farm population counts for 1910–1970: U.S. Bureau of the Census, *Historical Statistics of the United States, Colonial Times to 1970*, Bicentennial Edition, Part 1 (Washington, D.C.: U.S. Government Printing Office, 1975), 457. Farm population count for 1980: U.S. Bureau of the Census, *1980 Census of Population: Volume 1, Characteristics of the Population—United States Summary*, Part 1 (Washington, D.C.: U.S. Government Printing Office, 1983), Chap. C, Table 72. Farm population count for 1990: U.S. Bureau of the Census, *1990 Census of Population: Social and Economic Characteristics* (CP-2-1) (Washington, D.C.: U.S. Government Printing Office, 1993), Table 1.

1950 and 1960 tabulated urban and rural population counts both according to the old definition and the new). By 1920, less than half the population lived in rural areas. The pace of steady decline in the proportion of the population classified as rural was interrupted only twice in two hundred years. As noted by researcher Glenn V. Fuguitt, the decades of the 1930s and 1970s witnessed (for largely different reasons) substantial increases in the rural population.

Often overlooked in examining the widely recognized trend of a declining *proportion* of the population living in rural areas are two less well-known facts. First, overwhelmingly, the land area in the United States is rural. The 1990 census classified more than 97 percent of the 3.5 million square miles in the country as rural. Second, the number of people living in rural areas (almost 62 million persons in 1990) has been growing rather steadily. Indeed, were it not for the change in the definition of rural territory introduced in the 1950 census, today's rural population, shown in Figure 2, would be at an all-time high. However, the population living on farms (the definition of which has changed over time) is at an all-time low, at just under 4 million persons.

The decline of farming as the dominant rural activity, and twentieth-century changes in technology, communications, transportation, and levels of living, have mostly broken down the isolation and sense of solidarity that once characterized rural communities in America. As a consequence, many Americans who live in rural areas are able to lead lives not all that different from those of their urban counterparts. Indeed, many of them work and routinely take part in the larger commercial and cultural life of America's urban cities. It is the U.S. decennial census that has served as a principal source of data over the decades to document in considerable detail the characteristics of both urban and rural Americans.

See also *Agricultural censuses; Decennial censuses, 1920 census; Metropolitan areas; Urban areas.*

■ Paul R. Voss

Bibliography

Fuguitt, Glenn V. "The Nonmetropolitan Population Turnaround." *Annual Review of Sociology* 11 (1985): 259–280.

Fuguitt, Glenn V., David L. Brown, and Calvin L. Beale. *Rural and Small Town America.* New York: Russell Sage Foundation, 1989.

Hathaway, Dale E., J. Allan Beegle, and W. Keith Bryant. *People of Rural America.* 1960 Census Monograph Series. Washington, D.C., 1968.

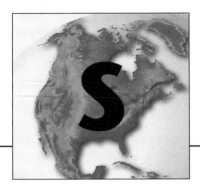

Sampling for content

Every census since 1940 has obtained responses for some content items from samples of the population selected with known probability. The role of sampling in the 1940 census was limited, but by 1960 the majority of population and housing items were asked on a sample basis.

The use of scientifically selected probability samples makes it possible to obtain accurate data at substantially less cost and burden on respondents compared with asking the entire population. Sampling adds error to the data, but the extent of this type of error (called sampling variability) can readily be assessed.

History

Prior to the 1930s and the demands for information to assess the Great Depression, the federal government made very little use of probability sampling. Surveys conducted before that time, such as consumer expenditure surveys during World War I, generally selected samples with, at best, limited regard for the laws of probability. Consequently, the error properties of the data could not readily be determined.

Application of probability sampling for federal government statistics required theoretical and practical developments. Jerzy Neyman, beginning in the 1920s, pioneered the theory of using probability methods to sample "finite populations," such as U.S. households. (Neyman was a Polish statistician who came to the United States in 1938.) In the 1930s, federal agencies began serious exploration of ways to implement probability samples for such purposes as obtaining statistics on unemployment, notably in a 2 percent survey of households on U.S. Postal Service routes conducted in 1937.

It was a logical next step to use sampling in the census. Almost from the beginning, the census has been a vehicle to obtain additional useful information beyond the minimum necessary for the constitutionally mandated head count for reapportionment and redistricting of seats in the U.S. House of Representatives. The 1930 census schedule included upwards of forty items (and schedules in some previous censuses were even longer), all of which were asked of the entire population. For 1940, there was pressure to add more questions on socioeconomic status and to include a new set of questions on the adequacy of housing. To accommodate these needs, the decision was made, for the first time, to ask six new questions of a 5 percent sample of the population instead of everyone.

The 1950 census extended the use of sampling for content and featured a fairly complex sample design. About two-fifths of the questions were asked on a sample basis. Sample sizes for population items were 20 percent and 3.3 percent. A matrix design was used for housing sample items—each 20 percent of households was asked one or two housing items in addition to the complete count housing questions.

In 1960, about three-fourths of the population items and two-thirds of the housing items were asked on a sample basis. Sample sizes were 25 percent for population items and 25, 20, and 5 percent for housing items. The 1960 census first used separate "short" (complete count) and "long" (sample) forms for each household. The Postal Service delivered unaddressed short forms containing the complete-count items to all households, which were to be filled out and held for an enumerator to pick up. At every fourth household in urban areas, the enumerator left one of two versions of a long form, containing additional sample items, for the household to fill out and mail back (in rural areas, enumerators obtained long-form answers on the spot).

The 1970 census employed a short form and two long forms. Because of the use of mailout-mailback techniques on a large scale, each long form included complete-count as well as sample population and housing items. Both versions of the long form included a common set of sample items that were asked of 20 percent of households. In addition, one version included a set of sample questions asked of 15 percent of households, while the other version included a set asked of 5 percent of households.

The 1980 census used a short form and one long form, but different fractions of households received the long form in different types of places: the long-form sampling rate was 1-in-2 in governmental units, such as towns and townships, estimated to have fewer than 2,500 people and 1-in-6 in all other areas, for an overall sampling rate of about 19 percent of households. In 1990, there was again a short form and one long form. Three sampling rates were used for the long form; these varied by estimated population size—1-in-2, 1-in-6, and 1-in-8—for an overall sampling rate of about 17 percent of households. In 2000, there were four long-form sampling rates—1-in-2, 1-in-4, 1-in-6, and 1-in-8—for an overall sampling rate similar to that of 1990.

The specific content on the long-form sample questionnaires has varied over time, but some items have been asked repeatedly (see *Long form*, Table 1, which lists population and housing items by type of form in the 1960–2000 censuses). The 1990 and 2000 long forms were somewhat shorter than the 1980 long form. In 2000, all housing items that were previously on the short form, except for the item on tenure (owner or renter), were moved to the long form; in previous censuses, seven to thirteen housing items were included on the short form along with five to six population items.

In 2010, the long form may be dropped from the census, which would use only a short form to obtain basic items for the head count. This would likely be done if the new American Community Survey (ACS) is implemented as planned. That survey is designed to obtain long-form-type data on a continuous monthly basis from large samples of households. Over a five-year period, the sample size from the ACS would be almost as large as the 2000 long-form sample size of about 18 million households.

Processing and Quality

Publications and other data products that contain just the short-form items are produced from the entire set of census records (complete count). Data products that include the sample items asked on the long form (together with responses to short-form items for households in the sample) are produced in a second pass of only the sample records. The sample records are first weighted by the inverse of the sampling rate to equal the total population and then reweighted to achieve consistency between the complete count and sample-based estimates of short-form characteristics (for example, age). The reweighting technique is called *iterative proportional fitting*, or *raking ratio estimation*. It forces agreement on basic characteristics, which reduces the sampling variability of the long-form estimates and likely reduces any biases that may have occurred in the sample selection.

Data products from the complete count are provided for geographic areas as small as individual city blocks; however, the smallest areas for which sample data products are provided are groups of blocks. The reason is the sampling variability in the long-form estimates, which can make it difficult to compare very small geographic areas reliably. Thus, long-form estimates for areas smaller than about 10,000–15,000 people should be used with caution. Other kinds of error in the long-form data, such as item nonresponse and misreporting, occur in the complete-count data as well. These sources of error are corrected in the census processing to the extent possible by routines that edit the data for consistency and supply missing data values through imputation techniques.

See also *American Community Survey; Content determination; Editing and imputation; Long form.*

■ Constance F. Citro

Bibliography

Anderson, Margo J. *The American Census: A Social History.* New Haven: Yale University Press, 1988.

Duncan, Joseph W., and William C. Shelton. *Revolution in United States Government Statistics, 1926-1976.* Office of Federal Statistical Policy and Standards. Washington, D.C.: U.S. Department of Commerce, 1978.

Sampling for follow-up of nonresponding households

Part of the Census Bureau's original Census 2000 Plan, sampling for follow-up of nonresponding households, or SNRFU (sampling for nonresponse follow-up), refers to a method of enumeration that employs a probability sample of nonresponding households to estimate the population of nonsample nonresponding households. Nonresponding households are those that have failed to return their census questionnaires. The advantage of this method of enumeration is that enumerators are required to visit only some nonresponding households to obtain census data rather than visit all such households.

For each decennial census since 1970, questionnaires have been delivered (mostly by mail) to all known households with a request that the completed questionnaire be returned by mail. (For a small and decreasing percentage of households, mainly in areas designated as "list/enumerate," completed questionnaires are returned by census enumerators rather than by mail.) Not every household, however, completes and returns its census questionnaire. For the 1990 census, approximately 74.1 percent of households returned their questionnaires by mail. (This percentage represents the *return* rate, which refers to the number of occupied households that returned their questionnaires, and is different from the oft-quoted 65-percent mail *response* rate, which refers to the rate of return of all households, including those that are occupied as well as vacant and nonexistent.)

To obtain information for the 25.9 percent of households that did not return their questionnaires in 1990, approximately 500,000 individuals were hired and trained as interviewers to go in person to each nonresponding household to obtain information. Many interviewers had to return to households on more than one occasion before they were able to obtain a complete response. Indeed, in a number of cases responses were obtained from neighbors and/or other community sources, creating additional concern about data quality. Follow-up visits to all nonresponding households are both expensive and time consuming.

Even after follow-up visits have been made to all nonresponding households, there are still persons who have been missed or incorrectly enumerated in the responding households, as well as persons who have been missed because they live in households that have been inadvertently left off of the Census Bureau's nationwide listing of addresses for all households. The official population count for the 1990 census was 248,709,873. This count was lower than both an independent count obtained from demographic analysis (253,393,786) and another count (252,712,921) obtained by combining results from a nationwide sample and statistical estimation with the official count.

The cost of the 1990 census was approximately $2.6 billion. In its efforts to control costs for Census 2000, the Census Bureau on February 28, 1996, announced its Census 2000 Plan. Included in that plan was sampling for follow-up of nonresponding households. Such sampling was to be conducted at the census tract level. (A census tract is a neighborhood of approximately 4,000 people. There were over 60,000 census tracts associated with the 1990 census.) Following repeated attempts (for example, via multiple-mailings to each address, advertising, outreach, and so on) to obtain responses from every household, a probability sample was to be selected from the collection of all nonresponding households in each tract. The information obtained from the sample of nonresponding households was to be used to help estimate the population of the nonsample nonresponding households. For tracts with an initial mail response rate of less than 85 percent, the sampling rate of the nonresponding households was to be large enough to have direct contact with 90 percent of all households in the tract; for tracts with at least an 85 percent response rate, the sampling rate of the nonresponding households was to be one in three.

Following is an illustration of how sampling for follow-up of nonresponding households would work: Assume a hypothetical census tract of 15 blocks with approximately 4,000 people in 1,500 households. Next, assume that conventional counting methods (listing addresses, mailbacks, counts received by telephone, special census forms, and so on), applied everywhere, result in 1,005 (or 67 percent) responding households. To ensure direct contact with at least 90 percent of the households in the tract, the Census Bureau would select, using randomization, 345 of the 495 nonresponding households for visits and interviews. Responses for the 150 (10 percent) remaining (nonresponding) households would be estimated using sample interview data from the sample of 345 households. Thus, an *initial estimate* of the population would be obtained by adding the count of persons from the 1,005 responding households, the count of persons from the 345 households selected for visits and interviews, and the count of persons statistically estimated for the remaining 150 households.

The method of statistically estimating the count of persons for the remaining 150 households would be the "nearest-neighbor" hot deck. The basic concept is that data for each of the 150 households would be obtained by substituting data from a nearby household selected from among the 345 households.

The original Census 2000 Plan also called for a nationwide quality check sample of about 750,000 households, for which an independent count of census-day residents would be obtained. A *final estimate* of the population was to be obtained by combining the data from this sample of 750,000 households with the initial estimate. The process of integrating information from several efforts into a final estimate was referred to in the original Census 2000 Plan as a "one-number census."

The Census Bureau first formally tested the concept of a one-number census in its 1995 Census Test conducted at three sites (Paterson, New Jersey; Oakland, California; and six parishes in northwest Louisiana). The second major test occurred during the Census 2000 Dress Rehearsal, conducted for the most part during 1998 at three sites (Sacramento, California; the city of Columbia, South Carolina, and eleven surrounding counties; and Menominee County, Wisconsin, and the Menominee Reservation).

While acknowledging that sampling for follow-up of nonresponding households would introduce sampling error, the Census Bureau felt that the anticipated error would have only a limited effect, if any, on data quality, especially at higher levels of geography and for larger population groups. But such sampling offered several advantages including:

1. *Overall costs controlled.* Following up on only some of the nonrespondents rather than all of them would procure clear financial savings as a result of putting forth an overall smaller-scale effort.
2. *Hiring needs controlled.* With extremely low unemployment rates nationwide, the Census Bureau was concerned about its ability to hire, train, and maintain an adequate staff to follow up on all nonresponding households. By following up on only a sample of nonresponding households, the Census Bureau's hiring needs could be reduced and oversight of those hired could be simplified.
3. *Time saved.* Following up on only a sample of nonresponding households would mean that resources could be focused on a smaller-scale effort that would require less time to complete. The time saved would permit additional time for the execution of the nationwide quality check sample.

In spite of these advantages, the use of sampling for obtaining the population count in Census 2000, including the use of sampling for follow-up of nonresponding households, was not acceptable to everyone. Congress expressed concern about the constitutionality of sampling, the possibility that the use of statistical methods would allow the data to be manipulated for political advantage, and the magnitude of sampling error in very small geographical areas (for example, at the block level). Almost two months after the beginning of fiscal year 1998, President Bill Clinton signed a compromise bill that, among other things, permitted the U.S. House of Representatives to sue the Census Bureau with the understanding that the case on the constitutionality of sampling in the census would be on a fast schedule to the U.S. Supreme Court. Lawsuits were filed, and two lower courts' rulings were promptly appealed to the Supreme Court.

On January 25, 1999, in a 5–4 decision, the Court announced that Section 195 of the Census Act (Title 13, U.S.C.) "prohibits the proposed uses of statistical sampling in calculating the population [of the United States] for purposes of apportionment [of the U.S. House of Representatives]." The Court also noted that when Congress amended Section 195 of the Census Act in 1976, it "changed a provision that permitted the use of sampling for purposes other than apportionment into one that required that sampling be used for such purposes if 'feasible'." The Court's decision implied that use of sampling for follow-up of nonresponding households had to be eliminated from the Census 2000 Plan and that there had to be follow-up of *all* nonresponding households. This decision was based on the wording of the Census Act and not on the U.S. Constitution. Hence, the constitutionality of sampling to help produce census counts remains unanswered. In its revised plan for Census 2000, announced on February

24, 1999, the Census Bureau stated that, while it would conduct follow-ups of all nonresponding households, it still planned to implement its nationwide quality check sample (of about 300,000 households) to provide an improved count that would be available for use for purposes other than apportionment, such as the distribution of federal funds and redistricting within the states.

■ Tommy Wright

Bibliography

Citro, Constance F., and M. L. Cohen, eds. *The Bicentennial Census: New Directions for Methodology in 1990.* Washington, D.C.: National Academy Press, 1985.

Edmonston, B., and C. Schultze, eds. *Modernizing the U.S. Census.* Washington, D.C.: National Academy Press, 1995.

Hogan, Howard. "The 1990 Post-Enumeration Survey: An Overview." *The American Statistician* 46 (1992): 261–269.

Killion, R. A. "Memorandum to J. H. Thompson: Decision to Increase Nonresponse Follow-up Sampling Rates for High Response Tracts." Census 2000 Decision Memorandum No. 34. U.S. Bureau of the Census, Washington, D.C., January 2, 1998.

———."Memorandum to J. H. Thompson: Decision to Use Hot Deck for Nonresponse Follow-up and UAA Vacant Estimation and Decision on Late Returns." Census 2000 Decision Memorandum No. 41. U.S. Bureau of the Census, Washington, D.C., January 28, 1998.

Robinson, J. G., B. Ahmed, P. Das Gupta, and K. A. Woodrow. "Estimation of Population Coverage in the 1990 United States Census Based on Demographic Analysis." *Journal of the American Statistical Association* 88 (1993): 1061–1071.

U.S. Bureau of the Census. "Assessment of Accuracy of Adjusted Versus Unadjusted 1990 Census Base for Use in Intercensal Estimates." In *Report of the Committee on Adjustment of Postcensal Estimates, Attachment 3.* Washington, D.C., August 7, 1992.

———.*1990 Census of Population: General Population Characteristics, United States* (1990 CP-1-1). Table 3. Washington, D.C.: Government Printing Office, 1990.

———. *1990 Census of Population and Housing: History—Part C* (1990 CPH-R-2C). Pages 1–24. Washington, D.C.: Government Printing Office, 1990.

———. *1990 Census of Population and Housing: History—Part D* (1990 CPH-R-2D). Appendix A, Tables 1 and 2. Washington, D.C.: Government Printing Office, 1990.

Vacca, E., M. Mulry, and R. A. Killion. "The 1995 Census Test: A Compilation of Results and Decisions." Memorandum 46, 1995 Census Test Results. U.S. Bureau of the Census, Washington, D.C., 1996.

Wright, Tommy. "Sampling and Census 2000: The Concepts." *American Scientist* 86 (1998): 245–253.

———."A One-Number Census: Some Related History." *Science* 283 (1999): 491–492.

Wright, Tommy, and Howard Hogan. "Census 2000: Evolution of the Revised Plan." *Chance* 12, no. 4 (1999): 11–19.

Sampling in the census

Scientific probability sampling procedures have contributed importantly to many aspects of census operations since the decision was made to ask some of the questions for the 1940 census on a sample basis. Sampling has been used in the census for content, coverage evaluation, coverage improvement, follow-on surveys, quality control of field operations, and processing, and testing and experimentation. Sampling was planned to be used in the 2000 census not only for such purposes as obtaining added content and conducting experiments, but also to help produce the census population totals for states for reapportionment of the U.S. Congress. However, a U.S. Supreme Court decision delivered in January 1999 stated that statistical sampling could not be used for the counts for reapportionment, so the plans to use sampling for this purpose were dropped.

New Methods

The 1940 census saw the first application of newly developed methods for population sampling to reduce census costs and the burden on the public by asking some questions of a sample of the population. In this census, most questions were asked of everyone, but six questions were asked of only a 5-percent sample of people. The use of sampling for content expanded greatly in subsequent censuses. In 1950 about two-fifths of the questions were asked on a sample basis. The 1960 census was the first to use the mails to assist the enumeration with separate short-form and long-form questionnaires. Long forms contain not only the short-form questions asked of everyone, but also the additional questions asked of only a sample. (See the entry for *Long form,* Table 1, which lists the short-form and long-form population and housing items for each census from 1960 to 2000.) Long-form sample sizes have varied across censuses. In the 2000 census, the long form was sent to about one-sixth of households overall (17 percent); sampling rates varied depending on the size of the area (from 13 to 50 percent).

Sample surveys have been used to evaluate the completeness of coverage of the population in every census since 1950. In the 1950, 1960, 1980, 1990, and 2000 censuses, a post-enumeration survey (PES) was conducted shortly after the census field enumeration and the results used to evaluate the census count (a PES was not conducted in 1970, but a match of census records with the Current Population Survey provided similar information). The methodology for designing and using post-enumeration surveys evolved to the point where the post-enumeration survey results in 2000 were to be used to correct the official census counts through an Integrated Coverage Measurement program (the corrected population totals would be obtained by matching the PES with the census records and applying a statistical technique called dual-system estimation). However, the Supreme Court ruled that existing law precluded the use of survey sampling for the population counts for states to be delivered by December 31, 2000, for purposes of congressional reapportionment. Hence, the plan is to use the results of an Accuracy and Coverage Evaluation Survey to evaluate and possibly correct the detailed census counts released after that date.

Programs for Improving Coverage

The 1970 census saw the first use of specific programs to improve population coverage by rechecking the address list and trying to find people who might be missed in the regular enumeration. Two of these procedures were carried out on a sample basis. One of the sample-based procedures was the National Vacancy Check, in which a sample of addresses initially designated as vacant or nonresidential were revisited by enumerators. The second such procedure was the Post Office Post-Enumeration Check. In this operation, the Postal Service identified addresses in selected areas of sixteen southern states that were missed in the enumeration, and Census Bureau staff revisited a sample of those addresses to determine whether there were people at these locations that should be included in the census. The results of both programs were used to impute additional people to the census count. For example, on the basis of the National Vacancy Check of a sample of units, 8.5 percent of all vacant units were reclassified as occupied and people were imputed to those units. The 1970 census is the only census in which statistical sampling procedures have been used to add people to the count.

For the 2000 census, the original plan was not only to implement Integrated Coverage Measurement to correct the count on the basis of a post-enumeration survey, but also to conduct nonresponse follow-up on a sample basis. Instead of sending enumerators to visit every household that did not mail back a census questionnaire and every address designated as vacant or nonresidential, the plan was to use sampling for these operations. The sampling rate for the check of vacant units would have been 30 percent; the sampling rate for following up households that did not mail back a questionnaire would have varied depending on the initial mail response rate. The rate chosen would have ensured that at least 90 percent of households in every census tract responded by mail or personal visit. Statistical imputation procedures would then have added people to the count to represent those addresses not contacted directly.

The expectation was that sampling for nonresponse follow-up would reduce not only census costs, but also the time to complete the enumeration, which, in turn, could make it possible to conduct a coverage evaluation survey in time to adjust the census counts by December 31, 2000. (A shorter time period could also perhaps improve the quality of the follow-up if fewer people were missed or counted twice due to moving.) Sampling for nonresponse follow-up would introduce sampling error, which would be larger for smaller geographic areas, but that error could be measured. However, consequent to the Supreme Court decision referenced above, the 2000 census plans were changed to follow up every nonresponding household and recheck every vacant unit.

Recent Censuses

Recent censuses have routinely used sampling for quality control of many aspects of census field and processing operations. The 1940 census first used sampling to verify the quality of work of coders and keypunchers. Also, crew leaders use sampling to recheck a sample of interviews conducted by an enumerator to uncover "curbstoning" (making up responses rather than interviewing the household) or other problems.

Recent censuses have also used sampling for testing questionnaires and operational procedures prior to taking the census and for experiments conducted as part of the census to try out procedures that could improve future censuses. Examples have included an experiment in the 1980 census in which a sample of nonresponding households were followed up by telephone calls using telephone directories organized by address; and extensive sample tests of alternative questionnaire formats and mailing packages prior to the 2000 census to identify formats that would encourage a higher mailback response rate.

Finally, sampling has been used in recent censuses for follow-on surveys that select respondents with particular characteristics in order to obtain more detailed information about them. For example, the National Science Foundation has sponsored a survey of people who reported their census occupation as scientist or engineer following the 1960, 1970, 1980, and 1990 censuses. Sometimes, such follow-on surveys are helpful in evaluating and improving the census itself, as when a disability survey after the 1970 census identified problems with the census information on disability.

See also *Accuracy and Coverage Evaluation; Capture-recapture methods; Census testing; Coverage evaluation; Coverage improvement procedures; Editing and imputation; Long form; Post-enumeration Survey; Sampling for content; Sampling for follow-up of nonresponding households.*

■ Constance F. Citro

Bibliography

Anderson, Margo, J. *The American Census: A Social History.* New Haven: Yale University Press, 1988.

Duncan, Joseph W., and William C. Shelton. *Revolution in United States Government Statistics, 1926–1976.* Office of Federal Statistical Policy and Standards. Washington, D.C.: U.S. Department of Commerce, 1976.

National Research Council, Committee on National Statistics, Panel on Decennial Census Methodology. *The Bicentennial Census: New Directions for Methodology in 1990.* Ed. by Constance F. Citro and Michael L. Cohen. Washington, D.C.: National Academy Press, 1985.

National Research Council, Committee on National Statistics, Panel on Alternative Census Methodologies. *Measuring a Changing Nation: Modern Methods for the 2000 Census.* Ed. by Michael L. Cohen, Andrew A. White, and Keith F. Rust. Washington, D.C.: National Academy Press, 1999.

Small Area Income and Poverty Estimates (SAIPE)

SAIPE is the Census Bureau's program to produce estimates of income and poverty—for states, counties, and school districts—that are more current than the most recent decennial census estimates.

Some Origins of the Program

When federal programs use decennial census income or poverty estimates to target funds and activities for an entire decade, the programs remain fixed on the old targets when income and poverty levels rise or fall. Over a decade, state and local poverty levels change both absolutely and relative to one another. For example, comparison of the 1980 and 1990 censuses shows that although state poverty rates in 1989 were, on average, 104 percent of their 1979 level, one quarter of the states had an increase of 15 percent or more and one quarter experienced a decrease of 10 percent or more.

The need for intercensal estimates of population and poverty in small areas (that is, at the subnational level) has long been recognized. Starting in the 1960s, the Census Bureau began to provide regular intercensal subnational population estimates. In the 1970s and 1980s the Census Bureau published annual estimates of per capita income for each of the 39,000 units of state and local government, for use in the federal revenue sharing program. In 1976, Congress authorized the use of the results of a mid-decade census—including sampling procedures and special surveys—in place of the most recent decennial census, for determining eligibility or amounts for any federal program providing benefits to state or local governments. Funds have never been appropriated for such a census. In 1976 the Census Bureau conducted the Survey of Income and Education, in response to a congressional requirement, to estimate the number of children age five to seventeen years in each state who were living in families classified below the poverty threshold (that is, "in poverty").

In 1994 Congress required the Department of Education to use the Census Bureau's most recent estimates of poverty to allocate more than $7 billion under its Title I program, unless the secretaries of education and commerce, with the advice of the National Academy of Sciences (NAS), decided against it. The SAIPE program then attempted to devise a means of estimating the number of related school-age children who were living in families in poverty in each county and school district—and to provide statistical evidence the NAS could use to cogently evaluate the estimates.

Challenges to Estimation

The complexity of the concept of poverty precludes estimating it from readily available measures of income. In order to decide whether a family's members are poor, one needs to know the family's size and the age of its head, in addition to its income. As a result, estimates of aggregate income or per capita income for a county do not provide useable estimates of poverty.

Direct survey estimates from the decennial census are available for all areas and have acceptable levels of uncertainty at the county level. But they go out of date, remaining fixed for ten years, and they are based on a definition of poverty that differs slightly from the "official" definition established by the Office of Management and Budget (OMB), which takes the Current Population Survey (CPS) estimates as the standard.

Direct estimates from the CPS are current (the CPS is conducted annually), and they are the official estimates for statistical purposes, but they are not available at all for about 2,000 counties, because there are no households in the CPS sample in these counties, and they are very uncertain in the other 1,200 or so counties, because of the small numbers of sampled households in each county.

Starting after 2003 the Census Bureau's American Community Survey will address the need for current estimates of a large number of characteristics, including poverty, by loosening the temporal precision of its estimates. The survey will provide direct estimates of several-year averages. The SAIPE program took a less expensive and more rapidly implemented approach. In future years the two approaches will be joined to provide even better small-area estimates of income and poverty for small areas.

Model-based Small-area Estimates

The SAIPE program models the relation between officially measured poverty and a small number of proxy measures of poverty from administrative records: the number of people from an area on tax returns with adjusted gross income below the poverty threshold, the difference between the population and the number of people on tax returns in the area, the number of participants in the federal food stamp program, and the estimated number of poor people in the preceding decennial census. The SAIPE program treats the 1,200 or so counties with households in the CPS sample as a representative sample on which to base its estimate of the relation between poverty, as measured in the CPS, and the proxy measures for counties. It then uses the county model and the proxy measures, which are available for all counties, to make regression predictions. For counties with no households in the CPS, the regression predictions are taken as the estimates. For counties with households in the CPS sample, the regression predictions are combined with the direct sample estimates in a way that reflects the relative uncertainty of each—the more uncertain the direct estimate is for a county relative to the model prediction, the less weight it gets in their combination. A separate but similar model is used to make estimates for all states.

The model predictions for each county or state "borrow strength," because they are based on the overall relationship of poverty to the proxy measures for all areas in the CPS sample. The modeling makes it possible to develop fairly reliable estimates for smaller areas for which the survey information is unreliable or does not exist. The model predictions are then combined with the information that is directly measured for each area in the survey, which is helpful for larger areas for which the survey data are more reliable. The statistical form of the models permits us to characterize the uncertainty in the estimates, which provides one basis for evaluating them. The entire set of estimates is forced to be internally consistent (counties sum to states, age groups sum to totals) and consistent with the official estimate of the number of poor people in the nation.

Estimates of the number of school-age children in families in poverty are made for all 15,000 school districts in the country by prorating each county's estimated number of poor children to its constituent school districts according to their shares of the county's poor children in the previous census. At present, this crude approach is used because, except for poverty measured in the previous decennial census, none of the proxies used to make state and county estimates is available for school districts.

Evaluating the Estimates

The 1990 census provides relatively precise estimates of poverty for counties in income year 1989 compared to the corresponding SAIPE model-based estimates. Although there are certainly more noise and uncertainty in the SAIPE estimates than in the census estimates, there is little evidence of systematic statistical bias in them. When a similar comparison is made for school districts, the results are more difficult to evaluate, though there can be no question that the SAIPE estimates for income year 1989 are far inferior to those from the 1990 census and that the proration using the 1980 census results is their major weakness.

Although no one would prefer the present SAIPE estimates to the census estimates of poverty in the census year, the choice is more difficult to make in intercensal years. The SAIPE estimates reflect changing conditions, and the census estimates do not. If economic conditions change greatly after the census, preference should swing toward the SAIPE estimates because of their currency, despite their imprecision. The NAS recommended that the 1993 county estimates of numbers of poor school-age children be used in the Title I allocations for the 1998–1999 school year. They concluded that these estimates were demonstrably superior to estimates from the outdated 1990 census because of major changes that had occurred in the distribution of poverty between 1989 and 1993. The evaluation of the 1995 poverty estimates for school districts (the first year for which school-district estimates were made) was less clear-cut. The NAS concluded that although they had potentially large errors for many (small) school districts, the SAIPE estimates were at least as good as the alternatives currently in use, such as 1990 census estimates not adjusted to the post-census county poverty estimates, and data from the school lunch program, which includes both poor and near-poor students and is thought to understate poverty among high school students. Given that some type of estimate had to be used, the SAIPE estimates would confer the advantage of a consistent set of estimates in a nationwide program.

The caution exercised by the Department of Education in reaching the decision to use the SAIPE estimates should be mirrored by others contemplating their use. The SAIPE program has gone to great lengths to provide evidence that can be used to evaluate the use of its estimates against some alternative. The prudent user will accept that all knowledge is imperfect and take the opportunity offered by the SAIPE program to judge the utility and appropriateness of its estimates for each potential application.

See also *American Community Survey; Federal administrative records; Income and poverty measures; Population estimates and projections; Sampling in the census.*

■ Paul Siegel

Bibliography

National Research Council, Committee on National Statistics, Panel on Estimates of Poverty for Small Geographic Areas. *Small-area Income and Poverty Estimates: Priorities for 2000 and Beyond,* edited by Constance F. Citro and Graham Kalton. Washington, D.C.: National Academy Press, 2000.

U.S. Bureau of the Census. *Small Area Income and Poverty Estimates: Intercensal Estimates for States, Counties, and School Districts.* (http://www.census.gov/hhes/www/saipe.html)

Staffing

The decennial census is the largest peace-time operation undertaken by the federal government. It is a complex operation that requires large numbers of temporary employees to carry out hundreds of interrelated tasks. During the 1990 census, 2.9 million applicants were tested to attain a peak staff of more than 500,000 employees.

Recruitment and Training

All decennial census workers must be recruited, hired, and trained to carry out their jobs within a very short period of time. One of the key historical factors that allowed the Census Bureau to successfully recruit large numbers of people who could handle complex, interrelated decennial census tasks was that the Census Bureau frequently was able to hire people who already had basic work skills. Supervisory experience was necessary for office or field supervisor positions. Temporary office clerks needed to know the basics of office clerical work. Field enumerators needed to be able to use a map to locate specific addresses. Enumerators also needed to have organizational skills for efficiently following up on missing interviews, and they had to be able to face rejection when working with the public. All decennial census workers had to be able to use a variety of reference manuals and materials, and they had to be able to read and follow directions.

In censuses before 1980, the Census Bureau often relied on people who were not actively seeking permanent employment. Many were attracted to temporary census jobs by the thought of earning extra money while helping with an important cause. Middle-aged women and housewives were the backbone of the decennial census staff. (Even today, the decennial census enumerator staff is predominantly composed of women.) This staff was supplemented with retirees, college students, and others who were usually unemployed at the time of recruitment.

Today a larger percentage of the total population is already in the labor force and that percentage continues to increase. Lifestyles, goals, and ambitions of working-age people have changed. Working-age women are becoming increasingly career-oriented and are more likely to join the permanent labor force than in the past. They are attracted by aspirations of career achievements or by the simple need to earn more money because of today's higher cost of living. Those who seek permanent employment find little attraction in a three- to six-week decennial census job.

Since 1960 the number of households in which both husband and wife are part of the labor force has increased significantly. The percentage participation in the labor force of married women with children under age six years has increased even more dramatically. This pattern of higher numbers of women already in the permanent work force means that fewer women are readily available to work on the decennial census.

The continuing increase in the cost of living is another factor that influences the availability of applicants who historically would have been part of the decennial census applicant pool. The elderly who live on Social Security or small retirement annuities and who need a supplement to their income often prefer permanent part-time jobs over decennial census jobs that last only three to six weeks. Permanent part-time work spreads earnings over the course of a year and generally produces a greater annual income supplement. Temporary census jobs provide an opportunity to earn a little spending money but can be inadequate for those who need a continuous monthly income supplement.

Thus, when the Census Bureau recruits for decennial census workers from the pool of applicants that historically have worked on the census, it must compete for large numbers of people who are already employed, seek retirees, or attract the unemployed, who may be looking for permanent work instead of a short-term job.

Pay and Workload

In the 1980 census, workers averaged seven to eight hours per day. In 1990 they averaged six hours per day, and in the 1995 census test they averaged five hours per day. Because an enumerator is paid portal to portal, and travel time from home to a given assignment area is the same whether the enumerator works one hour or eight, with shorter working hours the actual time available for enumeration is proportionally less as the number of hours worked per day decreases. Part of the reason for the shorter work day is the relatively fewer hours each day that respondents can be found at home, another trend that makes the enumeration job more difficult. Reduced employee hours increases staffing requirements and training costs. These increasing staff requirements, compiled by the National Research Council, are shown in Table 1.

In the 1970 and 1980 censuses, enumerators often quit because they were not paid in a timely manner. They were paid by the amount of work completed (by household, "vacant," or nonexistent housing unit), once or twice during the entire enumeration period. Hourly pay rates and weekly pay periods were instituted for all enumerators for the 1990 census. The hourly rates in 1990, ranging from $5.00 to $10.00 for enumerators, were keyed to local economic variables for each of the 449 field offices used to conduct the census. Census

Table 1. Census Bureau Personnel Taking the Census, 1960–1990

	1960	1970	1980	1990
Number of local cEnsus offices	399	393	412	449
Peak field staff	187,500	223,038	458,523	510,000
Processing staff	2,000	2,600	5,400	11,000
Average enumerator pay per hour	$1.60	$2.56	$4.03	$7.50

Note: Hourly pay rates in 1970 and 1980 are estimated based on average pieces of work (households, "vacants," or nonexistent housing units) completed per hour.

Source: National Research Council Panel on Census Requirements in the Year 2000 and Beyond, *Modernizing the U.S. Census,* Washington, D.C.: National Academy Press, 1995.

2000 plans included continuing the hourly pay methodology and an expansion of the 1990 program to implement locality-based pay. The larger program strengthened analysis of local economic variables and made available a wider range of pay rates. For Census 2000 the Census Bureau attempted to expand the labor pool from which it could recruit by negotiating with other federal and state agencies that manage retirement and income transfer programs (federal civilian and military retirement, Public and Indian Housing program, Welfare to Work, and so on) to reduce barriers and encourage recipients of the various programs to work for the Census Bureau.

Evaluations of the Census 2000 hourly pay structure, as used in the Census 2000 dress rehearsal, showed that the Census Bureau was able to hire and retain an adequate staff of enumerators. Productivity during the dress rehearsal, conducted in 1998, was highest among part-time employees, employees that had previous work experience, and individuals who were not part of the active labor force (such as retirees). The strength of this new pay structure, the effective assignment and supervision of work, and the administrative difficulty in the implementation of incentives led to a recommendation against using separate incentive payments for productivity in Census 2000.

■ Jay K. Keller and John M. Stuart

Bibliography

National Research Council, Committee on National Statistics, Panel on Census Requirements in the Year 2000 and Beyond. *Modernizing the U.S. Census.* Ed. Barry Edmonston and Charles Schultze. Washington, D.C.: National Academy Press, 1995.

Neece, Lorraine, and Janice Pentercs. *1970, 1980, 1990 Decennial Census Cost Comparison.* Washington, D.C.: U.S. Bureau of the Census, 1993.

Stuart, John. *2000 Decennial Census Labor Force Issues.* Washington, D.C.: U.S. Bureau of the Census, 1995.

U.S. Bureau of the Census. *Census 2000 Dress Rehearsal Evaluation Summary.* Washington, D.C., 1999.

U.S. Bureau of the Census. *Census 2000 Operational Plan.* Washington, D.C., 1998.

U.S. Bureau of the Census. *Statistical Abstract of the United States: 1998.* 118th edition. Washington, D.C., 1994.

State and local censuses

The federal government has taken a decennial census each decade since 1790 and, for the most part, state and local governments have relied on these census results for information about their populations. For much of the nineteenth century, however, many state governments also took periodic censuses, usually in years different from those of federal counts. Though census taking at the state level ceased about 1945 and is no longer a function of state government, its practices may be usefully compared with those of the federal effort. The state census data, both published and unpublished (in the surviving manuscript schedules), provide additional demographic, economic, and social information about the American population.

State censuses, which varied greatly in their scope, form, content, frequency, quality, and publication style, have been analyzed primarily by librarians and genealogists (for analyses prepared by two such specialists, see the bibliography at the end of this entry). Researchers interested in the quality and completeness of an individual state or local census, or in publications about it, should consult these experts or local state archival sources.

Like the federal census, state censuses were political instruments before they were demographic ones. Most commonly, they were mandated in state constitutions to provide the basis for apportioning representatives in the state legislature. In other cases, legislatures instituted censuses to serve state government functions, such as apportioning taxes or planning state economic policy. Territorial governments conducted censuses to demonstrate that they had sufficient population to apply for statehood.

Only eight states have never taken a state or territorial census: Connecticut, Idaho, Kentucky, Montana, New Hampshire, Ohio, Pennsylvania, and Vermont. Between 1810 and 1945 twenty-seven states took 160 separate censuses; forty-three territorial censuses were taken between 1801 and 1907. In two out of every three years in the nineteenth century, a state or territory commissioned a census somewhere in the continental United States.

Variety of Methods

States and territories used a wide variety of administrative mechanisms to collect, tabulate, and publish the data. Usually tax assessors collected the data and the secretary of state made a routine count of the population in a small number of categories in the field. These totals were sent to the state capitol to be published in a page or two of a legislative journal. Sometimes, though, states created full-scale census offices. State officials appointed enumerators to take the census and supervised elaborate tabulations and publication of several volumes of data. Some state constitutions mandated periodic censuses which were never taken. Others directed states to take repeated censuses at short intervals—sometimes as short as four years.

The duration of data collection efforts—when states began to collect census data and when they stopped—also varied from state to state. For some states, such as New York, one-hundred-year data series exist; for others, such as Maryland in 1776, single censuses exist that were never replicated.

Though diverse in practice and duration, state census taking conformed to definite patterns. Most obviously, the history of state censuses is tied to that of the states themselves: a census could not be taken unless a state or territory had been defined. Only six of the original thirteen states took complete count censuses after the nation's founding in 1787: Georgia, Massachusetts, New York, New Jersey, Rhode Island, and South Carolina. New York was the first to do so. Like the other original states, including Pennsylvania, Connecticut, and Vermont, New York first counted voters or taxables. It took the first complete count census in 1795 and repeated it in 1801 and 1807. Unlike these other states, however, New York in 1814 began counting the total population. By 1825 it had instituted a regular decennial census in the fifth year of the decade, which continued through 1875. It took no census in 1885. The series resumed in 1892, returned to the fifth year of the decade in 1905, and ended in 1925. Georgia began to collect census data in 1810 but stopped with the Civil War. The other original states did not begin taking censuses until well after their admission to the Union. Massachusetts, which became a state in 1788, started counting its population in 1837, while South Carolina, also admitted to the Union in 1788, began taking censuses in 1868. Except for New York, none of the original thirteen states built censuses into the fabric of their earliest political life.

Census taking in the "western states"—including the old northwest and south central regions—followed a different pattern. Although only six (46 percent) of the original thirteen states took censuses, twenty-one (60 percent) of the other thirty-five states in the continental United States took censuses at some time in their history. Twenty-one states also took censuses while they were territories. Sixteen of them continued to take censuses after becoming states.

The most common type of state census included a simple population count, with minimal publication of the results. States published one-half of the census results in documents of thirty pages or fewer and one-third of the results in documents of fewer than ten pages. Once a state invested in census taking, it could become a fairly elaborate exercise, one that grew for several decades in size and complexity. In a quarter of the censuses, the states published works between 275 and 4,800 pages. Prior to 1870 the mean number of pages published in state census publications was 84; after 1870, it climbed to 560, though page counts varied widely.

Regional Patterns

Regional patterns among the state censuses reflected the larger economic and political conditions. From the mid-nineteenth to the early twentieth centuries, the eastern industrial states of New York, New Jersey, Rhode Island, and Massachusetts used their censuses to monitor the growth of the industrial economy and to measure the proportion of natives and foreigners, workers and farmers. Midwestern states such as Michigan, Wisconsin, Iowa, and Kansas emphasized data on population, agriculture, and manufacturing. Kentucky, Tennessee, Ohio, and Indiana, admitted to the Union between 1792 and 1816, began collecting data on free male electors in the early nineteenth century and continued these counts into the early twentieth, never developing full-scale state censuses.

States once part of Mexico or the Spanish or French colonial empires (for example, Texas, New Mexico, California, Arizona, and Louisiana) have censuses dating from their common history with those nations. Both Hawaii and Alaska took censuses in the nineteenth century, long before they joined the Union in 1959.

States stopped taking censuses when they recognized that they could save money by using the federal data, which were of sufficient size and quality for state and local government purposes, or contract with the Census Bureau for special surveys as needed. In the 1920s state and local governments appealed to the federal government to provide them with local tabulations. In recent years the Census Bureau has worked closely with state demographic services, and state demographic agencies have republished state and local data from the federal enumeration.

See also *Census tracts; State data centers.*

■ Margo Anderson

Bibliography

Dubester, Henry J. *State Censuses: An Annotated Bibliography of Censuses of Population Taken after the Year 1790 by States and Territories of the United States.* 1948. Reprint, New York: Burt Franklin, 1969.

Lainhart, Ann S. *State Census Records.* Baltimore: Genealogical Publishing Co., 1992.

State Censuses. Microfiche collection of the sources cited in Dubester. Millwood, N.Y.: KTO Microform, 1977.

State and local governments: legislatures

Legislatures at the state and local levels have come to rely upon and perpetuate the use of decennial census data for a variety of reasons and a range of purposes— from compliance with reapportionment, redistricting, and voting and civil rights requirements to establishing program eligibility, allocating dollars, and assessing legislative proposals. Political and institutional events and trends have coincided with or precipitated the legislatures' applications of these data in recent decades.

With heightened state and local involvement, prominence, and stakes in the debates over the conduct and operations of the census and decennial data accuracy, it is easy to overlook the era when subnational legislatures were ill-equipped and even less inclined to attend to the quality or application of these data. Fewer than forty years have passed since the move to reform legislative operations and revitalize notions of legislative representation accelerated. Reapportionment, redistricting, and decennial census data played roles in the modernization and capacity-building of legislatures, especially at the state level.

Studies conducted by universities, foundations, the Citizens Conference on State Legislatures, and other reform groups found the institutions generally to be weak, ineffectual, and nonrepresentative. As long as they were malapportioned and not fully representative of their citizenry, little impetus existed to change antiquated structures and processes.

But reform picked up steam in the 1960s with the prospect that the legislatures might be forced to become more representative of the citizenry-at-large and presumably more responsive to increasingly complex needs and shifting intergovernmental relationships. State, and later local, legislatures' concerns about their reapportionment and redistricting responsibilities and their reliance on decennial population figures grew as a body of case law emerged in a series of U.S. Supreme Court decisions.

On the heels of *Baker v. Carr* (369 U.S. 186 (1962)), in which the Court ruled that redistricting cases were subject to the courts, came *Gray v. Sanders* (372 U.S. 368 (1963)) and *Wesberry v. Sanders* (376 U.S. 1 (1964)), in which the Court enunciated and then reiterated the "one-person, one-vote" principle; that is, as nearly as possible, one person's vote in a congressional election was to be worth as much as another's. In *Reynolds v. Sims* (377 U.S. 533 (1964)), the Court required reapportionment of both houses of state legislatures according to the "one-person, one-vote" principle. Substantial population equality among legislative districts must exist to afford equal protection under the Fourteenth Amendment.

The decisions contributed to a rush of apportionment activities. By 1970, every state had redistricted at least once, most for both houses, with all but three states using decennial census population data. Kansas conducted its last state census and reapportioned its legislative seats in 1979 and began using federal census data in 1990. For Hawaii, the state's redistricting population base did not switch from the total number of registered voters to the total number of permanent residents until the passage of three constitutional measures in 1992. In 1998, Massachusetts, which had been using a commonwealth-conducted census, moved to the federal census for determining the population base of its representative, senator, and councillor districts.

Local legislatures were touched as well. In *Avery v. Midland County* (390 U.S. 474 (1968)), the Court extended the "one-person, one-vote" dictum to local units of general government elected on a district basis. The Court held that, even when the state legislature is properly apportioned, the Fourteenth Amendment requires "that citizens not be denied equal representation in political subdivisions which also have broad policy-making functions."

This principle of legislative apportionment and the articulation of voting rights put the squeeze on state and local legislatures and on a Bureau of the Census already pressured by demands associated with the Great Society grants-in-aid programs. Accurate, detailed cross-tabulations of census data were becoming essential to fair, equitable state and local legislative apportionments and the administration and implementation of federal civil rights legislation, as Margo Anderson points out (in *The American Census: A Social History*, 1988).

After the 1970 census, state legislatures found that the small geographic area data did not coincide with their voting district boundaries, frustrating efforts to merge local voting behavior data with census counts and spawning a 1980 census program to meet the need. Public Law 94-171, enacted in 1975 to provide legislatures with small-area census population totals, further required the bureau to inform governors and state legislative leaders of the technical guidelines for obtaining population totals for their locally defined voting districts.

Policy makers and Census Bureau officials alike were beginning to understand the wider need for adequate census data and to acknowledge that seemingly technical issues such as the differential census undercount—in which certain segments of the population would likely be undercounted despite general improvements in the overall population count—were destined to be explosive political issues, ultimately affecting intergovernmental and legislative-constituent relationships.

The Changing Face of Legislatures and Representation

An early assumption about legislative reapportionment was that urban interests would overtake long-standing rural interests, with urban problems and needs becoming the dominant drivers in the states. After the 1970 census, however, reapportionment raised the legislative representation of suburban areas and the specter that cities would be forceful players in fighting census undercounts to ensure their cut of significant federal and state dollars allocated through decennial population-based formulas.

By the 1990s, the demographics of legislators had changed substantially in most parts of the country. The number of farmers and lawyers in the legislatures declined, while the number of educators, urban professionals, women, and racial minorities grew. Accounting for some of the increase, and for some of the questions about representation and the redistricting process

following the 1990 census, were the numbers of districts containing a majority of minority citizens.

The 1982 amendment to the Voting Rights Act of 1965, establishing the concept of discrimination as a "result" rather than an intent, and subsequent federal interpretations (as in *Thornburg v. Gingles*, 478 U.S. 30 (1986)) precipitated intricate use of the population data in drawing districts where minorities would have an open run at elected office. In the process of creating opportunity, unusual and extreme district maps emerged, ranging from a Mississippi House district, where a virtually all-white enclave of voters who could not be placed in any other district were put in the middle of a predominantly African American region, to Arizona, where the 1982 amendment was interpreted to mean creating as many districts as possible with Hispanic majorities, according to Alan Ehrenhalt (in *Democracy in the Mirror*, 1998).

Analysts such as Ehrenhalt suggest that the long-term consequences of contrived constituencies will be enormous, with voters unable to keep track of who their representatives are and representatives confused about who they represent. Community-of-place as the basis for political representation will continue to erode and will be supplanted by some different, perhaps less stable, concept of representation independent of geography.

Other State and Legislative Applications of Census Data

Despite their collective, significant impact on legislative and constituent life, more routine applications that incorporate decennial results get far less attention than those associated with redistricting or civil rights compliance.

Among the types of legislative provisions dependent on the census are determining classes and categories of municipalities; allocating municipal aid funds; planning and allocating funds for construction of new schools, other public buildings, police stations, and fire stations; calculating contribution formulas for county jails and other facilities based in part on proportions of at-risk populations; determining eligibility for enterprise zone designations; allocating library funds; determining "undue concentration" or the ratio of liquor and other licenses to census tract populations; determining eligibility for senior citizen and other special population housing developments; and determining eligibility for social services based on some level of neighborhood or community risk.

See also *Apportionment and districting; Grassroots groups; Litigation and the census.*

■ Deborah A. Gona

Bibliography

Anderson, Margo J. *The American Census: A Social History.* New Haven: Yale University Press, 1988.

Citizens Conference on State Legislatures. *The Sometime Governments.* Kansas City, Mo.: Citizens Conference on State Legislatures, 1973.

The Council of State Governments. *The Book of the States,* 1970–1971 to present. Lexington, Ky.: The Council of State Governments.

Ehrenhalt, Alan. *Democracy in the Mirror: Politics, Reform, and Reality in Grassroots America.* Washington, D.C.: Congressional Quarterly, 1998.

U.S. Congress. House. Committee on Post Office and Civil Service. *Review the Role of Local Governments in the 1990 Census and to Hear Recommendations for the 2000 Census. Hearing before the Subcommittee on Census and Population of the Committee on Post Office and Civil Service House of Representatives.* 102nd Cong., 1st Sess., June 15, 1991. Serial No. 102-17.

U.S. Congress. Senate. Committee on Governmental Affairs. *Adjustment Again? The Accuracy of the Census Bureau's Population Estimates and the Impact on State Funding Allocations. Hearing before the Committee on Governmental Affairs.* 102nd Cong., 2nd Sess., August 12, 1992.

State and local governments: use of census data

State and local governments are major users of census data for a wide variety of purposes, making them major stakeholders in the decennial census process. Census data are frequently a key part of demonstrating need on applications for funding at all levels of government. Governments prepare informational and comparative profiles about the size and characteristics of states' and communities' populations to attract new businesses, new residents, tourists, and students. Census data also form the basis for producing local population estimates and projections.

Allocation of Power and Money

The initial purpose of conducting the census was to provide the information needed to ensure that every state got its fair share of political power. This was done by providing a means of periodically changing the number of representatives that each state has in the House of Representatives. Over the centuries since the Constitution was first ratified, the application of this fairness principle has been expanded through legislation and court decisions so that every resident is equally represented at all levels of government. The adjustments that ensure equal representation are done through reapportionment and redistricting of legislative bodies at all governmental levels every decade when new population figures are released by the U.S. Census Bureau. Similarly, members of many local boards, commissions, and service districts are elected to represent geographic areas that are redrawn to recognize population growth and diversity using data from the most current census.

According to a 1999 study by the General Accounting Office, more than $180 billion is distributed by the federal government to state and local governments every year. This is often done through complex formulae that are at least partially dependent on census data. In addition, in many cases, the allocation of dollars to jurisdictions within states by state governments is based on formulae that use population, employment, income, or related data from the decennial census.

Many federal and state local assistance programs are targeted to specific types of communities, such as economically distressed areas. The enabling legislation for these programs often specifically states the minimum eligibility requirements. Frequently, eligibility for these programs is determined for small areas, such as census tracts, based on selected census characteristics, such as poverty or unemployment rates that exceed some threshold. These data come almost exclusively from the decennial census.

The allocation of money for a program is the first step in providing services to people. Just as important is placing a program into communities where it will reap the greatest benefits. One of the most wasteful acts of government is to direct services to the wrong geographic areas. For example, if a limited amount of money were available to educate a community about the dangers of lead paint to children, the local government would want to identify those areas where people were most at risk to the problem. To do this, community leaders could look at local census data to identify large concentrations of homes built before a certain date with large numbers of children.

Program Planning and Evaluation

A major function of state and local governments is to plan programs aimed at improving the quality of life for their residents. To do this, they need to have a clear understanding of their community. While they may have a general feel of the community's make-up and needs, they must have numbers to support these impressions. They get many of these numbers from the census.

While local governments are heavy users of census data, they also provide census data by answering written and telephone requests as well as by publishing agency newsletters, reports, and speeches. Some agencies staff information desks and provide access to census publications. Local governments are active in displaying, interpreting, and consulting on census data, providing comparisons with other communities, identifying and explaining population trends, and translating national census press releases into local terms.

Staff may provide workshops and training to help policy makers, government officials, the press, and the public to understand census data and use them appropriately. Census services range from simply looking up data to extensive, sophisticated custom data tabulations and consultations to support a legislative analysis or an executive or business decision. In one study done by Leonard M. Gaines in the mid-nineties, 134 organizations (twenty-three state government agencies, eighty local government organizations, and thirty-one university-based data providers) filled more than twenty-two thousand census data requests from within their own organizations in a one-year period, an average of 170 requests per organization. Many times this number of requests were answered for people outside their organizations.

The demand for census data is so acute because they are the only comprehensive source of information available for local areas. Frequently, census data are used by community planners to determine the severity of a problem. For example, factors that may deter residents from utilizing government services, such as English-language proficiency problems or low educational attainment, must be identified. By looking at the census data on English-language proficiency, language spoken at home, and years of school completed, these barriers can be identified, quantified, and overcome. Furthermore, census data on the location of residents with such difficulties are an essential part of effective program targeting and resource allocation.

Along with planning programs, government officials are responsible for evaluating existing programs. Often this is done with census data. Consider, for example, a community program aimed at reducing teen pregnancies. While the total number of teenagers who become pregnant over a number of years can be ascertained, these data do not tell the whole story. They must be evaluated relative to the number of teens in the community. That is, to determine whether the rate of teen pregnancies is dropping or rising, public health officials must chart any changes in the overall number of teens in the community. Thus, to determine what is really happening, data on pregnancies must be examined along with Census Bureau estimates of the population by sex and age.

Facility Planning

Census data are commonly used in decisions about the type and location of facilities the community needs. For example, a community might be experiencing growth in its population and in the number of jobs. Normally, this situation indicates a need to either build more roads or improve the community's mass transit system. However, this need does not necessarily exist. Journey to work data could reveal that the number of people traveling to work at any one time is well below the capacity of the highway system. If, however, the highways are being used close to their capacity, some action is needed. The data also could show that people are commuting to unexpected locations. This could suggest that different bus routes need to be designed. When information about the number of people commuting between two census tracts or traffic analysis zones, when they left home, how they traveled to work, and how long it took them is combined with local knowledge about the transportation network, employment data, and local surveys of commuters, a clear picture of the community's transportation needs emerges.

In many cases, the data are used in an indirect manner, which is invisible to the data user. For example, consider a growing community concerned about the need to provide additional classroom space for the students in the school system. To determine whether more schools or classrooms are needed, the community's planners would look at projections and estimates of the community's population over time. While the planners might not realize this, the estimates and projections are ultimately based on decennial census population and housing data.

Disaster Planning

Another area where census data are commonly used is emergency or disaster planning. In this governmental function, one of the largest concerns is how people are going to be relocated during an emergency. Two fundamental aspects of this problem can be answered by census data.

First, the government can figure out how many people might need to be moved and from where by looking at population data by the smallest geographic units available in the areas that might be affected by a disaster. For example, by matching census population data with specific areas that might be flooded, emergency planners can easily determine the number of people who would need to be evacuated from a flood plain if the area floods.

Second, the government can anticipate how to move these people by examining several characteristics of the community described by the data. In particular, the data will tell how many vehicles the residents have access to, the number of households without cars or trucks available to them, and who might need public transportation. Similarly, a community may need special transportation services for disabled residents.

Economic Development and Marketing

In an attempt to improve the economic opportunities for their residents, governments try to attract new businesses. While they frequently use a variety of incentives to do this and must have the types of facilities that a given business needs, they also must show that a community has the character that a business is looking for. A business might wonder if it can get the number of workers that it needs or if the area is sparsely or densely populated. Both of these questions can be answered based on data from the decennial census.

States can also use Census Bureau data on government finances to show business trends in total taxes for an area. Furthermore, a state can show a business that supporting industries already exist in the area. Using data from the economic census, County Business Patterns, and annual economic surveys, the cost of producing a certain amount of output in different geographic areas can be compared.

State and Local Governments as Stakeholders

The Census Bureau is responsible for conducting the decennial census, but state and local government employees often have extensive knowledge about local census data, changing population structures and trends, and characteristics of population changes stemming from births, deaths, and migration patterns. They are also aware of changing settlement patterns resulting from new subdivisions, special housing programs, shifts in land use and zoning, and changing physical and political features that affect census geography, such as new roads and updated city boundaries. Thus, local knowledge and expertise are used by the Census Bureau in the many preparations for conducting a decennial census.

The majority, and some of the most formalized, cooperative activities between the Census Bureau and local governments involve identifying or verifying local geographic features, such as streets, housing unit counts, and address information prior to conducting the census. State and local governments also provide valuable input for the Census Bureau's questionnaire content determination process. Local officials help the Census Bureau identify areas within their communities that may be difficult to count. They describe and locate areas where their residents experience linguistic isolation or have limited English-speaking ability, new immigrants reside, and the homeless congregate. They pinpoint special facilities, nursing homes, institutions, and other group quarters. They also provide introduction to community leaders and gatekeepers who will help the census enumerator gain access to difficult-to-count areas. Some government agencies are asked to help with efforts to recruit the enormous, temporary workforce needed to take the census. Sometimes, considerable local resources are utilized—an investment that many states and localities are willing to make because of the importance of an accurate census count.

See also *Apportionment and districting; Data dissemination and use; Federal agency uses of census data; Local involvement in census taking; State and local governments: legislatures.*

■ Leonard M. Gaines, Linda Gage, and
Joseph J. Salvo

Bibliography

Bryant, Barbara Everitt, and William Dunn. *Moving Power and Money: The Politics of Census Taking.* Ithaca, N.Y.: New Strategist Publications, 1995.

Gaines, Leonard M. "The Selection of Census Data in State Data Center/Business and Industry Data Center Organizations: A Gatekeeping-Based Model." Ph.D. dissertation, Rensselaer Polytechnic Institute, 1997.

Lavin, Michael. *Understanding the Census: A Guide for Marketers, Planners, Grant Writers, and Other Data Users.* Kenmore, N.Y.: Epoch Books, 1996.

Myers, Dowell. *Analysis with Local Census Data: Portraits of Change.* San Diego, Calif.: Academic Press, 1992.

Paez, Adolfo. "U.S. Census Data Uses." *Government Publications Review* 20 (March/April 1993): 163-182.

U.S. General Accounting Office. *Formula Grants: Effects of Adjusted Population Counts on Federal Funding to States.* Letter Report, GAO/HEHS-99-69. Washington, D.C., 1999.

State data centers

State data centers serve as statistical clearinghouses for census and related economic and demographic information, technical assistance, research and analysis. Dissemination of the results of the national census is a mammoth undertaking. After the release of the 1970 decennial census, it became evident to the Census Bureau that the systems for disseminating results were inadequate to meet the demand for data. This demand was largely driven by the need for local demographic, housing, and economic data for grant applications and business analysis. Because much of the census data was available only in computerized media, processing of the computer files required mainframe computer capability and specialized programming. Access to the data was costly and available only through organizations with significant resources and technical expertise. To alleviate this roadblock, the Census Bureau began a pilot project to explore the feasibility of establishing central, state-managed centers that would provide inexpensive and ready access to each state's data. The project drew quick acceptance and in 1978 the Census Bureau formalized the State Data Center (SDC) program and began the process of establishing centers in each state. By 1982, all fifty states were voluntarily participating. Currently, the program includes the fifty states, the District of Columbia, Puerto Rico, Guam, the Northern Mariana Islands, and the Virgin Islands. In 1988, the bureau announced an expansion of the data center concept to emphasize the economic census and other economic programs. This expansion established fifteen pilot sites for the new Business and Industry Data Center (BIDC) program. Currently, twenty-three states participate in the joint SDC/BIDC program. The BIDC program allowed for an expansion of the state network to include organizations providing services and outreach to the business community.

Program Objectives

The overall goal of the network is to provide the public with efficient access to U.S. Census Bureau data, as well as geographic and reference products. Access is provided to a range of data users that include state and local governments, businesses, the media, not-for-profit organizations, and the general public. Specific objectives include:

- Providing an institutional structure for the dissemination and maintenance of census statistical products within each state;
- Providing increased and comprehensive technical assistance in the access and use of census data;
- Creating value-added products while moderating the cost of access to census data;
- Providing education and training to users through workshops, presentations, and publications;
- Actively participating in census planning and operations to improve procedures and products;
- Increasing awareness of the importance of the decennial and economic censuses to the general public and businesses to improve response.

These objectives have been met over the twenty-year history of the program. This nationwide network is now a model of federal-state cooperation and is being studied by other federal agencies.

Program Structure

The organizational structure of the program varies from state to state, but all states provide services to meet the core objectives. The lead agency in each state is appointed by the governor and signs a formal agreement with the Census Bureau to outline the duties and responsibilities of the state and the Census Bureau and the resources devoted to the program. The lead agency is typically an executive-level agency such as labor, planning, economic development, or budget and may involve the state library or a major university. The lead agency may designate one or more coordinating agencies to share administrative responsibilities or serve in an advisory capacity to the network. The lead agency also designates affiliate organizations that generally serve a local, county, or regional area. Organizations such as county and regional planning agencies, public libraries, university centers, and councils of governments serve as affiliates. Affiliates participating through the BIDC program include trade organizations, chambers of commerce, small business development centers, and other organizations serving business needs or member organizations. Nationwide, the data center network includes more than 1,500 participating agencies.

Products and Services

The Census Bureau provides, without charge, copies of all printed reports, computer files in various media, and Internet access to all lead agencies. Coordinating and affiliate agencies also have access to print and computerized products and services through the lead agency. Internet access is available. Statistical resources for other state and federal agencies such as the U.S. Bureau of Economic Analysis, the Bureau of Labor Statistics, and state departments of labor, health, and education are often available through the network. Data centers provide a wide range of services to data consumers, including the following:

- *Technical Assistance and Consulting*—Information services range from providing a single statistic over the phone to creating customized data extracts from CD-ROM and Internet files. Nationally, the data center program responds to more than 1.5 million requests each year. Data centers also produce specialized value-added products in published and computerized media.
- *Training and Outreach*—The network provides general information on the census and training in the use of geographic and data products, research techniques, and demographic analysis.
- *2000 Census Planning*—Data centers act as liaisons between state and local government and the Census Bureau on planning and operations for the decennial census. Data centers provide detailed feedback to the Census Bureau on local operations, data content, and product development. The Data Center program has been instrumental in reviewing and commenting on prototypes for the American FactFinder dissemination system, the Census Bureau's Internet site for release of Census 2000 results.

It is important to note that there is no direct financing of state data center participants from the federal government. Likewise, affiliates and coordinating agencies provide services without direct funding from their respective state lead agencies; all support is in the form of in-kind products and services. As a result, state data center networks vary in the level of resources and staff devoted to the program. These factors can often limit the level of products and services provided but can also allow for substantial flexibility for states to determine how their data centers will operate. Newly adopted core competencies attempt to ensure that each state program provides an acceptable level of service.

Meeting the Challenge of Census 2000

The Census Bureau has changed significantly over the twenty years of the State Data Center program. Each state has had to incorporate those changes into their operation. Initially, the centers were "the place to go" for census data, support, and technical assistance. Data centers received the highest priority for release of products and they added value to the computerized tape files by creating print products beyond the Census Bureau's standard series. The advent of CD-ROM technology and its use for release of 1990 Census summary data allowed data users direct access to information that previously required mainframe tape processing. Census 2000 brings another major shift in how data consumers acquire census information and in the services and products that data centers provide. The centers' roles will shift from primary data processing to providing increased technical assistance and support. While users will have detailed census summaries at their fingertips, it will be increasingly important to have access to intermediaries who know about the census, how the data were gathered, what the limitations of the data are, how to use them, and most importantly, how not to use them. A large contingent of census experts has been cultivated throughout the nation in the twenty-year operation of the State Data Center program. After Census 2000, less of that expertise will be applied to processing data and more to the development of value-added products, education of census data users, and analysis of how the nation is changing.

See also *State and local governments: uses of census data.*

■ Robert Scardamalia

Bibliography

National Research Council, Committee on National Statistics, Panel on Census Requirements in the Year 2000 and Beyond. *Modernizing the U.S. Census.* Ed. Barry Edmonston and Charles Schultze. Washington, D.C.: National Academy Press, 1995.

Lavin, Michael R. *Understanding the Census: A Guide for Marketers, Planners, Grant Writers and Other Data Users.* Kenmore, N.Y.: Epoch Books, 1996.

Statistical policy and oversight

Perhaps more than that of any other industrialized nation, the federal statistical system of the United States stands as a hallmark of decentralization. Approximately seventy entities, scattered across all facets of government, conduct surveys and censuses, analyze returns, and disseminate results. In designating the Office of Management and Budget (OMB) as the agency responsible for statistical policy oversight, Congress, in the Budget and Accounting Procedures Act of 1950 and again in the Paperwork Reduction Act of 1980, as amended, and the president, via executive orders, have sought to ensure that the American public is well served in its statistics-gathering needs. It is the OMB's job to adopt common classifications, coordinate statistical activities, develop and implement professional statistical standards, and ensure that the trade-offs between the need for statistical information and the burden on the public are balanced.

Responsibilities of OMB

The director of OMB is charged with (1) developing and implementing government-wide policies, principles, standards, and guidelines concerning data collection procedures and methods, data classifications, statistical information presentation and dissemination, and statistical data sources for the administration of federal programs; (2) long-range planning for the improved performance of federal statistical programs; (3) reviewing the budget proposals of agencies to ensure their consistency with long-range planning; (4) coordinating the statistical functions of the federal government through budget review and other means; and (5) evaluating statistical program performance and agency compliance with government-wide policies and standards.

Despite this broad mandate, the statistical policy function at OMB is carried out by a relatively small office; for at least the past ten years it has numbered fewer than six staff. The survey clearance responsibilities of OMB, which are discussed in more detail below, are carried out in cooperation with other staff members of OMB who have specific agency responsibility for the review and clearance of proposed regulations. The authorization for OMB's regulatory activities is also provided by the Paperwork Reduction Act of 1980, as amended.

Minimizing Public Burden and Maximizing Utility. The congressional intent of the Paperwork Reduction Act of 1980, as amended, was, among other things, to minimize the paperwork burden for individuals; small businesses; educational and nonprofit institutions; federal contractors; state, local, and tribal governments; and other persons that resulted from the collection of information by or for the federal government, and to ensure the greatest possible public benefit from, and maximize the utility of information created, collected, maintained, used, shared, and disseminated by or for, the federal government.

The legislative history of the Paperwork Reduction Act and its predecessor, the Federal Reports Act of 1942, suggests that they were driven by a concern that agencies, left to their own devices, may impose unnecessary burdens on the public by designing forms that are either unnecessary or overlong, or both. Streamlining surveys and censuses also serves a valid statistical purpose. Evidence suggests that lengthy and intrusive questions can affect response rates and the quality of the response. The act sets up a tension, however, between OMB, as overseer, and the program or statistical agency collecting the data.

The act gives OMB broad authority to carry out this mandate by providing that any information collection imposed on more than nine persons or entities carry an OMB approval number. This applies to collection regardless of medium—oral interview, paper form, or electronic submittal—and whether or not it is compulsory. In effect, this means that virtually every survey and census proposed by a federal agency must be submitted to OMB for approval. Central to this review and approval process is the requirement for consultation with members of the public and affected agencies. Congress intended that this public notice should solicit comment to (1) evaluate whether the proposed collection of information is necessary for the proper performance of the functions of the agency, including whether the information shall have practical utility; (2) assess the accuracy of the agency's estimate of the burden of the proposed collection of information; (3) enhance the quality, utility, and clarity of the information to be collected; and (4) minimize the burden of the collection of information on respondents. While most of the burden in responding to government data collection requests does not come from statistical data collections, these collections are an important component of the federal government's data collection activities and are subject to the requirements of the Paperwork Reduction Act.

The authority of the director of OMB to provide leadership and standards for a decentralized statistical system combined with the director's ability to review and approve data collections provides OMB with extremely powerful tools in carrying out its statistical policy oversight mandate. There is one more authority that the director has that is central to defining OMB's involvement in all statistical activities, including the census, and that is OMB's role in the budget process.

OMB and the Federal Budget Process. One of the more important responsibilities of OMB concerns its involvement in the federal budget process. The director of OMB is responsible for preparing the federal budget for submission to Congress. This involves more than simply stapling together the various budget requests from the various federal agencies. OMB performs the traditional roles of a budget office in any government: it examines agency budget requests to ensure economy and efficiency—that is, it possesses the time-honored role of "guardian of the public purse." Additionally, it must ensure consistency with the policies and priorities of the current presidential administration. OMB asks questions relating to the cost and utility and feasibility of projects, their expected impact on the agency mission and on the public, and their relationship to other agencies. Finally, it must ensure that all of the numbers "add up."

Nature of OMB Involvement

OMB has a right—even a duty to the extent there is discretion—to question what agencies propose to do. This duty exists whether the agency proposal is a data collection, a rule making, or any other proposed budgetary expenditure. It uses standards based first in law, then policy (e.g., administration preferences and priorities), and then common sense. Defining OMB's role in deciding how something is to be done—a program or project, a rule, or a survey—involves thornier questions, such as the extent to which an organization like OMB should second guess (the inflammatory term is "micromanage") the technical judgments of the agencies. Statistical surveys are, in this respect, no different from other issues that come to OMB.

Whenever OMB examines a proposed statistical data collection, one question immediately presents itself: How far should an OMB statistician go in substituting his or her statistical judgment for agency judgment? Decisions about sampling and questionnaire design, survey and census planning, estimation, and minimization of error are not mere matters of casual opinion. These decisions are, or should be, dependent on professional experience and training. In terms of sheer numbers, the agencies employ two to three times the number of trained professionals that OMB itself employs. And in terms of expertise, OMB statisticians do not hold a decisive edge over statisticians employed elsewhere.

What, then, it is reasonable to ask, is the appropriate role of the OMB statistician? First, it is important that she or he be able to ask the right questions. Second, it is essential that he or she understand the answers. In fact OMB has written down the basic questions and published them. Statistical Policy Directives 1 and 2 address "Standards for Statistical Surveys" and "Standards for Publication of Statistics," respectively. Establishing that the data collection methods employed by statisticians in reviewed agencies and the publication of their results conform with OMB standards is a primary responsibility of the OMB statistician.

From a budget preparation perspective, too, OMB must know the correct questions. These include questions concerning the reliability of the cost estimates, the relationship of the benefits to the costs, the ability of the agency to carry out the project successfully, implications for other agencies, and the relationship of the project to the goals of the president.

Usually in the discussions between OMB and agencies about questions such as the intended use and utility of a data collection, the parties are able to reach mutual agreement on how to proceed. However, at times agreement is not achieved, and in those cases OMB does attempt to substitute its judgment for agency judgment. If OMB believes that an agency's methodology is clearly flawed and that the results of the data collection would be misleading, it will intervene. For example, one case concerned a proposal to collect data that relied on detailed recall of events thirty years in the past. While it agreed that the results of the survey would be very helpful, OMB decided, after consultation with outside experts, that those results would be unreliable and even misleading. In that case, OMB did not allow the data collection to proceed.

OMB and the Census

In many ways the OMB's involvement in the decennial census is typical of its oversight role in any other data collection endeavor. The census is subject to the same intense scrutiny as other data collection projects. Yet the census differs in important ways. It is both the most visible and the most costly of governmental statistical activities. The census is used to apportion seats in the U.S. House of Representatives, and it is explicitly mentioned in the Constitution. The following examples illustrate the range of issues that may be discussed in relation to the census. These issues are drawn specifically from the 1990 census.

- What is the justification for the questions that are proposed?
- Are there any ways to minimize the impact on the public?
- Will the census meet the needs of the other statistical/nonstatistical agencies?
- Are there alternatives to the mailout/mailback approach?
- What steps have been taken to ensure the accuracy of the address list?
- How reliable are the estimated census costs?
- Where can savings be accomplished?
- Is the planning sound and well thought out?
- Are the computer acquisitions on schedule?
- Will the dress rehearsal be a test of what will actually happen in 1990?
- Should more commercial off-the-shelf software be used rather than Census Bureau-developed software?
- Should the vacant/delete check be accomplished by sample or census?
- Should the results of a post-enumeration survey be used to adjust the census count?

The bulk of discussion takes place at the career staff level. Certainly, general guidance is obtained from political appointees. However, OMB career staff in general take pride in their political neutrality. Political appointees usually respect this attribute of OMB career staff and undertake decisions of a political nature themselves. Many of the questions noted above did not, in fact, reach the political level. Census Bureau and OMB staff were able to reach agreement. In the few cases where agreement or resolution could not be reached, the issues in question were put to the political appointees of both agencies for resolution.

It is not possible, within the limits of this article, to describe the nature of the discussions on all of the issues affecting the 1990 census. However, there is one issue that deserves special mention, and that is the issue of whether and how the census count should, and could, be adjusted. When the secretary of commerce—to whom the Census Bureau director reports—sent the draft criteria for determining whether an adjustment should be made to OMB for review and approval, the question of OMB review of what are essentially professional/technical judgments arose. On the one hand, no data collection of the federal government is more important than the census. It was clear that the decision to adjust or not could have enormous political ramifications because of an adjustment's potential effect on the allocation of seats in the House. (The economic importance of the decision, while widely trumpeted, was less clear.) It was also clear that the decision on adjustment would have important effects on the other agencies. These facts seemed to argue in favor of OMB involvement in the adjustment decision. On the other hand, it was also clear that broad public participation could be expected. This participation, coming as it did from Congress, nongovernmental organizations, and the academic community, seemed to ensure full public participation. As such, OMB concluded that its voice would be unlikely to add significant value to the debate, and in fact could detract from the debate by introducing a perspective that might be seen as politically motivated. For these reasons, OMB decided not to try to substitute its judgment for that of the Census Bureau and did not review or comment on the proposed criteria.

■ Hermann Habermann and Franklin S. Reeder

Summary Tape Files

Summary Tape Files (STFs) are computerized summaries of decennial census data. They include predefined data summaries (frequency counts or tabulations) for all geographic entities recognized or defined by the Census Bureau. For example, Table 1 is Summary Table P8 on race for the United States from the 1990 census STF 3, and the same table is included for all geographic areas on STF 3.

The first STFs, on magnetic tape for use on mainframe computers, were developed for the 1960 census, primarily as tools for internal Census Bureau research and a few specialized organizations. With the 1970 census, STFs became widely used standard products. The tabulations are predefined and include more detail than printed reports. The STFs for the 1980 and 1990 censuses were very similar to those for 1970, occupying

Table 1. Example of a U.S. Summary Table: Table P8 from 1990 STF 3

RACE

Universe: All Persons	
White	199,827,064
Black	29,930,524
American Indian, Eskimo, or Aleut	2,015,143
Asian or Pacific Islander	7,226,986
Other race	9,710,156

fewer tapes each decade as the technology became more sophisticated. In the early 1990s, after initial release on tape, the STFs were released on CD-ROM, ushering in the Census Bureau's transition to dissemination for personal computers. The STFs for the 2000 census were no longer tape files, but equivalent data summaries were distributed on CD-ROM and on the Internet, now referred to as electronic summary files.

Preparing Summary Files

To prepare most of the decennial census data products, the Census Bureau tallies, by computer, the basic record tapes containing individual information. This procedure produces specified summary statistics for various types of areas about persons, families, households, and housing units. The tabulated data are recorded on the Census Bureau's internal-use summary files, which are used to generate the contents of printed reports and public summary files.

STFs are generally organized into two basic file sets, one for the data collected from the complete count of the population on the short form, and one for the sample data collected on the long form. Within this framework, the files are organized to maximize the availability of data for any given geographic area while remaining within the legal limits that prevent disclosure of confidential information. For example, the smallest geographic level (city blocks or larger rural areas of similar populations) is not available for the sample data.

There are four basic STFs for the 1990 census. STF 1 includes about 1,000 items of data from the complete population and housing counts, presented for all geographic entities, including blocks. STF 2 includes more than 2,000 data items from the complete count, with such detail as single years of age and with separate iter-

ations for each race and Hispanic group, but the smallest geographic area is the census tract. STF 3 includes more than 3,000 items of sample population and housing characteristics for all geographic areas down to the block group. A special STF 3 file (STF 3B) includes data for zip codes, a popular geographic area that is not a traditional census geographic area. STF 4 is by far the most detailed, with more than 10,000 data items of sample population and housing characteristics and separate presentations for as many as forty-nine population groups defined by race or Hispanic origin. Census tracts are the smallest geographic area included in STF 4. For the 1970 and 1980 censuses, STF 5 was an extremely detailed file for larger geographic areas, with more than 100,000 data cells. By 1990 STF 5 was discontinued as the focus shifted to producing more specialized summary files.

Summary files typically contain data for many geographic levels in a single "file." Summary-level codes are used to differentiate the geographic levels. The 1990 STF 2 and STF 4 also include record type codes to distinguish among records for different racial or ethnic groups. Because of the inclusion of as many as forty-nine separate ethnic records for each geographic area, the structure of STF 2 and STF 4 is far more complex than the structure of STF 1 and STF 3.

On the summary files of past censuses, the data were stored as strings of digits, grouped into logical records. A printout of one of these files showed simply a mass of unlabeled characters. Specialized software was typically used to define and display the data, following location and definition information in the appropriate technical documentation of each file. When the first STFs from the 1970 census were released, the files required programmers to define and use them. A consortium of universities and other large-scale data users formed the Summary Tape Assistance, Research, and Training (START) community to share the costs of acquiring the files and developing software and documentation for using the STFs. Under the START Community's auspices and the leadership of John C. (Jack) Beresford, DUALabs (Data Use and Access Laboratories) developed the MOD-Series, a set of computer programs that defined the file structures and contents and produced formatted data reports. Using compressed data files and data dictionaries, the MOD-Series programs were highly innovative for their time. By the 1980s, other software entered the scene, including the Census Bureau's CENSPAC, but many of the larger users continued to use the MOD-Series. With the first CD-ROM summary files for the 1990 census, dBASE format files became an option and software to display the summary tables was included with the data.

In addition to the basic summary files, special summary files are typically produced. Most important is the PL 94-171 file, the very first summary of data to be released for each census. These files satisfy the legal requirement, established in 1975 by Public Law 94-171, that within a year of census day, the Census Bureau must send all state legislatures and governors the data they need to redefine districts for their state legislatures. These data also are usually used to delineate revised districts for the U.S. House of Representatives. The 1990 PL 94-171 data included basic population and housing counts for many geographic levels down to the block. Other special summary files have included an Equal Employment Opportunity file and a County-to-County Migration file. The 1990 Journey to Work file provided details on place of work specifically for residents of each county. Sometimes a special summary file can be requested and paid for by a user or group of users, provided that it does not violate the Census Bureau's confidentiality restrictions. The 1990 Census Transportation Planning Package (CTPP) was developed by the Census Bureau in conjunction with other federal and state agencies and nongovernmental organizations. Distributed by the Departments of Transportation of individual states and on CD-ROM by the federal Bureau of Transportation Statistics, the CTPP shows characteristics of workers presented by place of residence, cross-tabulated by place of work.

2000 Census Summary Files

The 2000 census electronic summary files will be distributed on the Internet through American FactFinder and on CD-ROM. There will be four major summary files, similar to the four basic 1990 STFs. In addition to tables for the total population, many of the tables will be presented separately for each major race group:

white, black or African American, American Indian and Alaska Native, Asian, and Native Hawaiian and Other Pacific Islander. Separate tables will be included for the Hispanic population. New racial and ethnic definitions will permit individuals to identify with multiple racial or ethnic groups, resulting in new complexities in the file structures of special race and Hispanic iterated files.

The geographic iterations on national files will include summary tabulations for the nation; regions; divisions; states; counties; county subdivisions; places; American Indian and Alaska Native Villages (AIANAs); Metropolitan Areas (MAs) or core-based statistical areas; Urbanized Areas (UAs); state parts of divided AIANAs, MAs, and UAs; and congressional districts. Separate files for each state will include states; counties; county subdivisions; places; census tracts; state parts of divided AIANAs, MAs, and UAs; block groups; congressional districts; Zip Code Tabulation Areas (ZCTAs); and blocks (for complete count data only). Some of the more detailed tables will not be presented for block groups or blocks.

With changing technology and new definitions, new formats of summary files are evolving. For example, some of the more frequently used tables will be available on the Internet as "Demographic Profiles" and "Quick Tables" from geographic summary files, permitting occasional users to avoid working with the larger summary files. In contrast, the increased detail on race and ethnicity will permit more in-depth analysis by experienced users.

■ Deirdre A. Gaquin

Bibliography

U.S. Bureau of the Census. *Census '80: Continuing the Factfinder Tradition.* Washington, D.C., 1980.

———. *1990 Census of Population and Housing: Guide, Part A. Text.* Washington, D.C., 1992.

———. *Census Catalog and Guide, 1997.* Washington, D.C., 1997.

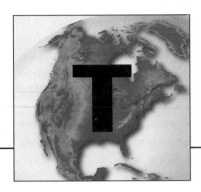

Tabulation geography

All census data analysis takes place in a geographic context. We look at the characteristics of people and housing in space, that is, a defined geographic area. The size of the areas for which data are available range from the United States as a whole to a city block. Many different types of geographic areas lie in-between.

The Census Bureau publishes its data at a wide variety of geographic levels. Some of these areas are political, some are statistical, and some are administrative. For some users and applications, the published geographic areas are sufficient. In other cases, users need to aggregate the published geography so that they can use data for user-defined geographic areas.

Political Geography

The term *political geography* refers to geographic areas that are defined in law and in which, usually, the government is run by elected officials. The most common political geographic areas are state, county, and county subdivision.

State. These are the fifty states of the United States. Some other areas are state equivalents, including the District of Columbia, Puerto Rico, and the outlying territories.

County. Almost every state has counties (called parishes in Louisiana). The number of counties in a state varies widely, ranging from 254 in Texas to 3 in Delaware. In four states (Maryland, Missouri, Nevada, and Virginia) independent cities are treated as county equivalents. The District of Columbia and Guam are also each considered the equivalent of a county. Counties or county-equivalent areas completely cover the territory of each state. At the time of the 1990 census, there were 3,141 county areas in the United States.

County subdivision. About half the states have legally defined minor civil divisions (MCDs), which are recognized in census data publications as county subdivisions. (In the remaining states, statistical areas called Census County Subdivisions are used in data publications.) Minor civil divisions vary widely in their level of importance as functioning governments. For this reason, they are treated differently in census data publications in different states. The major groupings are New England towns, the Mid-Atlantic states, and the upper Midwest.

In the six New England states (Maine, New Hampshire, Vermont, Massachusetts, Rhode Island, and Connecticut), government was organized in towns prior to the Revolutionary War. In these states, the towns deliver most of the governmental services, and counties are quite weak.

In the Mid-Atlantic states of New York, New Jersey, and Pennsylvania, a variety of labels describe minor civil divisions. These include town, township, borough, city, village, and district. Regardless of name, virtually all of them are functioning units of local government.

The states of the upper Midwest (Michigan, Minnesota, Wisconsin) divide their counties into cities and townships (called towns in Wisconsin). Although the township was designed as a rural form of government, many have large populations (in excess of 25,000) and have developed into full-scale municipal governments. All are functioning units of government.

Towns, townships, and other similar areas are not incorporated, but the MCDs in these twelve states are important units of government. For this reason, the Census Bureau now publishes data for them in the same way that data are published for incorporated areas of the same population size. Prior to 1980 these data were only published for the New England states.

Place. There are two kinds of places: incorporated places and census designated places (CDPs). Incorporated places are legally recognized entities. Naming conventions vary by state; some of the terms commonly used are *city, village, borough,* and *town.* More than one term may be used in a given state; if so, there are legal differences between them. Places may or may not be independent of MCDs. For example, in Michigan, cities are incorporated places that are independent of townships, whereas a village is an incorporated place that remains part of its township. Places may cross MCD boundaries (if they are not independent of MCDs) or county boundaries. This leads to hierarchical presentation in electronic census products (see the example of hierarchy).

Some other types of areas may appear to be political geography but are not. These include various types of political districts (congressional, state representative, state senate, county commissioner) and election areas, such as wards and precincts. Although this geography is used for political purposes, the areas are not actually general governmental units providing a variety of services to their residents. Census data may be published for them by the Census Bureau (congressional districts) or by data service organizations at the state and local levels as a convenience to the incumbent officeholders and to others wishing to link or analyze data for these areas.

Statistical Geography

The term *statistical geography* refers to geographic areas created expressly for aggregation and presentation of data. Statistical geography is entirely within the control of the Census Bureau or of the intermediaries who create these types of geographic areas for local use.

Census Tract. The best-known unit of statistical geography is the census tract. Census tracts were originally developed as a way of looking at small areas within large cities. The census tract program has been extended nationwide for publication of 2000 census data. Census tracts never cross county boundaries. In the strong MCD states (New England, Mid-Atlantic, and upper Midwest), census tract boundaries often match the MCD lines as well.

Census tracts are important in and of themselves, that is, to view data for a small area, but they are equally important as building blocks for administrative and service geography. Because some tracts are small (less than 1,000 housing units), and because response rates to the census long form are low in some areas, the long-form data for a single census tract often carry high sampling errors. This makes the information unreliable. However, they are still very useful in the building-block approach to data analysis.

Block Group. Block groups are subdivisions of census tracts, defined as the blocks beginning with a single digit. Thus, tract 3062 may have block group 1, block group 2, and so on. Block groups are designed to be about 400 housing units and 1,000 population, but many vary significantly from that ideal. The problems with data quality outlined earlier for census tracts apply even more strongly to block groups. Thus, they should only rarely be used as individual areas. Their main function is to serve as building blocks to larger-area geography.

Block. A census block is, strictly speaking, not statistical geography. It describes a physical area, bounded by visible features such as streets, railroads, and water. Occasionally, especially in rural areas, drainage ditches or power lines may be used to define blocks. Block data are often outdated before they are published. People and households move in and out, people die, and babies are born, continually. Because most blocks have small population and housing unit counts, only 100 percent data, or short-form data, are tabulated for them. The housing data items are much more reliable and consistent than the population items. Unfortunately, in 2000 the only housing data available were the housing unit counts, occupancy/vacancy rates, and tenure (rent or own).

As with block groups, the primary use of block data is as building blocks to other geography, especially voting precinct. Block data have also served an important function as the source of housing unit counts for sampling frames used in local surveys.

Metropolitan Areas (MAs). Metropolitan areas are groups of counties that are geographically contiguous and share common economic and social bonds. In New England, towns are used as the building blocks rather than counties. Responsibility for defining MAs lies with the federal government's Office of Management and Budget. Metropolitan areas are intended for statistical use only. However, over the decades they have taken on nonstatistical uses that were not originally intended. These uses include many federal laws that reference them, as well as various private sector applications.

Census County Divisions (CCDs). Census County Divisions are used in states where there are no minor civil divisions or where the MCDs are weak or unknown to the public. A total of twenty-one states defined CCDs for the 1990 census. Like census tracts and some other programs, they are a cooperative effort between the state and the Census Bureau.

Administrative Geography

The term *administrative geography* refers to areas that exist to deliver services. They are often independent of standard political geographic areas, except that they are unlikely to cross state lines. The Census Bureau published data in 1990 for three types of administrative areas: school districts, voting districts, and zip codes.

School districts are independent geographic areas in thirty-five to forty states. Elected school boards select school administrators. School districts are within the control of state governments. In 1980 and 1990, a special *School District Data Book* was created in cooperation with the National Center for Education Statistics, combining census data with administrative data for each school district.

Voting districts, called "voting precincts" in many states, are important geographic areas because voting data are tabulated by this geography. Linking census data with voting data is the core activity involved in *redistricting*, the process of redrawing congressional, state legislative, and other districts every ten years. The Census Bureau delivers voting district data under the

Example of Hierarchy

State
> *County A*
>> County subdivision 1 in county A
>>> Place within county subdivision 1 within county A
>>>> Tract 101 within Place
>>>>> Block Group 1 in Tract 101
>>>>> Block Group 2
>>>> Tract 102
>>>>> Block Group 1 in Tract 102
>>>>> Block Group 2
>>> Remainder of county subdivision 1
>>>> Tract 102 in the Remainder
>>>>> Block Group 3 in Tract 102
>> *County subdivision 2*
>>> (Iteration of records for place/remainder and tract repeated)
>> *County subdivision 3*
>>> (Iteration of records for place/remainder and tract repeated)

mandate of Public Law 94-171, passed in 1975. The data file is called the PL 94-171 file and is often referred to as "PL" for short. The law requires the file to be released, for every state, no later than April 1 of the year after the census. As such, it is the first data file to be released.

Zip codes are often called the "universal geo-code," because they are almost always attached to administrative or local data files that include addresses. Thus, a wide variety of users want to use census data tabulated by zip code. It is important to remember that zip codes are administrative units created by the U.S. Postal Service for the purpose of delivering mail. They need not even refer to a defined spatial land area. Even when they do, the boundaries are often difficult to discern. Their boundaries may not be on streets. Some roads may be served by more than one post office and, therefore, have overlapping zip codes.

Although the Census Bureau has published data for these three sets of geography, local data providers (often called "intermediaries") aggregate census tracts and/or block groups to produce and publish census data for local administrative or service geography. Examples in the public and nonprofit sectors include police precincts, health service areas, school attendance areas (within a school district), territories of neighborhoods and community organizations, rural water districts, and catchment areas for delivery of mental health services.

The private sector uses aggregation techniques for similar purposes. Examples include sales territories and radio listening and television viewing areas. Another frequent data application in the private sector is tabulation of demographic or economic profiles for the population located in a circle defined by a radius distance from a specific site of interest. A standard report may show the data for a one-mile radius, a three-mile radius, and a five-mile radius. A Geographic Information System (GIS) determines the census block groups that meet the distance criteria and aggregates them together for the profile.

Published Geographic Areas

Census printed reports usually present a group of like geographic areas together in one table. For example, in a typical decennial census report all counties in the state will be in one table, and places in the state will be in another. In the electronic products (currently CD-ROM disks), geographic areas are presented in hierarchical order, from the largest to the smallest (see the example of hierarchy on the previous page).

See also *Census tracts; Metropolitan areas.*

■ Patricia C. Becker

Bibliography

Association of Public Data Users. *A Guide to State and Local Census Geography, 1990 CPH-I-18.* Washington, D.C.: U.S. Bureau of the Census, 1993.

Tax records

See *Federal administrative records; Federal agency uses of census data; Income and poverty measures; State and local governments: use of census data.*

Three-fifths Compromise

The Three-fifths Compromise is the name given to the provision in the Constitution (1787) that mandated how members of the House of Representatives were to be apportioned among the states. The provision, in Article I, Section 2, based apportionment on a population count of the "whole Number of free Persons" and "three fifths of all other Persons"—that is, three fifths of the slaves. The provision resulted from an intense debate among members of the 1787 Constitutional Convention about the guiding principle for allocating House members. The Framers agreed that the sovereignty of the states derived from the "People of the United States." They therefore decided that state population sizes would determine how seats in the House would be allocated. They also built into the Constitution a requirement for a periodic population count, or census.

North versus South

As the Framers confronted the question of whether such a population count would include all people, including women, children, aliens, and slaves, who had no political rights, they considered whether the formula for apportioning representatives should differentiate among the population's demographic or civil classes. While northern states with few slaves opposed including slaves in the population to be counted, southern states supported doing so, claiming that although slaves were not "people" with political rights, they nevertheless contributed to the political and economic welfare of the states in which they resided. Southerners further argued that since the census would also be used to allocate direct taxes among the states, slaves should be counted as members of the taxable population.

The resulting compromise counted in the census both slaves and free persons. It "discounted" the size of a state's slave population to three-fifths of the total before adding it to the state's free population to produce the official apportionment population. The Framers chose the fraction after debating various ratios. As James Madison and Alexander Hamilton noted in The Federalist Papers, the "reasoning" behind the compromise "may appear to be a little strained in some points," but the three-fifths requirement proved "the least objectionable among the practicable rules."

Impact on the Census

From 1790 to 1860, therefore, the census questionnaire distinguished between the free and slave populations. Census reports listed the states' total and apportionment populations and generally included breakdowns for the slave and free populations of smaller geographic divisions and demographic groups. From the outset of the Republic, then, these requirements embedded a "race classification" in census questions, which yielded elaborate racial statistics. The compromise and the resulting census data provided fodder for antebellum debates about the future of slavery, the "peculiar institution." Racists proposed amending the Constitution to base House representation on the white population only. Opponents of slavery pointed to the compromise to rebut claims that the Constitution was silent on the legitimacy of slavery.

In 1865 the Thirteenth Amendment to the Constitution abolished slavery and the Three-fifths Compromise, but it did not grant political rights to freed persons. After the Civil War southern states reentering the Union were expected to receive the full apportionment for their former slaves. They also were slated to increase their relative weight in the House, while it was clear that they intended that politics would continue to be dominated by whites. The potential for the southern states' increased representation in the House and the electoral college prompted Congress to pass further provisions—particularly the Fourteenth Amendment (Section 2), the Fifteenth Amendment, and their implementing legislation—to reconstruct the Union and to give freed persons the right to vote.

After the war freed persons voted and participated in government, and postbellum censuses included questions on voter participation to monitor compliance with the newly enacted amendments. After the turn of the twentieth century, freed persons were effectively disenfranchised through seemingly colorblind provisions such as those authorizing the white primary, the poll tax, and literacy tests. During the Second Reconstruction of the 1950s and 1960s, Congress revisited the issue and passed the Voting Rights Act of 1965 to require racially unbiased political participation in the United States. Census statistics on race again became essential to answering the question of whether all people of the United States "counted" and were effectively participating in government.

See also *Civil War and the census.*

■ Margo Anderson

Bibliography

Ohline, Howard A. "Republicanism and Slavery: Origins of the Three-Fifths Clause in the United States Constitution." *William and Mary Quarterly* 28, no. 4 (1971): 563–584.

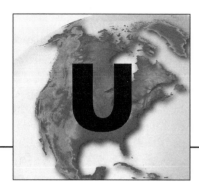

UNIVAC

See *Appendix, Glossary; Data capture; Dissemination of data: electronic products; Editing and imputation.*

Urban areas

The census defines urban areas and territory in order to provide statistics on the population living in cities and towns, or in city-like conditions, as opposed to rural or non-city territory. Prior to 1850 the census provided separate populations for many cities and towns but did not summarize them as a group. From 1850 to1870, limited data were presented on cities grouped by population size, but the term *urban* first appeared in the *Statistical Atlas* in 1874, when it was defined as comprising places with populations of at least 8,000.

From 1874 to 1930, the census used various cutoffs ranging from 8,000 down to 2,500 as the minimum size for defining an urban place. In 1940 data on the urban population based essentially on the 2,500 cutoff were presented for each census back to 1790, broken down by size of place. With minor revisions this series has been published in each subsequent census. In 1950, the urban category was expanded to include qualified census-designated (unincorporated) places and the entire population within urbanized areas, as discussed below, but this expansion was not carried back to earlier censuses.

While common usage in recent decades often has distinguished *urban* from *suburban*, U.S. census usage generally has defined urban as part of a dichotomy, with rural consisting of all territory and population not designated as urban.

Administrative Versus Geographic Boundaries

Before 1950, the urban category consisted only of incorporated municipalities (cities, towns, boroughs, villages, and so on) recognized by their states, provided they met the established size cutoff. This approach assumed that nearly all population clusters that had a city- or town-type character also had incorporated status, and that any urban development that overflowed city limits either would be quickly annexed or would achieve separate incorporation. These assumptions generally were correct until about 1900, although incomplete identification of incorporated municipalities produced gaps in the census list of urban places, especially prior to 1870.

A perennial problem with using municipalities as the basis for defining urban was that in New England the basic municipal unit is the town, an entity that typically includes both one or more population clusters and extensive open country. After the census had tried various alternatives, the urban series from 1790 first presented in 1940 treated New England towns as urban only if they were judged to contain a cluster of at least 2,500 population and to have more than half of their population in clusters. The 1790–1940 series also accepted certain densely settled townships in other states as urban in 1930 and 1940.

By the time this solution was adopted, however, urban overflow beyond city boundaries had become a more serious problem for the urban definition. Such development had existed on a small scale as early as

1790, notably around Philadelphia, but after about 1900 rapid population growth, improvements in public transportation, and increased automobile ownership had produced rapid suburban expansion at the same time that annexations by large cities had slowed. The result was the development of suburban areas that were not separately incorporated and that therefore were left out of the urban definition.

The 1950 census dealt with this problem by introducing the concept of the urbanized area (UA), providing a better separation of urban and rural population in the vicinity of the larger cities. A UA was defined to include each city of at least 50,000 and its contiguous densely built-up suburbs, incorporated or not. The UA boundary did not divide incorporated cities or villages, but included only the built-up parts of suburban townships and New England towns. All population within UA boundaries was defined as urban.

The 1950 UA delimitations were based on pre-census fieldwork and a density of at least 500 housing units per square mile; in 1960, the density limit was lowered slightly to 1,000 persons per square mile. Although emphasizing built-up continuity, the UA definitions always have permitted some gaps of up to one-and-a-half miles under specified circumstances. Some cities of less than 50,000 had UAs defined for 1970, and in 1980–1990 a UA was recognized for each area with a total population of 50,000, essentially irrespective of the size of its main community.

The UAs, defined by density and land use, contrast with the metropolitan areas, which are defined as functional areas centered on UAs. Almost invariably a UA's territory expands with each census, and its definition in terms of census blocks precludes same-area comparisons over time.

Also introduced in 1950 was the systematic recognition of significant population clusters outside UAs and lacking separate municipal status. These unincorporated places, known since 1980 as census-designated places (CDPs), were defined for clusters down to populations of 1,000, with those of at least 2,500 classed as urban. Together the UAs and CDPs added a net of 6.7 million to the urban population of 1950, increasing it from 59.6 to 64 percent of the national total, and a net of 12.2 million in 1960, an increase from 63 percent to 69.9 percent compared to what would have been the case under the urban criteria of 1940.

Since 1970 the "extended city" has excluded from UAs and the urban category the sparsely settled portions of incorporated places whose boundaries include large areas of open country. Pickard (1967) augmented the UA database by defining UAs of at least 50,000 for 1920–1960 using the 1970 census criteria.

Growth of the Urban Population

According to the current historical urban series, the 1790 urban population was 201,655, or 5.1 percent of the national total. In 1990, the urban total was over 187 million, more than nine hundred times as great as in 1790, while the rural population in 1990 was only sixteen times its 1790 total. The urban proportion first exceeded 10 percent in 1840, 25 percent in 1870, and 50 percent in 1920, and was 75.2 percent in 1990.

The level of urbanization has varied greatly by region. The populations of the New England and Middle Atlantic census divisions were more than half urban by 1880, and were joined by the East North Central and Pacific divisions in 1910. The West North Central, West South Central, and Mountain divisions first exceeded 50 percent urban in 1950; the South Atlantic in 1960; and finally the East South Central division in 1970. By 1990 the only states whose populations were less than half urban were Mississippi, Maine, West Virginia, and Vermont, the least urban at 32.2 percent.

The Middle Atlantic division has had a higher urban proportion than the rest of the nation since 1790, and this was true of New England until 1990. The Pacific division's population has been more urban than the nation's since 1870, while the East North Central division, with its extensive farming areas as well as many cities, did not exceed the national urban percentage until 1890 and fell slightly below it in 1990.

The Rationale for the Urban/Rural Classification

Census publications have offered little rationale for the choice of 2,500 or any other population cutoff. There always has been uncertainty about whether population clusters in roughly the 2,500–10,000 range should properly be seen as mainly like larger places, and hence urban, or mainly like the countryside, and hence rural. Similar questions have characterized efforts to define urban population in other countries, where the cutoffs adopted range from a few hundred up to 30,000. The United Nations has not recently tried to achieve international uniformity on the topic. However, the urban category is regularly summarized by population size category in census statistics, providing some data for those who prefer to adopt a different cutoff.

In 1990, as it had since 1950, the urban classification constituted a residence category reflecting population density. It quite closely comprises the population living at an urban density (1,000 or more per square mile) and in a cluster of at least 2,500 population. (The classification departs modestly from this norm in excluding overflow built-up areas around places too small to have UAs defined, and in including some sparse population within the boundaries of incorporated places.)

In an era in which urban densities are dropping, many city workers commute from the country, and the social and cultural distinctions between city and country people are seen as fading away, it is easy to overlook the extreme disparity in population density that continues to exist between urban and rural territory. The 75.2 percent of the nation's population classified as urban in 1990 lived on only 2.9 percent of the nation's area. The mean population density of urban territory in 1990 was 2,152 per square mile, or one hundred times that of all rural areas, 21.4 per square mile. (These comparisons omit Alaska.) Even in the most densely populated states like New Jersey and Rhode Island, urban density averages about fifteen times rural density. At the time the census first reflected the urban/rural dichotomy in the nineteenth century, few people questioned the major significance of the contrast between high-density urban and low-density rural living conditions. Today, although the density disparity remains great, its social and economic concomitants have changed substantially. But no alternative concept has acquired sufficient consensus to persuade the census to replace the existing classification.

Developments for 2000

Although plans will not be complete before summer 2000, there are indications that the 2000 census will define *settlement clusters* similar to the UAs for population concentrations of less than 50,000. Coverage may extend down to clusters of at least 10,000 or even 2,500. If such a plan is adopted, all population within such clusters would be classified as urban, transferring some additional population and territory out of the rural category and further emphasizing the density-based character of the current urban definition.

See also *Metropolitan areas*.

■ Richard L. Forstall

Bibliography

Pickard, Jerome P. *Dimensions of Metropolitanism* (Research Monograph 14; Appendixes, Research Monograph 14A). Washington: Urban Land Institute, 1967.

Truesdell, Leon E. *The Development of the Urban-Rural Classification in the United States: 1874 to 1949* U.S. Bureau of the Census, Current Population Reports, Series P-23, No. 1, August 1949.

U.S. Bureau of the Census. *1990 Census of Population and Housing. Population and Housing Units Counts. United States.* (1990 CPH-2-1). Washington: Government Printing Office, 1993, pp. A-11–A-12 and tables 4 and 23.

U.S. Census Office. *9th Census, 1870. Statistical Atlas of the United States based on the results of the Ninth Census.* New York: J. Bien, 1874.

U.S. insular areas

The United States currently has four insular areas: the Virgin Islands in the Caribbean near Puerto Rico constitute 134 square miles on three major islands—St. Croix, St. John, and St. Thomas. Guam is the southernmost of the Mariana Islands, south of Japan and east of the Philippines, and is 210 square miles. The rest of the Mariana Islands are the Northern Mariana Islands, an archipelago of more than twenty islands and 179 square miles, with Saipan being the largest in size and population, but with sizable populations also living on Rota and Tinian. American Samoa, the only U.S. insular area in the Southern Hemisphere, is 77 square miles, with most of the population living on Tutuila, but with populations also living on the three Manua Islands, Aunuu, and Swains Island.

The first insular area over which the United States gained jurisdiction was *Guam*, which was ceded to the United States by Spain in October 1898 by the Treaty of Paris, ratified in 1899. The United States acquired *American Samoa*, a group of seven islands, in accordance with a convention among the United States, Great Britain, and Germany, ratified in 1900. American Samoa annexed Swains Island in 1925. In 1917 the United States purchased the *Virgin Islands*, comprising fifty islands and cays, from Denmark.

The United States administered the *Northern Mariana Islands* between 1947 and 1986 as a United Nations strategic trust by an agreement approved by the UN Security Council and the United States. The

Table 1. Summary Population Statistics, United States and Insular Areas: 1990

Characteristic	United States	Virgin Islands	Guam	American Samoa	Northern Mariana Islands
Population	248,709,873	101,809	133,152	46,773	43,345
Median age	32.9	28.2	25.0	20.9	27.4
Persons per household	2.63	3.14	3.97	7.00	4.63
Children born per female 15 to 44	1.223	1.662	1.523	1.757	1.226
Percent 5 years and over:					
Living in same house in 1985	53.3	60.6	46.3	77.2	29.3
Living outside area in 1985	2.2	12.4	32.7	15.8	53.2
Speaking only English at home	86.2	76.1	37.3	3.0	4.8
Percent 25 years and over:					
High school graduate	75.2	56.5	73.3	54.5	66.3
Bachelor's degree or higher	45.2	31.3	39.9	22.6	31.1
Percent 16 years and over:					
In the labor force	65.3	67.6	72.7	50.7	81.8
Unemployed	6.3	6.7	3.8	5.1	2.3
Median family income in 1989	$35,225	$24,036	$31,178	$15,979	$21,275

Source: Adapted from U.S. Bureau of the Census, *Statistical Abstract of the United States, 1996* (Washington, D.C.: U.S. Government Printing Office, 1996), tables 1311 and 1312.

Northern Mariana Islands became a commonwealth in 1986.

Because characteristics of the insular areas differ, the presentation of census data for them is not uniform. The 1960 census of population covered the Virgin Islands and Guam. It excluded the Northern Mariana Islands because their census was conducted in April 1958 by the Office of the High Commissioner. The 1960 census of housing excluded American Samoa. The 1970, 1980, and 1990 censuses of population and housing covered all four insular areas. In 1990 the population of Guam was 133,152; the Virgin Islands, 101,809; American Samoa, 46,773; and the Northern Mariana Islands, 43,345. A summary of comparisons from the 1990 census appears in Table 1.

The 1959, 1969, 1978, and 1987 censuses of agriculture covered American Samoa, Guam, and the Virgin Islands; the 1964, 1974, and 1982 censuses covered only Guam and the Virgin Islands; and the 1969, 1978,

1987, 1992, and 1997 censuses included the Northern Mariana Islands. The census of agriculture was conducted in American Samoa and the Northern Mariana Islands in 1990 along with the population and housing censuses.

Beginning in 1967 Congress authorized the economic censuses to be taken at five-year intervals, for years ending in "2" and "7." Prior economic censuses were conducted in Guam and the Virgin Islands for 1958 and 1963. In 1972 the census of construction industries was added for the first time in the Virgin Islands and Guam. For 1982, 1987, and 1992 the economic censuses covered the Northern Mariana Islands. American Samoa is not included in the economic censuses. In 1992 the Virgin Islands had 2,932 business establishments, Guam had 1,955, and the Northern Mariana Islands had 1,266.

For mid-year 1999, the Census Bureau estimated the population of Guam to be 151,968; the Virgin Islands,

119,615; the Northern Mariana Islands, 69,216; and American Samoa, 63,781. The bureau bases its population estimates on births, deaths, and net migration.

■ Michael J. Levin

Bibliography

U.S. Bureau of the Census. *Statistical Abstract of the United States, 1999.* Washington, D.C.: U.S. Government Printing Office, 1999.

Uses of census data by the private sector

The U.S. census is a federal data collection undertaken for federal purposes. However, businesses use census information to increase efficiency and competitiveness, and private companies have developed census-based information products that are used widely in business applications.

Business Decision Making

The use of census data in strategic and tactical decision making by U.S. businesses has become widespread. These applications reflect businesses' increased awareness of demographic trends, improved technology for accessing and processing census data, and the underlying need to be competitive and responsive to increasingly diverse consumer and employee populations.

Census data are used by business both for broad strategic positioning and to better compete for customers and employees. As the U.S. population moved west and south, and to suburban locations, stores and services followed. As households and families became more diverse in terms of race, ethnicity, and socioeconomic status, business strategy shifted from a mass market, one-size-fits-all perspective to that of targeting specific segments or niches of the population. As competition for customers and employees intensified, the need to identify the size, location, and characteristics of consumer markets and employee populations became critical to profitability and survival in the business community. The census is particularly well suited to such targeting objectives because it provides data nationwide and for very small areas.

Many industries, such as consumer product manufacturers, retailers, financial services, housing, transportation, travel and entertainment, and health care, integrate census data into their business plans. Within these industries, census data inform decisions on target marketing, strategic planning, human resources planning and staffing, site location, merchandising and media, logistics and distribution networks, and financial forecasting.

Population size and change are key data elements in business plans. Census data are fundamental building blocks for analyzing the size of consumer segments and geographic areas. Data on the number of teenagers may be used to launch a new product nationwide or to develop a strategic plan for hiring part-time workers. The size and location of the Hispanic population is important for the placement of Spanish-language advertising, signing, and merchandising operations. Accurately identifying the year in which the population of a growing suburb will reach a company's threshold for building a new grocery store ensures that sales goals will be met.

Demographic characteristics are correlated with consumer behavior. The success of a product or service may be correlated with the presence of a particular age group, household income level, or educational profile. For example, families with teenagers in high school, incomes above $55,000, and with two working parents may be the more responsive target audience for a particular product or service. Launching a product in an area with few such families would not be successful. Combining internal company information on customers with census data further refines the business focus.

Many business applications of census data depend on small-area- or neighborhood-level information available primarily from the census. Data at the block, block group, tract, and zip code levels are used for site location, target mailings, merchandising, and hiring plans. The availability of small-area data and the development of user-friendly, affordable Geographic Information Systems (GIS) created explosive growth in mapping products in the 1990s. Such mapping products clearly identify market potential to business executives and support timely decisions on multimillion-dollar investments. An important byproduct of the census is the Topologically Integrated Geographic Encoding and Referencing (TIGER) system, which produces computer mapping files that have become an important component of business analyses of spatial data such as store and customer locations.

Computer technology has made possible the efficient access and sharing of census data across business divisions including local and wide-area networks, the Internet, and large-scale company databases. Easy-to-use and affordable data products from private suppliers have expanded the audience for census data within the business community. Census data, previously used primarily by those with academic training in large corporations, have become available to decision makers in businesses of all sizes. Many applications now extend beyond the use of census data to include supplemental data and estimates provided by private data suppliers and government agencies. However, small-area estimates of race, education, housing tenure, and other characteristics are subject to considerable uncertainty, and business decision making remains a difficult process. The American Community Survey, currently being developed by the Census Bureau, would greatly enhance the contribution of census data to business decision making by continuously measuring socioeconomic and demographic characteristics, and enabling the development of enhanced small-area estimates.

Private Sector Disseminators

The release of 1970 census data on computer tapes promoted the demand for demographic information, as businesses were quick to recognize the benefits of the applications described in the previous section. However, few companies were equipped to process the massive census files, and the Census Bureau was not equipped to respond to the demand for its data. In response, private companies bought the census tapes and established themselves as value-added disseminators.

In contrast to the limited options available from the Census Bureau, private suppliers provided quick and flexible access to the census—for a price. If a business needed income data only for selected neighborhoods, or reports comparing the demographics of alternative trade areas, private suppliers were the best source. One could define several areas and quickly identify their demographic characteristics or identify areas with selected characteristics—such as affluent families with children. Private suppliers also offered flexibility in area definition—providing data for "geometric" areas such as a one-mile radius around a store. Where standard census products are lacking, private suppliers have paid the Census Bureau to produce "special tabulations" of census data. For example, data for zip codes and small-area household income by age were first produced as special tabulations for private suppliers.

Repackaging of census data did not sustain the industry for long. Because business users need data more current than the aging census, private suppliers now produce small-area estimates of basic counts and characteristics. Similarly, because businesses need content beyond that provided by the census, these suppliers estimate noncensus items such as sales potential and wealth. Supplemental data on businesses and employment are added to identify commercial and workplace markets, and many businesses integrate their own data into private suppliers' products.

Most private suppliers use census data to develop lifestyle cluster systems—neighborhood types that are predictive of consumer behavior and provide a shorthand way of applying the census. Using neighborhood clusters, rather than detailed census tables, businesses can efficiently identify the characteristics of their customers, locate untapped concentrations of similar populations, and advertise to them though their preferred media.

Some private suppliers provide value-added geographic information. The census provides the basic framework of blocks, tracts, and associated spatial data, and the private suppliers turn this information into commercial products. Among these are boundaries for computer mapping, address coding systems that link addresses to geographic units or latitude/longitude coordinates, and cross-reference files used to build nonstandard areas (such as zip codes or cable television areas) from small-area census geography.

Dissemination technology is an essential and always changing part of the data business. Mainframe computer dissemination products were replaced in the 1980s by CD-ROMs for desktop systems. These systems have been expanded and upgraded over the years, and private suppliers have worked closely with GIS providers as these systems have become widely used. Dissemination through the Internet is the most recent trend.

The Census Bureau also is moving toward Internet dissemination, with products that are more flexible and user friendly. However, the role of private suppliers is secure, because few businesses seek only census data. The full array of proprietary estimates and private sector database products is expected by most business users, as are information products tailored to the needs of specific industries (for example, financial services, telecommunications).

Private suppliers have extended so far beyond the repackaging of census data that one can lose sight of how dependent they still are on the census. Many products are derivatives, several steps removed from the census, and used in conjunction with private sector resources. With competition focused on proprietary advantages, private suppliers have little incentive to tout the importance of the census on which they all rely.

The data suppliers also are making greater use of the large consumer databases compiled by marketing firms. With millions of frequently updated household records, these databases have long been valuable to businesses marketing to individual consumers. However, small-area data summarized from these databases are a supplement to census data—not a replacement for them.

The private data business is no longer about repackaging and disseminating the census, and it never really was. It is about providing businesses with valuable information and the tools and knowledge to efficiently apply this information. The business sector produces impressive resources of its own, but the census remains the indispensable statistical foundation for many business applications. The private suppliers, and the companies that use their value-added products, all have a major stake in the continued success of the U.S. census.

See also *Private sector*.

■ Joan Naymark and Kenneth Hodges

Bibliography

Kintner, Hallie, Thomas Merrick, Peter Morrison, and Paul Voss, eds. *Demographics: A Casebook for Business and Government*. Westport, Conn.: Westview Press, 1994.

Merrick, Thomas, and Stephen Tordella. "Demographics: People and Markets," *Population Bulletin*. 43 (February 1988).

Pol, Louis, and Thomas, Richard. *Demography for Business Decision Making*. Westport, Conn.: Quorum Books, 1997.

Russell, Cheryl. "The Business of Demographics." *Population Bulletin*. 39 (June 1984).

Thomas, Richard, and Russell Kirchner. *Desktop Marketing: Lessons from America's Best*. Ithaca, N.Y.: American Demographics Books, 1991.

Weiss, Michael. *The Clustering of America*. New York: Harper & Row, 1988.

Veterans' status

The information on veterans' status collected by the census is used by the Department of Veterans Affairs to calibrate its veteran population model. It is also available to the general population in the microdata releases from the Bureau of the Census.

Today, individuals interested in veterans and veteran issues take for granted the availability of veteran population data by gender, age, and period of military service down to the county level. These estimates, anchored to the previous census and updated annually for separations from the service, as well as estimates of mortality and migration, are prepared by and available from the Office of the Assistant Secretary for Planning and Analysis, U.S. Department of Veterans Affairs. However, as pointed out by Cowper, Heltman, and Dienstfrey (1994), this was not always the case.

History of the Veteran Status Question

The census of 1840 represented the first effort of the U.S. government to collect data on veterans. This information was used in updating the records of pensioners from the Revolutionary War. The next census to collect data on veterans was in 1890; data were collected on those who had served in the Union and Confederate Armies. While the censuses of 1910, 1930, 1940, and 1950 did include veteran status questions, the results were never published due to the relatively large nonresponse rate (U.S. Bureau of the Census, 1964).

When plans were made for the census of 1960, it became apparent that with the increasing numbers of veterans and programs available only to those who had served during specific periods of service, more accurate data were needed. Beginning in 1960, and continuing in each succeeding census, the veteran status questions have been refined to reflect more accurately the definition of who is a veteran as well as to meet the data needs of an increasing number of programs and services available to them. In 1960 the veteran status question was asked only of males age fourteen or older. Specifically, they were asked if they had served in "Army, Navy, or other Armed Forces of the United States," and if so, to indicate if that service had occurred during the Korean War, World War II, World War I, or any other time. Virtually the same question was used in 1970; the only change was the addition of the Vietnam Conflict to the list of periods of service.

The veteran status questions were changed dramatically for the census of 1980. First, the question was reworded to ask if the person was "a veteran of the active-duty military service in the Armed Forces of the United States." Specific mention of the Army and Navy was removed. In addition, those who had served only in the National Guard or Reserves were referred to the instruction guide. (Veteran status and associated benefits are available to those whose service was limited to the National Guard or Reserves *only* if they were called up to active duty.)

Second, the list of periods of service was changed. Specifically, the terms *Korean War* and *Vietnam Conflict* were relabeled as *Korean Conflict* and *Vietnam Era*. In addition, instead of having all peacetime service covered by the catch-all category "any other time," the periods between the Korean Conflict and the Vietnam Era, and after the Vietnam Era were specified since veterans of these periods could be eligible for different benefits. The new list included:

- May 1975 or later
- Vietnam Era
- February 1995 to July 1964
- Korean Conflict
- World War II
- World War I
- Any other time

Lastly, and perhaps most importantly, the 1980 census was the first to ask the veteran status of both men and women. As a result, the census attempted the first accurate count of the number of women veterans. (Subsequent analysis as a result of the findings of the *1984 Survey of Female Veterans* indicated that the census results may have overestimated the number of women veterans, particularly in World War II and peacetime periods prior to World War II. The overestimate may have resulted from the fact that organizations women served in were not granted veteran status.)

The veteran status questions were further refined for the census of 1990. Because it is difficult to distinguish between active-duty service and service in the reserves or National Guard, the question was revised to allow respondents to address the issue actively (through questions) rather than passively (through responding to instructions). The new question asked: Has this person ever been on active-duty military service in the Armed Forces of the United States or ever been in the United States military Reserves or the National Guard?

- Yes, now on active duty
- Yes, on active duty in the past but not now
- Yes, service in Reserves or National Guard only
- No

This query was followed by a question asking respondents to specify the periods in which their active-duty service occurred. This list was the same as that used in 1980, with the addition of a new peacetime category of "September 1980 or later." Also added was a question asking for the total number of years of active-duty military service with a space for the number to be entered. Those additions were in response to legislation effective September 1980, requiring twenty-four months of active-duty service before an individual is eligible for most veterans benefits. (This last question was further revised/simplified in 2000 by providing only two response categories: "Less than 2 years" and "2 years or more.")

Beginning in the 1980s the number of veterans began to decrease. Since that time the 16 million World War II veterans have seen mortality take a staggering toll; in recent years they have been dying at twice the rate of separations from the active-duty military. While our nation has participated in military combat since the end of Vietnam, the conflicts have not been associated with large-scale call-ups. As a result, the rolls of the active-duty military have stayed relatively constant. It is likely that this trend will continue.

Tabulating and Reporting the Number of Veterans

A note on how the Department of Veterans Affairs tabulates and reports the veteran population is in order. For tabulation purposes, individual veterans are considered to have served in *either* wartime or peacetime. If they have served in both, they are considered wartime veterans. A peacetime veteran is reported in only one peacetime period. If veterans have served in more than one peacetime period, they are counted in the most recent.

Veterans are counted in *all* wartime periods in which they served. Reports typically show all those who served in a particular wartime period (labeled "Total") as well as those who served only in that period (labeled "No Prior Wartime Service").

Estimates of the veteran population based on the previous census are published in a variety of sources, most notably the *Annual Report of the Secretary of Veterans Affairs*. They are also available upon request, at the county level by gender as well as age or period of service, from the Office of the Assistant Secretary for Planning and Analysis, U.S. Department of Veterans Affairs. This office is responsible for preparing projections of the veteran population until at least the next census.

Once the census has identified an individual as a veteran, the entire panoply of data collected is available for analysis. Using the microdata releases from the Bureau of the Census, veterans can be compared against their nonveteran counterparts on a host of characteristics.

However, the researcher is advised to keep in mind that veterans have an age and gender distribution very different from the population at large. In addition, the military occupations of men and women are quite different, particularly during wartime periods.

Sources of Data on Veterans

The most detailed source of data on veterans' status and their associated socioeconomic characteristics is the microdata releases from the decennial census. Annual updates on the estimated veteran population are made by the Office of the Assistant Secretary of Planning and Analysis. The Bureau of Labor Statistics produces monthly estimates of veteran unemployment, collected in the monthly Current Population Survey (CPS), though the user is cautioned to be mindful of the associated standard errors. The annual March CPS contains additional questions on veterans' status and characteristics.

In addition, The Office of the Assistant Secretary for Planning and Analysis (and its predecessors) have sponsored periodic surveys of the veteran population. Reports from these surveys are available to the public. General data on veterans' use of VA health services and benefits are available in the *Annual Report of the Secretary of Veterans Affairs*. Detailed data on veterans' use of VA health services are available at the VA Information Resources Center (Hines VA Hospital, P.O. Box 5000, Hines, IL 60141-5000) and detailed data on the use of veterans benefits are available from the Office of the Undersecretary for Benefits, U.S. Department of Veterans Affairs (810 Vermont Avenue, NW, Washington, DC, 20420).

■ Stephen J. Dienstfrey

Bibliography

Cowper, C. W., L. R. Heltman, and S. J. Dienstfrey. *The Concept of Veteran Status in the U.S. Decennial Censuses: 1960–90*. Princeton, N.J.: Association of Public Data Users, June 1994.

U.S. Bureau of the Census. *U.S. Census of Population: 1960 Subject Reports: Veterans*. PC(2)-8c. Washington, D.C.: U.S. Government Printing Office, 1964.

U.S. Bureau of the Census. *1970 Census of Population Subject Reports: Veterans*, PC(2)-6e. Washington, D.C.: U.S. Government Printing Office, 1973.

U.S. Bureau of the Census. *1980 Census of Population, Detailed Characteristics*, PC(1)-D. Washington, D.C.: U.S. Government Printing Office, 1984.

U.S. Bureau of the Census. *1990 Census of Population, Social and Economic Characteristics*, CP-2-1. Washington, D.C.: U.S. Government Printing Office, 1993.

U.S. Department of Veterans Affairs, Veterans Benefits Administration. *The Veterans Benefits Administration: An Organizational History: 1776–1994*. Washington, D.C.: U.S. Department of Veterans Affairs, November 1995.

Vital registration and vital statistics

In 1997 a total of 3,880,894 live births and 2,314,245 deaths were reported in the United States. These figures were obtained through vital record registration systems maintained in the fifty states, New York City, and the District of Columbia. Vital registration is the recording of events occurring to individuals, such as births, deaths, marriages, and divorces, on a continuous basis as those events occur. Vital statistics are the numerical data compiled from those records and include information on characteristics of the individuals having the events. A census, on the other hand, is based on enumeration or a count of a particular population and its characteristics at a point in time.

States register vital records of birth, death, marriage, and divorce under the legal authority of the individual state but use methods for registration and data collection that are comparable from state to state. All states then provide data from these records to the National Center for Health Statistics in the Department of Health and Human Services for compilation into national vital statistics for the United States. However, this system for obtaining national vital statistics data was developed only within the twentieth century.

Since the Constitution did not provide for vital registration, this process evolved as a state function in the United States in a different way from many other countries that have a national system for registering vital events. The first birth and death statistics published for the entire United States were based on information collected as part of the 1850 decennial census. Although these reports were inaccurate and incomplete, collection of birth and death statistics continued with each decennial census through 1900 when the system was changed to collect vital statistics information through the legal registration of these events. Improvements were made over time in the completeness and quality of information collected through the vital registration process. Today, vital statistics data are collected nationally by the National Center for Health Statistics through a cooperative arrangement with all states.

Early Collection of Vital Statistics

Vital registration began in churches, particularly in England, when clergy began keeping records of christenings, burials, and marriages. In 1639 the Massachusetts Bay Colony required courts to keep records of legal events including births, deaths, and marriages. This model of recording vital events as legal statements of fact to ensure the rights of individuals was followed in other colonies. Often, the recording of deaths included information on age and cause of death, so these records were useful for studying patterns of disease when epidemics occurred. As the relationship between causes of death and bad sanitary conditions became apparent, the need for better and more accurate collection of vital-events data and a better registration system was recognized. In 1842, Massachusetts adopted the first state vital registration law that contained provisions for collection of specified types of information including causes of death.

Perceiving the need for national data, officials in the Census Office added questions to the 1850 census to collect information on persons "Born within the year," "Married within the year," and "Disease, if died within the year." While it was known that people could not remember and report past events accurately, this system for collecting national vital statistics persisted until the early 1900s. Census counts of deaths for 1850, 1860, and 1870 are believed to be about 40 percent short of the actual number of deaths.

As the need for better public health information increased, physicians and others began pushing for a more aggressive vital registration system to obtain the statistics necessary to monitor disease outbreaks. While a number of cities and a few states had vital registration systems, they used different forms and collection methods. In 1879 Congress created the National Board of Health to promote complete and uniform registration of vital events.

For the 1880 census, the concept of "registration area" was developed for accepting registration records from areas having death records in satisfactory detail. Two states, Massachusetts and New Jersey, and several

large cities were able to meet the criteria to become part of the official registration area in 1880. Books of blank death certificates were provided to physicians to complete for each death they attended. The books were then collected by census takers and were used to improve the accuracy of death reporting.

Due to differences in collection methods, in forms used, and in the manner of recording data, the Census Office had difficulty tabulating death records obtained for the 1880 count. Therefore, the Census Office wrote to all states and cities with a population over 5,000 recommending a standard form of death certificate to be used for the 1890 census. Also in 1890 an attempt was made to monitor the probable registration completeness. Again for the 1900 census, intensive efforts were made to promote the use of a standard death certificate. By January 1900, twelve states adopted the standard form, six other states and the District of Columbia adopted it in part, and seventy-one large cities in other states adopted the form in some manner. The 1900 census included figures on deaths from states and cities that were believed to have at least 90 percent of the deaths registered.

Improvement of Vital Statistics Data

In 1902 the Bureau of the Census was made a permanent full-time agency of the federal government. The act creating the bureau authorized the director to obtain, on an annual basis, copies of records filed in vital statistics offices of states and cities with adequate birth and death registration systems. At this point, the effort to obtain counts of deaths as part of the decennial census was abandoned, and the development of an annual system for collection of vital statistics from the registration of vital events was begun.

To have a uniform system for registration of vital events, the Census Bureau began to develop a model law for vital registration, drafted standard forms, prepared instructions for physicians and others completing vital records, formulated rules for statistical practice including a system for mortality classification, and began establishing working relationships with state and local registrars. Promotional efforts helped states pass uniform legislation and become part of the death registration area. From 1913 the Census Bureau began locating agents in state health agencies to promote registration and to improve the quality of information about vital records.

The first annual report on mortality statistics, published by the Bureau in 1906, presented data for the five years from 1900 to 1904 as if they were separate annual reports. The volume included details on deaths for the registration states and cities by month of death, age at death, sex, color, and cause of death. In 1914 the Bureau published the first table separating resident deaths from nonresident. Prior to that time, published data was presented only by place where the event occurred.

In 1915 the birth registration area was formed and the Bureau began publishing annual statistical data on natality. The 1915 volume (published in 1917) contained data for 776,304 live births in the registration area containing ten states and the District of Columbia. Tables included data on month of birth, sex, color, parent nativity of white children, and deaths to children under one year of age.

Growth in the number of states included in the birth and death registration areas was slow. In 1924, the Bureau established a committee to bring all states into the registration area by 1930. An effort was made to educate boards of health, physicians, and citizens about the need for these data for public health. It was not until 1933 that all states were included in the registration areas for births and deaths.

After 1933, the Census Bureau began working to improve data on the records for all states and to research new fields of vital statistics. In 1935 births and deaths were reported by place of residence of the mother or decedent; this procedure greatly improved the usefulness of the data. Under the leadership of Halbert L. Dunn, a physician and biometrician, the Division of Vital Statistics within the Bureau was greatly strengthened to include more professional staff. Other innovations included a monthly reporting system to provide provisional figures on births, a series of special monographs, and the expansion of annual published volumes to include more extensive tabulations by socioeconomic groups and more analytical and interpretative material. Emphasis was also placed on expanding field work to improve the completeness and accuracy of the information reported on the original certificates, coordinating activities between the federal and state offices to eliminate duplication of effort, and stimulating research within the Division of Vital Statistics.

Collection of national marriage and divorce data was begun in 1940 by the Division of Vital Statistics following the pattern used for births and deaths. Transcripts of marriage and divorce records were collected from state vital statistics offices. Although national marriage data for 1939 and 1940 provided some detail other than numbers of occurrences, marriage records were available for only thirty states. Divorce data published for 1939 included only a dozen states. Efforts to collect marriage and divorce data were suspended during World War II, but in 1944 the Bureau resumed publishing the number of occurrences by state.

In 1942, the president of the United States acknowledged problems with national vital statistics data and asked the Budget Bureau to conduct a study and make recommendations for improvement. In 1943 the concept of a cooperative vital statistics system of state vital record offices and a national federal office was proposed. The national office would provide financial and technical aid to assist state vital record offices in correcting defects to achieve standardization of vital record agencies, methods, and requirements. The plan also called for transferring the Division of Vital Statistics from the Bureau of the Census to the Public Health Service as a separate organizational unit. These recommendations were accepted by the president; in 1946 the vital statistics functions were transferred to the Public Health Service, and the National Office of Vital Statistics was established. In 1960 the National Office of Vital Statistics merged with the National Health Survey to become the National Center for Health Statistics (NCHS).

Current Vital Statistics

Today the states and the NCHS work together through a cooperative agreement to develop standard forms, definitions, and procedures for data collection and uniform procedures for coding and processing data. The data are then transmitted electronically to NCHS, combined from all states, and included in the national database. Computer automation has greatly improved the timeliness and quality of vital statistics, and states continue to increase the use of automation so that electronic registration of births and deaths has become a reality. Dissemination of vital statistics data to the public has also improved, and along with published data, vital statistics are available in a variety of electronic formats and through the Internet.

In addition to the many uses of vital statistics for monitoring and assessing the health of the public, vital statistics are used to measure a variety of demographic and social issues such as teenage pregnancy and out-of-wedlock births. Death records contain items on the decedent's place of residence, age, race, sex, education, occupation, marital status, and cause of death. Birth record information has increased to include the mother's place of residence, age, race, Hispanic origin, marital status, education, and number of previous children as well as medical items about prenatal care and delivery. Birth records also contain birth weight and other medical information on the infant. For infants who die, birth and death records are linked together to study factors about the birth and the mother's medical and demographic information that may have a relationship to the infant's death.

At the Bureau of the Census, birth and death data are among the main components used in the Intercensal Population Estimates Program to develop annual estimates of the total population and its characteristics for the nation, states, and counties. Special counts of births and deaths by age, sex, race, and Hispanic origin for each county in the United States are compiled for the Bureau's use in preparing the estimates by NCHS from the national data base that contains data from all state vital record offices. These population estimates are in turn used as denominators in the calculation of vital statistics rates and as the basis for health and disease incidence rates as well as for many other program and planning purposes.

■ Dorothy S. Harshbarger

Bibliography

Birth Statistics for the Registration Area of the United States, 1915, First Annual Report. Washington, D.C.: Department of Commerce, Bureau of the Census, 1917.

Hetzel, Alice M. "U. S. Vital Statistics System: Major Activities and Developments, 1950–95." Hyattsville, Md.: U.S. Department of Health and Human Services, National Center for Health Statistics, February 1997 (DHHS Publication No. PHS 97–1003).

Mortality Statistics, 1900 to 1904, Special Reports. Washington, D.C.: Department of Commerce and Labor, Bureau of the Census, 1906.

Vital Statistics of the United States, 1950, Volume I, Chapter I, "History and Organization of the Vital Statistics System, Historical Development," 2–19. Washington, D.C.: U.S. Department of Health, Education and Welfare, National Office of Vital Statistics, 1954.

Voting Rights Act

See *African-origin population; Apportionment and districting; Race: questions and classifications.*

White or European-origin population

Since the first census in 1790, a question assessing the race of individuals has been asked every decade. While the racial categories used by the Census Bureau have changed over time, *White* has always been an included category.

European ethnicity, on the contrary, has been enumerated by the census in a variety of ways over the last two hundred years. The earliest estimates of the ethnicity of the U.S. population were based upon an analysis of the surnames of individuals. The 1850 census was the first to include a question about birthplaces; the 1880 census added a question about the birthplace of individuals' parents.

For the next century, only the first two generations of European immigrants could be identified by the census. In 1980, the inclusion of an ancestry question meant that all of those identifying with a particular national-origin group would be rightfully counted. The 1990 census kept the ancestry question but, as was the case in 1980, no longer kept the parental birthplace question.

The 2000 census follows the 1990 census with regard to the nativity and ancestry questions, but marks a major change in racial categorization. While *White* is still a category, individuals are able to choose multiple racial identifications. For the first time since the earliest censuses, which counted "mulattoes" and "half-breeds," individuals who are partly white will be officially reported in the census.

Direct Identifiers of Whites and European Origin Groups

Race has been asked of individuals in every census, and *White* has been an option in each. Before 1960, the census enumerator was responsible for recording a person's race; beginning with the 1960 census, individuals self-reported race. The 1990 and 2000 censuses explicitly asked respondents which race they "consider themselves to be."

The relative size of the white population in the United States has remained fairly consistent over the last two hundred years; the 1790 census indicated that 80.7 percent of Americans were white, while according to the 1990 census 83.9 percent of Americans are white. This is part of a downward trend in the percentage of the U.S. population that is whites, which had peaked at almost 90 percent in 1930 and 1940.

The identification of European origin groups falls into three broad categories: surnames, nativity, and ancestry. Surnames refer to the use of the surnames of individuals to impute their ethnic backgrounds. This was the method used in a Census Bureau-sponsored book, *A Century of Population Growth*, by William Rossiter, that used data from the 1790 census. The earliest estimates probably overestimated the size of those of English background, as names that were Anglicized upon immigration as well as names that had no other discernible ethnic origin were assigned to the English category. A subsequent re-estimate by the American Council of Learned Societies in 1931 found that roughly 60 percent of the U.S. white population in 1790 was of English extraction, with the next largest groups being the Scottish, Irish, and Germans. The other nationalities calculated were Dutch, French, Swedish, and Spanish.

Nativity questions refer to queries about the birthplace and citizenship of respondents and, in some years, their parents. The first census year in which an individual's place of birth was recorded was 1850. In 1870, a question was introduced that established whether one's parents were foreign or native-born, although it was not until 1880 that the specific parental birthplace question appeared on the census. The parental birthplace question was subsequently dropped in the 1980 and 1990 censuses.

From 1950 to 1980, respondents were explicitly instructed to record the place in which their mother resided when they were born (as opposed to the exact location at which they were born) as their birthplace, but this instruction was dropped in 1990. Before 1900, the country was recorded simply as the response of the individual who was surveyed. Beginning with the 1900 census, the birth country was recorded as "a region whose people have direct relation with other countries." In 1940, enumerators were instructed to record the birth country as it existed in 1937—this introduced an element of comparability given shifting political boundaries that had not been present in earlier census counts.

Ancestry questions were initially included on the 1980 census. For the first time, the census captured the full extent of the self-identified European-American population. Until this time, only those who were European immigrants themselves or the sons or daughters of European immigrants were enumerated by the census; the third generation (and beyond) was simply classified as native-born whites.

In 1980, individuals could respond with as many ancestry groups as they wished; the 1990 census restricted this to a maximum of two. Hence, one can know the number of "English-German" as opposed to those who identify solely as "English" or "German." The 1990 and 2000 questions include ethnic origin in the terms of the query, and both give examples of possible responses. Additionally, those whose ethnicity is "Canadian," "Australian," and so on are often whites, although they would not be counted as "European Americans."

The detailed instructions for the ancestry question note that a religious group should *not* be reported as an ancestry group. Hence, the number of Jewish Americans must be estimated via other means. Likewise, important distinctions between, for example, Irish Catholics and Irish Protestants, are not discernible with census data.

Factors Influencing the Variability of Racial and Ethnic Identification

While the racial identification of whites by the census is more straightforward than ethnic identification, some factors can influence the number of individuals who are officially counted as *White*. One of the chief factors is the composition of the other racial categories into which one may be assigned. There has been considerable variation throughout the years in these other categories; several of these labels have implications for who is counted as *White* by the Census Bureau. The mixed-race categories, in particular, have some obvious overlap with the single race category of *White*. While mulattoes would typically have been counted as *Black* if forced into a single-race category, there are some who would perhaps be identified as *White*. *Half-breed* was included as an option on earlier censuses; this group contained those who were part American Indian, part another race. While a small overall percentage of the population, this group no doubt contained some who would be identified as *White* on later censuses without the category.

Other as an option for responding to the race question also has some implications for those who identify as white. Groups such as Arabs, Hispanics, and multiracial individuals might be identified by others as white, but would be recorded by the census as *Other*. This is a particularly important factor in the earliest administrations of the census, when write-in categories were not permitted.

The 2000 census will witness big changes with regard to the ambiguity of racial identification, as those who had previously identified with a single race may now record all of the races with which they identify. This means that some respondents who had previously identified as white will now assign themselves to two or more racial groups. Since those who had previously identified as black or Asian or any other group may do the same, it will be difficult to ascertain which of the respondents who check off *White* as one of the racial groups with which they identify have been recorded as such in previous censuses. It will also be impossible to determine whether such individuals are considered as white or as another race by the people and institutions with which they have contact.

Another factor influencing the size of the tallied white population is the method by which the census is administered. Before 1960, census takers assigned respondents to a racial category. While this presumably was subject to the input of the individuals who were enumerated, it is possible that mistakes in classification were made. From 1960 onwards, racial classification has been based upon the self-identification of individuals.

Perhaps the biggest factor in recent years to influence white racial identification in the census is the way in which *Hispanic* has been enumerated by the Census Bureau. While a separate question addressing the Hispanicity of respondents has appeared on the census, *Hispanic* has never been an option to individuals answering the race question. Throughout the years, most Hispanics have been classified as *White*, although this has been influenced both by the design of the census and the shifting nature of Hispanic ethnic consciousness.

The censuses of 1940 and 1950 explicitly instructed enumerators to classify Hispanics as *White*. An *Other* race category was added in 1910; it is not clear how many Hispanics were counted as white or as other race between 1910 and 1940. Since the addition of a separate Hispanic question in 1970, a substantial number of Hispanics have identified as white. The Census Bureau made an effort to increase the appropriate identification of Hispanics by working with community organizations in anticipation of the 1980 and 1990 censuses; this may have decreased the number of Hispanics who self-identified as whites.

Difficult as it may be to assemble accurate racial estimates from the census, the measurement of European ancestry has been subject to even greater variability throughout the history of the census. As mentioned, the initial attempt to glean ethnicity from the 1790 census counts relied upon an analysis of the ethnic origin of surnames. While this was a reasonable way of estimating the ancestry of the population given the available data, it is likely the case that numerous individuals were misclassified. The Anglicization of names, name changes due to marriage, and the ambiguous ethnicity of names such as "Miller" or "Abraham" are factors contributing to the unreliability of these estimates.

While the introduction of nativity questions to the census in 1850 was a great advance over the surname method of ascertaining ethnicity, there were nonetheless some problems with the accuracy of the responses to this question. Chief among these was the variability of the political boundaries; national entities such as "Germany" and "Poland" took many different forms throughout the nineteenth and twentieth centuries. The response of individuals to the country of birth question could depend upon their age, political beliefs, and year of immigration to the United States. While the census gave precise instructions for handling these issues in certain years, in others the respondent or enumerator was free to answer the question with no constraints.

The ancestry question from the 1980 and 1990 censuses introduces different sources of inconsistency to the estimation of the ethnicity of Americans. For the first time, self-assessment and choice play a role in the assignment of ethnic identifiers. In the 1980 census, individuals could list as many ethnic origin groups as they wished, although only the first two were tabulated by the census. The exceptions were seventeen of the most common three-ethnicity combinations; these included ancestry groups such as English-German-Irish.

The chief difficulty in assessing the size of various European ethnic groups with this method is the variation in the detail of the terminology used to describe ancestry. Some respondents refer to ethnic groups, while others refer only to the nation of origin. For example, some "Yugoslavian" respondents specified their membership in certain ethnic groups within Yugoslavia, while others did not. The same type of dilemma holds true for the Swiss respondents.

Specific groups are likely to be undercounted using this method. As mentioned, the numbers and characteristics of Jewish Americans are difficult to assess based upon the census, as no religious information is recorded, even if it is indistinguishable from the ethnicity of the group. The Scotch-Irish are another problematic group. Scotch-Irish is a distinct ethnicity representing origins in Northern Ireland, especially prevalent among those living in several South Atlantic states. However, the 1980 census recorded this group as equivalent to those who had multiple Scotch and Irish ancestries. The 1990 census corrected this problem.

Conclusion

In summary, the U.S. census has included questions identifying the race of white Americans since the first census in 1790. Factors such as the inclusion of a variable number of other racial categories as well as the instructions given to census enumerators have influenced the count of whites. European ancestry has been directly measured by the census through either nativity or ancestry questions since 1850.

See also *Appendix, Standards for the Classification of Federal Data on Race and Ethnicity.*

■ Monica McDermott

Bibliography

Alba, Richard D. *Ethnic Identity: The Transformation of White America.* New Haven: Yale University Press, 1990.

Farley, Reynolds. *The New American Reality.* New York: Russell Sage Foundation, 1996.

Lieberson, Stanley, and Mary C. Waters. *From Many Strands.* New York: Russell Sage Foundation, 1988.

Ruggles, Steven, Matthew Sobek, et al. *Integrated Public Use Microdata Series: Version 2.0.* Minneapolis: Historical Census Projects, University of Minnesota, 1997.

White population of the United States

A question about the race of respondents has been included on the census since 1790. Additional information about the ethnicity, occupational, and educational characteristics of the white population was added in subsequent censuses.

Size and Geographic Distribution

The proportional size of the white population in the United States has remained fairly constant since the first census in 1790 (see Figure 1). The first census enumerated 3,140,531 white persons, or 80.7 percent of the total population. The 1990 census counted approximately 208,727,000 white persons, which was 83.9 percent of the population. The greatest percentage of whites in the population was reached in the census years of 1930 and 1940, when 89.8 percent of the population was identified as white.

The geographic concentration of the white population has always been quite skewed given the history of slavery and immigration. The nature of this distribution has exhibited little variation over the last two hundred years relative to many other variables. The South has characteristically been the area with the lowest con-

centration of whites in terms of percentage of the population. The entry of slaves into this part of the country logically led to a greater percentage of black Americans in this area than in the rest of the country.

In the 1790 census, South Carolina and Virginia were both less than 60 percent white, while all of the New England states were over 97 percent white. By 1850, the geographic distribution had become extreme; all of the New England states were now 99 percent white, while the slave states of Louisiana, Mississippi, and South Carolina were less than half white. Only 41.1 percent of South Carolina's population was white in 1850. Numerically, New York, Pennsylvania, and Ohio had the largest white population that year.

By 1900, both Louisiana and South Carolina were approximately 41 percent white. At the other end of the spectrum, eleven states were 99 percent white, including all of the New England states. Newly added states in the Midwest and West were also predominantly white; Wisconsin, Iowa, and Minnesota had the greatest percentage of whites (outside of New England) that year. The largest numbers of whites were in New York, Pennsylvania, and Illinois.

The 1950 census indicated the smallest percentages of whites in the Deep South. Mississippi now had the lowest white percentage (54.6 percent), although none of the Southern states any longer had a minority white population.

The 1990 census provided similar results, although Hawaii is now the state with the lowest proportion of its population white—33.4 percent (most of its residents are Asian). California, New York, and Maryland are comparable to the states of the Deep South in their relatively low percentage of whites—California and South Carolina have equivalent results (69 percent white). The upper New England states (New Hampshire, Vermont, and Maine) still have the highest percentage of whites, although Massachusetts and Connecticut are now both less than 90 percent white. California, New York, and Texas have the largest white population in terms of numbers.

Intermarriage rates can affect the overall size of the white population. Throughout most of the history of the United States, intermarriage rates have been quite low. However, recent censuses have witnessed nonnegligible intermarriage rates; 1.8 percent in 1980 and 3 percent in 1990. If this trend continues, it can be expected to have an impact upon the overall size of the white population as these couples have children who may or may not be considered "white."

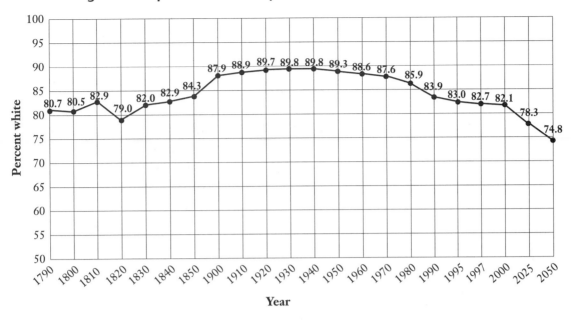

Figure 1. Proportion of U.S. Population That Is White, 1790–2050

Immigration and Ethnicity

The entire white population of the United States is composed of either immigrants or the descendants of immigrants. Throughout the nineteenth century, almost 90 percent of all immigrants were of European origin. The chief area of the world for white immigrants has been Europe, although Canada, Australia, and parts of Central and South America have also contributed to the white population. The numbers and sources of immigrants have a considerable impact upon the size of the white population. In the wake of decades of sizable migrations from Europe, the white population was at its highest level of almost 90 percent in 1930 and 1940. However, recent shifts in the countries of origin of most immigrants have led to a decline in the proportion of the U.S. population that is white.

While the first census in 1790 did not directly ask about ethnicity or birthplace, census recalculations in the early twentieth century based on the surnames of enumerated individuals found an overwhelming concentration of English origin—more than 80 percent. Subsequent recalculations of the same data using different methods found a more modest yet still sizable proportion of English-Americans, over 60 percent. Only Pennsylvania, with a population that was one-third German, had fewer than half of its residents of English extraction. New York and New Jersey both had sizable Dutch populations.

The introduction of the birthplace question in 1850 has led to more precise estimates of the ethnic composition of the U.S. white population. In 1850, over 92 percent of the foreign-born population was from Europe; by 1990, that number had declined to 22.9 percent. In 1998, only 8.6 percent of the U.S. white population was foreign-born, down from a high of 16.6 percent in 1910. Until the late nineteenth century, most immigrants were from northern and western Europe. Between 1880 and 1930, southern and eastern Europe came to lead immigration to the United States. Immigration from Europe has fallen off dramatically since the passage of the 1965 immigration law that enabled Asian and Latin American countries to send more of their numbers to the United States. While 99.8 percent of the U.S. foreign-born population was white in 1850, this number had fallen to an all-time low of 50.7 percent in the 1990 census.

The introduction of ancestry questions in the 1980 census gives the clearest picture yet of the ethnic distribution of the white population. In 1980, English and German predominated as the ancestries of the greatest number of Americans, with each ancestry being claimed by about one-quarter of Americans. The Irish were also a sizable group, with 21 percent claiming Irish ancestry.

French, Italian, and Scottish were each claimed by more than 5 percent of the individuals counted. In the 1990 census, English slipped to being the third-most-popular ancestry group, with German and Irish being the first and second, respectively.

Demographic Characteristics

Native-born whites are the oldest of any group in America. With a median age of thirty-five, the age distribution of whites is vastly different from that for native-born Hispanics or Asians, both of whom have median ages of eighteen. About 60 percent of white Americans age 18-64 live in husband-wife families; another 20 percent live alone. The large percentage of whites living alone is rivaled only by Asians; it is likely due to the large number of both groups enrolled in post-graduate education.

Native-born whites also stand out as having extremely low fertility rates. The number of lifetime births for white women is 1.76 (compared with 3.02 for Hispanic women; Farley, 1996). According to the 1990 census, 24 percent of married white women between the ages of 25 and 34 are childless; only Asians have a higher rate. The average number of children for these women was 1.5. Amongst never-married women in this age group, a full 87 percent of white women have never had a child. This compares with rates of 40 percent for black women and 58 percent for native-born Hispanic women.

Employment and Income

Whites have always had lower levels of unemployment than other races; this continues to be the case today. The unemployment rate for the U.S. white male population has hovered around 4 percent since 1960, with sharp spikes during the recessions of the mid-1970s and mid-1980s. The unemployment rate for white women has been closer to 6 percent, although the unemployment figures for 1990 indicate that white women have a slightly lower rate (4.0 percent) than white men (4.2 percent). Similarly, white men work more hours per year than any other group. In 1989, the average white man worked 2,172 hours, while the average white woman worked 1,683 hours—a relatively low figure.

The results of the 1990 census indicate that approximately 19 million white Americans live in poverty (9.5 percent of the total white population). This compares favorably with the U.S. poverty rate, which in 1990 was 12.8 percent. According to the 1990 census, the per capita income for the population as a whole was $14,420 in 1989; for whites, the figure was $15,687.

Future Projections

The white population is expected to decline as a proportion of the overall U.S. population. The Census Bureau projects that whites will be only 75 percent of the population by 2050. Fertility rates, age distribution, and immigration rates contribute to the declining proportion of whites (U.S. Bureau of the Census, 1996). Since the current white population has a low fertility rate, has a high median age relative to other groups, and is a declining percentage of immigrants to this country, non-Hispanic whites are projected to experience the greatest relative decline during the next fifty years. The decline is only in terms of proportion of the total population; the actual count of the U.S. white population is expected to steadily increase.

See also *Appendix, Standards for the Classification of Federal Data on Race and Ethnicity.*

■ Monica McDermott

Bibliography

Farley, Reynolds. *The New American Reality.* New York: Russell Sage Foundation, 1996.

Kivisto, Peter. *Americans All.* Belmont, California: Wadsworth Publishing Co., 1995.

Lieberson, Stanley, and Mary C. Waters. *From Many Strands.* New York: Russell Sage Foundation, 1988.

U.S. Bureau of the Census. "Population Projections of the United States by Age, Sex, Race, and Hispanic Origin: 1995 to 2050." *Current Population Report*, Feb. 1996.

Women in the decennial census

Since it was first taken in 1790, the decennial census has included information on the sex distribution of the population, and hence on the situation of women. Censuses from 1790 to 1840 gathered information on the number of people in households by sex and by age. The original census recorded the number of people per household who were free (white males age sixteen years and over, white males under age sixteen years, white females, and all other free people) and slaves. Although the age and racial categories changed, the census schedules for 1800 through 1840 contained similar household counts. In 1850 the census began recording the characteristics of individuals living in each household. Since then, data on sex have been collected separately from age or race.

In Census 2000, respondents were asked the following question for every household member: "What is this person's sex? Mark One Box. Male/Female." Because data are collected by sex, analyses can differentiate responses and determine, for example, the difference between personal income levels of women and men. Numerous social and economic characteristics of women can be examined, including age, race, Hispanic or Latino origin, educational level, occupation, income, family type, and poverty status. Responses to Census 2000 questions can be compared to previous census data to examine how women's characteristics have changed over time.

Historical analyses of women's lives are restricted, however, by three census enumeration procedures. First, for much of U.S. history, less information was collected about women than about men. For example, from 1790 to 1840, only the name of the household head was listed on the census form. Since women were considered dependents of men, as relatives or servants, it is rare to find women's names in censuses before 1850. Similarly, in 1790, free white males were divided into two age cohorts of under age sixteen years and age sixteen years and over, but no age breakdowns were available for the free white female population. An individual-level question on occupation was asked of males from 1850 onward; for females the question was first asked in 1860, and information on housekeeping duties, the most common occupation for women in the past, was not tabulated for wives, daughters, or other relations to the household head. Second, relationship to household head was not recorded for family members until 1880. Third, until 1980, women were never classified as heads of household in married couple families, if the husband was present. Although these limitations restrict certain analyses, they do not affect examination of women's lives from the 1980 census to the present.

Many federal agencies, including the Departments of Commerce, Education, Labor, and Justice, use decennial census information on women. Numerous federal statutes require the Census Bureau to collect information on sex in order to implement or evaluate social programs. Community planners at both the state and local levels also use census data, broken down by sex, to evaluate future needs for child care, education, and employment. At all levels of government, this information is used for equal opportunity purposes for women specified by civil rights acts.

Overall, the decennial census is one of the most important sources of information on the situation of American women, both in the past and today. Since the sex distribution of the U.S. population is generally close to 50 percent male and 50 percent female, the analysis of sex distributions is of interest when the patterns diverge from the norm. Such divergence is found in analyses of the greater number of widows than widowers, or when women appear to be behaving in ways that challenge traditional or so-called "appropriate" sex roles, for example, when women combine the roles of employed worker and wife and mother. For most of U.S. history, women's "appropriate" sphere was in the home; as a result, data tabulations and analyses focused on those roles, reporting for example, patterns of fertility. The census has been used to document women in nontraditional roles, particularly in the past generation as women have joined the labor force in large numbers even while raising small children.

Finally, the changing status of women over the centuries can be seen in the administration of the census itself. The census office began to employ women as enumerators and clerks to process census data in the late nineteenth century. In 1989, Barbara Everitt Bryant became the first woman to be appointed director of the Census Bureau, and she was succeeded by Martha Farnsworth Riche as director in 1994.

■ Gretchen A. Stiers

Bibliography

Bianchi, Suzanne, and Daphne Spain. *American Women in Transition.* New York: Russell Sage Foundation, 1986.

Spain, Daphne, and Suzanne Bianchi. *Balancing Act: Motherhood, Marriage, and Employment Among American Women.* New York: Russell Sage Foundation, 1996.

U.S. Bureau of the Census. *General Population Characteristics: Part I, United States Summary.* Washington, D.C.: Government Printing Office, 1983.

U.S. Bureau of the Census. *Planning for Census 2000: Questions Planned for Census 2000, Federal Legislative and Program Uses.* Washington, D.C.: Government Printing Office, 1998.

U.S. Bureau of the Census. *Twenty Censuses: Population and Housing Questions, 1790–1980.* Washington, D.C.: Government Printing Office, 1978.

Wright, Carroll D. *The History and Growth of the United States Census.* Washington, D.C.: Government Printing Office, 1900.

Appendix

Census Leadership, 1850–2000   374

U.S. Population and Area, 1790–2000   375

Center of Population, 1790–1990   376

Congressional Apportionment, 1789–1990   378

Percentage of the House of Representatives for Each State After Each
    Apportionment   379

Methods of Congressional Apportionment   381

Chronology of the States of the Union   382

Growth of the Decennial Census, 1790–1990   383

Cost of Taking the Census, 1790–2000   384

Census 2000 Questionnaires: Short and Long Forms   385

Standards for the Classification of Federal Data on Race and Ethnicity   400

Census on the Internet   403

Glossary   406

Census Leadership, 1850–2000

Superintendents of the Census Office, Department of Interior, 1850–1902

Joseph Camp Griffith Kennedy	1850–1853, 1858–1865
James D. B. DeBow	1853–1855
Francis Amasa Walker	1869–1871, 1879–1881
Charles W. Seaton	1881–1885
Robert Porter	1889–1893
William Rush Merriam	1899–1902

Directors of the Bureau of the Census, 1902–2000

Department of the Interior (1902–1903)

William Rush Merriam	1902–

Department of Commerce and Labor (1903–1913)

William Rush Merriam	–1903
Simon Newton Dexter North	1903–1909
Edward Dana Durand	1909–1913

Department of Commerce (March 1913 to date)

William Julius Harris	1913–1915
Sam Lyle Rogers	1915–1921
William Mott Steuart	1921–1933
William Lane Austin	1933–1941
Vergil Daniel Reed (acting)	Feb. 1941–May 1941
James Clyde Capt	1941–1949
Philip Morris Hauser (acting)	Aug. 1949–March 1950
Roy Victor Peel	1950–1953
Robert Wilbur Burgess	1953–1961
Albert Ross Eckler (acting)	March 1961–May 1961
Richard Montgomery Scammon	1961–1965
Albert Ross Eckler	1965–1969
George Hay Brown	Sept. 1969–1973
Vincent P. Barabba	1973–1976, 1979–1981
Robert L. Hagan (acting)	1976–1977, 1979
Manuel D. Plotkin	1977–1979
Daniel B. Levine (acting)	1979, 1981
Bruce K. Chapman	1981–1983
C. Louis Kincannon (acting)	1983, 1989
John C. Keane	1983–1989
Barbara Everitt Bryant	1989–1992
Harry Scarr (acting)	1993–1994
Martha Farnsworth Riche	1994–1998
James Holmes (acting)	1998
Kenneth Prewitt	1998–

U.S. Population and Area, 1790–2000

| Census date | Resident population | | | | Area (square miles) | | |
| | Number | Per square mile of land area | Increase over preceding census | | Total | Land | Water |
			Number	Percent			
1790 (Aug. 2)	3,929,214	4.5	NA	NA	891,364	864,746	24,065
1800 (Aug. 4)	5,308,483	6.1	1,379,269	35.1	891,364	864,746	24,065
1810 (Aug. 6)	7,239,881	4.3	1,931,398	36.4	1,722,685	1,681,828	34,175
1820 (Aug. 7)	9,638,453	5.5	2,398,572	33.1	1,792,552	1,749,462	38,544
1830 (Jun. 1)	12,866,020	7.4	3,227,567	33.5	1,792,552	1,749,462	38,544
1840 (Jun. 1)	17,069,453	9.8	4,203,433	32.7	1,792,552	1,749,462	38,544
1850 (Jun. 1)	23,191,876	7.9	6,122,423	35.9	2,991,655	2,940,042	52,705
1860 (Jun. 1)	31,443,321	10.6	8,251,445	35.6	3,021,295	2,969,640	52,747
1870 (Jun. 1)[1]	39,818,449[1]	13.4	8,375,128	26.6	3,021,295	2,969,640	52,747
1880 (Jun. 1)	50,155,783	16.9	10,337,334	26.0	3,021,295	2,969,640	52,747
1890 (Jun. 1)	62,947,714	21.2	12,791,931	25.5	3,021,295	2,969,640	52,747
1900 (Jun. 1)	75,994,575	25.6	13,046,861	20.7	3,021,295	2,969,834	52,553
1910 (Apr. 15)	91,972,266	31.0	15,977,691	21.0	3,021,295	2,969,565	52,822
1920 (Jan. 1)	105,710,620	35.6	13,738,354	14.9	3,021,295	2,969,451	52,936
1930 (Apr. 1)	122,775,046	41.2	17,064,426	16.1	3,021,295	2,977,128	45,259
1940 (Apr. 1)	131,669,275	44.2	8,894,229	7.2	3,021,295	2,977,128	45,259
1950 (Apr. 1)[2]	151,325,798	42.6	19,161,229	14.5	3,618,770	3,552,206	63,005
1960 (Apr. 1)	179,323,175	50.6	27,997,377	18.5	3,618,770	3,540,911	74,212
1970 (Apr. 1)[3]	203,302,031[3]	57.4	23,978,856	13.4	3,618,770[3]	3,540,023[3]	78,444
1980 (Apr. 1)[4]	226,542,199[4]	64.0	23,240,168	11.4	3,618,770	3,539,289	79,481
1990 (Apr. 1)[5]	248,718,291[5]	70.3	22,176,092	9.8[6]	3,717,796[6]	3,536,278[6]	181,518[7]
2000 (Apr. 1)[8]	275,000,000	—	—	—	—	—	—

Notes: Area figures represent area on indicated date including in some cases considerable areas not then organized or settled, and not covered by the census. Total area figures for 1790 to 1970 have been recalculated on the basis of the remeasurement of states and counties for the 1980 census, but not on the basis of the 1990 census. The land and water area figures for past censuses have not been adjusted and are not strictly comparable with the total area data for comparable dates because the land areas were derived from different base data, and these values are known to have changed with the construction of reservoirs, draining of lakes, and so on. Density figures are based on land area measurements as reported in earlier censuses.

NA = Not applicable

[1] Revised to include adjustments for underenumeration in southern states; unrevised number is 38,558,371 (13.0 per square mile).

[2] Figures for 1950 and following years include populations of Alaska and Hawaii.

[3] Figures corrected after 1970 final reports were issued.

[4] Total population count has been revised since the 1980 census publications. Numbers by age, race, Hispanic origin, and sex have not been corrected.

[5] The April 1, 1990, census count includes count resolution corrections processed through March 1994, and does not include adjustments for census coverage errors.

[6] Data reflect corrections made after publication of the results.

[7] Comprises Great Lakes, inland, and coastal water. Data for prior years cover inland water only.

[8] Population figure for 2000 is an estimate.

Source: U.S. Bureau of the Census, *Statistical Abstract of the United States: 1999* (Washington, D.C.: U.S. Government Printing Office, 1999), 8.

Center of Population, 1790–1990

Mean Center of Population, 1790–1990

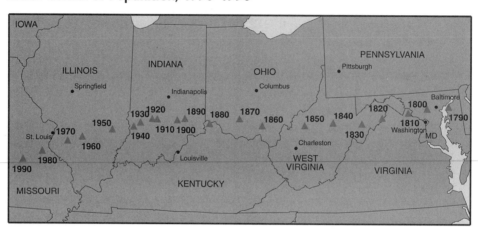

Median Center of Population, 1880–1990

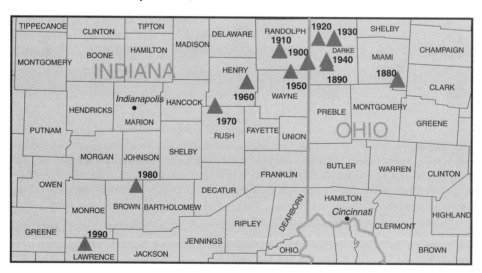

	Median center		Mean center		
Year	**North latitude**	**Longitude**	**North latitude**	**West longitude**	**Approximate location**
1790 (August 2)	NA	NA	39 16 30	76 11 12	In Kent County, Md., 23 mi. east of Baltimore, Md.
1850 (June 1)	NA	NA	38 59 00	81 19 00	In Wirt County, W.Va., 23 mi. southeast of Parkersburg, W.Va.[1]
1900 (June 1)	40 03 32	84 49 01	39 09 36	85 48 54	In Bartholomew County, Ind., 6 mi. southeast of Columbus, Ind.
1950 (April 1)	40 00 12	84 56 51	38 50 21	88 09 33	In Richland County, Ill., 8 mi. north-northwest of Olney, Ill.
1960 (April 1)	39 56 25	85 16 60	38 35 58	89 12 35	In Clinton County, Ill., 6.5 mi. northwest of Centralia, Ill.
1970 (April 1)	39 47 43	85 31 43	38 27 47	89 42 22	In St. Clair County, Ill., 5.3 mi. east-southeast of Mascoutah, Ill.
1980 (April 1)	39 18 60	86 08 15	38 08 13	90 34 26	In Jefferson County, Mo., 0.25 mi. west of DeSoto, Mo.
1990 (April 1)	38 57 55	86 31 53	37 52 20	91 12 55	In Crawford County, Mo., 10 mi. southeast of Steelville, Mo.

Notes: Before 1960, calculations exclude Alaska and Hawaii. The *median center of population* is located at the intersection of two median lines, a north-south line constructed so that half of the nation's population lives east and half lives west of it, and an east-west line selected so that half of the nation's population lives north and half lives south of it. The *mean center of population* is that point at which an imaginary, flat, weightless, and rigid map of the United States would balance if weights of identical value were placed on it so that each weight represented the location of one person on the date of the census. The maps and table illustrate the population's westward migration since 1790.

NA = not available.

[1] West Virginia was set off from Virginia on December 31, 1862, and was admitted as a state on June 19, 1863.

Source: U.S. Bureau of the Census, *Statistical Abstract of the United States: 1999* (Washington, D.C.: U.S. Government Printing Office).

Congressional Apportionment, 1789–1990

Year of Census[a]

	Constitution[b] (1789)	1790	1800	1810	1820	1830	1840	1850	1860	1870	1880	1890	1900	1910	1930[c]	1940	1950	1960	1970	1980	1990
Ala.				1[d]	3	5	7	7	6	8	8	9	9	10	9	9	9	8	7	7	7
Alaska																	1[d]	1	1	1	1
Ariz.														1[d]	1	2	2	3	4	5	6
Ark.						1[d]	1	2	3	4	5	6	7	7	7	7	6	4	4	4	4
Calif.							2[d]	2	3	4	6	7	8	11	20	23	30	38	43	45	52
Colo.										1[d]	1	2	3	4	4	4	4	4	5	6	6
Conn.	5	7	7	7	6	6	4	4	4	4	4	4	5	5	6	6	6	6	6	6	6
Del.	1	1	1	2	1	1	1	1	1	1	1	1	1	1	1	1	1	1	1	1	1
Fla.							1[d]	1	1	2	2	2	3	4	5	6	8	12	15	19	23
Ga.	3	2	4	6	7	9	8	8	7	9	10	11	11	12	10	10	10	10	10	10	11
Hawaii																	1[d]	2	2	2	2
Idaho												1[d]	1	1	2	2	2	2	2	2	2
Ill.				1[d]	1	3	7	9	14	19	20	22	25	27	27	26	25	24	24	22	20
Ind.				1[d]	3	7	10	11	11	13	13	13	13	13	12	11	11	11	11	10	10
Iowa							2[d]	2	6	9	11	11	11	11	9	8	8	7	6	6	5
Kan.									1	3	7	8	8	8	7	6	6	5	5	5	4
Ky.		2	6	10	12	13	10	10	9	10	11	11	11	11	9	9	8	7	7	7	6
La.				1[d]	3	3	4	4	5	6	6	6	7	8	8	8	8	8	8	8	7
Maine				7[d]	7	8	7	6	5	5	4	4	4	4	3	3	3	2	2	2	2
Md.	6	8	9	9	9	8	6	6	5	6	6	6	6	6	6	6	7	8	8	8	8
Mass.	8	14	17	13[e]	13	12	10	11	10	11	12	13	14	16	15	14	14	12	12	11	10
Mich.						1[d]	3	4	6	9	11	12	12	13	17	17	18	19	19	18	16
Minn.								2[d]	2	3	5	7	9	10	9	9	9	8	8	8	8
Miss.				1[d]	1	2	4	5	5	6	7	7	8	8	7	7	6	5	5	5	5
Mo.					1	2	5	7	9	13	14	15	16	16	13	13	11	10	10	9	9
Mont.												1[d]	1	1	2	2	2	2	2	2	1
Neb.									1[d]	1	3	6	6	6	5	4	4	3	3	3	3
Nev.									1[d]	1	1	1	1	1	1	1	1	1	1	2	2
N.H.	3	4	5	6	6	5	4	3	3	3	2	2	2	2	2	2	2	2	2	2	2
N.J.	4	5	6	6	6	6	5	5	5	7	7	8	10	12	14	14	14	15	15	14	13
N.M.														1[d]	1	2	2	2	2	3	3
N.Y.	6	10	17	27	34	40	34	33	31	33	34	34	37	43	45	45	43	41	39	34	31
N.C.	5	10	12	13	13	13	9	8	7	8	9	9	10	10	11	12	12	11	11	11	12
N.D.												1[d]	1	2	3	2	2	2	2	1	1
Ohio			1[d]	6	14	19	21	21	19	20	21	21	21	22	24	23	23	24	23	21	19
Okla.													5[d]	8	9	8	6	6	6	6	6
Ore.								1[d]	1	1	1	2	2	3	3	4	4	4	4	5	5
Pa.	8	13	18	23	26	28	24	25	24	27	28	30	32	36	34	33	30	27	25	23	21
R.I.	1	2	2	2	2	2	2	2	2	2	2	2	2	3	2	2	2	2	2	2	2
S.C.	5	6	8	9	9	9	7	6	4	5	7	7	7	7	6	6	6	6	6	6	6
S.D.												2[d]	2	2	3	2	2	2	2	1	1
Tenn.		1	3	6	9	13	11	10	8	10	10	10	10	10	9	10	9	9	8	9	9
Texas							2[d]	2	4	6	11	13	16	18	21	21	22	23	24	27	30
Utah												1[d]	1	2	2	2	2	2	2	3	3
Vt.		2	4	6	5	5	4	3	3	3	2	2	2	2	1	1	1	1	1	1	1
Va.	10	19	22	23	22	21	15	13	11	9	10	10	10	10	9	9	10	10	10	10	11
Wash.											1[d]	2	3	5	6	6	7	7	7	8	9
W.Va.										3	4	4	5	6	6	6	6	5	4	4	3
Wis.							2[d]	3	6	8	9	10	11	11	10	10	10	10	9	9	9
Wyo.												1[d]	1	1	1	1	1	1	1	1	1
Total	65	106	142	186	213	242	232	237	243	293	332	357	391	435	435	435	437[f]	435	435	435	435

Sources: Biographical Directory of the American Congress and Bureau of the Census.

a. Apportionment effective with congressional election two years after census.

b. Original apportionment made in Constitution, pending first census.

c. No apportionment was made in 1920.

d. These figures are not based on any census, but indicate the provisional representation accorded newly admitted states by Congress, pending the next census.

e. Twenty members were assigned to Massachusetts, but seven of these were credited to Maine when that area became a state.

f. Normally 435, but temporarily increased two seats by Congress when Alaska and Hawaii became states.

Percentage of the House of Representatives for Each State After Each Appointment

Census Apportionment

States	1790	1800	1810	1820	1830	1840	1850	1860	1870	1880	1890	1900	1910	1930	1940	1950	1960	1970	1980	1990
Alabama				1.4	2.1	3.1	3.0	2.5	2.7	2.5	2.5	2.3	2.3	2.1	2.1	2.1	1.8	1.6	1.6	1.6
Alaska[a]																	0.2	0.2	0.2	0.2
Arizona													0.2	0.2	0.5	0.5	0.7	0.9	1.1	1.4
Arkansas						0.4	0.9	1.2	1.4	1.5	1.7	1.8	1.6	1.6	1.6	1.4	0.9	0.9	0.9	0.9
California							0.9	1.2	1.4	1.8	2.0	2.1	2.5	4.6	5.3	6.9	8.7	9.9	10.3	12.0
Colorado										0.3	0.6	0.8	0.9	0.9	0.9	0.9	0.9	1.1	1.4	1.4
Connecticut	6.7	5.0	3.9	2.8	2.5	1.8	1.7	1.7	1.4	1.2	1.1	1.3	1.1	1.4	1.4	1.4	1.4	1.4	1.4	1.4
Delaware	1.0	0.7		0.5	0.4	0.4	0.4	0.4	0.3	0.3	0.3	0.3	0.2	0.2	0.2	0.2	0.2	0.2	0.2	0.2
Florida							0.4	0.4	0.7	0.6	0.6	0.8	0.9	1.1	1.4	1.8	2.8	3.4	4.4	5.3
Georgia	1.9	2.8	3.3	3.3	3.8	3.6	3.4	2.9	3.1	3.1	3.1	2.8	2.8	2.3	2.3	2.3	2.3	2.3	2.3	2.5
Hawaii[a]																	0.5	0.5	0.5	0.5
Idaho											0.3	0.3	0.5	0.5	0.5	0.5	0.5	0.5	0.5	0.5
Illinois				0.5	1.3	3.1	3.8	5.8	6.5	6.2	6.2	6.5	6.2	6.2	6.0	5.7	5.5	5.5	5.1	4.6
Indiana				1.4	2.9	4.5	4.7	4.6	4.5	4.0	3.7	3.4	3.0	2.8	2.5	2.5	2.5	2.5	2.3	2.3
Iowa							0.9	2.5	3.1	3.4	3.1	2.8	2.5	2.1	1.8	1.8	1.6	1.4	1.4	1.1
Kansas								0.4	1.0	2.2	2.2	2.1	1.8	1.6	1.4	1.4	1.1	1.1	1.1	0.9
Kentucky	1.9	4.3	5.5	5.6	5.4	4.5	4.3	3.7	3.4	3.4	3.1	2.8	2.5	2.1	2.1	1.8	1.6	1.6	1.6	1.4
Louisiana				1.4	1.3	1.8	1.7	2.1	2.1	1.8	1.7	1.8	1.8	1.8	1.8	1.8	1.8	1.8	1.8	1.6
Maine				3.3	3.3	3.1	2.6	2.1	1.7	1.2	1.1	1.0	0.9	0.7	0.7	0.7	0.5	0.5	0.5	0.5
Maryland	7.6	6.4	5.0	4.2	3.3	2.7	2.6	2.1	2.1	1.8	1.7	1.6	1.4	1.4	1.4	1.6	1.8	1.8	1.8	1.8
Massachusetts	13.3	12.1	11.0	6.1	5.0	4.5	4.7	4.1	3.8	3.7	3.7	3.6	3.7	3.4	3.2	3.2	2.8	2.8	2.5	2.3
Michigan						1.3	1.7	2.5	3.1	3.4	3.4	3.1	3.0	3.9	3.9	4.1	4.4	4.4	4.1	3.7
Minnesota								0.8	1.0	1.5	2.0	2.3	2.3	2.1	2.1	2.1	1.8	1.8	1.8	1.8
Mississippi				0.5	0.8	1.8	2.1	2.1	2.1	2.2	2.0	2.1	1.8	1.6	1.6	1.4	1.1	1.1	1.1	1.1
Missouri				0.5	0.8	2.2	3.0	3.7	4.5	4.3	4.2	4.1	3.7	3.0	3.0	2.5	2.3	2.3	2.1	2.1
Montana											0.3	0.3	0.5	0.5	0.5	0.5	0.5	0.5	0.5	0.2
Nebraska									0.3	0.9	1.7	1.6	1.4	1.1	0.9	0.9	0.7	0.7	0.7	0.7

Percent of House ■ Peak Representation ■ Lowest Representation

[a] Alaska and Hawaii retained the same percentage since their first census apportionment in 1960.

continued

Percentage of the House of Representatives for Each State After Each Appointment *continued*

Census Apportionment

States	1790	1800	1810	1820	1830	1840	1850	1860	1870	1880	1890	1900	1910	1930	1940	1950	1960	1970	1980	1990
Nevada									0.3	0.3	0.3	0.3	0.2	0.2	0.2	0.2	0.2	0.2	0.5	0.5
New Hampshire	3.8	3.5	3.3	2.8	2.1	1.8	1.3	1.2	1.0	0.6	0.6	0.5	0.5	0.5	0.5	0.5	0.5	0.5	0.5	0.5
New Jersey	4.8	4.3	3.3	2.8	2.5	2.2	2.1	2.1	2.4	2.2	2.2	2.6	2.8	3.2	3.2	3.2	3.4	3.4	3.2	3.0
New Mexico													0.2	0.2	0.5	0.5	0.5	0.5	0.7	0.7
New York	9.5	12.1	14.9	16.0	16.7	15.2	14.1	12.9	11.3	10.5	9.6	9.6	9.9	10.3	10.3	9.9	9.4	9.0	7.8	7.1
North Carolina	9.5	8.5	7.2	6.1	5.4	4.0	3.4	2.9	2.7	2.8	2.5	2.6	2.3	2.5	2.8	2.8	2.5	2.5	2.5	2.8
North Dakota											0.3	0.5	0.7	0.5	0.5	0.5	0.5	0.2	0.2	0.2
Ohio			3.3	6.6	7.9	9.4	9.0	7.9	6.8	6.5	5.9	5.4	5.1	5.5	5.3	5.3	5.5	5.3	4.8	4.4
Oklahoma													1.8	2.1	1.8	1.4	1.4	1.4	1.4	1.4
Oregon								0.4	0.3	0.3	0.6	0.5	0.7	0.7	0.9	0.9	0.9	0.9	1.1	1.1
Pennsylvania	12.4	12.8	12.7	12.2	11.7	10.8	10.7	10.0	9.2	8.6	8.4	8.3	8.3	7.8	7.6	6.9	6.2	5.7	5.3	4.8
Rhode Island	1.9	1.4	1.1	0.9	0.8	0.9	0.9	0.8	0.7	0.6	0.6	0.5	0.7	0.5	0.5	0.5	0.5	0.5	0.5	0.5
South Carolina	5.7	5.7	5.0	4.2	3.8	3.1	2.6	1.7	1.7	2.2	2.0	1.8	1.6	1.4	1.4	1.4	1.4	1.4	1.4	1.4
South Dakota											0.6	0.5	0.7	0.5	0.5	0.5	0.5	0.5	0.2	0.2
Tennessee		2.1	3.3	4.2	5.4	4.9	4.3	3.3	3.4	3.1	2.8	2.6	2.3	2.1	2.3	2.1	2.1	1.8	2.1	2.1
Texas							0.9	1.7	2.1	3.4	3.7	4.1	4.1	4.8	4.8	5.1	5.3	5.5	6.2	6.9
Utah												0.3	0.5	0.5	0.5	0.5	0.5	0.5	0.7	0.7
Vermont	1.9	2.8	3.3	2.3	2.1	1.8	1.3	1.2	1.0	0.6	0.6	0.5	0.5	0.2	0.2	0.2	0.2	0.2	0.2	0.2
Virginia	18.1	15.6	12.7	10.3	8.8	6.7	5.6	4.6	3.1	3.1	2.8	2.6	2.3	2.1	2.1	2.3	2.3	2.3	2.3	2.5
Washington											0.6	0.8	1.1	1.4	1.4	1.6	1.6	1.6	1.8	2.1
West Virginia									1.0	1.2	1.1	1.3	1.4	1.4	1.4	1.4	1.1	0.9	0.9	0.7
Wisconsin							1.3	2.5	2.7	2.8	2.8	2.8	2.5	2.3	2.3	2.3	2.3	2.1	2.1	2.1
Wyoming											0.3	0.3	0.2	0.2	0.2	0.2	0.2	0.2	0.2	0.2
Number of states at peak percentage	9	1	2	2	3	2	1	1	2	4	2	3	5	1	0	0	1	0	5	5
Number of states at lowest percentage	1	0	1	5	1	2	6	2	2	1	3	2	7	3	0	1	1	2	1	6
Total number of states at peak and lowest	10	1	3	7	4	4	7	3	4	5	5	5	12	4	0	1	2	2	6	11

Percent of House: ◼ Peak Representation ▢ Lowest Representation

Methods of Congressional Apportionment

All methods of apportionment require determining the population total and setting the size of the body. The U.S. House of Representatives currently has 435 members. The Constitution requires all states to receive at least one seat; therefore, 385 seats must be apportioned after each of the fifty states receives one. Because it is practically impossible to divide 385 into the total population and come up with integer results for all fifty states, each method must set a rule for treating fractions or remainders. What should be done if a state deserves 3.6, 4.2, or 43.7 representatives? Each of the four methods explained below provides an answer.

Thomas Jefferson's method. Find a number, a divisor, that will produce quotients for all the states that sum to the required total for the body. Disregard any fractions.

Alexander Hamilton's method. Calculate the proportion of each state's population of the total population to find its "quota" of seats. Give each state its quota in whole numbers, disregarding the fractions. If the allocation does not sum to the total, give the states with the largest remainders additional seats until all the seats have been allocated.

Daniel Webster's method. Find a number, a divisor, that will produce quotients for all the states that sum to the required total for the body, when fractions greater than 0.5 are rounded up, and fractions less than 0.5 are rounded down.

Joseph Hill's method. Find a number, a divisor, that will produce quotients for all the states that will minimize the relative difference in constituency size between any two states. In practice, Hill's method rounds a fraction up as it exceeds the geometric mean of the two integers (for example, the geometric mean of 1 and 2 is 1.41, compared with the arithmetic mean of 1.5).

Notes: For some years (for example, 1850-1900 and 1930) the same apportionment would have resulted from two different methods. Congress did not reapportion itself after the 1920 census. There are many other possible apportionment methods. For more information, see the entry *Apportionment and districting* in this encyclopedia. See also Michel Balinski and H. Peyton Young, *Fair Representation: Meeting the Ideal of One Man, One Vote* (New Haven: Yale University Press, 1982).

Chronology of the States of the Union

State	Date admitted to Union	State	Date admitted to Union
1. Delaware	Dec. 7, 1787	28. Texas	Dec. 29, 1845
2. Pennsylvania	Dec. 12, 1787	29. Iowa	Dec. 28, 1846
3. New Jersey	Dec. 18, 1787	30. Wisconsin	May 29, 1848
4. Georgia	Jan. 2, 1788	31. California	Sept. 9, 1850
5. Connecticut	Jan. 9, 1788	32. Minnesota	May 11, 1858
6. Massachusetts	Feb. 6, 1788	33. Oregon	Feb. 14, 1859
7. Maryland	Apr. 28, 1788	34. Kansas	Jan. 29, 1861
8. South Carolina	May 23, 1788	35. West Virginia	June 20, 1863
9. New Hampshire	June 21, 1788	36. Nevada	Oct. 31, 1864
10. Virginia	June 25, 1788	37. Nebraska	Mar. 1, 1867
11. New York	July 26, 1788	38. Colorado	Aug. 1, 1876
12. North Carolina	Nov. 21, 1789	39. North Dakota	Nov. 2, 1889
13. Rhode Island	May 29, 1790	40. South Dakota	Nov. 2, 1889
14. Vermont	Mar. 4, 1791	41. Montana	Nov. 8, 1889
15. Kentucky	June 1, 1792	42. Washington	Nov. 11, 1889
16. Tennessee	June 1, 1796	43. Idaho	July 3, 1890
17. Ohio	Mar. 1, 1803	44. Wyoming	July 10, 1890
18. Louisiana	Apr. 30, 1812	45. Utah	Jan. 4, 1896
19. Indiana	Dec. 11, 1816	46. Oklahoma	Nov. 16, 1907
20. Mississippi	Dec. 10, 1817	47. New Mexico	Jan. 6, 1912
21. Illinois	Dec. 3, 1818	48. Arizona	Feb. 14, 1912
22. Alabama	Dec. 14, 1819	49. Alaska	Jan. 3, 1959
23. Maine	Mar. 15, 1820	50. Hawaii	Aug. 29, 1959
24. Missouri	Aug. 10, 1821		
25. Arkansas	June 15, 1836		
26. Michigan	Jan. 26, 1837		
27. Florida	Mar. 3, 1845		

Source: Encyclopedia of American History: Bicentennial Edition (New York: Harper & Row, 1976), 616.

Growth of the Decennial Census, 1790–1990

Census year	Total U.S. population (millions)	Number of enumerators[a]	Maximum size of office force	Total pages in published reports	Total cost (thousands of dollars)	Cost per capita (cents)
1790	3.9	650[b]	[c]	56	44	1.1
1800	5.3	900[b]	[c]	74	66	1.2
1810	7.2	1,100[b]	[c]	469	178	2.4
1820	9.6	1,188	[d]	288	208	2.1
1830	12.9	1,519	43	214.	378	2.9
1840	17.1	2,167	28	1,465	833	4.8
1850	23.2	3,231	160	2,165	1,423	6.1
1860	31.4	4,417	184	3,189	1,969	6.3
1870	39.8[e]	6,530	438	3,473	3,421	8.8
1880	50.2	31,382	1,495	21,458	5,790	11.4
1890	62.9	46,804	3,143	26,408	11,547	18.3
1900	76.0	52,871	3,447	10,925	11,854	15.5
1910	92.0	70,286	3,738[f]	11,456	15,968	17.3
1920	105.7	87,234	6,301[f]	14,550	25,117	23.7
1930	122.8	87,756	6,825[f]	35,700	40,156	32.6
1940	131.7	123,069	9,987[f]	58,400	67,527	51.1
1950	151.3	142,962	9,233	61,700	91,462	60.4
1960	179.3	159,321	2,960	103,000	127,934	71.4
1970	203.3	166,406	4,571	200,000	247,653[g]	121.8
1980	226.5	457,523	9,481	300,000	1,247,653	486.0
1990	248.7	510,000	17,763	500,000[h]	2,600,000	1,045.0

NA = Not applicable.

[a] Designated as assistants to the marshals, 1790–1870.

[b] Estimated; records destroyed by fire.

[c] None employed.

[d] Amount expended for clerk hire: $925.

[e] Revised to include adjustments for underenumeration in southern states; unrevised number is 38,558,371.

[f] Includes all employees in years 1910–1940. Most of the 700 to 900 in the permanent force were probably actually engaged in decennial operations at the peak period.

[g] At July 1969 pay rates; covers some additional expenditures for tests of new procedures introduced in 1970.

[h] By 1990 the emergence of electronic forms of publication—for example, electronic tape, microfiche, CD-ROM, and Internet publications—made print pages published a weak indicator of census data distributed..

Sources: Adapted from A. Ross Eckler, *The Bureau of the Census* (New York: Praeger, 1972), 24; Barry Edmonston and Charles Schultze, eds., "Census Cost Increases and their Causes," in *Modernizing the U.S. Census* (Washington, D.C.: U.S. Government Printing Office, 1995), 44–58.

Cost of Taking the Census, 1790–2000

Census year	Total U.S. population (millions)	Census cost in current dollars (thousands)	Census cost in constant dollars (1999) (thousands)	Real cost per capita (dollars)
1790 (Aug. 2)	3.9	$44	$418	$0.106
1800 (Aug. 4)	5.3	66	627	0.118
1810 (Aug. 6)	7.2	178	1,837	0.254
1820 (Aug. 7)	9.6	208	2,196	0.228
1830 (June 1)	12.9	378	5,735	0.446
1840 (June 1)	17.1	833	12,651	0.741
1850 (June 1)	23.2	1,423	27,671	1.193
1860 (June 1)	31.4	1,969	35,464	1.128
1870 (June 1)	39.8	3,421	41,580	1.044
1880 (June 1)	50.2	5,790	100,524	2.004
1890 (June 1)	62.9	11,547	207,802	3.301
1900 (June 1)	76.0	11,854	230,273	3.030
1910 (Apr. 15)	92.0	15,968	287,437	3.125
1920 (Jan. 1)	105.7	25,117	235,734	2.230
1930 (Apr. 1)	122.8	40,156	380,416	3.098
1940 (Apr. 1)	131.7	67,527	787,874	5.984
1950 (Apr. 1)	151.3	91,462	621,641	4.108
1960 (Apr. 1)	179.3	127,934	710,802	3.964
1970 (Apr. 1)	203.3	247,653	1,093,932	5.383
1980 (Apr. 1)	226.5	1,247,653	2,400,436	10.598
1990 (Apr. 1)	248.7	2,600,000	3,390,620	13.633
2000 (Apr. 1)*	275.0	—	6,700,000	24.364

* Figures for 2000 are estimated.

Sources: Adapted from A. Ross Eckler, *The Bureau of the Census* (New York: Praeger, 1972), 24; Barry Edmonston and Charles Schultze, eds., "Census Cost Increases and their Causes," in *Modernizing the U.S. Census* (Washington, D.C.: U.S. Government Printing Office, 1995), 44–58.

Census 2000 Questionnaires: Short and Long Forms

Following are sample pages from the short and long form questionnaires used in the 2000 census. The editors have reprinted three representative pages from the short form (pages 1, 2, and 5) and all pages of the informational copy of the long form. Whereas the short form asks respondents only for basic demographic and housing information, the long form requests this basic information as well as other data on income, employment, education, veteran status, and transportation to work, among other topics. For the 2000 census, long forms were sent to about eighteen million (one in six) housing units.

Person 2

Your answers are important!
Every person in the Census counts.

What is Person 2's name? *Print name below.*
Last Name

First Name   MI

How is this person related to Person 1? *Mark* ☒ *ONE box.*

☐ Husband/wife
☐ Natural-born son/daughter
☐ Adopted son/daughter
☐ Stepson/stepdaughter
☐ Brother/sister
☐ Father/mother
☐ Grandchild
☐ Parent-in-law
☐ Son-in-law/daughter-in-law
☐ Other relative — *Print exact relationship.* →

If NOT RELATED to Person 1:
☐ Roomer, boarder
☐ Housemate, roommate
☐ Unmarried partner
☐ Foster child
☐ Other nonrelative

What is this person's sex? *Mark* ☒ *ONE box.*

☐ Male   ☐ Female

What is this person's age and what is this person's date of birth? *Print numbers in boxes.*

Age on April 1, 2000   Month   Day   Year of birth

▸ **NOTE: Please answer BOTH Questions 5 and 6.**

Is this person Spanish/Hispanic/Latino? *Mark* ☒ *the "No" box if **not** Spanish/Hispanic/Latino.*

☐ **No,** not Spanish/Hispanic/Latino   ☐ Yes, Puerto Rican
☐ Yes, Mexican, Mexican Am., Chicano   ☐ Yes, Cuban
☐ Yes, other Spanish/Hispanic/Latino — *Print group.* ↘

What is this person's race? *Mark* ☒ *one or more races to indicate what this person considers himself/herself to be.*

☐ White
☐ Black, African Am., or Negro
☐ American Indian or Alaska Native — *Print name of enrolled or principal tribe.* ↘

☐ Asian Indian ☐ Japanese   ☐ Native Hawaiian
☐ Chinese ☐ Korean   ☐ Guamanian or Chamorro
☐ Filipino ☐ Vietnamese   ☐ Samoan
☐ Other Asian — *Print race.* ↘   ☐ Other Pacific Islander — *Print race.* ↘

☐ Some other race — *Print race.* ↘

▸ **If more people live here, continue with Person 3.**

Person 3

Census information helps your community get financial assistance for roads, hospitals, schools, and more.

1. What is Person 3's name? *Print name below.*
Last Name

First Name   MI

2. How is this person related to Person 1? *Mark* ☒ *ONE box.*

☐ Husband/wife
☐ Natural-born son/daughter
☐ Adopted son/daughter
☐ Stepson/stepdaughter
☐ Brother/sister
☐ Father/mother
☐ Grandchild
☐ Parent-in-law
☐ Son-in-law/daughter-in-law
☐ Other relative — *Print exact relationship.*

If NOT RELATED to Person 1:
☐ Roomer, boarder
☐ Housemate, roommate
☐ Unmarried partner
☐ Foster child
☐ Other nonrelative

3. What is this person's sex? *Mark* ☒ *ONE box.*

☐ Male   ☐ Female

4. What is this person's age and what is this person's date of birth? *Print numbers in boxes.*

Age on April 1, 2000   Month   Day   Year of birth

→ **NOTE: Please answer BOTH Questions 5 and 6.**

5. Is this person Spanish/Hispanic/Latino? *Mark* ☒ *the "No" box if **not** Spanish/Hispanic/Latino.*

☐ **No,** not Spanish/Hispanic/Latino   ☐ Yes, Puerto Rican
☐ Yes, Mexican, Mexican Am., Chicano   ☐ Yes, Cuban
☐ Yes, other Spanish/Hispanic/Latino — *Print group.* ↘

6. What is this person's race? *Mark* ☒ *one or more races to indicate what this person considers himself/herself to be.*

☐ White
☐ Black, African Am., or Negro
☐ American Indian or Alaska Native — *Print name of enrolled or principal tribe.* ↘

☐ Asian Indian ☐ Japanese   ☐ Native Hawaiian
☐ Chinese ☐ Korean   ☐ Guamanian or Chamorro
☐ Filipino ☐ Vietnamese   ☐ Samoan
☐ Other Asian — *Print race.* ↘   ☐ Other Pacific Islander — *Print race.* ↘

☐ Some other race — *Print race.* ↘

→ **If more people live here, continue with Person 4.**

Persons 7 – 12

If you didn't have room to list everyone who lives in this house or apartment, please list the others below. *You may be contacted by the Census Bureau for the same information about these people.*

Person 7 — Last Name

First Name   MI

Person 8 — Last Name

First Name   MI

Person 9 — Last Name

First Name   MI

Person 10 — Last Name

First Name   MI

Person 11 — Last Name

First Name   MI

Person 12 — Last Name

First Name   MI

The Census Bureau estimates that, for the average household, this form will take about 10 minutes to complete, including the time for reviewing the instructions and answers. Comments about the estimate should be directed to the Associate Director for Finance and Administration, Attn: Paperwork Reduction Project 0607-0856, Room 3104, Federal Building 3, Bureau of the Census, Washington, DC 20233.

Respondents are not required to respond to any information collection unless it displays a valid approval number from the Office of Management and Budget.

Thank you for completing your official U.S. Census 2000 form.

United States
Census 2000

U.S. Department of Commerce
Bureau of the Census

This is the official form for all the people at this address. It is quick and easy, and your answers are protected by law. Complete the Census and help your community get what it needs — today and in the future!

The "Informational Copy" shows the content of the United States Census 2000 "long" form questionnaire. Each household will receive either a short form (100-percent questions) or a long form (100-percent and sample questions). The long form questionnaire includes the same 6 population questions and 1 housing question that are on the Census 2000 short form, plus 26 additional population questions, and 20 additional housing questions. On average, about 1 in every 6 households will receive the long form. The content of the forms resulted from reviewing the 1990 census data, consulting with federal and non-federal data users, and conducting tests.

For additional information about Census 2000, visit our website at **www.census.gov** or write to the Director, Bureau of the Census, Washington, DC 20233.

Start Here
Please use a black or blue pen.

① **How many people were living or staying in this house, apartment, or mobile home on April 1, 2000?**

Number of people

INCLUDE in this number:
- foster children, roomers, or housemates
- people staying here on April 1, 2000 who have no other permanent place to stay
- people living here most of the time while working, even if they have another place to live

DO NOT INCLUDE in this number:
- college students living away while attending college
- people in a correctional facility, nursing home, or mental hospital on April 1, 2000
- Armed Forces personnel living somewhere else
- people who live or stay at another place most of the time

➡ **Please turn the page and print the names of all the people living or staying here on April 1, 2000.**

If you need help completing this form, *call 1–800–XXX–XXXX between 8:00 a.m. and 9:00 p.m., 7 days a week. The telephone call is free.*

TDD – *Telephone display device for the hearing impaired. Call 1–800–XXX–XXXX between 8:00 a.m. and 9:00 p.m., 7 days a week. The telephone call is free.*

¿NECESITA AYUDA? *Si usted necesita ayuda para completar este cuestionario llame al 1–800–XXX–XXXX entre las 8:00 a.m. y las 9:00 p.m., 7 días a la semana. La llamada telefónica es gratis.*

The Census Bureau estimates that, for the average household, this form will take about 38 minutes to complete, including the time for reviewing the instructions and answers. Comments about the estimate should be directed to the Associate Director for Finance and Administration, Attn: Paperwork Reduction Project 0607-0856, Room 3104, Federal Building 3, Bureau of the Census, Washington, DC 20233.

Respondents are not required to respond to any information collection unless it displays a valid approval number from the Office of Management and Budget.

Form **D-61B**

OMB No. 0607-0856: Approval Expires 12/31/2000

List of Persons

→ **Please be sure you answered question 1 on the front page before continuing.**

② **Please print the names of all the people who you indicated in question 1 were living or staying here on April 1, 2000.**
Example — Last Name

| J | O | H | N | S | O | N | | | | | | | | | | |

First Name   MI

| R | O | B | I | N | | | | | | | | | | | | J |

Start with the person, or one of the people living here who owns, is buying, or rents this house, apartment, or mobile home. If there is no such person, start with any adult living or staying here.

Person 1 — Last Name

First Name   MI

Person 2 — Last Name

First Name   MI

Person 3 — Last Name

First Name   MI

Person 4 — Last Name

First Name   MI

Person 5 — Last Name

First Name   MI

Person 6 — Last Name

First Name   MI

Person 7 — Last Name

First Name   MI

Person 8 — Last Name

First Name   MI

Person 9 — Last Name

First Name   MI

Person 10 — Last Name

First Name   MI

Person 11 — Last Name

First Name   MI

Person 12 — Last Name

First Name   MI

→ **Next, answer questions about Person 1.**

FOR OFFICE USE ONLY			
A. JIC1	**B. JIC2**	**C. JIC3**	**D. JIC4**

Form D-61B

2

Person 1

Your answers are important! Every person in the Census counts.

1 What is this person's name? *Print the name of Person 1 from page 2.*

Last Name

First Name | MI

2 What is this person's telephone number? *We may contact this person if we don't understand an answer.*

Area Code + Number

3 What is this person's sex? *Mark* [X] *ONE box.*

☐ Male
☐ Female

4 What is this person's age and what is this person's date of birth?

Age on April 1, 2000

Print numbers in boxes.

Month   Day   Year of birth

→ NOTE: Please answer BOTH Questions 5 and 6.

5 Is this person Spanish/Hispanic/Latino? *Mark* [X] *the "No" box if not Spanish/Hispanic/Latino.*

☐ **No**, not Spanish/Hispanic/Latino
☐ Yes, Mexican, Mexican Am., Chicano
☐ Yes, Puerto Rican
☐ Yes, Cuban
☐ Yes, other Spanish/Hispanic/Latino — *Print group.* ↘

6 What is this person's race? *Mark* [X] *one or more races to indicate what this person considers himself/herself to be.*

☐ White
☐ Black, African Am., or Negro
☐ American Indian or Alaska Native — *Print name of enrolled or principal tribe.* ↗

☐ Asian Indian   ☐ Native Hawaiian
☐ Chinese   ☐ Guamanian or Chamorro
☐ Filipino
☐ Japanese   ☐ Samoan
☐ Korean   ☐ Other Pacific Islander —
☐ Vietnamese   *Print race.* ↗
☐ Other Asian — *Print race.* ↘

☐ Some other race — *Print race.* ↘

7 What is this person's marital status?

☐ Now married
☐ Widowed
☐ Divorced
☐ Separated
☐ Never married

8 a. At any time since February 1, 2000, has this person attended regular school or college? *Include only nursery school or preschool, kindergarten, elementary school, and schooling which leads to a high school diploma or a college degree.*

☐ No, has not attended since February 1 → *Skip to 9*
☐ Yes, public school, public college
☐ Yes, private school, private college

☞ Question is asked of all persons on the short (100-percent) and long (sample) forms.

2043

Person 1 (continued)

8 b. What grade or level was this person attending?
Mark ☒ ONE box.

- ☐ Nursery school, preschool
- ☐ Kindergarten
- ☐ Grade 1 to grade 4
- ☐ Grade 5 to grade 8
- ☐ Grade 9 to grade 12
- ☐ College undergraduate years (freshman to senior)
- ☐ Graduate or professional school *(for example: medical, dental, or law school)*

9 What is the highest degree or level of school this person has COMPLETED? *Mark ☒ ONE box.*
If currently enrolled, mark the previous grade or highest degree received.

- ☐ No schooling completed
- ☐ Nursery school to 4th grade
- ☐ 5th grade or 6th grade
- ☐ 7th grade or 8th grade
- ☐ 9th grade
- ☐ 10th grade
- ☐ 11th grade
- ☐ 12th grade, **NO DIPLOMA**
- ☐ **HIGH SCHOOL GRADUATE** — high school DIPLOMA or the equivalent *(for example: GED)*
- ☐ Some college credit, but less than 1 year
- ☐ 1 or more years of college, no degree
- ☐ Associate degree *(for example: AA, AS)*
- ☐ Bachelor's degree *(for example: BA, AB, BS)*
- ☐ Master's degree *(for example: MA, MS, MEng, MEd, MSW, MBA)*
- ☐ Professional degree *(for example: MD, DDS, DVM, LLB, JD)*
- ☐ Doctorate degree *(for example: PhD, EdD)*

10 What is this person's ancestry or ethnic origin?

(For example: Italian, Jamaican, African Am., Cambodian, Cape Verdean, Norwegian, Dominican, French Canadian, Haitian, Korean, Lebanese, Polish, Nigerian, Mexican, Taiwanese, Ukrainian, and so on.)

11 a. Does this person speak a language other than English at home?

- ☐ Yes
- ☐ No → *Skip to 12*

b. What is this language?

(For example: Korean, Italian, Spanish, Vietnamese)

c. How well does this person speak English?

- ☐ Very well
- ☐ Well
- ☐ Not well
- ☐ Not at all

12 Where was this person born?

- ☐ In the United States — *Print name of state.*

- ☐ Outside the United States — *Print name of foreign country, or Puerto Rico, Guam, etc.*

13 Is this person a CITIZEN of the United States?

- ☐ Yes, born in the United States → *Skip to 15a*
- ☐ Yes, born in Puerto Rico, Guam, the U.S. Virgin Islands, or Northern Marianas
- ☐ Yes, born abroad of American parent or parents
- ☐ Yes, a U.S. citizen by naturalization
- ☐ No, not a citizen of the United States

14 When did this person come to live in the United States? *Print numbers in boxes.*

Year

15 a. Did this person live in this house or apartment 5 years ago (on April 1, 1995)?

- ☐ Person is under 5 years old → *Skip to 33*
- ☐ Yes, this house → *Skip to 16*
- ☐ No, outside the United States — *Print name of foreign country, or Puerto Rico, Guam, etc., below; then skip to 16.*

- ☐ No, different house in the United States

Person 1 (continued)

15 b. Where did this person live 5 years ago?

Name of city, town, or post office

| | | | | | | | | | | | | | | | | | | | |

Did this person live inside the limits of the city or town?

☐ Yes
☐ No, outside the city/town limits

Name of county

| | | | | | | | | | | | | | | | | | | |

Name of state

| | | | | | | | | | | | | | | | | | | |

ZIP Code

| | | | | |

16 Does this person have any of the following long-lasting conditions:

	Yes	No
a. Blindness, deafness, or a severe vision or hearing impairment?	☐	☐
b. A condition that substantially limits one or more basic physical activities such as walking, climbing stairs, reaching, lifting, or carrying?	☐	☐

17 Because of a physical, mental, or emotional condition lasting 6 months or more, does this person have any difficulty in doing any of the following activities:

	Yes	No
a. Learning, remembering, or concentrating?	☐	☐
b. Dressing, bathing, or getting around inside the home?	☐	☐
c. (Answer if this person is 16 YEARS OLD OR OVER.) Going outside the home alone to shop or visit a doctor's office?	☐	☐
d. (Answer if this person is 16 YEARS OLD OR OVER.) Working at a job or business?	☐	☐

18 Was this person under 15 years of age on April 1, 2000?

☐ Yes → *Skip to 33*
☐ No

19 a. Does this person have any of his/her own grandchildren under the age of 18 living in this house or apartment?

☐ Yes
☐ No → *Skip to 20a*

b. Is this grandparent currently responsible for most of the basic needs of any grandchild(ren) under the age of 18 who live(s) in this house or apartment?

☐ Yes
☐ No → *Skip to 20a*

c. How long has this grandparent been responsible for the(se) grandchild(ren)? *If the grandparent is financially responsible for more than one grandchild, answer the question for the grandchild for whom the grandparent has been responsible for the longest period of time.*

☐ Less than 6 months
☐ 6 to 11 months
☐ 1 or 2 years
☐ 3 or 4 years
☐ 5 years or more

20 a. Has this person ever served on active duty in the U.S. Armed Forces, military Reserves, or National Guard? *Active duty does not include training for the Reserves or National Guard, but DOES include activation, for example, for the Persian Gulf War.*

☐ Yes, now on active duty
☐ Yes, on active duty in past, but not now
☐ No, training for Reserves or National Guard only → *Skip to 21*
☐ No, never served in the military → *Skip to 21*

b. When did this person serve on active duty in the U.S. Armed Forces? *Mark* ☒ *a box for EACH period in which this person served.*

☐ April 1995 or later
☐ August 1990 to March 1995 (including Persian Gulf War)
☐ September 1980 to July 1990
☐ May 1975 to August 1980
☐ Vietnam era (August 1964—April 1975)
☐ February 1955 to July 1964
☐ Korean conflict (June 1950—January 1955)
☐ World War II (September 1940—July 1947)
☐ Some other time

c. In total, how many years of active-duty military service has this person had?

☐ Less than 2 years
☐ 2 years or more

2045

Form D-61B

5

Person 1 (continued)

21 **LAST WEEK, did this person do ANY work for either pay or profit?** *Mark ☒ the "Yes" box even if the person worked only 1 hour, or helped without pay in a family business or farm for 15 hours or more, or was on active duty in the Armed Forces.*

☐ Yes
☐ No → *Skip to 25a*

22 **At what location did this person work LAST WEEK?** *If this person worked at more than one location, print where he or she worked most last week.*

a. Address (Number and street name)

| | | | | | | | | | | | | | | | | | | | | |

| | | | | | | | | | | | | | | | | | | | | |

(If the exact address is not known, give a description of the location such as the building name or the nearest street or intersection.)

b. Name of city, town, or post office

| | | | | | | | | | | | | | | | | | | |

c. Is the work location inside the limits of that city or town?

☐ Yes
☐ No, outside the city/town limits

d. Name of county

| | | | | | | | | | | | | | | | | | | |

e. Name of U.S. state or foreign country

| | | | | | | | | | | | | | | | | | | |

f. ZIP Code

| | | | | |

23 **a. How did this person usually get to work LAST WEEK?** *If this person usually used more than one method of transportation during the trip, mark ☒ the box of the one used for most of the distance.*

☐ Car, truck, or van
☐ Bus or trolley bus
☐ Streetcar or trolley car
☐ Subway or elevated
☐ Railroad
☐ Ferryboat
☐ Taxicab
☐ Motorcycle
☐ Bicycle
☐ Walked
☐ Worked at home → *Skip to 27*
☐ Other method

→ If "Car, truck, or van" is marked in 23a, go to 23b. Otherwise, skip to 24a.

23 **b. How many people, including this person, usually rode to work in the car, truck, or van LAST WEEK?**

☐ Drove alone
☐ 2 people
☐ 3 people
☐ 4 people
☐ 5 or 6 people
☐ 7 or more people

24 **a. What time did this person usually leave home to go to work LAST WEEK?**

| | : | | ☐ a.m. ☐ p.m.

b. How many minutes did it usually take this person to get from home to work LAST WEEK?

Minutes

| | | |

→ Answer questions 25–26 for persons who did not work for pay or profit last week. Others skip to 27.

25 **a. LAST WEEK, was this person on layoff from a job?**

☐ Yes → *Skip to 25c*
☐ No

b. LAST WEEK, was this person TEMPORARILY absent from a job or business?

☐ Yes, on vacation, temporary illness, labor dispute, etc. → *Skip to 26*
☐ No → *Skip to 25d*

c. Has this person been informed that he or she will be recalled to work within the next 6 months OR been given a date to return to work?

☐ Yes → *Skip to 25e*
☐ No

d. Has this person been looking for work during the last 4 weeks?

☐ Yes
☐ No → *Skip to 26*

e. LAST WEEK, could this person have started a job if offered one, or returned to work if recalled?

☐ Yes, could have gone to work
☐ No, because of own temporary illness
☐ No, because of all other reasons *(in school, etc.)*

26 **When did this person last work, even for a few days?**

☐ 1995 to 2000
☐ 1994 or earlier, or never worked → *Skip to 31*

Form D-61B

6

Person 1 (continued)

27 **Industry or Employer** — *Describe clearly this person's chief job activity or business last week. If this person had more than one job, describe the one at which this person worked the most hours. If this person had no job or business last week, give the information for his/her last job or business since 1995.*

a. For whom did this person work? *If now on active duty in the Armed Forces, mark* ☒ *this box →* ☐ *and print the branch of the Armed Forces.*

Name of company, business, or other employer

[ ]

[ ]

b. What kind of business or industry was this? *Describe the activity at location where employed. (For example: hospital, newspaper publishing, mail order house, auto repair shop, bank)*

[ ]

[ ]

c. Is this mainly — *Mark* ☒ *ONE box.*
- ☐ Manufacturing?
- ☐ Wholesale trade?
- ☐ Retail trade?
- ☐ Other *(agriculture, construction, service, government, etc.)?*

28 **Occupation**

a. What kind of work was this person doing? *(For example: registered nurse, personnel manager, supervisor of order department, auto mechanic, accountant)*

[ ]

[ ]

b. What were this person's most important activities or duties? *(For example: patient care, directing hiring policies, supervising order clerks, repairing automobiles, reconciling financial records)*

[ ]

[ ]

29 **Was this person** — *Mark* ☒ *ONE box.*
- ☐ Employee of a PRIVATE-FOR-PROFIT company or business or of an individual, for wages, salary, or commissions
- ☐ Employee of a PRIVATE NOT-FOR-PROFIT, tax-exempt, or charitable organization
- ☐ Local GOVERNMENT employee *(city, county, etc.)*
- ☐ State GOVERNMENT employee
- ☐ Federal GOVERNMENT employee
- ☐ SELF-EMPLOYED in own NOT INCORPORATED business, professional practice, or farm
- ☐ SELF-EMPLOYED in own INCORPORATED business, professional practice, or farm
- ☐ Working WITHOUT PAY in family business or farm

30 **a. LAST YEAR, 1999, did this person work at a job or business at any time?**
- ☐ Yes
- ☐ No → *Skip to 31*

b. How many weeks did this person work in 1999? *Count paid vacation, paid sick leave, and military service.*
Weeks

[ ]

c. During the weeks WORKED in 1999, how many hours did this person usually work each WEEK?
Usual hours worked each WEEK

[ ]

31 **INCOME IN 1999** — *Mark* ☒ *the "Yes" box for each income source received during 1999 and enter the total amount received during 1999 to a maximum of $999,999. Mark* ☒ *the "No" box if the income source was not received. If net income was a loss, enter the amount and mark* ☒ *the "Loss" box next to the dollar amount.*

For income received jointly, report, if possible, the appropriate share for each person; otherwise, report the whole amount for only one person and mark ☒ the "No" box for the other person. If exact amount is not known, please give best estimate.

a. Wages, salary, commissions, bonuses, or tips from all jobs — *Report amount before deductions for taxes, bonds, dues, or other items.*
- ☐ Yes   Annual amount — *Dollars*
  $ [ ] , [ ] .00
- ☐ No

b. Self-employment income from own nonfarm businesses or farm businesses, including proprietorships and partnerships — *Report NET income after business expenses.*
- ☐ Yes   Annual amount — *Dollars*
  $ [ ] , [ ] .00   ☐ Loss
- ☐ No

Person 1 (continued)

31 c. Interest, dividends, net rental income, royalty income, or income from estates and trusts — *Report even small amounts credited to an account.*

☐ Yes   Annual amount — *Dollars*

$ _____ , _____ .00   ☐ Loss

☐ No

d. Social Security or Railroad Retirement

☐ Yes   Annual amount — *Dollars*

$ _____ , _____ .00

☐ No

e. Supplemental Security Income (SSI)

☐ Yes   Annual amount — *Dollars*

$ _____ , _____ .00

☐ No

f. Any public assistance or welfare payments from the state or local welfare office

☐ Yes   Annual amount — *Dollars*

$ _____ , _____ .00

☐ No

g. Retirement, survivor, or disability pensions — *Do NOT include Social Security.*

☐ Yes   Annual amount — *Dollars*

$ _____ , _____ .00

☐ No

h. Any other sources of income received regularly such as Veterans' (VA) payments, unemployment compensation, child support, or alimony — *Do NOT include lump-sum payments such as money from an inheritance or sale of a home.*

☐ Yes   Annual amount — *Dollars*

$ _____ , _____ .00

☐ No

32 What was this person's total income in 1999? *Add entries in questions 31a—31h; subtract any losses. If net income was a loss, enter the amount and mark ☒ the "Loss" box next to the dollar amount.*

Annual amount — *Dollars*

☐ None   OR $ _____ , _____ .00   ☐ Loss

☞ Question is asked of all households on the short (100-percent) and long (sample) forms.

HOUSING QUESTIONS

➡ **Now, please answer questions 33—53 about your household.**

☞ **33 Is this house, apartment, or mobile home —**

☐ Owned by you or someone in this household with a mortgage or loan?
☐ Owned by you or someone in this household free and clear (without a mortgage or loan)?
☐ Rented for cash rent?
☐ Occupied without payment of cash rent?

34 Which best describes this building? *Include all apartments, flats, etc., even if vacant.*

☐ A mobile home
☐ A one-family house detached from any other house
☐ A one-family house attached to one or more houses
☐ A building with 2 apartments
☐ A building with 3 or 4 apartments
☐ A building with 5 to 9 apartments
☐ A building with 10 to 19 apartments
☐ A building with 20 to 49 apartments
☐ A building with 50 or more apartments
☐ Boat, RV, van, etc.

35 About when was this building first built?

☐ 1999 or 2000
☐ 1995 to 1998
☐ 1990 to 1994
☐ 1980 to 1989
☐ 1970 to 1979
☐ 1960 to 1969
☐ 1950 to 1959
☐ 1940 to 1949
☐ 1939 or earlier

36 When did this person move into this house, apartment, or mobile home?

☐ 1999 or 2000
☐ 1995 to 1998
☐ 1990 to 1994
☐ 1980 to 1989
☐ 1970 to 1979
☐ 1969 or earlier

37 How many rooms do you have in this house, apartment, or mobile home? *Do NOT count bathrooms, porches, balconies, foyers, halls, or half-rooms.*

☐ 1 room   ☐ 6 rooms
☐ 2 rooms   ☐ 7 rooms
☐ 3 rooms   ☐ 8 rooms
☐ 4 rooms   ☐ 9 or more rooms
☐ 5 rooms

Form D-61B

8

Person 1 (continued)

38 How many bedrooms do you have; that is, how many bedrooms would you list if this house, apartment, or mobile home were on the market for sale or rent?

☐ No bedroom
☐ 1 bedroom
☐ 2 bedrooms
☐ 3 bedrooms
☐ 4 bedrooms
☐ 5 or more bedrooms

39 Do you have COMPLETE plumbing facilities in this house, apartment, or mobile home; that is, 1) hot and cold piped water, 2) a flush toilet, and 3) a bathtub or shower?

☐ Yes, have all three facilities
☐ No

40 Do you have COMPLETE kitchen facilities in this house, apartment, or mobile home; that is, 1) a sink with piped water, 2) a range or stove, and 3) a refrigerator?

☐ Yes, have all three facilities
☐ No

41 Is there telephone service available in this house, apartment, or mobile home from which you can both make and receive calls?

☐ Yes
☐ No

42 Which FUEL is used MOST for heating this house, apartment, or mobile home?

☐ Gas: from underground pipes serving the neighborhood
☐ Gas: bottled, tank, or LP
☐ Electricity
☐ Fuel oil, kerosene, etc.
☐ Coal or coke
☐ Wood
☐ Solar energy
☐ Other fuel
☐ No fuel used

43 How many automobiles, vans, and trucks of one-ton capacity or less are kept at home for use by members of your household?

☐ None
☐ 1
☐ 2
☐ 3
☐ 4
☐ 5
☐ 6 or more

44 Answer ONLY if this is a ONE-FAMILY HOUSE OR MOBILE HOME — All others skip to 45.

a. Is there a business (such as a store or barber shop) or a medical office on this property?

☐ Yes
☐ No

b. How many acres is this house or mobile home on?

☐ Less than 1 acre → *Skip to 45*
☐ 1 to 9.9 acres
☐ 10 or more acres

c. In 1999, what were the actual sales of all agricultural products from this property?

☐ None
☐ $1 to $999
☐ $1,000 to $2,499
☒ $2,500 to $4,999
☐ $5,000 to $9,999
☐ $10,000 or more

45 What are the annual costs of utilities and fuels for this house, apartment, or mobile home? *If you have lived here less than 1 year, estimate the annual cost.*

a. **Electricity**

Annual cost — *Dollars*

$ [, | |].00

OR

☐ Included in rent or in condominium fee
☐ No charge or electricity not used

b. **Gas**

Annual cost — *Dollars*

$ [, | |].00

OR

☐ Included in rent or in condominium fee
☐ No charge or gas not used

c. **Water and sewer**

Annual cost — *Dollars*

$ [, | |].00

OR

☐ Included in rent or in condominium fee
☐ No charge

d. **Oil, coal, kerosene, wood, etc.**

Annual cost — *Dollars*

$ [, | |].00

OR

☐ Included in rent or in condominium fee
☐ No charge or these fuels not used

2049

Form D-61B

46 **Answer ONLY if you PAY RENT for this house, apartment, or mobile home — All others skip to 47.**

a. What is the monthly rent?

Monthly amount — *Dollars*

$ | | , | | | .00

b. Does the monthly rent include any meals?

☐ Yes
☐ No

47 **Answer questions 47a—53 if you or someone in this household owns or is buying this house, apartment, or mobile home; otherwise, skip to questions for Person 2.**

a. Do you have a mortgage, deed of trust, contract to purchase, or similar debt on THIS property?

☐ Yes, mortgage, deed of trust, or similar debt
☐ Yes, contract to purchase
☐ No → *Skip to 48a*

b. How much is your regular monthly mortgage payment on THIS property? *Include payment only on first mortgage or contract to purchase.*

Monthly amount — *Dollars*

$ | | , | | | .00

OR

☐ No regular payment required → *Skip to 48a*

c. Does your regular monthly mortgage payment include payments for real estate taxes on THIS property?

☐ Yes, taxes included in mortgage payment
☐ No, taxes paid separately or taxes not required

d. Does your regular monthly mortgage payment include payments for fire, hazard, or flood insurance on THIS property?

☐ Yes, insurance included in mortgage payment
☐ No, insurance paid separately or no insurance

48 **a. Do you have a second mortgage or a home equity loan on THIS property?** *Mark ☒ all boxes that apply.*

☐ Yes, a second mortgage
☐ Yes, a home equity loan
☐ No → *Skip to 49*

b. How much is your regular monthly payment on all second or junior mortgages and all home equity loans on THIS property?

Monthly amount — *Dollars*

$ | | , | | | .00

OR

☐ No regular payment required

49 **What were the real estate taxes on THIS property last year?**

Yearly amount — *Dollars*

$ | | , | | | .00

OR

☐ None

50 **What was the annual payment for fire, hazard, and flood insurance on THIS property?**

Annual amount — *Dollars*

$ | | , | | | .00

OR

☐ None

51 **What is the value of this property; that is, how much do you think this house and lot, apartment, or mobile home and lot would sell for if it were for sale?**

☐ Less than $10,000
☐ $10,000 to $14,999
☐ $15,000 to $19,999
☐ $20,000 to $24,999
☐ $25,000 to $29,999
☐ $30,000 to $34,999
☐ $35,000 to $39,999
☐ $40,000 to $49,999
☐ $50,000 to $59,999
☐ $60,000 to $69,999
☐ $70,000 to $79,999
☐ $80,000 to $89,999
☐ $90,000 to $99,999
☐ $100,000 to $124,999
☐ $125,000 to $149,999
☐ $150,000 to $174,999
☐ $175,000 to $199,999
☐ $200,000 to $249,999
☐ $250,000 to $299,999
☐ $300,000 to $399,999
☐ $400,000 to $499,999
☐ $500,000 to $749,999
☐ $750,000 to $999,999
☐ $1,000,000 or more

52 **Answer ONLY if this is a CONDOMINIUM —**

What is the monthly condominium fee?

Monthly amount — *Dollars*

$ | | , | | | .00

53 **Answer ONLY if this is a MOBILE HOME —**

a. Do you have an installment loan or contract on THIS mobile home?

☐ Yes
☐ No

b. What was the total cost for installment loan payments, personal property taxes, site rent, registration fees, and license fees on THIS mobile home and its site last year? *Exclude real estate taxes.*

Yearly amount — *Dollars*

$ | | , | | | .00

➡ **Are there more people living here? If yes, continue with Person 2.**

Person 2

Census information helps your community get financial assistance for roads, hospitals, schools and more.

1 **What is this person's name?** *Print the name of Person 2 from page 2.*

Last Name

First Name   MI

☞ **2** **How is this person related to Person 1?**
Mark ☒ ONE box.

- ☐ Husband/wife
- ☐ Natural-born son/daughter
- ☐ Adopted son/daughter
- ☐ Stepson/stepdaughter
- ☐ Brother/sister
- ☐ Father/mother
- ☐ Grandchild
- ☐ Parent-in-law
- ☐ Son-in-law/daughter-in-law
- ☐ Other relative — *Print exact relationship.*

If NOT RELATED to Person 1:

- ☐ Roomer, boarder
- ☐ Housemate, roommate
- ☐ Unmarried partner
- ☐ Foster child
- ☐ Other nonrelative

☞ Question is asked of Persons 2–6 on the short (100-percent) and long (sample) forms.

For Person 2, repeat questions 3-32 of Person 1.

INFORMATIONAL COPY

2051

Form D-61B

11

Person 3

1+1=2

Information about children helps your community plan for child care, education, and recreation.

For Persons 3–6. repeat questions 1-32 of Person 2.

NOTE – *The content for Question 2 varies between Person 1 and Persons 2–6.*

Thank you for completing your official U.S. Census form. If there are more than six people at this address, the Census Bureau may contact you for the same information about these people.

Standards for the Classification of Federal Data on Race and Ethnicity

The Office of Management and Budget (OMB) sets standards for statistical classifications. In 1977 OMB issued "Race and Ethnic Standards for Federal Statistics and Administrative Reporting," which specified four racial categories: "White," "Black," "American Indian and Alaskan Native," and "Asian and Pacific Islander." They also specified two ethnic categories: "Hispanic Origin" and "Not of Hispanic Origin." According to the standards, people of Hispanic origin could be of any race.

After the 1990 census the standards were criticized for no longer reflecting the increasing racial and ethnic diversity of the country. After soliciting extensive public comment, OMB in 1997 issued revised standards (popularly known as Statistical Directive 15). The text of the revised standards, which defined the questions for the 2000 census, appears below.

Standards for Maintaining, Collecting, and Presenting Federal Data on Race and Ethnicity

This classification provides a minimum standard for maintaining, collecting, and presenting data on race and ethnicity for all Federal reporting purposes. The categories in this classification are social-political constructs and should not be interpreted as being scientific or anthropological in nature. They are not to be used as determinants of eligibility for participation in any Federal program. The standards have been developed to provide a common language for uniformity and comparability in the collection and use of data on race and ethnicity by Federal agencies.

The standards have five categories for data on race: American Indian or Alaska Native, Asian, Black or African American, Native Hawaiian or Other Pacific Islander, and White. There are two categories for data on ethnicity: "Hispanic or Latino," and "Not Hispanic or Latino."

1. Categories and Definitions

The minimum categories for data on race and ethnicity for Federal statistics, program administrative reporting, and civil rights compliance reporting are defined as follows:

—*American Indian or Alaska Native.* A person having origins in any of the original peoples of North and South America (including Central America), and who maintains tribal affiliation or community attachment.

—*Asian.* A person having origins in any of the original peoples of the Far East, Southeast Asia, or the Indian subcontinent, including, for example, Cambodia, China, India, Japan, Korea, Malaysia, Pakistan, the Philippine Islands, Thailand, and Vietnam.

—*Black or African American.* A person having origins in any of the black racial groups of Africa. Terms such as "Haitian" or "Negro" can be used in addition to "Black or African American."

—*Hispanic or Latino.* A person of Cuban, Mexican, Puerto Rican, South or Central American, or other Spanish culture or origin, regardless of race. The term "Spanish origin" can be used in addition to "Hispanic or Latino."

—*Native Hawaiian or Other Pacific Islander.* A person having origins in any of the original peoples of Hawaii, Guam, Samoa, or other Pacific Islands.

—*White.* A person having origins in any of the original peoples of Europe, the Middle East, or North Africa.

Respondents shall be offered the option of selecting one or more racial designations. Recommended forms for the instruction accompanying the multiple response question are "Mark one or more" and "Select one or more."

2. Data Formats

The standards provide two formats that may be used for data on race and ethnicity. Self-reporting or self-identification using two separate questions is the preferred method for collecting data on race and ethnicity. In situations where self-reporting is not practicable or feasible, the combined format may be used.

In no case shall the provisions of the standards be construed to limit the collection of data to the categories described above. The collection of greater detail is encouraged; however, any collection that uses more detail shall be organized in such a way that the additional categories can be aggregated into these minimum categories for data on race and ethnicity.

With respect to tabulation, the procedures used by Federal agencies shall result in the production of as much detailed information on race and ethnicity as possible. However, Federal agencies shall not present data on detailed categories if doing so would compromise data quality or confidentiality standards.

a. Two-question format

To provide flexibility and ensure data quality, separate questions shall be used wherever feasible for reporting race and ethnicity. When race and ethnicity are collected separately, ethnicity shall be collected first. If race and ethnicity are collected separately, the minimum designations are:

Race:
   —*American Indian or Alaska Native*
   —*Asian*
   —*Black or African American*
   —*Native Hawaiian or Other Pacific Islander*
   —*White*

Ethnicity:
   —*Hispanic or Latino*
   —*Not Hispanic or Latino*

When data on race and ethnicity are collected separately, provision shall be made to report the number of respondents in each racial category who are Hispanic or Latino.

When aggregate data are presented, data producers shall provide the number of respondents who marked (or selected) only one category, separately for each of the five racial categories. In addition to these numbers, data producers are strongly encouraged to provide the detailed distributions, including all possible combinations, of multiple responses to the race question. If data on multiple responses are collapsed, at a minimum the total number of respondents reporting "more than one race" shall be made available.

b. Combined format

The combined format may be used, if necessary, for observer-collected data on race and ethnicity. Both race (including multiple responses) and ethnicity shall be collected when appropriate and feasible, although the selection of one category in the combined format is acceptable. If a combined format is used, there are six minimum categories:

   —*American Indian or Alaska Native*
   —*Asian*
   —*Black or African American*
   —*Hispanic or Latino*
   —*Native Hawaiian or Other Pacific Islander*
   —*White*

When aggregate data are presented, data producers shall provide the number of respondents who marked (or selected) only one category, separately for each of the six categories. In addition to these numbers, data producers are strongly encouraged to provide the detailed distributions, including all possible combinations, of multiple responses. In cases where data on multiple responses are collapsed, the total number of respondents reporting "Hispanic or Latino and one or more races" and the total number of respondents reporting "more than one race" (regardless of ethnicity) shall be provided.

3. Use of the Standards for Record Keeping and Reporting

The minimum standard categories shall be used for reporting as follows:

a. Statistical reporting

These standards shall be used at a minimum for all federally sponsored statistical data collections that include data on race and/or ethnicity, except when the collection involves a sample of such size that the data on the smaller categories would be unreliable, or when the collection effort focuses on a specific racial or ethnic group. Any other variation will have to be specifically authorized by the Office of Management and Budget (OMB) through the information collection clearance process. In those cases where the data collection is not subject to the information collection clearance process, a direct request for a variance shall be made to OMB.

b. General program administrative and grant reporting

These standards shall be used for all Federal administrative reporting or record keeping requirements that include data on race and ethnicity. Agencies that cannot follow these standards must request a variance from OMB. Variances will be considered if the agency can demonstrate that it is not reasonable for the primary reporter to determine racial or ethnic background in terms of the specified categories, that determination of racial or ethnic background is not critical to the administration of the program in question, or that the specific program is directed to only one or a limited number of racial or ethnic groups.

c. Civil rights and other compliance reporting

These standards shall be used by all Federal agencies in either the separate or combined format for civil rights and other compliance reporting from the public and private sectors and all levels of government. Any variation requiring less detailed data or data which cannot be aggregated into the basic categories must be specifically approved by OMB for executive agencies. More detailed reporting which can be aggregated to the basic categories may be used at the agencies' discretion.

4. Presentation of Data on Race and Ethnicity

Displays of statistical, administrative, and compliance data on race and ethnicity shall use the categories listed above. The term "nonwhite" is not acceptable for use in the presentation of Federal Government data. It shall not be used in any publication or in the text of any report.

In cases where the standard categories are considered inappropriate for presentation of data on particular programs or for particular regional areas, the sponsoring agency may use:

a. The designations "Black or African American and Other Races" or "All Other Races" as collective descriptions of minority races when the most summary distinction between the majority and minority races is appropriate;

b. The designations "White," "Black or African American," and "All Other Races" when the distinction among the majority race, the principal minority race, and other races is appropriate; or

c. The designation of a particular minority race or races, and the inclusion of "Whites" with "All Other Races" when such a collective description is appropriate.

In displaying detailed information that represents a combination of race and ethnicity, the description of the data being displayed shall clearly indicate that both bases of classification are being used.

When the primary focus of a report is on two or more specific identifiable groups in the population, one or more of which is racial or ethnic, it is acceptable to display data for each of the particular groups separately and to describe data relating to the remainder of the population by an appropriate collective description.

5. Effective Date

The provisions of these standards are effective immediately for all new and revised record keeping or reporting requirements that include racial and/or ethnic information. All existing record keeping or reporting requirements shall be made consistent with these standards at the time they are submitted for extension, or not later than January 1, 2003.

Source: "Revisions to the Standards for the Classification of Federal Data on Race and Ethnicity," *Federal Register* 62, no. 210 (October 30, 1997): 58782–58790.

Census on the Internet

Census data and background information on census questions and methods are increasingly available on the Web sites of national statistical agencies. To assist in the search for useful information, the editors have compiled the following list of sites on the census. The list was current at the time of the book's publication in July 2000. The editors attempted to choose sites that showed some degree of stability, but site addresses may change or sites may disappear altogether. The list is divided into four sections: (1) Census Information, (2) Census Bureau Sites, (3) Congressional Sites, and (4) Other Useful Sites.

Census Information

Current Population Survey

http://www.bls.census.gov/cps

This site has data and press releases related to the Current Population Survey, a monthly survey of about 50,000 households that is the primary source of information about the U.S. labor force.

FERRET

http://ferret.bls.census.gov

FERRET provides data from the Current Population Survey, the Survey of Income and Program Participation, and the National Health Interview Survey. FERRET also offers data about employment and unemployment, displaced workers, job tenure, race and ethnicity, school enrollment, income, and many other topics.

Geospatial and Statistical Data Center

http://fisher.lib.virginia.edu

The Geospatial and Statistical Data Center site offers numerous searchable databases containing data from the Census Bureau, Bureau of Economic Analysis, and other agencies. The site includes various editions of the Census Bureau's *County and City Data Book*, a database containing data from the Census Bureau's *County Business Patterns* reports, a database containing historical and forecasted levels for population and income for each state from 1969 to 2045 from the Bureau of Economic Analysis, the National Income and Products Accounts database from the Bureau of Economic Analysis, and the 1987 *Standard Industrial Classification Manual*, among other databases.

Government Information Sharing Project

http://govinfo.kerr.orst.edu

The Government Information Sharing Project provides a magnificent collection of online databases containing federal data on demographics, economics, education, and related subjects. The data are extracted from CD-ROMs published by the Bureau of the Census, Bureau of Economic Analysis, National Center for Education Statistics, and other organizations. The following databases are available:

- 1990 Census of Population and Housing
- Population Estimates by Age, Sex and Race: 1990–94
- 1992 Economic Census
- Census of Agriculture: 1982, 1987, 1992

U.S. Census Bureau

http://www.census.gov

The U.S. Census Bureau site offers a wealth of statistical information about the nation's people and economy. It has data about housing, health insurance coverage, income, poverty, the labor force, industrial production, international trade, agriculture, population, and county business patterns, among other subjects. The site features Map Stats, an interactive system that presents statistical profiles of states, congressional districts, and counties, as well as detailed maps for counties; up-to-the-second projections of the current population of the United States and the world; and the full text of the *Statistical Abstract of the United States*, software for analyzing Census Bureau data, press releases, links to other Internet sites that offer Census data, and more.

The Census Bureau operates four mailing lists that provide information about its products and services:

- censusandyou is an electronic version of the monthly newsletter *Census and You*, which has articles about new Census Bureau products and tips about how to use them.
- i-net-bulletin is a biweekly list of new data files, reports, and features on the Census Bureau's World Wide Web site.
- press-release distributes Census Bureau press releases, most of which provide news about new reports.
- product-announce has news about new printed reports, CD-ROMs, computer tapes, floppy disks, and other products available from the Census Bureau.

To subscribe to a mailing list, send an e-mail message to majordomo@census.gov. Include in the e-mail's message area the following text: **subscribe** *listname.*

United States Historical Census Data Browser
http://icg.fas.harvard.edu/census

This site provides U.S. Census data from 1790 to 1970. Data are available about the people and economy of each state and county. The types of data vary with each census, but frequently there are data on agriculture, churches, manufacturing, population, slave ownership, and real estate and personal property.

Census Bureau Sites

Census Field Divisions
http://www.census.gov/field/www/index.txt.html

Plans and directs the collection of national sample survey, census, and other data at the local level. Data are collected through regional offices in twelve major cities across the country. The offices employ part-time interviewers who gather data from households who have not returned their census forms. During major censuses, the division administers temporary regional census centers, district offices, and other offices.

Census Information Centers
http://www.census.gov/clo/www/cic.html

Represents the interests of racial and ethnic communities to make census information and data available to participating organizations for analysis and policy planning.

Census Regional Offices
http://www.census.gov/field/www/

Twelve permanent offices that collect economic and demographic data for an area that covers several million housing units.

Federal State Cooperative Program for Population Estimates
http://www.census.gov/population/www/coop/fscpe.html

Race and Ethnic Census Advisory Committees
http://www.census.gov/dmd/www/minority-2.html

African Americans
http://www.census.gov/dmd/www/dateaap.html

American Indians and Alaska Natives
http://www.census.gov/dmd/www/dateaian.html

Asians and Pacific Islanders
http://www.census.gov/dmd/www/dateapi.html

Hispanics
http://www.census.gov/dmd/www/datehis.html

State Data Centers
http://www.census.gov/sdc/www

A state agency or university facility identified by the governor of each state and state equivalent to disseminate census data to the public.

Congressional Sites

House Government Reform Committee, Subcommittee on the Census
http://www.house.gov/danmiller/census/

Census Monitoring Board
http://206.183.6.96/index.asp

Established by Congress in 1997, the Census Monitoring Board is an eight-member bipartisan oversight board charged with observing and monitoring all aspects of the preparation and implementation of the 2000 decennial census.

Other Useful Sites

Accessing Census Bureau Data
http://www.census.gov/mso/www/npr/access.html

Apportionment Spreadsheet
www.iupui.edu/it/ibrc/SDC/apportionment.html

This spreadsheet, prepared by Ryan Burson, demographer for the state of Missouri, calculates how many congressional representatives each state can expect to receive in the reapportionment following the 2000 census. The spreadsheet uses the current apportionment formula, known as the method of equal proportions.

Frequently Asked Questions
http://www.census.gov/dmd/www/faqquest.htm

Glossary of Census Terms
http://www.census.gov/dmd/www/glossary.html

Historical Census Data for the United States
http://www.ipums.umn.edu/

National and International Statistical Services Around the World

Census Bureau
http://www.census.gov/main/www/stat_int.html

Statistics Canada
http://www.statcan.ca/

United Nations Statistics Division
http://www.un.org/Depts/unsd/

Other U.S. Government Sites with Data on the American Population

Economic Statistics Briefing Room
http://www.whitehouse.gov/fsbr/esbr.html

Federal Interagency Council on Statistical Policy (FedStats)
http://www.fedstats.gov/

Social Statistics Briefing Room
http://www.whitehouse.gov/fsbr/ssbr.html

Demography
http://www.whitehouse.gov/fsbr/demography.html

Statistical Abstract of the United States
http://www.census.gov/statab/www

Glossary

Following is a selection of terms that arise frequently in discussions about the census. Far from comprehensive, the glossary nevertheless covers many of the concepts, statutes, processes, and phrases that may be unfamiliar to readers.

Accuracy and Coverage Evaluation (ACE). A coverage measurement method that will be used to determine the number of people and housing units missed or counted more than once in Census 2000.

Address control file (ACF). The 1990 residential address list used to label questionnaires, control the mail response check-in operation, and determine the nonresponse follow-up workload. See also *Master address file; Nonresponse follow-up.*

Address List Improvement Act of 1994 (P.L. 103-430). Permitted local governments to receive and review the address list used to mail questionnaires before the 2000 census, provided that reviewers sign an agreement not to disclose any information and to use it solely for the purpose of making the census more accurate. It also allowed for the transfer of address information between the postal service and the Census Bureau for decennial census purposes.

Address register. A book used by enumerators in a census that contains the street address and related information for every housing unit and special place listed or enumerated during the census. Now called an assignment area. See also *Special place.*

Address register area. A small geographic area, usually a block group or part of a block group, established by the Census Bureau as a basic unit for data collection by a single enumerator during the 1990 decennial census. Conceptually equivalent to a 1980 or earlier decennial census enumeration district.

Administrative geography. Areas that exist to deliver services. They are often independent of standard political geographic areas, except that they are unlikely to cross state lines. The Census Bureau published data in 1990 for three types of administrative areas: school districts, voting districts, and zip codes.

Administrative records. Records collected and maintained by federal, state, and local agencies for the purpose of program implementation, monitoring, and administration. Examples at the federal level include tax returns, demographic and earnings records of the Social Security Administration, and immigrant information from the Immigration and Naturalization Service. At the state and local level, records are kept on births, deaths, marriages, and divorces (much of this for reporting to higher governmental entities), as well as on driver's licenses, participation in programs for health and welfare, and on the size and characteristics of the housing stock. These data are useful because they can be used to check the quality of the decennial census, as a supplement to the census, or as a means of constructing population estimates and projections.

Advance census report. An unaddressed short-form census questionnaire with respondent instructions delivered by the U.S. Postal Service to housing units in sparsely populated areas. The respondent completes the questionnaire and retains it for pickup by an enumerator.

Advisory committee. A committee of members of the public who meet occasionally to give advice to the Census Bureau. The members may come from stakeholder groups, professional organizations, or state and local government. Examples include the Commerce Secretary's 2000 Census Advisory Committee and the American Statistical Association/American Economic Association Census Advisory Committee.

Apportionment. The process of dividing up the 435 memberships, or seats, in the House of Representatives among the fifty states.

Block group. A combination of census blocks that is a subdivision of a census tract or BNA (block numbering area). A block group consists of all blocks whose numbers begin with the same digit in a given census tract or BNA. The block group is the lowest level of geography for which the Census Bureau has tabulated sample data. All areas had census tracts in 2000.

Block numbering area. An area delineated by state officials or the Census Bureau for the purpose of grouping and numbering decennial census blocks in counties or statistically equivalent entities in which census tracts have not been established. Thus, a BNA is equivalent to a census tract in the Census Bureau's geographic hierarchy.

Census block. The smallest entity for which the Census Bureau collects and tabulates decennial census information; bounded on all sides by visible and non-visible features shown on Census Bureau maps. Occasionally, especially in rural areas, drainage ditches or power lines may be used to define blocks. Because most blocks have small population and housing unit counts, only 100-percent data, or short-form data, are tabulated for them. See also *Short form.*

Census Day. Since 1930, April 1 of years ending in zero.

Census designated place. A statistical area defined for a census as a densely settled concentration of population that is not incorporated but which resembles an incorporated place in that it can be identified with a name. See also *Incorporated place.*

Census feature class code. An alphanumeric code that uniquely identifies the basic characteristics of a map feature in the Census Bureau's TIGER file. See also *TIGER (Topologically Integrated Geographic Encoding and Referencing System).*

Census tract. A small, relatively permanent, homogenous subdivision of metropolitan areas and selected nonmetropolitan counties, delineated for the purpose of presenting census data. See also *Metropolitan area.*

Census Transportation Planning Package (CTPP). Aggregate data on the number and characteristics of workers presented for the full hierarchy of census geography down to the block group level and organized as summary files. Files from the CTPP in 1990 (and in earlier censuses back to 1970) were created through a cooperative effort that included federal, state, and local transportation agencies. While data for 1990 and 2000 are available for all areas of the nation, earlier data were available only for selected areas, based on contractual agreements with local groups of transportation officials. These files are unique in that they provide users with data on workers (as opposed to residents) for small areas and, as such, are used extensively by local planning organizations.

Computer assisted interviewing (CAI). A group of methods for using computers to assist with data col-lection. CAI surveys can be either interviewer-administered (conducted in person using a laptop computer or by telephone using a shared computer) or self-administered (conducted using surveys disseminated to respondents by telephone, by the Internet, or on a computer disk).

Coverage evaluation. Statistical studies conducted to evaluate the level and sources of coverage error in censuses and surveys.

Current Population Survey. Monthly sample survey of the U.S. population that provides employment and unemployment figures as well as current data about other social and economic characteristics of the population. Collected for the Bureau of Labor Statistics by the Census Bureau.

Data capture. The process by which survey responses are transferred from written questionnaires to an electronic format for tabulation. Currently done by optical scanning; from 1960 to 1990, by FOSDIC; from 1890 to 1950, using punch cards. See also *FOSDIC.*

Enumeration district. A geographic area, often used as a work unit or unit of measure, into which counties are divided for the purpose of taking a census. Enumeration districts (also referred to as enumeration areas) were replaced with address register areas as the data collection units in the 1990 census and with block groups for data tabulation. See also *Address register; Block group.*

Enumerator. A census field operations employee. A person who collects information by interviewing.

Erroneous enumeration. A person counted incorrectly in the census, for example, because the person is counted more than once or because the person is counted at the wrong location, according to census residence rules. A college student living in a dormitory away from home on April 1 would be an erroneous enumeration if the student was listed on the questionnaire as a resident of the parental home. See also *Omission; Overcount; Undercount.*

Federal depository library. A cooperative venture between the U.S. Government Printing Office (GPO) and America's library community, the purpose of which is to make government information readily accessible to the general public at no cost to the user. Under the provisions of the program, the GPO provides participating libraries with publications and databases at no charge; in exchange, the libraries agree to provide the public with access to these materials.

Follow-up. A secondary census or survey operation, predominantly in data collection, carried out to successfully complete an initial operation. It is most often a telephone or personal visit interview to obtain missing data or clarify original responses.

FOSDIC (Film Optical Sensing Device for Input to Computers). From 1960 to 1990 census questionnaires were microfilmed. The answers were read from the microfilmed questionnaires using FOSDIC and converted to electronic codes in computer tape format.

Geographic center of area of the United States. The point at which the surface of the United States would balance if it were a plane of uniform weight per unit of area. In early 2000 that point fell in Butte County, South Dakota, as it has since the 1960 census, after Alaska and Hawaii became states. The geographic center of the coterminous United States (forty-eight states and the District of Columbia) is in Smith County, Kansas.

Geographic tabulation unit base. A geographic record containing a unique combination of geographic codes. It is the smallest unique area required for tabulation purposes above the block group level. See also *Block group*.

Gross error. The sum of the erroneous enumerations and the omissions in the census. See also *Erroneous enumeration; Omission; Overcount; Undercount*.

Group quarters. A place where people live that is not a housing unit. There are two types of group quarters: institutional (for example, nursing homes, mental hospitals, and correctional institutions) and noninstitutional (for example, college dormitories, ships, hotels, group homes, and shelters).

Housing unit. A house, apartment, mobile home or trailer, group of rooms or single room occupied as a separate living quarters or, if vacant, intended for occupancy as a separate living quarters. The definition of separate living quarters for the 2000 census is that the occupants live separately from any other individuals in the building and have direct access from outside the building or through a common hall. Additional criteria, such as the presence of a kitchen or cooking equipment for the exclusive use of the occupants, were used to define a housing unit in previous censuses.

Impute. To assign answers to questions with missing responses on the basis of information from other respondents. Sometimes people are added to the census count by imputation.

Incorporated place. Legally recognized entities. Naming conventions vary by state; some of the terms commonly used are *city, village, borough,* and *town*. More than one term may be used in a given state.

Integrated coverage measurement. A coverage measurement technique that combines estimates of missed persons with enumeration results before producing a single set of official census results.

IPUMS (Integrated Public Use Microdata Series). A coherent individual-level national database that describes the characteristics of the American population in thirteen census years spanning the period from 1850 through 1990. It combines nationally representative probability samples produced by the Census Bureau for the period since 1940 with new high-precision historical samples produced at the University of Minnesota and elsewhere. See also *PUMS (Public Use Microdata Sample)*.

List/enumerate. A method of enumeration in which enumerators canvass a geographic area, list each residential address, and collect a questionnaire from or enumerate the household.

List/leave. A method of enumeration in which enumerators list each residential address and at the same time deliver the census forms for return by mail.

Local Update of Census Addresses (LUCA). A product of the Address List Improvement Act of 1994, this program was established to elicit review and feedback from representatives of local and tribal governments on the Bureau-compiled address list for the 2000 census.

Long form. The decennial census questionnaire containing 100-percent (short form) and sample questions. Sent to a sample of addresses in the census, long forms typically contain the short-form person and housing items that all households are asked to provide, together with additional items that only the households in the long-form sample are asked to provide. Whereas short-form items are generally limited to basic demographic and housing questions, long-form items cover such topics as income, employment, veteran status, transportation to work, education, and others.

Mailout-mailback. Descriptive of the enumeration method in which the post office delivers decennial census questionnaires to specific addresses and the respondents mail them back to the district office or processing office for processing. Mailout-mailback is the primary method of data collection for censuses today.

Master address file. The Census Bureau's permanent list of addresses for individual living quarters that is linked to the TIGER data base. See also *TIGER (Topologically Integrated Geographic Encoding and Referencing System)*.

Median center of population. The intersection of two median lines: one a north-south line (a meridian of longitude) chosen so that half the population lives east of it and half west, and the other an east-west line (a parallel of latitude) selected so that half the population lives north of it and half south. The median center of population for the 1990 census resided in Indiana.

Metropolitan area (MA). A collective term established by the Office of Management and Budget (OMB) to refer to metropolitan statistical areas, consolidated metropolitan areas, New England county metropolitan areas, and primary metropolitan statistical areas. The OMB designates MAs based on the concept of functional integration between core and periphery areas, using data on commuting. In most areas of the nation (for example, outside of New England), MAs are composed of whole counties.

Metropolitan statistical area (MSA). Designated by the Office of Management and Budget for use by federal statistical agencies. This geographically based entity is a core area with a large population nucleus. It also includes adjacent communities with a high degree of economic and social integration with the core.

National content test. Mail survey of a large sample of housing units conducted several years before the census. A national content test is used to test alternative question wording and the feasibility of including proposed new or modified questions.

Nonresponse follow-up. A decennial census operation in which enumerators visit addresses from which no questionnaires have been returned by mail.

Numident file. Also known as the SSA Numident file, the Numident contains data collected from applications for Social Security numbers and replacement cards as well as applications to change the name associated with a previously issued number. Data recorded on the Numident include the Social Security number, date of birth, sex, race, Hispanic origin, country of birth, and all names associated with that number.

Omission. A person missed in the census. See also *Erroneous enumeration; Overcount; Undercount.*

Overcount. The total number of people counted more than once or otherwise enumerated erroneously in the census. See also *Erroneous enumeration; Omission; Undercount.*

P.L. 94-171. The public law that requires the Census Bureau to provide the decennial census data required for congressional redistricting to the states by April of the year following the year of the census enumeration.

Political geography. Geographic areas that are defined in law and in which, usually, the government is run by elected officials. The most common political geographic areas are states, counties, and county subdivisions.

Post-enumeration Survey (PES). A coverage measurement survey that is conducted several months after the April census date and is designed to identify the number of people missed, counted twice, or counted at the wrong location. From the results of the survey, the Census Bureau calculates corrected population counts for local areas of the country.

PUMS (Public Use Microdata Sample). Computerized files containing a sample of individual long-form decennial census records showing most population and housing characteristics. See also *IPUMS (Integrated Public Use Microdata Series).*

Redistricting. The process of redrawing congressional, state legislative, and local political boundaries every ten years using population counts provided to the states by the Census Bureau.

Schedule. Also called forms or returns, schedules are the questionnaires, listing individuals by name, that are filled out by census takers.

Shelter/street-night. An enumeration conducted before Census Day in which enumerators visit shelters, missions, and any other areas where emergency housing has been set up, to enumerate each resident. Enumerators also visit pre-identified street locations to enumerate those people living on the street.

Short form. The decennial census questionnaire requesting basic demographic and housing information. See also *Long form.*

Simplified questionnaire test. A test conducted in 1992 to determine the effects of form length, respondent-friendly construction, and a request for the respondent's Social Security number on mail responses.

Source and accuracy statement. Published by the Census Bureau with each survey, this statement documents the level of sampling error and its impact on survey-based estimates. Typically, estimates are provided with a variety of statistics that indicate the estimates' degree of uncertainty, such as confidence intervals or standard errors, and are suppressed from publication if deemed unreliable based on these measures.

Special census. A federal census conducted at the request and cost of a local government to obtain population figures between decennial censuses.

Special place. A place where people live or stay that is different from the usual private house, apartment, or mobile home and that requires different decennial census procedures. Examples are hospitals, prisons, hotels, motels, orphanages, nursing homes, dormitories, marinas, military installations, and large rooming or boarding houses. See also *Group quarters*.

State data center. A state agency or university research center that acquires Census Bureau data products through a special cooperative agreement and disseminates these data to clientele through a network of statewide affiliate agencies and organizations.

State economic area. A single county or group of counties within a state that have similar economic and social characteristics as determined by various governmental agencies.

Statistical geography. Geographic areas, such as census tracts, created expressly for aggregation and presentation of data.

Summary Tape File. Tabulations of complete count and sample population and housing data presented as aggregates for a hierarchy of geographic areas ranging in size from census blocks to totals for the nation and regions.

Survey of Income and Program Participation (SIPP). A continuing longitudinal survey that obtains detailed information about sources and amounts of income, participation in public and private transfer programs, asset holdings, and related topics. The survey follows members of originally sampled households over time, with interviews every four months; a new sample (panel) is introduced periodically. Since the beginning of SIPP in 1983, the number of interviews and the sample size for each panel have varied, as has the frequency with which a new sample is introduced.

TIGER (Topologically Integrated Geographic Encoding and Referencing System). A computer database that contains all census-required map features and attributes for the United States and its possessions, plus the specifications, procedures, computer programs, and related input materials required to build and use it.

Title 13 of the U.S. Code. Originally enacted in 1954, the law under which the Census Bureau operates. It also protects the confidentiality of census information and establishes penalties for disclosing this information.

Undercount. The total number of people missed in the census. The difference between the overcount and the undercount is the net undercount.

UNIVAC (Universal Automatic Computer). The first nondefense computer, UNIVAC was developed by the Census Bureau in conjunction with the National Bureau of Standards (now the National Institute of Standards and Technology) and the Eckert-Mauchly Computer Corporation in the late 1940s. The first UNIVAC was delivered to the Census Bureau's Data Tabulation Office in Philadelphia on March 31, 1951. Initially, UNIVAC sped up the tabulation process and increased the capacity for more elaborate data tabulations.

Update/leave. A method of enumeration in which the enumerators deliver decennial census forms for return by mail and at the same time update the census mailing list.

Urbanized area. An area identified by the Census Bureau that contains a central place surrounded by a closely settled incorporated and unincorporated area. An urbanized area has a combined population of at least fifty thousand.

Index

A

Abstract of the Fourteenth Census, 138
Accuracy and Coverage Evaluation (ACE),
    3–5, 164, 296, 299, 306, 328
    coverage improvement and, 64, 103, 270
A. C. Nielsen, 309
ACRs (advance census reports), 202
Adams, John, 117
Adams, John Quincy, 93, 119, 121
Address Coding Guide (ACG), 7, 154,
    200–201
Address Control File (ACF), 7–8, 12, 60,
    202
Addresses, 6–13, 65, 102–103, 248, 297–298.
    See also Local Update of Census Addresses
    (LUCA); Mailout-mailback census; Master
    Address File (MAF)
        1970 census, 200–201
        commercial mailing lists, 154, 201
        early coding efforts, 6–8
        GBF/DIME files, 8
        post-enumeration survey, 304
        Puerto Rican, 59, 60–61
        TIGER database, 8–9
Address List Improvement Act (1994). *See*
    Census Address List Improvement Act (P.L.
    103-430, 1994)
Administrative geography, 349–350, 352–353
Administrative Procedure Act (APA, 1946),
    269
Administrative records, 287, 301, 317, 318
    federal, 213–216
Administrative Services Division records, 287
Advance Census Reports (ACRs), 200, 202
Advance Post Office Check, 7, 9, 103, 202
Advertising, 13–14, 204, 298
Advertising Council, 13, 14
Advisory committees, 14–18, 135, 291
        minority, 16
        National Academy of Sciences review
    panels, 16–17
        professional, 15–16
Advocacy groups, 291
Affirmative action cases, 85
African American Census Advisory Commit-
    tee, 16
African Americans, 73, 79–80, 123, 313–314,
    346
        apportionment prescriptions and, 19, 336
        undercounts and, 3, 160
African-origin population, 18–22. *See also*
    Slaves
        household censuses and, 19
        migration of, 19–21

Age Discrimination and Employment Act, 22
Age distribution, 75–76
    2000 census, 162
    Asian and Pacific Islander Americans
    (API), 47
        of educational attainment, 294
        of foreign-born population, 231*t*
        Hispanics, 242
        by major life-cycle age groups,
    1880–2050, 76*t*
        by median age, 76*t*
        of veterans, 361
Age heaping, 22
Age questions, 22–23, 91, 117, 371
Age Search Service, 109
"Age/Sex Distribution of the Population 1905
    to 2025" (film), 288
Agricultural Atlas of the United States, 26
Agricultural census, 23–26, 92, 181, 320
        availability/uses of, 26
        farm definition for, 24–25
        farms by market value of products sold,
    1969 to 1997, 25*t*
        insular areas in, 355
        percentage of farms and of market values
    of products sold (1997), 25*t*
        questionnaire, 23–24
Agricultural Economics and Land Ownership
    Survey, 23
Alabama Paradox, 36–37
Alaska Natives, 16, 28–31. *See also* American
    Indians
        American Indian and Alaska Native Vil-
    lages (AIANAs), 346
Alho, J. M., 99
Allen, Thomas, 123
Allocation, 196
Alternative Census Methodologies, Panel on,
    17
American Antiquarian Society, 168
The American Census: A Social History (Ander-
    son), 336
American Community Survey (ACS), 26–28,
    63, 93, 179, 319
        addresses for, 203, 248
        business applications for, 357
        development of, 26–27
        IPUMS and, 267
        long form and, 277, 324
        poverty estimates from, 330
        Puerto Rican census and, 62
        quality of data findings by, 302
American Congressional Dictionary, 34
American Council of Learned Societies, 15, 366

American Economic Association, 15, 93
American FactFinder (AFF), 82, 114, 299, 310,
    346
        Economic Census reports in, 192
        evolution of, 178
        race data on, 317
        State Data Centers and, 341
American Geographical and Statistical Society,
    15
American Housing Survey (AHS), 220*t*
American Indian and Alaska Native advisory
    group, 16
American Indian and Alaska Native Villages
    (AIANAs), 346
American Indians, 20, 28–31, 163, 313, 314
American Institute of Planners, 14
American Marketing Association, 15
American Philosophical Society, 116
American Samoa, 354–356
Americans overseas, 31–33, 299
        1900–1990, 33*t*
        instructions for inclusion of, 1860–1990,
    32*t*
American Statistical Association (ASA), 15, 67,
    93, 110, 140
Americans with Disabilities Act, 171, 217
"America's Uncounted People" (1972), 17
Ancestry questions, 91, 366, 369
Anderson, Margo, 49, 54, 336
Annual Report of the Secretary of Veterans Affairs,
    360, 361
Anthropology, American Indian questions and,
    29
Antiterrorism and Effective Death Penalty Act
    (1996), 254
Any-Address Matching, 304
API. *See* Asian and Pacific Islander Americans
Applied Urbanetics, 186
Apportionment bias, 35, 37
Apportionment prescriptions, 16, 34–42, 108,
    109, 299
        from 1790 to 1910, 34–37
        1870 presidential election and, 36
        1990 census, 159
        Accuracy and Coverage Evaluation and,
    3–4
        districting, 38–42
        equal representation and, 84
        military and maritime enumeration for, 205
        politics and, 42
        sampling and, 323, 326–327
        state and local governments and, 335
        Thirteenth Amendment and, 128
        twentieth century, 37–38

undocumented aliens and, 259
Appropriations, census, 86–87
  coverage improvement and, 102
Arbitron Company, 309
Archival access to census data, 42–45
  data types, 42–43
  issues of using, 44
  sources, 43
Area offices, 145
Asian Americans, 79–80. *See also* Asians
  1990 census data content and, 93–94
  among API category, 45
  changing ethnic composition of, 46*t*
  classification of, 313–314
  country of origin and, 88–89
  SSA Numident file and, 215
Asian and Pacific Islander Americans, 45–48,
  88–89, 313–314
  changing composition of, 46–47, 46*t*
  distribution of, 47–48
  growth of, 1970 to 1997, 45*t*
  by nativity and generation, 1990 to 2040,
  47*t*
Asian and Pacific Islander Census Advisory
  Committee, 16
Asian and Pacific Islander Center for Census
  Information and Services, 240
Asian Indians, 46
Asians, 229, 232, 253, 294
Association of Public Data Users, 94, 110
Asylees, 258
Attainment, educational, 198, 293–294
Aunuu (island), 354
Austin, William Lane, 140, 141, 142
Automobiles, 251
Avery v. Midland County (1968), 335

B
Baby boom, WWII, 152, 153
Baker v. Carr (1962), 38, 39, 335
Baldrige v. Shapiro (1982), 58, 81
Balinski, Michael L., 37, 38
Barabba, Vincent, 113, 157
Barbados colonial census, 73
Bar codes, 65, 159
Be Counted program, 104, 206, 298
Bell, William R., 53
Benchmarks, independently derived, 226,
  300–301
Beresford, John C. (Jack), 113, 155, 173, 176, 345
Bias
  apportionment, 35, 37
  correlation, 53, 99
  head-of-household gender, 149
  survey, 226
"The Bicentennial Census: New Directions
  for Methodology in 1990" (1985), 17
BIDC (Business and Industry Data Center),
  110, 340–341
Biennial population estimates, 300
Bierce, Ambrose, 262
Biggers, John D., 141
Bilingual voting data, 217
Billings, John Shaw, 106
Birthplace, 91, 227, 365–366, 369

Birth statistics, 73, 235, 301, 363, 364
  out-of-wedlock, 363
  registration study, 64
Bishop, Yvonne M. M., 53
Blacks, 18–22. *See also* African Americans;
  African-origin population
Blair & Rives, 123
Blind Population of the United States, 138
Block groups, 348–349
Block-numbering areas (BNAs), 67
Blocks, census, 40, 42, 114, 348–349
  PL 94-171 Reapportionment-Redistrict-
  ing Act file and, 156
Blood quantum, 30
Boarding school students, 200
Board of Trade, British, 74
Bogue, Donald, 289
Boroughs, 348
Bradburn, Norman, 17
Bridge between NAICS and SIC (1997), 194, 195
Brown, Lawrence D., 54
Brownrigg, L. A., 100
Bryant, Barbara Everitt, 159, 371
Budget and Accounting Procedures Act
  (1950), 342
Building permits, 301
Bureau of Economic Analysis (BEA), 319
Bureau of Health Manpower Area Resources
  Files, 288–289
Bureau of Indian Affairs, 29
Bureau of Labor Statistics, 216, 318–319
Bureau of the Budget, 143, 149, 261
Bureau of the Census, 83, 157. *See also* Ameri-
  can FactFinder (AFF); Decennial censuses
  1910 census and, 135–136
  archives of, 285–287
  Bureau of the Census Catalog, 183
  Committee on Adjustment of Postcensal
  Estimates, 98
  congressional authorization for, 85
  Data Access and Use Laboratory
  (DAUL), 173
  economic product classification by, 188
  local liaisons for tract program and, 67
  management structure of, 139–140,
  296–297
  National Services Program, 239
  Permanent Census Act and, 134
  printed publications of, 179, 180–181
  publishing program, 147
  punching and tabulating machines of, 308
  Research, Evaluation, and Experimental
  (REX) Program of, 62
  Vital Statistics Division of, 363
  women employees of, 371
  World Wide Web site confidentiality, 82
Bureau of Transportation Statistics, 185
Burr, Aaron, 117
Bush, George, 158
Business and Industry Data Centers (BIDC),
  110, 340–341
Business census, 92
Businesses, census data usage by, 85, 356–357
Business Expenses, Economic Census Reports,
  192
Butz, William P., 178

C
Calhoun, John C., 123
Cambodian Americans, 46
Canada, 21, 27, 70, 96–97, 107
  foreign-born population of U.S. from,
  228–229
Capture-recapture methods, 49–55
  census counting and, 51–52, 52*t*
  dual systems for, 52–53
  dual-systems modification for, 53–54
  fish in a lake example, 49–51, 50*t*, 51*t*
Card-to-tape tabulation machines, 106
Carey v. Klutznick (1980), 269
Cartographic data files, 289
Casing check, 7
Casual Count, 102
Catalog of United States Census Publications, 183
CD-ROMs, 109, 114, 236, 310, 341, 357
  1990 census, 161, 177
  2000 census on, 314, 346
  agricultural census data, 26
  Economic Census reports on, 192, 195
  Summary Tape Files (STFs) on, 345–346
CENSPAC (computer program), 158, 345
Census, 218, 361. *See also* Accuracy and Cov-
  erage Evaluation
  in other countries, 68–71
Census, House Subcommittee on the, 86
Census, Statistics, and Postal Personnel,
  House Subcommittee on, 85
Census 2000. *See* Decennial censuses
*Census 2000: Summary Population and Housing
  Characteristics*, 182
*Census 2000: Summary Population and Housing
  Unit Counts*, 182
*Census 2000: Summary Social, Economic, and
  Housing Characteristics*, 182
Census Act of 1954 (P.L. 83-740), 88, 93
Census Address List Improvement Act (P.L.
  103-430, 1994), 12, 58, 60–61, 203, 272
  confidentiality and, 81
Census Advisory Committee(s), 15–16, 93, 287
Census Advisory Committee of Professional
  Associations, 15, 17
Census Advisory Committee of the Population
  Association of America, 15
Census and Population, House Subcommittee
  on, 85
Census Board, 1850 census and, 124
Census Bureau. *See* Bureau of the Census
Census Bureau and Statistics Canada, 21
Census Catalog and Guide, 185
Census County Divisions (CCDs), 349
Census Coverage Survey (CCS), U.K., 70
Census-designated places (CDPs), 40, 348, 353
Census employees, litigation against, 268
Census enumeration district maps
  in National Archives, 287–288
Censuses, decennial. *See* Decennial censuses
Census Information Center Program, 240
Census law, 55–58
  1790 to 1870, 56
  U.S. Constitution, 55
Census Monitoring Board, 87, 296, 299
Census of Agriculture Act (1997), 24
Census Office, 83, 180

Act of March 6, 1902 (32 Stat. 51), 57
Census of Outlying Areas, Economic Census Reports, 192
Census plus process, 99
Census pretest policy, 227
Census Requirements in the Year 2000 and Beyond, Panel on, 17
Census returns, 234
Census schedules
    digital imaging of, 236
    in National Archives, 287
    publication of, 234–235
Census testing, 62–66
Census Tract Reports, 1960 census, 152
Census tracts, 40, 66–68, 348
    data products, 112
    electronic summary files on, 346
    origin and use of 1947–1952, 287*t*
    redistricting and, 42
    small-area data and, 273
    SNRFU in, 325–326
Census Tract Statistics, 1950 census, 146
Census Transportation Planning Package (1990), 157, 185, 346
Census Users Conference, Little Rock, Ark. (1980), 288
Census User's Guide, 113
Center for Economic Studies, 193
Center for Research Libraries, 113
Center of population, 71–72
A Century of Growth (Rossiter), 365
Characteristics by Age, Marital Status, Relationship, Education, and Citizenship, 181
Characteristics of Displaced Homemakers and Single Parents File, STP 89, 185
Characteristics of the Population, 181
    1950 census, 146
    1960 census, 151
Check census, 141
Child Labor in the United States, 184
Child Labor Laws, 292
Children, 210–211
    census form inclusion of, 235
    in shared custody, 31, 162
Children in Gainful Occupations at the Fourteenth Census of the United States, 138, 184
China, foreign-born originating from, 229
Chinese Americans, 46
    classification of, 313
Chinese Exclusion Act (1882), 45, 229, 253
Church of Jesus Christ of Latter-day Saints (LDS), 267
Cities, 40, 348. *See also* Local governments
Citizens Conference on State Legislatures, 335
Citizenship
    immigration and, 253
    question on, 91
City Blocks, 1960 census, 151
City governments
    grassroots groups and, 239
The City of New York et al. v. U.S. Department of Commerce et al. (1988), 158
Civilian employees of government overseas, 32
Civil Rights Act, 315

Civil service, census employees and, 136–137, 140
Civil War, 18, 72–73, 351
    census publications during, 184
    demographics and, 126–127
Claritas Corporation, 310
Clark, Rebecca L., 259
Clean Air Act, 185
Cleveland, Ohio, census tracts in, 67
Clinton, Bill, 84, 326
Clinton v. Glavin (1999), 34
Close-out procedures
    1960 census, 200
Cluster analysis, market research and, 310
Coale, Ansley, 166
Code of Federal Regulations, 28–29
Coding, improvements in, 65–66
Cognitive techniques
    pretesting research and, 227
COGSIS (Committee on Government Statistics and Information Services), 15, 140
Cohabitation, 211
Cohen, M. L., 54
Cohort-component method, population projections, 302–303
Cold deck method of imputation, 196
Colgrove, Kenneth, 38–39
Colgrove v. Green (1946), 39
College students, 31, 146, 198, 200, 248
    National Survey of College Graduates (NSCG), 222*t*, 224–225, 318–319
    National Survey of Recent College Graduates, 318
Colonial censuses, 73–75
Colonialism, international census and, 263
Colonias, 163
Colorado Springs Census District Office, FBI and, 81
Commercial mailing lists, 6–7, 154, 201
Commission on Civil Rights, 288
Committee on Census Enumeration, ASA, 67
Committee on Government Statistics and Information Services (COGSIS), 15, 140
Committee on National Statistics (CNSTAT). *See also* National Academy of Sciences, 17
Committee on Population Statistics, 14
Committee on Problems of Census Enumeration, 16–17
Communications, directorate for, 280, 296
Communist sympathizers, attorney general's request on, 81
Community Address Updating System, 27
Community Development Block Grants, 90
    census data uses by, 217
Community Services Administration
    records of, 288
Commuting, 91
Compendium of the Seventh Census, 125, 307
Compensatory Education Study, NIE, 1975–1980, 288
Complete Count Committees, 201, 272
Component method, demographic analysis, 301
Components of Inventory Change, 1960 census, 152
Composite list, 97
    methodology strengths/weaknesses, 99
Composition, population, 75–80

age, 75–76
    nativity, 77–78, 77*t*
    race and ethnicity, 78–80
    sex, 76–77, 77*t*
Compromise of 1850, 72
Computer assisted interviewing (CAI), 225
Computer-Assisted Personal Interviewing (CAPI), 5
Computers
    1960 microdata files and, 175
    1970 census data and, 176
    1980 census data and, 176–177
    1990 census data and, 177–178
    address list development and, 6–8
    client/server models, 178
    congressional districts and, 40
    data capture and, 106–108
    data dissemination and, 108–109, 159, 172–179
        GBF/DIME file, 8, 201, 289
        imputation and, 197
        personal, 177, 310
        Summary Tape Files and, 345
        TIGER database, 8–9, 60, 62, 297
Condominiums, 249
Conference of European Statisticians
    global census information/experience and, 264
Confidentiality, 80–83
    1790 census, 110
    1880 census, 57
    1960 census, 174
    advertising on, 204
    challenges to/defenses of, 268–269
    in Economic Census, 187
    federal administrative records and, 216
    nondisclosure of census information, 286
    Public Use Microdata Sample (PUMS), 178–179
    Summary Tape Files and, 109, 155, 177, 345
    Title 13 of U.S. Code and, 57–58, 272
Congress, 83–90. *See also* Apportionment prescriptions
    on 1790 data content, 92–93
    appropriations, 86–87
    authorization, 85
    Census 2000 operations, 299, 326–327
    data content decisions, 88–89
    grassroots groups' lobby efforts, 238–239
    independent agencies/organizations and, 87–88
    Indian Affairs committees, 28–29
    oversight by, 85–86
    programmatic use of data, 89–90
    usual place of residence for, 31
Congressional districts, 38–42, 346
    as census districts, 145
    depository libraries in, 168
    gerrymandering in 1990s: North Carolina, 41*t*
    one-person, one-vote requirements, 39–40
    Voting Rights Act (1965) and, 40–42
Congressional Research Service (CRS), 88
Connecticut Academy of Arts and Sciences, 116

Consistency checks, 167
Consolidated metropolitan statistical areas (CMSAs), 282
Constituent groups, 84–85
Consumer behavior, 356
Consumer databases, 358
Consumer Expenditure Survey (CE), 219, 220t
Consumer Price Index for all urban consumers (CPI-U), 261
Content, census data, 90–92
    response rate and, 89
Content determination, 92–94. *See also* Questionnaires
Content edit, 197
Continental Congress, 271
Continuous measurement program, 26, 27
Contract rent information, 250
Conventional enumeration, 6
Cook, Kevin L., 183
Cooperative housing, 249–250
Core Business Statistics, Economic Census Reports, 191
Cornbury, Lord Edward Hyde, 74
Correlation bias, 53, 99
Coterminous geographic center of population, 72
Council for Foreign Plantations, 74
Council of Professional Associations on Federal Statistics, 31, 110
Count and Public Use Sample data, 113
Counties, 40, 347. *See also* Census County Divisions (CCDs); Local governments
"Counting People in the Information Age" (1994), 17
Counting procedures
    dual systems and, 51–52, 52t
    litigation on, 269
"Counting the Jobless" (film), 288
"Counting the People in 1980: An Appraisal of Census Plans," 17
Count Question Resolution, 12
Country of origin
    of Asian and Pacific Islander Americans, 88–89
    of legal immigrants, 1951–1960 to 1991–2000, 256t
Counts, 113
County and City Data Book, 182
County and City Data Book electronic files, 288
County Business Patterns, 339
County population estimates, 301
County subdivisions, 347–348
County-to-County Migration file, 346
Coverage, 63, 64, 93. *See also* Accuracy and Coverage Evaluation of Census
Coverage Edit Program, 197, 299
Coverage evaluation, 95–101. *See also* Accuracy and Coverage Evaluation of Census
    for agricultural census, 24
    demographic analysis, 95
    dual-systems estimation, 51–54, 64, 95–96
    history of, 97–98
    methodology strengths/weaknesses, 98–100

post-enumeration surveys, 52, 95–96, 269
reverse record check, 96–97
undercoverage causes, 100–101
undercoverage trends, 100
Coverage improvement procedures, 101–104
Coxe, Tench, 117, 118, 119
Crew leader districts, 150
Crew leaders, qualifications for, 145
Cross-sectional surveys, 225
Cuba, foreign-born originating from, 229
Cuomo v. Baldrige (1987), 269
Curbstoning, 328
Current Population Survey (CPS), 221t, 318
    1950 census comparison with, 147
    Asian and Pacific Islander data, 47
    coverage evaluation and, 97
    disability questions on, 172
    as dual-systems method, 52
    interactive use of, 178
    IPUMS and, 267
    poverty estimates from, 221t, 261, 330
    reports from, 186

D

Darroch, John N., 53
Data Access and Dissemination System (DADS), 178
Data and Statistical Service, Princeton University, 114
Database dictionary of electronic census data, 43–44
Data capture, 105–108, 297. *See also* Tabulation
Data collection
    Census 2000, 298–299
    Economic Census, 187–188
    federal household surveys, 224–225
Data definitions, 44, 181
    1950 geographic, 281–282
    for agricultural census, 24–25
    group quarters, 247
    households, 144, 210
Data dissemination, 108–110, 299. *See also* Data users; Dissemination
    data products, 108–109
    data uses, 109–110
    electronic products, 153–154, 172–179
    printed publications, 179–183
    State Data Centers for, 340–341
Data Extract System (DES), 114
Data products, 110–115
    centralized census office, 111
    electronic, 153–154, 172–179
    printed publications, 179–183
    secondary, 183–186
    as service, 112–114
    U.S. Bureau of the Census, 111–112
Data sources. *See* Archival access to census data
Data transmission, 299
Data Use and Access Laboratories (DUALabs), 113, 176, 345
Data users, 94, 109–110, 290–291. *See also* Data dissemination
    1970 census, 155
    Census Users Conference, Little Rock, Ark. (1980), 288

Census User's Guide, 113
confidentiality and, 81–82
grassroots groups, 240
international coordination and, 264
for media reports, 280
of Puerto Rican data, 61
state and local governments, 337–340
Data uses, 26, 109–110, 301
    Community Development Block Grants, 217
    by federal agencies, 216–217
    by private sector, 310, 356–358
Data vendors, 309
Daughters of the American Revolution (DAR), 286
David v. Bandemer, 34
dBase format data, 346
Deaf-Mute Population of the United States, 138
Deaf-Mutes in the United States, 184
Death certificates, standardized, 362
Death statistics, 362–363
    genealogy and, 235
    population estimates and, 301
    scope of, 363–364
DeBow, James D. B., 125, 307
"Decade Census Program," 27
Decennial census. *See also specific years of*
    directorate for, 296
    dual-systems modification for, 53–54
    federal household surveys and, 219
    local involvement in, 270–273
    questions on, 1960–2000, 274–276
    records and schedules archives of, 287–289
    stakeholders to, 290–291, 339
    systematic undercount of, 49
    undocumented aliens in, 259
Decennial censuses
    1790 census, 56, 90, 115–116, 292
        report from, 108, 110, 179
        U.S. House of Representatives state gains/losses, 115
    1800 census, 56, 116–118, 292
        reports from, 110, 179
        U.S. House of Representatives state gains/losses, 117
    1810 census, 56, 118–119
        manufactures census, 92, 187
        reports from, 110–111, 179
        U.S. House of Representatives state gains/losses, 118
    1820 census, 56, 119–120, 306
        reports from, 111, 179–180
        U.S. House of Representatives state gains/losses, 119
    1830 census, 56, 120–122, 180, 292, 306
        data content of, 93, 171
        U.S. House of Representatives state gains/losses, 121
    1840 census, 56, 122–123, 180, 293, 359
        tabulation of, 306–307
        U.S. House of Representatives state gains/losses, 122
    1850 census, 56, 72, 123–125, 235
        birth and death statistics in, 361, 362
        data capture, 105

data content, 93
data products, 111
methodology changes for, 124–125
tabulation of, 307
U.S. House of Representatives state gains/losses, 124
1860 census, 29, 56, 72, 125–127
reports from, 111, 180
tabulation of, 307
U.S. House of Representatives state gains/losses, 126
1870 census, 56, 105–106, 111, 127–130, 271
U.S. House of Representatives state gains/losses, 72, 128
1880 census, 56–57, 130–131, 267, 362
reports from, 111, 180
Seaton Machine tabulation of, 307
U.S. House of Representatives state gains/losses, 130
1890 census, 19, 29, 57, 72, 132–133
data capture, 106
data products, 111
destruction of, 234
fraud during, 271
Hollerith machine tabulation of, 307–308
U.S. House of Representatives state gains/losses, 132
vital registration in, 362
1900 census, 19, 57, 106, 133–135, 184
Hollerith machine tabulation of, 307–308
U.S. House of Representatives state gains/losses, 134
1905 Manufacturers Census, 187, 281
1910 census, 57, 106, 112, 135–136, 308
census tracts in, 66
U.S. House of Representatives state gains/losses, 135
1920 census, 19, 57, 106, 136–138, 184
nonapportionment after, 137–138, 237
1930 census, 20, 57, 93, 139–140, 184
length of, 323
unemployment supplemental schedule for, 15, 92
U.S. House of Representatives state gains/losses, 139
1940 census, 20, 67, 112, 140–143, 260
demographic analysis, 166
housing questions, 246
imputation in, 197
reports from, 181, 184
sampling in, 323
U.S. House of Representatives state gains/losses, 38, 141
1950 census, 143–148, 197, 260, 323
data collection, 145–146
data products, 112, 146–147, 181, 184
demographic analysis, 166
geographic definitions in, 281–282
planning, 143–144
post-enumeration survey of, 147, 303–304, 328
questionnaire, 144–145
race question on, 20, 30

selected findings from, 147–148
U.S. House of Representatives state gains/losses, 144
1954 Economic Census, 187
1960 census, 148–153, 260, 273, 323–324, 359
data collection, 150–152
data dissemination, 174–175
data products, 113, 151–152, 172–173, 181–182, 184
demographic analysis, 166
enumeration, 6, 199–200
evaluation, 152
litigation, 152
planning, 148–149
post-enumeration survey of, 303, 304, 328
questionnaire, 150
race question on, 20, 30
selected findings from, 152–153
U.S. House of Representatives state gains/losses, 149
1970 census, 20, 153–155, 246–247, 260. See also Mailout-mailback census
American Indians and Alaska Natives in, 29
coverage improvement procedures in, 101–102
data capture, 107
data dissemination, 175–176
data products, 113, 173, 182, 184
demographic analysis, 166
enumeration procedures, 200–201
Hispanic/Latino identifiers in, 244–245
poverty estimates from, 288
sampling in, 324
short and long forms for, 276
Summary Tape Files from, 309
U.S. House of Representatives state gains/losses, 154
1980 census, 20, 29–30, 155–158, 247, 260–261
addresses for, 8
coverage improvement procedures in, 102–103
data capture, 107
data products, 114, 157, 182, 184
demographic analysis, 166
enumeration procedures, 201–202
Equal Employment Opportunity (EEO) Special File, 185
post-enumeration survey, 304–305, 328
sampling in, 324, 329
short and long forms for, 277
Summary Tape Files, 288
topcoding of incomes in, 262
undercount, 49, 269
U.S. House of Representatives state gains/losses, 156
veteran status questions on, 359–360
1990 census, 158–161, 247–248, 261, 288, 360
addresses for, 9, 12
Census Transportation Planning Package (CTPP), 346
cost of, 159

coverage improvement procedures in, 103
data capture, 107
data dissemination, 177–178
data products, 182, 184
demographic analysis, 166
dual-systems estimation for, 49
enumeration procedures, 202–203
Equal Employment Opportunity (EEO) Special File, 185
litigation and controversy, 158–159
organization and administration of, 295
post-enumeration survey, 3, 53–54, 305–306, 328
in Puerto Rico, 60
PUMS file types from, 311–312
race questions on, 20–21
SAIPE model-based estimates from, 319, 331
Shelter and Street Night (S-night), 206
short and long forms for, 277
Subject Summary Tape Files (SSTFs), 185
Summary Tape Files, 288
technological triumphs, 159–160
TIGER files, 289
undercount, 159
U.S. House of Representatives state gains/losses, 159
2000 census, 161–163, 206, 248, 261, 325–326
addresses for, 12–13
advertising, 13
advisory committees, 17–18
coverage improvement procedures in, 103–104
data capture, 108
data content, 92
data products, 114, 182
dress rehearsal, 4, 167, 326
enumeration procedures, 203–204
federal administrative records and, 213, 215–216
household diversity, 162
Integrated Coverage Measurement (ICM) program, 4
on Internet, 297
long form, 27, 91–92, 171, 277
Monitoring Board, 18
organization and administration of, 295
partisan dispute over, 87
Partnership Program, 239
planning, 325, 341
post-enumeration survey, 4, 306, 328
Promotional Office, 298
in Puerto Rico, 60, 62
race questions on, 21, 314–315
settlement clusters, 354
short forms, 91, 277
undercount issues for, 84
2010 census, 27, 28, 33, 215–216, 324
Decennial Census Improvement Act (1991), 17
Decennial Census Methodology, Panel on, 17
Decennial Census of Population and Housing, 112, 246
Decennial Census Plans, Panel on, 17

Decennial Management Division (DMD), 296
Decennial Programs Coordination Branch, 185
Decennial Statistical Studies Division (DSSD), 296
Decennial Systems and Contracts Management Office (DSCMO), 296, 299
Dedrick, Calvert L., 140, 141, 142
DeFonso, Teresa K., 49
De la Puente, M., 100
Delivery Sequence File, USPS, 12, 60, 203, 248
Deming, W. Edwards, 52, 142, 197
Democracy in the Mirror (Ehrenhalt), 336
Demographic analysis (DA), 95, 98, 159, 164–168, 296
    age group components, 164
    component method for population estimates, 301
    description, 164–165
    historical estimates development, 165
    history, 166–167
    limitations, 165
    methodology strengths/weaknesses, 98
    net undercount estimates, by race, 1940–1990, 165*t*
    net undercount estimates, for blacks, 1960–1990, 165*t*
    trends, 165–166
    of white population, 370
Denmark, census in, 69
Department of Commerce v. House of Representatives (1999), 58, 270
Depository libraries, 168–171
Depository Library Act (1962), 168
Depository Library Program, 168
Desegregation, 85
Detailed Characteristics, 1960 census, 151
Developing countries, census methods in, 264
Diary Survey of Consumer Expenditure Survey (CE), 220*t*
Differential (net) undercount, 95
Digital Versatile Disks (DVD), 177
Directive 15, 157, 245
Direct-mail marketing, 309–310
Directory of Data Files, 185
Disability, 91, 171–172, 329
Disaster planning, 339
Disease patterns, 362, 364
Dissemination. *See also* Data dissemination
    1960 census, 174–175
    1970 census, 175–176
    1980 census, 176–177
    1990 census, 177–178
    electronic products, 153–154, 172–179
    printed publications, 179–183
    secondary products, 183–186
    technology for, 174
Districting, 38–42. *See also* Apportionment prescriptions
District offices, 150
Divisor (apportionment) methods, 38
Divorce, 211, 363
Domestic abuse shelters, 248
Draft evaders, census data on, 80–81
Dress rehearsal, 4, 167, 186, 326
DUALabs (Data Use and Access Laboratories), 155, 173, 345

Dual-systems estimation (DSE), 49, 50*t*, 51–52, 51*t*, 52*t*
    assumptions for, 52–53
    coverage evaluation and, 64, 95–96, 98
    methodology strengths/weaknesses, 99–100
        modifications for 1990 census, 53–54
        post-enumeration survey and, 304–306
Dubester, Henry J., 183
Dubester's U.S. Census Bibliography with SuDocs Class Numbers and Indexes (Cook), 183
Du Bois, W. E. Burghardt, 184
Dunn, Halbert L., 363
Durand, Edward Dana, 135, 271

E

Earned Income Tax Credit, 262
Eckert-Mauchly Computer Corporation, 174
Economic Census, 92, 181, 187–195, 320
    basic concepts, 188
    commercial mailing lists for, 6–7
    coverage of, 189
    data collection, 187–188
    geographic comparability of, 194–195
    geographic depth of, 189–190, 190*t*
    historical reports from, 193
    industry classification for, 188
    industry comparability in, 194
    insular areas included in, 355
    microdata access issues of, 193
    report formats, 192
    report timing, 192, 192*t*
    report types, 190–192, 191*t*
    scope of, 194
    time series data from, 193
Economic Commission for Europe, 264
Economic development, 339
Economics and Statistics Administration, 83
Editing, 65–66, 195–197
Education, 91, 198–199, 292–295, 329–330
Educational Attainment by Economic Characteristics and Marital Status, 184
Edwards, Alba M., 142
Ehrenhalt, Alan, 336
1800–1890 censuses. *See* Decennial censuses
Elderly. *See* Older Americans
Electric tabulating machine, 307–308
Electronic Information Access Enhancement Act (1993), 170
Electronic products. *See* Dissemination
Elementary and Secondary Education Act, Title 1, 187, 216–217, 300, 329–330
Employment discrimination cases, 217
Employment status, 91, 242, 370
Encyclopedia of American Government, 34
England, colonial census taking by, 73–75
Enumeration, 199–204
    conventional, 6
    erroneous, 206, 208–209, 208*t*
    self-enumeration, 149
    special problems, 204–206
    street book for, 134
    underenumeration issues, 44
Enumeration districts, 131, 145, 150, 287–288, 289

Enumerators, 58, 121, 129, 131, 296
    1960 census, 150, 151, 199–200
    examinations for, 134
    FOSDIC and, 107
    Hispanic/Latino identification by, 244
    housing questions, 247
    litigation against, 268
    qualifications, 145
    race questions and, 20, 314
    recruitment of, 331–332
    training for, 136, 331–332
    undercount theory and, 101, 149, 206, 207
    women as, 371
Epidemics, 362
Equal Employment Opportunity (EEO) Special File, 185
Equal Employment Opportunity file, 157, 184, 315, 346
Equal opportunity, 371
Equal proportions apportionment method, 16, 37, 38
Equal representation decisions, 84, 101
Ericksen, Eugene P., 49, 100
Error sources/measures, 206–209, 262
    1840 census, 123
    1940 census, 142
    composite list, 99
    demographic analysis, 98
    dual-systems estimation (DSE), 99–100
    editing and imputation, 196
    erroneous inclusions, 303
    erroneous enumerators, 101, 149, 206, 207
    genealogical data and, 235, 236
    mail-back rate and, 208–209
    omissions, 207, 303
    Parolee/Probationer Check, 103
    in Puerto Rican census, 61
    reverse record check, 98–99
    sampling variability, 323, 324
    SNRFU, 326
    super census process, 98
    systematic observation process, 98
    undercount challenges and, 269
    Vacant/Delete Check, 103
E-sample, 5, 96, 97–98, 303–304
Estimates, population. *See* Population estimates and projections
Estimation techniques, survey, 226–227
Ethnic groups, 78–80, 291
Europe, censuses in, 69
European-origin population, 228–229, 365–368
Evaluate Alternative Census Methods, Panel to, 17
Exchange visitors, 227
Expert review, pretesting research and, 227

F

Facility planning, 338
Factor analysis, market research and, 310
Fair Housing Act, 315
FAIR v. Klutznick (1980), 259, 269
Families, 210–211
Family composition, 144, 210–213
    census data limitations on, 212–213

future trends in, 212
Hispanic, 242
recent trends in, 211–212
Family household, 210
Farm Housing Characteristics, 1950, 146–147
Farm Population of the United States: An Analysis of the 1920 Farm Population Figures Especially in Comparison with Urban Data, 184
Farm residences, 91–92
Farrell, Raymond, 258
Fay, Robert E., 49, 52
Fecundity of Immigrant Women, 184
Federal administrative records, 213–216
limitations of, 214–215
Federal Advisory Committee Act (1972), 14, 16
Federal agencies, census data uses by, 216–217
Federal budget, OMB and, 343
Federal Bureau of Investigation, 81
Federal Depository Libraries, 26, 110. *See also* Depository libraries
Federal Depository Library Directory, 170
Federal Depository Library Program (FDLP), 168, 169
Federal household surveys, 218–227, 317, 318–319
considerations for using, 218–219
data collection, 224–225
decennial census effect on, 219
estimates derived from, 226–227
focus, 222–224
history, 219–220, 222
repetition/cycle of, 225
sampling error in, 225–226
Federal marshals, 105, 116, 129
assistant, 121
Federal programs, 94, 173–174, 184, 301, 371
advisory committees and, 17
age information, 22
state and local census data uses and, 90, 338
Federal Property and Administrative Services Act (1950), 286
Federal Records Center, 286
Federal Register, 14, 315
Federal Reports Act (1942), 342
Federal-State Cooperative Program for Local Population Estimates (FSCPE), 300, 319
Federal Transit Act, 217
FERRET, 114
Field Division, 296–297
Field operations, 296
Field studies, 302
Fienberg, Stephen E., 49, 52, 53
Fifteenth Amendment, 129, 351
Fifth Count, 113, 176
Filipino Americans, 46, 229
Filmstrips, 288
Final estimate, SNRFU, 326
Finance and administration directorate, 296
Financial Survey of Urban Housing, 219–220
Finland, census in, 69
First Count, 113, 175–176
Focus groups, 227
Follow-up, nonresponse, 207, 298–299, 325–327
Food Stamp Program records, 214, 318
Ford Foundation, 155

Foreign-born population, 227–233
1850–1990, 228*t*
1850–1998, 257*t*
1890 to 1930 and 1960 to 1970, 229*t*
birthplace and parentage trends, 228
demographic characteristics of, 229, 231, 231*t*
geographic origin of, 228–229, 230*t*
Hispanic, 241
number/percentage of for U.S. regions: 1850–1990, 232*t*
and percentage of total population, 1850–2050, 78*t*
region and state of residence, 231–233
by region of residence: 1850, 1920, and 1990, 233*t*
source countries of, 1850, 1920, and 1990, 230*t*
states with highest share of: 1820, 1920, and 1990, 233*t*
trends, 256–257
Foreign stock, 227
Foreign students, 227
Formula grant programs, 90, 216–217
Forsyth, John, 122, 307
Fortier, J. Michael, 178
Forward Trace Study, 98
FOSDIC (Film Optical Sensing Device for Input into Computers), 64, 65, 107, 174
1960 census, 150, 199, 200
1970 census, 155
Fourteenth Amendment, 55, 128–129, 335, 351
Fourth Count, 113, 176
Frankfurter, Felix, 39
Franklin, Benjamin, 75
Franklin, William, 73, 74
Franklin v. Massachusetts (1992), 269
Freedom of Information Act, 81
Fringe benefits, income measures and, 261
FSCPE. *See* Federal-State Cooperative Program for Local Population Estimates (FSCPE)
Fuguitt, Glenn V., 322
Future Census Methods, Panel on, 17

G
GACI (Geographic Area Code Index), 113
Gaines, Leonard M., 338
Gallatin, Albert, 117
Gang punch tabulation machine, 106
Gannett, Henry, 129
Garfield, James A., 93, 128–129
GBF-DIME file, 8, 201, 289
Gender distribution
of educational attainment, 294
of veterans, 361
Genealogy, 58, 234–236
General Accounting Office (GAO), 18, 163, 296, 299, 337
General Characteristics, 1950 Housing Census, 146
General Revenue Sharing, 277, 300
General Social and Economic Characteristics, 1960 census, 151
Gentlemen's Agreement (1907), 45–46, 253

Geo-coding questionnaires, 201
Geographic Area Code Index (GACI), 113
Geographic area data, 44, 186, 291, 346
Geographic Area Series, Economic Census Reports, 191, 191*t*
Geographic Base File/Dual Independent Map Encoding (GBF/DIME), 8, 201, 289
Geographic center of population, 72
Geographic coding of questionnaires, 202–203
Geographic Information Systems (GIS), 108–109, 203, 310, 350
1990 census, 160–161
business applications for, 356
Geographic reference files, 8
Geography, 39–40, 181, 236–237, 287. *See also* Census tracts; Tabulation geography
apportionment prescriptions and, 84
Puerto Rican census and, 61
Geography Division, 7, 12, 287, 296, 297–298
"Geometric" areas, 357
Germany, foreign-born from, 142–143, 229
Gerry, Elbridge, 41–42
Gerrymandering in 1990s: North Carolina, 41*t*
Gingrich, Newt, 270
GIS. *See* Geographic Information Systems (GIS)
Glavin v. Clinton (1998), 270
Global census, 262–264
GO (information retrieval program), 177
Government census, 92
Government Reform and Oversight, House Committee on, 85
GPO Access, 170
Grandchildren responsibility, 91
Grassroots groups, 238–240
Gray v. Sanders (1963), 335
Great Britain, foreign-born from, 229
Great Compromise. *See* Three-fifths Compromise
Great Depression, 237, 255
Green, Duff, 121
Green, Howard Whipple, 67
Gross errors, 303
Group quarters, 204–205, 247, 248, 301
Grover, Wayne C., 286
Guam, 354–356
Guide to the Economic Census, 195

H
Hamilton, Alexander, 34, 35*t*, 350
Hamilton, Archibald, 74
Hansen, Morris H., 140, 174
Harris, William J., 135
Hauser, Philip M., 26, 142
Hayes, Rutherford B., 36*t*
Head-of-household gender bias, 149
Heads of Families at the First Census of the United States taken in the Year 1790, 110
Health and Disability Interagency Working Group, 172
Health Care Financing Administration (HCFA), 214, 318
Health Insurance Master Record, 214
Health Resources and Services Administration, 288–289
Herriot, Roger, 27

Heterogeneity, capture probabilities and, 53
Hill, Joseph A., 16, 37, 184
Hispanics, 79–80, 215, 241–243, 367
    apportionment prescriptions and, 336
    educational attainment, 294–295
    electronic summary files on, 346
    ethnicity and identifiers, 243–246
    origin question, 91, 94
    population estimates and projections, 319
Historical Census Projects, University of Minnesota, 311
Historical estimates development, 165
Hogan, Howard, 53, 100
Holland, Paul W., 53
Hollerith, Herman, 106, 111, 133, 174, 307
Homeless people, 103, 206, 215, 248
Home Mortgage Disclosure Act, 184
Hoover, Herbert, 138
Hopkins, Albert Jarvis, 37
Hopkins, Harry, 142
Hospitals, long-term care, 248
Hot deck method of imputation, 196
Hours usually worked per week last year, 91
House Appropriations Committee, 86
Householder, 210, 371
Households, 116, 144, 162, 210, 301. *See also*
    Family composition; Federal household
    surveys
        refusing to respond, 268
        summaries *versus* individual data, 93
        surveys of, 317, 318–319
        undercoverage of, 217
House of Representatives. *See also* Apportionment prescriptions
        census-related committees/subcommittees, 85–86
        nonapportionment of 1920s, 137–138, 237
        population and apportionment of, 1790–2000, 36t
        sampling and, 58, 326
House v. U.S. Department of Commerce (1998), 270
Housing, 92, 246–252, 355
        American Housing Survey (AHS), 220t
        censuses, 142, 146, 263
        costs, 251–252
        data items, 249–252
        data tabulation, 248–249
        facilities, 251
        unit concept of, 247–248
Housing and Household Economic Statistics Division (HHES), 185
Housing and Home Finance Agency, 184
Housing Censuses, 142, 146, 263
Housing of Senior Citizens, 1960 census, 152
Housing Special Reports Series H-46, 184
Hunt, William, 106
Huntington, Edward, 37–38
Hypo-descent rule, 20

I

IBM, 106, 174, 299
ICPSR (Inter-university Consortium for Political and Social Research), University of Michigan, 43, 44

Illegal Immigration Reform and Immigrant Responsibility Act (1996), 81, 254
Illiterates, 253, 293
Immigrants and Their Children, 184
Immigration, 184, 215, 253–260. *See also* Nativity
        1821–1830 to 1991–2000, 255t
        1890 census, 132
        1960 census, 152
        1970 census, 153
        Asian and Pacific Islander Americans, 45–46
        foreign-born population, 1850–1998, 257
        foreign-born population trends, 256–257
        Hispanic, 163, 241, 242–243
        immigrant population legal status, 258–259
        origins of legal, 1951–1960 to 1991–2000, 256t
        policy for, 253–254
        stocks and flows, 227, 254–256
        undocumented, 257–258
        year of, 91
Immigration Act (1990), 254, 256
Immigration and Nationality Act Amendments (1965), 46, 228, 229, 254, 255–256
        foreign-born population distribution and, 232, 369
Immigration and Naturalization Act (1924), 255
Immigration and Naturalization Service (INS), 81, 217, 301
Immigration Reform and Control Act (IRCA, 1986), 254, 258
Improving America's Schools Act (1994), 300
Imputation, 195–197, 227
Income measures, 91, 145, 260–262, 370
        concept and quality issues in, 261–262
        population estimates and, 301
        poverty measures, 261
Incorporated places, 348
Indexes, census schedules, 234
India, census in, 69
Indian Americans, 46, 47
Indian Citizenship Act (1924), 29
IndianNet Information Center, 240
Industrial statistics, 1810 census, 118–119
Industry of current employment, 91
Industry Series, Economic Census Reports, 191
Infant card, 146
"Information About the National Archives for Researchers," 285
Information technology, 296
Initial estimate, SNRFU, 326
In-kind benefits, income measures and, 261–262
Inspectors, 136, 137
Integrated Coverage Measurement (ICM) program, 4, 103, 328
Integrated Public Use Microdata Series (IPUMS), 264–267, 311
        availability of, 266
        characteristics of, 265, 267
Intercensal Population Estimates Program, 28, 364
Interest groups, 84–85, 93
Intermarriage, 244, 368
Internal Migration: Color and Sex of Migrants, 184
Internal Revenue Service (IRS), 213, 215, 318

International Business Machines (IBM), 106, 174, 299
International coordination, 262–264, 267
International Labour Organization, 263
International Statistical Institute (ISI), 262
Internet, 114, 177–178, 236, 310, 357
        agricultural census data, 26
        assistance on, 298
        confidentiality issues with, 82–83
        data dissemination on, 43, 44, 109, 341
        decennial census data on, 13, 14, 161, 297, 346
        depository libraries and, 169–170
        Economic Census reports on, 192, 195
        GPO Access, 170
        NARA, 285
Inter-university Consortium for Political and Social Research (ICPSR), University of Michigan, 43, 44
Interviewed units, survey estimates and, 226
Ireland, foreign-born from, 229, 366
Italy, foreign-born from, 142–143, 229
Iterative proportional fitting, 324

J

Japan, Gentlemen's Agreement with, 45–46, 229, 253
Japanese-Americans, 46, 81, 143
Jaro, Matthew, 52
Jarvis, Edward, 123
Jefferson, Thomas, 34–35, 56, 116, 117, 292
        apportionment proposal by, 35t
        on data dissemination, 179
Jewish Americans, 366, 367
Jones Act (1917), 244
Journalists, 279–280
Journey to Work file (1990), 346
Judicial districts. *See* Federal marshals

K

Kadane, Joseph B., 53
Karcher v. Daggett (1983), 40–41
Kennedy, Joseph C. G., 15, 72, 307
        1850 census, 124, 125
        1860 census, 127
Keyfitz, Nathan, 17
Keypunch machines, 106
King, Benjamin, 17
King, Rufus, 117
Kirkpatrick V. Preisler (1969), 40
Kish, Leslie, 26
"Know Your U.S.A." (film), 288
Korean Americans, 46, 47
Kr'otki, Karol J., 52

L

The Labor Force, 181
        (Sample Statistics) Employment and Family Characteristics of Women, 184
Laidlaw, Walter, 66, 67
Language, 91, 243
Laotian Americans, 46
Laptop computers, 65

Latin Americans, 229, 243–246
LCOs (Local Census Offices), 279–280, 296, 297
League of Latin American Citizens, 243–244
League of Nations, 263
Legal permanent residents (LPRs), 258–259
Legislatures, 335–337
Libraries. *See* Depository libraries
Library of Congress, 88
Lifestyle cluster systems, 357
Lincoln, Abraham, 125
List independence, dual-systems, 52, 53, 99
Literacy, questions on, 91, 198
Litigation, 268–270
Local censuses, 333–335
Local Census Offices (LCOs), 279–280, 296, 297
Local governments, 183–184, 291, 335–337, 349–350
    review for census coverage, 63
    use of census data by, 173–174, 337–340
Local involvement, 270–273
    1960 census, 199–200
    1970 census, 201
    1980 census, 201–202
Local Review Program, 201, 202–203, 272
    1980 census, 102, 156
    1990 census, 103
    address list development and, 12
Local Update of Census Addresses (LUCA), 12, 103, 203, 272, 297–298
    state FSCPE agencies' data and, 301
Lockheed Martin, 297
Logistic regression, 99
Long forms, 247, 273–277, 324, 327. *See also* Sampling
    1960 census, 150, 200
    1970 census, 154–155, 200–201
    1980 census, 156–157, 202
Longitudinal Research Database (LRD), 193
Longitudinal surveys, 222*t*, 225
Lookup, 114
Louisiana Territory, 118
LUCA. *See* Local Update of Census Addresses

M

Machine Readable Records Division, National Archives, 286
Madison, James, 179, 350
    on questionnaire scope, 92, 115–116, 117, 292
Magnetic tape, 174, 175, 176, 177
Mail-back rate, errors and, 208–209, 208*t*
Mail-order catalogues, 309–310
Mailout-mailback census, 6, 58, 153–154, 200–201, 298
    for agricultural census, 24
    decline in return from, 203
    housing questions, 246–247
    race questions and, 20, 314
    testing for, 62–63
Major fractions apportionment method, 16, 37
Majority-minority districts, 41–42
Manpower Administration, U.S. Labor Department, 16

Manpower and Human Resources, House Subcommittee on, 85
Manua Islands, 354
Manufactures census, 92, 179
Maps, 13, 60, 65, 180, 287–288
        Geographic Base File/Dual Independent Map Encoding (GBF/DIME), 8, 201, 289
        Metropolitan Map Series, 7–8
Map spotting, 8
March Current Population Survey, 221*t*, 261, 319
Mariana Islands, 354
Marital status, question on, 91
Maritime personnel, 200, 202, 205. *See also* Merchant seamen
Marketing for business, states', 339
Market segmentation, 174, 309
Market Statistics, 309, 310
Mark-sense schedules, 107
Marriage, 211, 235, 363
Marshall, John, 117
Massachusetts 1885 census, 106
Master Address File (MAF), 12, 203, 215–216, 248, 277
        1990 census, 159, 161
        American Community Survey and, 27, 28
        compilation of, 297–298
        Puerto Rican census and, 60, 62
Master Address Register (MAR), 248
Master Enumeration District List files, 289
Master trace sample, 299
McCarran-Walter Act (1952), 255
McCoy, Donald R., 285
"Measuring a Changing Nation—Modern Methods for the 2000 Census" (1999), 17
Media, 278–281, 299
        post-census coverage, 280–281
        variety of coverage by, 279–280
Median age of population, 75–76
Medians, computation of, 114
Medicaid records, 216, 318
Medical Expenditure Panel Survey, 219
Medicare records, 64, 214, 301, 318
Megalist process, 97
Merchant seamen, 32. *See also* Maritime personnel
Mercur, Ulysses, 36–37
Merriam, William R., 133
Methodology and standards directorate, 296
Metropolitan American Housing Survey (AHS), 220*t*
Metropolitan areas (MAs), 47–48, 281–284, 346, 349
Metropolitan Housing, 1960 census, 151
Metropolitan Map Services, 7
Metropolitan statistical areas (MSAs), 217, 282
Mexican American Legal and Defense Education Fund, 18, 239
Mexican Americans, classification of, 313–314
Mexico
        foreign-born from, 245
        immigration from, 229, 232, 241, 258
Meyer, Michael M., 53
Microdata files, 82. *See also* Integrated Public Use Microdata Series (IPUMS); Public Use Microdata Sample (PUMS)

Microfiche data files, 109, 114, 157
Microfilm, census, 65, 107, 109, 113, 286
Microfilm Rental Program, NARA, 285
Midwest, foreign-born population in, 231, 232, 233
Migration estimates, internal, 215, 302
Military personnel, 200, 202, 205
        overseas, 32
Mining census, 92
Minneapolis/St. Paul, census fraud in, 271
Minor civil divisions (MCDs), 40, 281, 282, 314, 347–348
Minority advisory committees, 16
Minority community organizations, 239
Missed Person campaign, 102
Missouri Compromise (1820), 119
Mixed races, identification of, 19–20, 314–315
"Modernizing the U.S. Census" (1995), 17
MOD Series (computer) programs, 155, 345
Money, allocation of, 337
Monitoring Board, 18
Monthly Catalog of U.S. Government Publications, 169
Monthly Report on the Labor Force, 220, 222. *See also* Current Population Survey (CPS)
Mortality statistics, 362–364
Mosaic, 178
Mosbacher, Robert A., 159, 270
Motion picture film archives, 288
Move, people who, 99, 102, 207, 304
Mulattos, 19–20, 314
Mulry, Mary H., 54
Multilist process, 97
Multiple responses, unduplication of, 299

N

Natality statistics, 363, 364
National Academy of Sciences (NAS), 37, 88, 163, 261, 299
        census organization and administration study by, 295–296
        post-enumeration surveys and, 84
        review panels, 16–17
        Title 1 funding and, 329–330, 331
National Agricultural Statistics Services (NASS), 24
National American Housing Survey (AHS), 220*t*
National Archives and Records Administration (NARA), 43, 285–290
        census enumeration district maps, 287–288
        census schedules in, 109, 234
        confidentiality and, 81
        Machine Readable Records Division, 286
        records and schedules archives, 287–289
        Summary Tape Files (STFs), 286–287, 288–289
National Archives and Records Service, 286
National Association for the Advancement of Colored People, 239
National Board of Health (1979), 362
National Bureau of Standards, 65
National Census Information Centers, 110
National Center for Education Statistics (NCES), 185

National Center for Health Statistics (NCHS), 214, 216, 318, 361, 363
Intercensal Population Estimates Program, contribution to 364
National Center for Supercomputer Applications (NCSA), 178
National Clearinghouse for Census Data Services, 110
National Content study, 64
National Content Test, 94
National Council of La Raza, 240
National Crime Victimization Survey (NCVS), 221t, 225
National Health Interview Survey (NHIS), 219, 222t, 225, 318
National Health Survey, 220, 363
National Institute of Education (NIE), 288
National Institutes of Health, 311
National Longitudinal Surveys (NLS), 222t
Nationally representative probability samples, 264
National Office of Vital Statistics, 363
National Planning Data Corporation (NPDC), 309, 310
National Processing Center (NPC), 108, 297
National Research Council (NRC), 16–17, 54, 88, 261, 332
National Science Foundation, 288, 311, 329
National Security, International Affairs, and Criminal Justice, House Subcommittee on, 86
National Services Program, 239
National Survey of College Graduates (NSCG), 222t, 224–225, 318–319
National Survey of Fishing, Hunting, and Wildlife-Associated Recreation (FHWAR), 223t
National Survey of Recent College Graduates, 318
National Urban League, 240
National Vacancy Check, 102, 208, 328
Native Americans, 79, 92, 120, 346. See also American Indians
Nativity, 77–78, 77t, 366
from 1850 to 2050, 78t
Naturalized citizens, 227, 258
Navajo, photographs of enumeration of, 288
The Negro Population, 1790–1915, 184
Neighborhood-level data, 356
Net coverage errors, 303
Net undercount, 95, 206–207
New Construction program, 12
Newfoundland colonial census, 73
New Jersey colonial census, 74
Newspaper coverage, 279
New state paradox, 37
New York (state), 334
colonial census, 73
New York City, 66, 272, 305
Housing Vacancy Survey (NYCHVS), 223t, 224
New York Federation of Churches, 272
Population Research Bureau of, 66
New Zealand, census in, 69
Neyman, Jerzy, 323
911 emergency services system, 161, 203

1900–1990 censuses. See Decennial censuses
Nondisclosure of census information, 286
Non-English-speaking residents, 201
Nonfamily household, 210
Nonfarm Housing Characteristics, 1950, 146
Nonhousehold Sources Program, 102
Nonimmigrant residents, 258, 259
Noninterviews, nonsampling error and, 227
Nonmetropolitan population, 281
Non-Response Follow-up (NRFU), 207, 298–299
sampling for (SNRFU), 325–327
Nonsampling error, 149, 226
North, Simon N. D., 133
North American Industry Classification System (NAICS), 188
Bridge between NAICS and SIC report, 194
coverage of in 1997 Economic Census, 189t
hierarchic structure of, 188t
Manual, 195
North Carolina, 1990s gerrymandering in, 41t
Northeast, foreign-born population in, 231–232, 233
Northern Mariana Islands, 354–356
Norway, census in, 69, 70–71
Norwood, Janet, 17
Not-for-profit organizations, 290–291
Number of Inhabitants, 181
1950 census, 146
1960 census, 151
Nursery schools, 198
Nursing homes, 248

O

Occupation, 91, 120, 142, 292–295
requests to include, 115, 116, 117
Occupation cards, 106
Occupations of the First and Second Generations of Immigrants in the United States, 184
O'Connor, Sandra Day, 34
Office of Management and Budget (OMB), 217, 298, 330, 342–344
census content and, 88, 94
Directive 15, 157, 245
metropolitan areas definition by, 281, 282, 283
Race and Ethnic Standards for Federal Statistics and Administrative Reporting, 20, 21, 214–215, 314–315, 315t
Standard Occupational Classification (SOC), 293
Office of the Assistant Secretary for Planning and Analysis, U.S. Department of Veterans Affairs, 359
Office of the Associate Director for Decennial Census, 296
Office of the Associate Director for Field Operations, 297–298
Office of the Inspector General, 296
Ogilvy and Mather, 14
Older Americans, household composition and, 211
Older Americans Act, 22

Omissions, 206, 207, 208–209
mail-back rate and, 208t
One-drop rule, 20
O'Neill, Michael, 290
One-number census, 326
One-person, one-vote requirements, 39–40, 84, 101, 335
Optical character recognition (OCR), 108
Optical mark recognition (OMR), 65
Optical scanning, 65, 108, 203
Organization and administration, 295–299
data capture, 297
major operations, 297–299
management structure, 296–297
research, 297
Organization of American States, 264
Orshansky, Mollie, 261
Other race, classification of, 314–317
Two or More Races combination tabulation, 316t
Overcounts, coverage evaluation and, 95
Overseas federal civilian and military employees, 299
Own children, 210–211

P

Pacific Islanders, 45, 47, 294. See also Asian and Pacific Islander Americans
Paperwork Reduction Act (P.L. 96-511, 1980), 88, 218, 342
Parentage questions, 227–228
Parochial schools, 198
Parolee/Probationer Check, 103
Parolees, 258
Partnership agreements, 298
Passel, Jeffrey S., 259
Paupers in Almshouses, 1910, 184
Pay, census worker, 332–333
Peel, Roy V., 286, 288
Per capita personal income estimates, 301
Perfect matching, dual-systems, 52
Permanent Census Act (1902), 134
Permanent resident aliens, 227
Personal Responsibility and Work Opportunity Reconciliation Act (1996), 254
Persons of color, undercounting of, 291
Person weights, survey estimates and, 226
Philippines, foreign-born from, 46, 229
Pickard, Jerome P., 353
Pickering, Thomas, 117
Pidgin, Charles, 106
Pierce, Franklin, 125
PL 94-171 Reapportionment-Redistricting Act file, 39, 156, 157, 177, 349
Places, census designated, 40, 320, 346, 348
Planning, 238, 291
1950 census, 143–144
1960 census, 148–149
2000 census, 325, 341
Census Transportation Planning Package (CTPP), 157, 346
Planning, Research, and Evaluation Division (PRED), 297, 299
Poland, foreign-born from, 229
Political geography, 42, 347–348

European, 367
Population, center of, 71–72
Population adjustment requests, 291
Population and Housing, 1950 census of, 112, 143, 286
Population Association of America, 14, 15
Population-based federal assistance, 90. *See also* Federal programs
Population composition. *See* Composition, population
Population estimates and projections, 300–303, 317, 318–319
    estimate methods, 301–302
    projection methods, 302–303
    uses of, 301
Population Information in Nineteenth Century Census Volumes (Schulze), 183
Population Information in Twentieth Century Census Volumes, 1900–1940 (Schulze), 183
Population Information in Twentieth Century Census Volumes, 1950–1980 (Schulze), 183
Population paradox, 37
Population Statistics, Census Advisory Committee on, 15
Porter, Robert P., 131
Postcensal Estimates Program, 306
Post-Enumeration Post Office Check, 102, 327
Post-Enumeration Program (PEP), 97–98
Post-enumeration survey (PES), 52, 96*t*, 269, 303–306, 328
    1990 census, 159
    coverage measurement and, 64, 95–96
    dual-systems estimation and, 304–306
    history of, 303–304
    methodology strengths/weaknesses, 99–100
    undercounts and, 84
Posters in National Archives, 288
Post Office and Civil Service, House Committee on, 85
Poverty, 242, 261, 288. *See also* Rural areas; Urban areas
    SAIPE estimates of, 317, 319, 329–331
Povey, Thomas, 74
Powell, Lewis F., Jr., 34
Power, allocation of, 337
Pratt, John, 17
Precanvass, 8
Precensus local review, 103
Pre-computer tabulation systems, 306–308
Pre-enumeration survey, 64
Prelisting, 63
Pretesting research, 227
Price, Daniel O., 166
Primary metropolitan statistical areas (PMSAs), 282
Princeton University, 114
Principles and Recommendations for Population and Housing Censuses (United Nations), 263
Printed publications, 29, 179–183, 285
    nineteenth century, 179–180
    resources on, 182–183
    technology and, 182
    twentieth century, 180–182
Prior residence, 91–92
Prisoners and Juvenile Delinquents in the United States, 1910, 184

Prisons, 248
Privacy, 14, 110, 204, 216. *See also* Confidentiality
Privacy and Confidentiality, Census Advisory Committee on, 15
Private citizens overseas, 32
Private schools, 198
Private sector, 309–311, 357–358
Processing Centers, 107
Program grants. *See* Federal programs
Projections, population. *See* Population estimates and projections
Promotional Office, 298
P-sample, 4–5, 96, 303
Publications, electronic. *See* Data products
Publications of the U.S. government, 289. *See also* Printed publications
Public Documents Library, 289
Public Health Act, 315
Public Health Service, 363
Public Information Office, 298
Public Law 94-171, 39, 288, 299, 336, 346
    Two or More Races combination tabulation, 316*t*
Public Law 103-430, 12, 58, 60–61, 203, 272
Public Use Microdata Sample (PUMS), 43, 109, 286–287, 288, 311–312
    1960 census, 172–173
    1970 census, 155, 176
    1980 census, 156, 157, 176–177
    1990 census, 177–178
    on CD-ROMs, 114
    confidentiality of, 178–179
    contents of, 311
    interactive use of, 178
    topcoding of incomes in, 262
    use of, 174
Public Use Samples, 1960 census, 113, 152
Puerto Rico, 59–62, 241, 288, 299
    enumeration methodology in, 60–61
    Hispanic/Latino identifiers and, 244
Punched cards, 106, 133

Q

Quality check, 4
Quality of data, population estimates and, 302
Quarterly Interview Survey of Consumer Expenditure Survey (CE), 220*t*
Questionnaires, 64, 65, 159, 298. *See also* Content determination

R

Race/racial groups, 91, 214–215, 245, 313–317
    apportionment prescriptions and, 336
    census form inclusion of, 72, 235, 350–351
    composition of, 78–80
    composition of, 1850–2050, 79*t*
    data tabulation, 315–317
    early classifications, 313–314
    educational attainment of, 294–295
    electronic summary files on, 346
    Fifty-seven Combinations of Two or More Races, 316*t*

mixed races, 19–20, 314–315
    primary publications on, 184
    SSA Numident files classifications, 214–215
    undercounting, 291
    white or European-origin, 365–368
Radio coverage, 14, 279
Radio-navigational system, 65
Raking ratio estimation, 324
Ranking of States and Counties, 26
Ratio-raking adjustment, for population estimates, 302
Reagan, Ronald, 84, 89, 157
Reapportionment-Redistricting Act file, PL 94-171 (PL), 349
Record Group 29 (R.G. 29), 287–289
    County and City Data Book electronic files, 288
Record Group 287 (R.G. 287), 289
Record Group 381 (R.G. 381), 288
Record Group 419 (R.G. 419), 288
Record Group 453 (R.G. 453), 288
Record Group 512 (R.G. 512), 288
Records, National Archives, 285
Recruitment, census worker, 298, 331–332
Redistricting. *See also* Apportionment prescriptions
    census data uses by, 217
    PL 94-171 Reapportionment-Redistricting Act file, 39, 349
Reed, Vergil D., 142
Reform and Oversight Committee, House Government, 86
Refugee Act (1980), 254, 256
Refugees, 258
Regional Census Centers (RCCs), 202, 296, 297, 298
Regional Depository Libraries, 168–169
Regional Offices (ROs), 296, 297
Regional Records Facilities, NARA, 285
Related data sources, 317–320
    administrative records, 318
    household surveys, 318–319
    other censuses, 320
    population estimates and projections, 319
    Small Area Income and Poverty Estimates (SAIPE), 319
Remington-Rand Univac processing system, 173
Rent information, 250
Repeated cross-sectional surveys, 225
Report on Indians Taxed and Not Taxed in the United States, Except Alaska, 29
Representation, 336
Reproducer tabulation machine, 106
Research, census, 184, 297, 299
Research, Evaluation, and Experimental (REX) Program, 62
    content error studies by, 64
    demographic analysis and, 64
    processing operations and, 65–66
Residence, 31, 207, 251
Residential Finance, 1960, 152
Residential Financing, 1950, 147
Residential Financing, survey of 92, 145
Resolution E/1995/7 (2000 World Population and Housing Census Programme), 263

Response rate, 13, 89, 325
Response Variance Study, 63
Return rate, 325
Reverse record check, 96–97
    methodology strengths/weaknesses, 98–99
Review periods, pre-census and post-census, 291
Review the 2000 Census, Panel to, 17
Reynolds v. Sims (1964), 335
Rice, Stuart A., 15, 140
Riche, Martha Farnsworth, 371
Ridge v. Verity (1989), 259, 269
Rockefeller Foundation, 140
Roemer, Mark, 226
Rogers, Samuel L., 135, 136
Rooms (housing question), 251
Roosevelt, Franklin D., 140, 246
Rossiter, William, 365
Rota (Pacific island), 354
Roybal Resolution (P.L. 93-311), 245
Rural areas, 203, 207, 291, 320–322
    apportionment prescriptions and, 38, 336
    metropolitan areas and, 282–283
    percentage, 1790–1990, 321*t*
    radio-navigational system and, 65
    total rural population and farm population, 1790–1990, 321*t*
Russell, Archibald, 15, 124
Rust, Keith F., 17, 54

S

St. Croix, 354
St. John, 354
St. Regis Paper Co. v. United States, 81
St. Thomas, 354
Saipan, 354
SAIPE (Small Area Income and Poverty Estimates), 28, 317, 319, 329–331
Sales and Marketing Management Magazine (S&MM), 309
Salvage ethnography, 29
Sampling, 112, 219–220, 327–329. *See also*
    American Community Survey
    1940 census, 141, 142
    1950 census, 145, 147
    2000 census, 163
    in agricultural census, 23
    capture-recapture methods and, 49–55
    census data content and, 91
    challenges to, 268, 270, 296
    for content, 323–325
    content determination and, 93
    coverage evaluation and, 97
    coverage improvement and, 102
    fish in a lake example, 49–51, 50*t*, 51*t*
    Integrated Coverage Measurement (ICM) program, 4, 103
    master trace, 299
    non-profit organizations on, 291
    partisan dispute over, 87
    post-enumeration counts and, 100
    testing for, 63
    Title 13, Sect. 195, Amendments (P.L. 94-521) and, 34, 58
    University of Minnesota high-precision

census samples, 264
Sampling error, 149, 174, 225–226
Sampling for nonresponse follow-up (SNRFU), 325–327
Schedules, National Archives, 285
Schenker, Nathaniel, 52
School District Data Base, 157
School District Data Book, 349
School district reports, 186
School enrollment, 198
Schultze, Charles, 17
Schulze, Suzanne, 182–183
Scotch Irish, 367
Seaton, Charles W., 105, 130, 131, 307
Seaton Device, 105
Seaton Machine, 307
Secondary data products, 183–186
Second Count, 113, 175–176
Second War Powers Act (1942), 142
Secret Service, census data request by, 81
Sekar, C. Chandra, 52
Selected Area Reports, 1960 census, 151
Selective Depository Libraries, 168, 169
Self-identification, 20, 30, 150, 244–245, 314
Senate Committee on Governmental Affairs, 86
Senate Subcommittee on Energy, Nuclear Proliferation, and Federal Services, 86
Senate Subcommittee on Government Information and Regulation, 86
Senior Citizens and How They Live: An Analysis of 1960 Census Data, 184
Service-Based Enumeration (SBE), 206
Settlement clusters, 354
1790 census. *See* Decennial census
Seventy-two year rule, 286
Sex distribution, 47, 370
Sex question, 91
Sex ratios, 76–77, 98
    of foreign-born population, 231*t*
    by nativity groups, 77*t*
Shares method, demographic analysis, 301–302
Shattuck, Lemuel, 15, 124
Shaw v. Reno (1993), 42
Shelter and Street Night (S-night), 206
Sherman, William Tecumseh, 72
Short forms, 91, 273, 276, 277, 324
    1960 census, 150
    1970 census, 154
    1980 census, 156
Siegel, Jacob S., 166
Simple random sample, 226
Single-race tabulation, 315
Sixteenth Amendment, 55
Sixth Count, 113, 176
Slade, William, 122
Slaves, 18–19, 292, 368
    census form inclusion of, 72, 120, 235, 350–351
Slide presentations, 288
Small-area data, 112, 217, 272–273, 356
    Accuracy and Coverage Evaluation and, 5
    Special Tabulation Program (STP), 185
    Summary Tape Files and, 345
    target marketing and, 309

Small Area Data Notes, 113
Small Area Income and Poverty Estimates (SAIPE), 28, 317, 319, 329–331
SNRFU (sampling for nonresponse follow-up), 325–327
Social and human service-oriented not-for-profits, 291
Social Science Research Council (SSRC), 15, 140, 152
Social Security, analysis of, 301
Social Security Administration (SSA), 261, 318
    IRS records and, 213
    Master Beneficiary Record, 213–214
    Numident files, 213, 214–215
    population projections by, 300, 302–303
    20-percent Numident files, 302
Soundex indexes, 234, 285
Sound recordings, 288
Source and Accuracy Statements, 225–226
South, foreign-born population in, 231, 232, 233
Southeast Asian Americans, 46, 47
Southeastern Legal Foundation, 270
Southwestern Spanish surname public use microdata sample files, 288
Soviet Union, foreign-born from, 229
Spanish language questionnaire, 202
Spanish surname as Hispanic identifier, 244
Special Advisory Panel, 16
Special Place Facility Questionnaire Operation, 205
Special places, 248, 249, 299
Special Reports, 1950 census, 146
Special Reports for Local Housing Authorities, 1960 census, 152
Special Tabulation for Local Housing Authorities, Series HC-6, 184
Special Tabulation Program (STP), 185, 357
Spencer, Bruce D., 54
Sprizzo, John, 269
Staffing, 331–333, 331*t*
Stakeholders, decennial census, 290–291, 339
Standard consolidated areas (SCAs), 282
Standard Industrial Classification (SIC), 142, 188
    Bridge between NAICS and SIC report, 194
Standard metropolitan areas (SMAs), 281–282
Standard Metropolitan Statistical Areas (SMSAs), 112, 282, 288
Standard Occupational Classification (SOC), 293
Standards for Publication of Statistics, 343
Standards for Statistical Surveys, 343
START Community, 345
State and Local Area Statistics, Census Advisory Committee on, 15–16
State and Local Fiscal Assistance Act (1972), 277, 300
State Data Centers (SDC), 43, 44, 110, 340–341
    1980 census, 157
    agricultural census data, 26
    depository libraries and, 169
State governments, 173–174, 337–340, 362.
    See also States

administrative geography of, 349–350
censuses by, 333–335
FSCPE agencies of, 300–301
legislatures, 335–337
records from federal programs, 215
redistricting and, 41
secondary products and, 183–184
undercounts and, 291
State income tax records, 318
State population estimates, 301
States, 40, 346, 347
States and Small Areas, 1960 census, 151
Statistical Abstract of the United States, 182, 183
Statistical Atlas, 352
Statistical Atlas of the United States (1920 census), 138
Statistical geography, 348–349
Statistical matching, imputation and, 197
Statistical policy and oversight, 342–344
Statistical summary data files, 183
STAT-USA database, 170
Steelville, Mo., 71
Steering committee, 296
Stephan, Frederick F., 142
Steuart, William Mott, 136, 139
STF files. *See* Summary Tape Files (STFs)
Stiles, Ezra, 75
Still picture records, 288
Stock, 30, 227, 254–256
Stratification, capture probabilities and, 53
Street book, 134
Structural type, housing, 250
Study of Consumer Purchases, 220
Subject reports, 183
Subject Reports, 1960 census, 151
Subject Series, Economic Census Reports, 191
Subject Summary Tape Files (SSTFs), 1990, 185
Subject Summary Tapes (SSTs), 114
Substitution, 196
Suburban areas, 8, 352
Suburbanization, 237
Summary data files, 43
Summary Reports by Sector, Economic Census Reports, 191
Summary Tape Assistance, Research, and Training (START) Community, 345
Summary Tape Files (STFs), 109, 114, 286–287, 288–289, 344–346
1960 census, 172–173
1970 census, 155, 175–176
1980 census, 156, 157, 176–177
1990 census, 177
CENSPAC (computer program), 158
example, 345t
STF3 ZIP Code file, 157
use of, 174
Super census process, 97, 98
Supervisors, census, 131, 136, 137, 140
Supervisors' districts, 131
Supplementary Analysis and Derivative Tables, Twelfth Census of the United States, 184
Supplementary Reports, 1960 census, 151
Survey bias, 226
Survey of Buying Power, 309
Survey of Change and Residential Finance (SCARF), 304
Survey of Components of Change, 150
Survey of Doctorate Recipients, 318–319
Survey of Income and Education, 329
Survey of Income and Program Participation (SIPP), 172, 224t, 225, 319
Survey of Minority-Owned Business Enterprises, 192
Survey of Residential Financing, 92, 145, 150
Survey of Women (SW), 222t
Surveys *versus* census, 218
Swains Island, 354
Systematic observation process, 97, 98

T
Tabulating machines, 108, 134, 288, 307–308
card-to-tape tabulation machines, 106
Hollerith Electric, 111, 133
Seaton, 105, 307
Tabulation, 176, 360–361. *See also* Data capture
pre-computer, 105–106, 306–308
Tabulation geography, 181, 347–350
administrative, 349–350
political, 347–348
statistical, 348–349
Tacoma, Wash., overcount in, 268, 271
Taiwanese Americans, 89
Talk show coverage, 14
Tallying machines. *See* Tabulating machines
Tape Address Register (TAR), 7, 8, 201
Target marketing, 309
Tax assessors, state, 334
Taxes, income measures and, 262
Tax lists, 235–236
Tax Reform Act of 1986, 213
Technical documentation of electronic census data, 43–44
Technical Panel on the Census Undercount, 15
Technologies Management Office (TMO), 296, 297, 299
Technology, 65, 357
confidentiality issues and, 82–83
information technology directorate, 296
Teenage pregnancy, 363
Telephone assistance, 298
Television shows, 279, 288
Tenure, housing, 249
"The Negro Farmer" (Du Bois), 184
"There's A Man Going 'Round Taking Names" (sound recording), 288
Third Count, 113, 175–176
Thirteenth Amendment, 128, 351
Thornburg v. Gingles (1986), 41, 336
Three-fifths Compromise, 55, 350–351
TIGER System, 9, 160–161
map, 10–11
TIGER (Topologically Integrated Geographic Encoding and Referencing) database, 8–9, 154, 289, 297
business applications for, 356–357
Census 2000 improvements, 12–13
data dissemination and, 108–109
Puerto Rican census and, 60, 62
Tilden, Samuel J., 36t
Time-of-delivery check, 7
Time series surveys, 225
Tinian (Pacific island), 354
Title 1, Elementary and Secondary Education Act, 329–330
census data uses by, 216–217
population estimates for, 300
Title 13 of U.S. Code, Census Act (68 Stat. 1012), 57, 83
1960 census and, 148
on confidentiality, 80, 272
Economic Census mandate in, 187
Sect. 195 Amendments (P.L. 94-521) and, 34, 58
Tobey, Charles W., 142
Topologically Integrated Geographic Encoding and Referencing (TIGER)/Line files, 1990 census. *See* TIGER (Topologically Integrated Geographic Encoding and Referencing) database
Towns, 348
Training, census worker, 136, 137, 298, 331–332
Transients, 200, 205, 299
Transportation census, 92
Transportation Planning Data for Urbanized Areas based on 1960 census, 184
Transportation to work, 91
Treaty of Paris (1898), 354
Triple-system estimation, 99
Tri-racial groups, 314
Truesdell, Leon, 142
Truman, Harry S., 81
Tukey, John W., 53
Tutuila (island), 354
Twin-city pairs, 282
Two or More Races tabulation, 315, 316t, 317
2000 census. *See* Decennial censuses
Tydings-McDuffie Act (1934), 46

U
"Uncle Sam Calling—Story of the 1940 Census" (sound recording), 288
Undercounts, 64, 100. *See also* Accuracy and Coverage Evaluation; Post-enumeration survey (PES)
1870 census, 129, 271
1950 census, 147
1970 census, 201
1980 census, 157
1990 census, 158–159, 161t
2000 census, 162–163
capture-recapture methods and, 49, 52
confidentiality and, 81
coverage evaluation and, 95
dual-systems estimation technique and, 53–54
homeless people, 206
housing stock and, 249
litigation on, 268, 269–270
mail-back rate and, 208t
non-profit organizations and, 291
Special Advisory Panel, 16
Underenumeration issues, 44
Underreporting, independently derived benchmarks and, 226
Undocumented aliens, 84, 98, 243, 257–258, 259

Unduplication of multiple responses, 299
Unemployed persons, 15, 92
Unemployment census, 141
Unemployment insurance benefit records, 318
Unincorporated places, 144, 320, 353
Unique-Address Matching, 304
United Kingdom, census in, 69–70
United Nations
    international census and, 263
        Northern Mariana Islands strategic trust
        and, 354–355
    on urban areas, 353
United Nations Economic and Social Council,
    263
United Nations Statistical Commission, 263
United States Summary (agricultural census
    data), 26
United States v. William Rickenbacker
    (1961–1963), 152
UNIVAC I computer, 173, 174, 197
Universal geo-codes, 349
University of Michigan, Inter-university Con-
    sortium for Political and Social Research,
    43, 44
University of Minnesota
    high-precision census samples at, 264
    Historical Census Projects, 311
Update/leave techniques, 12, 203–204, 298
Urban areas, 137, 237, 320, 346, 352–354
    1950 census, 143, 144
    apportionment prescriptions and, 37, 336
    congressional districts in, 38
    in metropolitan areas, 281
    undercounts, 291
Urban Transportation Planning Package (1970
    and 1980), 185
U.S. Bureau of Economic Analysis, 216, 217
U.S. Coast Guard, 205
U.S. Constitution, 55, 83, 313, 350–351
U.S. Department of Agriculture, 24, 320
U.S. Department of Commerce, 24, 83, 136,
    139
    census advisory committees, 17–18
    fire of January 1921 at, 285
    on post-enumeration survey, 84, 269
    Special Advisory Panel and, 16
    STAT-USA database, 170
U.S. Department of Commerce and Labor,
    83, 110–111, 135
U.S. Department of Defense, 33, 205
U.S. Department of Education, 329, 331
U.S. Department of Health and Human
    Services. *See* National Center for Health
    Statistics
U.S. Department of Interior, 57, 83, 111, 130,
    132, 133
U.S. Department of Justice, 40, 41–42, 217,
    296
U.S. Department of Labor, 16, 219
U.S. Department of State, 33, 121, 123
U.S. Department of Transportation, 157, 217
U.S. Department of Veterans Affairs, 359
U.S. Equal Employment Opportunity Com-
    mission

EEO file, 157, 184, 185, 315, 346
    small-area data for employment discrim-
    ination cases, 217
U.S. General Accounting Office (GAO),
    87–88, 90, 272
U.S. Geological Survey (USGS), 160–161
U.S. Government Printing Office, 152, 168,
    169, 170
    library collection, 289
U.S. insular areas, 354–356
U.S. Labor Department, 16, 219
U.S. Maritime Administration, 205
U.S. Office of Civil Rights, 157
U.S. Office of Economic Opportunity, 16
U.S. Office of Management and Budget
    (OMB). *See* Office of Management and
    Budget (OMB)
U.S. Postal Service
    1937 survey by, 323
    1960 census and, 6, 273, 324
    1970 census and, 7, 58
    1990 census and, 9
    address check by, 7, 9, 103, 202
    census coverage testing and, 63
    Delivery Sequence File, 12, 60, 203, 248
    Master Address File and, 12, 297
    Post-Enumeration Check, 102, 327
    Puerto Rican census and, 62
    zip codes of, 349
U.S. Supreme Court, 4, 296, 299, 326–327, 328
    1990 undercount and, 159
    redistricting cases, 40–41
U.S. War Department, 59
Users. *See* Data users
Uses. *See* Data uses
USGenWeb Census Project, 236
Usual place of residence, 31, 207

V

Vacant/Delete Check, 63, 102, 103, 202
    National Vacancy Check, 102, 208, 328
    New York City Housing Vacancy Survey
    (NYCHVS), 223*t*, 224
Value, housing, 250
Value-added geographic information, 357–358
Van Buren, Martin, 23, 121, 306
Veterans' status, 92, 196, 359–361
Vietnam War, 46
Villages, 348
Vinton, Samuel Finley, 35
Virginia colonial census, 73–74
Virgin Islands, 354–356
Vital registration and statistics, 361–364
    census use of, 214, 318
    history of, 362
    quality of data of, 302
    uses of, 363–364
Vocational schooling, 198–199
Voting precincts, 348–349
Voting Rights Act (1965), 17, 40, 217, 315,
    336, 351
    Directive 15 and, 157
Voting rights cases, 85

W

Walker, Francis Amasa, 111, 129, 130, 133,
    271
    procedural innovations by, 131
Warrantee card information, 310
Washington, George, 34, 35, 95, 115–116, 179
Weaver, William A., 122, 123
Webster, Daniel, 16, 35–37, 123
Weeks worked last year, question on, 92
Weighting, for survey estimates, 175, 226,
    301, 324
Welfare records, 318
Wells v. Rockefeller (1969), 40
"Were You Counted?" campaign, 102, 103,
    200, 201, 202
Wesberry v. Sanders (1964), 39, 335
West, foreign-born population in, 231, 232
"We: The People" (film), 288
White, A. A., 54
White/European-origin population, 365–368
White population, 313, 346, 368–370
    apportionment prescriptions and, 336
    Hispanics as part of, 244
    percentage of total population,
    1790–2050, 369*t*
White v. Weiser (1973), 40
Wigglesworth, Edward, 75
Willcox, Walter, 16, 37
William C. Velazquez Institute, 240
Winsborough, Halliman, 113
Wisconsin v. City of New York (1996), 270
Wolfgang, G. S., 53
Women, 136, 235, 360, 370–371
    Survey of Women (SW), 222*t*
Women in Gainful Occupations, 1870–1920, 184
Worker class, 91, 141–142
Workload, census worker, 332–333
Workplace, question on, 91
World War II, 142–143
World Wide Web, 177–178. *See also* Internet
Wright, Carroll D., 24, 132

Y

Year built (housing), 250
Year last worked, 92
Years of school, 199
Young, H. Peyton, 37, 38
Young and Rubicam, 14
Young v. Klutznick (1980), 269

Z

Zaslavsky, Alan M., 53
Zelnik, Melvin, 166
Zip codes, 157, 203, 310, 349–350
Zip Code Tabulation Areas (ZCTAs), 346
Zip Code Tabulation of Selected Items, 26
Zip Code Statistics, Economic Census
    Reports, 191

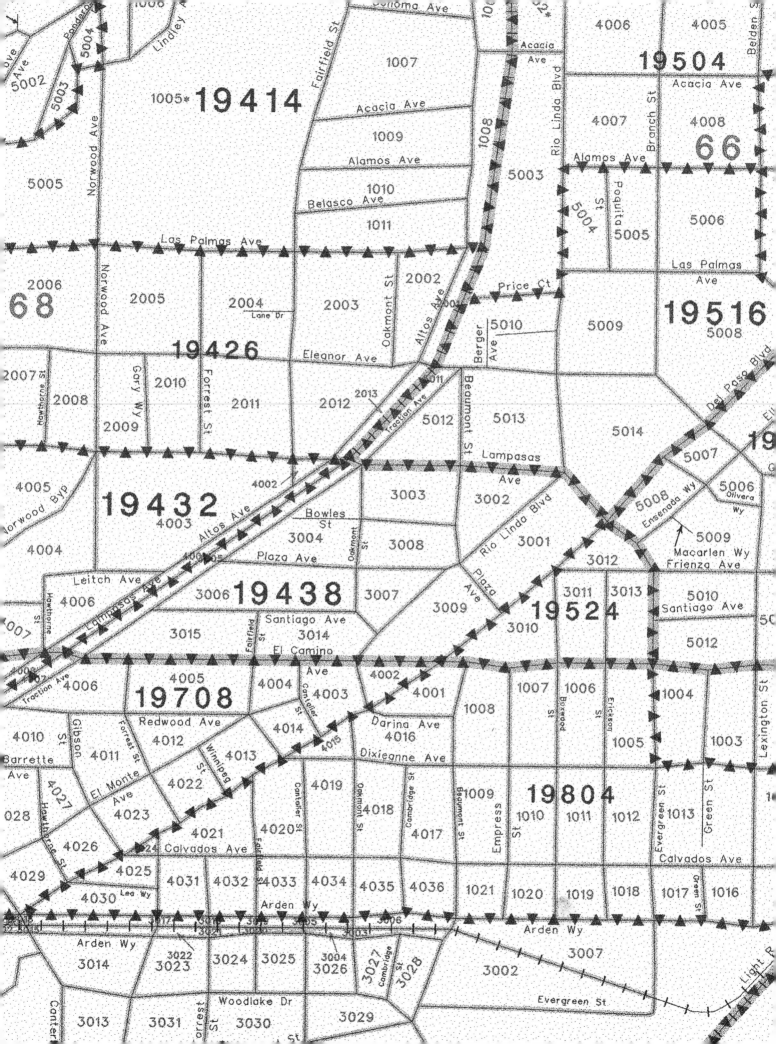